1992

Understanding Universal Health Programs

1992

Understanding Universal Health Programs

Issues and Options

Edited by
David A. Kindig
and
Robert B. Sullivan

Health Administration Press
Ann Arbor, Michigan   1992

96 95 94 93 92   5 4 3 2 1

Library of Congress Cataloging-in-Publication Data

Understanding universal health programs : issues and options / edited by David A.
Kindig   and Robert B. Sullivan
       p.   cm.
    Consists of 34 articles from various health care journals.
    Includes bibliographical references and index.
    ISBN 0–910701–86–5 (soft-bound) : alk. paper)
    1. Medicine, State—United States. 2. Insurance, Health—Government policy—United
States. 3. Medical policy—United States. I. Kindig, David A. II. Sulivan, Robert B.
    [DNLM: 1. Health Services—organization & administration—United States—collected
works. 2. National Health Insurance, United States—collected works. 3. National Health
Programs—collected works. 4. State Medicine—United States—collected works. W 275
AA1 U104]
RA412.5.U6U48   1992
362.1'0973—dc20
DNLM/DLC for Library of Congress   92-49882 CIP

The paper used in this publication meets the minimum requirements of American
National Standard for Information Sciences—Permanence of Paper for Printed Library
Materials, ANSI Z39.48-1984. ∞ ™

Health Administration Press
A division of the Foundation of the
   American College of Healthcare Executives
1021 East Huron Street
Ann Arbor, Michigan 48104-9990
(313) 764-1380

Contents

Foreword

Periodically, but unpredictably, the United States has flirted with national health insurance since the early twentieth century, when Theodore Roosevelt advocated the idea—much like Lloyd George and Winston Churchill, in the belief that no country could be strong whose people were poor and sick. Regrettably for advocates of universal insurance, Roosevelt's defeat by Woodrow Wilson in the presidential election of 1912 postponed for another two decades further consideration of broader protections against the financial consequences of disease. Ever since, though not often, presidents (most prominently Franklin D. Roosevelt, Harry S. Truman, and Richard M. Nixon) and other ranking government officials have raised the banner on behalf of various forms of national health insurance, based more on an individual's medical need than economic standing. Taking such action in any society is a political act. Not to take such action, which has obviously been the pattern over time, also equates to politics and the absence of a consensus over what society's role should be in providing health insurance to its citizens.

Once again, a variety of legislative proposals have been advanced in Washington that address the subject of universal health coverage. Only a year or two ago, a publisher would have had serious reservations about producing an anthology that related to this subject because national health insurance had remained on Washington's back burners since the mid-1970s. That changed rather suddenly in late 1991 in a way that says a lot about the modern politician. The flash point was not a concern over soaring costs (they have been soaring for 20 years) nor the uninsured (many millions have been uninsured for decades, too), but rather the defeat of a Republican establishment politician, Richard Thornburgh, who had resigned as President Bush's attorney general to seek elective office in his native Pennsylvania. Thornburgh was upset in his bid for a U.S. Senate seat by Democrat Harris Wofford, who ran on a platform of national health insurance now. That November 5 result moved President George Bush, who had previously ignored these issues, to pledge in an off-hand comment to a group of businessmen on December 13: "I will have a (health insurance) proposal in the State of the Union message. . . . I do think the time has come for the administration to come forward with a comprehensive program."

The study of a subject as broad and complex as universal health programs is best illuminated by a diverse selection of readings that shed light on a range of issues and that enliven the debate. David A. Kindig and Robert B. Sullivan have compiled such an anthology of key articles from the research and policy literature, primarily for the use of faculty and students teaching and learning about these vexing issues. But it will be of great value to policymakers and researchers as well. Following a brief historical section, they present eighteen "issues" papers from the areas of changing demographics and efficacy, financing strategies, access and rationing, and the delivery system. The editors chose to present issues before proposals so that the readers will have an understanding of the major components of policy prior to approaching the review of specific proposals. Since we may have time to reflect more carefully before full action and implementation of universal coverage, this approach has obvious merits. The second section contains a selection of key articles relating to international experiences, the process of change and implementation, and several current domestic proposals. Whereas many specific proposals are not included due to space limitations, the ones selected represent the continuum from managed competition to "pay or play" to a Canadian-style national health program. The inclusion of one additional long-term care proposal is important since the current debate is almost exclusively limited to the acute care system.

It is extremely difficult to choose articles for inclusion in a volume such as this, since, as the editors indicate, almost all health services and health policy research has some bearing on the questions posed by universal coverage. While the articles selected are all of critical relevance, the editors indicate in the introductory sections several of the most critical omissions from the original 1,000 citations. At the least the editors have simplified the task for many faculty members who are teaching or planning to teach in this area. Beyond that, their approach to consider history and basic issues first has broader implications and will, it is hoped, encourage policymakers to pause and reflect a little more in specific proposal design and negotiation.

John K. Iglehart

Preface

This volume is the outgrowth of two years of research and discussion by the Faculty Task Force on National Health Plans, sponsored by the Wisconsin Consortium for Health Services Research at the University of Wisconsin–Madison. With financial support from UW's LaFollette Institute of Public Affairs, the Task Force formed as a multidisciplinary group of faculty knowledgeable about various aspects of the issues underlying existing and proposed health plans. Its main purpose was to stimulate individual and team research relating to universal health care and to plan a research agenda conference on this topic. In the course of its activities, the Task Force compiled a literature data base with about 1,000 citations.

This anthology is our attempt to assemble a sample of the most challenging and relevant thinking on national and state health plans. As public awareness of these issues mounts, we expect the number of courses and seminars on health program options to increase. We are thus directing this volume primarily toward students, although we believe that anyone interested in the topic will find the contents relevant, including faculty, policy analysts, and health services researchers. Wherever possible, therefore, we have selected papers not so much for their theoretical sophistication as for their clarity and value to graduate and upper-level undergraduate students.

The organization of the anthology arose from early debate and discussion among Task Force members. Two general approaches appeared feasible. The initial preference was to review the various international and proposed domestic plans, debate their strengths and weaknesses, and see if something appropriate for our culture and political structure emerged from this analysis. The other option was to examine national health plans and proposals in the light of several key groups of issues that underlie them. We finally adopted the latter course. Since health plans and proposals are the product of both explicit and implicit policy perspectives and political considerations, we agreed that understanding the underlying issues should precede attempts to evaluate a spectrum of specific proposals with a variety of combinations and emphases. The initial issue areas around which we organized our discussions were benefits and coverage, financing, the delivery system, and administration and implementation.

One of our goals for the collection is to challenge our readers' assumptions by presenting articles arguing variously for economics and values, entertaining both incremental and radical changes, and promoting systems and proposals from both the U.S. and abroad. In Sections I and II, we treat background and issues that we would want our students to become familiar with, so that their subsequent analysis of specific plans will be an informed one. Section I, Historical Perspectives, presents the background essential to any theoretically sound analysis of present structures and future potentials. As will be spelled out more completely in the introduction to Section II, The Issues, and its four parts, it is a formidable task to select a few papers that are representative of the social-policy debate, since in one sense all of health services research has some bearing on these questions. Nevertheless, with the help of our editors, we have made choices with an eye to breadth as well as depth.

We also treat aspects of existing and proposed plan. Section III, Universal Health Programs Abroad, examines selected national health systems in place in Canada, Germany, Scandinavia, and Japan. Section IV, Domestic Universal Health Plans, has two parts. The first discusses issues of political implementation in the United States and includes a number of timely commentaries on political strategies for and obstacles to reform during the 1990s. The second part presents some of the proposals currently under consideration for reforming the U.S. system.

Although we have covered a great deal of academic and policy territory in this volume, we have of necessity omitted many useful and significant articles. When faced with difficult choices, we asked, "Should this article be required reading for a graduate course on universal health plans?" As will be covered more fully in the section introductions, some articles were too long, some too technical and esoteric, and some redundant. In other instances, little material other than newspaper articles could be found (on the Hawaiian state plan, for example). Neither were we able to reproduce major commission reports such as the National Leadership Commission, the President's Commission on Access, or the Pepper Commission report. Some critical items that were omitted are cited in the introductory pieces; supplemental references to much of the germane literature can also be found in the notes to the articles presented.

We hope that this volume will itself play a role in the process of reform toward universal coverage in the United States. On the one hand, we could have focused our selections more narrowly on proposals for financing coverage for the currently uninsured, which from one perspective might be the most pressing priority for the country. On the other hand, opportunities for major reform do not arise often, and proposals and plans that do not anticipate or that, at the worst, preclude future developments in health services (e.g., the shift from acute to chronic disease, the changing role of the hospital, and the paradigm shift to health outcomes) should not pass unchallenged. In presenting the issues before the plans, we hope that these considerations will be taken into account in both incremental and radical proposals for reform, either as they are initially adopted or as they are modified in future iterations. Because we recall the failure of the Kennedy-Mills proposal in 1974, in which "the best became the enemy of the good," our consideration of the broad issues is not intended to inhibit the chances of realistic and reasonable incremental proposals. Our aim is rather to help ensure that they and their descendants recognize needs and provide incentives for a twenty-first–century system that features universal access at reasonable cost while promoting health status and quality of life for all Americans.

David A. Kindig
Robert B. Sullivan

Acknowledgments

This volume is one product of the Faculty Task Force on National Health Programs at the University of Wisconsin–Madison, School of Medicine, which met from fall 1989 to fall 1991. The editors would like to express their appreciation to the LaFollette Institute of Public Affairs at the University of Wisconsin–Madison, which furnished partial support to the Task Force and project staff for this volume. We are indebted to Task Force members Dave Kreling, Ken Rentmeester, Pam Spohn, Earl Thayer, Daniel Wikler, and Barbara Wolfe for the spirited intellectual interchange that inspired this project. Mary Schuster and Monica Brown provided invaluable clerical assistance.

Daphne Grew, Ed. Kobrinski, and Christina Bych of Health Administration Press offered constructive critiques that smoothed the publication process. We would also like to thank Ronald L. Numbers, William Coleman Professor of the History of Science and Medicine, University of Wisconsin–Madison, for illuminating the potential pitfalls that often attend the publication of an anthology. Apart from his extensive familiarity with the history of national health insurance, Ron's experience as author and editor of nearly twenty books on the history of medicine, of science, and of religion proved an inspiration in helping us complete what at times seemed an unending project.

David Kindig would like to express special appreciation to Victor Sidel, with whom he had collaborated on a paper for the 1971 Eilers and Moyerman National Health Insurance Conference at Wharton, which was titled "Proposed National Health Programs: Impact on Consumers." It has taken a long time to return to this subject—it is hoped less time will elapse before some concrete reform is produced.

I
Historical Perspectives

Introduction

Robert B. Sullivan

If history is the study of change, few fields in American health care policy afford the student more fertile opportunities for analysis than the national health insurance debate. For more than 75 years, American politicians, physicians, and health care consumers have proposed, promoted, declaimed, rejected, and revised an array of programs designed to make health services more affordable, accessible, and effective. Congress has even enacted plans covering limited segments of the American populace. But it has been the manifold attempts—and failures—to reach consensus on a comprehensive, universal plan that have made the campaigns for and against national health insurance such engrossing history.

The historical appeal of the subject has not gone unnoticed, although historians have certainly not had a monopoly on it. Since the 1920s, and particularly in the past two decades, political scientists, health services researchers, ethicists, physicians, sociologists, and economists have joined historians in producing a host of articles, studies, and monographs on national health insurance[1] in America and abroad. So vital have investigators considered a knowledge of historical antecedent to be that virtually all have grounded their approaches, whatever the parent discipline, in an interpretation of history. Indeed, at least one writer has questioned whether national health insurance should have occupied so prominent a place in the health policy landscape.[2]

Few can dispute that historical awareness should inform any serious appraisal of the tenor and tempo of the current debates over the feasibility and form of national health insurance proposals. Because the scope of this collection extends well beyond historical analyses, space considerations have forced us to limit this section to two articles. We believe, however, that the authors selected present unusually illuminating histories of encounters among national health insurance stakeholders.

In "Transformation in Defeat: The Changing Objectives of National Health Insurance, 1915–1980," Paul Starr presents a useful framework for conceptualizing the struggle for national health insurance in America. To view the periodic national health insurance initiatives over the past eight decades as no more than the ebb and flow of a protracted offensive is to miss crucial shifts in emphasis, Starr argues.

Each attempt to improve access and expand coverage for health services has sought to blunt the impact of different combinations of social and individual, and direct and indirect, costs. Whereas early proposals included provisions both to reduce financial hardships from lost earnings due to sickness and to compensate patients for some medical expenses, later proposals concerned themselves almost exclusively with insuring individual patients and families against the actual costs of care. The last two decades have pushed concerns over the spiralling social costs of health care to the fore.

Starr uses this cost matrix to segment his analysis into three periods: the early years of the century and advocacy of "progressive" health insurance; an era of more sophisticated financing, growing provider power, and extensions of access across socioeconomic classes ("expansionary" health insurance, from the 1930s into the 1960s); and the present period of "containment" insurance, a vehicle for cost control and system reform. In discussing the objectives of the reforms proposed during each period, Starr cites parallels in the broader social and political context. For example, unlike the European countries, the impetus for reform in the United States, he observes, did not come from political circles. Economic fluxes, such as the Depression and the recession of 1974–1975, also influenced American receptivity to overtures by national health insurance proponents to a great extent.

Although never far from center stage in the concerted campaign waged by organized medicine against national health insurance, financial motivations, as Ronald L. Numbers points out in "The Specter of Socialized Medicine: American Physicians and Compulsory Health Insurance," do not alone explain the collective or individual aversion of physicians to national health insurance proposals. In fact, in an effort to stabilize or increase physician incomes, a number of American Medical Association (AMA) and state medical society leaders supported social insurance reforms on the eve of World War I. Fears of loss of professional autonomy, anticipated declines in quality of care, and presumed violation of patients' rights to choose a physician, compounded by popular sentiment against Germany (which had instituted compulsory health insurance three decades earlier), gradually turned the majority of doctors against government-sponsored health plans during the war. Mixed experiences with payment under the new workers' compensation plans also acted to exacerbate organized medicine's expectations that compensation would drop under what they termed "socialized medicine" (although few proposals actually favored making physicians state employees). Numbers goes on to trace the role of the AMA in opposing voluntary health insurance in the early 1930s, before it turned its efforts once more toward blocking national health insurance initiatives under Roosevelt, Truman, Eisenhower, Kennedy, and Johnson. The article concludes with a synopsis of the reasons that physicians have traditionally marshalled to justify their antipathy toward national health insurance.

It is impossible to mention here all the articles meriting attention that were excluded from this collection, but several might be profitably considered. One of the earliest historical accounts is Odin Anderson's "Health Insurance in the United States, 1910–1920." [3] Ronald L. Numbers offers an excellent overview of the rise of health insurance in its various forms in "The Third Party: Health Insurance in America." [4] For readers interested in the link between history and present-day policy, Stacey T. Cyphert and James E. Rohrer ("A National Medical Care Program: Review and Synthesis of Past Proposals") recap the issues and summarize arguments against national health insurance before presenting eleven criteria for evaluating six types of proposals that have appeared since the 1930s. [5] In "National Health Insurance—The Triumph of Equivocation," Samuel Levey and James Hill present a sobering portrait of the "long tradition of equivocation" on national health insurance policy in the United States. After reviewing the reasons for past defeats, the authors find few signs that privilege and special-interest lobbies are on the verge of yielding to the "larger interests of society" or, for that matter, that the American medical community and its public are prepared to curtail their demands for more and more expensive medical interventions. [6]

Interested readers may wish to supplement these readings with full-length sources on the historical intricacies of the national health insurance controversy. Sociologist Paul Starr's Pulitzer Prize–winning history of the medical establishment, *The Social Transformation of American Medicine*, is a comprehensive work that nevertheless accords ample treatment to the origins and direction of voluntary and compulsory health insurance in America. [7] Medical historian Ronald L. Numbers, in *Almost Persuaded: American Physicians and Compulsory Health Insurance, 1912–1920*, concentrates on the years when providers first seriously considered social insurance for illness, a time during which organized medicine advanced and then withdrew its support for the program. [8] Daniel S. Hirshfield's *The Lost Reform: The Campaign for Compulsory Health Insurance in the United States from 1932 to 1943* also circumscribes a particular phase of the legislative contest. It covers the unsuccessful drive to write health insurance into the Social Security Act during the New Deal and renewed attempts at enactment during the first half of World War II, culminating in the Wagner-Murray-Dingell

bill. [9] In *Harry S. Truman Versus the Medical Lobby: The Genesis of Medicare*, Monte M. Poen examines the years following the war and President Truman's spirited, if frustrated, advocacy of national health insurance, which had a host of unanticipated repercussions—including arousing what may have been the AMA's most concerted campaign against a political initiative and preparing the way for the passage of Medicare in 1965. [10]

To be sure, not all writers have presented or perceived the history of national health insurance in the same way. Daniel M. Fox has decried what he sees as a tendentious consensus on the subject among historians. [11] The majority of them, he has repeatedly alleged, have devoted their attention to American policymakers' rejection of proposed plans for universal health insurance coverage—largely ignoring the measures taken that did respond to the growing demand for medical care. Although history comprises both those debates that bear policy fruit and those that do not, Fox's work should remind us that national health insurance has yet to prove itself inevitable in the United States. At this point, that may well be the sole indisputable conclusion that we can draw from the literature.

Notes

1. The term "national health insurance" did not gain much currency until after a 1937 Supreme Court ruling on the constitutionality of federally sponsored social insurance plans. Discussions of "compulsory health insurance" during the 1910s, 1920s, and 1930s generally referred to state-level plans, although the term was used in later years to refer to national plans. For the sake of simplicity, however, we will refer to national health insurance throughout. See *Compulsory Health Insurance: The Continuing American Debate*, ed. Ronald L. Numbers (Westport, CT: Greenwood Press, 1982), x.
2. Daniel M. Fox, "The Decline of Historicism: The Case of Compulsory Health Insurance in the United States," *Bulletin of the History of Medicine* 57, no. 4, (Winter 1983): 596–610.
3. Odin Anderson, "Health Insurance in the United States, 1910–1920," *Journal of the History of Medicine and Allied Sciences* 5 (1950): 363–96.
4. Ronald L. Numbers, "The Third Party: Health Insurance in America," in *The Therapeutic Revolution: Essays in the Social History of American Medicine*, edited by Morris J. Vogel and Charles E. Rosenberg (Philadelphia: University of Pennsylvania Press, 1979), 177–200. For a concise overview of the waxing and waning of national health insurance in America, see the preface to Numbers's *Compulsory Health Insurance: The Continuing American Debate* (Westport, CT: Greenwood Press, 1982).
5. Stacey T. Cyphert and James E. Rohrer, "A National Medical Care Program: Review and Synthesis of Past Proposals, *Journal of Public Health Policy* (Winter 1988): 456–72.
6. Samuel Levey and James Hill, "National Health Insurance: The Triumph of Equivocation," *New England Journal of Medicine* 321, no. 25 (December 21, 1989): 1750–154.

7. Paul Starr, *The Social Transformation of American Medicine*, (New York: Basic Books, 1982).

8. Ronald L. Numbers, *Almost Persuaded: American Physicians and Compulsory Health Issues, 1912–1920* (Baltimore: Johns Hopkins University Press, 1978).

9. Daniel S. Hirshfield, *The Lost Reform: The Campaign for Compulsory Health Insurance in the United States from 1932 to 1943* (Cambridge, MA: Harvard University Press, 1980).

10. Monte M. Poen, *Harry S. Truman versus the Medical Lobby: The Genesis of Medicare* (Columbia: University of Missouri Press, 1979).

11. Fox, "The Decline of Historicism." For a more detailed statement and a comparison of the role of national health insurance in the historiography of health policy in Britain and the United States, see also Daniel M. Fox, *Health Policies, Health Politics: The British and American Experience, 1911–1965* (Princeton, NJ: Princeton University Press, 1986).

1

Transformation in Defeat:
The Changing Objectives of
National Health Insurance, 1915–1980

Paul Starr

The persistence of a social movement over a long period sometimes obscures slow changes in its underlying purposes and sources of inspiration and support. The campaign for a government-sponsored program of health insurance in the United States has stretched over nearly three-fourths of a century, but insofar as it still continues it is no longer the same struggle it started out to be. As American political life and the economics of health care have changed, the objectives of reform have subtly shifted, and the idea of health insurance as a public program has undergone a complete transformation. National health insurance[1] has always been concerned with relieving the economic problems of sickness. However, there are different types of cost associated with sickness, and reformers have gradually shifted their focus of concern from one type to another. The costs of sickness for individual households have two principal components: the cost of lost earning and disruption of family life (sometimes termed "indirect" costs), and the cost of medical care. These costs fall not only upon individuals, but also in their aggregate upon society at large, which experiences costs in diminished production and lost national income as well as a total medical bill. Accordingly, sickness creates costs of four general kinds: individual income and other indirect losses,

the indirect social costs of sickness, individual medical costs, and the social costs of medical care.[2]

During the twentieth century, reformers have shifted their attention, at the individual level, from lost earnings to medical costs, as health insurance has become more concerned with health care financing than income maintenance. Second, they have dropped their initial emphasis on the indirect social costs of sickness, which they originally expected insurance would reduce, as health insurance has become increasingly divorced from public health. And, third, in recent years they have begun fundamentally to recast health insurance as a means of controlling and perhaps even reducing the social costs of medical care as national health insurance has become increasingly viewed as an instrument of institutional reorganization and (social) cost containment.

These changes have taken place for two sorts of reasons—first, enormous changes in the economics of health and medical care; and second, more general changes in American society that inevitably affect the politics and ideology of reform. This history can be conveniently divided into three periods: (1) the early twentieth century, or Progressive era, when health insurance was introduced in America as a program of income maintenance for wage earners and, its advocates maintained, disease prevention and increased national efficiency; (2) the period from the 1930s to the 1960s when health insurance became a program primarily of medical care financ-

ing to distribute individual risks and expand the access of lower- and middle-income groups to increasingly expensive services; and, finally, (3) the most recent period beginning in the 1970s, when health insurance evolved into a program of cost control and institutional reform as well as universal coverage.

For convenience, I shall call these three phases Progressive Health Insurance, Expansionary Health Insurance, and Containment Health Insurance.

Progressive Health Insurance

The historical origins of health insurance as a public program are linked more to concerns about income maintenance, national economic power, and political stability than they are to the financing of medical care. Prior to any national programs, many workers in both Europe and America were insured through sickness funds sponsored by mutual societies, unions, and employers; the principal function of these funds was to provide cash benefits in sickness ("sick pay") to make up for lost wages. When European governments first made such insurance compulsory for wage earners or began subsidizing voluntary funds, compensating for individual wage losses was still their principal function; paying for medical care was secondary. Sickness insurance (as it originally was called) was instituted as part of a general program of social insurance against the chief risks that interrupted continuity of income: industrial accidents, sickness and disability, old age and unemploy-

Reprinted with permission from the *American Journal of Public Health* 72, no. 1 (January 1982), pp. 78–88. Copyright © 1982 American Public Health Association.

ment (typically covered by governmental programs in that sequence). [3] Bismarck in Germany and other leaders elsewhere were consciously seeking to attach the loyalty of workers to the state and to deny socialism its sources of appeal; thus social insurance was a defensive program, inaugurated first by authoritarian and later by liberal regimes, to integrate workers into the society and stabilize the political order. [4] Political leaders also believed there would be a dividend in the increased health and efficiency of the labor force and the army. As England's Lloyd George put it in a memorable phrase, "You can not maintain an A-l empire with a C-3 population."[5] For all these reasons—income maintenance, the preemption of socialism, increased efficiency and power—social insurance programs, including sickness insurance, were extended initially to wage earners and only later to their dependents and other people.

This background colored the campaign for health insurance in the United States, which began in earnest about 1915, after most of the major European countries had adopted either a compulsory program or subsidies to voluntary plans. As in Europe, interest in health insurance developed soon after the passage of insurance against industrial accidents. In America, however, reformers outside government, rather than political leaders, took the initiative in advocating health insurance. Some were socialists—indeed, the Socialist Party in 1904 was the first to endorse health insurance—and even those who were not, such as the members of the American Association for Labor Legislation (AALL), the leading organization in the campaign, generally supported the rights of trade unions. Hence the proposal did not come into political debate in America under anti-socialist sponsorship, as it had in both Germany and England. Yet the AALL's bill followed European precedent in placing an income ceiling on participation and aiming to improve workers' health on grounds of industrial efficiency as well as social equity. Its program applied only to manual workers and others, except for domestic and casual employees, earning less than $1,200 a year. The benefits included both medical aid and sick pay (at two-thirds wages for up to 26 weeks, except during hospitalization, when it fell to one-third wages). Dependents were eligible for the medical benefits. The costs, estimated at four percent of wages, were to be divided among employers and workers, each of whom was to pay two-fifths, and the state, which would contribute the remaining one-fifth. The employers' share increased for the lowest-income workers. A worker earning $600 a year, the AALL estimated, would pay eighty cents a month out of a premium of two dollars. [6]

The reformers formulated the case for health insurance in terms of two objectives. They wanted, first, to relieve poverty caused by sickness by distributing individual wage losses and medical costs through insurance. And, second, they wanted to reduce the social costs of illness by providing effective medical care and creating monetary incentives for disease prevention. This mixture of concerns was typical of the social Progressives. On the one hand, in emphasizing the relief of poverty, they made an appeal to moral compassion; on the other, in emphasizing prevention and increased national efficiency, they made an appeal to economic rationality. [7] Combining social meliorism with the ideals of efficiency fitted perfectly into Progressive ideology. It also reflected the political conditions of a democratic capitalist society, which made it incumbent upon reformers to gain the support of both the public and powerful business interests. Progressive health insurance was shaped by these political realities as well as the economics of sickness and health care of the time.

For the Progressives, the economic problem at the individual level involved both lost earnings and medical costs. Among individual workers, income losses appeared then to be greater than health care costs, but for families as a whole they were about the same. In a 1913 study, I. M. Rubinow—a doctor and actuary, a socialist, a founder of the AALL, and a leading authority on social insurance—put the average daily wage loss at $1.50 and average medical costs at $1.00 a day[8]; in 1916, B. S. Warren and Edgar Sydenstricker of the U.S. Public Health Service estimated the daily wage loss at $2.00 and medical costs at $1.00. [9]

The most exhaustive empirical investigation of the period, conducted for an Illinois health insurance commission, found that among wage earners sick one week or more, lost wages were four times the costs of medical care. However, for families with disabling illnesses in the course of a year, the difference was not as great because of the additional medical expenses of dependents: lost wages averaged $54.95 and direct outlays for medical care $43.03 (4.2 and 3.3 percent, respectively, of average annual incomes of $1,300). Among all families, including those that had no disabling illnesses, the wage loss and medical costs were about the same. [10]

The case for insurance rested on the unequal distribution of individual losses. The Illinois commission showed that a small proportion of families suffered large losses of income; one in seven men sick one week or more lost more than 20 percent of annual earnings, not counting medical costs. Many such households were already at the edge of poverty when the breadwinner was healthy. The proportion who could not "make ends meet" increased to 16.6 percent among families with serious illness, compared to 4.7 percent among those without. Advocates of health insurance also cited data from charities indicating that sickness was the leading immediate cause of poverty; the Illinois commission, making one of the most conservative estimates, found it to be the chief factor in one-fourth to one-third of the charity cases in the state. [11]

To "eliminate sickness as a cause of poverty," as Rubinow defined the chief aim of health insurance, a compulsory system would distribute the losses not only among workers, but also among employers and the state since workers were not alone responsible for the conditions that caused sickness. Such a program had to be compulsory, he argued, to make it universal (that is, among low-income wage earners) and to secure contributions from employers and the public. A voluntary scheme would miss the majority of workers in need of income protection who simply could not afford the mutual benefit plans of fraternal societies and unions, much less the little commercial health insurance that was then available. [12] Yet most reformers were not advocating any radical transfer of income; they spoke of health insurance, like all social insurance, as a program primarily of income stabilization rather than income redistribution. The interest they claimed to represent was a public interest in preventing poverty and disease, not a special interest of labor. In fact, to their political embarrassment, the American Federation of Labor (though not all its member unions or state federations) opposed the program. Samuel Gompers, president of the AFL, repeatedly denounced compulsory health insurance as an unnecessary, paternalistic reform that would create a system of state supervision of the people's health. Gompers, who always insisted that workers had to rely on their own economic power rather than the state, was concerned that a government insurance system would weaken unions by denying them the function of providing social benefits, which in his own experience was a key to building trade union solidarity. [13]

There was, indeed, a solicitous, if not paternalistic, attitude implicit in the second half of the reformers' case for health insurance. In the language of the AALL's letterhead, health insurance had as its aim the "conservation of human resources," seen as analogous to conservation of natural resources. Irving Fisher, then one of the country's most eminent economists, argued in a presidential address to the AALL in 1916 that health insurance would have its greatest value in stimulating preventive measures and hence was needed not just "to tide workers over the grave emergencies incident to illness," but also "to reduce illness itself, lengthen life, abate poverty, improve working power, raise the wage level, and diminish the causes of industrial discontent." [14] Warren and Sydenstricker expected that by assigning insurance contributions to industry, workers, and the community, a compulsory insurance scheme would induce them to adopt public health measures to prevent disease and save money. [15] Reformers were, in short, suggesting that despite additional expenditures for treatment, prevention, and sick pay, health insurance would yield a net savings in social costs and accordingly greater economic efficiency.

This argument was meant to appeal to business. Earlier in the decade, many employers had concluded that the benefits of compulsory insurance against industrial accidents outweighed its costs. The increasing unpre- dictability of liability judgments had convinced them to accept a system of compensation that would limit and stabilize their losses. No such direct economic advantage interested them in health insurance, which they saw as a de facto rise in wages, and this difference decisively affected their response. The National Industrial Conference Board, a research organization established by major industrial trade associations, agreed that sickness was a serious handicap on the "social well-being and productive efficiency of the nation," but argued that direct investment in public health measures would have a higher return than investment in cash benefits for the sick. Compulsory health insurance would not "materially reduce the amount of sickness"; the incentives for prevention would not work because the responsibility for most sickness could not be fixed. Indeed, days lost from work might increase because sick pay encouraged malingering; the board cited statistics indicating days lost from work on account of sickness had increased in Germany after insurance was enacted. Nor would health insurance greatly reduce poverty. The figures suggesting sickness caused poverty ignored other causes; also, many charity cases would not have had health insurance because they were casual workers, self-employed, or unemployed. The large sums spent on health insurance would benefit only part of the population; in New York, the board calculated, the insurance bill would cover only one-third of the population. [16]

In response to criticism that health insurance was too costly, Progressive reformers answered that it involved no new cost at all. It merely distributed over society the income losses and medical costs that individual families already faced. Reformers did not talk of any need to spend more money or recognize any likelihood that health insurance might inadvertently increase social costs. They believed, however, that health insurance had to be properly designed to prevent abuses. In particular, sick

pay represented a potentially serious cost-control problem. If patients were certified for sick pay by their doctor and had free choice of physician, certification might be all too easy to come by. Consequently, the AALL proposal recommended separating treatment from certification; the local funds charged with administering insurance were to employ physicians to do nothing but verify sick pay claims. In addition, reformers recommended that doctors be paid on a capitation basis rather than by visit; or, if paid by visit, that the local fund make such payments out of a fixed budget determined by the number insured in its area. European experience had clearly indicated that per capita arrangements were critical in maintaining limits on expenditures. [17]

The Progressive reformers also hoped to use health insurance to bring about even more radical changes in medical service than had been attempted elsewhere. Rubinow saw health insurance as an opportunity to encourage a shift from individual general practice to specialized group practice under governmental control. [18] Michael M. Davis. Jr., director of the Boston Dispensary, also advocated more specialism and organization. The initially positive response in 1915 of leaders of the American Medical Association to the AALL's approaches on health insurance encouraged Davis that America might be able to "improve on" Britain and Germany. In a letter to the AALL's John Andrews, he wrote that "we ought to aim to get started in such a way that we are not tied to a system of individualized private practice without creating a definite opening for development along the lines of cooperative medical work in diagnosis and treatment." Davis added that he had "a good many ideas on organization" since visiting the Mayo Clinic. [19]

But physicians were unlikely to be enthusiastic about such ideas. They strongly objected to any form of "contract practice" (i.e., capitation payment) as a result of their experience with fraternal lodges and industrial firms that forced them to bid against each other for group business. Workmen's compensation had biased many of them against any kind of insurance. As private practitioners learned more about health insurance, their opposition mounted, and capitation payment, much less group practice, became politically unrealistic. Reformers attempted to placate professional opposition by surrendering to virtually all the physicians' demands, but the concessions were futile. The organized profession, which had shown an early interest in health insurance, became instrumental in its defeat. [20]

Reformers ran into perhaps their most implacable opponent, the insurance industry, also partly because of their desire to achieve new efficiencies in social organization. Progressive health insurance plans included a death or "funeral" benefit, amounting to $50 or $100. Today, the inclusion of such a benefit must seem odd, but it was crucial at the time. In the early twentieth century, life insurance companies sold "industrial" policies to working-class families that provided lump-sum payments at death generally used to pay for funerals and the expenses of the final illness. This industrial life insurance was the backbone of commercial insurance; both Metropolitan Life and Prudential had risen to the top of the industry by successfully marketing industrial policies. Out of small payments of 10, 15, and 25 cents a week, two of the largest financial institutions of the day had been built. But because the premiums were paid on a weekly basis and lapses were frequent, industrial insurance had to be marketed by an army of insurance agents who visited their clients, usually the women of the family, as soon after payday as possible. Consequently, the administrative costs of industrial insurance were staggering; the workers who bought the policies received in benefits only about 40 cents of every dollar they paid in premiums. [21] Yet the fear of a pauper burial was so great that the policies were extremely popular. According to Warren and Sydenstricker, a 1901 Bureau of Labor study of 2,567 families disclosed that 65.8 percent had annual expenditures for such insurance averaging $29.55 per family, while 76.7 percent had expenditures for sickness and death averaging $26.78 per family. Compulsory insurance would have entirely eliminated the huge cost of marketing industrial policies, not to mention the profits. Hence

reformers claimed that they could finance much of the cost of health insurance out of the money wasted on industrial insurance policies. [22] In effect, instead of paying insurance agents to visit them weekly, wage-earning families could pay for doctors and nurses to visit them in sickness. So the inclusion of funeral benefits was not an idiosyncratic choice by Progressive reformers; it was part of their general program for increased social efficiency. Probably no other measure stimulated more opposition, since compulsory insurance would have pulled the rug from under the multimillion dollar industrial life insurance business. Ironically, compulsory health insurance failed to win the support of business and financial interests, not only because they found unpersuasive the claims for an efficiency dividend from effective prevention and treatment, but also because the greater efficiency of compulsory insurance threatened to eliminate an important source of profit for the insurance industry and of investment capital for American business.

Expansionary Health Insurance

The economic objectives and rhetorical appeals, as well as the content of health insurance proposals, changed by the time the idea was revived during the New Deal and even more so after World War II.

Between the 1930s and 1960s, reformers made several distinct efforts to enact compulsory health insurance. During the early New Deal, the planners of social security tried to persuade President Franklin D. Roosevelt to include health insurance in the new system. In the late 1930s, many of the same people backed renewed proposals for federal sponsorship of health insurance at the state level, where campaigns were also in progress. Then with the Wagner-Murray-Dingell bill, first introduced in Congress in 1943, and President Harry Truman's health program of 1945, advocates of government health insurance moved to a genuinely national plan. Finally, limiting their efforts to the aged and the poor, they ultimately secured the passage of Medicare and Medicaid in 1965. But despite important changes

in strategy and substance, the insurance proposals throughout this period rested on some common assumptions about individual and social costs that distinguish them from plans of the Progressive era and those that emerged later in the 1970s.

First of all, reformers dropped the funeral benefit, to which they attributed much of the responsibility for the defeat of health insurance in the Progressive era. It no longer seemed worth the fight.

Second, by the 1930s reformers had become more concerned with medical costs than lost wages. The creation in 1927 of the Committee on the Costs of Medical Care (CCMC) underlined the shifting emphasis, even in its name. I.S. Falk, a member of the staff, estimated that medical costs were 20 percent higher than lost earnings for families with incomes under $1,200 a year and nearly 85 percent higher for families earning between $1,200 and $2,500. The relatively higher cost of medical care was "a new condition, different from what prevailed in other times and in other countries when they faced the problem of planning for economic security against sickness." [23] Reformers such as Falk continued to advocate cash benefits in sickness, but they proposed that it be entirely separated from health insurance, which now became almost exclusively concerned with medical services. Writing in 1937, Michael Davis commented, "The development of health insurance has shown a steady but slow change from the economic to the medical emphasis." Not only was medical care now a bigger item in family budgets than wage losses, but "medical care is also more important than income protection because the provision of adequate medical service, curative and preventive, holds large possibilities for relieving suffering and for the positive promotion of health and economic efficiency." [24]

Such premises led to a somewhat altered justification for health insurance. Two considerations now prevailed—increasing medical costs and unmet medical "needs." The costs of services were rising to the point that not only wage earners, but also people of "moderate means," were finding them hard to meet. And as a result of this economic barrier, society was failing to meet individuals' health care needs.

The rise in medical costs had its origins before the Progressive proposals had been made, but the impact of change was not yet fully felt nor clearly understood until the 1920s. The increase came in the costs of both physicians' services and hospital care, but especially the latter. The rise in physicians' costs had two sources: improvement in the quality of services, as a result of scientific advance and increased investment in required education, and increasing monopoly power, as a result of licensing restrictions and other practices that by the 1920s were giving doctors significantly higher returns than their investment in education would have justified.[25] The rise in hospital costs had its origins in the complete transformation in the nature of hospital care. Before 1870, hospitals were caretakers for the chronically ill, operating on a low-budget basis as charities, but as they became centers for surgery and acute medical work, their construction and operating costs soared beyond the capacity of charity to support them. As hospital care became more common and as hospitals increasingly derived more of their income from services to patients, hospital charges grew.[26] But their cost was still relatively low when the insurance plans of the Progressive era were formulated. Among 211 families surveyed in 1918 in Columbus, Ohio, by the U.S. Bureau of Labor Statistics, hospital costs averaged only 7.6 percent of a total medical bill averaging $48.41 (of which about half went to physicians).[27] Consequently, the Progressives gave relatively little attention to hospital costs or the problems of hospital reimbursement. By 1929, according to the CCMC, hospital costs (not including doctors' and private nurses' hospital bills) were 13 percent of a total family medical bill averaging $108.[28] In 1934, Davis put hospital bills and physicians' bills for in-hospital services at 40 percent of total family medical costs. However, the key point, as Davis observed, was not just the growing average cost of medical care, but the increasing *variance* of costs as a result of exceptionally high hospital bills in a small number of serious illnesses. This new situation was respon-

sible for the middle-class complaints that had focused attention on the problem of rising medical costs *before* the Depression. "In former years," Davis wrote, "when the range of sickness costs was lower, and few illnesses caused high expenditures, families with middle-class incomes felt financial pinch due to sickness much less frequently than today. Now, people who are economically secure, humanly speaking, are not secure against the costs of sickness. Thus, the economic problems of medical care now implicate not merely wage earners but the whole population, except the 5 percent with the largest incomes."[29]

It was, of course, precisely in this period that voluntary insurance primarily against hospital costs began to emerge as the predominant form that health insurance would take in America—a far cry from what Progressive reformers had intended. But as hospital charges were rising for patients, the hospitals in the Depression faced a financial crisis of their own, and they actively cooperated in creating Blue Cross plans as a means of meeting it.[30] In fact, it might be said that while advocates of a government program were trying to improve the access of patients to medical care, the founders of Blue Cross succeeded in improving the access of hospitals to patients.

Most advocates of health insurance regarded the social costs of medical care, estimated by the CCMC at about four percent of national income, as not at all excessive.[31] Indeed, the reformers believed that people needed more medical care than they were receiving. Beginning with the CCMC, policy analyses typically began with estimates of the "need" for medical care or the "health needs" of the nation.[32] According to the CCMC, the need for medical care, as defined by professional standards, was higher than the rate of utilization even among the highest income group[33]; thus, presumably everyone needed more, and America would have to devote more of its resources to health care. In fact, instead of health insurance merely being a means of covering existing costs, as the Progressives had seen it, reformers now spoke of insurance as a way of budgeting larger expenditures. In the Introduction to the CCMC's final staff

report, committee chairman Ray Lyman Wilbur wrote, "More money must be spent for medical care; and this is practicable if the expenditures can be budgeted and can be made through fixed, periodic payments—even as people are enabled to spend more for other commodities by installment than by outright purchase."[34] Falk, too, wrote that "the same procedures which will distribute sickness costs . . . will enable people to budget them and therefore spend more money for useful health and medical services, and will also provide larger and more assured incomes for those who render medical services."[35] And President Truman, introducing his program in 1945, cited the estimate that Americans spent four percent of their income on medical care and declared, "We can afford to spend more for health."[36]

Thus health insurance was evolving from a means of distributing wage losses and medical costs into an expansionary financing measure. Its chief concern became increasing access to health care rather than income protection. And whereas the Progressives had been thinking of insurance for low-income workers, reformers now had in mind the middle class as well. By Truman's proposal national health insurance was to cover salary as well as wage earners, self-employed businessmen, professionals, domestic and farm workers, and the poor in one comprehensive system.[37]

The proposals became expansionary in another sense: they dropped the cost-controls that the Progressives had wanted, such as capitation payment, and the earlier interest in organizational reform. Stung by the successful opposition of the medical profession in 1918–1920, reformers during the New Deal and after promised repeatedly that health insurance would not mean "socialized medicine." The Falk of 1936 did not sound like the Rubinow of 1916. Whereas Rubinow openly suggested that a state-administered medical system was ultimately the best solution, Falk insisted that health insurance was antithetical to state medicine: "Health insurance is not a system of medical practice. . . . It is always and everywhere consistent with the private practice of medicine."[38]

Truman stated that under his plan "our people would continue to get medical and hospital services just as they do now." Hospitals and doctors would be permitted to choose whatever method of remuneration they desired; and, furthermore, doctors would have a right to expect higher average incomes. [39]

The desirability of expanding medical services and a general willingness to accommodate the interests of doctors and hospitals characterized almost all public and private programs in this period. National health insurance proposals only reflected the general climate. Especially after World War II, when the federal government began extensively subsidizing hospital construction and medical research, public policy took as its principal objective the expansion of needed medical resources. Rather than correcting distributional inequities, the policies favored growth—a characteristic of most American social policy, particularly in the postwar era.

The same expansionary premises characterized the private health insurance system and the policies the federal government adopted toward it. The government aided the spread of private insurance by excluding health insurance benefits from wage controls during World War II and by excluding employers' contributions to health insurance from taxable income. The tax exemption for employers' contributions (now worth about 40 percent of the value of health insurance premiums to the average family, making it one of the largest federal expenditures on health care) became a growing insurance subsidy primarily for the middle class and unionized workers. The effect of the exemption was to encourage employees to take wage increases in fringe benefits for health insurance rather than cash; the exemption thus pumped money into medical care. Moreover, the private insurers, competing with one another, exerted no countervailing power against physicians and hospitals: antitrust laws forbade them from joining together to limit fees and rates. It was easier for insurance companies to raise their own rates than to pursue effective cost controls; besides, the higher the total volume of expenditures, the greater their profits. The long-run outcome was a system of

health insurance that channeled a growing proportion of national income into health care and in no way infringed on the physicians' prerogatives to set prices and control their work.

Medicare and Medicaid did not fundamentally change this pattern. Although the government filled some of the gaps in the private insurance system, it followed the same pattern of accommodation to professional and institutional interests by not challenging the established payment system. Medicare, in particular, provided extremely favorable terms for reimbursing both doctors and hospitals. Payment to physicians was based on the history of their past charges and the level of fees in their communities; hence doctors had every incentive to push up their fees to raise the allowable levels of reimbursement. They could also choose to charge patients more than Medicare would pay. Medicare reimbursed hospitals on the basis of their costs, and allowed the hospitals to choose whichever of two means of computing their costs was most favorable to them. By paying hospitals according to their costs, Medicare did not discourage them from having higher costs, since higher costs would mean higher reimbursements. [40] Medicaid allowed nursing homes to figure depreciation into their costs and encouraged an elaborate legal game of buying and selling homes at increasingly extravagant prices to jack up their rates. [41] That such arrangements contributed to a surge in medical, hospital, and nursing home costs—from 5.9 to 9.1 percent of the gross national product (GNP) between 1965 and 1979—should have surprised no one. [42]

Not all of the increase in social costs in the decades after World War II can be attributed to the insurance system. The new public investment programs in hospitals and research played a part, as did the general growth in technological development and public expectations. In the same period, almost all the major industrial nations saw dramatic increases in the share of their resources devoted to medical care. But two sources of evidence indicate that financial and organizational structures matter a great deal. The most dramatic exception to the inflationary pattern in medical costs

has been Great Britain. With a national health service providing free care to its entire population, the British have nonetheless been able to hold medical costs to about five percent of their GNP. (Nor does the existence of a private sector in British medicine contradict the pattern of containment: private services account for only about five percent of the total.) The medical budget in Britain is set at the national level and must compete for funds with defense, education, and other areas; in America, medical expenditures are fragmented and even much of the public expenditure, under Medicare and Medicaid, is administratively uncontrollable.

The other dramatic example of successful cost containment has, of course, been the American prepaid health plan (or "health maintenance organization"), where costs have run 20 to 30 percent below fee-for-service medicine, primarily because of reduced hospitalization. [43] Like the British system, the prepaid plans have a single fixed budget that places constraints on professional decision-making; they also have to negotiate rates with large groups of subscribers. The evidence suggests that without the constraints provided by concentrated budgeting and countervailing power, whether at the national or organizational levels, costs are almost impossible to control. [44]

But America turned away from the type of system that would have provided these cost-control mechanisms. Earlier in the century there were alternatives to private insurance for spreading individual medical costs. The prepayment systems, such as contract practice in mutual benefit societies and later prepaid group practice plans, represented nongovernmental health services with fixed budgets. But these forms were bitterly opposed by private practitioners, partly because they gave organized consumers greater countervailing power in the market. "Contract practice" survived only as long as there were struggling young physicians willing to take positions. As the profession's market power increased with the falling supply of doctors in the wake of the Flexnerian cutback in medical education, there were fewer practitioners willing to accept contracts with fraternal lodges and employers; the fraternal and company plans also suffered because of their status as second-class medicine. The prepaid group practice plans, which began in the 1930s as medical cooperatives, aroused boycotts and blacklists by local medical societies. Even though these actions resulted in a conviction of the AMA under the Sherman Antitrust Act, professional resistance generally succeeded in preventing prepaid plans from proliferating. The plans also faced difficulties in meeting start-up costs, as did Blue Cross. But Blue Cross plans had the aid of hospitals in underwriting their risks, cooperation from the medical profession, and favorable state legislation. Some states, under professional pressure, outlawed prepaid group practice plans entirely.[45]

Whether national health insurance would have controlled costs more effectively than private insurance depends on when it might have been enacted and what direction it would have taken. A plan enacted along the lines of the earlier Progressive proposals, with capitation payment and/or fixed local budgets for medical services, might have held down physicians' costs. But like the English system, it would have later faced difficulties in its relations to hospitals; and only if the principle of fixed budgeting had been maintained might it have been able to control costs. On the other hand, the health insurance plans of the expansionary phase might well have landed us in as deep water as we are in now, though such a system would have made the costs more politically visible earlier and might have prompted a more effective response.

The campaign for health insurance in America failed, in any event, because the political conditions that brought about its adoption in Europe were not replicated here. In Europe social insurance emerged from the conflict between socialist movements and conservative regimes with a paternalistic tradition of social legislation. In America, there was neither the powerful socialist movement from below nor the paternalistic or authoritarian regime above. And, indeed, the history of health insurance betrays a lack of both popular support from underneath and unified elite sponsorship from on top. The calculations of

cost partly derive from political conditions: had there been more of a socialist challenge here, business might have changed its estimate of the benefits of health insurance.

But the repeated defeat of national health insurance did not prevent the United States from gradually adopting a national health insurance policy. By the end of the expansionary phase, the U.S. had a program of tax subsidies for the middle- and upper-income employees with private insurance; a program of compulsory hospital insurance and subsidized voluntary medical insurance for the aged; and a noncontributory, federally subsidized state insurance program for the poor. This system was not universal, and it certainly was not progressive. Perhaps one-tenth of the population still had no insurance, and much of the private insurance provided inadequate coverage. Still, it was a system, and with only marginal changes it could cover the entire population. But before it could be made universal, it was overtaken by the problems of social cost that it had helped create.

Containment Health Insurance

In the mid-1970s, America entered a new stage in the history of health insurance. Many people may be puzzled by that remark. After all, no national health insurance program was adopted, nor was there any fundamental reorganization of medical services. One might well be impressed by the continuity of historical experience: the recurrence once again in the 1970s of campaigns for reform and the expectation that their triumph was inevitable, followed by their defeat and the persistence of existing institutions. This continuity is unmistakable. But while Americans continued discussing national health insurance and the economic problems of medical care, what they were discussing once again changed. The center of debate moved from distributing individual medical costs to controlling the social costs of medicine, and with that shift came fundamental changes in their assumptions and outlook for the future.

Until recently, there was little thought that the share of national in-

come going to health care was excessive. Government and foundation reports well into the 1960s generally presumed the wisdom of increased investment in health care. Hospital construction, medical research, and medical education continued to receive subsidies for expansion. The problem of medical costs was understood fundamentally to be a problem of their uneven incidence over individuals and over time—the solution for which was insurance.

The dispute over the extent and control of insurance obscured a more basic consensus in the postwar period that third-party, fee-for-service payment was an appropriate and sufficient means of managing medical expenses. In the 1970s that belief broke down, and many concluded that the method we use to spread individual costs increases social costs unacceptably. Even though the problem of equitably distributing costs (and services) remains, the chief preoccupation now is how social costs may be limited.

It hardly needs pointing out that the concern with cost control reflects the condition of the economy and particularly the uneasiness over inflation. As one of the four most inflationary sectors of the economy (the others have been energy, food, and housing), medical care is an inevitable target of anti-inflation policies. But even if fiscal and inflationary pressures were to subside, the search for cost restraints in medical care would persist. For medical costs cause concern not only because of their magnitude, but also because of increasing skepticism about their legitimacy. The studies, frequently reported in the press, of unnecessary surgery, excess hospital capacity, duplication of technology, and so on reflect a crisis of confidence in the value of medical services and methods of resource allocation. Similar doubts now surround education, welfare programs, and many other areas of social policy. Rising costs and diminished confidence set the debate about health insurance today in a new context: the old reformers, as well as the physicians, took the value of medical care for granted. They just wanted more of it for everybody. Now reformers want less of some services, more of others, but most of all, control of what it all adds up to.

The rising costs of medical care have also now begun to disturb some powerful institutions that feel the brunt of them. Corporations object to the burgeoning costs of fringe benefits for health care; General Motors, for example, has been widely (though mistakenly) publicized as paying more to Blue Cross than to any steel manufacturer or other supplier. Unions, too, are uneasy: they find it harder to secure pay increases for their members because the "fringes" soak up so much of their gains. Faced by these pressures, both corporations and unions have been agitating for effective cost controls. The federal government has also faced fiscal pressures as a result of soaring costs in uncontrollable health programs. Medicare and Medicaid both provide an entitlement to coverage without limitation as to total cost. By fiscal year 1977, for example, Medicare and Medicaid outlays were double what they had been only three years earlier. Nor was the problem restricted to the federal government. In Los Angeles County, medical costs to the indigent increased from 24 to 42 percent of property tax revenues between 1968–69 and 1975–76. The rise of medical costs thus played a part in the California tax revolt of the late 1970s. State after state was forced to make cutbacks in health programs as medical costs increased.[46]

In the debate on national health insurance, which revived at the close of the 1960s, the social costs of medical care became a dominant concern only during and after the 1974–75 recession. The early 1970s saw a profusion of expansionary health insurance proposals. Sensing public pressure, the Nixon Administration presented its own alternative to the comprehensive public insurance system advocated by Senator Edward M. Kennedy. The Nixon plan would have mandated coverage by private employers—a regulatory approach to expanding health insurance that relied on copayments and other benefit limitations to control expenditures. Even the AMA felt obliged to advance a proposal for income-scaled tax credits to cover the premium cost of the "catastrophic" portion of health insurance.

Unlike the Administration's proposal, the AMA approach would have kept private insurance voluntary. This plan, as well as a proposal supported by the American Hospital Association, had few significant cost controls.[47]

With all sides acknowledging the need for change, observers widely believed that passage of some plan was imminent and that the only question was which kind. There appeared to be clear progress toward a political compromise. Between 1971 and 1974, the Nixon Administration moved toward a plan that was significantly more liberal in its benefits. By 1974, the estimated cost was about equal to the plan proposed by Senator Kennedy. "I consider the total [cost] as not a very significant figure," said Caspar Weinberger, Secretary of Health, Education, and Welfare (HEW), at a press conference in February 1974.[48] For his part, Senator Kennedy had joined with Representative Wilbur Mills, then the powerful chairman of the House Committee on Ways and Means, to support a plan that was more accommodating to the private insurance industry. In June 1974 Senator Kennedy announced, "A new spirit of compromise is in the air" and suggested a bill could reach the President's desk by the fall.[49] But the Watergate crisis prevented its enactment and soon the careers of both President Nixon and Representative Mills ended in political scandal. In addition, Kennedy had been unable to swing labor behind the Kennedy-Mills proposal; without any support from its natural constituency, the compromise plan had no chance in Congress.

During the second half of the 1970s, a stalling economy stalled the movement for national health insurance. In 1975, President Gerald Ford did not resubmit the Nixon health insurance plan on the grounds that it would exacerbate inflation. That same year, the AMA withdrew its support for the tax credit proposal. Labor and other supporters of a public insurance system decided to pass up opportunities for incremental legislation (e.g., to cover the unemployed) in the hope of a breakthrough after the next election. But even though presidential candidate Jimmy Carter had pledged to a universal health insurance plan, President Carter was

reluctant to press for a specific proposal because of inflation and slow economic growth. Ambivalent and timid, the Carter Administration let health insurance get backed up behind its proposals for welfare reform and hospital cost containment.[50]

However, during these years of impasse, the positions of liberals and conservatives underwent further evolution. On both sides there emerged proposals to combine national health insurance with a more general reorganization of the medical industry in the interests of cost control. In 1979, Senator Edward Kennedy—this time with the support of the AFL-CIO and other liberal organizations—introduced a compromise proposal that would have provided universal coverage while retaining private insurance plans. The new Kennedy initiative—basically a voucher system—incorporated many of the suggestions of market-oriented critics of the health industry aimed at fostering greater competition and rational decision making. Yet it also retained redistributive and planning mechanisms to achieve equity as well as cost containment. Introducing the proposal, Senator Kennedy predicted a "cross-over point" four years after enactment when the new system would cost less than if Congress allowed the present, incomplete insurance system to continue.[51]

Unwilling to accept Kennedy's leadership and under pressure to come up with its own plan, the Carter Administration finally adopted an incremental proposal to phase in national health insurance gradually as economic conditions permitted. It also included new regulatory and incentive mechanisms to contain costs, but there was a basic difference in outlook from the Kennedy plan. Kennedy saw national health insurance as an opportunity to reconstitute the health system on a new framework of incentives and bargaining relationships; improvements in cost control would accompany improvements in access. Hence national health insurance could resolve problems of individual and social cost simultaneously. Carter, on the other hand, regarded national health insurance as an onus the system could bear only if cost controls preceded it and the economy prospered. Hence the administration approached a plan reluctantly and never actively sought its enactment.

A more strictly market approach to national health insurance was meanwhile presented by Alain C. Enthoven, a Stanford economist and member of the Reagan transition team who developed his proposal originally as a consultant to HEW Secretary Joseph Califano. The basic principles of the Enthoven proposal—modeled after the Federal Employees' Health Benefits Program are: (1) multiple choice among competing private insurance and prepayment plans; and (2) "fixed-dollar" public subsidies to consumers through vouchers and tax credits. "The subsidy might be more for the poor than for the nonpoor, for old than for young, for families than individuals, but not more for people who choose more costly health plans," Enthoven wrote in his book *Health Plan*, modestly subtitled "The Only Practical Solution to the Soaring Cost of Medical Care."[52] Indeed, so vigorous have Enthoven's efforts been to associate the proposal with cost containment that some who have heard of it may not realize it is a national health insurance plan which, in its basic assumptions, is not significantly different from Kennedy's most recent proposal and from analogous "voucher" plans for education often favored by left-wing critics of the public schools.

At the end of the 1970s, all the major new national health insurance proposals were almost inseparably plans for cost containment. In the early 1970s, conservative proposals either echoed trade association views or offered limited additions to private insurance. By the late 1970s, some conservative health advisors adopted a market model of national health insurance that involved extensive structural change in the health industry. And, whereas at the beginning of the decade Senator Kennedy had favored a public insurance system with regulation from the "top" to control costs, by the decade's end he too accepted a system of private plans with a greater emphasis on incentives.

But while a new conception of national health insurance was emerging at the close of the 1970s, the bottom dropped out of the movement's political support. In the wake of Ronald Reagan's election, all such plans are off the national agenda. Conservatives no longer feel obliged to propose any version of national health insurance, and a good part of the progressive coalition has abandoned the idea in favor of a national health service. Ironically, both conservatives and many radicals agree that national health insurance would be unable to restrict cost increases. The conservatives see more health insurance as likely to reduce the cost-consciousness of patients, while the radicals lay the blame not on patients, but on the power and profit-mindedness of the providers. Between these convergent antagonists are the weary and divided advocates of national health insurance, trying to redefine the movement for an era of cost containment and conservative skepticism of social reform.

From the beginning, advocates of health insurance have tried to make a case for its economic rationality. In the Progressive era, the case rested on promised reductions in the social costs of illness and insurance and improvements in the productive efficiency of labor. This argument did not win reformers the support they anticipated. During the expansionary phase of health insurance, reformers still referred to the gains in efficiency from improved health, but the point became less central and the gains were expected to come from better treatment of illness rather than financial incentives for public health or the elimination of industrial insurance. Recently, health insurance supporters have revived the notion that reform will yield savings, but the savings now are to come primarily from eliminating unnecessary medical services rather than a more efficient and healthy population.

This new phase, however, creates its own distinct tensions. To make national health insurance into an instrument of cost containment—or, to use the voguish term, "rationing"—threatens its popular appeal. For however important questions of efficiency have been, questions of equity have always been the true moral basis of health insurance as a social movement. Today, however, health insurance seems less like a moral cause than an argument about economic management. What once would have been a statement of social equality is now, if carried out, likely to be an effort of financial rationalization. Like some of its advocates, the idea of national health insurance has passed from an idealistic youth to a kind of grim maturity.

Notes

1. I use the current term "national health insurance" in a generic sense to cover the various government-sponsored health insurance programs proposed since the Progressive era, even though the earliest plans were introduced into state legislatures rather than Congress.
2. These terms require explanation.

    (1) "Individual income and other indirect losses" should ideally include the unpaid time of family members lost in caring for the sick as well as income lost during sickness and from diminished earning capacity thereafter; however, estimates cited below include only lost wages. Moreover, individual losses, as usually conceived, include only those losses from sickness in an individual's own household, not the indirect losses from sickness in other households. Consequently, the sum of individual income losses does not equal the social costs of sickness. The costs to society would include reduced productivity among temporarily sick workers who nevertheless receive their customary wages. On the other hand, there is no social cost if one worker loses income on account of sickness but is replaced by another, otherwise unemployed, unless the new worker needs to be trained or is less productive.

    (2) Most estimates of individual medical costs cited below include only private medical expenditures (i.e., payments out of pocket and for insurance), whereas estimates of the social costs of medical care also include tax revenues spent on medical services. A more complete estimate of the social cost might include the opportunity cost of capital invested in the health sector that might be more productively invested elsewhere.
3. See Flora P. et al.: "On the Development of the Western European Welfare States," paper prepared for the International Political Science Association, Edinburgh, August 16–21, 1976, p. 22.
4. Rimlinger GV: *Welfare Policy and Industrialization in Europe, America and Russia* (New York: John Wiley, 1971).
5. Gilbert BB: *British Social Policy*. 1914–1939 (London: B.T. Batsford, 1970), p. 15; see

also Gilbert's earlier book. *The Evolution of National Insurance in Great Britain* (London: Michael Joseph, 1966), chapters 6 and 7.

6. For the AALL's "standard bill," see American Labor Legislation Review 6 (1969), 239–68. On the background of the AALL, see Irwin Yellowitz: *Labor and the Progressive Movement in New York State, 1897–1916* (Ithaca, NY: Cornell University Press, 1965), pp. 55–59. For a general treatment of the entire Progressive social insurance movement, see Roy Lubove: *The Struggle for Social Security 1900–1935* (Cambridge: Harvard University Press, 1970).

7. Yellowitz: *Labor and the Progressive Movement*, p. 85. Progressivism contained quite divergent tendencies, of which the "social Progressives" represent only one —and even they are difficult to characterize. For some major accounts of the Progressive period, see Hofstadter R: *The Age of Reform: From Bryan to F.D.R.* (New York: Random House, 1955); Mowry GE: *The Era of Theodore Roosevelt and the Birth of Modern America, 1900–1912* (New York: Harper & Row, 1958); and Weinstein J: *The Corporate Ideal in the Liberal State: 1900–1918* (Boston: Beacon Press, 1968); and for a contentious essay arguing that Progressivism was too diverse to be described as a movement, see Filene PG: An Obituary for The Progressive Movement, *American Quarterly* 22 (1970), pp. 20–34.

8. Rubinow IM: *Social Insurance* (New York: Henry Holt, 1916), p. 214.

9. Warren BS, Sydenstricker E: Health Insurance: Its Relation to Public Health, *Public Health Bulletin*, No. 76 (March 1916), p. 6.

10. Report of the Health Insurance Commission of Illinois, May 1, 1919, pp. 15–17, 204–11.

11. Ibid., pp. 18–22.

12. Rubinow: *Social Insurance*, pp. 264, 248–49, 281–98.

13. For an acrimonious confrontation between the socialist and conservative union viewpoints, see the testimony of Rubinow and Gompers and the exchanges between them in U.S. Congress, House Committee on Labor, Hearings Before the Committee on H.J. Resolution 159 . . . April 6 and 11, 1916, 64th Cong., 1st sess., pp. 36–45, 122–89. For Gompers' position, see also Samuel Gompers: Trade Union Health Insurance, *America Federationist* 23 (November 1916), 1072–74; Compulsory Sickness Insurance, *The National Civic Federation Review* 5 (April 1, 1920), p. 8; and Philip Taft: *The A.F. of L. in the Time of Gompers* (New York: Harper

and Row, 1957), pp. 364–65.

14. Fisher I: The Need for Health Insurance, *American Labor Legislation Review* 7 (March 1917), pp. 17–23.

15. Warren and Sydenstricker: Health Insurance: Its Relation to Public Health, p. 5. For the suggestion that the costs of sickness be calculated on the basis, not of lost earnings and medical expenses, but of the cost of "the services and equipment that suffice to prevent sickness," see Haven Emerson: The Social Cost of Sickness, American Labor Legislation Review 6 (March 1916).

16. National Industrial Conference Board: Sickness Insurance or Sickness Prevention? Research Report No. 6, May 1918. For similar arguments, see Frank F. Dresser: Suggestions Regarding Social Insurance, An Address Before the Conference on Social Insurance, Washington, DC, Dec. 4–9, 1916, National Association of Manufacturers pamphlet 46.

17. Alexander Lambert, medical advisor to the AALL and chairman of the AMA's social insurance committee, favored payment by visit under a fixed budget for physicians' services. See Lambert: Organization of Medical Benefits and Services Under the Proposed Sickness (Health) Insurance System, in: U.S. Department of Labor, Proceedings of the Conference on Social Insurance (Washington, DC: Govt Printing Office, 1917), pp. 655–59. The California insurance commission recommended capitation payment. See Report of the Social Insurance Commission of the State of California, March 1919 (Sacramento: California State Printing Office, 1919), p. 11.

18. Rubinow: *Social Insurance*, pp. 271–72.

19. Davis MM Jr, to Andrews JB, July 21, 1915, in *Papers of the American Association for Labor Legislation, 1905–1945* (Glen Rock, NJ: Microfilm Corporation of America, 1973), Reel 14.

20. See Numbers R: *Almost Persuaded: American Physicians and Compulsory Health Insurance, 1912–1920* (Baltimore: John Hopkins University Press, 1978).

21. Rubinow: *Social Insurance*, p. 420; Marquis James: *The Metropolitan Life: A Study in Business Growth* (New York: The Viking Press, 1974), pp. 73–93. As of 1915, Metropolitan held 34 percent and Prudential 39 percent of all industrial business. James, pp. 171–72.

22. Warren and Sydenstricker: *Health Insurance*, p. 54; Rubinow: *Social Insurance*, p. 420.

23. Falk IS: *Security Against Sickness* (Garden City, NY: Doubleday, Doran & Co., 1936), pp. 14–16.

24. Davis MM Jr, preface to Millis HA: *Sick-*

ness and Insurance (Chicago: University of Chicago Press, 1937), p. v.

25. Friedman M, Kuznets S: *Income from Independent Professional Practice* (New York: National Bureau of Economic Research, 1945); for an analysis of the process by which physicians transformed their growing cultural authority into economic power—a much more complex process than just limiting entry into the market—see my analysis in *The Social Transformation of American Medicine* (New York: Basic Books, 1982).

26. For a contemporary account of rising costs, see Goldwater SS: The Cost of Modern Hospitals, *National Hospital Record* 9 (November 1905), pp. 39–48.

27. Ohio Health and Old Age Insurance Commission: *Health, Health Insurance, Old Age Pensions* (Columbus, Ohio, 1919), p. 116.

28. Falk IS, Rorem R, Ring MD: *The Cost of Medical Care* (Chicago: University of Chicago Press, 1933), p. 89. The estimate was only for private expenditures; figuring in tax money spent on hospital care, the proportion of social costs for hospital care rose to 23 percent (p. 19).

29. Davis MM Jr: The American Approach to Health Insurance, *Milbank Memorial Fund Quarterly* 12 (July 1934), p. 211, 214–15.

30. Reed LS: *Blue Cross and Medical Service Plans* (Washington, DC: Federal Security Agency, 1947).

31. E.g., Falk, *Security Against Sickness*, p. 20.

32. See Falk, Rorem and Ring: *The Cost of Medical Care*, pp. 25–58, 70–79; Reed LS, *Health Insurance: The Next Step in Social Security* (New York: Harper and Brothers, 1937), pp. 21–33: Interdepartmental Committee to Coordinate Health and Welfare Activities: A National Health Program: Report of the Technical Committee on Medical Care, in *Proceedings of the National Health Conference, Washington, DC, July 18–20, 1938* (Washington, DC: Govt Printing Office, 1938), 29–64; National Health Assembly, American's Health: *A Report to the Nation* (New York: Harper and Brothers, 1949), passim.

33. Falk, Rorem and Ring: *The Cost of Medical Care*, pp. 73–76; Committee on the Cost of Medical Care: *Medical Care for the American People* (Chicago: University of Chicago Press, 1932), p. 7.

34. Introduction, in Falk, Rorem and Ring: *The Cost of Medical Care*, pp. vi-vii.

35. Falk: *Security Against Sickness*, p. 358.

36. A National Health Program: Message from the President, *Social Security Bulletin* 8 (December 1945), p. 8.

37. Ibid.

38. Falk: *Security Against Sickness*, p. 359.

39. National Health Program, p. 11; Altm-

eyer AJ: How Can We Assure Adequate Health Service to All the People? *Social Security Bulletin* 8 (December 1945), p. 15.

40. On the accommodation of the hospitals and doctors, see Marmor TR: *The Politics of Medicare* (Chicago: Aldine, 1973), pp. 85–88; and Feder JM: *Medicare: The Politics of Federal Hospital Insurance* (Lexington, MA: Lexington Books, 1978).

41. See Vladeck B: *Unloving Care: The Nursing Home Tragedy* (New York: Basic Books, 1980).

42. Worthington NL: National Health Expenditures, 1929–74, *Social Security Bulletin* 38 (1975), p. 5; the estimate for 1979 was a preliminary figure from Rice D, National Center for Health Statistics, October 1979. On the general origins of health care inflation, see Enthoven AC: Consumer-Choice Health Plan, *N Eng J Med* 298 (March 23, 1978), pp. 650–58. For an expanded version of the argument presented here, see Starr P and Esping-Andersen G: Passive Intervention, Working Papers for a New Society (July/ August 1979), pp. 15–25.

43. The exact reasons for reduced hospitalization are subject to dispute. For views on the question, see Roemer MI, Shonick W: HMO Performance: The Recent Evidence, *Health and Society* 51 (September 1973), pp. 271–318; Gaus C, Cooper BS, Hirshman CG: Contrasts in HMO and Fee-for Service Performance, *Social Security Bulletin* 39 (May 1976), pp. 3–14; and Luft HS: How Do Health Maintenance Organizations Achieve their 'Savings'; Rhetoric and Evidence, *N Eng J Med* 298 (June 15, 1978), pp. 1336–43.

44. For more on this point, see my discussions in The Undelivered Health System, *The Public Interest* (Winter 1976), pp. 66–85; and Controlling Medical Costs Through Countervailing Power, *Working Papers for a New Society* 5 (Summer 1977), 10 ff.

45. On the aid to Blue Cross, see Reed: *Blue Cross and Medical Service Plans*; on prepaid group practice, Hansen HR: Group Health Plans: A Twenty-Year Legal Review, *Minnesota Law Review* 42 (1958), 527–48.

46. Enthoven: *Consumer-Choice Health Plan*,

p. 650; Iglehart J: The Rising Cost of Health Care—Something Must be Done, But What? *National Journal* (October 16, 1976), 1458–65.

47. Davis K: *National Health Insurance* (Washington, DC: The Brookings Institution, 1975), ch. 5.

48. *The New York Times*, Feb. 8, 1974.

49. Insuring the Nation's Health, *Newsweek*, June 3, 1974. See also Rivlin AM: Agreed: Here Comes National Health Insurance, *The New York Times Magazine*, July 21, 1974.

50. For an inside account, see Heineman BW Jr, Hessler CA: *Memorandum for the President* (New York: Random House, 1980), 266–301.

51. Press conference, May 14, 1979.

52. Enthoven AC: *Health Plan* (Reading MA: Addison-Wesley, 1980), xxii.

53. A proposal for a national health service was introduced in the U.S. House of Representatives in March 1979 by Rep. Ronald Dellums and eight cosponsors. See HR 2969, 96th Congress, 1st Session, and Congressional Record, March 19, 1979, H1453-1457.

2

The Specter of Socialized Medicine: American Physicians and Compulsory Health Insurance

Ronald L. Numbers

No special-interest group has influenced the American debate over compulsory health insurance more than organized medicine. Time after time since World War I, the American Medical Association (AMA) and its constituent societies have played key roles in turning back the forces of reform and preventing the passage of state or national compulsory health-insurance legislation. Although few proponents of such measures ever entertained the possibility of making physicians employees of the state, the medical profession came to regard compulsory health insurance, even when it allowed doctors to practice on a fee-for-service basis, as socialized medicine,

which the AMA House of Delegates defined in 1948 as "a system of medical administration by which the government promises or attempts to provide for the medical needs of the entire population or a large part thereof."[1]

No single factor adequately explains the suspicion and hostility with which many physicians have regarded compulsory health insurance. Critics of organized medicine have often described the doctors' motives solely in terms of economic self-interest; but money, as we shall see, accounts for only part of the medical profession's antagonism. Also important were its fears about the possible negative consequences of govern-

ment involvement in medicine, particularly the anticipated loss of individual freedom and the decline of high-quality medical care.

I recognize, of course, that the AMA and its affiliates have not spoken for all physicians in the United States and that not even all AMA members have always agreed with that body's policies. The Physicians Forum, for example, has since the 1940s "supported every major proposal for a strong and comprehensive national health insurance system."[2] The American Public

Health Association, the Association of American Medical Colleges, the National Medical Association, the American Osteopathic Association, and various specialty groups have also departed at times from the AMA's position.

Nevertheless, the AMA has represented the overwhelming majority of "the active, private-practice, office-based physicians in this country," as one AMA trustee described his constituency, and these doctors have since 1920 consistently and effectively opposed compulsory health insurance.[3]

From Support to Opposition

Before 1920 substantial segments of organized medicine, including AMA leaders and state medical societies, actively supported compulsory health insurance at the state level. Although Americans paid little attention to this social reform before the passage of the National Insurance Act in Great Britain in 1911, the British example prompted the American Association for Labor Legislation (AALL), an organization

founded by reform-minded social scientists, to create a Committee on Social Insurance to prepare a model bill for introduction in state legislatures. By the fall of 1915, this committee had completed a tentative draft and was laying plans for an extensive legislative campaign. Its bill required the participation of virtually all manual laborers earning $100 a month or less, provided both income protection and complete medical care, and divided the payment of premiums among the state, the employer, and the employee.[4]

The medical profession's initial response to this proposal bordered on enthusiasm. Three physicians—Alexander Lambert, Isaac M. Rubinow, and S. S. Goldwater—had served on the drafting committee, and for a brief period after the turn of the century, organized medicine reflected the country's progressive mood. Upon receiving a copy of the AALL's bill, Frederick R. Green, secretary of the AMA's Council on Health and Public Instruction, informed the bill's sponsors that their plan for compulsory health insurance was "exactly in line with the views that I have held for a long time regarding the methods which should be followed in securing public health legislation. . . . Your plans are so entirely in line with our own that I want to be of every possible assistance." Specifically, Green wanted to give the AALL "the assistance and backing of the American Medical Association in some official way," and he proposed setting up an AMA Committee on Social Insurance to cooperate with the AALL in working out the medical provisions of the bill.[5] As a result of his efforts, the AMA Board of Trustees early in 1916 appointed a three-man committee, with Lambert as chairman. He, in turn, hired Rubinow, a Socialist, as executive secretary and set up committee headquarters in the same building with the AALL.

The *Journal of the American Medical Association (JAMA)* hailed the appearance of the model bill as "the inauguration of a great movement which ought to result in an improvement in the health of the industrial population and improve the conditions for medical service among the wage earners."[6] In the editor's opinion, "No other social movement in modern economic development is so pregnant with benefit to the public."[7] At the AMA's annual session in June 1916, President Rupert Blue called compulsory health insurance "the next step in social legislation," and Lambert, as chairman of the Committee on Social Insurance, presented a report that stopped just short of endorsing the measure.[8]

Physician support at the state level showed similar strength. In 1916 the state medical societies of both Pennsylvania and Wisconsin formally approved the principle of compulsory health insurance, as did the Council of the Medical Society of the State of New York.[9] Reasons for favoring health insurance varied from physician to physician. According to the *Journal of the American Medical Association*, the most convincing argument was "the failure of many persons in this country at present to receive medical care"; but the average practitioner, who earned less than $2,000 a year, was probably more impressed by the prospect of a fixed income and no outstanding bills.[10] Besides, the coming of health insurance appeared inevitable, and most doctors preferred cooperating to fighting. "Whether one likes it or not," wrote the editor of the *Medical Record*,

social health insurance is bound to come sooner or later, and it behooves the medical profession to meet this condition with dignity. . . . Blind condemnation will lead nowhere and may bring about a repetition of the humiliating experiences suffered by the medical profession in some of the European countries.[11]

By early 1917, however, medical opinion was beginning to shift, especially in New York, where the AALL was concentrating its efforts. One after another of the county medical societies voted against compulsory health insurance, until finally the council of the state society rescinded its earlier endorsement.[12] Both friends and foes of the proposed legislation agreed on one point: the medical profession's chief objection was monetary. As the exasperated secretary of the AALL saw it, the "crux of the whole problem" was that physicians were constantly hearing the lie that the model bill would limit them to $1,200 a year.[13] "If you boil this health insurance matter down, it seems to be a question of the remuneration of the doctor," observed one New York physician.[14] Another New York practitioner, who opposed the AALL's bill, described all other objections besides payment as "merely camouflage for this one crucial thought." Medical opposition would melt away, he predicted, if adequate compensation were guaranteed.[15]

America's entry into World War I in April 1917 not only interrupted the campaign for compulsory health insurance, but touched off an epidemic of anti-German hysteria. Patriotic citizens lashed out at anything that smacked of Germany, including health insurance, which was reputed to have been "made in Germany." As the war progressed, Americans in increasing numbers began referring to compulsory health insurance as an "un-American" device that would lead to the "Prussianization of America."[16]

Shortly before the close of the war, California voters, in the nation's only referendum on compulsory health insurance, soundly defeated the measure by a vote of 358,324 to 133,858 and dampened the hopes of insurance advocates.[17] Their spirits revived briefly in the spring of 1919, when the New York State Senate passed a revised version of the model bill, but the bill subsequently died in the Assembly. By 1920 even the AALL was rapidly losing interest in an obviously lost cause.

As the prospects for passage of the model bill declined, the stridency of anti-insurance doctors increased. "Com-

pulsory Health Insurance," declared one Brooklyn physician, "is an Un-American, Unsafe, Uneconomic, Unscientific, Unfair and Un-scrupulous type of Legislation [supported by] Paid Professional Philanthropists, busybody Social Workers, Misguided Clergymen and Hysterical women."[18] In 1919 he and other critics launched a campaign to have the AMA's House of Delegates officially condemn compulsory health insurance. They failed on their first attempt, but the following year the delegates overwhelmingly approved the following resolution:

That the American Medical Association declares its opposition to the institution of any plan embodying the system of compulsory contributory insurance against illness, or any other plan of compulsory insurance which provides for medical service to be rendered contributors or their dependents, provided, controlled, or regulated by any state or the Federal Government.[19]

This repudiation of compulsory health insurance was not, as one writer has suggested, the result of "an abdication of responsibility by the scientific and academic leaders of America medicine."[20] Nor was it primarily the product of a rank-and-file takeover by conservative physicians disgruntled with liberal leaders.[21] The doctors who rejected health insurance in 1920 were by and large the same ones who had welcomed—or at least accepted—it only four years earlier. For example, Frederick Green, the person most responsible for the AMA's early support of compulsory health insurance, was by 1921 describing it as an "economically, socially and scientifically unsound" proposition favored only by "radicals."[22]

Many factors contributed to such reversals. Opportunism no doubt motivated some, and the political climate surely affected the attitudes of others. But even more important was the growing conviction that compulsory health insurance would lower the incomes of physicians rather than raise them, as many practitioners had earlier believed. The profession's recent experience with workmen's compensation, probably the most common form of health insurance in America from the 1910s to the 1940s, also undermined physician support for third-party plans. Beginning in 1911, many states passed laws making employers legally responsible for on-the-job injuries, but few of the early compensation acts provided comprehensive medical benefits. During World War I, however, most states added such provisions or liberalized existing ones, giving American doctors their first taste of social insurance. For many, it was not pleasant. Employers often took out accident insurance with commercial companies, which either contracted with physicians to care for the injured or paid local practitioners according to an arbitrary fee schedule.[23] Neither arrangement pleased the medical profession, which complained that the abuses resulting from such practices "were akin to mayhem and murder."[24] It was evident from this experience, reported the AMA, that "pus and politics go together."[25]

With each legislative defeat of the AALL's model bill, the coming of compulsory health insurance seemed less and less inevitable, and the self-confidence of the profession grew correspondingly. "[T]his Health Insurance agitation has been good for us," concluded one prominent New York physician as the debate drew to a close. "If it goes no farther it will have brought us more firmly together than any other thing which has ever come to us."[26]

In 1925 the New York State Medical Society reported that compulsory health insurance "is a dead issue in the United States. . . . It is not conceivable that any serious effort will again be made to subsidize medicine as the hand-maiden of the public."[27] The victorious New York physicians had every reason to be confident, but they failed to reckon with economic disaster. The Great Depression invalidated many assumptions about American society—and resurrected the specter of socialized medicine.

During the first few years of the Depression, organized medicine devoted its energies to fighting *voluntary* health insurance, initially promoted by financially stricken hospitals. It was not until 1934, when President Franklin D. Roosevelt appointed a Committee on Economic Security to draft legislation for a social-security program, that the AMA, fearing medical care might be included,

renewed its struggle against compulsory health insurance. In February 1935, the House of Delegates met in special session—the first since World War I—to reaffirm its opposition to "all forms of *compulsory* health insurance."[28] Under pressure from organized medicine, the president dropped health care from the bill he sent to Congress in 1935, although members of his administration continued throughout the 1930s to agitate for compulsory health insurance. The AMA remained adamant in its opposition, and not even the threat of blackmail by the attorney general's office (in the form of prosecution for violation of the Sherman Anti-Trust Act) could budge it.[29]

World War II diverted attention away from compulsory health insurance, but the coming of peace and the arrival of Harry S. Truman in the White House allowed the issue to flare again. Since his days as a county judge in Missouri, Truman had been concerned about the health needs of the poor, and within a few weeks of assuming the presidency, he decided to lend his support to a campaign for national compulsory health insurance. Following a strategy session with the president in 1945, Senators Robert Wagner and James Murray and Representative John Dingell introduced a bill providing medical and dental insurance to all persons paying social-security taxes, as well as to their families.[30]

This development terrified the AMA, which viewed the Wagner-Murray-Dingell Bill as the first step toward a totalitarian state, where American doctors would become "clock watchers and slaves of a system."[31] To head off passage of such legislation, the AMA in 1946 began backing a substitute bill, sponsored by Senator Robert A. Taft, which authorized federal grants to the states to subsidize private health insurance for the indigent.[32]

Truman's surprise victory in 1948, at the close of a campaign that featured health insurance as a major issue, convinced the AMA that it was time to declare all-out war. Shortly after the election returns were in, the House of Delegates voted to assess each member $25 to raise a war chest for combatting

what the physicians called socialized medicine. Within a year $2,250,000 had been raised, and the public relations firm of Whitaker and Baxter was putting it to effective use in an effort to "educate" the American people. The showdown came in 1950 when organized medicine won a stunning victory in the off-year elections, forcing many candidates to renounce their earlier support of compulsory health insurance and defeating "nearly 90 percent" of those who refused to back down.[33]

Throughout this controversy, representatives of organized medicine insisted that the country did not need compulsory health insurance, just as they had insisted in the early 1930s that voluntary insurance was unnecessary. "There is no health emergency in this country," said a complacent AMA president in 1952. "The health of the American people has never been better."[34] If some individuals could not afford proper medical care, it was probably the result of self-indulgence rather than genuine need.

Since one out of every four persons in the United States has a motor car, one out of two a radio, and since our people find funds available for such substances as liquors and tobacco in amounts almost as great as the total bill for medical care, one cannot but refer to the priorities and to the lack of suitable education which makes people choose to spend their money for such items rather than for the securing of medical care.[35]

The election of a Republican administration in 1952 effectively ended the debate over compulsory health insurance, and organized medicine breathed a sigh of relief. "As far as the medical profession is concerned," wrote the AMA president, "there is general agreement that we are in less danger of socialization than for a number of years. . . . We have been given the opportunity to solve the problems of health in a truly American way."[36] The "American way," it went without saying, was the way of voluntary health insurance.

During the Eisenhower years, advocates of government health insurance abandoned their campaign for a compulsory and universal system and focused instead on proposals that limited coverage to social-security beneficiaries. To organized medicine, even such restricted coverage amounted to "creeping socialism," and the physicians would have none of it. [37] Their only concession was to approve a government plan providing assistance to "the indigent or near indigent," which would benefit physicians as much as the poor. [38] Thus in 1960 Congress, with AMA approval, passed the Kerr-Mills amendment to the Social Security Act granting federal assistance to the states to meet the health needs of the indigent and the elderly who qualified as "medically indigent."

If the medical profession hoped to forestall the coming of compulsory health insurance by this small compromise, John F. Kennedy's election to the presidency that fall soon convinced them otherwise. Upon occupying the White House, he immediately began laying plans to extend health-insurance protection to all persons on social security, whether or not "medically indigent." The AMA denounced his plans as a "cruel hoax," [39] but Congress nevertheless in 1965 voted to include health insurance as a social-security benefit (Medicare) and to provide for the indigent through grants to the states (Medicaid). Although the medical profession benefitted handsomely from these government plans, [40] organized medicine has continued to oppose compulsory health insurance into the 1980s.

Selfishness or Social Concern?

How, then, do we explain the fervor with which American physicians have opposed compulsory health insurance since 1920? Although the struggle has spanned seven decades and involved a variety of proposals, the arguments of the medical profession have remained remarkably similar. "No matter what the year—1937, 1950, 1960—the issue remains the same," observed an editor of *JAMA*. [41] As seen by organized medicine, compulsory health insurance was unnecessary, unsuccessful, and uneconomical. But even worse, it threatened to affect adversely the income of physicians, to strip them of their freedom, and, consequently, to reduce the quality of medical care. These are the issues on which the medical opposition focused.

Despite repeated protests from the leaders of organized medicine denying "selfish" intent, economic considerations have demonstrably influenced, both positively and negatively, the attitudes of physicians toward compulsory health insurance. Early in the century when, according to one report, "hardly more than 10 percent of the physicians in the United States [were] able to earn a comfortable income," doctors tended to discuss their financial affairs more openly and candidly than they would feel comfortable doing today. [42] In language that would make present-day physicians blush, a Wisconsin practitioner in 1914 explained his motives for entering medicine: "Like the vast majority of medical men I took up the study of medicine purely as a means to an end—wealth and social position. A life of service to my fellow men and ethics were purely secondary considerations." [43] A few years later, a prominent New York doctor estimated that "ninety-nine out of one hundred men will say that they took up the practice or the profession of medicine as a means of earning a livelihood." [44] Given such attitudes, it is not surprising to find participants in the first debate over compulsory health insurance arguing that "The one thing in which doctors as a whole are most interested, and in which they should be interested, is what return for their services may they look forward to." [45]

Ironically, much of the physician *support* for compulsory health insurance during the years before America's entry into World War I stemmed from the promise of high incomes. Early reports from England, carried in *JAMA* and the state medical society journals, told of markedly increased fees under the National Insurance Act of 1911, and many American practitioners began thinking wistfully of "no charity work and no uncollectible bills." [46]

More recently, representatives of both the liberal Physicians Forum and the black National Medical Association (NMA) have appealed to higher physician incomes as a legitimate reason for supporting government health insurance. [47] The prospect of more money partially explains why the nation's black physicians broke with the AMA in the 1960s to support Medicare legislation, and why they have, unlike the white medical establishment, continued to favor compulsory health insurance. Testifying before a Senate committee in 1970, Dr. Julius W. Hill, president of the NMA, argued for the extension of federally subsidized health insurance on the grounds that it was needed to attract good physicians to practice among the poor. A doctor, he said, "must be able to make a reasonable living for himself and his family. He will not practice under the most difficult possible conditions if it means he must also make a financial sacrifice." Of course, the NMA's "primary concern" was the plight of millions of black Americans unable to afford adequate medical care. [48]

If the lure of additional income has prompted some physicians to endorse compulsory health insurance, the fear of diminished revenues has led even more to oppose the measure. As we have already noted, the prospect of reduced fees played a major role in reversing organized medicine's position on health insurance in the late 1910s. By 1917 reports were beginning to circulate that European physicians, instead of benefitting monetarily from insurance, had been "markedly reduced financially and many of them completely beggared." [49] False rumors that compulsory health insurance would limit American doctors to 25 cents a visit also began making the rounds. [50] American physicians reacted predictably. "[T]he time has arrived," declared the alarmed president of the American Surgical Association in 1918, "when the financial status of medical men should be amply safeguarded. . . . The dollar sign is not and should not be our hall mark, but in the interests of professional dignity and of justice it is clearly our right, our duty, to conserve and protect our economical welfare." [51]

Understandably, many doctors felt ill at ease about using personal gain to determine social policy. Thus they couched their objections to compulsory health insurance in altruistic language, convincing themselves, as Charles H. Mayo said in his 1917 presidential address to the AMA, that "Anything which reduces the income of the physician will limit his training, equipment and efficiency, and in the end will react on the people."[52] The editor of a midwestern medical journal in 1920 stated the case another way:

Much has been said for and against Compulsory Health Insurance, but in the main, the physicians of the United States are opposed to it, largely through reasons that have to do with their own economic welfare though they should oppose it for other reasons equally valid. Very naturally, we are inclined to protect ourselves first and the other fellow afterward, and this leads to the assumption that our attitude is a selfish one rather than one inclined to be considerate of the interests of others as well as our own. In the discussion of Compulsory Health Insurance we must take into consideration not only the injustice that the scheme will have on the economic welfare of the medical profession, but the injustice and unfairness with which the plan will operate for working man.[53]

As the century progressed, American physicians heeded this advice, emphasizing the dire consequences that low physician income would have on the quality of medical care while downplaying any hint of selfishness. For example, when testifying before a congressional committee in 1963, AMA representatives argued that compulsory health insurance would lead to price fixing by the federal government, which in turn would undermine the financial incentive to practice medicine and discourage bright young people from entering the profession. The net result would be "a deterioration of the quality of health care."[54] This argument became a favorite of organized medicine in a period when conspicuously high physician income made any effort to defend personal wealth appear unseemly at best.

It would be a mistake, however, to conclude that economic self-interest alone explains the medical profession's long-standing antipathy to compulsory health insurance. As Roy Lubove has pointed out in his analysis of the AMA's opposition to national health insurance in the 1930s, such simplistic explanations fail to recognize that "the average physician would have benefited substantially from a national health program."[55] Many physicians, especially the most successful, have doubted the promised financial rewards, but others have realized, as a North Carolina pe-

diatrician wrote in 1943, that "Health insurance has always brought more money to the doctors," a principle spectacularly confirmed by Medicare.[56] Nevertheless, these same physicians often opposed compulsory health insurance, because, said one AMA official, they did "not desire the promised increase in medical incomes under government control."[57] Given such evidence, we must, I think, take seriously the medical profession's noneconomic objections to compulsory health insurance.

According to the AMA, its "basic objection" to such a system has been "that it will lead to controlled medicine with its accompanying loss of freedoms and deterioration of medical care."[58] Certainly, this has been organized medicine's most oft-repeated criticism of compulsory health insurance, one that has appeared time and again in professional journals and in statements for the general public.

From the earliest protests to the present, concerned physicians have predicted that compulsory health insurance would turn them into mere "cogs" in a giant government-controlled medical machine. Government insurance, they believed, would demote them to employee status—like schoolteachers—robbing them of their professional identity and respect. It would "enslave, burden and belittle all parties to it."[59] One physician writing in the 1930s no doubt described the feelings of many colleagues when he said: "Let the big business men who would reorganize medical practice, the efficiency engineers who would make doctors the cogs of their governmental machines, give a little of their sixty horse power brains to a realization of the fact that Americans prefer to be human beings."[60]

Many physicians feared that working conditions under compulsory health insurance would be a "nightmare" in which a medical dictator in Washington would treat physicians and patients as "inanimate units" and would regiment every aspect of the physician's practice. As a result, American doctors "would become clock watchers and slaves of a system."[61] Their valuable time would be squandered preparing voluminous reports—"in triplicate"—instead of spent

ministering to the sick. Such apprehensions of being buried by paperwork did not lessen with the coming of Medicare and Medicaid.[62]

A survey of American medical students in the early 1960s revealed that 84 percent of those polled preferred not to work under compulsory health insurance, largely because of the restrictions they thought it would impose on them. "I would not want to become a civil servant and surrender my independence in the profession," said a first-year student at Columbia University. "I chose medicine as a career because I wanted a profession which offered me a chance to work with people and still left me the right to be my own supervisor," explained a third-year student at George Washington University. A fourth-year student at the University of Minnesota expressed concern that government-controlled medicine would result in "bureaucracy, ineptness, and most of all control of the private physician."[63] For individuals attracted to medicine because of the freedom it offered, such considerations loomed large.

Undoubtedly, some of the rhetoric about bureaucratization and regimentation reflected a suspicion that the government would control fees as well as other aspects of medical practice, but I think we should not dismiss the medical profession's repeated pleas for freedom as mere camouflage. As one exasperated pro-insurance doctor explained to Senator Robert F. Wagner in 1939, he could not convince his colleagues to support the senator's bill, because "Many honestly believe that physicians will be regimented . . . [and] under bureaucratic control of laymen."[64]

In addition to having qualms about the effects of government intervention on their own lives, the opponents of compulsory health insurance also believed that it would adversely affect the quality of medical care by denying patients the freedom to choose their own doctors. Once the element of choice disappeared, predicted some physicians, practitioners would—consciously or unconsciously—treat their patients differently and less effectively. "There is an intangible something," wrote Dr. Frank H. Lahey in 1946, that lay people laugh at in medicine that makes doctors want to do it, that makes them willing to get up at night. It makes them willing to do charity without vanity. If you make medicine into a commodity, doctors will never want to do those things with the same willingness. If they do them, they will do them because they will have to and not because they want to.[65]

American physicians repeatedly cited the experience with contract practice at home and compulsory health insurance abroad as proof that such arrangements dehumanized medical service, causing doctors to view patients as "mere numbers."[66] "There is no other service so individual and so personal as medical service," explained one practitioner. "The conscientious physician who feels that he is called on to treat a patient who he knows has come to him only because he is compelled to and not because he wants to, unconsciously fails to give that patient the best that is in him. The finer sensibilities of both parties are offended."[67]

Proponents of compulsory health insurance, including some physicians, viewed "free choice" as nothing but a shibboleth and pointed out that the primary beneficiaries of such insurance—the millions of poor black and white Americans—had no medical freedom to loose. Decades ago, W. Montague Cobb, the distinguished black physician, reminded a Senate committee that individuals who have never had medical care, or who have received unsatisfactory care in overcrowded clinics from impersonal staff, cared little about ideal doctor-patient relationships.[68] Such logic, however, failed to persuade the leaders of organized medicine, who continued to equate quality medical care with personalized service.

Although many physicians genuinely feared the intrusion of the government into the practice of medicine, the attitude of organized medicine toward federal subsidies for charity medical care suggests that such scruples could be set aside when the rewards were sufficiently high and the perceived risks low. The American medical profession has long taken pride in its willingness to provide care regardless of a patient's ability to pay; at the same time, it has resented society's failure to provide relief from "the financial burdens thrown

upon the medical professions by the immense proportion of unpaid, gratuitous, unremunerative, charitable work done by the profession."[69] In the early 1930s, for example, the AMA denounced national health insurance while simultaneously calling for state intervention "to give complete and adequate medical care to the indigent." The minority report of the Committee on the Costs of Medical Care, which the AMA endorsed, identified charity care as "one of the greatest burdens on the medical profession . . . a burden which should be borne by the entire community and not by the medical profession alone."[70]

Doctors who practiced primarily among the poor felt especially abused. In 1960 the president of the National Medical Association "bitterly" disagreed with the view, expressed by an AMA trustee, "that doctors will gladly give their services to those unable to pay." "No allowances are made by bill collectors for the charity doctor," pointed out the black physician.[71] That same year, the AMA approved the Kerr-Mills amendment to the Social Security Act. Although the Kerr-Mills program opened the door to government regulation, it retained the principle of free choice of physician and thus, in the eyes of America's doctors, posed little threat to the independence of the professions or to the quality of medical care.

It should be apparent by now that there is no simple answer to the question of why organized medicine has so forcefully and persistently fought the passage of compulsory health insurance legislation. Although the themes of money, freedom, and quality have dominated the seventy-year-old debate, they have also confused it. American physicians, as we have seen, feared the economic consequences of compulsory health insurance but, after 1920, failed to support the measure even when it promised higher incomes. They protested vehemently about the inevitable loss of freedom that a partnership with the government would entail, but eagerly sought assistance with the burden of caring for the poor. They deplored the inferior medical care that compulsory health insurance would bring, yet at times showed little concern for those who could afford no medical care at all.

In their own minds, however, the doctors saw the issues clearly. "I am frank to admit that the practice of Medicine is highly individualistic, and as individuals we may be as selfish as members of any other group," testified the president of the Colorado State Medical Society in 1946, "but I deny that our main reason for opposition is based on selfishness. We are opposed to socialized medicine because it leads to an inferior type of medical care."[72]

The author is indebted to William J. Orr, Jr., for his research assistance and to Judith Walzer Leavitt for her criticisms and encouragement.

Notes

1. *1846–1958 Digest of Official Actions: American Medical Association* (Chicago: American Medical Association, 1959), p 331. A recent proposal that would make physicians employees of the state is Congressman Ronald V. Dellums' Health Service Act, introduced in Congress in 1978.
2. Testimony of Victor W. Sidel, M.D., "National Health Insurance Proposals," Hearings before the Committee on Ways and Means, House of Representatives, 92nd Cong., 1st Sess., Oct. 19–Nov. 19, 1971 (Washington, DC: Government Printing Office, 1972), p. 2720.
3. Ibid., Testimony of Dr. Max H. Parrott, p. 1951. Elton Rayack also concluded that the AMA generally reflects the attitudes of American physicians in his *Professional Power and American Medicine: The Economics of the American Medical Association* (Cleveland: World Publishing Co., 1967), p. 17.
4. The following account of the first phase of the American debate over compulsory health insurance is based on the author's monograph *Almost Persuaded: American Physicians and Compulsory Health Insurance, 1912–1920* (Baltimore: Johns Hopkins University Press, 1978), and closely follows his summary, "The Third Party Health Insurance in America," in *The Therapeutic Revolution: Essays in the Social History of American Medicine*, ed. Morris J. Vogel and Charles E. Rosenberg (Philadelphia: University of Pennsylvania Press, 1979), pp. 177–200.
5. F. R. Green to J. B. Andrews, Nov. 11, 1915, American Association for Labor Legislation Papers, Cornell University, Ithaca, NY. Hereafter cited as AALL Papers.

6. "Industrial Insurance," *JAMA* 1916, 66: 433.

7. "Cooperation in Social Insurance Investigation," *JAMA*, 1916, 66: 1469–70.

8. Rupert Blue, "Some of The Larger Problems of the Medical Profession," *JAMA*, 1916, 66: 1910; Report of the Committee on Social Insurance, pp. 1951–85.

9. Proceedings of the Medical Society of the State of Pennsylvania, Sept. 18–21, 1916, *Pennsylvania Medical Journal*, 1916, 20: 135, 143; Proceedings of the House of Delegates, State Medical Society of Wisconsin, Oct. 5, 1916, *Wisconsin Medical Journal*, 1916, 15: 288; Minutes of the Council, Medical Society of the State of New York, Dec. 9, 1916, *New York State Medical Journal*, 1916, 17: 47–48.

10. "Social Insurance in California," *JAMA*, 1915, 65: 1560. Income statistics are scarce for this period, but a 1915 survey of physicians and surgeons in Richmond, Virginia, showed that "the very large proportion of physicians were earning less than $2,000," and income tax records for Wisconsin in 1914 indicated that the average income of taxed physicians was $1,488. Committee on Social Insurance, *Statistics Regarding the Medical Profession*, Social Insurance Series Pamphlet No. 7 (Chicago: American Medical Association, n.d.), pp. 81, 87.

11. "Opposition to the Health Insurance Bill," *Medical Record*, 1916, 89: 424.

12. Report of the Committee on Legislation, *New York State Journal of Medicine*, 1917, 17: 234.

13. J. B. Andrews to New York Members of the AALL, Nov. 3, 1919, AALL Papers.

14. "A Symposium on Compulsory Health Insurance Presented before the Medical Society of the County of Kings, Oct. 21, 1919," *Long Island Medical Journal*, 1919, 13: 434.

15. M. Schulman to J. B. Andrews, Feb. 22, 1919, AALL Papers.

16. See Roy Lubove, *The Struggle for Social Security, 1900–1935* (Cambridge: Harvard University Press, 1968), pp. 66–90.

17. On the California debate, see Arthur J. Viseltear, "Compulsory Health Insurance in California, 1915–1918," *Journal of the History of Medicine and Allied Sciences*, 1969, 24: 151–82.

18. "A Symposium on Compulsory Health Insurance," p. 445.

19. Minutes of the House of Delegates, *JAMA*, 1920, 74: 1319.

20. John Gordon Freymann, "Leadership in American Medicine: A Matter of Personal Responsibility," *New England Journal of Medicine*, 1964, 270: 710–15.

21. Rayack, *Professional Power and American Medicine*, pp. 143–46. For a similar view, see Carleton B. Chapman and John M. Talmadge, "The Evolution of the Right to Health Concept in the United States," *Pharos*, 1971, 34: 39.

22. Frederick R. Green, "The Social Responsibilities of Modern Medicine," *Transactions*, Medical Society of the State of North Carolina, 1921, pp. 401–3.

23. On the early history of workmen's compensation in America, see Harry Weiss, "The Development of Workmen's Compensation Legislation in the United States" (Ph.D. diss, University of Wisconsin, 1933); Lubove, *The Struggle for Social Security*, pp. 45–65; and James G. Burrow, *Organized Medicine in the Progressive Era: The Move Toward Monopoly* (Baltimore: Johns Hopkins University Press, 1977), pp. 133–39.

24. Bureau of Medical Economics, *An Introduction to Medical Economics* (Chicago: American Medical Association, 1935), p. 80.

25. Committee on Social Insurance, *Workman's Compensation Laws*, Social Insurance Series Pamphlet No. I (Chicago: American Medical Association, [1915]), p 60.

26. Henry Lyle Winter, "Social Insurance," *New York State Journal of Medicine*, 1920, 20: 20.

27. Report of the Committee on Medical Economics, *New York State Journal of Medicine*, 1925, 25: 789.

28. Minutes of the Special Session, Feb. 15–16, 1935, *JAMA*, 1935, 104: 751.

29. Patricia Spain Ward, "The United States of America v. The American Medical Association: The Medical Anti-Trust Case of 1938–1943," Paper delivered at the 52nd annual meeting of the American Association for the History of Medicine, Pittsburgh, Pa., May 4, 1979. The fullest account of the second phase of the debate over compulsory health insurance is Daniel S. Hirshfield, *The Lost Reform: The Campaign for Compulsory Health Insurance in the United States from 1932 to 1943* (Cambridge: Harvard University Press, 1970). But see also Roy Lubove, "The New Deal and National Health," *Current History*, Aug 1963, 45: 77–86; Edwin E. Witte, *The Development of the Social Security Act* (Madison: University of Wisconsin Press, 1962); Arthur J. Altmeyer, *The Formative Years of Social Security* (Madison: University of Wisconsin Press, 1966); and James G. Burrow, *AMA: Voice of American Medicine* (Baltimore: Johns Hopkins Press, 1963), pp. 185–252.

30. Monte M. Poen, *Harry S. Truman versus the Medical Lobby: The Genesis of Medicare* (Columbia, Mo.: University of Missouri Press, 1979).

31. "The President's National Health Program and the New Wagner Bill," *JAMA*, 1945, 129: 950–53. See also "Senator Wagner's Comments," *JAMA*, 1945, 128: 667–68.

32. Burrow, *AMA*, p. 347.

33. Ibid., pp. 361–64; Minutes of the Interim Session, Nov. 30 - Dec. 1, 1948, *JAMA*, 1948, 138: 1241; "A Call to Action against Nationalization of Medicine," ibid., pp. 1098–99; "Reply by Officers and Trustees," *JAMA*, 1949, 139: 532; R. Cragin Lewis, "New Power at the Polls," *Medical Economics*, Jan. 1951, 28: 76.

34. John W. Cline, "The President's Page: A Special Message," *JAMA*, 1952, 148: 208.

35. "A Call to Action against Nationalization of Medicine," p. 1098. This comment was made in response to the federal security administrator's statement that millions of Americans could not afford proper medical care. See Oscar R. Ewing, *The Nation's Health: A Report to the President* (Washington, DC, September, 1948). See also Council on Medical Service, "Consumer Expenditures," *Voluntary Health Insurance vs Compulsory Sickness Insurance: A Compilation of Articles from Various Sources* (Chicago: American Medical Association, 1946), p. 99.

36. Louis H. Bauer, "The President's Page, *JAMA*, 1952, 150: 1675. Stephen P. Strickland, *Politics, Science, and Dread Disease: A Short History of United States Medical Research Policy* (Cambridge: Harvard University Press, 1972), points out that Congress subsequently developed an alternative national health policy based on the trickle-down effects of health research.

37. J. H. Houghton, "President's Message to the House of Delegates," *Wisconsin Medical Journal*, 1965, 64: 208.

38. "New Drive for Compulsory Health Insurance," *JAMA*, 1960, 172: 344-45. See also Edward R. Annis, "House of Delegates Report," *JAMA*, 1963, 185: 202.

39. Donavan F. Ward, "Are 200,000 Doctors Wrong?" *JAMA*, 1965, 191: 661–63; *The Case against the King-Anderson Bill* (H.R. 3820) (Chicago: American Medical Association, 1963), pp. 17, 118–19.

40. Numbers, "The Third Party," pp. 192–94.

41. "New Drive for Compulsory Health Insurance," p. 344.

42. Report of the Judicial Council, *JAMA*, 1913, 60: 1998.

43. W. F. Zierath, "The Socialization of Medicine," *Wisconsin Medical Journal*, 1915, 13: 306.

44. "A Symposium on Compulsory Health Insurance," p. 434.

45. M. Schulman to J. B. Andrews, Feb. 22, 1919, AALL Papers.

46. "Transactions of the Seventieth Annual Meeting of the State Medical Society of Wisconsin," *Wisconsin Medical Journal*, 1916, 15: 227. After visiting with the secretary of the British Medical Association, a South Carolina physician reported "that the income of the general practitioner had been, in many instances, quadrupled"; E. A. Hines, Report of Delegate to the AMA, *Journal of the South Carolina Medical Association*, 1916, 12: 260.

47. Testimony of Ernst P. Boas, chairman of the Physicians Forum, "National Health Program," Hearings before the Committee on Education and Labor, U.S. Senate, 79th Cong., 2nd Sess., April 2–16, 1946 (Washington, D.C.: Government Printing Office, 1946) p 738. Boas went on to explain (p. 761) that "although the lot of the average doctor would be improved by a bill such as this, the very large incomes of some surgeons and specialists would in the long run be deflated."

48. "Joint Statement of the American Medical Association and the National Medical Association before the Committee on Finance, United States Senate, June 15, 1970," *Journal of the National Medical Association*, 1970, 62: 399–400.

49. John V. Woodruff, Letter to the Editor, JAMA, 1917, 68: 796.

50. J. B. Andrews to the New York Members of the AALL, Nov. 3, 1919, AALL Papers.

51. Thomas W. Huntington, "Address of the President," *Transactions*, American Surgical Association, 1918, 36: 8.

52. Charles H. Mayo, "War's Influence on Medicine," *JAMA* 1917, 68: 1674.

53. "Compulsory Health Insurance," *Journal of the Indiana State Medical Association*, 1920, 13: 274.

54. *The Case against the King-Anderson Bill*, pp. 17, 119.

55. Roy Lubove, "The New Deal and National Health," *Current History*, 1977, 72: 226.

56. Wilburt C. Davison, "Should American Medicine be Socialized?" *JAMA*, 1943, 122: 1069.

57. *Voluntary Health Insurance vs Compulsory Sickness Insurance*, p. 5.

58. "Reasons for Opposing Administration Bill on Health Care for the Aged," *JAMA*, 1961, 176: 18.

59. "The Epstein State Health Insurance Bill," *JAMA*, 1935, 104: 401; Ralph S. Cone, Letter to the Editor, *JAMA*, 1917, 68: 1141. For examples of the "cog" metaphor, see Eden V. Delphey, "Compulsory Health Insurance from the Point of View of the General Practitioner," *New York State Journal of Medicine*, 1916, 16: 601; and the testimony of S. A. Cooney, president of the Montana State Medical Association, "National Health Program," p. 2099.

60. "The Report of the Committee on the Costs of Medical Care," *JAMA*, 1932, 99: 2035.

61. "Does American Medicine Need a Dictator?" *JAMA*, 1943, 123: 564; "The President's National Health Program and the New Wagner Bill," pp. 950–53; Elmer L. Henderson, "Statement on Truman Health Plan," *JAMA*, 1949, 140: 114; E. B. P[erry], "We and the Wagner Bill," *Journal of the National Medical Association*, 1944, 36: 63.

62. Testimony of H. F. Connally, president of the State Medical Association of Texas, "National Health Program," p. 606; Testimony of Joseph McGovern, Jr., chairman of the Doctors' Commission for American Health, "National Health Insurance Proposals," p. 2341.

63. "Future Doctors Oppose Federal Medicine," in *Federalized Health Care for the Aged? A Critical Symposium* (Chicago: American Medical Association, 1963), pp. 77-85. The survey was conducted by *Nation's Business*, and results published in June 1962.

64. John A. Kenney to Robert F. Wagner, June 8, 1939, *Journal of the National Medical Association*, 1939, 31: 176.

65. Frank H. Lahey, "An Appraisal of State-Controlled Medicine," in *Voluntary Health Insurance vs Compulsory Sickness Insurance*, p. 71.

66. Testimony of Thomas G. Dorrity, president of the Association of American Physicians and Surgeons, "National Health Insurance Proposals," p. 2194.

67. M. L. Harris, "Effects of Compulso-ry Health Insurance on the Practice of Medicine," *JAMA*, 1920, 74: 1041.

68. W. Montague Cobb, "Statement in Support of National Health Bill, S. 1606, on Behalf of the National Association for the Advancement of Colored People," *Journal of the National Medical Association*, 1946, 38: 136.

69. Report of Committee on Compulsory Health Insurance, *California State Journal of Medicine*, 1917, 15: 195. According to the president of the AMA in 1938, "It is a fundamental tenet of the American Medical Association that the poverty of a patient should demand the gratuitous services of a physician"; "Address of President Irvin Abell," *JAMA*, 1938, 111: 1193.

70. *Medical Care for the American People: The Final Report of the Committee on the Costs of Medical Care* (Chicago: University of Chicago Press, 1932), pp. 171–72. The AMA House of Delegates formally approved the minority report as representing "the collective opinion of the medical profession"; Minutes of the 84th Annual Session, June 12–16, 1933, *JAMA*, 1933, 100: 48.

71. Testimony of Edward C. Mazique, president of the NMA, "Health Needs of the Aged and Aging," Hearings before the Subcommittee on Problems on the Aged and Aging of the Committee on Labor and Public Welfare, U.S. Senate, 86th Cong., 2nd Sess., April 4–6, 11–13, 1960 (Washington, DC: GPO, 1960), p. 232.

72. Testimony of George A. Unfug, president of the Colorado State Medical Society, "National Health Program," p. 2177. For a discussion of how organized medicine's opposition to compulsory health insurance influenced its public image, see John C. Burnham, "American Medicine's Golden Age: What Happened to It?" *Science*, 1982, 215: 1474-9.

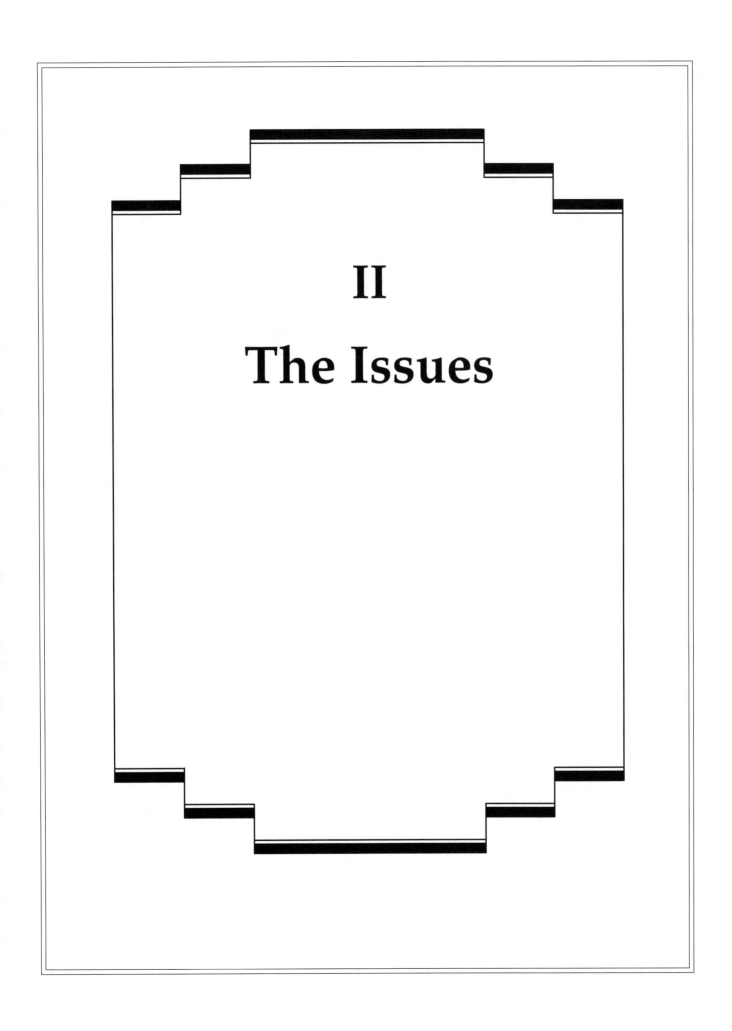

II

The Issues

Introduction

David A. Kindig

In the preface we discussed the rationale for first presenting a series of readings dealing with the fundamental issues underlying national and state universal health plans before approaching the existing or proposed plans themselves. For both our Faculty Task Force discussions and for the teaching of a graduate seminar, it is our opinion and preference that some understanding of the breadth and depth of issues precede specific plans (which are really aggregations of decisions or preferences on multiple issues) so that the consideration and critique can be informed by the issues and that the thinking about a preferred American solution can evolve inductively. Even if the process of moving toward a universal system is incremental and not all of the issues can be dealt with at one time, they still serve to guide the refinement process that will take place in future policy iterations.

Changing Paradigms of Morbidity and Efficacy

The first group of issues in this section is examined in four articles that present several different considerations about how underlying patterns of disease and our thinking about health outcomes may evolve in future decades. This issue may be the most important of all since major system change occurs infrequently and the risk of reinforcing underlying approaches that might retard new paradigms is considerable. The first article deals with the implications of the aging of the population and the shift of major attention in health care from young to old and from acute to chronic care. Edward Schneider and Jack Guralnik, in "The Aging of America: Impact on Health Care Costs," also call for research on prevention and the early treatment of diseases such as dementia and hip fractures, believing those actions to be fundamentally more cost saving than rationing or other administrative cost containment measures; they state that if we had relied solely on cost containment and rationing for tuberculosis, "we might still have tuberculosis sanatoriums and iron lungs." Jeff Goldsmith, "Chronic Illness and the Technologic Transformation of American Health Care," looks at how technology may evolve to change the ways health institutions provide services in a mainly chronic care environment, and specifically how hospitals will have to adapt to a lessened acute care role toward a "base station for

a network of community based services and information transmittal which stretches beyond the hospital . . . into remote ambulatory facilities and physicians offices."

The second two readings in this section do not discuss changing patterns of morbidity, but rather changes in ways we think about what the health care system produces or is responsible for. In Paul Ellwood's Shattuck lecture, "Outcomes Management: A Technology of Patient Experience," he again coins a new term—"outcomes management"—and defines it as a "technology of patient experience which is designed to help patients, payers, and providers make rational medical care related choices based on better insight into the effects of these choices on the patients' life." Our view of health care has been considerably influenced and limited by having to settle for structural and process indicators of quality and impact, since outcome measures have been largely unavailable, certainly at the system level.

Space prohibits inclusion of the seminal work by John Wennberg on variations in utilization of medical care, but the article by Mark Chassin et al., "Does Inappropriate Use Explain Geographic Variations in the Use of Health Care Services?," demonstrates substantial levels of inappropriate utilization for the three procedures evaluated and that geographic differences do not explain these variations. Other new methodologies of importance not covered here include cost benefit and effectiveness analysis (e.g., reform in Oregon), quality-adjusted life-year estimation, and population-based measures of health and functional status.

If the promise of these efforts is realized, purchasers of health care (public and private) could ultimately move to contracting for units of health status for beneficiaries rather than for amounts of health service. Such a development would certainly be a paradigm shift and have enormous implications for the health care financing and delivery system of the future. Any system of universal coverage in the short run should anticipate such a possibility and at the very least not include elements or incentives that would retard moving in this direction.

Financing Strategies and Incentives

The second group of articles deals with strategies and incentives for financing universal health plans. In writing on cross national health spending, George Schieber and Jean-

Pierre Poullier, in "International Health Spending: Issues and Trends," present comparative data in terms of per capita health expenditures, percentage of GDP devoted to health expenditures, and relative health spending growth rates for 24 OECD member countries. In addition to presenting current data which place the United States at the top in all three categories, they comment on the lack of standard definitions and information on institutional features of cross national health systems which are necessary to interpret such differences correctly. We have not been able to include the basic work of Joseph Newhouse and colleagues at RAND on the health insurance experiment in which utilization of both inpatient and ambulatory services was shown to increase for individuals with full coverage insurance policies in relation to income-related catastrophic policies; further analysis showed little negative impact on health status with the exception of ambulatory and preventive services for low-income individuals. This experiment is important in thinking about copayment policies in any universal plan, as well as considering whether any copayment provision is intended to control inappropriate utilization, or raise funding for the plan, or both. "Mandating Health Coverage for Working Americans," by Alan Monheit and Pamela Farley, is a very important policy analysis of mandating that employers provide health coverage to various categories of workers and dependents; they estimated that approximately two-thirds of the uninsured population would be covered by mandates for employees working 20 or more hours per week. Estimates of the employment impact of such mandates suggest that 2.5 percent of the workforce, or 847,000 workers, would have their jobs jeopardized. Several of the current national reform proposals include employer mandating and small group reform as key aspects of their approach. Stuart Butler, of the Heritage Foundation, presents the argument in "A Tax Reform Strategy to Deal with the Uninsured" that tax exclusion of company-based insurance plans has caused cost escalation and uninsurance because of inequity in tax assistance, job mobility disincentives, and inflationary pressure. Based on this analysis, he presents a proposal for a system of refundable market-based tax credits.

We have included the consumer choice competition approach of Alain Enthoven in a later section on current proposals (Chapter 32), but it could have been presented here as important thinking on financial incentives. The same consideration applies to both the Kevin Grumbach et al. (Chapter 33) and Karen Davis (Chapter 31) proposals which embody different approaches to financing mechanisms and incentives. The article by Brian Biles, Carl Schramm, and J. Graham Atkinson ("Hospital Cost Inflation Under State Rate-Setting Programs") is included to remind us that there has been and may still be a role for federal and state regulatory policies in system reform; many of these experiences tend to be forgotten or discarded out-of-hand in the current competitive context. Finally, Daniel Wikler introduces us to the often-discussed issue of using financial incentives to reform unhealthy and expensive health behaviors in "Persuasion and Coercion for Health." Missing from

the literature seems to be a clear and concise comparison of the relative advantages and disadvantages of these alternative financial strategies and incentives for universal coverage; it is hoped that such an analysis will be available in the future. Finally, we have omitted, but commend, the article by Uwe Reinhardt entitled "Does Spending by American Business on Health Care for Employees Erode this Nation's Competitive Position?" where he argues that the high health insurance premiums paid voluntarily by American businesses do not necessarily inhibit their competition in international markets since it is a part of total compensation and that health expenditures do not necessarily displace investment in other areas of productive capital.

Access, the Uninsured, and Rationing

The third group of issue articles contains five works on three related topics which, along with increased costs, have raised the potential for health system reform to its current level. Howard Freeman and colleagues reported in 1987 on the 1986 Robert Wood Johnson access survey in "Americans Report on Their Access to Health Care." Key findings from this survey were that there was an overall decline in visits to physicians and hospitals from 1982 and deterioration in access to the poor, minorities, and the uninsured. High percentages of pregnant women and individuals with hypertension did not receive appropriate care in all population groups, with higher rates in the minority and low-income groups. The AMA Council on Ethical and Judicial Affairs found disparities in access and treatment between black and white Americans, and they have had similar findings for Hispanic populations as well ("Black–White Disparities in Health Care"). Nicole Lurie et al. report from a RAND study that higher levels of cost sharing were associated with fewer childhood immunizations and fewer pap smears, but indicate that physician and patient factors also may contribute to the results ("Preventive Care: Do We Practice What We Preach?"). We were not able to include several important papers documenting health impacts of delay in care due to lack of insurance as well as the transfer of uninsured patients from emergency rooms in unstable condition.

On the topic of the uninsured, Emily Friedman summarizes why this dilemma has become a crisis in "The Uninsured: From Dilemma to Crisis." We have not included the important work of Gail Wilensky on this subject ("Viable Strategies for Dealing with the Uninsured"), nor the studies which indicate that half of uninsured spells end within four months and that employed persons are more likely to have uninsured spells (Katherine Swartz and Timothy McBride, "Spells Without Health Insurance: Distributions of Durations and Their Link to Point-in-Time Estimates of the Uninsured") and the role that state risk pools play in covering an important subgroup of the uninsured (Susan Laudicina, "State Health Risk Pools: Insuring the 'Uninsurable'").

The remaining article in this subsection deals with the topic of rationing. Aaron and Schwartz pose two definitions of rationing ("Rationing Health Care: The Choice Before Us): price rationing to deny goods to those who cannot afford them (the 15 percent uninsured) and the denial of commodities to those who can afford them (the 85 percent with health insurance). While not denying the importance of the former category, they focus on the latter and discuss it in the context of the inability to contain costs. They suggest that rationing is the only way such costs will be contained, and suggest that we look to Great Britain where past experience with such rationing "delineates the type of choices we may have to make." Of current interest in this regard is the reform proposal under discussion in Oregon which is attempting to use cost-benefit techniques mentioned previously to reallocate resources from ineffective to more effective services (William Stason, "Oregon's Bold Medicaid Initiative"; Norman Daniels, "Is the Oregon Rationing Plan Fair?"; R. Steinbrook and B. Lo, "The Oregon Medicaid Demonstration Project—Will it Provide Adequate Medical Care?").

The Delivery System and Administration

The reason for including this final set of articles is that any national or state health proposal will have to consider whether it will simply finance access to services in the existing delivery system or whether the proposals themselves will require or provide incentives for delivery system changes. We have omitted—but commend—an article by Donald Madison and Thomas Konrad ("Large Medical Group-Practice Organizations and Employed Physicians: A Relationship in Transition") where they describe large medical group practices with employed physicians and argue that the shift from "small scale individualistic to the large scale bureaucratic organization of medical practice is a rapid and irreversible historic transition which qualifies as a revolution." They suggest that such organizations will be the "building blocks of a number of private health care systems—both regional and national—or provide the experiences necessary for the construction of a public system."

The article by Will Manning et al. ("A Controlled Trial of the Effect of a Prepaid Group Practice on Use of Services") demonstrates that prepaid group practices provide 40 percent fewer hospitalizations than fee for service counterparts when both serve comparable populations with comparable benefits. Also commended is the paper by Joseph Newhouse ("Are Fee-for-Service Costs Increasing Faster than HMO Costs?") because it demonstrates that HMO costs have been rising as rapidly as fee-for-service costs, even though HMOs have lower costs at a point in time. The entire fall 1991 issue of *Health Affairs* is devoted to managed care, and is important given the high profile of managed care in reform discussions. It is essential to remember that most of the research on managed care has been done in the staff model mode whereas most growth is in IPA or other "looser" managed care arrangements.

Bruce Hillman et al. ("Frequency and Costs of Diagnostic Imaging in Office Practice") demonstrate that utilization of services increases dramatically when physicians have own-

ership interest, and underlies the importance of "safe harbor" regulations recently issued. In addition, the article points generally toward the advantages of a capitated or global budget rather than an à la carte fee-for-service approach in a capitalist economy. The American Society of Internal Medicine spells out the newly emerged "hassle factor" issue ("The Hassle Factor Defined"), which is having important ramifications on physician attitudes about medicine, the organizations of medicine, and their patients. We wish there were a succinct piece from the consumer perspective on how patients, often poor but sometimes not, fall daily between the financial and organizational cracks of our fragmented system and suffer from morbidity and lost productive time as a result.

Space precludes an article on long-term care, although we include one domestic proposal in the final section. The tendency is to consider acute and long-term care as separate sectors or plans, and current financial structures certainly reinforce this, but to patients there are no sharp boundaries between primary, acute, chronic, and community care. In our opinion, plans for universal coverage should move to integrate these boundaries. Certainly, if health status is the desired outcome, many community and social services may prove to be more effective than some of the acute procedures currently under evaluation. The social HMO idea has much conceptual appeal, and further research and policy analysis is certainly indicated. Another important reading on boundaries is the chapter by Paul Starr, "The Boundaries of Public Health" in the *Social Transformation of American Medicine*.

Finally, we include the important article by Steffie Woolhandler and David Himmelstein on administrative inefficiency of the current system in the United States—"The Deteriorating Administrative Efficiency of the U.S. Health Care System." If as much as 20 percent of health care expenditures are spent in administration, reform proposals which argue for simplification deserve serious study. This certainly has linkages to the "hassle factor" for physicians but is experienced by other providers and patients as well. The potential for cost savings in a single payer system has significant appeal, but threatens the private health insurance industry; it is important that more research and analysis be devoted to this important issue from both advocates of reform and the insurance industry.

In conclusion, we repeat our hope that considering this broad scope of issues before moving to specific plans will be useful for students and policymakers grappling with the important task of analyzing and creating an American system of universal coverage for the twenty-first century. Choices need to be made regarding changing epidemiology and health outcomes, on the most efficient and equitable financial incentives, on providing full access to the un- and underinsured, and to changes in delivery system and program administration which facilitate these goals. Some can be implemented in the short run; others will likely have to wait for further analysis and political will. In sum, they define a challenging agenda for both academic relevance and political action for the years ahead.

References

Daniels, Norman. "Is the Oregon Rationing Plan Fair?" *Journal of the American Medical Association* 265 (May 1, 1991): 2232–35.

Laudicina, Susan S. "State Health Risk Pools: Insuring the 'Uninsurable.'" *Health Affairs* (Fall 1988): 97–104.

Madison, D. L. and T. R. Konrad. "Large Medical Group-Practice Organizations and Employed Physicians: A Relationship in Transition." *Milbank Quarterly* 66 (2): 240–82.

Newhouse, Joseph P., et al. "Are Fee-for-Service Costs Increasing Faster Than HMO Costs?" *Medical Care* 23 (August 1985): 960–66.

Reinhardt, Uwe E. "Does Spending by American Business on Health Care for Employees Erode This Nation's Competitive Position?" *Journal of Medical Practice Management* 6 (Fall 1990): 90–98.

Starr, Paul. "The Boundaries of Public Health." In: *Social Transformation of American Medicine.* New York: Basic Books, 1982.

Stason, William B. "Oregon's Bold Medicaid Initiative." *Journal of the American Medical Association* 265 (May 1, 1991): 2237–38.

Steinbrook, R., and B. Lo. "The Oregon Medicaid Demonstration Project—Will It Provide Adequate Medical Care?" *New England Journal of Medicine* 326 (January 30, 1992): 340–44.

Swartz, Katherine, and Timothy D. McBride. "Spells Without Health Insurance: Distributions of Durations and Their Link to Point-in Time Estimates of the Uninsured." *Inquiry* 27 (Fall 1990): 28–88.

Wilensky, Gail R. "Viable Strategies for Dealing with the Uninsured." *Health Affairs* (Spring 1987): 33–46.

II

The Issues

**A   Changing Patterns of Morbidity
and Efficacy**

B Financing Strategies and Incentives

C Rationing, Access to Health Care
Services, and the Uninsured

D The Delivery System and System
Administration

3

The Aging of America: Impact on Health Care Costs

Edward L. Schneider and Jack M. Guralnik

Escalating health care costs are of increasing concern to local, state, and federal governments, corporations, and individual citizens. In the 11 years from 1976 to 1987, spending for medical care exceeded inflation by almost 80 percent.[1] In 1987, national health expenditures were $0.5 trillion, 11.1 percent of the gross national product.[2] Spending for federal Medicare and Medicaid programs has grown from $70 billion in 1982 to $111 billion in 1987.[2] Concern regarding health care costs is not confined to the United States; even countries with vastly different health care systems, such as Great Britain, are experiencing a rapid rise in their cost for health care.[3] In the 5-year period between 1981 and 1986, spending on the British National Health Service increased nearly 48 percent.[3]

Many factors contribute to rising health care costs: inflation of hospital and health care provider costs, the emergence of new diseases and disorders, and the development of new diagnostic and therapeutic modalities. In this article we will examine another factor that will have a substantial impact on health care costs in the upcoming decades: the aging of the aged. An unprecedented number of individuals are entering the ninth and tenth decades of life. This group, often referred to as the "oldest old" and defined as those aged 85 years and above, is now and will likely continue to be the fastest-

growing age group in the United States and other developed nations.[4]

Not anticipating the marked decline in mortality at older ages that has occurred in the past two decades, previous U.S. Census Bureau projections underestimated the growth of the oldest age groups, which surpassed even projections based on the lowest mortality assumptions.[5] The low-mortality assumption in the most recently published Census Bureau projections is more optimistic than previous projections.[6] We will therefore use current low- (series 9) as well as high- (series 19) and middle- (series 14) mortality Census Bureau projections for the growth of our older age groups to create projections for the costs for Medicare, nursing homes, and specific diseases that have an impact on these age groups.

Projections for Life Expectancy and for Growth of Older Populations

Life expectancies for men and women in the United States between 1900 and 1980 and the most recent projections by the Census Bureau for increases in life expectancy are presented in Figure 1.[6] The middle Census Bureau projection, the most frequently cited projection, predicts that by the year 2020, the average life expectancy will be 82.0 years for women and 74.2 years for men, and by the year 2040, the average life expectancy will rise to 83.1 years for women and 75.0 years for men. To examine the range of possibilities, we also present the Census Bureau's low- and high-mortality series (Figure 1).

The projected growth of those aged 65 years and above and those aged 85 years and above is presented in Figure

2. Current Census Bureau middle-mortality series projections predict that the number of individuals over age 65 years will increase to 52 million by the year 2020 and to 68 million by the year 2040. The low-mortality series projection results in the growth of this age group to 57 million by the year 2020 and to 83 million by 2050.[6] However, an examination of the projected growth of those over age 85 years is even more impressive. The middle Census Bureau projection, which is most frequently quoted, forecasts 6.7 million Americans age 85 years and over by the year 2020 and 12.2 million by the year 2040.[6] The low-mortality series projection results in 8.6 million Americans in this age group by the year 2020 and 17.8 million by the year 2040, a nearly 50 percent increase over the Census Bureau middle-mortality projection. This low-mortality series also projects over 1 million Americans 100 years and older in the year 2040. While there is always the possibility that new epidemics or failure to constrain the acquired immunodeficiency syndrome might result in lower numbers of older Americans than any of these projections, we believe it is more likely, given the rapid pace of biomedical research, that the actual numbers will surpass all three Census Bureau projections.[5]

Impact of Increasing Age on Disability and Institutionalization

As individuals enter the last decades of life, their needs for long-term care and the resultant costs increase exponentially. The increase with age in disability and the need for long-term care are presented in Figure 3. Because commu-

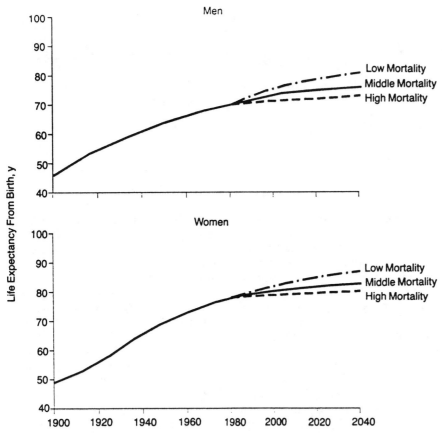

Fig 1.—Life expectancy for men and women from 1900 to 2040. From 1900 to 1980, the line represents actual life expectancy at birth. Projections are based on low- (series 9), middle- (series 14), and high- (series 19) mortality assumptions from the US Bureau of the Census.[6]

nity surveys do not include individuals residing in nursing homes, they substantially underestimate the prevalence of disease and disability in the overall older population. To approximate the burden of disability in the entire older population, the rates for nursing home use from the 1985 National Nursing Home Survey[7] and the rates for older persons living at home but needing the help of another person, from analyses done using *The Supplement on Aging to the 1984 National Health Interview Survey*,[8] were applied to the 1985 population (Figure 3). The percentage of all individuals aged 65 years and over who reside in nursing homes is 3 percent for men and 6 percent for women. For specific age groups, the percentage increases from 1 percent of men and women aged 65 to 74 years to 15 percent of men and 25 percent of women aged 85 years and above. The percentage of women in the population who live at

home and need the help of another person increases from 10 percent for those aged 65 to 74 years to 37 percent for those aged 85 years and above. For men, the corresponding numbers are 9 percent for those aged 65 to 74 years and 31 percent for those aged 85 years and above. Thus, the majority of women (62 percent) and a substantial proportion of men (46 percent) aged 85 years and above either reside in nursing homes or need assistance to live at home.

Limitations on Projecting Health Care Costs of Older Age Groups

There are many limitations on accurately projecting future health care costs for older persons. Projections must take into account several variables: the projected number of individuals age 65 years and older and their distribution within specific age groups, the estimated prevalence of disease and disabil-

ity at specific ages, and the estimated costs of providing health care at different ages for specific conditions.

Previous projections of health care costs have used the Census Bureau middle-mortality series projections for population growth.[9] These projections have been extremely useful in alerting policymakers to future increases in health care costs. However, it is useful to employ alternative Census Bureau projections for both higher and lower mortality.

Several factors may influence projections of the prevalence of diseases and disorders in specific age groups. Postponement of disease through preventive measures could lower age-specific disease prevalence, particularly in the younger segment of the population 65 years of age and older. Therefore, the use of current disease prevalence rates for those 65 to 74 years old may lead to an overprojection of the number of affected individuals in this age group. On the other hand, we may underproject the number of affected individuals aged 85 years and above for diseases whose prevalence increases exponentially with age. Within this open-ended age category, mean age will increase in the future, potentially leading to a higher prevalence of a disease whose frequency increases rapidly with aging. Furthermore, the costs associated with certain disorders, such as hip fractures, may be higher for those aged 85 years and above than for younger age groups. Elimination or reduction in the incidence of certain lethal diseases would result in more individuals surviving to older ages and developing other diseases. For example, declines in mortality from heart disease in the 65- to 74-year and/or 75- to 84-year age groups could lead to the survival of a larger population at risk for developing Alzheimer's disease or sustaining hip fractures in those aged 85 years and older.

It is difficult to predict the future levels of health care costs for specific conditions. While new efficiencies may be achieved that lower costs, the introduction of new diagnostic and/or therapeutic modalities may raise costs. If current trends oriented toward capping health care costs continue, it is probable that the average cost of the provision of

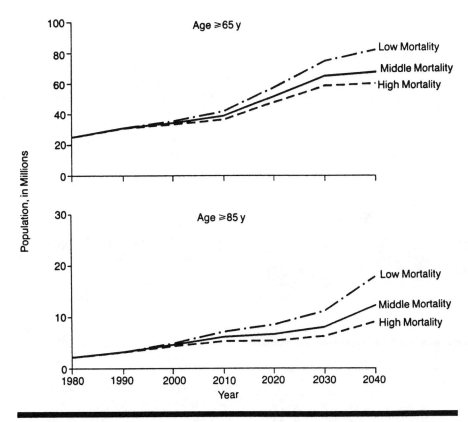

Fig 2.—Projected growth of the population aged 65 years and above and 85 years and above. Projections are based on low- (series 9), middle- (series 14), and high- (series 19) mortality assumptions from the US Bureau of the Census.[6]

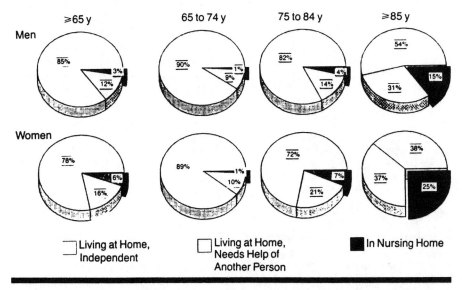

Fig 3.—Percentage of the population by age group and sex that (1) live at home independently, (2) live at home but require the help of another person, or (3) reside in a nursing home. The percentages of older persons in nursing homes by age group are from the 1985 National Nursing Home Survey.[7] The percentages of persons living at home and needing assistance are from analyses of data from *The Supplement on Aging to the 1984 National Health Interview Survey,*[8] applied to the total population. Assistance is defined as needing help with one or more of the following activities: eating, dressing, bathing, transferring from bed to chair, using the toilet, walking, cooking, shopping, managing money, using the telephone, and performing light housework.

health care for specific diagnosis related groups will remain relatively constant, with adjustments probably limited to the levels of inflation. In the projections to be presented, costs in 1985 or 1987 dollars are used.

Projected Medicare Costs for the Next Century

Medicare, which pays the majority of health care costs for older Americans, represents the largest health care expenditure for the federal government. However, in analyzing projections for Medicare costs it is important to keep in mind that the majority of the costs for long-term care are not covered under this entitlement. Nevertheless, Medicare costs are a useful reflection of the overall costs for health care for older Americans.

Average annual Medicare costs per person increase substantially with age, from $2017 for individuals aged 65 to 74 years to $3215 for those aged 85 years and above (Figure 4).[10] When Census Bureau middle series projections are used, the projected total cost of Medicare rises impressively during the upcoming decades, nearly doubling (in 1987 dollars) by the year 2020 (Figure 4). The greatest proportional increases are observed in the oldest age groups (75 to 84 and [is greater than or equal to] 85 years, Figure 4). In 2031, the first "baby boomers" will turn 85 years old. By 2040, the average age of a baby boomer will be 85 years, and the level of Medicare spending for the population age 65 years and above could range from $147 to $212 billion (in 1987 dollars).

Projected Nursing Home Costs for the Next Century

Currently, there are more residents of nursing homes than total available hospital beds.[7,11] Occupancy rates are also higher in nursing homes than in hospitals. In 1985, costs for nursing home care averaged $23,600 per resident, or a total of $31.1 billion for the 1.3 million nursing home residents aged 65 years and older.[12] While hospitals will have increasing trouble filling their beds, more nursing homes will have to be built to

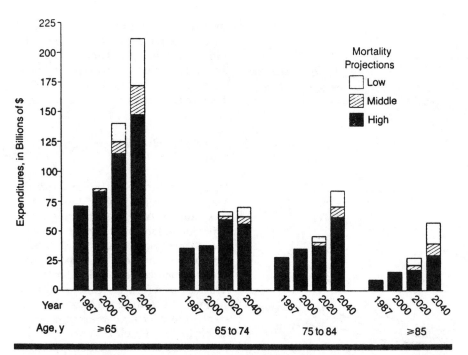

Fig 4.—Actual (1987) and projected Medicare expenses in 1987 dollars by age group. Average Medicare expenses per person were obtained from data from the Health Care Financing Administration.[10] Cost projections are based on low- (series 9), middle- (series 14), and high- (series 19) mortality assumptions from the US Bureau of the Census.[6]

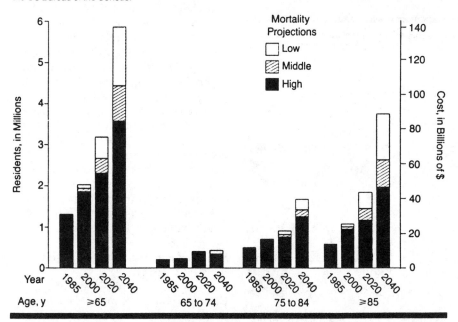

Fig 5.—Actual (1985) and projected numbers of US nursing home residents and costs in 1985 dollars by age group. The numbers of nursing home residents in 1985 are from the National Nursing Home Survey,[7] and the costs per resident are from the Health Care Financing Administration.[12] Projected numbers of residents and costs are based on low- (series 9), middle- (series 14), and high- (series 19) mortality assumptions from the US Bureau of the Census[6] and 1985 costs.

accommodate the increasing numbers of potential nursing home residents. Forty-five percent of elderly nursing home residents are 85 years and older.[7] Therefore, it is not surprising that al-

most half of current nursing home costs are consumed by those aged 85 years and above. As the number of individuals aged 85 years and above grows, assuming that the level of disability and

utilization of nursing home beds in this group remains stable, we will need large numbers of additional nursing home beds. By 2040, the number of nursing home residents aged 65 years and above may be between 3.6 and 5.9 million, 2.0 to 3.8 million of whom will be aged 85 years and above (Figure 5). Thus, there may be two to three times as many individuals aged 85 years and above in nursing homes in 2040 as there are individuals aged 65 years and above in nursing homes today!

The cost of nursing home care could rise between $84 and $139 billion (in 1985 dollars) by the year 2040 (Figure 5). Approximately 40 percent of current nursing home costs are reimbursed by the government through Medicaid. If this program continues and the number of nursing home residents rises to almost 6 million, the cost to the government could be as high as $56 billion (in 1985 dollars).

Projecting Costs of Specific Diseases and Disorders of Aging

Dementia

It is useful to examine two specific age-dependent disorders that contribute significantly to disability, nursing home admissions, and the need for long-term care: the dementias and hip fractures. Before projecting prevalence of dementias, we must emphasize the limitations of these projections. First, most prevalence studies have identified all causes of dementia without specifically diagnosing underlying causes, such as Alzheimer's disease.[13] Second, Alzheimer's disease, the most common form of dementia, manifests few distinctive signs or symptoms in the initial years, leading to an underestimate of the prevalence of this disorder.[13]

To project numbers of affected individuals, age-specific rates of dementia are needed for both community-dwelling individuals and nursing home residents. A number of studies have found age-dependent increases in dementia in community dwelling populations around the world.[14] To create our projections we have selected the median age-specific prevalences for moderate to severe dementia from several of these studies that provide age-specific rates beyond age 80 years.[14,15] This median prevalence of dementia increases rapidly with age, from 2.8 percent at ages 65 to 74 years to 9 percent at ages 75 to 84 years and 28 percent at age 85 years and above. A recent report by Evans et al.[16] suggests that the prevalence of dementia may be substantially higher than previously reported. The prevalence of dementia in nursing homes is much higher than among community-dwelling older Americans, ranging from 47 percent to 56 percent.[7,17] For our calculations we chose the average of the studies, 51.5 percent.

To project future costs of caring for those with dementia, we used estimates made by Hu and Cartwright[18] that the average cost of caring for a dementia patient is $22,458 per year in a nursing home and $11,735 per year at home. We used current age-specific rates for nursing home usage to project the future number of nursing home residents.

Costs for moderate to severe senile dementia were estimated in 1985 to be $35.8 billion to care for 2.4 million affected Americans (Figure 6). As seen in Figure 6, the costs of this condition will rise substantially in the upcoming decades. In 2040, when large numbers of baby boomers are in their 80s, there could be between 6.1 and 9.8 million Americans with moderate to severe dementia, requiring between $92 and $149 billion for their care (in 1985 dollars). These numbers approach the magnitude of current federal deficits.[19] If the expenditures for all levels of dementia were used for these calculations instead of those for just moderate to severe dementia, the future costs for this condition would exceed the largest federal deficits.

Hip Fractures

The risk of hip fracture increases exponentially with age.[20] In white women aged 85 years and above, the incidence of hip fractures is approximately 2 percent per year.[20] Hip fractures are a particularly important problem in older women, since approximately 20 percent of women who experience a hip fracture do not survive the first year after the fracture, and another 20 percent do not regain the ability to walk without assis-

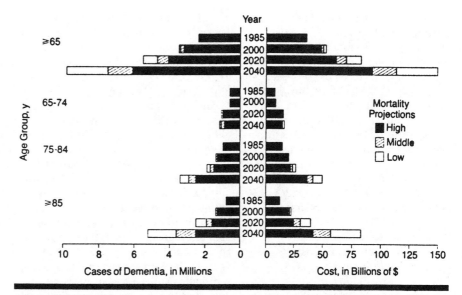

Fig 6.—Actual (1987) and projected numbers of individuals with moderate and severe dementia and costs in 1985 dollars for care by age group. These numbers are calculated by applying estimated age-specific prevalence rates of dementia in the community[14,15] and in nursing homes.[7,17] Costs for dementia are calculated for cases both in the community and in nursing homes.[18] Projected numbers of affected individuals and costs are based on low- (series 9), middle- (series 14), and high- (series 19) mortality assumptions from the US Bureau of the Census[6] and 1987 costs.

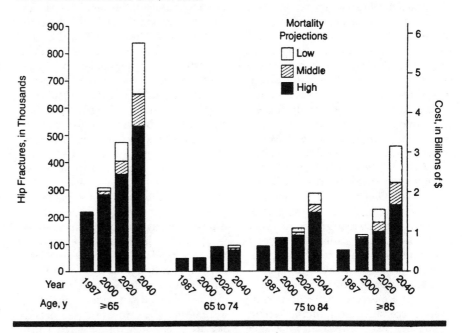

Fig 7.—Actual 1987 and projected hip fractures and costs in 1987 dollars by age group. Age-specific prevalence rates for hip fractures are from the National Hospital Discharge Survey,[27] and the costs were calculated from Medicare payment schedules for this diagnosis. The costs include only acute hospitalization and surgeons' fees. Projected numbers of hip fractures and costs are based on low- (series 9), middle- (series 14), and high- (series 19) mortality assumptions from the US Bureau of the Census[6] and 1987 costs.

tance.[21,22] In Figure 7, the projected number of hip fractures and the future health care costs associated with them are presented. These cost estimates are conservative; they represent only acute hospitalization costs, based on 1987

prospective Medicare payment schedules for this diagnosis, and surgeons' fees. If specific nursing home or home care costs for hip fractures were obtainable, they would add significantly to these costs. A review of projected costs for hip fractures reveals that the costs for those aged 85 years and above will almost equal the costs for all other age groups combined (Figure 7). The number of hip fractures is projected to increase from 220,000 in 1987 to approximately 300,000 by the year 2000 and to between 530,000 and 840,000 by the year 2040 (Figure 7). The costs for this condition, even under these modest estimates, are projected to increase from approximately $1.6 billion in 1987 to over $2 billion in 2000 and as much as $6 billion in 2040 (in 1987 dollars).

Responding to the Projected Increase in Health Care Costs for Our Aging Population

We have presented some projections for costs of Medicare, nursing homes, dementia, and hip fractures. These projections are based on many assumptions: that the age-specific prevalence of disease and disability will remain relatively constant, that costs for medical care will remain stable, and that population growth will be somewhere between the Census Bureau low- and high-mortality series projections. While many adjustments may need to be made in the future, these projections clearly demonstrate that the growing number of individuals reaching their 80s will have a significant impact on health care costs.

What is the best response to the forthcoming projected increases in health care costs? One obvious option is to reduce reimbursement for health care. In response to the rising Medicare costs of the last two decades, the federal government is now reimbursing for defined diagnosis related groups by specific fixed prospective payments. This approach appears to have been relatively successful at continuing certain health care costs.[1] However, if the age-specific frequencies of conditions such as hip fractures remain constant, capping the costs for the diagnosis related groups that cover these conditions will not prevent massive increases in overall cost as the number of affected individuals increases rapidly. While cost containment should be pursued vigorously, other approaches to limiting future health care costs are needed.

Increasingly vocal suggestions that we consider rationing health care for older Americans are an ominous reflection of the desperate fears associated with rising health care costs. Ex-Governor Richard D. Lamm of Colorado and Daniel Callahan, Ph.D., director of the Hastings Institute, Briarcliff Manor, NY, have suggested that after the completion of a "natural life span," somewhere in the late 70s or early 80s, medical care should be provided only to relieve suffering.[23] There are many pitfalls to rationing health care by age: (1) It would be extremely difficult to reach a consensus on what age denotes the completion of a "natural life span." (2) The heterogeneity that occurs with aging[24] makes chronological age a poor basis for any decision to bar someone from medical care. (3) It would promote and encourage age discrimination.[25] (4) Last and most important, the decision to withhold care should be based on criteria other than age: the desires of the patient and his/her family and the patient's health status. However, if health care costs for older Americans increase as projected, these unpopular and inadequate proposals may be hard to derail.

One positive approach to reducing health care costs is to mobilize research resources on common diseases and disorders that lead to long-term disability in the oldest old. Today, between 0.1 and 0.2 cents are spent on basic research on Alzheimer's disease for every dollar spent on care for victims of Alzheimer's disease.[26] Considering the enormous future projected cost of this disorder, it is imperative that this disease receive a more appropriate level of research support. Application of the tools of molecular genetics to the study of Alzheimer's disease is already providing important insights into the nature of this disorder. We must accelerate this research, since delays could result in the unnecessary expenditure of hundreds of billions of dollars for services as well as the exposure of millions of Americans and their families to this tragic disease. Additional research support is also needed for other diseases that disable the oldest old: Parkinson's disease, osteoarthritis, hip fractures, and peripheral vascular diseases.

In conclusion, unless we make substantial advances in the prevention and treatment of the diseases that cause the greatest disability, the aging of our oldest age groups will have a major impact on future health care costs. There will be large increases in the costs for Medicare, nursing homes, dementia, and hip fractures, in large part resulting from projected growth in the numbers of the oldest old. These increased costs will more than offset potential gains from cost-containment strategies. For example, even if the care of a dementia patient could be reduced in the future by 50 percent, which would be a significant reduction, the projected 300 percent to 500 percent increase in the number of affected individuals would still result in a 150 percent to 250 percent increase in the overall cost for this disorder.

A more successful long-term approach is to prevent and/or cure the most common cause of dementia, Alzheimer's disease. Other diseases have produced large numbers of disabled Americans in this century: tuberculosis and polio. Research on these diseases led to antibiotics and vaccines that have significantly reduced the incidence and costs of these conditions. If, instead of research, we had relied solely on cost containment or rationing, we might still have tuberculosis sanitoriums and iron lungs. Even in today's difficult financial climate, we must not be myopic but instead should look for long-term solutions for projected increases in health care costs.

Dr. Schneider receives support from the John D. and Catherine T. MacArthur Foundation Network on Successful Aging and the Retirement Research Foundation. We thank Freddie Segal-Gidan for her research assistance and Gitta Morris and Donna Polisar, M.A., for technical help in preparation of the manuscript.

Notes

1. Altmann SH, Rodwin MA. Halfway competitive markets and ineffective regulation: the American health care system. *J Health Polit Policy Law.* 1988;13:323–339.
2. Levit KR, Freeland MS. Datawatch. *Health Aff.* 1988;5:124–136.

3. *Social Trends*. London, England: Central Statistics Office, Dept of Health and Social Security; 1987:17.

4. Rosenswaike IA. Demographic portrait of the oldest old. *Milbank Q*. 1985;63:187–205.

5. Guralnik JM, Yanagishita M, Schneider EL. Projecting the older population of the United States: lessons from the past and prospects for the future. *Milbank Q*. 1988;66:283–308.

6. Spencer G. *Projections of the Population of the United States by Age, Sex and Race: 1988 to 2080*. Washington, DC: US Bureau of the Census; 1989. Current Population Reports. Series P-25. No. 1018.

7. Hing E. *Use of Nursing Homes by the Elderly: Preliminary Data From the 1985 National Nursing Home Survey*. Hyattsville, Md: US Public Health Service; 1987. U.S. Dept of Health and Human Services publication (PHS) 87-1250. Advance Data From Vital and Health Statistics. No. 135.

8. *The Supplement on Aging to the 1984 National Health Interview Survey*. Hyattsville, Md: National Center for Health Statistics; 1987. Vital and Health Statistics. Series 1. No. 21.

9. Rice DP, Feldman JJ. Living longer in the United States: demographic changes and health needs of the elderly. *Milbank Q*. 1983;61:362–396.

10. Waldo DR, Sonnefeld ST, McKusick DR, Arnett RH III. Health expenditures by age group, 1977 and 1987. *Health Care Finance Rev*. 1989;10: 111–120.

11. *Hospital Statistics*. Chicago, Ill: American Hospital Association; 1987.

12. Lazenby H, Levit KR, Waldo DR. *National Health Expenditures*, 1985: No. 6. Washington, DC: Office of Research and Demonstrations, Health Care Financing Administration; 1986. Publ. (HCFA) 03232.

13. Schoenberg BS. Methodologic approaches to the epidemiologic study of dementia. In: Mortimer JA, Schuman L, eds. *The Epidemiology of Dementia*. New York, NY: Oxford University Press; 1981:117-131.

14. Evans JG. The epidemiology of dementias in the elderly. In: Brody JA, Maddox GL, eds. *Epidemiology and Aging: An International Perspective*. New York, NY: Springer-Verlag NY Inc; 1988:36–53.

15. Mortimer JA, Hutton JT. Epidemiolgy and etiology of Alzheimer's disease. In: Hutton JT, Kenny AD, eds. *Senile Dementia of the Alzheimer Type*. New York, NY: Alan R Liss Inc; 1985:177–196.

16. Evans DA, Funkenstein HH, Albert MS, et al. Prevalence of Alzheimer's disease in a community population of older pesons: higher than previously reported. *JAMA*. 1989;261: 2551–2556.

17. Rovner BW, Kafonek S, Filipp L, Lucas MJ, Folstein MF. Prevalence of mental illness in a community nursing home. *Am J Psychiatry*. 1986;143:1446–1449.

18. Hu T, Cartwright WS. Evaluation of the costs of caring for the senile demented elderly: a pilot study. *Gerontologist*. 1986;26:158–163.

19. *Historical Tables: Budget of the US Government: Fiscal Year, 1989*. Washington, DC: Executive Office of the President, Office of Management and Budget; 1989.

20. Farmer ME, White LR, Brody JA, Bailey KR. Race and sex differences in hip fracture incidence. *Am J Public Health*. 1984;74:1374–1380.

21. Miller CW. Survival and ambulation following hip fracture. *J Bone Joint Surg Am*. 1978;60:930–934.

22. Kenzora JE, McCarthy RE, Lowell JD, Sledge CB. Hip fracture mortality: relation to age, treatment, preoperative illness, time of surgery, and complications. *Clin Orthop*. 1984;186:45–56.

23. Callahan D. *Setting Limits*. New York: Simon & Schuster Inc Publishers; 1987.

24. Finch CE, Schneider EL, eds. *Handbook of the Biology of Aging*. New York, NY: Van Nostrand Reinhold Co; 1985.

25. Jecker NS, Pearlman RA. Ethical constraints on rationing medical care by age. *J Am Geriatr Soc*. 1989;37:1067–1075.

26. *Special Report on Alzheimer's Disease*. Bethesda, Md: National Institute on Aging; 1988.

27. Havlik RJ, Liu BM, Kovar MG, et al. *Health Statistics on Older Persons, United States, 1986*. Washington, DC: US Public Health Service; 1987:66. US Dept of Health and Human Services publication (PHS) 87-1409. Vital and Health Statistics. Series 3. No. 25.

4

Chronic Illness and the Technologic Transformation of American Health Care

Jeff Goldsmith

We would like to begin our conference by speculating a little bit on the shape of the future of our health care system. One of the things that I've discovered about futurism, besides reaffirming Henry Kissinger's maxim that there's virtue in ambiguity, is that you're not supposed to quote specific figures or name a date by which something is supposed to happen. I have concluded that people like thinking about the future for the very same reason we like watching Evel Knievel attempt to jump the Grand Canyon—because we knew he wasn't going to make it. But thinking about the future is very different from jumping the Grand Canyon. The further out you go, the safer it is. Completely the opposite from the Evel Knievel dynamics. How did I learn this? Well, about three years ago, I was asked to write an article about "American Medicine in 50 Years." I remember getting this phone call and hearing, "Would you write an article about what the health care system's going to be about in 50 years?" My first reaction was to hold the phone up and go, "Are you nuts? I mean, how do I know?" And then, a little light bulb went on. And I realized that not only would I be dead in the year 2036. but so would every single person who read the article. So it is in that spirit that we're going to talk about the twenty-first century. It hasn't happened yet, so we're all on equal ground and we can all speculate freely without fear of the

consequences. One of the things that I did learn from Evel Knievel is that it helps to start as far back from the canyon wall as you can to get a good run at it. And so, with that thought in mind, I believe that when we look back on this century from the vantage point of the year, let us say, 2020, we will see that our nation's health care system underwent two historic transformations in the nature of what was wrong with people and how we dealt with them— the first transformation in about the first 40 years of the century and the second beginning about 1970.

I've taken a lot of this material from James Fries, who is a fascinating and controversial student of the changing nature of human illness, and one of the things that Fries points out in his work "Vitality and Aging" is that during the first four decades of this century, our society basically vanquished whole categories of human illness. What's so interesting is that these are infections borne by bacteria. We didn't really have definitive treatments for any of these diseases until about 1940. So a lot of the progress that was made in reducing mortality from these infectious diseases is the product of other things: public health measures, improved living standards and nutritional standards, and growing awareness of health hazards on the part of the population. No one really knows. But we did in fact, change the profile of what was wrong with Americans during this period of time. And this transformation, students of epidemiology tell us, is common to all modernizing nations: at some point, a

modernizing nation goes through this transformation and defeats these diseases. Now, infectious diseases are still with us, but it is the most difficult infectious diseases—viral illnesses, like AIDS and hepatitis—that I think are going to be with us for a while. These diseases help shape our concept of disease—the idea of something caused by an external agent that you can't see that comes out of nowhere, throws your body into violent disequilibrium, creates a life threat and crisis, and either passes or terminates you, one or the other. And we carried that model of disease well on into this century, past the point where these types of diseases really are dominant medical problems. Another thing to say about this period is that the hospital, the acute care hospital as we see it, was a creature of this era. It was created to diagnose these diseases, to isolate the infected patient from the community, to hold the patient's hand, because until 1940 there really wasn't a heck of a lot you could do about any of them, other than send the patients home after a couple of weeks or to send them on to the next life.

And a lot of what we've done to the hospital in the intervening 40 or 50 years is retool that basic acute care mainframe to deal with an entirely different set of medical problems. The first 30 or so years of that retooling were interesting from an epidemiological standpoint because there was a period of pause here, a cessation of progress in reducing overall mortality rates in the society and an equally interesting cessation of progress in reducing infant mortality. Begin-

Reprinted with permission from *Decisions in Imaging Economics* (February 1989), pp. 4-13.

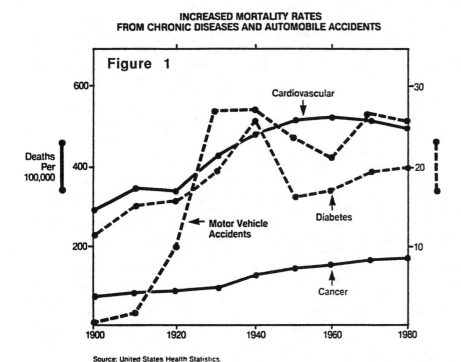

**INCREASED MORTALITY RATES
FROM CHRONIC DISEASES AND AUTOMOBILE ACCIDENTS**

Figure 1

Source: United States Health Statistics.

ning in the 1950s and up through about 1970, the nature of what was wrong with Americans and what people died of was changing, as indicated in Figure 1. Now, we got the bonus from this substantial reduction in mortality rates. We got to live about another 20 years, on the average, but the reward for living the additional years was perverse—we got to die of even more intractable and horrible illnesses later in our lives. What emerged underneath that pattern of declining causes of death from acute illness and, in fact, really emerged in part as a result of the decline in acute illness was that chronic illnesses, systemic diseases of our body's organ systems, became our nation's dominant health care problem, and today, better than 80 percent of all deaths and 90 percent of all morbidity in the country is associated with these, what one might term, degenerative diseases, such as cancer, diabetes, and heart disease. Radicals, like Fries, balk at calling these diseases. They don't like associating chronic illness with the idea of an acute episode. Their point is that what we call chronic illness is really not so much a

disease as a natural process of the breakdown of our body's systems, our abilities to function in a world or environment that constantly challenges them. Chronic illness, Fries and others argue, is systematically different. We are roughly comparably at risk for contracting these diseases. They are universal, meaning that we all, to some extent, have them in various stages.

All the people in this room are in various stages of degenerative diseases of their circulatory systems, but how far along they are is an interesting question. As we age and as our body's systems—the circulatory system, the mechanism for cellular reproduction, the endocrine system—become less resilient, they become more prone to breaking down, and it is the breakdown of those systems that results in chronic illness. One of the other things that students of these diseases point out to us is that we have them for many years before they reach a life threat, that there is a sort of a steadily rising threshold of acuity of the diseases, and that only at a certain point do they reach a life-threatening position. Why is this impor-

tant? Well, it's because this model of disease is fundamentally different from the model of a disease caused by an external agent that comes out of nowhere and precipitates a crisis and throws the body into violent disequilibrium, etc. Chronic disease is inherent in the aging process. It is inevitable, though there is a lot of dispute over whether the degeneration is genetically programmed, [or] is a function of just the wearing out of our cells or organs. But there are other emerging causes of death and disability, such as motor vehicle accidents and the rising prevalence of homicide and suicide and diseases from drug abuse and drug addiction, which emerged as major causes of human misery during this period of time.

Our nation's health care system as it is presently organized uses an acute care model to respond to chronic illness. That is, it tends systematically to ignore the disease process until it has reached a life-threatening stage. Then a helicopter lands on your lawn and spirits you away to a coronary care unit where you are stabilized, catheterized evaluated for possible open heart surgery, kept a short time in the hospital, rehabilitated, and then dumped out on the street. The disease is still there. You still have heart disease. But the acute care episode is past, and the interest of our health care system in continuing to care for you is sharply diminished. And you can tell this sharp diminution by the language that hospitals use to describe getting rid of the patient who is no longer acutely ill. The process is called "discharge planning."

If you think about the language a little bit, discharge planning is really something you do with toxic waste, isn't it? But in the hospital it's more like throwing the patients over the wall into the chronic care world without really caring all that much what happens to them once they're out of your immediate orbit. Our health care system, in a perverse way, concentrates an extraordinary amount of resources on an extremely narrow band of that chronic illness and as a result, many people believe, is not making a very effective use of overall societal resources.

Nevertheless, this mission, this use of our health care system, is being undercut not only by changing technology and medical practice patterns but by a growing awareness of a mismatch between our society's needs and what our health care system offers people. And you can see the beginnings of the transformation, if you look closely, in the late 1960s. You can see the seeds of that second transformation in our health care system's needs and response. The bending of the curve for cardiovascular disease mortality does not adequately display the more than 20 percent reduction that's taken place since about 1970 in deaths from heart disease of all kinds, and almost a 50 percent reduction in deaths from strokes. Even within cancer—the epidemiologists don't like you to do this, but if you took lung cancer out—the curve would have bent in cancer as well in the early or mid 1970s. Of course the argument against taking lung cancer out is that here was an eminently preventable disease; if we just educated people enough and maybe taxed cigarettes, they wouldn't have smoked all of them and they wouldn't be dying in record numbers from lung cancer.

But my point is, if you take lung cancer out, deaths from other forms of cancer have been going down, and for some forms of cancer, fairly dramatically. What is wrong with us and what our society needs to do to take care of it in the first part of the twenty-first century could look very different than what it does today.

Let us speculate a little bit about how the patterns of treatment for three complex illnesses that our society is worrying about right now are likely to change in the next few years. Let's start with heart disease, because this is the one where the most significant progress has been made. In 1970, frankly, there wasn't a lot we could do about this disease because, typically, people ended up in the emergency room in extremis, in acute M.I. or stroke situation. That was often the diagnostic event, that they appear blue in the emergency room. The periods of hospitalization were relatively lengthy, the ability to repair the damage done by the heart attack or stroke relatively modest, and the patient would typically die of the disease in a later episode. In 1988 we

have vastly complicated and, some people believe, improved the treatment for this disease. Most importantly, at least in my lay person's judgment, is that we're catching it a lot earlier. We're diagnosing it earlier, and as a consequence of major advances in knowledge about how behavior leads to vulnerability to heart disease and, particularly, the drugs that were developed in the 1970s to control hypertension, we're able to intervene to bend the curve—that is, to bend off that rapid rise in life threat that the disease represented.

We've also got a whole array of technologies that can be used to bring to bear on the disease to the point where it does become symptomatic. If patients have angina, we can catheterize them, we can replace defective coronary arteries with arteries from the leg or wherever, the patients stay in the hospital a week, maybe, after open heart surgery and are back on the street. If they come in with an acute episode, we could administer a lytic agent, like TPA or streptokinase, to try to restore circulation before the heart or the brain is damaged. Or, with some controversy about how effective the results are, we can use second-generation technologies, like angioplasty, to restore circulation. Whether people really live longer as a result of these technologies being brought to bear, we don't really know. We do know that there is a longer period of time when they're free of symptoms. But remember, from 1970 to 1988, as a result of drugs and dietary changes and increased awareness of the risk factors associated with heart disease, we have seen a sharp reduction in the death rate from heart disease in that period of time.

By 1995, I think the time line will look something like that in Figure 2. We will have the capability by 1995 of diagnosing the disease to the point where it is completely asymptomatic, and which of the three competing technologies emerges as the definitive diagnostic tool for this disease is anybody's guess. Lance Gould would tell you that it will be PET (positron emission tomography); other people will tell you it will be MRI (magnetic resonance imaging), cinematically enhanced; yet others, ultrasound. One of those technologies

will probably have evolved by 1995 to the point where we can detect the narrowing of the coronary or carotid arteries, the major arteries, with as little as perhaps 20 percent occlusion.

Many cardiologists believe that in animal models you can reverse the progress of the disease, not merely slow it down, but reverse the progress and the occlusion of the arteries. If people don't take the drugs to lower cholesterol levels or change their strategy for managing the risk factors, then we'll have third- and fourth-generation catheter-delivered technologies like laser angioplasty or atherectomy.

For those of you who have been wondering about this process; it's a little bit like peeling back the layers of an onion. We peeled back the diseases of childhood and got the diseases of early adulthood, many of those infectious diseases, like syphilis. We peeled those back and underneath was heart disease. And every time you peel back a layer, you get disease.

You can see a similar pattern with AIDS. In 1984 the disease was diagnosed again at the point where the actual symptoms of the infection had already materialized, namely the opportunistic infections themselves, Kaposi's sarcoma or pneumocystis pneumonia, and the futile course of treatment—there was typically no more than 18 months to two years from diagnosis to death—was a course of lengthening and deepening hospitalizations. If you believe what we are learning in San Francisco and other West Coast cities about the management of the disease, the 1990 profile for AIDS will look something like that in Figure 3. The disease will be diagnosed again asymptomatically. A person who is a part of the risk group will have tests done that will detect the presence of the AIDS virus in the form of its antibodies well in advance of the infection emerging. And with drugs like AZT that help the body's immune system fight the infection, it is believed—although we don't really know how long—that this time line is going to be lengthened. It could be two, three, four years, but we really won't know for sure until we've been able to evaluate the survival rates of cohorts of patients that have taken AZT or drugs like it for some

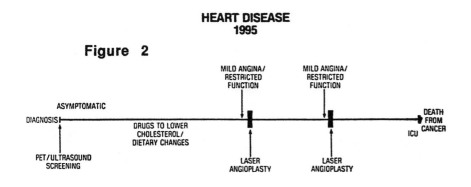

HEART DISEASE
1995

Figure 2

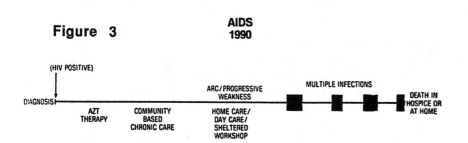

Figure 3

AIDS
1990

time. We will also have, by then, drugs that will be developed to fight the specific opportunistic infections as well, so that you'll be increasing the period of morbidity but, again, bending the curve, slowing the progression of the disease to the point where it reaches a life threat. During that period of time, the health care system's role in treating the AIDS patient will focus around what we've called here "community-based chronic care," a lot of ambulatory treatment, home health care services, day care, sheltered workshops for AIDS patients who have been fired from their jobs. In other words, a whole complex of services that basically help patients remain ambulatory and help them continue to lead a productive and meaningful life. A result of these services—we've already seen this in San Francisco—is the sharp reduction in inpatient length of stay for this disease, so when the patients die, they're as likely to die in a hospice or in a home as they are to die in a hospital.

With cancer, a similar pattern exists. In 1970, our health care system

wasn't doing a very effective job of treating this disease, primarily because it caught the disease so late that surgery was the principal remedy. You did a biopsy; if the biopsy showed malignancy, you cut it out—a very large part of the organ system. You tried to prevent recurrence with crude radio- or chemotherapy, but the disease would inevitably, except for miracle kinds of interventions, reoccur and the patient would die from the illness. Recognizing that there are thirty-some kinds of cancer, I think the pattern in 1985 looked a little better. Again, with a more sophisticated patient population and better diagnostics, we were able to detect the disease earlier with better and more focused radio- and chemotherapy. With new drugs like cisplatin, the disease could be suppressed or at least the tumor shrunk to the point where, when you did have to have surgery, the patient wasn't really compromised; you didn't lose the whole organ—you would do a lumpectomy instead of taking off the whole breast, etc. The period of recuperation postsurgery was typically

a lot shorter, but we're still losing the vast majority of the people who have the disease. By the year 2010—and here we are nearing the far side of the canyon—a lot of people think the pattern will look something like that in Figure 4. The disease, or at least the predisposition of the disease, will be diagnosed at birth or before by taking a sample of the patient's genetic material and subjecting it to a genetic screen that will evaluate, if you will, the competence of the patient's genetic apparatus to produce a whole, viable organ for a long period of time. We have been able to tie genetic defects to vulnerability to specific kinds of cancers and other diseases. We'll be able to identify all sorts of vulnerabilities besides just the vulnerability to cancer. We will have this embarrassing lapse, and it could be as long as 20 years from now, between the time when we have the ability to do that screening and the ability to treat any of the diseases thus identified. So I went out to 2010, by which time there is a chance, at least, that we will have technologies for correcting the genetic defects. One that's really intriguing to me is the idea of transfection, that is, of using a genetically engineered virus to carry new genetic information into the body—to basically change the genetic makeup of the individual; to eliminate the vulnerability to cancer or whatever the genetically influenced disease is; to provide the person a level playing field for life. People are still going to get cancer from all sorts of other causes: toxins, bad diet, living too close to nuclear power plants, whatever it is, but there is also going to be not only a mechanism for detecting the cancer when it's in the system much earlier—probably much earlier than the formation of a lesion—but also, with outpatients at home, chemotherapy with the use of biotherapeutic agents. Monoclonal antibodies or substances like interferon, which our body makes but which we're now manufacturing outside the body, can be put in in greater concentrations to deal with the disease. People will still die of cancer in the year 2010, but I believe that we will sharply reduce its prevalence and that there is a greater likelihood that people will die of misadventure or just sort of running down and falling apart than from the disease.

What's the common element in these three disease patterns? You are detecting chronic illnesses and diseases like AIDS that behave like chronic illnesses earlier and earlier in the disease process at lower levels of acuity, far in advance of a life threat, with technologies that permit, in effect, the medical care system to intervene earlier, with progressively more effective methods of therapy that bend the curve, that reduce the progression of the disease to the point of life threat. There's a prolongation of the life span from the point of diagnosis. But also, it's important to add, a prolongation of the period of morbidity. I guess you could argue the morbidity was there before you diagnosed it, but we tend not to believe something unless we've gotten scientific evidence that we have a disease based on genetic makeup and information and a sampling of blood cholesterol levels and a sonogram. And it'll be up to me as a manager of my own destiny to figure out how I deal with this looming threat to my existence. The role of the acute inpatient part of the hospital is sharply diminished, again as a direct function of catching the diseases earlier. You're not getting the patient so late in the disease process that the patient is already compromised from a strategic standpoint, and I think this is equally important for the people who pay for health care as much as it is for the people who deliver it. It's really important to control the diagnosis because if you don't make the diagnostic decision, you probably do not participate in the planning for the care and intervention and continuing interaction with the patient that result. There's also an interesting cost benefit issue of how much that screening process costs. What is the social impact of every woman at risk for breast cancer getting a mammogram every year or every five years or whatever it is? We're clearly not, as a society, going to be able to afford to screen every individual in the country for heart disease with cinematic magnetic resonance imaging. So we've also got interesting cost issues about how the payers for care are going to intervene here as the diagnosis moves earlier and earlier into the time line of the disease. And finally, one of the benefits, I guess, of getting the

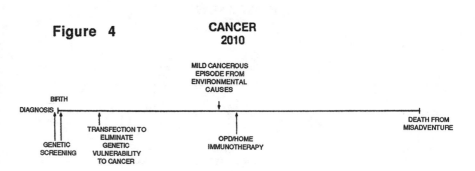

Figure 4   CANCER 2010

disease earlier from a societal standpoint is that the focus of the health care system changes from curing the symptoms, transplanting damaged heart or kidney, to helping patients live with the illness and helping them modify their behavior and the environment in which they function to help, again, bend the curve short of producing a life threat.

The problem a hospital has in all of this is, I think, pretty obvious, which is that as long as the hospital continues to define its principal business as the rendering of inpatient hospital care, it's going to preside over a shrinking empire and be fighting over a pie that's getting smaller and smaller. It is possible to construct a path of treatment for many forms of cancer that completely bypasses the hospital, as shown in Figure 5. I think that the only reason a lot of these paths pass through the hospital today is what I would term sociological: medical oncologists tend to cluster in hospitals and the density of consultative resources, rather than the technology itself, is what is driving cancer care through hospitals today. But in fact, all of these technologies—biopsy, radio- and chemotherapy, home infusion therapy—all of those things, at least from a technological standpoint anyway, are detachable from that building and could be delivered to a population if the critical mass is sufficient in any number of ways, including ambulatory care facilities. The cataract operation has virtually disappeared from most hospitals. In Southern California you just don't see them in the hospital anymore. They're done in physicians' offices or in freestanding surgical facilities. Ditto with technologies like arthroscopy. And the more effective, noninvasive diagnostic/

therapeutic modalities we develop, the more options there will be for where those critters are located and how much overhead we need in order to pay for them. Paying triple the direct cost of the cataract operation because it happens to be performed in a hospital may not be a socially beneficial use of the dollars. The hospital in particular has begun, as a result of the beginning decline in utilization, to realize that it needs to reposition itself.

The sharp decline in inpatient hospital utilization that we experienced during this decade was, I believe, directly related to the processes that we have been talking about here: the rise in outpatient visits, a function of a larger number of technologies that can be administered in a lower-risk, noninvasive or minimally invasive environment at a lower unit cost. Of course, we've completely lost control of the volume of services because every time one of these technologies comes out, we broaden the range of disease that we can treat. We don't really have a good way of balancing the social benefits associated with doing more arthroscopies, more lithotripsy, etc., against the increased cost of using these services. You've seen an explosion in ambulatory surgery: a 136 percent increase in hospital-based ambulatory surgery in just five years. And during that same period of time, hospitals surrendered about 18 percent of the surgical marketplace to nonhospital-based services. That is, out-of-hospital ambulatory surgery also grew, but at an even more explosive rate during this time so that, despite growing 136 percent, hospitals lost surgical market share during that five-year period. And then, finally, the most significant explosion of

NEW DIAGNOSTIC/TREATMENT PATHS BYPASS HOSPITAL

Figure 5

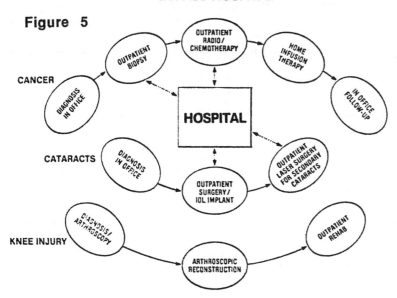

all—the explosive adoption and growth of noninvasive or minimally invasive imaging technologies that have dramatically expanded our ability to diagnose human illness without cutting the patient all the way open.

I believe that these changes in our health care system and in the nature of the illnesses that our society is going to be dealing with present a number of challenges to the health care delivery system. For one thing, it is entirely possible that by the early part of the next century, the home and the residential community, not the hospital, will be the center of our health care system and that the hospital will account—even with its outpatient departments—for as little as a third of total health care spending. And part of what's going to be driving this shrinkage in the hospital's resources is the societal dilemma that the only way we're going to be able to increase our investment in chronic care services— not only medical services, but social and human services—is to finance them, at least in part, by reducing or moderating the rate of increase in the financing of acute care hospital services. We must try rigorously to focus what the acute care hospital does with all of that cost and overhead on that relatively narrow range of conditions that cannot be man-

aged in any other setting. The hospital's role is likely to be reshaped by our payment system in technologies to be, in effect, the community's trauma center—the place for the multiple system failure, for the burn victim, for the accident victim, but also a base station for a network of community-based services and information transmittal that stretches beyond the hospital core physical plant into remote ambulatory facilities and directly into the physician's office. The hospital will become the hub, as we've suggested in our articles, of an electronic network that conveys in both directions clinical and economic information about the patient and that provides a safety net for the practitioner who may be as many as 200 miles away from the hospital, but who can still participate in the hospital's data bases and use artificial intelligence and expert systems to aid in the diagnosis and treatment of patients.

The role of the health care system in the face of this change in technological focus will be twofold: One, to prevent or retard the onset of disease, and two, the societal bottomless pit, to maximize the function of the individual in the face of emerging disability. And the reason I say this is a bottomless pit is that resolving an acute life threat is vastly

more quantifiable and capturable in a statistical methodology than improving the quality of someone's life. Distinguishing between those two things and figuring out how to measure them—the new changes in the quality of somebody's life relative to the infusion of large amounts of societal dollars—are, I suspect, a good portion of what the conference's ultimate agenda is going to be wrestling with. The transformation in our health care financing and delivery system required to bring about a system for treating chronic illness more effectively will be painful and wrenching. And it is entirely possible that our own institutions and physicians may well, for reasons of fear, inertia, and vested economic interests, be the principal barriers in the transition. The current status system of our large institutions' medical staffs does not give us a lot of comfort that the acute care approach to medicine is going to go quietly in the night. Preventive medicine, community medicine, family practice, are typically at the bottom of the status hierarchy at most medical centers and in the medical communities that they serve. The pinnacle of most medical communities, at least the ones that I've worked in anyway, seems to be the transplant surgeon—the person who's right there catching the patients just before they drop off the edge from the threat of chronic illness.

How we move ourselves from a societal mindset and a resource allocation mode is, I think, a very significant challenge and one that, as a person of social science training, I don't have a lot of answers for. I tend to feel that behavior is a function of incentives; until the incentive structure changes and our society stops rewarding late intervention and starts rewarding early intervention in the way in which it reimburses hospitals and physicians, we're going to have a very difficult time making that transformation. What I think is really going to hurt us more than the status hierarchy in our medical communities, though, is the lack of a chronic care paradigm. We can say to ourselves, "Wait a minute. We know that the acute care model we've been using to treat illness fits less and less well that nature of our society's needs."

But we do not have a handy paradigm for thinking about how to intervene in and finance the management of chronic illness, and for the movement away from acute medicine and toward behavioral medicine and the effect on people's lifestyles that is going to be essential to fight chronic illness effectively. I think we've got our work cut out for us, ladies and gentlemen, but the fact is that I believe that our society will be better off when we have begun to grapple with that transformation. The question will not be so much one of resources, the aggregate resources available in our society, but whether we have the courage to reallocate them in a way that more closely meets our society's needs.

5

Outcomes Management:
A Technology of Patient Experience

Paul M. Ellwood

We pay dearly for the possession of the intricate machinery which gives us our vivid imagination, our retentive memory, and that power by which we are able to grasp at each moment all the threads of our past experience and to weave them into a new fabric for the service of the present. Mischief begins when the demands of this service cannot be properly met.—James J. Putnam, M.D., Shattuck Lecture, 1899.[1]

When the President proclaimed in 1969 that our nation faced a health care crisis, it was not news to the medical community. Costs were surging. Patients were beginning to challenge the authority of doctors, and doubts were being raised about the efficacy of some expensive medical procedures. The response to the crisis was a bold federal policy aimed at restructuring the organization and incentives of the entire American health care enterprise. The policy to restructure provoked first a trend and then a mass movement toward a health care system influenced by market forces, incentive-based payment arrangements, and aggregations of providers. Group practice is flourishing, because it provides physicians with leadership, organizational support, economic security, and a power base. The number of multispecialty groups with more than 100 physicians jumped from 46 to 168 between 1980 and 1986.[2,3] In 1986, the number of hospital inpatient days hit an 18-year low, but the number of surgical operations hit an 18-year high.[4] Access has improved for some patients but deteriorated for others; care is less costly for those using managed-care organizations, but overall expenditures for medical care continue to rise. The health maintenance organization (HMO) movement, after spawning numerous kindred "products," has become the managed-care industry.

The most destabilizing consequence of the restructuring of the health system has also been, in my view, the most desirable one: patients, payers, and executives of health care organizations now have both higher expectations and greater power. The democratization of choice and the proliferation of decision makers in the American health care system will perpetuate and accelerate the restructuring of medicine, even after universal health coverage is adopted. But what physicians find most troubling about restructuring is not so much sharing decision making and power with patients and others; it is the nagging, not entirely arrogant or paternalistic, belief that nonphysicians simply do not have the information necessary to make rational decisions about medical care. The physician's capacity to make sound decisions is also jeopardized by the increasing complexity of medical practice and the growing number of chronically ill patients. The fine line between chaos and democracy is rationality of choice. It is the seeming irrationality of choices that has put the restructured American health care system on today's chaotic course. The problem is that what has not changed about American medicine is more important than what has. The next phase will determine the future roles of physicians and the fates of patients.

The intricate machinery of our health care system can no longer grasp the threads of experience. The mischief that began long before the health care crisis of the 1970s is progressively disabling the vast machinery of medicine. Too often, payers, physicians, and health care executives do not share common insights into the life of the patient. We acknowledge that our common interest is the patient, but we represent that interest from such divergent, even conflicting, viewpoints that everyone loses perspective. As a result, the health care system has become an organism guided by misguided choices; it is unstable, confused, and desperately in need of a central nervous system that can help it cope with the complexities of modern medicine. The problem is our inability to measure and understand the effect of the choices of patients, payers, and physicians on the patient's aspirations for a better quality of life. The result is that we have uninformed patients, skeptical payers, frustrated physicians, and besieged health care executives.

Uninformed Patients

For patients, the results of the health reforms of the 1970s have been mixed. Most who joined managed-care organizations express high levels of satisfaction. At the same time, some are concerned about the impersonality of "corporate medicine," and their fears are growing that payers', health executives', and physicians' intensified sensi-

Reprinted with permission from *The New England Journal of Medicine* 318, no. 23 (June 9, 1988), pp. 1549-56. Copyright © 1988 by the Massachusetts Medical Society.

Presented as the 99th Shattuck Lecture to the Annual Meeting of the Massachusetts Medical Society on May 21, 1988.

tivity to costs may reduce the quality of medical care. As they did before restructuring, patients say that they are too uninformed to make appropriate health care choices. Meanwhile, states are passing diagnosis-specific laws requiring that an informed choice between clinical options be based on documentation in "layman's language." But patients are still forced to judge medical care on the basis of the quality of amenities (the physician's manner, the waiting time, and so forth) because they rarely have the knowledge or suitable information to base it on anything else. Doctors think that patients' opinions about quality relate poorly to actual quality in medical care. As a result, patients claim that they are told what kind of care they will receive, rather than being given real choices. In the end, consumers believe that the only power they have is to choose a physician, hospital, or health plan, yet they still have no way of making an informed choice because they have no way of knowing which choice will yield the best results.

Skeptical Payers

Those who pay for most medical care, the group buyers of health care benefits—the government, unions, and businesses—express some satisfaction with the greater voice that restructuring has given them. But the majority are convinced that medical care is still not a consistently good value. The private-sector payers are exercising their newly found market power to purchase what they choose to define as value.

Group payers are particularly perplexed by John Wennberg's repeated demonstration of wide variations in practice style between geographic areas, without corresponding differences in health outcomes.[5] Sick-fund directors in The Netherlands, national health insurance leaders in Australia, and employee-benefits managers throughout the United States all ask me the same tough questions: What value do we get from these mounting expenditures on medical care? Will technology continue to bring us high costs and uncertain results? Differences in national health policies, cultures, payment arrangements, and organizational

structure do not seem to affect the payers' perception of the problem. The payers are increasingly skeptical of medicine's willingness or ability to resolve issues of effectiveness and cost, and are emboldened to seek answers on their own, with or without the acquiescence of medicine. Without compelling information on the quality of life, the bottom line will continue to be money.

Frustrated Physicians

Physicians are convinced that the financial concerns of payers are jeopardizing the care of their patients. Physicians today are often responsible for patients with multiple chronic conditions who have seen several subspecialists and gotten conflicting advice. Often, too, the potential for relief in such cases carries with it the risk of serious side effects. This all-too-common situation defies previous experience and makes it virtually impossible to offer an accurate prognosis.

Some of the tension that has surfaced between primary physicians and referral specialists with the proliferation of primary care-gatekeeper arrangements has stemmed from doubts about the capacity of primary physicians to perform this decisive management function. At the same time, primary physicians express concern about referral specialists' lack of recognition of the broader needs of the patient. Physicians need a powerful management tool to enable them to anticipate and to evaluate the impact of medical care on the patient's quality of life. This will supply the missing ingredient in optimal patient care.

Besieged Health Care Executives

Executives of health care organizations express the same frustrations as individual physicians do about the compromises and uncertainty of the present medical environment. As money becomes tighter, health care executives report increasing difficulty in resolving differences of opinion about the purchase of costly technology and the compensation of those in one specialty as compared with another. Their concerns about health outcomes parallel those of

the payers, particularly as health executives observe the inconsistencies in practice patterns in their own organizations. Even some of the more tightly controlled group practices acknowledge that they are detecting an unexplained increase and more variations in the frequency of such interventions as cesarean sections, endoscopy, and coronary arteriography. The executives believe that we have struck an unhealthy balance between health outcomes and economic outcomes. They also recognize that a better, more professionally uplifting bond than money is needed to hold health care organizations together. Thus, they need a management tool that calculates health outcomes for the patient as a "bottom line" of greater importance than the economic wealth of the organization.

In an effort to wed greater understanding of medical interventions to financial considerations, health care organizations are installing computerized information systems to record what the organization is doing for patients and how much it costs. Unfortunately, such systems rarely record why the interventions were done and how well they worked. Technically, it would not be difficult to add health outcomes to the data bases, but abiding by a new set of accounts that calculates health outcomes for the buck rather than episodes for the buck involves the potentially fatal organizational risks of selling something different from what the payer is buying.

A Technology of Patient Experience

In the absence of any system of general reporting of all diseases by all physicians to any central health authority, I can think of no way in which we can arrive at any approximate idea of *the morbidity of this city.*—Richard C. Cabot, M.D., Shattuck Lecture, 1911.[6]

Despite the inability of the newly franchised decision makers of restructured medicine to reach a common understanding, they do share a common language-money, politics, goods, and services. Its vocabulary includes coronary-artery bypass grafts, malpractice premiums, waiting times, diagnosis-related-group (DRG) codes, intensive care-unit hours, compulsory disclosure, capitation rates, and the Tax Equity and Fiscal Responsibility Act. This negotiation has been garbled by the wrong language, leading inevitably to the wrong choices. Health care goals have been drowned out by the noise of commerce. Shared responsibility demands a new universal language to communicate hurting, functioning, working, interacting, and living.

Our national heritage, our strength, has been our ability to convert the intangible, even divisive concepts of individualism and liberty into consensus and collaborative action. In medicine, we already have a consensus that our unifying goal is the good of the patient. To support this philosophy, I propose that we adopt a technology for collaborative action. Since one of my proclivities is giving old ideas new labels, let's label this technology "outcomes management." Outcomes management is a technology of patient experience designed to help patients, payers, and providers make rational medical care-related choices based on better insight into the effect of these choices on the patient's life. Outcomes management consists of a common patient-understood language of health outcomes; a national data base containing information and analysis on clinical, financial, and health outcomes that estimates as best we can the relation between medical interventions and health outcomes, as well as the relation between health outcomes and money; and an opportunity for each decision-maker to have access to the analyses that are relevant to the choices they must make.

Outcomes management would draw on four already rapidly maturing techniques. First, it would place greater reliance on standards and guidelines that physicians can use in selecting appropriate interventions. Second, it would routinely and systematically measure the functioning and well-being of patients, along with disease-specific clinical outcomes, at appropriate time intervals. Third, it would pool clinical and outcome data on a massive scale. Fourth, it would analyze and disseminate results from the segment of the data base most appropriate to the concerns of each decision maker. This should also allow the entire outcomes-management system to be modified continuously and improved with advances in medical science, changes in people's expectations, and alterations in the availability of resources.

Outcomes management's closest relative is the clinical trial. The clinical trial consists of the same steps: a carefully designed and scrupulously followed protocol, measurements of results, data pooling, analysis, and dissemination. Unlike the typical clinical trial, outcomes management would be a "clinical-trial machine"—a routine part of medical care that would never stop. Outcomes management lacks the purposeful randomization of a clinical trial, but it would generate information about the results of the natural, seemingly random variations in practice style. It differs from a clinical trial in another important way: with outcomes management, standards and outcome measures would be constantly subject to modification based on the results of analysis and feedback. The statistical hazards of conclusions based on series can be mitigated with use of a national outcomes-management system for the conduct of classic randomized clinical trials.

Timing

In science the credit goes to the man who convinces the world, not to the man to whom the idea first occurs.—Sir Francis Darwin, *Eugenics Review*, 1914.[7]

Speaking from experience, I can say that the most important ingredients in applying someone else's great idea are great timing and luck. The good news is that a number of recent trends are paving the way for outcomes management, making it a more practical potential tool than ever before. The components of outcomes management are widely accepted. The lifelong efforts of three persons stand out in the establishment of the foundations of contemporary medical-quality management systems. Avedis Donabedian gave it a vocabulary; John Williamson and his "health-accounting" collaborators at Johns Hopkins anticipated and explored most of the concepts that shape the field; and Robert Brook and his associates at Rand conducted the step-by-step critical research that allows outcomes management to be considered as a nationwide undertaking. There have been many pioneering efforts to install integrated management-information systems that assist physicians in making decisions, record patient outcomes, and then feed the results to various decision makers. Some of these efforts, such as Lawrence Weed's problem-oriented record, have caught the imagination of the media and the medical profession. Some continue to be perfected and expanded, such as the computerized medical record systems of Octo Barnett, Homer Warner, and Clement McDonald. Some, such as Edward Shortliffe's MYCIN, involve the computer-age promise of artificial intelligence. None have grown with the speed the problem demands, and as far as I can determine, few have relied as heavily on functional outcome and well-being measures derived independently from medical records as does the outcomes-management system I'm proposing.

I have sought advice of the pioneering developers of medical-management technology. They are optimistic that the time is right for the widespread application of their systems. They base their opinions largely on improvements in our ability to manage information with computers and on the demonstration, particularly by DRGs, of the effect an expanded data base can have on integrating medical and financial information. I would add to these reasons the remarkable independent maturation of the four basic ingredients of an outcomes-management system: reliable outcomes, better standards, powerful data bases, and promising analyses. Integration of these four factors affords us the opportunity to proceed immediately.

Measuring the Quality of Life

The centerpiece and unifying ingredient of outcomes management is the tracking and measurement of function and well-being or quality of life. Although this sounds like a hopelessly optimistic undertaking, I believe that we already have the ability to obtain crucial, reliable data on quality of life at minimal cost and inconvenience.

Still, major questions surround attempts to measure the impact of medical care on the quality of life; these involve reliability, sensitivity, specificity, and whether patients' subjective opinions about well-being can be treated as objectively as direct pathophysiologic observations. The interpretation of outcomes is further complicated by the need to make adjustments for comorbidity and the intensity and stage of the patient's illness—a far from trivial undertaking. When dealing with the more prolonged and elusive effects of common conditions, the persistence of pain, the curves of decay in chronic illnesses, and the overlapping effects of comorbidity, we need to make our largest investment in follow-up.

Like other facets of outcomes management, the measurement of functional outcomes is being rapidly developed and perfected. The Sickness Impact Profile, the Index of Well-being, and several others are sound psychometric instruments that measure functional outcome.[8] General use of these instruments, however, is time-consuming and largely impractical. During the past several years, John Ware and his colleagues at Rand have been developing and testing increasingly practical instruments for measuring outcome and consumer satisfaction. Alvin Tarlov anticipated the urgent need for an index for assessing quality of life by organizing a national medical-outcomes study, which was led by Ware, in Chicago, Los Angeles, and Boston. The study, which used modified measures of function and well-being and a set of clinical descriptors developed by Sheldon Greenfield, established the value of a general, short health survey in various practice settings for a range of chronic illnesses. The form is particularly appealing for widespread use in outcomes management because it is reliable, self-administrable, and comprehensive. It takes approximately five minutes to answer questions about roles, social interactions, physical function, emotions, and perceptions of health and pain. Since the survey instrument is so short, it may turn out to be insufficiently sensitive to detect subtle changes in health status. Or we may find it needs to be expanded to cover such important aspects as sleep

and patients' feelings about their energy level. Whatever functional outcome measures we choose, we will need to obtain clinical follow-up measures that are time- and illness-specific.

Better Standards

Perhaps the most controversial element in the outcomes-management concept is the starting point—the increasing reliance on standards or assessments for medical interventions. A system of appropriate medical standards, guidelines, and hard-and-fast rules that can be used by physicians in caring for their patients—referred to by many physicians as "cookbook medicine"—continues to be devastatingly controversial, providing a bonanza for litigators, a conundrum when patients do not fit the standards, a bureaucrat's paradise, and the last stand for free physicians. To avoid controversy, the developers of standards have clothed their products with euphemistic labels. Congress speaks of "technology assessments"; the National Institutes of Health of "the Consensus Development Program"; the American College of Physicians of the "Clinical Efficacy Assessment Project"; David Eddy, for the Council of Medical Specialty Societies, of "clinical policies"; and the American Medical Association of "DATTA."[9] But those who are devising these aids for physicians are responding to a real problem— the need to sort out and apply more rigorous analysis to the combinations of conflicting technology, changing technology, halfway technology, and unempirical technology in modern medical practice. The Institute of Medicine's Council on Health Care Technology has identified more than 60 groups engaged in producing assessments. More than 3,000 assessments have been conducted to date, and the Institute of Medicine, with Congress' urging, has formed a clearinghouse on health-technology assessments.[10]

Most of those involved in assessing medical interventions emphasize the importance of flexibility, branching, and judgment in their application. In situations in which no formal assessments exist, which may describe most medical encounters, outcomes management will

need to rely on encounter forms or computerized lists of observations and choices to ensure the entry of reliable data. The current state of ambulatory medical records and the problem of moving reliable data from them into a computerized data base is perhaps the most serious technical barrier to outcomes management.

The technology assessors acknowledge that their work is largely necessitated by a paucity of data on outcomes. Outcomes management can help to circumvent this weakness by creating an opportunity for continuous improvement through a feedback of outcomes. It can be used to assess and, where appropriate, to modify initial standards. Standards, then, are not some rigid laws to be followed blindly forever; they are a starting point—data elements and recommendations that respond continually to what is learned from application and subsequent research.

Powerful Data Bases

The crucial element that would link the actions and observations of thousands of health professionals with millions of patients is a massive, computerized data base. We seek from this data base the inhuman capacity of computers to cope with information gathered over time from multiple sources and to provide on-line feedback to a variety of users. We're not expecting a technology that thinks better than human beings. We need a technology that keeps track of more participants and remembers better than we do. Advances in the use of computers have led data pooling and management to be the most rapidly moving yet the most immature science in outcomes management.

The current proliferation of medical data bases demonstrates how large in size and broad in scope they can become and how fragmented and fragile they are to maintain. The Mayo Clinic data base covering the medical histories of the residents of Olmsted County has been maintained for 81 years and contains comprehensive medical records on 4 million encounters.[11] Virgil Slee's PAS/CPHA system, at its high point, covered 2,300 hospitals, and it contains 220 million discharge abstracts. The National Cancer Institute's Surveillance Epidemiology and End Results system has collected information on over a million patients with cancer. In fact, more than a thousand cancer registries, recording the diagnoses in 55 to 60 percent of all cases of cancer each year, have been approved by the American Cancer Society's Commission on Cancer.[12]

Major data bases have not been limited to cancer; they also exist for cardiovascular disease (Duke, Seattle Heart Watch), arthritis (ARAMIS), strokes (BUSTOP), angioplasties (National Heart, Lung, and Blood Institute), renal dialysis, head injuries, hypertension, hepatitis, glaucoma, and many other disorders.[9,12,13] Each data base represents an advance in its own field, but perhaps because of the fragmentary and proprietary nature of the data and the difficulty of converting medical records across systems, clinical data base development is now held hostage by our tendency to create information repositories independently of each other. This incompatibility in data systems, rooted in history, function, pride, and money, creates added urgency to adopt a uniform subset of health outcomes data.

Data-base developers emphasize some hard-learned lessons from the recent information explosion. First and most important, they tell us that the goals of an information system must be established in advance to define the appropriate data to be collected. Second, the numbers need to be large enough to detect important phenomena but not so detailed that the quality of input information deteriorates. Third, the information may be structured in a variety of ways and collected in a decentralized fashion, but some mechanism for centralizing information is essential. Progress in coding and integration of operating systems should facilitate this process. Fourth, experienced developers of data bases have suggested that the data bases must extend beyond the hospital. Our present data bases are largely hospital bound, cover only fragmentary episodes of an illness, and give the briefest glimpses into the changing functions of the patient. Finally, many data bases have not survived because they were set up as one-time exercises

or because they lacked long-term funding. A decision to pay for the maintenance of the outcomes-management system with patient care revenues is a necessary assumption in the health-outcomes strategy.

Promising Analyses

Ultimately, outcomes management can serve us by generating facts and insights that help people make sounder decisions. Many of those with whom I've discussed outcomes management claim that "informatics" and "decision theory" are the "hot topics," whereas the real excitement and breakthroughs will be experienced as outcomes management illuminates totally novel insights. Before we jump to any conclusions about the brilliant future of this concept, some disclaimers are necessary about the utility of large data bases drawn from medical practice. Rarely can we reach clear-cut conclusions on the basis of a small series of cases. At the outset, outcomes-management lacks a denominator. It is based only on observations made of people who happen to use medical care. It will not always contain enough information about the natural history of untreated conditions. Except in circumstances in which an outcomes-management data base is used to conduct a formal clinical trial, extraordinary care will be required to reach conclusions about efficacy and other factors.

Most clinical trials attempt to eliminate cofactors, such as multiple illnesses, which are rare in real medical practice. Complex cases in the data base complicate and potentially weaken the conclusions that can be drawn from even the huge amount of information that may be accumulated. It is these technical factors, not the length of time required to install a system to track health outcomes, that should make us cautious about the ability of outcomes management to produce dramatic, immediate results. It seems appropriate to predict that in 5 to 10 years we can apply this technology in a widespread, valuable way. I suspect that the most immediately discernible results will be in the more subjective realm—in a sense of participation, a dispelling of suspicion, and progress toward a

fairer, more effective health care system.

To break the impasse and move medicine forward as a sound applied biologic and social science, adoption of a technology like outcomes management is essential. The promise will be worth the wait. More accurate prognostic information will become available to patients in a video format for study at home. The potential value of costly equipment and the legion of technicians it requires will be easier to sort out. Better answers will be available on the questions of what and whom technology displaces and whether a machine will produce better end results than what is already installed. Conflicting and rapidly changing diagnostic and therapeutic problems, like those involving myocardial infarctions, should get resolved more quickly and decisively. Doctors will find that they need to depend less on their memories, that the records of patient progress will be more complete, that the statistics on which they base decisions will be more robust, and that the recommendations of their colleagues can be cross-checked. Outcomes management can help every doctor become a better doctor; as Dr. Edward Augustus Holyoke said, "Indeed the joint efforts of many engaged, in the same design, may accomplish, in a few years, what would be impracticable to a few individuals, though employed for ages."[14]

A Strategy for the Medical Profession

If the medical profession could agree to establish a common national technology that measured the effect of medical care on health outcomes, could we move cooperatively toward implementation of outcomes management? The American health care system is the most dynamic and flexible in the world. But moving even a substantial fraction of it in a common direction is difficult. Where is the forum for the medical profession to consider new policies? The Shattuck Lecture, the *New England Journal of Medicine*, and several other journals have become American medicine's town-meeting halls.

There is no powerful leader or group that can command reforms in health systems. There are no dominant health care firms that can lead the way. The largest health care firm, Kaiser Permanente, accounts for 1 percent of the country's health care expenditures. Normally, in devising health policies, we are pragmatically inclined to think small and to act smaller—independently. We are faced with a health and professional crisis that compels us to think big and to act bigger—together. The most aggressive national health policy is incremental. The surest routes are those relying on trial and error. Even health policies that appear massive in scope are refinements, not solutions. This proposed policy touches everyone associated with health care. It demands such a high level of trust and collaboration that its success will depend on a combination of unselfish leadership from the health sector, the government, foundations, businesses, and consumer groups.

We can learn something about leadership and change from the current restructuring, which represents one of those occasions when thinking broadly was followed by substantial change. During the restructuring experience, we observed that the President can articulate goals but that the private sector is more likely to take bold action.

The restructuring strategy for health maintenance called for people receiving Medicare to be permitted immediately to join HMOs. The legislation to capitate Medicare at 95 percent of per capita costs passed the House of Representatives in 1970, but the United States Senate took 15 years to pass similar measures. In the meantime, 256 HMOs were started by the private sector, and 9.6 million people joined them.[15] Perhaps the next president might be persuaded to support a health-outcomes strategy, but it is safest to assume that the private sector will initiate the action.

Concepts need to be converted into something tangible: definable, traceable activities and organizations. At the same time, the definitions ought to be sufficiently flexible to permit continuing innovation and to avoid a divisive ideologic conflict that attracts attention but kills long-term reform. In the case of restructuring, the HMOs were sufficiently defined to allow InterStudy to follow and publicize their spread. Defining outcomes management as a "permanent national medical data base that uses a common set of definitions for measuring quality of life to enable patients, payers, and providers to make informed health choices" provides an entity that is tangible enough to follow and evaluate.

The restructuring also taught us that proprietary approaches in medical care attract inordinate distrust and distortions, along with desirable growth and private capital. This is a situation in which competition can impede progress. Outcomes management is absolutely dependent on the participation and cooperation of the entire health enterprise. Its internal architecture needs to be open so that everyone can understand how it reaches conclusions. Open architecture will also encourage its wider use for research purposes. But even an open and nonproprietary architecture does not preclude competition and innovation. Competition will develop around how well organizations use the information that outcomes management produces. I suspect that a whole new set of profit and nonprofit activities will develop around manipulating, displaying, researching, auditing, litigating, and responding to the data. Serious efforts will need to be made to prevent the data from exploitation by the already ravenous litigation industry. This is a technology of choice, not of exploitation or regimentation.

The restructuring both succeeded and faltered in its attempts to become a part of mainstream medical care and traditional insurance. Managed care has too rarely given mainstream physicians the chance to be better doctors. It continues to grow because it is now part of the traditional insurance system and is flexible enough to continue to attract those who are interested in improving the performance of the health care system. The health-outcomes strategy has purposefully been designed to appeal from the outset to academic health centers and leading health care organizations because it allows them to evaluate their performance and it facilitates the conduct of clinical trials and research at relatively low cost. Start-up money might come from a coalition of foundations and government grants, but the technology won't succeed unless it is perceived and paid for as a part of routine patient care.

Finally, we learned from restructuring how impatient Americans are for tangible results. Instant drops in hospital admissions and length of stay were the rallying cry of the restructured health system. Outcomes management may not have an important effect on the American health care system for 5 or 10 years—maybe even longer. The people who pay the bills will need some evidence of success—lower costs and favorable health outcomes—right from the outset. Carotid endarterectomy is costing the country about $1.5 billion a year. Yet its benefits, as measured in terms of better function through stroke prevention, are unverified. Successfully evaluating the effectiveness of this one procedure early can provide outcomes management the impetus needed to carry it through the build-up period, until it becomes more widely useful.

Impetus to Change

After past experience has been applied to the health-outcome strategy, what actions are capable of stimulating what Burns calls the ultimate test of leadership, "the real changes that meet people's enduring needs?"[16] I wish I could persuade the medical profession to take the initiative in applying the health-outcomes strategy. Some individual persons and organizations have moved well along in that direction. Donald Berwick has devised and installed throughout the entire Harvard Community Health Plan a system that integrates computerized medical records with quality-improvement techniques developed outside the health industry to create what is perhaps the most advanced operational health-quality-measurement system in the United States. Paul Griner has established an office of clinical-practices analysis at Strong Memorial Hospital. The Joint Commission on Accreditation of Health Care Organizations under the leadership of Dennis O'Leary is successfully nudging some very powerful elements of the health system along the outcome route. Walter McClure's "buy-right" philosophy has invigorated the demand side and alerted the supply side in response to the need to solve the problem of better data for better decisions. But I'm concerned that the slow, piecemeal, even conflicting activities of the health care system will not satisfy the demands for immediate action of patients and payers.

Medicine can accelerate the use of outcomes management by adding a uniform set of life measures as a new data element to any preexisting computerized clinical data base that has the capacity to relate clinical observations to outcomes. Such an approach will allow the rapid participation of any organization or person involved in the practice of medicine. Integration of data bases can be conducted incrementally. An open health systems corporation might be created, which would be similar to organizations that exist in the fields of telecommunications and computers, to ease the integration of data bases.

Payers, insurers, and managed-care organizations, through their proliferating case-management programs, are likely to exert early pressures for outcomes management. The basic method and source of leverage in case management is to channel very sick patients to so-called "centers of excellence." Such centers are typically the country's best-known health organizations. If payers make the installation of outcomes-management technology a condition for referral for "big-deal" procedures—transplants, cardiac surgery, the care of low-birth-weight infants—they will get such technology. As a result, the famous, most emulated research- and education-oriented health organizations will be the first to get involved in the implementation process. The health centers' roles in perfecting and ultimately relying on outcomes management will expand to include everyone else as the techniques are applied to less costly interventions in typical practice situations. The catch is that the case-management movement itself is fragmented. The integration of the information needs of case managers is but one more challenge to the health-outcomes strategy. The government, as a stan-

dardizer of information systems, could become crucial.

The government's role, if we can judge by what has occurred with respect to HMOs and DRGs, is to standardize data just by asking for it. For their programs, Medicare instantly created a new data base for hospitals with DRGs and has had the same standardizing effect on other aspects of Medicare reporting. The federal professional-review-organization program is searching for innovative methods beyond the analysis of hospital records and the detection of outliers to stimulate improvements in the quality of care for Medicare recipients. In this case, the Health Care Financing Administration (HCFA) could take the lead in defining the content of the quality-of-life data set.

The process of installing outcomes-management programs can proceed in stages—according to industry segment, region of the country, clinical entity, or component of the system. The job could be facilitated by a series of regional outcomes-management resource centers that would provide consultation and education while functioning as sites for data analysis and interpretation.

Who Wins?

Some physicians might adopt this technology grudgingly in order to preempt one more threat to the control of medicine. By the control of medicine, I'm not referring to the current concerns of physicians about the control of the structure of health care organizations or payment procedures. I'm referring to the loss of control over the science of medicine when someone else knows more about the impact of physicians' work than they do. That threat is real. For example, quality-of-life information can be gathered directly from the patient through a self-administered questionnaire. Any payer can obtain this information and match it with claims data on diagnosis and treatment. If the data are pooled with those of other payers, adjusted, modeled, and objectively analyzed, the payers will succeed in circumventing whatever exclusive legitimacy medicine claims to have as a

profession. Payers will be the first to possess information on effectiveness. This cannot be allowed to happen.

The recent release of mortality data by HCFA demonstrates how close to losing professional control medicine is moving. HCFA brilliantly demonstrated its latent evaluative capacity by combining Medicare claims data with information on deaths. In the process, they began to develop an information technology that can assess the impact of medical interventions. Although HCFA has been criticized for its methods, they are improving. HCFA has demonstrated its insights through the release of data showing which patients died up to one month after discharge from the hospital. Such actions have not yet had a profound effect on the behavior of either consumers or providers, but the message is clear—the government's agency had at its disposal more information about the impact of medical care on life and death than did many of those who were responsible for providing that care. If physicians want to remain in control of their profession, they must have the motivation to track and evaluate health outcomes routinely.

The positive reasons for supporting outcomes management are more important than the negative ones. If our logic is sound, the health-outcomes strategy could bring order and predictability to the American health system. Even more compelling, it could lead to a more satisfying relationship with patients. It will allow economic choices to be made on the basis of facts that have been derived more openly. It will be possible for personal and societal values to be weighed while health care decisions are made.

If the health care system is out of control because of irrational and conflicting decisions by legitimate parties to health transactions, then putting those decisions (value-laden and empirical) in a common patient-driven framework could help to create order and a greater sense of justice. It will not automatically favor a decrease or increase in health care expenditures, nor will it predictably favor one specialty over another or one organizational arrangement over another.

Third parties can independently employ this technology as a powerful but blunt instrument of compliance. Only physicians have the full opportunity to use outcomes management as a technology of experience to enhance their own knowledge of the decisiveness of science and the subtlety of caring to bring a better quality of life to their patients.

Notes

1. Putnam JJ. Shattuck Lecture—Not the disease only, but also the man. *Boston Med Surg J* 1899; 141:53–6, 77–80.
2. Group practice data base. Chicago: American Medical Association, 1987.
3. Medical groups in the U.S., 1980. Chicago: American Med. Association, 1982.
4. Health Care Financing Administration, Division of National Cost Estimates, Office of the Actuary. National health expenditures, 1986– 2000. *Health Care Financ Rev* 1987; 8(4):1–36.
5. Wennberg JE. The paradox of appropriate care. *JAMA* 1987; 258: 2568–9.
6. Cabot RC. Shattuck Lecture—Observations regarding the relative frequency of the different diseases prevalent in Boston and its vicinity. *Boston Med Surg J* 1911; 165:155–70.
7. Darwin F. Francis Galton, 1822–1911. *Eugen Rev* 1914; 6:1–17.
8. Stewart A, Haynes R, Ware J. The MOS short form general health survey: reliability and validity in a patient population. *Med Care* (in press).
9. Institute of Medicine. Assessing medical technologies. Washington, DC: National Academy Press, 1985.
10. *Council on Health Care Technology Newsletter*. Vol. 2. No. 1. Washington, D.C.: National Academy Press, 1988:3–5.
11. Mayo Clinic fact sheet. Rochester, Minn.: Mayo Clinic, 1987.
12. Laszlo J. Health registry and clinical data base technology: with special emphasis on cancer registries *Chronic Dis* 1985; 38:67–78.
13. Pryor DB, Califf RM, Harrell FE Jr, et al. Clinical data bases: accomplishments and unrealized potential. *Med Care* 1985; 23:623–47.
14. Holyoke EA. An account of the weather . . . 1786. In: Medical papers communicated to Massachusetts Medical Society, 1787; 1:19.
15. National HMO census June 30, 1982. Excelsior, Minn.: InterStudy, 1983.
16. Burns JM. *Leadership*. New York: Harper & Row, 1978:461.

6

Does Inappropriate Use Explain Geographic Variations in the Use of Health Care Services? A Study of Three Procedures

Mark R. Chassin, Jacqueline Kosecoff, R. E. Park,
Constance M. Winslow, Katherine L. Kahn, Nancy J. Merrick,
Joan Keesey, Arlene Fink, David H. Solomon, and Robert H. Brook

Many researchers have documented large and significant geographic variations in the use of a variety of health care services.[1-11] Much of this work has been done using the technique of small-area analysis.[2-7,10,11] Previously we reported that geographic differences are just as great across large geographic areas, such as medium-sized states or large portions of large states.[12]

Many explanations for these differences have been proposed. These range from differences among geographic areas in the number of available physicians[1-3,6] or hospital beds,[1,3,6] to differences in the sociodemographic composition of patient populations,[5,11] to differences in the degree of uncertainty facing physicians regarding the use of different procedures.[7,13]

We were concerned about whether such geographic variations might be explained by differences in the appropriateness with which physicians use medical and surgical procedures. The hypothesis was that a high rate of inappropriate use might accompany and explain a high overall use rate in a particular geographic area. We report

Reprinted with permission from *JAMA, The Journal of the American Medical Association* 258, no. 18 (November 13, 1987), pp. 2533-37. Copyright © 1987 American Medical Association.

herein the results of a study in which we measured how appropriately physicians performed coronary angiography, carotid endarterectomy, and upper gastro-intestinal (GI) tract endoscopy in the elderly Medicare population in 1981 in areas of the United States characterized by high, average, and low use of the procedures.

Methods

Site Selection

We have previously described the methods by which we measured population-based rates of use of health care services in our 13 sites.[12] Briefly, we obtained complete files of physician claims for the year 1981 from Medicare insurance carriers in Arkansas, Colorado, Iowa, Massachusetts, Montana, Pennsylvania, South Carolina, and northern California. We divided both northern California and Pennsylvania into three smaller areas and Massachusetts into two smaller areas, choosing the area boundaries to minimize the number of patients that crossed them to receive health care services.

We calculated population-based rates of use for 153 procedures (accounting for 87 percent of total physician charges to Medicare in these sites) by counting the frequency with which

physicians practicing in each site provided services to Medicare beneficiaries who resided therein. We calculated rates by dividing this count by the number of Medicare part B enrollees who lived in each site in 1981. We excluded claims for patients living outside an area who came into it for services, as well as services performed for residents of an area by physicians practicing outside the area. Rates were adjusted for age and sex differences among sites. Statistically significant differences were demonstrated among sites for all procedures.[12]

Table 1 gives the rates of use in the sites we selected for the study reported herein. For each procedure, we selected one high-use site and one low-use site. The selection of the third study site was based on a different strategy for each procedure.

For coronary angiography we studied two low-use sites, because they represented geographic areas with notably different characteristics (site 3 is a relatively rural site, while site 2 is considerably more urban). For carotid endarterectomy, we chose a site with an average rate so that at least one of our sites would not represent an extreme rate. For upper GI tract endoscopy, we chose two high-use sites, because different kinds of physicians reported doing the endoscopies in the two sites; in site 2, physicians who described them-

Table 1.—Rates of Use of Study Procedures in Study Sites

Site No.	Rates of Procedures*		
	Coronary Angiography	Carotid Endarterectomy	Upper GI Tract Endoscopy†
1	50	23	102
2	23	6	144
3	22	NS‡	NS‡
4	NS‡	16	NS‡
5	NS‡	NS‡	149
Range, all sites	22-51	6-23	94-153

*Procedure rate (age and sex adjusted) per 10 000 elderly.
†GI indicates gastrointestinal.
‡NS indicates appropriateness of use was not studied for this procedure in this site.

selves to the insurance carrier as gastro-enterologists performed 72 percent of the endoscopies, whereas in site 5, internists performed 61 percent.

Procedure Selection and Appropriateness Rating

From among all the health care services for which we found significant variation in use rates among sites, we selected the three listed above for this study. These procedures were selected because each is frequently performed in the Medicare population and each consumes substantial resources.

For each of these procedures we prepared reviews of the medical literature that summarized existing knowledge concerning the circumstances under which each procedure has been proved to be efficacious, its risks, its costs, and opinions concerning when it ought to be used. [14-16] From these reviews we developed comprehensive and detailed lists of indications or specific clinical situations in which the use of each procedure might be considered.

Panels of expert physicians rated each indication on a nine-point scale of appropriateness (where 9 indicates extremely appropriate; 5, equivocal; and 1, extremely inappropriate). We defined appropriateness as present to the extent that the expected health benefits of a procedure exceed its expected negative consequences by a sufficiently wide margin that the procedure is worth doing. We explicitly excluded considerations of monetary costs from this definition. Panelists were given our literature reviews and specifically instructed to

rate indications for the performance of these procedures in 1981.

The process by which the panels were constituted and conducted has been reported elsewhere. [17,18] Briefly, each panel rated and revised the initial set of indications by mail, then met at The Rand Corporation, Santa Monica, California, reviewed and finalized the list of indications, reviewed summaries of first-round ratings, discussed the clinical areas in which disagreement among panelists was prominent, and "re-rated" all indications. The lists of final, rated indications are available elsewhere. [14-16] (Reports are available at nominal cost on request from The Rand Corporation.) Final indications rated by the panels number 300 for coronary angiography, 864 for carotid endarterectomy, and 1,058 for upper GI tract endoscopy.

Our consensus method did not force panelists to reach agreement on appropriateness. As we have described elsewhere, significant degrees of disagreement for specific indications persisted after the meetings. [17,18] We considered indications appropriate if their median ratings were from 7 to 9 without disagreement. We considered indications inappropriate if their median ratings were from 1 to 3 without disagreement. We considered indications equivocal if their median ratings were from 4 to 6, or if panelists disagreed on the appropriateness of performing the procedure for that specific indication. For this purpose, we defined disagreement as occurring when at least three panelists rated the indication appropriate (ratings of 7 to 9) and at least three panelists rated the indication inappropriate (rat-

ings of 1 to 3), regardless of the median rating.

Data Collection

We selected a random sample of cases of each of the three study procedures in each study site. These samples were drawn directly from the claims data that had been used to calculate each site's rates of utilization. We have described in detail in the next article in this series the complex, three-tiered approach we employed to recruit the participation of this community-based sample of 913 physicians who performed the 5,411 study procedures. [19] Ninety percent, or 819 physicians, participated in the study; they performed 4,988 (92 percent) of all sampled procedures. We recruited the participation of 227 (99 percent) of the 230 hospitals at which the sampled procedures had been performed. We have also described our data collection methods, as well as the methods and results of the studies we did of the validity of the indications assigned to each case by these methods. We obtained complete clinical data on 96 percent of eligible cases. [19]

Statistical Methods

We sampled roughly equal numbers of cases for each procedure in each site, to maximize the power to detect differences among sites. With approximately 500 sample cases for each procedure in each site, we could expect to detect a true difference of eight percentage points in appropriate or inappropriate use in at least 80 percent of repeated trials.

Although the sample sizes were approximately equal, the population sizes differed greatly. For some procedures in some sites, all of the population cases were sampled; for one procedure in one site, fewer than 10 percent of the population cases were sampled. To obtain unbiased estimates of appropriate or inappropriate use across all sites, we used inverse sample-probability weights when we calculated statistics for all sites.

We tested for differences in the distribution of appropriateness ratings across sites using chi^2 tests on unweighted sample frequencies.[20]

Results

Table 2 gives the appropriateness of use of each of our three study procedures in each of the geographic sites in which we collected clinical data. For each procedure, it lists the percent of cases in each site in each of the three appropriateness categories: appropriate, equivocal, and inappropriate. It also gives the rate of use of each procedure in each site as determined by our previous analysis of Medicare claims data. More detailed data on appropriateness are presented in Table 3, including confidence intervals on all estimates of appropriateness and one additional significant figure on all estimates.

We found small, but statistically significant differences in appropriateness among the three sites studied for each procedure. For coronary angiography, the highest-use site had the lowest rate of appropriateness (72 percent) and the lowest-use site had the highest rate of appropriateness (81 percent). For carotid endarterectomy, there were no significant differences between the high- and low-use sites. The average-use site, however, had a significantly higher rate of inappropriate procedures (40 percent) than either of the other two (30 percent and 29 percent, respectively). For upper GI tract endoscopy, the low-use site had the lowest rate of inappropriate procedures (15 percent), compared with the two sites with higher rates of use (18 percent and 19 percent, respectively).

As given in Table 2, across all sites we found that coronary angiography was performed appropriately 74 percent of the time, carotid endarterectomy, 35 percent, and upper GI tract endoscopy, 72 percent. Overall, the three procedures were performed for equivocal indications in 9 percent, 32 percent, and 11 percent of cases, respectively. Finally, inappropriate cases accounted for 17 percent of coronary angiographies across all sites, 32 percent of carotid endarterectomies, and 17 percent of upper GI tract endoscopies.

Table 2.—Appropriateness and Geographic Variations in Three Procedures

Procedure	Site No.	Sample Size, No.	Appropriateness Category, %			Rate per 10 000 Elderly*
			Appropriate	Equivocal	Inappropriate	
Coronary angiography†	1	628	72	10	18	50
	2	514	77	7	17	23
	3	535	81	4	15	22
Total	All sites	1677	74	9	17	...
Carotid endarterectomy‡	1	600	37	34	30	23
	4	492	30	30	40	16
	2	210	42	29	29	6
Total	All sites	1302	35	32	32	...
Upper GI tract endoscopy§‖	5	509	71	11	18	149
	2	462	73	8	19	144
	1	614	72	14	15	102
Total	All sites	1585	72	11	17	...

*1981 rates are adjusted for age and sex differences among sites.[12]
†$P<.01$ for differences in appropriateness among all sites and for differences between site 1 and sites 2 and 3 combined.
‡$P<.01$ for differences in appropriateness among all sites, and $P\geq.05$ for differences between site 1 and site 2.
§GI indicates gastrointestinal.
‖$P<.05$ for differences in appropriateness among all sites and for differences between site 1 and sites 5 and 2 combined.

Table 3.—Appropriateness of Use of Three Procedures by Site With 95% Confidence Intervals (CI)

Procedure	Site No.	Sample Size, No.	Appropriateness Category, %		
			Appropriate (95% CI)	Equivocal (95% CI)	Inappropriate (95% CI)
Coronary angiography	1	628	71.7 (68.1-75.2)	10.0 (7.7-12.4)	18.3 (15.3-21.3)
	2	514	76.8 (73.2-80.5)	6.6 (4.5-8.8)	16.5 (13.3-19.8)
	3	535	80.7 (77.4-84.1)	4.5 (2.7-6.2)	14.8 (11.8-17.8)
Total	All sites	1677	74.0 (71.9-76.1)	8.5 (7.2-9.9)	17.4 (15.6-19.3)
Carotid endarterectomy	1	600	36.5 (32.7-40.4)	33.9 (30.1-37.7)	29.5 (25.9-33.2)
	4	492	29.7 (25.6-33.7)	30.1 (26.0-34.1)	40.2 (35.9-44.6)
	2	210	41.9 (35.2-48.6)	29.0 (22.9-35.2)	29.0 (22.9-35.2)
Total	All sites	1302	35.3 (32.7-37.9)	32.3 (29.8-34.9)	32.4 (29.8-34.0)
Upper GI tract endoscopy*	5	509	70.9 (67.0-74.9)	11.2 (8.5-13.9)	17.9 (14.5-21.2)
	2	462	72.9 (68.9-77.0)	7.6 (5.2-10.0)	19.5 (15.9-23.1)
	1	614	71.6 (68.1-75.2)	13.5 (10.8-16.2)	14.9 (12.1-17.7)
Total	All sites	1585	72.0 (69.7-74.2)	10.8 (9.3-12.4)	17.2 (15.4-19.1)

*GI indicates gastrointestinal.

Table 4 lists the two most frequent appropriate indications for each procedure across all three sites and the percent of cases of each procedure accounted for by each. Table 5 does the same for the most frequent equivocal indications. Table 6 lists the most frequent inappropriate indications.

Table 4.—Most Frequent Appropriate Indications for Three Procedures

Procedure	Indication	% of All Cases
Coronary angiography	Patient's primary cardiac abnormality is valvular disease	18
	Patient hospitalized for unstable angina, pain is controlled during admission, angiography performed during admission	12
Carotid endarterectomy*	Patient has had multiple carotid transient ischemic attacks, has never received medical therapy, has medium surgical risk, and 70%-99% stenosis of artery ipsilateral to symptomatic hemisphere	6
	Patient is asymptomatic, has low stroke risk, low surgical risk, and 70%-99% stenosis of the artery operated on	4
Upper GI tract endoscopy†	Patient has dysphagia, previous barium swallow shows an anatomic lesion	12
	Patient has had previous roentgenographic examination of the upper GI tract within 3 mo that suggests a malignant lesion	9

*Our panel defined a carotid transient ischemic attack as any transient unilateral neurologic deficit lasting less than 24 hours. We defined medical therapy as any anticoagulant or platelet-inhibiting agent at any dose. We defined surgical risk as low, medium, or high according to the criteria defining the Goldman index, the Dripps-American Society of Anesthesiologists criteria, or both. Stroke risk was defined as normal if the risk of stroke was less than 10% within eight years, using data from the Framingham study. A full and detailed list of definitions and indications is available elsewhere.[16]
†GI indicates gastrointestinal.

Table 5.—Most Frequent Equivocal Indications for Three Procedures

Procedure	Indication	% of All Cases
Coronary angiography*	Patient has chronic stable angina (class III or IV), has received less than maximal medical therapy, and has undergone no exercise tests	2
	Patient has chronic stable angina (class I or II), is 65 years or older, has received maximal medical therapy, and has undergone no exercise tests	1
Carotid endarterectomy	Patient is asymptomatic, has low stroke risk, medium surgical risk, and 70%-99% stenosis of the artery operated on	8
	Patient has had at least one vertebrobasilar transient ischemic attack within 3 mo, medium surgical risk, and 70%-99% stenosis of the artery operated on	3
Upper GI tract endoscopy†‡	Patient has uncomplicated peptic symptoms that persist on inadequate medical therapy, no history of peptic disease, and upper GI tract roentgenograms not performed.	2
	Patient has had a roentgenographic examination of upper GI tract within 3 mo that shows an antral deformity (no ulcer), and endoscopy performed for immediate diagnostic confirmation	1

*Our panel used the Canadian Cardiovascular Society's definitions of angina class. Our panel defined maximal outpatient management of angina as the use of any long-acting nitrate and any β-blocker (or a documented history of intolerance to either). We defined angina as present if any three of the following four conditions were met: chest pain present in typical location (eg, substernal, left side of chest), pain of typical quality (eg, pressing or tight), pain typically produced by exertion, and pain typically relieved by sublingual nitroglycerin therapy. A full and detailed list of all definitions and indications is available elsewhere.[14]
†GI indicates gastrointestinal.
‡Our panel defined adequate therapy for peptic symptoms as consisting of any antacid or any H_2-receptor antagonist in any dose with any daily frequency. Adequacy also depended on the duration of treatment; this criterion varied with the nature of the finding on previous upper GI tract roentgenograms. If previous upper GI tract roentgenographic studies were normal or not done, at least two weeks of therapy was considered adequate. If a gastric ulcer was shown at least six weeks was considered adequate. Peptic symptoms were considered uncomplicated if unaccompanied by GI tract bleeding, a weight loss greater than 4.5 kg, or the symptom complex of anorexia, weight loss, and early satiety. A full list of definitions and indications is available elsewhere.[15]

Comment

We measured the appropriateness of performing three procedures in a randomly selected, community-based sample of cases from five sites across the United States in 1981. The sites were selected because they represented high, average, or low use for each of the procedures studied. We found small, but statistically significant differences in appropriateness among sites in each of the procedures we studied.

Although these differences were in the direction supporting the hypothesis (i.e., less appropriate or more inappropriate procedures in areas of high use), in no case can differences in appropriateness explain the large differences in overall rates previously reported. Thus, we did not find evidence to support the hypothesis that areas with high use of medical and surgical procedures show these high rates primarily or to any meaningful extent because physicians in these areas perform procedures more often for inappropriate indications than their counterparts in areas of lower use.

While further research is needed to explain geographic variations in health care service use, we believe our data suggest several new approaches. First, we must begin to examine the question of underuse more scientifically. Our study design did not permit us to measure directly the extent of underuse, if any, and its contribution to geographic differences. Second, we should also begin to look more closely at regional differences in disease incidence as possible partial explanatory factors. Third, regional social and cultural differences may produce differences among geographic areas in the stage of illness at which patients seek health care. And fourth, we should give more attention to the role of primary care physicians in determining which patients eventually receive specialized procedures such as the ones we studied. Openness of referral channels and the threshold for referral might be important factors in explaining regional differences in utilization rates for procedures.

We believe our method of cataloging and rating indications for these procedures using expert physician panels has produced valid data on appropriateness. We have discussed this issue in detail elsewhere for carotid endarterectomy.[21] We also believe the data in Tables 4 to 6 provide further evidence that this method does distinguish clinically meaningful differences in appropriateness. For example, the data in Table 4 show that the most frequent appropriate indication for upper GI tract endoscopy was for patients with dysphagia in whom a previous upper GI tract roentgenographic study had shown an anatomic lesion, such as an esophageal stricture or ulcer. Few, if any, physicians would deny that this is a clearly appropriate indication for upper GI tract endoscopy.

Table 6.—Most Frequent Inappropriate Indications for Three Procedures

Procedure	Indication	% of All Cases
Coronary angiography	Patient has chest pain that is not anginal, no exercise test performed	3
	Patient's only cardiac abnormality is congestive heart failure	2
Carotid endarterectomy	Patient is asymptomatic, has low stroke risk, medium surgical risk, and 50%-69% stenosis of the artery operated on	1
	Patient had completed stroke within 3 wk, has medium surgical risk, and 70%-99% stenosis of artery ipsilateral to symptomatic hemisphere	1
Upper GI* tract endoscopy	Patient has uncomplicated peptic symptoms persistent on inadequate medical therapy, no history of peptic disease, and upper GI tract roentgenogram is normal	2
	Patient has dysphagia with normal immune system; neither manometry nor upper GI tract roentgenogram performed	2

*GI indicates gastrointestinal.

The indication listed in Table 5 as the most frequently occurring equivocal indication for upper GI tract endoscopy would be more likely to provoke controversy. Under what circumstances should patients with uncomplicated peptic symptoms who have received inadequate medical therapy and who have not had upper GI tract roentgenographic studies receive endoscopy? It seems likely that physicians will differ (as did our panel) far more on this issue than on the appropriateness of the procedure for patients with dysphagia.

Similarly, the most frequent inappropriate indication for upper GI tract endoscopy, listed in Table 6, is clearly less appropriate than the equivocal indication. Should patients with uncomplicated peptic symptoms and normal upper GI tract roentgenographic studies who have received inadequate medical therapy ever undergo upper GI tract endoscopy before receiving a trial of adequate medical treatment? Perhaps there are rare special circumstances that might justify the procedure under these conditions, but we believe most physicians would agree that ordinarily endoscopy is inappropriate.

In two of the three procedures, we found most use to be for clearly appropriate indications over all sites: 74 percent for coronary angiography and 72 percent for upper GI tract endoscopy. For carotid endarterectomy, however, 35 percent of procedures across all sites were performed for clearly appropriate indications. Carotid endarterectomy was again different, with 32 percent of cases performed for equivocal indications.

In all three procedures we found substantial numbers of procedures performed for inappropriate indications. Over all sites, 17 percent of coronary angiographies, 17 percent of upper GI tract endoscopies, and 32 percent of carotid endarterectomies were inappropriate, judged against our expert panels' ratings.

These findings are especially worrisome, because we constructed our method of assigning indications to give cases higher appropriateness ratings where information was ambiguous. Many of the definitions we used leaned in the same direction. For example, our definition of maximal medical therapy for angina was met if the patient was receiving any long-acting nitrate and any β-blocker in any dosage schedule. Many clinicians might regard this definition as insufficiently stringent. Similarly, we classified any transient unilateral neurologic deficit as a carotid transient ischemic attack no matter how vaguely described. If differing opinions about degree of carotid stenosis were recorded in the medical record, we used the highest recorded degree of stenosis. Our panel's definition of maximal medical therapy for peptic symptoms was met if the patient was receiving any antacid or any H_2-receptor antagonist, regardless of daily dosage schedule. All of these decisions tended to result in higher ratings of appropriateness than would the application of stricter standards. The results of our validity studies are also consistent with this observation. [19]

Our definition of appropriateness excluded consideration of cost from the negative consequences of performing procedures because we wanted the definition to be a purely medical one. Had we asked our panelists to include cost considerations, their ratings of appropriateness might have been lower.

Several factors might mitigate the generalizability of our findings. We studied only three procedures; results might differ for other health care services. We studied common procedures, however, and did not select ones generally perceived to be of no medical benefit. On the contrary, we selected procedures generally agreed—at least under some circumstances—to be beneficial. We studied procedures performed by a variety of physicians as well as diagnostic an therapeutic procedures.

Another factor that might limit the applicability of our findings is that we studied practice in 1981. Medicine has changed since then, and an appropriateness study of current practice might yield different results. While some important changes have occurred—e.g., the advent of coronary angioplasty—we do not believe the bulk of community-based practice, which is the subject of this study, has changed sufficiently to render these results outdated.

While detailed data on rates of use, comparable with the data we published previously, are not routinely available, the existing data suggest that the use of the procedures we studied has increased since 1981. For example, the National Center for Health Statistics reported an increase of 34 percent in the overall rate of use of cardiac catheterization per 100,000 population between 1981 and 1984. [22,23] Similarly, the rate of open heart surgery increased by 41 percent during the same period. In 1984, the same data source reported a national rate of coronary artery bypass surgery of 25 per 10,000 population for persons aged 65 years or older. This rate is greater than the rate we reported for our highest-use site in 1981 (23 per 10,000). We believe that, in the main, the way these procedures are used in the community has changed little since 1981. We know of no evidence to suggest that the appropriateness of use of any of these procedures has improved between 1981 and 1987.

A third limiting factor is that we studied the use of these procedures only among elderly Medicare beneficiaries. Might the results have been different in a younger population? We have no reason to believe so. If a bias exists in studying the elderly, it may be in the direction of revealing less inappropriate use than the same study of a younger population. To the extent that physicians may tend to be somewhat less aggressive with these procedures in the elderly, we might find even more inappropriate use in a younger group.

We believe these results may have important implications for current health care policy. Our findings should be replicated for other procedures, for populations who are not elderly, and for more recent periods. A consistent finding of significant inappropriate use would challenge us to find ways of selectively eliminating these practices as a method of substantially improving the quality of care we provide and perhaps simultaneously controlling costs.

This work was supported by the Commonwealth Fund, New York, the John A. Hartford Foundation, New York, the Health Care Financing Administration of the U.S. Department of Health and Human Services, Washington, DC, the Pew Memorial Trust, Philadelphia, and The Robert Wood Johnson Foundation, Princeton, New Jersey.

The authors are deeply grateful to all of the physicians who participated in this study and to the efforts of their staffs who facilitated its work. The efforts of the medical records staffs of the participating hospitals were also indispensable. The study could not have been accomplished without the tireless endeavors of the many data collectors who provided the information on which these analyses depend. We also wish to thank Mary-Frances Flynn, MPH, Lois McCloskey, MPH, Barbara J. Genovese, and Carole Oken, MA, for their perseverance in overseeing the completion of the fieldwork. Mary Stout and Elizabeth Sullivan deserve special thanks for their talent and commitment in preparing our manuscripts.

We are also indebted to the members of our Policy Advisory Board whose contributions throughout the study were vital to its success: Robert J. Adolph, M.D., John D. Alexander, M.D., Richard Berman, MPH, Gerald E. Bisbee, Ph.D., Ernie Chaney, M.D., John H. Dawson, Jr., M.D., Linda K. Demlo, Ph.D., Neil J. Elgee, M.D., Ronald G. Evens, M.D., Donald S. Frederickson, M.D., Paul F. Griner, M.D., Anthony M. Imparato, M.D., John M. Lowe, Douglas B. McGill, M.D., Francis D. Moore, M.D., Melvin Schapiro, M.D., Marvin Shapiro, M.D., Thomas L. Stern, M.D., and Richard S. Wilbur, M.D.

Notes

1. Lewis CE: Variations in the incidence of surgery. *N. Engl J Med* 1969;281:880–884.

2. Wennberg J, Gittelsohn A: Small-area variations in health care delivery. *Science* 1973;182:1102–1108.

3. Stockwell H, Vayda E: Variations in surgery in Ontario. *Med Care* 1979; 17:390–396.

4. Roos NP, Roos LL Jr, Henteleff PD: Elective surgical rates—do high rates mean lower standards?: Tonsillectomy and adenoidectomy in Manitoba. *N Engl J Med* 1977; 297:360–365.

5. Roos NP, Roos LL Jr: Surgical rate variations: Do they reflect the health or socioeconomic characteristics of the population? *Med Care* 1982;20:945–958.

6. Wennberg J, Gittelsohn A: Variations in medical care among small areas. *Sci Am* 1982;246:120–135.

7. McPherson K, Wennberg JE, Hovind OB, et al.: Small-area variations in the use of common surgical procedures: An international comparison of New England, England, and Norway. *N Engl J Med* 1982; 307:1310–1314.

8. Gornick M: Medicare patients: Geographic differences in hospital discharge rates and multiple stays. *Soc Secur Bull* 1977;40:22–41.

9. Deacon R, Lubitz J, Gornick M, et al.: Analysis of variations in hospital use by Medicare patients in PSRO areas: 1974–1977. *Health Care Finance Rev* 1979;1:79–108.

10. Connell FA, Day RW, LoGerfo JP: Hospitalization of Medicaid children: Analysis of small-area variations in admission rates. *Am J Public Health* 1981;71:606–613.

11. Roos NP: Hysterectomy: Variations in rates across small areas and across physicians' practices. *Am J Public Health* 1984;74:327–335.

12. Chassin MR, Brook RH, Park RE, et al.: Variations in the use of medical and surgical services by the Medicare population. *N Engl J Med* 1986; 314:285–290.

13. Wennberg JE, Barnes BA, Zubkoff M: Professional uncertainty and the problem of supplier-induced demand. *Soc Sci Med* 1982;16:811–824.

14. Chassin MR, Kosecoff J, Park RE, et al.: *Indications for selected medical and surgical procedures: A Literature Review and Ratings of Appropriateness: Coronary Angiography*, publication R-3204/1-CWF-HF-HCFA-PMT-RWJ. Santa Monica, Calif, The Rand Corp, 1986.

15. Kahn KL, Roth CP, Kosecoff J, et al.: *Indications for Selected Medical and Surgical Procedures: A Literature Review and Ratings of Appropriateness: Diagnostic Upper Gastrointestinal Endoscopy*, publication R-3204/4-CWF-HF-HCFA-PMT-RWJ. Santa Moni-ca, Calif, The Rand Corp, 1986.

16. Merrick NJ, Fink A, Brook RH, et al.: *Indications for Selected Medical and Surgical Procedures: A Literature Review and Ratings of Appropriateness: Carotid Endarterectomy*, publication R-3204/6-CWF-HF-HCFA-PMT-RWJ. Santa Monica, Calif, The Rand Corp, 1986.

17. Park RE, Fink A, Brook RH, et al.: Physician ratings of appropriate indications for six medical and surgical procedures. *Am J Public Health* 1986;76:766–772.

18. Park RE, Fink A, Brook RH, et al.: *Physician Ratings of Appropriate Indications for Six Medical and Surgical Procedures*, publication R-3280-CWF-HF-PMT-RWJ. Santa Monica, Calif, The Rand Corp, 1986.

19. Kosecoff J, Chassin M, Fink A, et al.: Obtaining clinical data on the appropriateness of medical care in community practice. *JAMA* 1987; 258:2538–2542.

20. *SAS User's Guide: Statistics*. ed 5. Cary, NC, SAS Institute Inc, 1985.

21. Merrick NJ, Fink A, Park RE, et al.: Derivation of clinical indications for carotid endarterectomy by an expert panel. *Am J Public Health* 1987;77:187–190.

22. Graves E, Haupt BJ: *Utilization of Short-Stay Hospitals: United States, 1981*, annual summary. Vital and Health Statistics Series 13, No. 72. US Dept of Health and Human Services publication (PHS) 83–1733. National Center for Health Statistics, 1983.

23. Graves EJ: *Utilization of Short-Stay Hospitals: United States, 1984*, annual summary. Vital and Health Statistics Series 13, No. 84, US Dept of Health and Human Services publication (PHS) 86–1745. National Center for Health Statistics, 1986.

II

The Issues

7

International Health Spending: Issues and Trends

George J. Schieber and Jean-Pierre Poullier

Comparative Data

Comparative data on health spending are developed on an ongoing basis by the secretariat of OECD [Organization for Economic Cooperation and Development], a Paris-based international organization. These data are based on national income and product account principles, gradually being implemented by all nations. Definitions of health spending and taxation concepts are based on the *Classification of the Functions of Government*, developed by the United Nations and embodied in OECD's *National Accounts*.[1]

Total health expenditures are the sum of public and private health consumption and investment netted for transfers as published for most of the twenty-four OECD member countries in *National Accounts*. To the extent that this source does not provide data for all countries, it is complemented by other national statistics approximating the desired national income and product account concept.[2] Data developed by the secretariat are verified by the member countries. However, the secretariat does not simply accept individual countries' recommended changes unless they are consistent with the underlying functional classification. The problem is even more difficult for disaggregate expenditure information, because reporting of this information in many countries often does not conform to the national income and product account concepts that may be employed to develop total national health expenditures. Thus, there

is a continuous process to generate subaggregate data that are based on the same national accounts principles and therefore more comparable. All this aside, substantial gray areas still exist, such as the boundary between health and social services, as well as deviations in reporting that lead us to urge caution in not attributing too much precision to these data. Moreover, figures for the most recent years are estimates and are frequently revised after the fact, and countries often redo their historical baseline estimates, necessitating complete revisions of published data.

This methodological discussion is prompted by a spate of recent efforts to develop comparative data and what we perceive to be some fundamental misunderstandings about these OECD data. These data have the advantages of being based on an internationally accepted functional classification; receiving direct comment and input from the statistical offices of the countries; and having the methodology, sources and underlying assumptions widely disseminated. This is not to suggest that major improvements are unnecessary or that other conceptual bases are inferior. However, comparative data development must be based on some objective classification. The reported administrative statistics of individual countries may provide information, but it will be based on the different definitions and concepts inherent in the reporting systems for each country. Moreover, there are no internationally accepted definitions of hospital, physician, nursing home, or other services.

In this DataWatch, we present and analyze internationally comparable data on health expenditures for the twenty-

four OECD countries for 1970–1989. These data update the information provided in our Fall 1989 DataWatch, but also reflect revisions in the series for Austria (from 1975), Australia (all years), Belgium (from 1977), Germany (all years), Iceland (all years), Italy (from 1980), Norway (from 1981), Spain (all years), and the United States (all years). These revisions, with the exceptions of those for Spain, Germany, and Italy, generally have little effect on levels of spending or rates of change. All components of the Spanish data are now based on official government estimates. The German health expenditure data have been revised upward by about 5 percent as a result of obtaining more complete data on private investment. The information for Italy reflects more complete data on private investment and private hospital expenditures, but only back to 1980. Thus, there is serious discontinuity in the Italian data, necessitating a cautious interpretation of any pre- and post-1980 comparisons for Italy.

Health Expenditure Levels and Trends

Health expenditures across countries can be analyzed in terms of each country's national currency or compared based on one numeraire currency. Expenditures can be adjusted for population and inflation; they can be compared at a point in time or over time. The most widely used measure based on national currencies is the ratio of health to gross domestic product (GDP), which provides an indication of the percentage of total output in each country that is devoted to health spending. Analyses of this ratio in terms of both level and

Reprinted by permission of *Health Affairs*, Chevy Chase, MD (Spring 1991), pp. 106–16.

changes over time must take into account both the health expenditure and GDP components. While levels of health expenditures in national currencies in any given year cannot be directly compared, changes over time can be. Thus, rates of growth in nominal health expenditures, real (inflation-adjusted) health spending, and real and nominal health spending per person can be compared across countries. Other important economic and demographic factors, such as GDP growth, health care inflation, and overall inflation, can also be compared. Such analyses provide information on differential growth in health services spending and health system-related demographic and economic factors across countries. However, it is important to bear in mind that the comparisons are only as good as the underlying data. In this regard, perhaps one of the weakest areas of international comparisons of health systems is in the questionable comparability and validity of the various health care price indices, thus making it difficult to determine real health spending growth.[3]

Comparing both absolute levels and trends in health spending when expenditures are denominated in a single numeraire currency is even more difficult given the dearth of reliable indices to account for differences in price structures and mix of services within a country. In the absence of better measures, purchasing power parities (PPPs)—indices that relate the prices of a market basket of goods in one country to the prices in a comparative group of countries—are used. More troubling is that, since health PPPs are unreliable, GDP PPPs are generally used to convert health spending across countries into a single numeraire currency. These types of comparisons should be treated with caution.

Our inability to measure health outcomes except in gross terms and difficulties in performing behavioral analysis limit our ability to make definitive policy assessments concerning comparative health expenditure performance. This is further confounded by the lack of detailed information on the institutional features of different health care financing and delivery systems. Nevertheless, for even descriptive analyses of health systems' performance to be meaningful, several measures of performance should be employed.[4] Furthermore, results from such analyses may be quite sensitive to the base years and time spans chosen.

Health-to-GDP Ratios

In 1989, the health-to-GDP ratios ranged from 5.1 percent in Greece to 11.8 percent in the United States, with an OECD average (excluding Turkey) of 7.6 percent. Canada and Germany, two countries currently under intense scrutiny vis a vis U.S. reform, had GDP shares of 8.7 percent and 8.2 percent, respectively. Once again, the data show a growing U.S. share relative to stability or even decline (particularly dramatic in Sweden) in the OECD average and for most other countries in recent years (Exhibit 1).

Exhibit 2 graphs the health-to-GDP ratios for six of the major OECD countries: Canada, France, Germany, Japan, the United Kingdom, and the United States. During 1970–1989, Canada's health-to-GDP ratio increased from 7.1 percent to 8.7 percent, an increase of 23 percent; Germany's share increased from 5.9 percent to 8.2 percent, an increase of 39 percent; the U.S. share increased from 7.4 percent to 11.8 percent, an increase of 59 percent. Particularly striking is the widening of the gap between the Unit-ed States and the other countries, especially since 1985. Given the current disparity in their health-to-GDP ratios, the virtual equivalence of the Canadian ratio to the U.S. ratio in 1971 and the near equivalence of the German and U.S. ratios in 1975 are remarkable. Unfortunately, this ratio tells only part of the story. The following analysis of nominal health spending and nominal GDP growth paints a rather different picture.

Nominal Health Spending in National Currencies

Indices of cumulative and annual growth for 1970–1989, with 1970 as the base year, are shown for the six major OECD countries in Exhibit 3. For the cumulative index, the value for each year is the per capita health spending figure for that year divided by the 1970 base year

figure. Thus, the value of the index for 1970 is always 1, and the value for subsequent years is 1 plus the percentage increase over the base year. For example, since the index for the United States for 1975 is 1.79, 1975 per capita health spending is 79 percent higher than (or 1.79 times) 1970 base year spending.[5] As these values are plotted on a semilogarithmic scale, the slope from year to year represents the annual rate of growth (Exhibit 4).[6] This type of visual display has the advantage of showing trends in the rates of growth across several countries and for all subperiods within the overall period. Year-to-year changes can be compared visually by simply comparing the slopes of the trend lines for each country between the two desired years.

From 1970 to 1989, the United Kingdom had the highest rate of growth in nominal per capita health expenditures, with 1989 per capita spending 12.85 times the level in the 1970 base year for a compound annual rate of growth of 14.4 percent. If growth in nominal per capita health spending is the measure of expenditure performance, Germany had the lowest rate of growth by far, while Canada had a higher rate of growth than Germany and the United States (Exhibit 4). Analysis of year-to-year changes in health spending, while possible, requires detailed institutional knowledge of the individual systems, information on major policy changes, and consideration of the overall economic environment.

While these data are useful in illustrating how well individual countries controlled health expenditure growth per person, they provide no information about real inflation-adjusted health expenditure growth, health expenditure performance relative to overall economic performance, or the absolute levels of health spending and their growth across countries. For example, other analyses have shown that after adjusting for health care inflation, Canada had the lowest growth in real per capita health spending, slightly below the United States, Germany, and the United Kingdom, while Japan and France had substantially higher rates.[7]

Growth in health spending relative to overall economic performance can be

Exhibit 1
Total Health Expenditures As A Percentage Of Gross Domestic Product, 1970–1989

	1970	1975	1980	1985	1986	1987	1988	1989
Australia	4.9%	5.5%	6.5%	7.0%	7.1%	7.1%	6.9%	7.0%
Austria	5.4	7.3	7.9	7.6	8.3	8.4	8.3	8.2
Belgium	4.1	5.9	6.3	6.9	7.2	7.3	7.3	7.2
Canada	7.1	7.2	7.4	8.5	8.8	8.8	8.6	8.7
Denmark	6.1	6.5	6.8	6.3	6.0	6.3	6.4	6.3
Finland	5.7	6.3	6.5	7.2	7.4	7.4	7.2	7.1
France	5.8	7.0	7.6	8.5	8.5	8.5	8.6	8.7
Germany	5.9	8.2	8.5	8.6	8.5	8.6	8.9	8.2
Greece	4.0	4.1	4.3	4.9	5.4	5.2	5.1	5.1
Iceland	5.2	6.2	6.5	7.4	7.8	7.9	8.5	8.6
Ireland	5.6	7.6	9.0	8.3	8.3	8.0	7.9	7.3
Italy	5.2	6.1	6.8	7.0	6.9	7.3	7.6	7.6
Japan	4.4	5.5	6.4	6.5	6.7	6.8	6.7	6.7
Luxembourg	4.1	5.6	6.8	6.8	6.7	7.2	7.3	7.4
Netherlands	6.0	7.7	8.2	8.2	8.1	8.5	8.4	8.3
New Zealand	5.2	6.7	7.2	6.6	6.9	7.3	7.4	7.1
Norway	5.0	6.7	6.6	6.4	7.1	7.5	7.4	7.6
Portugal	–	6.4	5.9	7.0	6.6	6.4	6.5	6.3
Spain	3.7	4.8	5.6	5.7	5.6	5.7	6.0	6.3
Sweden	7.2	7.9	9.5	9.3	9.0	9.0	9.0	8.8
Switzerland	5.2	7.0	7.3	7.6	7.6	7.9	8.0	7.8
Turkey	–	3.5	4.1	–	–	3.5	–	–
United Kingdom	4.5	5.5	5.8	6.0	6.0	5.9	5.9	5.8
United States	7.4	8.4	9.3	10.6	10.8	11.1	11.3	11.8
Mean[a]	5.4	6.5	7.1	7.4	7.4	7.6	7.6	7.6

Source: *Health OECD, Facts and Trends* (Paris: OECD. forthcoming).
[a] Mean excluding Turkey.

Exhibit 2
Total Health Expenditures As A Percentage Of Gross Domestic Product, Selected OECD Countries, 1970–1989

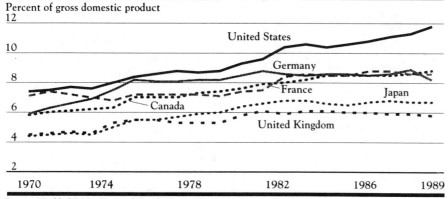

Source: *Health OECD, Facts and Trends* (Paris: OECD, forthcoming).

assessed by comparing rates of growth in nominal (or real) per capita health spending with growth in nominal (or real) per capita GDP. We examined the compound annual rates of growth in nominal per capita health spending relative to nominal per capita GDP for 1970–1989 and for 1970–1980 and 1980–1989

for the six countries. These nominal elasticities measure the relationship between percentage changes in health spending and in GDP.[8] Thus, the elasticity of 1.3 for the United States over the entire period means that nominal per capita health spending grew 30 percent faster than nominal per capita GDP;

alternatively, every 10 percent change in nominal per capita GDP was associated with a 13 percent change in nominal per capita health spending.

For the entire 1970–1989 period, Germany, Japan, and the United States (all 1.3) had the highest annual rates of increase, with nominal per capita health spending increasing 30 percent faster than nominal per capita GDP. France (1.2) ranks next, wherein health spending increased 20 percent faster than GDP. Canada and the United Kingdom (each 1.1) had the lowest increases, with health spending increasing only 10 percent faster than GDP. During 1970–1980, Germany (1.5) and Japan (1.3) had the highest elasticities, Canada (1.0) and the U.K. (1.1) had the lowest, and France and the United States (both 1.2) were in between. This period was a time of very rapid growth in Germany's health-to-GDP ratio (see Exhibit 1), resulting in the enactment of a series of cost containment measures.[9] In contrast, over the 1980–1989 period, Germany, Japan, and the United Kingdom had the lowest elasticities (all 1.0), significantly below those of the previous decade. France (1.2) showed little change, while Canada (1.2) and the United States (1.3) faced significantly higher growth than in the previous decade.

Health Expenditures per Capita in U.S. Dollars

While the previous analyses provide information about health expenditure growth within countries, they provide no information about the absolute levels of health spending denominated in a single currency. In 1970, spending ranged from $62 per person in Greece to $346 in the United States, with an OECD average of $175 (Exhibit 5). In 1989, health spending ranged from $371 per person in Greece to $2,354 in the United States, with an OECD average of $1,094. U.S. spending was over double the OECD average; 40 percent higher than Canada, the second-highest country; and 71 percent higher than Switzerland, the third-ranked country. Exhibit 6 graphically shows the widening gap over time in absolute terms between the United States and the five other major countries. Over this period, spending

Exhibit 3
Cumulative And Annual Growth In Nominal Per Capita Health Spending, 1970–1989

	Canada	France	Germany	Japan	United Kingdom	United States
1970	1.0	1.0	1.0	1.0	1.0	1.0
1971	1.14 (13.8)	1.16 (15.5)	1.19 (19.4)	1.13 (12.9)	1.14 (13.5)	1.11 (10.7)
1972	1.25 (9.4)	1.32 (14.2)	1.36 (14.0)	1.32 (17.2)	1.30 (14.3)	1.24 (12.1)
1973	1.39 (11.7)	1.52 (15.2)	1.60 (17.2)	1.57 (18.6)	1.48 (14.3)	1.38 (11.0)
1974	1.64 (17.5)	1.77 (16.6)	1.85 (15.8)	2.05 (31.0)	1.89 (27.7)	1.56 (13.3)
1975	1.96 (20.0)	2.21 (24.6)	2.12 (14.5)	2.51 (22.2)	2.49 (31.5)	1.79 (14.5)
1976	2.26 (15.1)	2.58 (16.7)	2.28 (7.9)	2.82 (12.3)	2.95 (18.5)	2.05 (14.5)
1977	2.48 (9.8)	2.91 (13.0)	2.44 (6.7)	3.22 (14.2)	3.35 (13.5)	2.31 (13.1)
1978	2.76 (11.3)	3.44 (18.1)	2.65 (8.7)	3.67 (13.8)	3.84 (14.8)	2.60 (12.4)
1979	3.10 (12.6)	3.98 (15.7)	2.89 (9.0)	4.06 (10.7)	4.48 (16.7)	2.91 (12.0)
1980	3.63 (17.0)	4.60 (15.4)	3.16 (9.5)	4.72 (16.4)	5.74 (28.1)	3.35 (15.0)
1981	4.26 (17.4)	5.39 (17.3)	3.40 (7.7)	5.13 (8.7)	6.62 (15.4)	3.88 (15.9)
1982	4.98 (16.9)	6.26 (16.0)	3.45 (1.3)	5.53 (7.8)	7.08 (6.8)	4.35 (12.2)
1983	5.52 (10.8)	7.07 (13.1)	3.57 (3.7)	5.82 (5.2)	8.01 (13.2)	4.79 (10.0)
1984	5.97 (8.1)	8.03 (13.5)	3.81 (6.7)	6.00 (3.1)	8.48 (5.9)	5.20 (8.7)
1985	6.46 (8.3)	8.61 (7.2)	3.98 (4.4)	6.30 (5.0)	9.10 (7.3)	5.65 (8.5)
1986	7.08 (9.6)	9.31 (8.2)	4.16 (4.4)	6.66 (5.7)	9.79 (7.7)	6.08 (7.7)
1987	7.67 (8.2)	9.82 (5.5)	4.34 (4.5)	7.10 (6.6)	10.75 (9.7)	6.62 (8.9)
1988	8.27 (7.9)	10.63 (8.3)	4.72 (8.6)	7.47 (5.2)	11.81 (9.9)	7.32 (10.5)
1989	8.97 (8.5)	11.57 (8.9)	4.63 (−1.8)	7.79 (4.3)	12.85 (8.8)	8.12 (11.1)
1970–80[a]	13.8%	16.5%	12.2%	16.8%	19.1%	12.9%
1980–89[a]	10.6	10.8	4.3	5.7	9.4	10.3
1970–89[a]	12.2	13.8	8.4	11.4	14.4	11.7

Source: *Health OECD, Facts and Trends* (Paris: OECD, forthcoming).
Note: Numbers in parentheses are the annual rate of growth from the previous year.
[a] Compound annual rate of growth over the time period.

Exhibit 4
Relative Growth Index In Nominal Per Capita Health Expenditures, Selected OECD Countries, 1970–1989 (Semilogarithmic Scale)

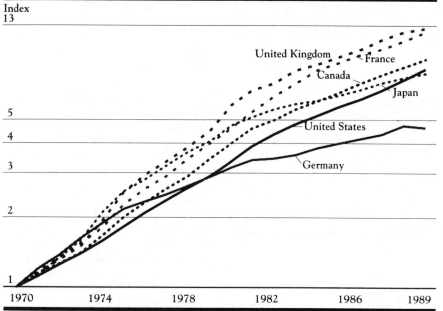

Source: *Health OECD, Facts and Trends* (Paris: OECD, forthcoming).

increased the least in the United Kingdom (9.6 percent compound annual growth), followed by Canada (10 per-cent), Germany (10.1 percent), France (10.5 percent), the United States (10.6 percent), and Japan (11.7 percent). In

1970, U.S. spending per person exceeded Canada by 26 percent, France by 80 percent, Germany by 74 percent, Japan by 175 percent, and the United Kingdom by 137 percent. By 1989, U.S. per capita spending exceeded Canada by 40 percent, France by 85 percent, Germany by 91 percent, Japan by 127 percent, and the United Kingdom by 182 percent. Accounting discrepancies explain only a relatively small part of these differences.

Future Directions

Improved international comparisons of health systems hinge on better data, detailed information on the institutional features of health systems, and better methodological tools for analysis. First, regarding better data, standard definitions and functional classifications need to be developed. National income and product account principles represent a useful approach. Unfortunately, no standardized definitions exist in national income and product accounts for health subaggregates such as hospitals, physicians, nursing homes, and the like. Even if standard definitions did exist, a second problem emerges, namely, that the administrative reporting systems of individual countries reflect the reporting needs of different institutional structures, such that in some countries, inpatient physician services would be treated as hospital expenditures, whereas in others, they would be treated as physician expenditures. A third problem is that even with standard agreed-upon definitions, reporting practices may differ, as has been the case in infant mortality and cause-specific reporting of death rates.[10] A fourth problem is obtaining accurate data on private health expenditures, which are usually obtained from periodic household surveys and are generally not part of the administrative reporting systems of government health programs.[11]

A second set of problems in evaluating the performance of health systems is the lack of readily accessible information, in a standardized format, of the institutional features of different health systems. We need information on (1) the underlying economic incentive aspects of the system; (2) public health

Exhibit 5
Per Capita Health Spending In U.S. Dollars, 1970–1989

	1970	1975	1980	1985	1986	1987	1988	1989
Australia	$176	$321	$ 528	$ 846	$ 895	$ 955	$ 986	$1,032
Austria	149	336	618	821	922	983	1,041	1,093
Belgium	123	286	513	749	801	853	924	980
Canada	274	478	806	1,315	1,427	1,507	1,581	1,683
Denmark	209	335	571	770	778	839	870	912
Finland	163	305	513	826	876	943	998	1,067
France	192	365	656	991	1,036	1,088	1,173	1,274
Germany	199	422	749	1,046	1,082	1,139	1,250	1,232
Greece	62	110	196	292	334	333	347	371
Iceland	152	321	638	964	1,115	1,252	1,350	1,353
Ireland	99	225	448	577	585	607	639	658
Italy	147	270	541	761	792	889	982	1,050
Japan	126	252	515	785	828	907	978	1,035
Luxembourg	150	319	616	879	921	1,053	1,146	1,193
Netherlands	207	418	707	931	954	1,033	1,076	1,135
New Zealand	174	354	523	667	722	796	811	820
Norway	154	350	624	900	1,046	1,147	1,214	1,234
Portugal	–	158	252	385	385	405	438	464
Spain	82	186	322	437	454	500	571	644
Sweden	274	475	864	1,187	1,192	1,266	1,328	1,361
Switzerland	247	477	734	1,104	1,143	1,244	1,323	1,376
Turkey	–	58	103	–	–	144	–	–
United Kingdom	146	272	454	658	697	747	793	836
United States	346	592	1,059	1,700	1,813	1,955	2,140	2,354
Mean[a]	175	332	585	852	904	976	1,042	1,094

Source: *Health OECD, Facts and Trends* (Paris: OECD, forthcoming).
[a] Mean excluding Turkey.

Exhibit 6
Per Capita Health Spending In U.S. Dollars, Selected OECD Countries, 1970–1989

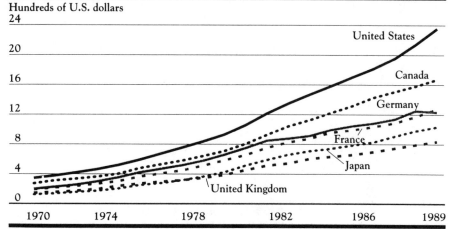

Source: *Health OECD, Facts and Trends* (Paris: OECD, forthcoming).

activities, the delivery system, health personnel, quality assurance programs, financing, reimbursement arrangements, and the integration of health and other social programs; (3) nongovernmental programs and their interface with the public system; (4) legal systems in terms of antitrust, malpractice, limitations on private insurance, and so on; and (5) recent and current policy initiatives. Developing such information for a large number of countries is no easy task, since a taxonomy for describing systems is needed. We need to be able to collate information that exists in many different languages and update this information as health systems change. This undertaking is not simple. Even in the United States, a mecca of health services data and research, it is difficult to find a detailed description of the U.S. health system that enables the analyst to understand the incentives inherent in the payment policies of the multitude of consumers, providers, and payers.

The third set of problems in national and international comparisons is methodological. Evaluating medical and cost effectiveness requires measurement of health outcomes and economic efficiency, both areas of conceptual and methodological difficulty. While strides are being made in these areas, much remains to be done, and much of the progress to date is based on the use of even more micro-level data, such as those available in clinical records. Moreover, behavioral analysis of specific policies is notoriously difficult.

In conclusion, several observations can be made. First, we hope that governments and international organizations will give higher priority to the issue of improved data than they have in the past. Second, the need exists for a handbook of the detailed institutional features of different health systems, updated on a regular basis (OECD's forthcoming *Health Care Reforms in Seven Countries* is a promising start). Third, intensive research on small groups of countries, where data can be standardized and more micro comparisons on expenditures and outcomes can be made, has the potential for significant advancements in our knowledge base.

U.S. health spending is the highest in the world and continues to increase more rapidly than in virtually all other countries. Gross outcome measures are poor; however, certain more refined outcome measures, such as infant mortality by birthweight and certain cause-specific mortality measures, appear to paint a slightly better picture of U.S. performance. [12] Perhaps the United States is getting favorable outcomes from some of its expensive and extensive technologies. To what extent do health systems costs really reflect social costs (such as teenage pregnancy, substance abuse, and violence), as opposed to waste and inefficiency in the health system? These are important questions to answer as U.S. health spending approaches 12 percent of GDP and one trillion dollars.

Notes

1. United Nations, *Classification of the Functions of Government* (New York: U.N., 1980); Organization for Economic Cooperation Development, *National Accounts, Main Aggregates* (Paris: OECD, 1991).

2. See OECD, *Measuring Health Care* (Paris: OECD, 1985); and OECD, *Health OECD, Facts and Trends* (Paris: OECD, 1991)

3. J.-P. Poullier, "Health Data File: Overview and Methodology," *Health Care Financing Review* (Annual Supplement 1989) 111–18.

4. G. J. Schieber, "Health Expenditures in Major Industrialized Countries," *Health Care Financing Review* (Summer 1990): 159–67.

5. The compound annual rate of growth from 1970 to year 1970 plus n can be obtained by taking the nth root of the cumulative spending ratio.

6. OECD, *National Accounts, Main Aggregates.*

7. Schieber, "Health Expenditures in Major Industrialized Countries."

8. The elasticities are obtained by double logarithmic regressions for each country for each of the three periods.

9. M. Schneider, "Cost Containment in Health Care in Federal Republic of Germany," *Health Care Financing Review* (Spring 1991).

10. C. Percy and C. Muir, "International Comparability of Cancer Mortality Data," *American Journal of Epidemiology* 129, no. 5 (1989): 934–46.

11. Methods for obtaining this type of information for U.S. health accounts are described in detail in HCFA Office of National Cost Estimates, "National Health Expenditures, 1988" and "Revisions to the National Health Accounts and Methodology," *Health Care Financing Review* (Summer 1990): 1–54.

12. H. J. Hoffman, P. Bergsjo, and D. W. Denman, "Trends in Birth Weight-Specific Perinatal Mortality Rates: 1970–83," *Proceedings of the International Collaborative Effort on Perinatal and Infant Mortality,* vol. II (Hyattsville, Md.: National Center for Health Statistics, 1990).

8

Mandating Health Coverage for Working Americans

Alan C. Monheit and Pamela Farley Short

Since the 1950s, most Americans have received health insurance coverage at the workplace. Increasingly, those seeking to extend health insurance to more people have proposed an expansion of employer-based coverage. Working Americans and their dependents comprise roughly three-quarters of the uninsured population.[1] Thus, extending employment-related coverage to this group has the appeal of targeting the largest component of the uninsured while avoiding the costs of a new government insurance program and further pressure on public budgets. To date, a variety of approaches designed to expand work-related coverage have been proposed or implemented. These include recent federal legislation requiring continuation of employment-related coverage as part of the Consolidated Omnibus Budget Reconciliation Act (COBRA) of 1985, proposals to continue tax incentives for health insurance available to small businesses and the self-employed under the Tax Reform Act of 1986, and efforts to encourage health insurance pools through voluntary coalitions of employers, unions, insurers, and medical providers.

Most prominent among these approaches, and the subject of continuing controversy, have been recent efforts to mandate minimum health insurance benefits for most workers, either directly as in the Minimum Health Ben-

efits for All Workers Act (S. 1265) introduced by Sen. Edward Kennedy (D–MA) and Sen. Lowell Weicker (R–CT) and in the expanded version of this proposal (S. 768), or indirectly in the system of mandatory employer surcharges on unemployment insurance contributions adopted by Massachusetts.[2] A number of states also have adopted a mandated approach to health insurance coverage by requiring employers to offer specific health insurance benefits, and forty states now require employers to offer continuation or conversion privileges to persons who otherwise would lose employment-related coverage.[3]

Mandating health insurance benefits on behalf of employees is not a new public policy approach. Its origins can be traced to the national health insurance debate of the Nixon administration, and it has reappeared periodically in other policy discussions since that time. As Charles Phelps notes, the appeal of a mandate is threefold.[4] First, mandated benefits are an off-budget item and therefore do not appear as direct public expenditures. Next, the approach is market-oriented since it maintains an active role for private insurers, relies upon the existing private health insurance system, and gives the appearance of minimum government intervention. Finally, since mandated coverage only sets a "floor" on the scope of health insurance benefits, employers can still offer several health insurance options, and employees can still negotiate for more generous health

insurance benefits. A mandatory approach also has the appeal of allowing employers and employees to take advantage of the current favorable tax treatment of employment-related health insurance and is seen in some quarters as possibly the only way to ensure that certain kinds of employers provide coverage to their workers.[5]

Critics of a mandate have charged that its advantages may be illusory at best and, at worst, may perversely harm the very persons it was intended to help. Although the costs of mandated coverage would not appear directly in the federal budget, the favorable tax treatment of newly created employees health plans will result in forgone tax revenues that will indirectly affect the level of federal expenditures. Uwe Reinhardt has characterized mandated coverage as a "hidden tax" (analogous to a payroll tax) whose short-run consequences may yield reduced employment, higher product prices, and business failures, especially for small firms with high employee turnover.[6] The latter type of firm would be affected especially adversely because of the relatively high cost of administering health insurance over a small and unstable employee base. Others fear that the effects on the employment of workers at or near the minimum wage would be particularly severe, since there is little latitude for adjusting the wages of these workers to compensate for the increased cost of employing them.[7] Finally, mandated benefits may be viewed as a paternalistic imposition on those em-

Reprinted by permission of *Health Affairs*, Chevy Chase, MD (Winter 1989), pp. 22–38.

ployees who prefer wages to noncash health insurance benefits.

It is also important to recognize that a mandated approach would affect the health insurance choices of those now insured through employers. Unlike at present, employees would not be able to waive the coverage offered by their own employer in favor of coverage as a dependent under a spouse's plan. In this respect, health insurance choices would become more limited under a mandate.

In other respects, the opportunities for choice would be widened. For example, under the Kennedy-Weicker proposal, employees earning less than $4.19 per hour are not required to contribute toward their coverage, and employee contributions are otherwise limited to 20 percent of the monthly actuarial rate.[8] As a result, family coverage could become an affordable option for those employees now unable to pay the additional costs.[9] In addition, families with more than one worker would have the chance to select coverage from several employers. Since dependent coverage would be available from several sources, more families may be able to select a plan that is consistent with their preferences. However, the number of persons with coverage from multiple sources may also increase.

Finally, mandated employer-provided health insurance coverage also would shift the burden of financing health care for the working elderly covered by Medicare from the public to the private sector. The Tax Equity and Fiscal Responsibility Act (TEFRA) of 1982, the Deficit Reduction Act (DEFRA) of 1984, and COBRA 1985 made Medicare the secondary payer for active workers and their spouses age sixty-five and older who are covered by employment-related plans. A mandate that required all elderly workers to have such coverage would continue the trend toward increased reliance on employers to finance health care for the elderly and reduce the burden on the Medicare trust fund.[10]

Data and Methods

In this article we examine how mandating health insurance for particular work-

ers in terms of hours worked, establishment size, and earnings, is likely to reduce the size of the uninsured population and affect workers who are insured through their employers. We do so with data from a new source, the 1987 National Medical Expenditure Survey (NMES), sponsored by the National Center for Health Services Research (NCHSR). NMES is a one-year panel survey of the medical care use, expenditures, and health insurance coverage of the U.S. population, including both the civilian, noninstitutionalized population and residents of nursing homes and facilities for the mentally retarded. The data used in this analysis were derived from the first round of interviews of the NMES household component, which surveyed approximately 15,000 households consisting of 36,000 individuals in the civilian, noninstitutionalized population.[11] The estimates presented in this article are point-in-time estimates for approximately the first quarter of 1987 and should be considered preliminary.

This analysis makes a number of specific assumptions about the provisions of a mandate. First, we assume that all eligible employees (except dependent children covered by a parent's employment-related plan) would have to accept coverage from their own employers for themselves and for their spouses and dependent children not covered under another employment-related plan. Second, we assume that dependents are defined as spouses and children either under age eighteen or age eighteen to twenty-three and full-time students.[12] Third we assume that the self-employed would only be subject to the mandate if they employed other people who were not members of their families. In contrast to the Kennedy-Weicker proposal, we assume no other exclusions from the mandate, such as for domestic or seasonal workers or other workers not covered by the Fair Labor Standards Act, and we use twenty hours a week as the minimum hours eligibility requirement.[13] We also assume that otherwise eligible workers and their families now covered under public financing programs (CHAMPUS/CHAMPVA, Medicare, and Medicaid) would be required to accept an employer's plan.

Finally, while our intent is to examine the number and characteristics of workers affected by a mandate, it is important to note that our analysis is distinctly very short-run in nature. In particular, our tabulations ignore any unintended employment effects resulting from any adjustments in the demand for labor (such as substitution of part-time for full-time workers or substitution of capital for labor) that might occur as employers respond to the costs of a mandate. We do not consider any labor supply adjustments should individuals alter their labor force participation, choice of jobs, or hours of work in response to the availability of health insurance or to a decline in real wages as a share of total compensation over the longer run. We also do not consider any indirect effects on employment resulting from any reduction in product demand should employers attempt to shift the costs of the mandate forward to consumers. Consequently, our results should be viewed as an upper bound of the effect of a mandate on both uninsured and insured workers.

Targeting the Employed Uninsured

To begin our examination of the effects of an employer mandate, it is instructive to identify the targeted employee population: workers who are uninsured and those not covered by employer-provided health insurance. Exhibit 1 reveals that about 14 percent of all employed persons (excluding the self-employed who do not employ others) are uninsured, while over three-quarters of employees have work-related health insurance. Only about 2 percent of workers obtain coverage exclusively through public programs.

Workers most likely to lack health insurance include young adults age nineteen to twenty-four, members of minority groups, and those employed in small firms (especially establishments with fewer than ten workers). Low-wage earners are particularly at risk of being without any health insurance; those earning five dollars an hour or less are twice as likely to be uninsured than high-wage earners. Part-time workers (fewer than thirty-five hours per week) are also far more likely to be uninsured

Exhibit 1
Health Insurance Status Of Employed Persons, First Quarter 1987

| Employee characteristic | Population[a] | Type of insurance | | | |
		Uninsured	Employment related	Other private	Public only
Total[b]	109,476	14.4%	77.2%	6.1%	2.2%
Age in years					
Under 19	4,259	16.9	75.6	4.0	3.5
19–24	16,639	26.5	63.3	7.9	2.3
25–54	75,243	12.8	80.9	4.5	1.8
55–64	10,629	9.5	80.5	8.3	1.8
65 and over	2,705	1.9[c]	48.8	34.7	14.6
Sex					
Male	59,281	15.6	76.6	6.2	1.6
Female	50,195	13.3	77.9	6.1	3.0
Race/ethnicity					
White	87,182	11.8	79.8	6.6	1.9
Black	11,088	20.9	70.9	3.9	4.3
Hispanic	7,796	31.7	60.8	4.1	3.5
Size of establishment					
Under 10	25,909	24.0%	59.0%	13.4%	3.6%
10–25	18,170	17.2	73.9	6.8	2.2
26–100	22,760	12.0	82.9	3.3	1.8
101–500	18,968	6.6	89.2	2.9	1.3
Over 500	16,610	5.6	91.8	1.7	0.9
Hourly wage					
Under $3.50	8,592	27.1	56.4	9.6	6.9
$3.50–$5.00	19,843	25.9	61.1	9.0	4.1
$5.01–$10.00	42,485	13.4	78.9	6.0	1.7
$10.01–$15.00	22,773	6.6	89.0	3.7	0.7
Over $15.00	14,730	5.6	89.5	4.2	0.8[c]
Hours per week					
10 or fewer	5,073	15.9	63.0	14.6	6.6
11–20	8,680	17.6	66.4	11.2	4.7
21–30	7,724	22.6	62.7	9.4	5.4
31–34	1,665	24.6	58.0	12.4	5.1
35 or more	85,437	12.9	81.1	4.7	1.3
Industry					
Agriculture	2,135	29.6	43.5	24.7	2.2[c]
Mining	723	9.9	88.1	1.3[c]	0.6[c]
Construction	5,914	28.2	62.8	7.5	1.5
Manufacturing	20,235	10.0	85.6	3.5	0.8
Transportation, utilities	8,016	9.6	86.0	3.3	1.1
Sales	22,158	20.9	68.7	7.3	3.1
Finance	7,068	6.8	86.6	4.6	2.0
Repair services	5,941	20.1	69.1	6.6	3.4
Personal services	3,447	26.8	56.8	11.6	4.8
Entertainment	1,404	27.3	63.7	7.4	1.6[c]
Professional services	23,713	8.5	82.4	6.6	2.4
Public administration	5,687	6.1	89.7	2.2	2.0[c]
Occupation					
Professional	18,464	7.2	86.4	5.5	1.0
Managerial and administrative	15,541	7.5	85.7	5.3	1.5
Sales	11,391	15.4	71.5	9.8	3.3
Clerical	17,403	9.5	83.4	4.9	2.2
Craftsmen and foremen	12,073	16.9	77.3	4.8	1.0
Operatives	7,439	14.0	80.5	3.7	1.8
Transport operatives	4,568	17.0	77.1	5.2	0.7[c]
Service workers	14,099	26.1	61.7	7.3	5.0
Laborers, not farming	4,588	28.0	64.9	4.3	2.8
Farm owners and managers	585	16.2[c]	37.3	45.2	1.3[c]
Farm laborers and foremen	1,343	35.6	48.2	13.7	2.6[c]

Source: National Center for Health Services Research and Health Care Technology Assessment, National Medical Expenditure Survey, Household Survey, round one, 1987.
[a] Thousands.
[b] Includes employees with other race/ethnicity or unknown size of establishment, wage, hours, industry, or occupation, not shown.
[c] Relative standard error greater than 30 percent.

than full-time workers. Persons employed in industries characterized by seasonal or transitory employment, a low-skilled or less technical work force, and little unionization (such as agriculture, construction, repair, entertainment, and personal services) are far more likely to be uninsured than workers in industries that provide stable, year-round employment to a skilled work force (such as manufacturing, transportation, communication and utilities, the finance and insurance sectors, professional services, and government). These findings also reveal a remarkable stability in the characteristics of the employed uninsured population over the past decade. [14]

Exhibit 2 describes the composition of the uninsured population in early 1987 in terms of employment status and relationship of family members to employed persons. When all employed and self-employed persons are considered, almost half of the uninsured are employed persons, and over three-quarters of the uninsured (77.9 percent) are employed persons and their dependents. These results are also strikingly similar to empirical findings we have reported using data from 1977 and 1980. [15] Consequently, targeting the employed uninsured and their dependents through a universal employer-based strategy potentially could insure all but a fifth of the uninsured population. Note, however, that an employer mandate that excluded self-employed persons who do not employ anyone outside the household would leave 29 percent of the uninsured without coverage.

In actual practice, however, an employer mandate is likely to exclude some hired employees as well as the self-employed. Eligibility criteria are likely to be imposed to minimize the effects on the employment of marginal, low-wage, or part-time workers or to avoid imposing undue employment costs on small and marginally profitable firms. Exhibit 3 illustrates how alternative eligibility criteria associated with an employer mandate would affect the size of the uninsured population. As the exhibit reveals, the choice of minimum establishment size would have an important impact on the number of uninsured workers and dependents affected by a mandate.

An employer mandate (similar to the Kennedy-Weicker bill) that includes part-time employees who work twenty or more hours per week would extend coverage to roughly two-thirds of the uninsured population.[16] If the mandate were restricted to full-time employees only (thirty five or more hours per week), four million fewer persons (9 percent) would be eligible for coverage. The difference in the effect of the mandate is more pronounced when small business establishments are excluded. Excluding establishments with fewer than ten employees would mean that the mandate would affect only 40 percent of the uninsured, reflecting the predominance of the working uninsured in small establishments. Restricting a mandate to larger establishments would only affect a relatively small minority of the uninsured. Finally, excluding workers earning below $3.50 per hour would still affect almost two-thirds of the uninsured, but limiting the mandate to employees earning at least $5 per hour would leave half of the uninsured without employment-related coverage. Consequently, relatively small changes in eligibility criteria would significantly affect both the population covered and the cost of a mandate.

Exhibit 4 extends this analysis by examining the sources of the coverage acquired by the uninsured under a mandate requiring coverage of hired employees working at least twenty hours per week. As noted in Exhibit 3, such a mandate would reduce the size of the uninsured population by two-thirds. The majority of those affected would be employees themselves, representing 14.2 million persons or 39 percent of the uninsured. Note that seven million children, representing almost a fifth of the uninsured, also would obtain coverage.

The mandate would have its greatest impact on employees of small firms, where almost ten million such workers and dependents, or 25 percent of the uninsured, would obtain coverage. Thus, excluding small establishments would severely limit the effect of the mandate. For example, limiting the mandate to medium and large firms (twenty six or more workers) would extend coverage to only a fifth of the uninsured. Consequently, if the costs of mandated insurance borne by small employers in the short run are considered prohibitive, subsidies or alternative strategies designed to include workers in these establishments may be necessary. Finally, most of the coverage acquired by the uninsured would be drawn from workers earning between five and ten dollars per hour. Insuring these workers would reduce the size of the uninsured population by almost half. Relatively few (7 percent) would gain coverage from workers earning at or near the minimum wage.[17] Finally, most of the newly acquired coverage would come from the construction, manufacturing, services, and sales sectors, particularly the latter.

Impact on Insured Workers and their Dependents

The coverage of over twenty-six million insured persons would be altered by a mandate extending coverage to all employees working twenty hours or more

Exhibit 2

Percent Distribution Of The Uninsured According To Relationship To Employed Persons, First Quarter 1987

Relationship to employee	Number (thousands)	Percent distribution
Including the self-employed as employees		
Total[a]	36,765	100.0%
Self	17,790	48.4
Spouse	2,508	6.8
Child		
Under 18	7,974	21.7
18–23 and full-time student	383	1.0
None of the above	8,110	22.1
Excluding the self-employed as employees		
Total[a]	36,765	100.0
Self	15,812	43.0
Spouse	2,554	6.9
Child		
Under 18	7,390	20.1
18–23 and full-time student	356	1.0
None of the above	10,652	29.0

Source: National Center for Health Services Research and Health Care Technology Assessment, National Medical Expenditure Survey, Household Survey, Round One, 1987.
[a] Persons are assigned to the first applicable category.

Exhibit 3

Estimates Of Uninsured Persons Affected By A Mandate Under Alternative Eligibility Criteria, First Quarter 1987

Alternative eligibility criteria	Number affected (thousands)	Percent of uninsured
Minimum hours per week[a]		
20 hours	24,391	66.4%
35 hours	20,171	57.6
Minimum establishment size[b]		
10 workers	15,078	41.0
26 workers	10,037	27.3
101 workers	4,974	13.5
Minimum hourly wage[c]		
$3.50 per hour	23,506	64.0
$4.20 per hour	20,258	55.1
$5.00 per hour	17,955	48.9

Source: National Center for Health Services Research and Health Care Technology Assessment, National Medical Expenditure Survey, Household Survey, Round One, 1987.
[a] Includes 1 percent of uninsured with missing hours for all working family members as affected.
[b] Excludes 8 percent with missing establishment size for all working family members as affected.
[c] Includes 1 percent of uninsured with missing wages for all working family members as affected.

per week. About two million persons who are now covered by Medicaid would gain private insurance from employers, as would about three million others with public (mainly Medicare) but not private insurance. Another eight million with private insurance obtained directly from insurance companies or from nonemployer groups (including some Medicare enrollees with Medigap coverage) would switch to employer-sponsored plans. The largest single group experiencing a change in coverage would be the thirteen million employees now covered by a spouse's employment-related insurance who would be required to accept the coverage offered by their own employers.[18] In addition, the spouses and children of these thirteen million new policyholders would have the option of coverage under their plans.

Exhibit 5 provides further description of the changes in coverage under the mandate. Overall, twenty million currently insured employees would newly enroll in plans offered by their employers. The majority (63.2 percent) already are covered by the employment-related insurance of a spouse Thus, the number of affected employes who already have employment-related insurance through a spouse (almost thirteen million) is almost as large as the number of uninsured employees who would be affected (fourteen million) and amounts to about a third of all affected employees.

The shift from other insurance to employment-related coverage under a mandate would be more pronounced among employees in small firms (and their dependents). Almost half of insured persons affected by mandated coverage of employees in establishments with fewer than ten workers would change from other private to employment-related insurance, as would about 1.4 million persons covered by Medicaid. In establishments of 500 workers or more, there would be a relatively larger shift in enrollment of persons now covered by other public programs (mainly Medicare beneficiaries who would gain employer-sponsored insurance).

Coverage Options under a Mandate

About 180 million persons would be covered by employment-related plans

Exhibit 4

Estimates Of Uninsured Persons Affected By Mandated Coverage Of Employees Working Twenty Or More Hours Per Week, First Quarter 1987

Family relationship and employee characteristics	Number affected (thousands)	Percent of uninsured
Total[a]	24,391	66.4%
Relationship to employee[b]		
Self	14,165	38.5
Spouse	2,575	7.0
Child		
Under 18	7,138	19.4
18–23, student	513	1.4
Size of establishment[c]		
Under 10	9,285	25.3
10–25	4,745	12.9
26–100	4,222	11.5
101–500	2,211	6.0
Over 500	1,717	4.7
Hours per week[c]		
Under 35	4,053	11.0
35 or more	19,960	54.3
Hourly wage[c]		
Under $3.50	2,734	7.4
$3.50–$5.00	7,202	19.6
$5.01–$10.00	9,629	26.2
$10.01–$15.00	2,847	7.7
Over $15.00	1,579	4.3
Industry[c]		
Agriculture	1,050	2.9
Mining	144	0.4
Construction	3,216	8.8
Manufacturing	3,570	9.7
Transportation, communications	1,434	3.9
Sales	6,091	16.6
Finance, insurance	901	2.5
Repair services	1,834	5.0
Personal services	1,157	3.2
Entertainment	420	1.1
Professional services	2,899	7.9
Public administration	840	2.3

Source: National Center for Health Services Research and Health Care Technology Assessment, National Medical Expenditure Survey, Household Survey, Round One, 1987.
[a] Includes unknown establishment size, hours, wage, or industry not shown below.
[b] Persons are assigned to the first applicable category.
[c] Job and firm characteristics are defined from the job of family member eligible for mandated coverage. The father's job characteristics are shown for children of two working spouses.

under mandated insurance for employees working twenty hours a week or more (Exhibit 6). This amounts to approximately a 20 percent increase in enrollment, compared to the 153 million persons currently covered by employment-related plans.[19] As we have already suggested, the potential increase in the amount of insurance obtained from employers might be even greater than these figures imply. Unless dual coverage is prohibited under a mandate, many families with more than one eligible employee would have the option employer.

More than half of those covered under the mandate would be eligible employees, 26.2 percent of them with spouses who were also eligible and who could elect to be covered under both plans. About half of the ineligible children covered under the mandate could be covered by two parents. Young adults eligible for coverage through their parents as well as under their own plans would constitute a small proportion of all persons enrolled, but they could elect coverage from as many as three employers. All in all, nearly half of all persons covered by

Exhibit 5

Estimates Of Currently Insured Persons Affected By Mandated Coverage Of
Employees Working Twenty Or More Hours Per Week, By Type Of Insurance,
First Quarter 1987

	Number affected (thousands)	Type of insurance			
		Employment related	Other private	Medicaid	Other public
Total[a]	26,307	48.2%	31.9%	7.8%	12.2%
Relationship to employee[b]					
Self	20,041	63.2	27.3	3.7	5.8
Spouse	2,071	–[c]	54.9	10.7	34.4
Child					
Under 18	3,964	–[c]	40.0	27.4	32.6
18–23, student	232[d]	–[e]	–[e]	–[e]	–[e]
Size of firm[f]					
Under 10	10,223	40.9	45.0	7.3	6.8
10–25	4,582	51.2	32.3	5.5	11.1
26–100	4,073	58.1	20.4	10.3	11.3
101–500	3,183	56.4	21.5	8.2	13.9
Over 500	2,382	50.7	13.8	3.4[d]	32.1
Hours per week[f]					
Under 35	6,859	54.7	27.2	9.5	8.6
35 or more	19,059	46.0	33.7	7.1	13.2
Hourly wage[f]					
Under $3.50	2,732	34.4	31.8	15.7	18.1
$3.50–$5.00	6,470	49.1	28.7	13.3	8.9
$5.01–$10.00	10,659	49.5	32.4	5.5	12.7
$10.01–$15.00	3,654	55.7	30.6	3.2[d]	10.6
Over $15.00	2,263	46.1	41.9	0.8[d]	11.1[d]
Industry[f]					
Agriculture	1,150	21.7	69.1	7.9[d]	1.2[d]
Mining	194[d]	–[e]	–[e]	–[e]	–[e]
Construction	1,682	42.4	44.6	7.7	5.3[d]
Manufacturing	2,717	52.7	34.5	8.1	4.7
Transportation, utilities	1,148	53.9	29.6	9.7	6.9[d]
Sales	5,828	49.0	32.2	9.6	9.2
Finance	1,548	58.4	28.1	5.2[d]	8.6[d]
Repair services	1,631	49.9	28.5	10.8	10.8
Personal services	1,128	46.1	30.2	8.9[d]	6.8[d]
Entertainment	301[d]	–[e]	–[e]	–[e]	–[e]
Professional services	6,134	57.3	29.0	6.5	7.2
Public administration	2,134	22.6	10.9	1.5[d]	64.9

Source: National Center for Health Services Research and Health Care Technology Assessment, National Medical Expenditure Survey, Household Survey, Round One, 1987.
[a] Includes missing size of establishment, hours, wage, or industry not shown below.
[b] Persons are assigned to the first applicable category.
[c] Not applicable.
[d] Relative standard of error greater than 30 percent.
[e] Population is too small to make estimates.
[f] Job and firm characteristics are defined from the job of the family member eligible for mandated coverage. The father's job characteristics are shown for children of two working spouses.

employers (43 percent) would have access to coverage from more than one employer.

Employment Effects of Mandated Health Insurance

Thus far, our analysis of mandated health insurance has not considered how the added costs borne by employ-ers would affect the employment status of eligible workers. Such a mandate would have little or no effect on employment if employee wages were perfectly flexible and could be adjusted so that total employee compensation (including the mandated health insurance benefit) remained the same. However, in the short run, it is unlikely that employers could shift the entire cost of the mandate back to employees through reduced wages, especially if employee earnings are at or near the minimum wage or if employees are low-wage earners not covered by minimum wage legislation. Even in the longer run, given the declining rate of growth in employees' real wages over the past decade, workers might be unwilling to trade wages for the health insurance benefits that employers are legally ob-ligated to provide. Consequently, some decline in the employment of workers eligible for the mandate should be expected.

To predict potential employment effects, we first compute mean hourly wages for two groups: low-wage work-ers (earning less than $4.19 per hour) and higher-wage workers. Aver-age hourly earnings for the former are $3.30; average hourly earnings for the latter are $9.06. Following the Kennedy-Weicker proposal, all of the estimated average premium costs of mandated coverage, $ 1,186, is applied to the hourly wages of low-wage earners and 80 percent of the estimated premium to the average wages of higher-wage work-ers.[20] This raises the hourly cost of employing low-wage earners by 19.7 percent and that of higher-paid workers by 5.3 percent. To examine the effects on employment, we apply estimates of the sensitivity (elasticity) of labor demand to changes in employment costs from the labor economics literature.[21] The relatively low elasticity estimates sug-gest that the mandate would jeopardize the jobs of at most 2.5 percent of affected employees (approx. 847,000 workers).[22]

Conclusions and Policy Implications

This article has examined how an em-ployer mandate is likely to affect both uninsured and insured workers and their families. Among the latter, thir-teen million people who already have employment-related insurance would be affected if all eligible employees (including those now covered by a spouse's employment-related plan) are required to accept the plans of their own employers. In addition, the mandate would expand the choice of health in-surance for many two-worker families and, unless specifically prohibited, the possibility of double coverage on rela-

Exhibit 6
Percent Distribution Of Persons Insured Under Mandated Coverage Of Employees
Working Twenty Or More Hours Per Week By Relationship To Eligible Employee,
First Quarter 1987

	Number (thousands)	Percent distribution
Total[a]	180,446	100.0%
Eligible adult		
With eligible spouse	47,249	26.2
Without eligible spouse	56,346	31.2
Ineligible adult with eligible spouse	17,818	9.9
Eligible child[a]		
With one eligible parent	2,811	1.6
With two eligible parents	3,070	1.7
Ineligible child[a]		
With one eligible parent	28,760	15.9
With two eligible parents	24,393	13.5

Source: National Center for Health Services Research and Health Care Technology Assessment, National Medical Expenditure Survey, Household Survey, Round One, 1987.
[a] Child is defined as under age 18, or age 18–23 and a full-time student.

tively favorable terms under the mandated premium contributions of employees and employers. Substantial increases in dual coverage would have obvious and undesirable implications for efficiency and cost containment.

Our analysis suggests that roughly two-thirds of the uninsured population (twenty-four million eligible workers and their dependents) would obtain employment-related coverage through an employer mandate directed at employees working twenty or more hours per week. This estimate, however, critically depends on the inclusion of workers in small establishments. If the costs of an employer mandate are prohibitively expensive for small employers, so that workers in establishments with fewer than ten employees are excluded, then the mandate will have a much smaller impact and only affect about 35 percent of the uninsured population (about thirteen million persons). Although much concern has been expressed about the employment effects of a mandate, especially with regard to workers at or just above the minimum wage, we estimate this effect to be small.

Finally, it is important to recognize that even if the mandate were to include all eligible employees (working twenty or more hours per week), it would not affect one-third of the uninsured population. Consequently, it is likely that providing health insurance for those who lack it will call for a mix of policy options.

We wish to thank Lita Manuel of Social and Scientific Systems, Inc., of Bethesda, Maryland, for skillful and diligent computer programming.

Notes

1. See A. C. Monheit et al., "The Employed Uninsured and the Role of Public Policy," *Inquiry* (Winter 1985): 348–64; and P. F. Short, A. C. Monheit, and K. Beauregard, *A Profile of Uninsured Americans*, DHHS Pub. no. (PHS)89-3443, National Medical Expenditures Survey Research Findings I, National Center for Health Services Research and Health Care Technology Assessment (Rockville, MD: DHHS, September 1989).

2. The Kennedy-Weicker proposal would amend the Public Health Service Act and the Fair Labor Standards Act of 1938 (FLSA). Employers covered by FLSA would be required to enroll all employees working 17.5 hours or more per week in an employment-based health insurance plan. Participation by employees would be mandatory, regardless of their current insurance status, and employers would also be required to offer coverage for dependents of employees. An employee could, however, waive coverage for the latter if his/her dependent was enrolled in another employment-related plan. The Kennedy-Weicker proposal also would require employers to pay all premium costs for employees earning hourly wages less than $4.19 and 80 percent of premium costs for higher-paid workers. The plan also specifies that employers provide a minimum set of health benefits for hospital and physician services or their

actuarial equivalent. Full details of the Kennedy-Weicker proposal (S. 1265) are described in the *Congressional Record— Senate*, 21 May 1987, S. 7075–7081. In April 1989, Senator Kennedy introduced S. 768, the Basic Health Benefits for All Americans Act, which extends the scope of S. 1265. For a full description of the Massachusetts program, see *Health Care for the Uninsured: Program Update* (Washington, DC: Alpha Center, July 1988).

3. M. E. Lewin and L. S. Lewin, "Health Care for the Uninsured," *Business and Health* (September 1984): 34–38.

4. C. E. Phelps, "National Health Insurance by Regulation: Mandated Employee Benefits," in *National Health Insurance: What Now, What Later, What Never?* ed. M. V. Pauly (Washington, DC: American Enterprise Institute, 1980), pp. 52–73.

5. K. Ignani, "Labor Forum: Unions' Views Vary on Mandated Benefits but not on Access to Care," *Business and Health* (February 1987): 54–55.

6. U. E. Reinhardt, "Should All Employers be Required by Law to Provide Basic Health Insurance Coverage for their Employees and Dependents?" *Government Mandating of Employee Benefits* (Washington, DC: Employee Benefits Research Institute, 1987), 121–33; and U. E. Reinhardt, "Are Mandated Benefits the Answer?" *Health Management Quarterly* (First Quarter 1988): 10–14.

7. Phelps, "National Health Insurance by Regulation." See also W. K. Viscusi, "Comments on Phelps," in *National Health Insurance*, ed. Pauly, pp. 80–82.

8. Under the Kennedy-Weicker plan, the monthly actuarial rate is defined as the average monthly per enrollee amount estimated by the employer as necessary to pay for yearly total benefits under the plan (including administrative costs and contingency margin). See the *Congressional Record*, 21 May 1987, S. 7079.

9. Using Bureau of Labor Statistics health insurance benefits data for medium and large firms, Gail Jensen and colleagues report substantial differences between family and individual out-of-pocket premium costs. For example, in 1985, 65 percent of employees had individual coverage premiums fully paid, compared to 45 percent of employees with family coverage. On average, employees with individual coverage were required to contribute $11.47 per month toward coverage, compared to $37 for family coverage (these were roughly the same percentage of premiums, approximately 24 percent). See G. A. Jensen, M. A. Morrisey, and J. W. Marcus, "Cost-Sharing and the Changing Pattern of Employer-Spon-

sored Health Benefits," *The Milbank Quarterly* 65, no. 4 (1975): 521–550.

10. See the discussion in P. F. Short and A. C. Monheit, "Employers and Medicare as Partners in Financing Health Care for the Elderly," in *Lessons from the First Twenty Years of Medicare: Their Implications for Public and Private Sector Policy*, ed. M. V. Pauly and W. Kissick (Philadelphia: University of Pennsylvania Press, 1989), pp. 301–320.

11. For a more complete discussion of methodology, write the authors at: Division of Intramural Research, National Center for Health Services Research and Health Care Technology Assessment (NCHSR), U.S. Department of Health and Human Services, 5600 Fishers Lane, Rm 18-A-55, Rockville, Maryland 20857.

12. Spouses and children who are employed but do not meet the employment eligibility requirements for insurance under the mandate through their own jobs are considered dependents in our analysis.

13. Unlike in the Kennedy-Weicker proposal, the population considered by our analysis is not restricted to workers covered by FLSA. In particular, our analysis includes executive, administrative, and professional workers not covered by FLSA as well as exempt, nonsupervisory workers found predominantly in agriculture, wholesale and retail trades, service industries, and the finance, insurance, and real estate sectors. The minimum-wage provisions of FLSA now cover about 80 percent of all nonsupervisory workers. Most studies of the impact of an employer mandate do not exclude non-FLSA workers and therefore somewhat overestimate the effect of the mandate. Estimates of the number of workers exempt from FLSA are reported in *Minimum Wage and Maximum Hours Standards Under the Fair Labor Standards Act* (Washington, DC: U.S. Department of Labor, Employment Standards Administration, 1986), 31–32, Table 8.

14. See results reported in Monheit et al., "The Employed Uninsured and the Role of Public Policy," using the 1977 National Medical Care Expenditure Survey and 1980 National Medical Care Utilization and Expenditure Survey.

15. Ibid.

16. This finding is identical to that reported in S. J. Long, "Public versus Employment-Related Health Insurance: Experience and Implications for Black and Non-black Americans," *The Milbank Quarterly* 65, Supplement I (1987): 200–212, using the 1985 Current Population Survey to assess the effect of an employer mandate for uninsured workers (including the self-employed) who work at least 17.5 hours per week.

17. This may reflect the "surprisingly weak relationship between being a worker whose hourly wage is low and being a member of a family whose annual income is low." Many such workers may obtain health insurance through other working family members so that extension of the mandate to persons at or near the minimum wage may not significantly reduce the size of the uninsured population. The quote is from C. Brown, "Minimum Wage Laws: Are They Overrated?" *Journal of Economic Perspectives* 2, no. 3 (Summer 1988): 133–45.

18. NMES estimates of the number of uninsured and insured persons affected by an employer mandate are similar to estimates derived from the March 1987 Current Population Survey. See E. Gramlich, Acting Director, Congressional Budget Office, statement before Senate Committee on Labor and Human Resources, 4 November 1987.

19. Short et al., "Uninsured Americans."

20. The premium costs for coverage under the Kennedy-Weicker proposal used in this analysis was estimated by Gordon R. Trapnell of the Actuarial Research Corporation and is an average of individual and family premium estimates. See the *Congressional Record—Senate*, 21 May 1987, S. 7801.

21. Labor demand elasticities describe the percentage change in labor demand associated with a given percentage change in employment costs. Applying estimates of these elasticities to the percentage increase in employment costs due to the mandate yields an estimate of the decline in employment. The elasticity estimates used (reported in Note 22) are from the following sources: for minimum-wage workers, C. Brown, C. Gilroy, and A. Kohen, "The Effects of the Minimum Wage on Employment and Unemployment," *Journal of Economic Literature* (June 1982): 487–528; short- and long-run elasticity estimates, for manufacturing workers, K. B. Clark and R. B. Freeman, "How Elastic Is the Demand for Labor?" *Review of Economics and Statistics* 62, no. 4 (1980): 509–520.

22. Applying an upper bound elasticity estimate of -.12 for minimum wage earners to our low-wage workers yields a 2.4% decline in employment (about 197,000 workers) for employees earning hourly wages below $4.19. Using a short-run elasticity estimate of -.2 for higher-paid workers yields a decline in employment of 1.1% (286,000 employees), while application of a long-run elasticity estimate, -.48, results in lost employment for 2.5% of higher wage employees (650,000 such workers). Using the estimate for low-wage workers and the latter estimate for high-wage workers yields the estimated employment effects reported in the text. These estimated employment effects should be interpreted cautiously since they rely upon elasticity estimates from secondary sources and since they abstract from possible actions by employees and employers that could mitigate the effect of a mandate upon employment (e.g., a reduction in weekly work hours by employees and the use of more part-time or shift workers by employers).

9

A Tax Reform Strategy to Deal with the Uninsured

Stuart M. Butler

Almost 90 percent of Americans say that fundamental changes are needed in the nation's health care system. Dissatisfaction centers on the shortcomings of health insurance.[1] One of the most pronounced deficiencies of this system, of course, is that as many as 37 million Americans lack health insurance.

Policymakers tend to assume that the only way to correct the problem is to construct a national health care system in which tighter regulation is used both to control providers and to constrain the appetites of consumers. Whether such policymakers favor a government-run Canadian-style system, or one requiring employers to provide universal access to health insurance, the assumption is that normal consumer choice within free and open markets can have no major role. This assumption is erroneous. Policymakers should recognize that the deficiencies in today's U.S. health care system are due in large part to powerful and perverse incentives resulting from the current tax treatment of health care. By correcting those incentives it would be possible to construct a system based on consumer-driven markets, in which the problem of uninsurance is solved and resources are used more efficiently with little or no increase in government expenditures.

How the Tax System Leads to Uninsurance

The vast majority of American families receive medical insurance through their employer. The tax code strongly encourages such employer-provided coverage as a fringe benefit because such plans are excludable without limit from the employee's taxable income. While limited tax relief is also available to the self-employed and those incurring unusually heavy medical costs, for most Americans the company plan is the only way of receiving a tax break for medical costs.

The tax exclusion for company-based plans undoubtedly has encouraged the spread of health insurance and eased the financial worries of millions of families. But it is also a major cause of uninsurance and rapidly escalating health costs. There are three reasons for this:

1. *Inequity in tax assistance.* A tax exclusion provides the employee with tax relief from all taxes (including payroll tax) at his or her marginal tax bracket. Thus, the tax benefit is highest for employees in the highest bracket with the most expensive health plans. A highly paid executive can easily receive a tax subsidy worth over 40 percent of the cost of a generous package, when state and local tax relief is considered. Meanwhile, an employee in the same firm, with children, making $10,000, may be below the tax threshold and receive no income tax break at all. Worse still is the individual who has no company plan, or a plan not covering his or her family. This person normally must pay in aftertax dollars for his or her family's insurance or out-of-pocket medical expenses.

Thus, the tax code gives virtually no help to Americans at the bottom of the income ladder who are not covered by company plans, while it can mean thousands of dollars in tax subsidies for higher-paid individuals. It is little wonder that approximately three quarters of the uninsured (those lacking private insurance or eligibility for public programs) are workers or the dependents of workers, concentrated heavily among lower-paid employees.[2] Moreover, a company-provided plan does not have to contain any specific features, such as preventive medical care, family coverage, or catastrophic protection, to be eligible for the tax exclusion. So it is not unusual to find workers with a very expensive plan paying for all routine dental care, and yet lacking catastrophic protection.

2. *Job mobility disincentives.* A job change of any kind, whether voluntary or forced, usually requires a family to change its insurer because coverage is employer-based. This often means waiting periods and preexisting condition clauses in the new plan, and possibly some change in benefits that the family would not have freely chosen. For families with severe health problems this can mean that moving to a better job is impossible, and a layoff can be a disaster.

3. *Inflationary pressure.* With health care largely paid for by the employer (completely so in the case of first dollar coverage, which covers all costs), an employee has little or no incentive to be economical when seeking services. If the employee does try to economize, it is the employer who normally will gain the vast bulk of the savings (assuming the annual deductible has been exceeded). Knowing that the patient has little incentive to economize, physicians and hospitals also have little incentive to hold down costs. Providing the per-

Reprinted with permission from *JAMA, The Journal of the American Medical Association* 265, no. 19 (May 15, 1991), pp. 2541–44. Copyright © 1991 American Medical Association.

ceived value of a service is greater than the copayment—if any—faced by the patient, the patient will have no cause to challenge the price charged the insurer and ultimately the employer.

This lack of concern for price is, of course, a recipe for inflation. This in turn adds to the number and plight of the uninsured. Rising costs force more companies to reduce coverage or drop dependents from plans. The annual survey of corporate health insurance conducted by the New York City benefits consulting firm of A. Foster Higgins & Co, for instance, found employees facing an average increase of $20 per month in 1990 for their share of family health plan costs, and more firms encouraging employees to accept restrictions on their choices of medical care (*Wall Street Journal*, January 29, 1991:B1). Higher insurance rates cause more families without company plans to forgo insurance while facing higher out-of-pocket costs.

How a Market-based National Health Care System Would Work

Proposals that would mandate employers to provide insurance for employees and their families or pay a payroll tax for public insurance (so-called play-or-pay proposals) simply would force all employers into today's flawed system. The result would be higher labor costs and fewer employment opportunities for workers whose low skills and whose insurance or health payroll tax costs would be high compared with their output. In addition, if employers were prohibited from reducing benefits or coverage, they would resort to even tighter controls over the most basic health care decisions of American families. A Canadian-style system similarly would use regulation rather than markets to determine access and to allocate resources. As we now see in the Canadian system, just as with its forerunner the British National Health Service, removing market prices as the primary regulator of demand leads to chronic overdemand when compared with supply and to waiting lines and shortages. [3,4]

The alternative to such systems based on curbing consumer choice and expanding regulation, which implicitly

remove consumer-driven markets from health care, is to address the perverse incentives that lead to today's shortcomings, and to construct a system based on an active consumer-driven market. Such a system has been developed by The Heritage Foundation. [5]

The Heritage Foundation proposal is based on a reform of the tax treatment of health care, designed to achieve two goals. First, by changing the structure of existing tax relief, it would provide more help to the uninsured to obtain health care and insurance, and less to those who do not need generous tax subsidies. The available pool of forgone tax revenues at the federal level alone is estimated by the Congressional Budget Office to be worth $48 billion in 1991. [6] Second, the new structure of tax relief would provide stronger incentives for consumers to challenge provider costs and to seek the best insurance value for their money.

The Heritage Foundation proposal calls for two principal steps:

1. *Replace today's tax exclusion with a new system of refundable tax credits for health expenses.* The current tax exclusion for company-provided health benefits would be phased out over several years. Any health package received by a worker would be included as taxable income on the employee's W2 tax form. If a company were to discontinue or scale back its health plan, it would have to add the cash value of the reduced benefits to employee paychecks. Over the same period, however, a new system of tax credits in the personal tax code would be introduced for family health care costs (out-of-pocket costs, insurance premiums, and prepaid plans). These credits would be "above-the-line," meaning they would be available to those who do not itemize deductions on their tax returns. They would also be "refundable." This means that if the total credit exceeded the family's tax liability, the Internal Revenue Service would remit the difference.

The size of the credit (in percentage terms) would depend on the family's total annual health care spending compared with its income; the higher that ratio, the higher the percentage credit. Thus, a typical family incurring insurance and direct medical costs (including

any employer-paid benefits) equal to 10 percent of its annual income, might be eligible for a 20 percent credit. If that same family faced unusually high costs, e.g., 30 percent of income, the credit might rise to 50 percent. Higher costs would mean a still larger percentage credit, such that the actual costs to the family, net of the tax credit, would be manageable. Similarly, if the family's annual costs were low compared with its income, the percentage credit would be lower than 20 percent, and perhaps phased out entirely above a certain income. The credit would be designed to ensure that these net costs would not normally exceed 10 percent of family income. By comparison, the most comprehensive analysis of family health expenditures currently available, based on the National Medical Care Expenditure Survey of 1977, showed that out-of-pocket premium and direct service expenses averaged 10.1 percent of family income for families earning less than $12,000 per annum, falling to 2.5 percent for families earning more than $20,000. [7]

2. *Establish a "Health Care Social Contract."* Under this "social contract," each head of household would be required, by law, to enroll all family members in a health plan containing at least a federally prescribed basic package of features. These would include catastrophic stop-loss insurance (which limits out-of-pocket costs to a fixed dollar amount), hospital and physician coverage for all family members, and routine preventive care. The out-of-pocket deductible and copayment in the health plan could not normally exceed 10 percent of adjusted gross income. Health plans would be required to offer a series of premiums, based on different out-of-pocket costs, and consumers would be required to choose a plan meeting at least the 10 percent requirements. While this would mean lower-income families typically would face higher premiums, reflecting the out-of-pocket limit, this in turn would be offset by the larger tax credit available to them.

The federal government would in turn guarantee to make it financially possible for each household to discharge this legal responsibility in one of the following two ways: through the system of refundable tax credits or by granting access to Medicaid or Medicare. Thus under The Heritage Foundation proposal, all Americans would have at least a basic package of medical care, paid for by themselves or by the federal government.

This two-pronged market strategy would have significant effects on the American health care system. First, it would guarantee basic health coverage to all Americans, irrespective of their place of employment—or whether they were employed at all.

Second, government help to offset medical costs would be based on medical expenses as a proportion of income, not on the family's marginal tax rate. Thus a part-time employee of Joe's Bar and Grill would be eligible for exactly the same structure of tax help as a senior executive with Megacorp Inc, but the part-time employee—or the chronically sick individual—would receive more cash help by virtue of his or her income and likely medical expenses.

Third, the credit system would introduce a powerful tool to curb rising health care costs, since families would have a strong incentive to seek the best value for their money in their health care decisions and to avoid overutilization. One reason for this is that the individual purchaser of insurance or services would keep any savings (net of the credit) gained through prudent buying, rather than these savings going to the employer. This incentive would be strongest for those eligible for only a small credit (generally the more healthy and affluent buyers), and weakest for those eligible for a large credit. Another reason is that an employee no longer would effectively be locked into the plan provided through the employer. Thus, the employee could "shop around" for a plan with the necessary services at the best price. That in turn would intensify competition among insurers and service providers. A family might choose more services than their company plan used to offer. Or it might mean fewer extra services, if a healthy employee had been overinsured, leaving the family with extra cash income.

Fourth, the consumer-driven model would drastically reduce the need for expensive administrative regulation by insurers and employers. Most critics of the current U.S. health care system point out, correctly, that it is probably the most bureaucratized and administratively top-heavy of systems. [8] This did not just "happen." In the rest of the U.S. economy, consumer choices based on real prices spur efficiency and force providers to compete by streamlining overhead costs. But in health care provision, the actual cost of services is largely irrelevant to consumer decisions. Thus, the immediate payers of medical bills—insurers and employers—have been forced to install a system of administrative controls and paperwork in an effort to allocate resources reasonably efficiently *in spite of* consumer demands. Consumer choice is a far more effective method of regulating prices and encouraging efficiency. It does not require a vast superstructure of resource planners trying to manage consumers. It is the individual decisions of consumers themselves that achieve an efficient system.

Fifth, a tax system allowing Americans to select from a full range of competing plans would end most of the employment mobility problems plaguing today's system (and inherent in employer-mandated proposals) because a family would not change plans merely because the head of the household changed jobs. Moreover, because the employer would not be responsible for providing health coverage under The Heritage Foundation proposal, there would not be an incentive for firms to avoid hiring individuals who would pose high insurance costs—another major drawback of mandated-benefits schemes.

Sixth, reforming the tax code would allow the uninsured to be protected at a far lower cost to the government than other approaches. Indeed, it might well be accomplished without any net increase in the federal deficit. The Congressional Budget Office estimates that if the current tax exlusion for company-based plans were ended and replaced with a flat 20 percent income tax credit for insurance costs up to $250 per month for families ($100 for individuals), the federal government would collect an additional $89.4 billion in net additional income and payroll taxes over 5 years. [6] This means that the basic 20 percent credit considered by the Congressional Budget Office could be expanded by additional credits in the amount of nearly $18 billion per year and still remain budget neutral. The U.S. Treasury has analyzed a limited version of a plan similar to The Heritage Foundation proposal. If the monthly exclusion for company-provided plans were capped at $400 per family ($160 per individual), the treasury estimates that the extra revenue would, by 1995, finance an annual refundable credit of $200 per individual (up to $600 per family) for families lacking company plans. If the monthly cap were placed at $300 per family ($120 per individual), the credit would still leave the treasury with a net annual surplus of $15.8 billion by 1995. This financial cushion would permit more generous credits to needy

Revenue Estimates of Options for Limiting the Tax Exclusion for Company-Based Health Plans and Introducing a Credit in the Personal Code*

	1991	1992	1993	1994	1995
Monthly limit on exclusion†					
$400 for families/$160 for individuals					
Total receipts, $ in billions	1.5	3.1	4.5	6.7	9.6
Affected recipients, %	15	16	19	22	26
$300 for families/$120 for individuals					
Total receipts, $ in billions	5.4	10.1	13.6	18.4	23.6
Affected recipients, %	32	35	39	40	42
Annual refundable credit‡					
$200 per individual, up to $600 per household					
Total cost, $ in billions	-0.4	-6.1	-6.6	-7.3	-7.8
Permanent 25% deduction for self-employed, $ in billions	-0.2	-0.4	-0.5	-0.5	-0.6

*Estimates assume that contributions to cafeteria plans for health care will be included in the computation of employer contributions. Data from Department of the Treasury, Office of Tax Analysis.[10]

†The monthly exclusion limit and the value of the refundable credit for 1991 and beyond are indexed by the consumer price index for all items.

‡The refundable credit is available to persons who do not have employer-provided insurance or public health insurance.

families and finance the refundable credits envisioned in The Heritage Foundation proposal. A summary of the treasury's estimates is provided in the table.[9]

Seventh, the tax credit system would reduce Medicaid and welfare costs. Since The Heritage Foundation proposal includes a system of refundable tax credits for lower-income individuals, it would eliminate the current disincentive for many welfare recipients receiving Medicaid to take a job with few or no medical benefits. The Medicaid program would be retained under The Heritage Foundation proposal as an integral part of the welfare system. Subsidized risk pools and similar state-based innovative strategies would also be encouraged as a safety net to deal with unusual situations,[10] although the number of uninsurable Americans would decline under the proposal (see below).

Eighth, the strong consumer incentives in The Heritage Foundation proposal would reduce pressure for medically unnecessary state mandates on insurers. Such mandates are a significant factor in rising insurance costs. Moreover, according to a statistical study by Goodman and Musgrave,[11] as many as 9.3 million Americans lack health insurance specifically because of the additional costs due to mandates. With families paying directly for insurance, rather than these costs being "hidden" in company plans, there would be far less voter acceptance of pressure from provider groups to add new services to state mandates. The same political dynamic would help offset providers' lobbying at the federal level to expand the legally required basic package.

There are a number of understandable concerns about such a consumer-driven system based on individual choice of a medical plan, including the following:

1. *Can average Americans really make informed choices about health care?* The more informed and technically sophisticated a consumer is, the more likely he or she is to make sound decisions regarding a medical plan. But there are two reasons why individuals with little medical knowledge can be confident buyers in the system envisioned under The Heritage Foundation proposal.

The first is that any comprehensive plan would, under federal law, have to include at least the basic set of services. The second reason is that a system based on individual buyers does not in any way rule out the formation of group buyers. Indeed, most individuals probably would join groups, both to gain bargaining power as organized buyers, and to delegate detailed purchasing decisions to an organization they trusted. Such groups would negotiate plans with providers and insurers on behalf of their members, much as companies do today. The important difference is that consumers would be able to choose a buyer group they really trusted and still obtain tax benefits; today they are effectively restricted to a group organized by their employer.

Various groups can be imagined participating in a system like The Heritage Foundation proposal. A trade union, a professional organization, or a state farm bureau might manage a plan on behalf of its members. Churches, university alumni groups, and school associations also might act as brokers. Other groups might comprise those who suffer from particular ailments, such as diabetics, who would be seeking the most economical plans supplying additional specialized services. The Heritage Foundation proposal, unlike the mandated benefits approach, would make it very easy for these specialized plans to develop.

2. *Wouldn't adverse selection undermine The Heritage Foundation proposal?* Active consumer choice is considered the key to the workings of other segments of the economy. In the health sector it is usually deemed adverse. The reason for this is that the principal method we use to subsidize working Americans facing high medical costs is equal premiums for company-based group plans. In this way the healthy subsidize the unhealthy. Naturally, a problem immediately arises if healthy consumers are permitted to opt out of the group and choose a lower-cost plan reflecting their better health risk. Hence, elaborate steps are included in managed care proposals to restrict or guide consumer choices.[12]

The Heritage Foundation proposal avoids this problem by cross-subsidizing through the tax code, rather than through premium setting. Under The Heritage Foundation proposal there would indeed be a tendency for healthy individuals to purchase lower-priced plans, leaving higher-risk individuals to face steeper premiums. But the higher-risk consumers would receive large credits to offset the higher costs, financed by U.S. Treasury savings achieved from lower revenue losses on the leaner plans chosen by healthy individuals. This method of cross-subsidy is not just more precise and consistent, and less expensive to the taxpayer, than the necessarily wide variations in subsidy levels with company groups. It would also reduce the problem of uninsurable individuals. Today such individuals cannot be insured except at rates they or their employer cannot afford. With the sliding scale credit in The Heritage Foundation proposal, however, realistic premiums could in many instances be charged and paid.

3. *Would a tax credit system be difficult for the consumer to operate?* Employees would instruct the payroll department of their employer to adjust their withholding to reflect their anticipated credit. If the employee was eligible for a refundable credit, credit would be added to the paycheck each pay period. At the end of the year the total credit would be adjusted when the family filed its tax return.

Variants of this basic mechanism would deal with most potential difficulties. If anticipated costs were to rise unexpectedly, the employee could change the number of exemptions claimed (as an individual would do if he or she were to take on a larger mortgage for a home). If the individual became unemployed, or a sudden outlay exceeded the family's immediate ability to pay, despite catastrophic protection, federal regulations could require providers to wait for payment until the appropriate refundable credit was processed by the Internal Revenue Service. In addition, to ensure regular premium payments, a requirement could be placed on larger employers to make a payroll deduction on behalf of their employees and to remit it to the insurance company chosen by the employee, as many firms currently do for 401K savings plans.

The primary tool to assure compliance with the mandate for families would be to require proof of basic insurance to be attached to the annual tax return. Insurance companies or health plans providing the basic comprehensive package would be required to send enrollees a statement indicating the period of coverage (if an employee switched companies, the statement would indicate the change). There would be fines for families failing to include proof of insurance with their tax return. While some families would still evade the requirement, just as some evade taxes, this system would reduce the problem to an acceptable level.

Conclusion

A structural change of this kind might seem politically unrealistic, but there are several reasons to believe otherwise. It is certainly less radical than replacing the entire system with a Canadian-style system. It can also be introduced gradually. A specific credit to cover one segment of the uninsured, for instance, could be paid for with a modest cap on the current exclusion. When consumers and insurers had grown accustomed to that change, the credit could be expanded and the cap reduced.

Moreover, the idea of individual tax credits to help certain categories of Americans to purchase medical insurance or services is not new or unique to

The Heritage Foundation proposal. The 1991 budget passed by Congress in October 1990, for instance, contains a new program granting a 50 percent refundable tax credit for low-income families purchasing insurance to cover children not covered under company plans.

Capping or limiting the exclusion of company plans also is not a new idea. It was routinely proposed as a deficit reduction measure during the Reagan administration. It made little headway then because workers saw no advantage in supporting such a measure. Blending a phaseout of the exclusion with a new system of tax credits leads to a very different political equation, however, since millions of employees would gain from such an exchange, including many workers currently with generous plans. In today's climate of deficit reduction and concern about rising unemployment, a "balanced budget" proposal that does not mean huge new federal outlays or additional payroll costs for business has a distinct attraction.

Notes

1. Blendon RB, Leitman R, Morrison I, Donelan K. Satisfaction with health systems in ten countries. *Health Aff.* 1990;9(2):185–192.

2. Short P, Cornelius L, Goldstone D. Health insurance of minorities in the United States. *J Health Care Poor Underserved.* 1990;1(1):15–16.

3. Walker M. Why Canada's health care system is no cure for America's ills. *Heritage Found Int Briefing;* no. 19.

4. Globerman S, Hoye L. *Waiting Your Turn: Hospital Waiting Lists in Canada.* Vancouver, British Columbia: Fraser Institute; 1990.

5. Butler S, Haislmaier E, eds. *A National Health System for America.* Washington, DC: The Heritage Foundation; 1989.

6. *Reducing the Deficit: Spending and Revenue Options, Part II.* Washington, DC: Congressional Budget Office; 1990:143–146.

7. National Center for Health Services Research and Health Care Assessment. A summary of expenditures and sources of payment for personal health services from the National Health Care Expenditure Survey. In: *National Health Care Expenditures Study, Data Preview 24.* Washington, DC: US Dept. of Health and Human Services; 1987:Table 12.

8. Himmelstein DU, Woolhandler S. Cost without benefit: administrative waste in US health care. *N Engl J Med.* 1986;314: 441–445.

9. Department of the Treasury, Office of Tax Analysis. *Financing Health and Long-term Care.* Washington, DC: US Dept of the Treasury; 1990:88.

10. Wasley T. Health care for the poor, unemployed, and high-risk. In: Butler S, Haislmaier E, eds. *A National Health System for America.* Washington, DC: The Heritage Foundation; 1989:119.

11. Goodman J, Mungrave G. *Freedom of Choice in Health Insurance.* Dallas, Tex: National Center for Policy Analysis; 1988.

12. Enthoven A, Kronick R. A consumer-choice health plan for the 1990s. *N Engl J Med.* 1989;320:29-37, 94–101.

Hospital Cost Inflation under State Rate-Setting Programs

Brian Biles, Carl J. Schramm, and J. Graham Atkinson

Over the past decade, a number of states have established programs to set hospital rates on a prospective basis as a response to rapid increases in health-care expenditures. During this period, several authorities have viewed the evidence on the effectiveness of these programs as inconclusive.[1-4] In a recent survey article, for example, Hellinger states: "Although firm conclusions regarding rate-setting programs should not be drawn from existing evaluations, few policy makers feel that state rate-setting commissions are capable of controlling health-care costs."[5] Others have taken a disparaging view of the ability of these regulatory agencies to limit increases in health care costs in general.[6] Enthoven captures the view of the pessimistic observers in his comment: "The weight of evidence, based on experience in many other industries, as well as in health care, supports the view that such regulation is likely to raise costs and retard beneficial innovation."[7]

Because most studies of the effectiveness of hospital rate-setting programs are based on their performance before 1975, when many programs were still in their early phases and were not yet regulating actively, more recent data are required for a valid assessment of the effectiveness of the programs. Data for the period from 1970 to 1978, presented here, show that substantial reductions in the rate of increase in the

cost of a hospital stay can be attributed to the cost-containment programs.

State Programs

According to the traditional reimbursement system, hospitals are paid after services are rendered, either on the basis of a schedule of charges (charge reimbursement) or, for selected third-party payers, at the actual cost of the service (cost reimbursement). In contrast, prospective rate-setting programs attempt to set the amount that hospitals can charge for services before the period for which the rate is to apply.

The approximately 25 prospective rate-setting programs now operating in the United States vary in authority, from mandatory rate setting by a legislatively established public agency to advisory budget review by nongovernmental associations. In addition, programs differ in the types of payers whose rates are subject to regulation—ranging from only Medicaid patients to all payers (Medicaid, Medicare, Blue Cross, commercial insurance, and out-of-pocket payers).

For this analysis, states are classified as rate-setting states only if they meet the following criteria: the rate-setting program is operated directly by a state agency, compliance by hospitals is mandatory, a majority of non-Medicare hospital expenses are subject to regulation, and the agency has been regulating rates actively since 1976 or earlier. The six states that meet these criteria are Connecticut, Maryland, Massachusetts, New Jersey, New York, and

Washington. Although a majority of non-Medicare hospital expenses are affected by rate setting in each of the six states, the states vary in the coverage that their programs provide. The types of coverage range from that of Connecticut, where rate setting applies only to persons with commercial insurance and persons who pay out of pocket, to those of Maryland and Washington, where rate setting applies to everyone.

In these states, the appropriate state agency establishes daily rates as well as a schedule of rates for the other revenue centers (e.g., laboratory, operating room, and radiology) in each hospital. These become the only schedules that the provider may use to compute bills. Thus, the hospital's annual operating budget may be computed by multiplying the projected volume of standardized units that are delivered in each revenue center by the schedule of rates. Payers pay the provider for services rendered to subscribers according to the schedule. This renders the traditional distinctions among costs, charges, and reimbursement irrelevant. For this reason, we use the term "expense" to refer to money actually paid to the hospital. Some states allow discounts from the scheduled rates to Blue Cross and Medicaid because of economies of scale in processing claims, certain contractual assurances to pay without challenge, and promptness of payment. Table 1 lists the year of passage of rate-setting legislation and the year in which regulation effectively began in each rate-setting state. The periods between the year of legislation and the year when

Reprinted with permission from *The New England Journal of Medicine* 303, no. 12 (September 18, 1980), pp. 664–68. Copyright © 1980 by the Massachusetts Medical Society.

Table 1. Delayed Regulatory Activity in Six Rate-Setting States.*

STATE	YEAR STATUTE ENACTED	YEAR AGENCY BEGAN TO REGULATE
Connecticut	1973	1976
Maryland	1971	1975
Massachusetts	1968	1975
New Jersey	1971	1974
New York	1969	1971
Washington	1973	1975

*Excludes six states with rate-setting programs that do not meet the listed criteria. In Arizona, Minnesota, and Wisconsin, participation in the review process is mandatory, but compliance with the proposed rates is voluntary. Rhode Island's program is a mandated process of negotiation and contract among the state government, Blue Cross, and the hospitals. Colorado's early program was restricted to Medicaid patients, and although comprehensive rate-setting legislation was enacted in 1977, controls were not imposed until 1978. Illinois, which passed enabling legislation in 1978, has not yet begun to regulate rates. (Source: interviews with state agencies.)

regulation became effective reflect start-up periods of various lengths.

In order to examine the impact of state rate-setting programs on the rate of increase in hospital costs, this analysis compares the rates of increase in expense per equivalent admission for community hospitals in the six rate-setting states with those rates for hospitals in the 44 non-rate-setting states and in Washington, D.C. during the years 1970 to 1978.

Data

Data for this study were drawn from the past 10 annual surveys of the nation's hospitals conducted by the American Hospital Association (AHA) and published in the 1970 through 1979 editions of the AHA's *Hospital Statistics*.[8] The survey questionnaire, which is sent to all hospitals registered in the United States, is usually returned by more than 90 percent of the hospitals.

We took the raw data from tables in the annual editions of *Hospital Statistics* and obtained the number of admissions and the total expenses for community hospitals in the individual states and in the United States as a whole from the tables entitled "Utilization, Personnel, and Finances." For 1972 and subsequent years, the data are presented as a total for the nation in Table 5A of the series and by state in Table 5C; for the years before 1972, these data are presented in Table 3. Inpatient gross revenue data for community hospitals were obtained from the table entitled "Revenue for Community Hospitals." This

table is now presented as Table 11 of *Hospital Statistics* and was presented before 1972 as Table 8.

The category of "community hospitals" was chosen to represent the kind of hospital typically subject to state regulation. Community hospitals denote all nonfederal hospitals except psychiatric institutions, tuberculosis hospitals, long-term general hospitals, and other special hospitals. The category includes nongovernmental, nonprofit hospitals, investor-owned, profit-making hospitals, and state and local governmental hospitals. After 1970 the AHA narrowed its definition of community hospitals to exclude "hospital units of institutions," primarily prison and college infirmaries. This change decreased the size of the category by less than 1 percent and does not affect the results of this study.

The expense per inpatient admission and the expense per inpatient day are the two measures of hospital output that are used most often to measure the major goal of state cost-containment programs—reduction in the rate of increase in inpatient costs. The fact that hospitals can maintain or increase current levels of spending and still show a reduction in per diem costs by extending the average length of stay limits the value of the per diem expense as a measure of cost savings. Therefore, we chose the expense per equivalent admission, which reflects the average cost of treating each hospitalized patient, as the best index with which to compare rates of cost increase in rate-setting and non-rate-setting states.

Methods

In order to study the effect of state rate-setting programs on the rate of increase in hospital costs, the average increase in the expense per admission was calculated for all hospitals in each state and the District of Columbia for each year from 1970 to 1978.

Calculation of increases in total hospital expenses requires a technique to measure a hospital's output of both inpatient and outpatient services. Admissions are a natural unit for inpatient treatment, whereas patient visits are the natural unit for outpatient services. In order to obtain an aggregate volume of services, it is common to calculate "equivalent inpatient" services by converting outpatient visits into a fraction of inpatient services. The fraction used is the ratio of the average revenue per outpatient visit to the average revenue per inpatient unit measured. This approach, which the AHA employs to compute adjusted patient days,[8] was used in this study to compute the number of equivalent admissions.

We then obtained the expense per equivalent admission (EPEA) by dividing the total expenses by the number of equivalent admissions. The number of equivalent admissions is the sum of the number of inpatient admissions plus the product of the number of outpatient visits times the ratio of revenue per outpatient visit to revenue per inpatient admission:

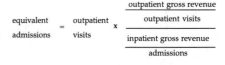

$$\begin{aligned}\text{equivalent} \atop \text{admissions} &= \text{outpatient} \atop \text{visits} \times \frac{\dfrac{\text{outpatient gross revenue}}{\text{outpatient visits}}}{\dfrac{\text{inpatient gross revenue}}{\text{admissions}}} \\ &\quad + \text{inpatient admissions}\end{aligned}$$

The expense per equivalent admission was then calculated as the total expenses divided by the number of equivalent admissions.

The EPEA was thus calculated each year from 1969 to 1978 for each of the 50 states and the District of Columbia. The EPEA was also calculated for the six rate-setting states as a group and for the 44 non-rate-setting states and the District of Columbia as a group. The rates of the increase from year to year, expressed as a percentage of the previous year, were then calculated; the mean rates of increase in EPEA for the rate-setting states were compared with the mean rates of increase in the non-rate-setting states and the District of Columbia (Figure 1). In addition, the rates of increase in EPEA for each of the six rate-setting states were compared with the mean performance of the non-rate-setting states and the District of Columbia (Figure 2).

Because both the sample sizes and the variances were significantly different, the Behrens-Fisher statistic[9] was used to compare the mean rates of increase in EPEA of the rate-setting states with those of the non-rate-setting states and the District of Columbia.

Results

Figure 1 compares the rates of increase in EPEA for the rate-setting and non-rate-setting states from 1970 to 1978. The annual rates of increase in EPEA show no discernible pattern of difference between rate-setting and non-rate-setting states until 1976, when they begin to diverge. The Behrens-Fisher test shows that the differences in EPEA between the rate-setting and non-rate-setting states were significant in 1976

$(P<0.05$, degrees of freedom $= 5,44)$ and highly significant in 1977 and 1978 $(P<0.005$, degrees of freedom $= 5,44)$.

Figure 2 compares the rate of increase in EPEA from 1974 to 1978 for the non-rate-setting states with that of each rate-setting state. The individual graphs show that of the six rate-setting states only Washington had a rate of increase above the national average in 1976, and that in 1978 all six rate-setting states had smaller increases in EPEA.

Discussion

Although comprehensive, legally mandated rate-setting programs have been in effect for as long as eight years, it is only in the past three years that notable differences between rates of cost infla-

tion in rate-setting and non-rate-setting states have emerged.

One explanation for the difference between the findings reported here and those reported in earlier studies is that because the state programs were only established between 1970 and 1975, earlier reporting periods did not allow them adequate time to become effective. There are indications that state programs and officials refine their administrative procedures and gain political skill in the early years of operation. [10,11] For example, although the Maryland Health Services Cost Review Commission was established on July 1, 1971, and given regulatory authority on July 1, 1974, only one hospital had been fully reviewed by July 1, 1975. It was not until July 1, 1977, that the rates of all Mary-

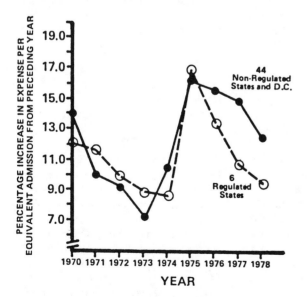

Figure 1. Annual Percentage Increases in Expense per Equivalent Admission (EPEA) of Rate-Setting and Non-Rate-Setting States, 1970-1978.

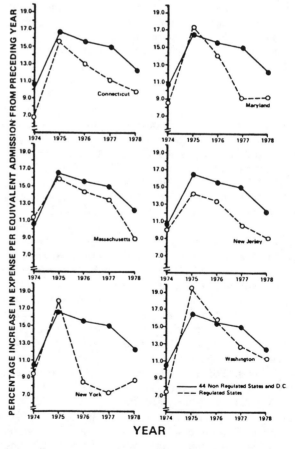

Figure 2. Annual Percentage Increases in Expense per Equivalent Admission (EPEA) for Each Rate-Setting State Compared with Increases in EPEA for Non-Rate-Setting States, 1974-1978.

land hospitals had been approved by the commission.

A second explanation for the recent trend is that only in the past few years has the concern with high rates of increase in hospital costs become a sufficiently visible public problem to give the officials of state programs the incentive (and perhaps the political support) to reduce the rate of cost increase. The high rate of increase nationwide during the early part of this period—16.9 percent in 1975 and 13.7 percent in 1976—may have increased the commitment of both the public and the state employees to improvement of the programs. In addition, the introduction of the Carter administration's hospital cost-containment proposal in early 1977 and the subsequent consideration of that proposal by Congress may have increased the states' interest and the regulators' ability to restrain cost increases.

Finally, it must be noted that the Nixon administration's Economic Stabilization Program operated from August 1971 to April 1974 and included specific rules to limit cost increases in hospitals nationwide. By reducing the rate of increase in hospital costs in non-rate-setting states, the Economic Stabilization Program may have masked any effect of state programs during this period.

With the recent Congressional rejection of the federal cost-containment bill, state initiatives to control hospital cost increases have taken on added importance. The data reported in this paper reveal a statistically significant reduction in average annual cost increases in rate-setting states as compared with non-rate-setting states from 1976 to 1978. These data are consistent with the view that mandatory rate-setting programs that establish rates prospectively and cover most patients can effectively contain increases in hospital costs.

Further analysis of the effects of state rate setting is of course necessary. The precise effects of rate setting on per capita use, the intensiveness of hospital services, the salaries of hospital employees, the prices paid by hospitals for goods and services, and a wide variety of other factors are all matters of interest. Ultimately, information on the relation between differences in per capita hospital expenditures and the health status of population groups will be desirable. Such analysis, when available, will permit the development of even more sophisticated hospital payment policies. Meanwhile, we believe that the results of this analysis support a more optimistic view of the effectiveness of state hospital rate-setting programs than that of the studies that covered earlier reporting periods.

We are indebted to Mr. Steven Renn and Dr. Susan Horn for assistance with the computer and statistical analyses, and to Ms. Janet Archer for her comments on the manuscript.

Notes

1. Bauer KG. Hospital rate setting—this way to salvation? Milbank Mem Fund Q. 1977; 55:117–58.
2. Berry RE Jr. Prospective rate reimbursement and cost containment: formula reimbursement in New York. Inquiry. 1976; 13:288–301.
3. Dowling WL. Hospital rate-setting programs: how, and how well, do they work? Top Health Care Financ. 1979; 6(1):15–23.
4. Gaus CR, Hellinger FJ. Results of prospective reimbursement. Top Health Care Financ. 1976; 3(2):83–96.
5. Hellinger FJ. Hospital rate-regulation programs and proposals: a survey and analysis. Top Health Care Financ. 1979; 6(1):5–14.
6. Noll RG. The consequences of public utility regulation of hospitals. In: Controls on health care. Washington, D.C.: National Academy of Sciences, 1975:25–48.
7. Enthoven AC. Consumer-choice health plan: inflation and inequity in health care today: alternatives for cost control and an analysis of proposals for national health insurance. N Engl J Med. 1978; 298:650–58.
8. Hospital statistics: annual ed. Chicago: American Hospital Association, 1979.
9. Fisher RA, Yates F. Statistical tables for biological, agricultural and medical research. 5th ed. New York: Hafner, 1957, tables VI, VI_1, VI_2.
10. Summary of testimony presented on the President's hospital cost-containment proposal—H.R. 2626: 96th Congress, first session (Committee Print 96-IFC 22). Washington, DC: Government Printing Office, 1979.

11

Persuasion and Coercion for Health: Ethical Issues in Government Efforts to Change Lifestyles

Daniel I. Wikler

What should be the government's role in promoting the kinds of personal behavior that lead to long life and good health? Smoking, overeating, and lack of exercise increase one's chances of suffering illness later in life, as do many other habits. The role played by lifestyle is so important that, as stated by Fuchs (1974): "The greatest current potential for improving the health of the American people is to be found in what they do and don't do for themselves."

Over the past two decades, North American governments have widened the scope of their involvement in lifestyle reform. In the 1970s, major prospective health policy documents of both the United States (Department of Health, Education, and Welfare, 1975) and Canadian governments (documented by Lalonde, 1974) announced a change of orientation in this direction. One factor involved in this shift was an increasing share of ill health attributed to chronic illnesses and accidental injuries that are aggravated by living habits. This development led to increased interest in preventive behavioral change, abetted by a wave of "therapeutic nihilism," an attitude that questions the effectiveness of many medical interventions and is more friendly to health efforts that begin and end at home.

That lifestyle reform should be undertaken by the *government*, rather than by private individuals or associations, is part of the general emergence of the government as health-care provider. Encouragement of healthful living may also have a budgetary motive. Government officials may find that lifestyle reform is one of the most cost-effective ways of delivering health, especially if more effective change-inducing techniques are developed. Indeed, the present cost-containment crisis may propel lifestyle reform to a central place in health planning before the necessary scientific and policy thinking has taken place.

Further pressure on the government to take strong steps to change unhealthy lifestyles might come from those who live prudently. All taxpayers have a stake in keeping federal health costs down, but moderate persons may particularly view others' self-destructive lifestyles as a kind of financial aggression against them. They may be expected to intensify their protest in the event of a national health insurance plan or national health service.

Involvement of the government in legislating healthful patterns of living is not wholly new; there have been public health and labor laws for a long time. Still, with the increased motivation for government action in lifestyle reform, it is time to reflect on the kinds of interventions the public wants and should have to accept. Various sorts of behavior change measures need to be examined

to see if they might be used to induce healthier living. But that is not enough; goals must also be identified and subjected to ethical examination.

The discussion below will be concerned with those behavior change measures that are likely to be unpleasant and unwelcome. Since most techniques now used or contemplated for future use do not have such properties, there is little need to justify or focus on them.

Considerably more debate, however, would arise over a decision to use stronger methods. For example, a case in point might be a government "fat tax," which would require citizens to be weighed and taxed if overweight. The surcharges thus derived would be held in trust, to be refunded with interest if and when the taxpayers brought their weight down. This pressure would, under the circumstances, be a bond imposed by the government upon its citizens, and thus can be fairly considered as coercive.

Though rarely acknowledged as such, the primary motivation for such government programs is paternalism, premised on the reasonable claim that health is valued by every rational person. Indeed the health planner may attempt to argue for coercive reforms of health-destructive behavior with a line of reasoning that recalls Pascal's wager. [1] Since death, which precludes all good experience, must receive an enormously negative valuation, contemplated action that involves risk of death will also receive a substantial negative value af-

Adapted from an article that appeared in *Milbank Quarterly* 56, no. 3 (1978), pp. 303–38. Reprinted with permission of the Milbank Memorial Fund. Copyright © 1978 The Milbank Memorial Fund.

ter the good and bad consequences have been considered. And this will hold true even if the risk is small, since even low probability multiplied by a very large quantity yields a large quantity. Hence anyone who risks death by living dangerously must, on this view, be acting irrationally. This would be grounds for suspecting that the life-threatening practices were less than wholly voluntary and thus created a need for protection. Further, this case would not require the paternalistic intervenor to turn away from pluralistic ideals, for the unhealthy habits would be faulted not on the basis of deviance from paternalistic values, but on the apparent lapse in the agent's ability to understand the logic of the acts.

This argument, or something like it, may lie behind the willingness of some to endorse paternalistic regulation of the lifestyles of apparently competent adults. It is, however, invalid. Its premises may sometimes be true, and so too may its conclusion, but the one does not follow from the other. Any number of considerations can suffice to show this. For example, time factors are ignored. An act performed at age 25 that risks death at age 50 does not threaten every valued activity. It simply threatens the continuation of those activities past the age of 50. The argument also overlooks an interplay between the possible course of action: if every action that carries some risk of death or crippling illness is avoided, the enjoyment of life decreases. This makes continued life less likely to be worth the price of giving up favorite unhealthy habits.[2] Indeed, although it may be true that death would deny one of all chances for valued experiences, the experiences that make up some people's lives have little value. The less value a person places on continued life, the more rational it is to engage in activities that may brighten it up, even if they involve the risk of ending it. Craig Claiborne (1976), food editor of *The New York Times*, gave ebullient testimony to this possibility in the conclusion of his "In Defense of Eating Rich Food":

I love hamburgers and chili con carne and hot dogs. And foie gras and sauternes and those small birds known as ortolans. I love banquettes of quail eggs with hollandaise sauce and clambakes with lobsters dipped into so much butter it dribbles down the chin. I like cheesecake and crepes filled with cream sauces and strawberries with creme fraiche. . . .

And if I am abbreviating my stay on this earth for an hour or so, I say only that I have no desire to be a Methuselah, a hundred or more years old and still alive, grace be to something that plugs into an electric outlet.

The assumption that one who is endangering one's health must be acting irrationally and involuntarily is not infrequently made by those who advocate forceful intervention in suicide attempts; and perhaps some regard unhealthy lifestyles as a sort of slow suicide. The more reasonable view, even in cases of imminent suicide, seems rather to be that *some* unhealthy or self-destructive acts are less-than-fully voluntary but that others are not. Claiborne's diet certainly seemed to be voluntary, and suggests that the case for paternalistic intervention in lifestyle cannot be made on grounds of logic alone. It remains true, however, that much of the behavior that leads to chronic illness and accidental injury is not fully under the control of the persons so acting. My thesis is merely that, first, this involuntariness must be shown (along with much else) if paternalistic intervention is to be justified; and, second, this can only be determined by case-by-case empirical study. Those who advocate coercive measures to reform lifestyles, whose notices are purely beneficent, and who wish to avoid paternalism except where justified, might find such study worth undertaking.

Any such study is likely to reveal that different practitioners of a given self-destructive habit act from different causes. Perhaps one obese person overeats because of an oral fixation over which he has no control, or in a Pavlovian response to enticing television food advertisements. The diminished voluntariness of these actions lends support to paternalistic interventions. Claiborne had clearly thought matters through and decided in favor of a shorter though gastronomically happier life; to pressure him into changing so that he may live longer would be a clear imposition of values and would lack the justification provided in the other person's case.

The trouble for a government policy of lifestyle reform is that a given intervention is more likely to be tailored to practices and habits than to people. Although we may someday have a fat tax to combat obesity, it would be surprising indeed to find one that imposed charges only on those whose obesity was due to involuntary factors. It would be difficult to reach agreement on what constituted diminished voluntariness; harder still to measure it; and perhaps administratively impractical to make the necessary exceptions and adjustments. We may feel, after examining the merits of the cases, that intervention is justified in the compulsive eater's lifestyle but not in the case of Claiborne. If the intervention takes the form of a tax on obesity per se, we face a choice: Do we owe it to those like Claiborne *not* to enforce alien values more than we owe it to compulsive overeaters to protect them from self-destruction? The general right of epicures to answer to their own values, a presumptive right conferred by the pluralistic ethic spoken of earlier, might count for more than the need of compulsive overeaters to have health imposed on them, since the first violates a right and the second merely confers a benefit. But the situation is more complex than this. The compulsive overeater's life is at stake, and this may be of greater concern (everything else being equal) than the epicure's pleasures. Then, too, the epicure is receiving a compensating benefit in the form of longer life, even if this is not a welcome exchange. And there may be many more compulsive overeaters than there are people like Claiborne. On the other hand, the positive causal link between tax and health for either is indirect and tenuous, while the negative relation between tax and gastronomic pleasure is relatively more substantial. (For a fuller discussion of this type of trade-off, see Bayles [1974].) Perhaps the firmest conclusion one may draw from all this is that a thoroughly reasoned moral rationale for a given kind of intervention can be very difficult to carry out.

Another concern is that the true motive for intervention may be less defensible than paternalism. There is some possibility that what would be advertised as concern for the individual's welfare (as that person defines it) would turn out to be simple legal moralism, i.e., an attempt to impose the society's or authorities' moral prescriptions upon those not following them. In Knowles's call for lifestyle reform (1976) the language is suggestive:

The next major advances in the health of the American people will result from the assumption of individual responsibility for one's own health. This will require a change in lifestyle for the majority of Americans. The cost of sloth, gluttony, alcoholic overuse, reckless driving, sexual intemperance, and smoking is now a national, not an individual responsibility.[3]

All save the last of these practices are explicit *vices;* indeed, the first—sloth and gluttony—use their traditional names. The intrusion of nonmedical values is evidenced by the fact that of all the living habits that affect health adversely, only those that are sins (with smoking excepted) are mentioned as targets for change. Skiing and the football produce injuries as surely as sloth produces heart disease; and the decision to postpone childbearing until the thirties increases susceptibility to certain cancers in women (Medawar, 1977). If it is the unhealthiness of "sinful" living habits that motivates the paternalist toward reform, then ought not other acts also be targeted on occasions when persons exhibit lack of self-direction? The fact that other practices are not ordinarily pointed out in this regard provides no argument against paternalistic lifestyle reform. But those who favor pressuring the slothful to engage in physical exercise might ask themselves if they also favor pressure on habits which, though unhealthy, are not otherwise despised. If enthusiasm for paternalistic intervention slackens in these latter cases, it may be a signal for reexamination of the motives.

Moreover, the involuntariness of some self-destructive behavior may make paternalistic reform efforts ineffective. To the extent that the unhealthy behavior is not under the control of the individual, we cannot expect the kind of financial threat involved in a "fat tax" to exert much influence. Paradoxically, the very conditions under which paternalistic intervention seems most justified are those in which many of the methods available are least likely to succeed. The result of intervention under these circumstances may be a failure to change the life-threatening behavior, and a needless (and inexcusable) addition to the individual's woes through the unpleasantness of the intervention itself. A more appropriate target for government intervention might be the commercial and/or social forces that cause or support the life-threatening behavior.

Although the discussion above has focused on the problems attendant to a paternalistic argument for coercive health promotion programs, I have implicitly outlined a positive case for such interventions as well. A campaign to reform unhealthy habits of living will be justified, in my view, so long as it does not run afoul of the problems I have mentioned. It may indeed be possible to design such a program. The relative weight of the case against paternalistic intervention can be lessened, in any case, by making adjustments for the proportion of intervention, benefit, and intrusion. Health-promotion programs that are only very mildly coercive, such as moderate increases in cigarette taxes, require very little justification; noncoercive measure such as health education require none at all. And the case for more intrusive measures would be stronger if greater and more certain benefits could be promised. Moreover, even if the paternalistic rationale for coercive reform of health-related behavior fails completely, there may be other rationales to justify the intrusion. It is to these other sorts of arguments that I now turn.

Fair Distribution of Burdens

The problem of health-related behavior is sometimes seen as a straightforward question of collective social preference:

The individual must realize that a perpetuation of the present system of high cost, after-the-fact medicine will only result in higher costs and greater frustration. . . . This is his primary critical choice: to change his personal bad habits or stop complaining. He can either remain the problem or become the solution to it; Beneficent Government cannot—indeed, should not—do it for him or to him (Knowles, 1977).

A good deal of the controversy is due, however, not to any one person's distaste for having to choose between bad habits and high costs, but rather some people's distaste for having to accept both high costs and someone *else's* bad habits. In the view of these persons, those who indulge in self-destructive practices and present their medical bills to the public are free riders in an economy kept going by the willingness of others to stay fit and sober. Those who hold themselves back from reckless living may care little about beneficence. When they call for curbs on the expensive health practices of others, they want the government to act as their agent primarily out of concern for their interests.

The demand for protection from the cost of calamities other people bring upon themselves involves an appeal to fairness and justice. Both the prudent person and the person with unhealthy habits, it is thought, are capable of safe and healthy living; why should the prudent have to pay for neighbors who decide to take risks? Neighbors ought not set fire to their houses if there is danger of its spreading. With the increasing economic and social connectedness of society, the use of coercion to discourage the unhealthy practices of others may receive the same justification. As the boundary between private and public becomes less distinct, and decisions of the most personal sort come to have marked adverse effects upon others, the state's protective function may be thought to give it jurisdiction over any health-related aspect of living.

This sort of argument presupposes a certain theory of justice; and one who wishes to take issue with the rationale for coercive intervention in health-related behavior might join the debate at the level of theory. Since this debate would be carried out at a quite general level, with only incidental reference to health practices, I will accept the argument's premise (if only for argument's sake) and comment only upon its applicability to the problem of self-destructive behavior. A number of considerations lead to the conclusion that the fairness argument as a justification of coercive intervention, despite initial appearances, is anything but straightforward. Underlying this argument is an empirical premise that may well prove untrue of at least some unhealthy habits: that those who take chances with their health do place a significant financial burden upon society. It is not enough to point to the cost of medical care for lung cancer and other disease brought on by individual behavior. As Hellegers (1978) points out, one must also determine what the individual would have died of had he not engaged in the harmful practice, and subtract the cost of the care which that condition requires. There is no obvious reason to suppose that the diseases brought on by self-destructive behavior are costlier to treat than those that arise from "natural causes."

Skepticism over the burden placed on society by smokers and other risk-takers is doubly reinforced by consideration of the nonmedical costs and benefits that may be involved. It may turn out, for all we know prior to investigation, that smoking tends to cause few problems during a person's productive years and then to kill the individual before the need to provide years of social security and pension payments. From this perspective, the truly burdensome individual may be the unreasonably fit senior citizen who lives on for 30 years after retirement, contributing to the bankruptcy of the social security system, and using up savings that would have reverted to the public purse via inheritance taxes had an immoderate lifestyle brought an early death. Taken at face value, the fairness argument would require taxes and other disincentives on *non*smoking and other healthful personal practices which in the end would sap the resources of the healthy person's fellow citizens. Only detailed empirical inquiry can show which of these practices would be slated for discouragement were the argument from fairness accepted; but the fact that we would find penalties on healthful behavior wholly unpalatable may weaken our acceptance of the argument itself.

A second doubt concerning the claim that the burdens of unhealthy behavior are unfairly distributed also involves an unstated premise. The risk taker, according to the fairness argument, should have to suffer not only the illness that may result from the behavior but also the loss of freedom attendant to the coercive measures used in the attempt to change the behavior. What, exactly, is the cause cited by those

complaining of the financial burdens placed upon society by the self-destructive? It is not simply the burden of caring and paying for care of these persons when they become sick. Many classes of persons impose such costs on the public besides the self-destructive. For example, diabetics, and others with hereditary disposition to contract diseases, incur unusual and heavy expenses, and these are routinely paid by others. Why are these costs not resisted as well?

One answer is that there *is* resistance to these other costs, which partly explains why we do not yet have a national health insurance system. But even those willing to pay for the cost of caring for diabetics, or the medical expenses of the poor, may still bridle when faced by the needs of those who have compromised their own health. Is there a rationale for resisting the latter kinds of costs while accepting the former? One possible reason to distinguish the costs of the person with a genetic disease from those of the person with a lifestyle-induced disease is simply that one can be prevented and the other cannot. Health behavior change measures provide an efficient way of reducing the overall financial burden of health care that society must shoulder, and this might be put forward as the reason why self-destructive persons may have their presumptive rights compromised while others with special medical expenses need not.

But this is not the argument we seek. The medical costs incurred by diseases caused by unhealthy lifestyles may be preventable, if our behavior-modifying methods are effective; but this fact shows only that there is a utilitarian opportunity for reducing costs and saving health-care dollars. It does *not* show that this opportunity makes it right to burden those who lead unhealthy lives with governmental intrusion. If costs must be reduced, perhaps they should be reduced some other way (e.g., by lessening the quality of care provided for all); or perhaps costs should not be lowered and those feeling burdened should be made to tolerate the expense. The fact that money could be saved by intruding into the choice of lifestyles of the self-destructive does not

itself show that it would be particularly fair to do so.

If intrusion is to be justified on the grounds that unhealthy lifestyles impose unfair financial burdens on others, then, something must be added to the argument. That extra element, it seems, is fault. Instead of the avoidability of the illnesses and their expenses, we point to the responsibility for them, which we may believe falls upon those who contract them. This responsibility, it might be supposed, makes it unfair to force others to pay the bills and makes it fair for others to take steps to prevent the behaviors that might lead to the illness, even at the cost of some of the responsible person's privacy and liberty.

The argument thus depends crucially on the premise that the person who engages in an unhealthy lifestyle is responsible for the costs of caring for the illness that it produces. "Responsible" has many senses, and this premise needs to be stated unambiguously. Since responsibility was brought into the argument in hopes of contrasting lifestyle-related diseases from others, it seems to involve the notions of choice and voluntariness. If the chronic diseases resulting from lifestyle were not the result of voluntary choices, then there could be no assignment of responsibility in the sense in which the term is being used. This would be the case, for example, if a person contracted lung cancer from breathing the smog in the atmosphere rather than from smoking. But what if it should turn out that even a person's smoking habit were the result of forces beyond the smoker's control? If the habit is involuntary, so is the illness; and the smoker in this instance is no more to be held liable for imposing the costs of treatment than would, say, the diabetic. Since much self-destructive behavior is the result of suggestion, constraint, compulsion, and other factors, the applicability of the fairness argument is limited.

Even if the behavior leading to illness is wholly voluntary, there is not necessarily any justification for intervention *by the state*. The only parties with rights to reform lifestyles on these grounds are those who are actually being burdened by the costs involved. A wealthy man who retained his own medical facilities would not justifiably be a target of any of these interventions, and a member of a prepaid health plan would be liable to intervention primarily from others in his payments pool. He would then, of course, have the option of resigning and continuing his self-destructive ways; or he might seek out an insurance scheme designed for those who wish to take chances but who also want to limit their losses. These insured parties would join forces precisely to pool risks and remove reasons for refraining from unhealthy practices; preventive coercion would thus be out of the question. Measures undertaken by the government and applied indiscriminately to all who indulge in a given habit may thus be unfair to some (unless other justification is provided). The administrative inconvenience of restricting these interventions to the appropriate parties might make full justice on this issue too impractical to achieve.

This objection may lose force should there be a national health insurance program in which membership would be mandatory. Indeed, it might be argued that existing federal support of medical education, research, and service answers this objection now. But this only establishes another ground for disputing the responsibility of the self-destructive individual for the costs of his medical care. To state this objection, two classes of acts must be distinguished: the acts constituting the lifestyle that causes the disease and creates the need for care; and the acts of imposing financial shackles upon an unwilling public. Unless the acts in the first group are voluntary, the argument for imposing behavior change does not get off the ground. Even if voluntary, those acts in the second class might not be. Destructive acts affect others only because others are in financial relationships with the individual that cause the medical costs to be distributed among them. If the financial arrangement is mandatory, then the individual may not have *chosen* that his acts should have these effects on others. The situation will have been this: an individual is compelled by law to enter into financial relationships with certain others as a part of an insurance scheme; the arrangement causes the individual's acts to have effects on oth-

ers that the others object to; and so they claim the right to coerce the individual into desisting from those acts. It seems difficult to assign to this individual responsibility for the distribution of financial burdens. He or she may (or may not) be responsible for getting sick, but not for having the sickness affect others adversely.

This objection has certain inherent limitations in its scope. It applies only to individuals who are brought into a mandatory insurance scheme against their wishes. Those who join the scheme gladly may perhaps be assigned responsibility for the effect they have on others once they are in it; and certainly many who will be covered in such a plan will be glad of it. Further, the burden imposed under such a plan does not occur until persons who have made themselves sick request treatment and present the bill to the public. Only if treatment is mandatory and all financing of care taken over by the public can the imposition of burden be said to be wholly involuntary.

In any case, certain adjustments could be made in a national health insurance plan or service that would disarm this objection. Two such changes are obvious: the plan could be made voluntary, rather than mandatory; and/or the public could simply accept the burdens imposed by unhealthy lifestyles and refrain from attempts to modify them. The first of these may be impractical for economic reasons (in part because the plan would fill up with those in greatest need, escalating costs), and the second only ignores the problem for which it is supposed to be a solution.

There is, however, a response that would seem to have more chance of success: allowing those with unhealthy habits to pay their own way. Users of cigarettes and alcohol, for example, could be made to pay an excise tax, the proceeds of which would cover the costs of treatment for lung cancer and other resulting illnesses. Unfortunately, these costs would also be paid by users who are not abusers: those who drink only socially would be forced to pay for the excesses of alcoholics. Alternatively, only those contracting the illnesses involved could be charged; but it would be difficult to distinguish illnesses result-

ing from an immoderate lifestyle from those due to genetic or environmental causes. The best solution might be to identify persons taking risks (by tests for heavy smoking, alcohol abuse, or dangerous inactivity) and charge higher insurance premiums accordingly. This method could be used only if tests for these behaviors were developed that were nonintrusive and administratively manageable.[4] The point would be to have those choosing self-destructive lifestyles assume the true costs of their habits. I defer to economists for devising the best means to this end.[5]

This kind of policy has its good and bad points. Chief among the favorable ones is that it allows a maximum retention of liberty in a situation in which liberty carries a price. Under such a policy, those who wished to continue their self-destructive ways without pressure could continue to do so, provided that they absorbed the true costs of their practices themselves. Should they not wish to shoulder these costs, they could submit to the efforts of the government to induce changes in their behavior. If the rationale for coercive reform is the burden the unhealthy lifestyles impose on others, this option seems to meet its goals; and it does so in a way that does not require loss of liberty and immunity from intrusions. Indeed, committed immoderates might have reason to welcome the imposition of these costs. Although their expenses would be greater, they would thereby remove at one stroke the most effective device held by others to justify meddling with their "chosen" lifestyles (Detmer, 1976).

The negative side of this proposal stems from the fact that under its terms the only way to retain one's liberty is to pay for it. This, of course, offers very different opportunities to rich and poor. This inequality can be assessed in very different ways. From one perspective, the advantage money brings to rich people under this scheme is the freedom to ruin their own health. Although the freedom may be valued intrinsically (i.e., for itself, not as a means to some other end), the resulting illness cannot; perhaps the poor, who are denied freedom but given a better chance for health, are coming off best in the transaction. From another perspective, however, it seems that such a plan simply adds to the degradation already attending to being poor. Only the poor would be forced to submit to loss of privacy, loss of freedom from pressure, and regulation aimed at behavior change. Such liberties are what make up full citizenship, and one might hold that they ought not to be made contingent on one's ability to purchase them.[6]

The premise that illnesses caused by unhealthy habits impose financial burdens on society, then, does not automatically give cause for adopting strong measures to change the self-destructive behavior. Still, it *may* do so, if the underlying theory of justice is correct and if its application can skirt the problems mentioned here. Besides, justification for such programs may be derived from other considerations.

Indeed, there is one respect in which the combined force of the paternalistic rationale and the fairness argument is greater than the sum of its parts. The central difficulty for the fairness argument, mentioned above, is that much of the self-destructive behavior that burdens the public is not really the fault of the individual; various forces, internal and external, may conspire to produce such behavior independently of the person's will. Conversely, a problem for the paternalist is that much of the harm from which the individual would be "protected" may be the result of free, voluntary choices, and hence beyond the paternalist's purview. The best reason to be skeptical of the first rationale, then, is doubt over the *presence* of voluntariness; the best reason to doubt the second concerns the *absence* of voluntariness. Whatever weighs against the one will count for the other.

The self-destructive individual, then, is caught in a theoretical double-bind: whether the behavior is voluntary or not, there will be at least prime facie grounds for coercive intervention. The same holds true for partial voluntariness and involuntariness. This consideration is of considerable importance for those wanting to justify coercive reform of health-related behavior. It reduces the significance of the notion of voluntariness in the pro-intervention arguments, and so serves to lessen concern over the intractable problems of defin-

ing the notion adequately, and detecting and measuring its occurrence.

Public Welfare

Aside from protecting the public from unfair burdens imposed by those with poor health habits, there may be social benefits to be realized by inducing immoderates to change their behavior. Health behavior change may be the most efficient way to reduce the costs of health care in this country, and the benefits derived may give reason to create some injustices. Further, lifestyle reform could yield some important collective benefits. A healthier work force means a stronger economy, for example, and the availability of healthy soldiers enhances national security.

There may also be benefits more directly related to health. If the supply of doctors and curative facilities should prove relatively inelastic, or if the economy would falter if too much of our resources were diverted to health care, it may be impossible to increase access to needed medical services. The social goal of adequate treatment for all would then not be realizable unless the actual need for medical care were reduced. Vigorous government efforts to change lifestyles may be seen as the most promising means to this end.

The achievement of these social goals—enhanced security, improved economic functioning, and universal access to medical care—could come at the price of limits to the autonomy of that segment of society that indulges in dangerous living. If we do not claim to find fault with them, it would be unreasonable to insist that the immoderate *owed* the loss of some of their liberties to society as a part of some special debt—while continuing to exempt from special burden those with involuntary special needs due to genes or body chemistry. The reason for society to impose a loss upon the immoderate rather than upon the diabetic would be, simply, that it stood to benefit more by doing so.

Whether it is permissible to pursue social goods by extracting benefits from disadvantageously situated groups within society is a matter of political ideology and justice. Our society routinely compromises certain of its citizens' interests

and privileges for the public good; others are considered inviolate. The question to be decided is whether the practices that we now know to be dangerous to health merit the protection given by the status of right. The significance of this status is that considerations of utility must be very strong before curbing the practice can be justified. Unfortunately, I see no decisive argument that shows that smoking, sloth, and other dangerous enjoyable pastimes are or are not protected by rights. It is worth mentioning, however, that many behaviors of interest to health planners are almost certainly of too trivial significance to aspire to such protection; freedom to drive at 65 miles per hour rather than 55 is an example, as is the privilege of buying medicine in nonchildproof containers. Consideration of social utility would seem to justify much that is being currently overlooked in prevention of injury and illness through behavior change.

Even those whose ideology would not ordinarily warrant government intervention on these grounds might make an exception for reform of unhealthy habits. Even if the real motivation for the reform efforts were to achieve the social goals mentioned above, some of the intervention might in fact be justifiable on paternalistic grounds; and even the intervention that is not thus justified confers some benefit in the form of promise of better health.

The author acknowledges support of the Joseph P. Kennedy, Jr., Foundation and of the Institute of Medicine, National Academy of Sciences; helpful suggestions from Lester Breslow, Don Detmer, Edmund Pellegrino, Michael Pollard, Bernard Towers, members of the Institute's Social Ethics Committee, and *Health and Society*'s referees; and numerous points and ideas from Norman Fost, Gerald MacCallum, John Robertson, Norma Wikler, and, particularly, David Mechanic.

Notes

1. The agnostic should adopt the habits which would foster his own belief in God. If he does and God exists, he will receive the infinite rewards of paradise; if he does and God does not exist, he was only wasting the efforts of conversion and prayer. If he does not try to believe in God, and religion is true, he suffers the infinitely bad fate of hell; whereas if God

does not exist he has merely saved some inconvenience. Conversion is the rational choice even if the agnostic estimates the chances of God's existing as very remote, since even a very small probability yields a large index when multiplied against an infinite quantity.

2. Readers of the previous footnote might note that a similar difficulty attends Pascal's wager. If the agnostic took steps to foster belief in every deity for which the chance of existing was greater than zero, the inconvenience suffered would be considerable, after all. Yet such would be required by the logic of the wager.

3. Elsewhere, however, Dr. Knowles emphasized that "he who hates sin, hates humanity" (Knowles, 1977). Knowles's argument in the latter essay is primarily nonpaternalistic.

4. It may be that the only way to separate smokers and drinkers taking risks from those not taking risks is to wait until illness develops or fails to develop. Perhaps smokers could save their tax seals and cash them in for refunds if they reach 65 without developing lung cancer!

5. The reader may sense a paradox by this point. Taxes on unhealthy habits would avoid inequities involved in lifestyle reform measures, such as taxes on unhealthy habits. And it is true that some of the steps that might be taken to permit those with unhygienic lifestyles to assume the costs incurred might resemble those that could be used to induce them to give the habits up. Despite this, and despite the fact that the two kinds of programs might even have the same effects, I believe that they can and ought to be distinguished. The imposition of a fat tax has a behavior change as its goal. It is this goal that made it a topic for discussion in this paper. It would not be imposed to cover the costs of diseases stemming from unhealthy lifestyles—indeed, as the reader will recall, the funds obtained through the tax were to be kept in trust and returned later if and when the behavior changed. In contrast, the taxes being mentioned as part of a "pay-as-you-go" plan would not be imposed as a means to changing behavior. Such a proposal would constitute one way of financing health costs, a topic I am not addressing in the present paper. These taxes would, of course tend to discourage the behavior in question; but this (welcome) effect would not be their purpose nor provide their rationale (more precisely, *need* not be their purpose). Any program, of course, can serve multiple needs simultaneously. The "pay-as-you-go" tax would succeed as a program even

if no behavior change occurred, and the behavior-modifying tax would succeed if behavior did change even if no funds were raised. In any case, surcharges and taxes would be but a few methods among many that might be used to induce behavior change; while they could constitute the whole of a policy aimed to impose costs upon those incurring them.

6. It might be possible to devise charges that would be assessed proportionately to income, so that the "bite" experienced by rich and poor would be about the same. This has not been the pattern in the past; all pay the same tax on a pack of cigarettes. In any case, this adjustment is in no way mandated by the fairness argument. The purpose of the charges would be to permit self-destructive individuals to "pay their own way" and hence remain free to indulge in favored habits. Reducing the amounts charged to low-income persons fails to realize that end; the costs of medical treatment for the poor are not any lower than for the rich. Indeed, being poor may increase the likelihood that the costs of treatment would have to be borne by the public. This suggests a scheme in which charges are assessed *inversely* proportional to income.

References

American Public Health Association. 1975. Statement on Prevention. *The Nation's Health* 5 (10): 7–13.

Bayles, M. D. 1972. A Concept of Coercion. In Pennock, J. R., and Chapman, J. W., eds., *Coercion*. pp. 16–29. Chicago/New York: Aldine Atherton, Inc.

——————. 1974. Criminal Paternalism. In Pennock, J. R., and Chapman, J. W., eds., *The Limits of Law: Nomos XV*. New York: Lieber-Atherton.

Claiborne, C. 1976. In Defense of Eating Rich Food. *The New York Times*. December 8.

Department of Health, Education and Welfare. 1975. *Forward Plan for Health FY 1977–81*. (June). Washington, DC: U.S. Government Printing Office.

Dershowitz, A. 1974. Toward a Jurisprudence of "Harm" Prevention. In Pennock, J. R., Chapman, J. W., eds., *The Limits of Law: Nomos XV*. New York: Lieber-Atherton.

Detmer, D. E. 1976. A Health Policy, Anyone? or What This Country Needs is a Market Health Risk Equity Plan! *The Public Affairs Journal* 6 (3): 101–2.

Dworkin, G. 1971. Paternalism. In Wasserstrom, R., ed., *Morality and the Law*. Belmont, CA: Wadsworth Publishing Co.

Feinberg, J. 1973. *Social Philosophy*. Englewood Cliffs, NJ: Prentice-Hall.

Fuchs, V. R. 1974. *Who Shall Live?* New York: Basic Books, Inc.

Gert, G., and Culver C. 1976. Paternalistic Behavior. *Philosophy &Public Affairs* 6(1):45-57.

Haefner, D. P., and Kirscht, J. P. 1970. Motivational and Behavioral Effects of Modifying Health Beliefs. *Public Health Reports* 85 (5): 478–84.

Haggerty, R. J. 1977. Changing Lifestyles to Improve Health. *Preventive Medicine* 6 (2): 276–89.

Held, V. 1972. Coercion and Coercive Offers. In Pennock, J. R., and Chapman, J. W., eds. *Coercion*. pp. 49–62. Chicago/New York: Aldine Atherton, Inc.

Hellegers, A. 1978. Personal communication.

Hodson, J. 1977. The Principle of Paternalism. *American Philosophical Quarterly* 14 (1): 61–69.

Knowles, J. II. 1976. The Struggle to Stay Healthy. *Time*: August 9.

——————. 1977. The Responsibility of the Individual. In Knowles, J. II., ed., *Doing Better and Feeling Worse*. New York: W. W. Norton.

Lalonde, M. 1974. *A New Perspective on the Health of Canadians*. Report (April). Ottawa: Government of Canada.

MacCallum, G. C. 1966. Legislative Intent. *Yale Law Journal* 75 (5): 754–87.

McKeown, T., and Lowe, C. R. 1974. *An Introduction to Social Medicine*. Second edition. Oxford: Blackwell's.

Mechanic, D. 1977. Personal communication.

Medawar, T. B. 1977. Signs of Cancer. *New York Review of Books* 24 (10): 10–14.

Milio, N. 1976. A Framework for Prevention: Changing Health-Damaging to Health-Generating Life Patterns. *American Journal of Public Health* 66 (5): 435–39.

Murphy, J. G. 1974. Incompetence and Paternalism. *Archiv für Rechts und Sozialphilosophie* LX (4): 465–86.

Nozick, R. 1969. Coercion. In Morganbesser, S.; Suppes, P.; and White, M.; eds., *Philosophy, Science and Method: Essays in Honor of Ernest Nagel*. New York: St. Martin's Press.

Pennock, J. R. 1972. Coercion: An Overview. In Pennock, J. R., and Chapman, J. W., eds., *Coercion*. pp. 1–15. Chicago/New York: Aldine Atherton, Inc.

Pomerleau, O., Pass F., and Crown, V. 1975. Role of Behavior Modification in Preventive Medicine. *The New England Journal of Medicine* 292 (24): 1277–82.

Rosenstock, I. M. 1960. What Research in Motivation Suggests for Public Health. *American Journal of Public Health*. 50 (3): 295–302.

Terris, M. 1968. A Social Policy for Health. *American Journal of Public Health* 58 (1): 5–12.

Ubell, E. 1972. Health Behavior Change: A Political Model. *Preventive Medicine* 1 (2): 209–21.

Walzer, M. 1978. Review of C. Lindblom, *Politics and Markets*. In *New York Review of Books*, July 20.

Bibliography: Additional Resource Materials Related to This Field

Barry, P. Z. 1975. Individual Versus Community Orientation in the Prevention of Injuries. *Preventive Medicine* 4: 47–56.

Beauchamp, D. E. 1975. Federal Alcohol Policy: Captive to an Industry and a Myth. *The Christian Century* (September 17): 788–91.

_____. 1975. Public Health: Alien Ethic in a Strange Land? *American Journal of Public Health* 65: 1338–39.

_____. 1976. Public Health as Social Justice. *Inquiry* 13: 3–14.

Becker, M. H., Drachman, R. H., and Kirscht, J. P. 1972. Motivations as Predictors of Health Behavior. *Health Services Reports* 87: 852–62.

Belloc, N. B. 1973. Relationship of Health Practices and Morality. *Preventive Medicine* 2: 67–81.

_____, and Breslow, L. 1972. Relationship of Physical Health Status and Health Practices. *Preventive Medicine* I: 409–21.

Biener, K. J. 1975. The Influence of Health Education on the Use of Alcohol and Tobacco in Adolescence. *Preventive Medicine* 4: 252–57.

Breslow, L. 1973. Research in a Strategy for Health Improvement. *International Journal of Health Services* 3: 7–16.

Brody, H. 1973. The Systems View of Man: Implications for Medicine, Science, and Ethics. *Perspectives on Biological Medicine* (Autumn): 71–92.

Brotman, R., and Suffet, F. 1975. The Concept of Prevention and Its Limitations. *The Annals of the American Academy of Political and Social Science* 417: 53–65.

Charrette, E. E. 1976. Life Styles: Controlled or Libertarian? (Letter to the Editor.) *The New England Journal of Medicine* 294: 732.

Cooper, J. D. 1966. A Nonphysician Looks at Medical Utopia. *Journal of the American Medical Association* 97: 105–7.

Dingle, J. H. 1973. The Ills of Man. *Scientific American* 299: 77–84.

Freeman, R. A., Rowland, C. R., Smith, M. C., et al. 1976. Economic Cost of Pulmonary Emphysema: Implications for Policy on Smoking and Health. *Inquiry* 13: 15–22.

Goldstein, M. K., and Stein, G. H. 1976. Regarding RF Meenan's Article "Improving the Public's Health—Some Further Reflections." (Letter to the Editor.) *The New England Journal of Medicine* 294: 732.

Greenberg, D. S. 1975. Medicine and Public Affairs: Forward, Cautiously, with the Forward Plan for Health. *The New England Journal of Medicine* 293: 673–74.

Grover, P. L., and Miller, J. 1976. Guidelines for Making Health Education Work. *Public Health Reports* 91: 249–53.

Haddon, W., Jr. 1970. On the Escape of Tigers: An Ecologic Note. *American Journal of Public Health* 60: 2229–34. (Originally published in *Technology Review* 72 (2), 1970.)

Higginson, J. 1976. A Hazardous Society? Individual versus Community Responsibility in Cancer Prevention. *American Journal of Public Health* 66: 359–66.

Kalb, M. 1975. The Myth of Alcoholism Prevention. *Preventive Medicine* 4: 404–16.

Kass, L. R. 1975. Regarding the End of Medicine and the Pursuit of Health. *The Public Interest* 40 (Summer): 11–42.

McKnight, J. 1975. The Medicalization of Politics. *The Christian Century* (September 17).

Meenan, R. F. 1976. Improving the Public's Health—Some Further Reflections. *The New England Journal of Medicine* 294: 45–46.

Ogden, H. G. 1976. Health Education: A Federal Overview. *Public Health Reports* 91: 199–217.

Outkn, G. 1974. Social Justice and Equal Access to Health Care. *Journal of Religious Ethics* 2 (1): 11–32.

Pennock, J. R., and Chapman, J. W., eds. 1972. *Coercion*. Chicago/New York: Aldine Atherton, Inc.

Pierce, C. 1975. Hart on Paternalism. *Analysis* 205–7.

Preventive Medicine USA: Health Promotion and Consumer Health Education. 1976. A Task Force Report sponsored by the John E. Fogarty International Center for Advanced Study in the Health Sciences, National Institutes of Health, and The American College of Preventive Medicine, New York: PRODIST.

Rabinowitz, J. F. 1976. *Review of The Limits of Law: Nomos XV*, by Pennock, J. R., and Chapman, J. W., eds. (New York: Lieber-Atherton, 1974), *Philosophical Review* 85: 244–50.

Regan, D. H. 1974. Justifications for Paternalism. In: Pennock, J. R., and Chapman, J. W., eds. *The Limits of Law: Nomos XV*. New York: Lieber-Atherton.

Roccella, E. J. 1976. Potential for Reducing Health Care Costs by Public and Patient Education. *Public Health Reports* 91: 223–24.

Sade, F. 1971. Medical Care as a Right: A Refutation. *The New England Journal of Medicine* 285: 1288–92.

Somers, A. R. 1971. Recharting National Health Priorities: A New Canadian Perspective. *The New England Journal of Medicine* 285: 415–16.

Somers, H. N. 1975. Health and Public Policy. *Inquiry* 12: 87–96.

Thomas, L. 1975. Notes of a Biology-Watcher: The Health-Care System. *The New England Journal of Medicine* 293: 1245–46.

Water Supply. 1976. *The United States Law Week* 44: 2480–81.

Whalen, R. P. 1977. Health Care Begins with the I's. *The New York Times* (April 17).

White, K. L. 1973. Life and Death and Medicine. *Scientific American* 229: 23–33.

White, L. S. 1975. How to Improve the Public's Health. *The New England Journal of Medicine* 293: 773–74.

Wilson, F. R. 1976. Regarding RF Meenan's article "Improving the Public's Health—Some Further Reflections." (Letter to the Editor.) *The New England Journal of Medicine* 294: 732–33.

Wriston, H. M. 1976. Health Insurance. *The New York Times* (May 23).

II
The Issues

A Changing Patterns of Morbidity and Efficacy

B Financing Strategies and Incentives

C Rationing, Access to Health Care Services, and the Uninsured

D The Delivery System and System Administration

12

Americans Report on Their Access to Health Care

Howard E. Freeman, Robert J. Blendon, Linda H. Aiken,
Seymour Sudman, Connie F. Mullinix,
and Christopher R. Corey

In developing its initial grantmaking program in the early 1970s, The Robert Wood Johnson Foundation chose to emphasize improving access to health care in the United States. There were many press accounts at the time about the difficulties Americans experienced obtaining medical care, but there was little timely and systematic information about the overall magnitude of the problem, its distribution among various population groups, and changes over time. To acquire this information, the Johnson Foundation supported three independent national studies in 1976, 1982, and 1986 to measure the extent to which individuals were experiencing problems obtaining medical care.[1] These surveys built on a research approach first implemented by the Committee on the Costs of Medical Care in the early 1930s, which was later extended and refined by Odin Anderson, Ronald Andersen, and their colleagues at the University of Chicago.[2]

This paper highlights results from the recently completed 1986 survey of access to and use of health services.[3] Six findings are of particular significance: (1) Between 1982 and 1986, Americans' overall use of medical care declined in terms of hospitalization and per capita physician visits. (2) Access to physician care for individuals who were poor, black, or uninsured decreased between 1982 and 1986, particularly for those in poor health. (3) Hospitalizations have also declined for these disadvantaged

groups, but the reduction is comparable to that experienced by the entire population. However, the uninsured and black and Hispanic Americans continue to receive less hospital care than might be appropriate given their higher rates of ill health. (4) Though much has been written about the overuse of medical care, this study found signs of underuse of important health services among key population groups. (5) The long-standing gap in receipt of medical care between rural and urban residents appears to have been eliminated. (6) Most Americans continue to be highly satisfied with their physician and inpatient hospital care. In addition, emergency care, which was a source of some dissatisfaction in 1982, received higher marks in 1986.

Methods

Data reported in this article come from two telephone surveys conducted in 1982 and 1986, using similar research instruments and design. Each respondent was interviewed for approximately twenty-five minutes about various aspects of access to medical care: the availability of a personal physician or usual source of care; the actual use of doctors, other health professionals, and hospitals; self-reports of health status; the presence of serious health conditions; problems in paying for care; and the degree of satisfaction with the care received. Supplemental face-to-face interviews were conducted in 1986 with a small sample of people without telephones in three geographically dispersed

communities. The findings of this survey confirm, as others have concluded, that if households without telephones were added to those surveyed by telephone, the findings would not be significantly different.[4]

The 1986 study consisted of interviews with 10,130 people in the continental United States, 76 percent of those selected for interviews.[5] People with chronic and serious illnesses were oversampled; the study group was weighted, however, so that the findings represent the U.S. population. Proxy interviews with a parent were conducted in order to obtain information on children under age seventeen. Also in cases where the respondent was too sick or otherwise unable to be interviewed, a proxy interview with another person in the household was completed.

The 1982 data are from the previous foundation-supported survey undertaken by Louis Harris and Associates in conjunction with the University of Chicago.[6] The study group consisted of approximately 6,700 adults and children. The 1982 sample was reweighted for the purposes of this analysis to be consistent with the procedures used for the 1986 sample; thus, there are small differences in the 1982 results reported here and in previous publications from the study.

The average number of physician visits reported in these two surveys differs somewhat from those reported by the National Center for Health Statistics because telephone consultations are not counted as visits in our two surveys. Also, the interviewers in our surveys

Reprinted by permission of Health Affairs, Chevy Chase, MD (Spring 1987), pp. 6–18.

Exhibit 1
The Use Of Medical Care By Americans, 1982 And 1986

	1982	1986
Percent without a physician visit in the past year	19%	33%
Average number of per person physician visits within the past year	4.8	4.3
Percent hospitalized during the past year	9%	7%
Percent without a usual source of care	11%	18%

probed to gain information on all visits to specialists, including mental health professionals, in 1986, which is not usually done in other national surveys.

Decline in the Use of Medical Care

Between 1982 and 1986, the average use of medical care declined across all population groups. As illustrated in Exhibit 1, the percentage of Americans hospitalized one or more times in the year prior to the survey declined by 22 percent. One-third of Americans did not visit a physician even once in the year prior to the survey, a major change since 1982. Average per capita visits to physicians declined by 10 percent, a consequence of the reduced portion of the population with any ambulatory contacts in 1986. It should be noted, however, that mean physician visit rates reported in the 1982 survey were higher than other studies undertaken that year, including the Health Interview Survey.[7] Hence, the difference in visits between our 1982 and 1986 data may overstate somewhat the actual decline in physician utilization.

Over the past two decades, a larger proportion of Americans have reported having access to a regular source of care, usually a particular private physician.[8] Studies have suggested that patients may receive more appropriate and effective health care when they have a single source for care—a place where there is some continuing knowledge of their health status and problems over time.[9] However, as Exhibit 1 shows, a larger proportion of Americans in 1986 compared with 1982 report having no single usual source of care (18 percent compared to 11 percent). Even among people who report having a usual source of care, there appears to be more use of multiple physicians and settings. For example, of those who had a particular

personal physician in 1982, 95 percent reported seeing that doctor on their last visit. In 1986, only 79 percent went to their regular doctor on their last visit.

The surveys do not provide data that permit a full explanation of the reduced use of physician and hospital care. The changes are consistent, however, with a number of trends in health care nationally including greater use of coinsurance and deductibles in private health insurance plans, increased out-of-pocket medical care costs, more widespread use of hospital preadmission screening, an increase in ambulatory surgery, and the rapid growth of urgent care centers.

Deteriorating Access for the Poor, Minorities, and Uninsured

Data on the number of visits people make to doctors' offices and hospitals do not tell us all we wish to know about the accessibility of health care in the United States. For example, visit rates tell us little about the appropriateness of treatment received. Visit rates do provide one window, however, on the accessibility of personal health services to different groups in the country. Moreover, the usefulness of this measure of

accessibility can be enhanced by taking into account individuals' relative need for health care. The President's Commission for the Study of Ethical Problems in Medicine and Biomedical and Behavioral Research in its 1983 report recommended that adjustments be made for health status in all comparisons of physician utilization rates between groups.[10] Earlier studies have shown that a person's self-assessment of health status is a reasonably sensitive indicator of actual need for medical care, including the presence of chronic conditions and disabilities, the number of specific health problems and symptoms, sensory impairment and immobility, and limitations of normal activities due to illness.[11]

The following exhibits, then, report utilization of physician and hospital care by health status for the poor, minorities, and the uninsured. Two types of comparisons are made: (1) the percent change between 1982 and 1986; and (2) the gap in receipt of care between different groups. The gap is the percent difference between two groups using the majority group as the standard against which the other is compared.

Low-Income Americans

The earliest access study, undertaken in 1931, found that people with low incomes saw physicians 50 percent less frequently than did those with higher incomes.[12] This gap was of particular concern because of evidence that serious illness was more common among the poor. By the mid-1970s, after decades of gradual progress, this inequity in the frequency of use of physician

Exhibit 2
Mean Number Of Physician Visits By Income And Health Status, 1982 And 1986

Income	Fair and poor health		Percent change
	1982	1986	1982 to 1986
Poor and near poor[a]	9.1	8.4	−8%
Noonpoor	8.1	11.5	+42%
Gap (percent)[b]	+12%	−27%	
	Excellent and good health		
Poor and near poor	4.1	3.3	−20%
Noonpoor	4.2	3.8	−10%
Gap (percent)	−2%	−13%	

[a]Less than 150 percent of poverty level.
[b]Percent difference in visits by poor compared to nonpoor.

services had been largely eliminated. Indeed, individuals from lower income groups were actually seeing physicians slightly more often than those of higher incomes, which reflected their higher burden of illness.[13]

However, between 1982 and 1986, this improved situation changed, particularly for low-income groups who were in poorer health. The nation's low-income citizens received less physician care, on average, in 1986 than comparable groups did in 1982. Between 1982 and 1986 as shown in Exhibit 2, physician visit rates for low-income individuals in poorer health declined by 8 percent while visit rates for the nonpoor of similar health status increased by 42 percent. This widened a gap that had all but disappeared. By 1986, the poor had 27 percent fewer physician visits than did the nonpoor of the same health status. This suggests a significant reversal in the longstanding trend toward greater equity in the accessibility of physician care.

Low-income adults, particularly those under age sixty-five, have experienced marked declines in physician visits since 1982 (Exhibit 3). The average number of physician visits declined by 30 percent for poor adults under age sixty-five while no change was found for the nonpoor. By 1986, poor and nonpoor adults under age sixty-five were seeing physicians at roughly the same rates even though almost three times more of the poor reported themselves in only fair or poor health. If poor and nonpoor adults had comparable access to physicians, we would expect the poor to see physicians more often because a larger proportion are in ill health. The same trends in access are noted for the elderly. Poor and nonpoor elderly saw physicians at the same rates in 1986 despite a higher proportion of poor elderly reporting themselves in ill health. Access to physician care for poor children remained about the same over the period, but physician use rates for poor children do not reflect that more poor children than nonpoor children are in ill health.

A number of changes in the organization and financing of hospital care occurred between 1982 and 1986. There has been much speculation about how

these changes affected low-income Americans. The national decline in hospital use mentioned earlier is reflected in a reduction of hospitalization among both poor and nonpoor Americans, as indicated in Exhibit 4. The poor were more likely than the nonpoor in both 1982 and 1986 to have been hospitalized at least once in a year, which appears to be justified in view of the larger proportion of low-income individuals in ill health. Our data do not permit an assessment, however, of whether the levels of hospital use by the poor in either 1982 or 1986 were appropriate to their actual levels of need.

Exhibit 3
Mean Number Of Physician Visits And Perceived Health Status By Age And Income, 1982 And 1986

	Physician visits		Percent change	Percent in fair/poor health
	1982	1986	1982–1986	1986
Children below 17:				
Poor/near poor	3.8	3.9	+3%	13%
Nonpoor	4.5	3.8	−16	4
Gap (percent)	−16%	+3%		
Adults 17-64:				
Poor/near poor	6.7	4.7	−30	21
Nonpoor	4.5	4.5	0	8
Gap (percent)	+49%	+4%		
Elderly 65+:				
Poor/near poor	6.0	4.8	−20	42
Nonpoor	5.7	4.9	−14	25
Gap (percent)	+5%	−2%		

Exhibit 4
Percent Hospitalized One Or More Times In Year And Perceived Health Status By Income, 1982 And 1986

Income	Percent hospitalized		Percent in fair/poor health
	1982	1986	1986
Poor and near poor	10.4	7.9	22%
Nonpoor	8.8	6.2	8
Gap (percent)	+18%	+27%	

Exhibit 5
Mean Number Of Physician Visits By Ethnicity And Health Status, 1982 And 1986

Race	Fair and poor health		Excellent and good health	
	1982	1986	1982	1986
Black	7.6	6.8	4.5	2.8
White	8.6	10.1	4.2	3.8
Gap (percent)	−12%	−33%	+7%	−26%
Hispanic	9.7	9.8	3.9	3.9
White	8.6	10.1	4.2	3.8
Gap (percent)	+13%	−3%	−7%	+3%

Access for Minorities

An important measure of equity of access is the frequency of the use of health services by minorities. Hispanics, on average, see physicians at about the same rate as whites. For black Americans, however, the 1986 survey portrays a picture of diminishing access to medical care. As indicated in Exhibit 5, physician visit rates for blacks declined between 1982 and 1986. Thus, by 1986, there was a difference of 33 percent between physician visit rates of blacks and whites in ill health, and about the same for those in good health.

Exhibit 6
Percent Hospitalized One Or More Times In Year By Ethnicity, 1982 And 1986

Ethnicity	Percent hospitalized		Percent in fair/poor health
	1982	1986	1986
Black	7.6	6.2	15.3%
White	10.2	6.8	10.6
Gap (percent)	−25%	−9%	
Hispanic	6.3	4.5	19.4
White	10.2	6.8	10.6
Gap (percent)	−38%	−34%	

Exhibit 7
Mean Number Of Physician Visits, Percent Hospitalized, And Perceived Heath Status By Insurance Coverage For Persons Under 65, 1982 And 1986

Insurance coverage	Physician visits		Percent in fair/poor health
	1982	1986	1986
Uninsured	3.8	3.2	12%
Insured	4.7	4.4	9
Gap (percent)	−19%	−27%	
	Percent hospitalized		
Uninsured	5.2	4.6	12
Insured	8.5	5.7	9
Gap (percent)	−39%	−19%	

The growing gap in physician visits between blacks and whites is of particular concern in view of the evidence recently assembled by the National Institutes of Health showing that black Americans have a considerably higher mortality rate than whites have. [14]

All ethnic groups were affected by the overall national decline in hospital use (Exhibit 6). However, the study shows that in both 1982 and 1986 there were significant gaps in receipt of hospital care for Hispanics compared to whites despite a greater proportion of Hispanics in ill health. Blacks were also less likely than whites to be hospitalized given their poorer health status.

Access for the Uninsured

Health insurance continues to be an important factor influencing access to medical care. The nation's uninsured population contains a somewhat larger share of people in fair or poor health than is found among those with health insurance. Thus, if there were no economic barriers to care, the receipt of physician services and hospital care by the uninsured would be expected to exceed that received by the insured. As

can be seen in Exhibit 7, the uninsured had fewer physician visits and were less likely than the insured to be hospitalized in both 1982 and 1986. [15] The gap between the uninsured and the insured in average number of physician visits widened substantially in 1986, suggesting that the uninsured are experiencing greater difficulty obtaining physician care. While the gap in receipt of hospital care narrowed over the period, a 19 percent difference still remains between the uninsured and the insured. In both 1982 and 1986, a smaller proportion of the uninsured were hospitalized than their higher burden of illness suggests might be appropriate.

Those surveyed were also asked if they had ever failed to obtain needed medical care for economic reasons. The results, presented in Exhibit 8, closely parallel the other findings. Of those interviewed, 6 percent, representing approximately 13.5 million Americans, reported not receiving medical care for financial reasons. An estimated 1 million individuals actually tried to obtain needed care but did not receive it. The majority of Americans experiencing these difficulties were poor, uninsured, or minorities.

Underuse Of Medical Care

Growing concerns about the nation's rising health care bill have led to an almost exclusive focus by public and private sector policymakers on how to reduce the unnecessary overuse of costly health care. Less attention has been directed to the possibility of serious underuse of medical care by some people. The results from this study point to particular problems of underuse across the country.

Exhibit 9 presents data providing measures of potential underuse of medical care by different groups in the country. One in six Americans who had an identifiable chronic and serious illness (such as cancer, heart disease, diabetes, and stroke) did not see a physician even once during the year. Many physicians would agree that patients with such illnesses should be seen by a doctor at least annually.

The survey also asked respondents whether, over the past thirty days, they had experienced one or more symptoms judged by a panel of physicians to warrant care in most instances, and if so, whether they sought medical attention. These serious symptoms were adapted from an instrument developed by the University of Chicago, and subsequently modified for use in the Rand Health Insurance Experiment. [16] Of those respondents who had at least one physician visit in the year, 41 percent reported the occurrence of one or more of five serious symptoms and did not see or tell a physician about the problem. These symptoms included bleeding, other than nosebleeds or menstrual periods, not caused by accidents; shortness of breath after light exercise; loss of consciousness fainting, or passing out; chest pain when exercising; and weight loss of more than ten pounds (except for dieting). The large proportion of people who failed to visit or telephone a physician in the face of having these symptoms is of concern.

Likewise, the large proportion of pregnant women who did not seek prenatal care in the first three months of their pregnancy is troubling. Infant mortality has been reduced by half since 1960, but the rates of infant death in the

United States still exceed those of many other comparable industrialized countries. A recent Institute of Medicine study concluded that early prenatal care leads to improved maternal and infant outcomes.[17] It is therefore of concern to find that one in seven pregnant women surveyed in 1986 did not seek medical care early in their pregnancy.

The study also found signs of underuse of medical care for persons diagnosed as having hypertension. This disease is associated with two of the nation's major killers—heart disease and stroke. Thus, it is of concern that 20 percent of people with diagnosed hypertension surveyed in 1986—and almost one third of blacks and Hispanics with this condition—did not have their blood pressure checked at least once during the year.

Americans have traditionally underused dental services, and this trend appears to have continued. Thirty-eight percent of all respondents had not visited a dentist in a year; only half of low-income individuals reported a dental visit.

These data taken together suggest that a substantial number of Americans may not be getting as much health care as they need. The reasons may include social and cultural factors as well as financial barriers. However, the presence of signs of underuse among all segments of the population also suggests a lack of understanding of appropriate use of medical care and a need for improved public education.

Other Findings

Improved Access for Rural Americans

A positive finding in the 1986 survey is that rural Americans, on average, appear to be receiving as much medical care as their urban counterparts, as indicated in Exhibit 10. Closing the rural/urban gap in access to health services has been a national goal for many years. That goal now appears to have been achieved. This is not to say, of course, that residents of some isolated rural communities do not still experience problems obtaining timely medical care. The same is true for some inner-

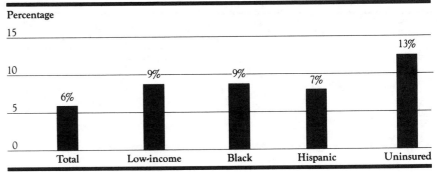

Exhibit 8
Percent Of Americans Not Receiving Care For Economic Reasons, 1986

Exhibit 9
Indicators Of Potential Underuse Of Medical Care, 1986

Problem	U.S.	Low-income	Black	Hispanic	Uninsured
Percent with chronic illness without physician visit in a year	17%	18%	25%	22%	20%
Among persons with one or more physician visits in year, percent with serious symptoms who did not see or contact a physician	41	42	39	53	67
Percent pregnant women without first trimester prenatal care	15	30	17	27	20
Percent of persons with hypertension without blood pressure check in a year	20	15	30	30	22
Percent without a dentist visit in a year	38	57	50	47	–

city residents. However, it is clear that major strides have been made in improving the geographic accessibility of physician and hospital services.

Satisfaction with Medical Care

Despite substantial disparities between various groups in their access to medical care, most Americans remain highly satisfied with the care they receive from physicians and hospitals. Even the modest levels of dissatisfaction with emergency care found in 1982 had declined by 1986 (Exhibit 11).

Conclusion

The results of the 1986 University of California, Los Angeles, survey, the largest supported by The Robert Wood Johnson Foundation to date, are both surprising and disturbing. Many of the nation's forecasters in health have clearly not been on the mark. An aging popu-

lation, a growing supply of physicians, and more and better medical technologies have not, as predicted, led to significant increases in use of health care per person. Rather, this study suggests that there has been a decline in visits to physicians and in the proportion of people hospitalized. This trend cuts across all groups within our country and is difficult to fully explain. Some will obviously associate this with the many changes now occurring in health care arrangements that emphasize lower utilization of health care resources, including health maintenance organizations, preferred provider organizations, utilization review, and diagnosis-related groups.

This study cannot answer the critical questions of whether Americans are sicker or remain in ill health longer because they receive less medical care today than they did in 1982. There are, however, significant numbers of individuals who have serious and poten-

Exhibit 10
Mean Physician Visits, Percent Hospitalized, And Perceived Health Status
For Urban And Rural Residents, 1982 And 1986

Residence	Physician visits		Percent in fair/poor health
	1982	1986	1986
Rural	4.4	4.4	14%
Urban	5.0	4.3	11
Gap (percent)	−12%	+2%	
	Percent hospitalized		
Rural	9.7	8.0	14
Urban	9.1	6.0	11
Gap (percent)	+7%	+33%	

Exhibit 11
Percent Dissatisfied With Their Use Of Medical Care, 1982 And 1986

Type of visit	Percent dissatisfied	
	1982	1986
Most recent emergency visit	11%	5%
Most recent physician visit	3	2
Most recent hospitalization	4	4

tially life-threatening illnesses who do not appear to use health care appropriately. This may prove to be a problem requiring more public education or it may reflect unrecognized financial or professional barriers to care.

On the positive side, after many years of national attention to achieving a more equitable geographic distribution of health resources, rural Americans, on average, appear to be receiving as much medical care as urban residents. While some isolated rural communities clearly have continuing problems that should not be overlooked, we can take some pride in knowing that medical care is reasonably accessible nationwide. Also on a positive note, Americans continue to express a high level of satisfaction with the medical care they receive.

Clearly, the most disturbing findings relate to the signs of deterioration in access to medical care for the nation's poor, minorities, and the uninsured. In particular, the poor and black Americans have experienced a reversal of the gains in access to physician care made over the previous two decades, moving us further from securing more equitable access to care for all.

This study was supported by a grant from The Robert Wood Johnson Foundation to the Institute for Social Sciences Research, University of California, Los Angeles.

Notes

1. The Robert Wood Johnson Foundation, "Access to Health Care," *Special Report* (Princeton, NJ: The Robert Wood Johnson Foundation, 1978, 1983, 1987).

2. I. S. Falk, M. C. Kelm, and N. Sinai, *The Incidence of Illness and the Costs of Care Among Representative Family Groups* (Chicago: University of Chicago Press, 1933); R. Andersen, J. Kravits, and O. W. Anderson, *Two Decades of Health Services Social Survey Trends in Use and Expenditure* (Cambridge, MA: Ballinger, 1976); and L. A. Aday, G. V. Fleming, and R. Andersen, *Access to Medical Care in the U.S.: Who Has It, Who Doesn't* (Chicago: Pluribus Press, 1984).

3. This study was conducted by University of California, Los Angeles, with grant support from The Robert Wood Johnson Foundation. Overall findings of the 1986 survey are available in the *Special Report on Access to Medical Care*, no. 2 (1987), from The Robert Wood Johnson Foundation, P.O. Box 2316, Princeton, NJ 08540.

4. A. C. Marcus and L. A. Crane, "Telephone Surveys in Public Health Research," *Medical Care* (February 1986): 97–112; and M. J. Banks and R. M. Andersen, "Estimating and Adjusting for Nonphone Noncoverage Bias Using Center for Health Administration Studies Data," *Health Survey Research Methods*, DHHS Pub. no. (PHS)84-3346 (Washington, DC: U.S. Department of Health and Human Services, 1984).

5. The field work for the UCLA study was undertaken by the Survey Research Laboratory of the University of Illinois in collaboration with the Survey Research Laboratory of University of Wisconsin.

6. Aday et al., *Access to Medical Care in the U.S.: Who Has It, Who Doesn't*.

7. National Center for Health Statistics, "Current Estimates from the National Health Interview Survey, United States, 1982," *Vital and Health Statistics*, Series 10, no. 150, DHHS Pub. no. (PHS)85-1578 (Washington, DC: U.S. Government Printing Office, 1985).

8. L. H. Aiken et al., "The Contribution of Specialists to the Delivery of Primary Care: A New Perspective," *The New England Journal of Medicine* 300 (14 June 1979):1363–70.

9. Citizens Commission on Graduate Medical Education, *The Graduate Education of Physicians* (Chicago: American Medical Association, 1966).

10. President's Commission for the Study of Ethical Problems in Medicine and Biomedical and Behavioral Research, *Securing Access to Health Care* (Washington, DC: U.S. GPO, 1983).

11. A. R. Davies and J. E. Ware, *Measuring Health Perceptions in the Health Insurance Experiment* (Santa Monica, CA: Rand Corporation, 1981); J. Yergan et al., "Health Status as a Measure of Need for Medical Care: A Critique," *Medical Care* 19, Suppl. 12 (December 1981): 57–68; and G. Maddox and E. Douglass, "Self-Assessment of Health: A Longitudinal Study of Elderly Subjects," *Journal of Health and Social Behavior* 14 (1983):87–93.

12. Committee on the Costs of Medical care, *Medical Care for the American People* (New York: Arno Press, 1972), 8.

13. President's Commission for the Study of Ethical Problems in Medicine and Biomedical and Behavioral Research, *Securing Access to Health Care*.

14. U.S. Department of Health and Human Services, *Black and Minority Health*, vol. 1 (Washington, DC: DHHS, 1985).

15. The elderly were omitted from these analyses by insurance status since most are covered by Medicaid. Nevertheless, our estimates of the number of uninsured in both 1982 and 1986 are lower than those reported in federal government studies.

16. L. A. Aday and R. Andersen, *Development of Indices of Access to Medical Care* (Ann Arbor, MI: Health Administration Press, 1975); and M. F. Shapiro, J. E. Ware, and C. D. Sherbourne, "Effects of Cost Sharing on Seeking Care for Serious and Minor Symptoms," *Annals of Internal Medicine* 104 (February 1986):246–51.

17. Institute of Medicine, *Preventing Low Birthweight* (Washington, DC: National Academy Press, 1985).

13

Black-White Disparities in Health Care

Council on Ethical and Judicial Affairs

There are persistent, and sometimes substantial, differences in the quality of health among Americans. Despite improvements in health care for black Americans since the 1960s, blacks have twice the infant mortality rate of whites and a life expectancy that is 6 years shorter than the life expectancy of white Americans (*New York Times*, March 16, 1989:B15). Black men younger than 45 years have a 45% higher rate of lung cancer and 10 times the likelihood of dying from hypertension than white men younger than 45 years (*New York Times*, July 17, 1989:A11). Underlying the racial disparities in the quality of health among Americans are differences in both need and access. Blacks are more likely to require health care but are less likely to receive health care services.

The disparity between blacks and whites in access to health care reflects the continuing disparities in their income, education, and other characteristics that correlate with the receipt of any complex and expensive service. But medical care is a unique and essential service and subtantial disparities cannot be tolerated. Equal access to basic medical care by all Americans is a longstanding policy of this country and the American Medical Association.

Moreover, recent studies have suggested that even when blacks gain access to the health care system, they are less likely than whites to receive certain

Reprinted with permission from *JAMA, The Journal of the American Medical Association* 263, no. 17 (May 2, 1990), pp. 2344–46. Copyright © 1990 American Medical Association.

surgical or other therapies. These studies vary in their purpose, depth, and validity, but they cannot be ignored. This report reviews the recent studies and discusses their significance.

Many of the disparities that exist for black patients also exist for other racial minorities, although there has not been the same degree of documentation in such cases. The concerns expressed in this report apply equally to other racial minorities.

Evidence of Disparities in Medical Treatment

Recent studies have suggested that the use of specific medical treatments differs between black and white patients. These studies have examined treatments in several areas, including cardiology and cardiac surgery, kidney transplantation, general internal medicine, and obstetrics.

In a national survey of patients who were discharged from hospitals with a diagnosis of anterior myocardial infarction, black men had a rate of anterior myocardial infarction that was three fourths of the rate for white men. However, the black men were only half as likely to undergo angiography and one third as likely to undergo bypass surgery as the white men.[1] On the other hand, mortality rates suggested that the severity of illness was comparable between blacks and whites at the time of admission. Nineteen percent of the whites and 18% of the blacks died while hospitalized for their anterior myocardial infarction. Long-term survival rates were not measured.

Another study reviewed data on all patients discharged from Massachusetts hospitals in 1985 with a preliminary diagnosis of circulatory system disease or chest pain.[2] While blacks and whites had similar rates of hospitalization, whites were one third more likely to undergo coronary angiography and more than twice as likely to be treated with bypass surgery or angioplasty. The racial disparities persisted even after differences in income and the severity of disease were taken into account. In a study of all patients who underwent coronary angiography between 1970 and 1978 at a major tertiary care center, whites were two to three times more likely to undergo bypass surgery than blacks who had similar clinical characteristics.[3] Similarly, in a study of data from the Coronary Artery Surgery Study, which enrolled patients in 1974 through 1979 from 15 geographically diverse academic institutions, a large differential between blacks and whites in the rate of bypass surgery could not be explained by differences in clinical or angiographic characteristics.[4] In that study, surgery was recommended for whites more often than for blacks and, among those for whom surgery was recommended, whites were more likely to have the surgery performed. In addition, among those for whom medical treatment was recommended, whites were more likely than blacks to undergo bypass surgery.

Racial status has also been found to correlate with the likelihood that a patient with kidney disease will receive long-term hemodialysis or a kidney transplant. Racial disparities in access to long-term hemodialysis are on the order of 5% to 15%; the most favored person is the white man aged 25 through 44 years.[5]

Several studies have documented racial disparities among patients who undergo kidney transplantation. In one study, the researchers reviewed all patients who received long-term dialysis in the United States in 1983 and all patients who received long-term dialysis in the upper Midwest between 1979 and 1985. Nonwhite dialysis recipients were two thirds as likely as white patients to receive a kidney transplant.[6]

A review of patients with end-stage renal disease who were covered by Medicare benefits from 1977 through 1985 revealed that blacks accounted for 33% of patients with end-stage renal disease, but only 21% of patients who received kidney transplants.[7] In a national survey of nearly 15,000 patients who began treatment for end-stage renal disease between 1981 and 1985 and who were therefore covered by Medicare benefits, researchers found that the likelihood of receiving a kidney transplant correlated with race and income and that the effects of race and income were independent of each other.[8] Patients who were treated at institutions that served a predominantly white population and that were located in high-income areas were almost twice as likely to receive a transplant as patients who were treated at institutions that served a predominantly black population and that were located in low-income areas.

While the patients in these studies were covered by Medicare, differences in income were still important. Until 1987, Medicare did not pay any of the bills for outpatient drugs, which, in the case of the immunosuppressive drug cyclosporine, could cost as much as $5,000 annually. In addition, for patients who do not live near a transplant center, transportation costs may be substantial.[8]

The evidence of racial disparities in treatment decisions also appears in general internal medicine. A study of treatment for patients hospitalized because of pneumonia found that the patient's race correlated with the intensity of care provided.[9] The researchers reviewed all patients hospitalized with a primary diagnosis of pneumonia in 17 hospitals between 1970 and 1973. The hospitals were selected in a manner designed to ensure that they varied in size, teaching status, and expenditures per patient. The study showed that, after controlling for differences in clinical characteristics and income, blacks were less likely to receive medical services, particularly intensive care.[9]

In a review of 65,000 deliveries in four New York, NY, hospitals during a 5-year period, researchers found that private patients were more likely than clinic patients to have a cesarean section, even though the private patients were less likely to have medical problems or to be delivered of low-birth-weight babies.[10] The disparity in cesarean section rate between private and clinic patients carried over to the subgroup of patients who were considered to be at low risk for a cesarean delivery. While 47% of the clinic patients were black, 22% of the private patients were black. Thus, blacks were probably less likely than whites to receive cesarean sections even when clinically comparable.

Racial disparities in treatment decisions have been documented previously. In a study of hospital admissions from the emergency department of a major tertiary care hospital during 1968, researchers found that blacks were more likely to be classified as ward patients and whites to be classified as private patients, even when there was a comparable ability to pay for care.[11] In addition, ward patients were less frequently admitted to the hospital even when clinical characteristics were similar. Studies from the psychiatric literature in the 1960s indicated that black patients were less often accepted for psychotherapy, more often assigned to inexperienced therapists, and seen for shorter periods and with less intensity.[12]

The racial disparities in treatment decisions are consistent with studies of patient perceptions. A national telephone survey conducted in 1986 found that blacks were more likely than whites to report that their physician did not inquire sufficiently about their pain, did not tell them how long it would take for prescribed medicine to work, did not explain the seriousness of their illness or injury, and did not discuss test and examination findings.[13] In addition, blacks were less likely than whites to be satisfied with the care provided during their most recent hospitalization or ambulatory care visit. Similar results were found in a survey of patients with hypertension in Edgecombe County, North Carolina.[14] Compared with white patients, the black patients reported more general difficulties getting into the health care system and greater dissatisfaction with medical care services.

Reasons for Racial Disparities

It is difficult to draw firm conclusions from these studies regarding the role of race in decisions to treat patients. With regard to bypass surgery, for example, while the studies tried to control for incidence and severity of disease, they generally did not control for other relevant variables that may account for the differences between blacks and whites. In the Massachusetts study, where the data were adjusted for differences in age, gender, severity of disease, income, and type of insurance, and racial disparities in the frequency of bypass surgery were still found, the researchers did not have actual income data but used the patient's residence as a proxy for income.[2] That is, they assumed that the patient's income was the average household income for people living in the patient's ZIP code. With more precise data, there might be a decrease in the extent of the racial disparities.

Some of the disparity in kidney transplantation rates may be explained by medical or biologic differences. For example, most of the kidneys donated for transplantation come from whites and intraracial antigen matching is often more favorable than interracial matching.[8] However, it is unlikely that medical differences account for all of the disparities. Whites not only are more likely to receive transplants, but they appear disproportionately on waiting lists for transplants.[8]

Income differences are probably the most important explanation for the disparities. Race and income are highly correlated and patients with higher incomes are better able to bear the direct and indirect costs of expensive medical procedures.

Some medical experts have also suggested that physicians are more likely to treat aggressively patients who are wealthier, more productively employed, and more assertive (*New York Times*, January 24, 1989:C1).[15] Such patients might be viewed as more likely to respond successfully to therapy. It has also been suggested that they might be viewed as more valuable to society.[8] In addition, there is a natural tendency to respond to those who are persistent in their requests for services.

Other factors, of course, such as education and the skills that come from it, inevitably restrict the ability of some blacks to gain access to and to negotiate effectively for the best medical treatment available. Commentators have also speculated that blacks and whites may differ in terms of their treatment preferences, although such a difference has not been documented.

Disparities in treatment decisions may reflect the existence of subconscious bias. This is a serious and troubling problem. Despite the progress of the past 25 years, racial prejudice has not been entirely eliminated in this country. The health care system, like all other elements of society, has not fully eradicated this prejudice.

Significance and Response

Whether the racial disparities in treatment decisions are caused by differences in income and education, sociocultural factors, or failures by the medical profession, they are unjustifiable and must be eliminated. Not only do the disparities violate fundamental principles of fairness, justice, and medical ethics, they may be part of the reason for the poorer quality of health of blacks in the United States.

The Council recognizes the complexity of the problem and the efforts within and outside organized medicine to address it. The Council emphasizes three approaches that it believes should be given high priority:

1. Greater access: The studies discussed in this report underscore the need for ensuring that black Americans without adequate health care insurance are given the means of access to necessary health care. The American Medical Association has recommended several measures to increase access to health care for the uninsured.[16,17] These include (a) a requirement that employers provide health insurance for all full-time employees and (b) for individuals who are not employed on a full-time basis), (1) reform of the Medicaid program to ensure adequate coverage for all Americans with incomes below the federal poverty level, (2) establishment of state risk pools to provide health insurance through the private sector at group rates for individuals earning between 100% and 200% of the poverty level of income, with provision of publicly funded vouchers on a sliding scale to those earning between 100% and 150% of the poverty level of income, and (3) publicly funded, state indigent-care funds to finance health care for patients who remain without adequate insurance coverage.

2. Greater awareness: Because racial disparities may be occurring despite the lack of any intent or purposeful efforts to treat patients differently on the basis of race, physicians should examine their own practices to ensure that inappropriate considerations do not affect their clinical judgment. In addition, the profession should help increase the awareness of its members of racial disparities in medical treatment decisions by engaging in open and broad discussions about the issue. Such discussions should take place as part of the medical school curriculum, in medical journals, at professional conferences, and as part of professional peer review activities.

Awareness of and responsiveness to the sociocultural factors underlying the disparities in treatment can also be enhanced by increasing the numbers of black Americans in medical school faculties and student bodies. The American Medical Association has recommended a number of measures to increase minority representation in medicine: (1) expansion of recruitment efforts, including special premedical and precolle-

giate programs for minority students, (2) greater government financial aid to those in need at both the collegiate and medical school levels, (3) affirmative action in medical school admission and faculty-hiring decisions, (4) more supportive academic programs for minority students (through tutorials and other academic assistance, decelerated schedules as required, and early orientations), and (5) competent and sensitive student counseling and advisory services.[18,19] The American Medical Association is currently developing new strategies to increase the recruitment and retention of minority medical students and faculty members.[20]

3. Practice parameters: The racial disparities in treatment decisions indicate that inappropriate considerations may enter the decision-making process. The efforts of the specialty societies, with the coordination and assistance of the American Medical Assciation, to develop practice parameters should include criteria that would preclude or diminish racial disparities.

Notes

1. Ford E, Cooper R, Castaner A, Simmons B, Mar M. Coronary arteriography and coronary bypass surgery among whites and other racial groups relative to hospital-based incidence rates for coronary artery disease: findings from NHDS. *Am J Public Health.* 1989;79:437-440.

2. Wenneker MB, Epstein AM. Racial inequalities in the use of procedures for patients with ischemic heart disease in Massachusetts. *JAMA.* 1989;261:253-257.

3. Oberman A, Cutter G. Issues in the natural history and treatment of coronary heart disease in black populations: surgical treatment. *Am Heart J.* 1984;108:688-694.

4. Maynard C, Fisher LD, Passamani ER, Pullum T. Blacks in the Coronary Artery Surgery Study (CASS): race and clinical decision making. *Am J Public Health.* 1986;76:1446-1448.

5. Kjellstand CM, Logan GM. Racial, sexual, and age inequalities in chronic dialysis. *Nephron.* 1987;45:257-263.

6. Kjellstrand CM. Age, sex, and race inequality in renal transplantation. *Arch Intern Med.* 1988;148:1305-1309.

7. Eggers P. Effect of transplantation on the Medicare end-stage renal disease program. *N Engl J Med.* 1988;318:223-229.

8. Held PJ, Pauly MV, Bovbjerg RR, Newmann J, Salvatierra O. Access to kidney transplantation: has the United States eliminated income and racial differences? *Arch Intern Med.* 1988;148:2594-2600.

9. Yergan J, Flood AB, LoGerfo JP, Diehr P. Relationship between patient race and the intensity of hospital services. *Med Care.* 1987;25:592-603.

10. de Regt RH, Minkoff HL, Feldman J, Schwarz RH. Relation of private or clinic care to the cesarean birth rate. *N Engl J Med.* 1986;315:619-624.

11. Perkoff GT, Anderson M. Relationship between demographic characteristics, patient's chief complaint, and medical care destination in an emergency room. *Med Care.* 1970;8:309-323.

12. Levy DR. White doctors and black patients: influence of race on the doctor-patient relationship. *Pediatrics.* 1985; 75: 639-643.

13. Blendon RJ, Aiken LH, Freeman HE, Corey CR. Access to medical care for black and white Americans: a matter of continuing concern. *JAMA.* 1989;261:278-80.

14. James SA, Wagner EH, Strogatz DS, et al. The Edgecombe County (NC) high blood pressure control program, II: barriers to the use of medical care among hypertensives. *Am J Public Health.* 1984;74:468-472.

15. Eisenberg JM. Sociologic influences on decision-making by clinicians. *Ann Intern Med.* 1979;90:957-959.

16. Board of Trustees. *Covering the Uninsured*. Chicago, Ill: American Medical Association; 1989. Report Q.

17. Board of Trustees. Covering the uninsured (Report JJ). In: *Proceedings of the House of Delegates*. Chicago, Ill: American Medical Association; 1989:118-123.

18. Council on Medical Education. Minority representation in the medical profession (Report C). In: *Proceedings of the House of Delegates*. Chicago, Ill: American Medical Association; 1982:124-129.

19. Council on Medical Education. Minority under-representation in medicine (Report A). In: *Proceedings of the House of Delegates*. Chicago, Ill: American Medical Association; 1978:213-214.

20. Board of Trustees. Minority students and faculty in U.S. Medical schools (Report F). In: *Proceedings of the House of Delegates*. Chicago, Ill: American Medical Association; 1989:41.

14

Preventive Care: Do We Practice What We Preach?

Nicole Lurie, Willard G. Manning, Christine Peterson, George A. Goldberg, Charles A. Phelps, and Lee Lillard

Introduction

In recent years, increasing attention has focused on providing services that may prevent or reduce the social and economic costs of some diseases. In 1979 the Canadian Task Force on the Periodic Health Examination[1] outlined a set of targeted preventive procedures, along with recommended frequencies of administration. In the following years, the American Cancer Society (ACS),[2] the American College of Physicians,[3] and the American Academy of Pediatrics[4] issued their own sets of preventive care recommendations.

Little is known about the amount of preventive care that most Americans receive or about the determinants of that care. Data from the Center for Disease Control (CDC)[5] indicate that two-thirds to three-fourths of one-year-olds have not had a complete set of immunizations. The National Center for Health Statistics[6] provides 1973 data on self-reported receipt of a limited number of preventive procedures. Several investigators have found poor compliance with preventive care standards for patients seen in university-based group practices[7-9] and Romm et al.,[10] found wide variation but generally low use of preventive procedures in their examination of practices of 39 volunteer physicians in North Carolina. Canadian studies based on physician self-report

Reprinted with permission from *American Journal of Public Health* 77, no. 7 (July 1987), pp. 801–4. Copyright © 1987 American Public Health Association.

yield similar results,[11,12] while a recent study by McPhee et al.,[13] suggests that some physicians may overestimate the amount of preventive care they provide. A patient survey done for the American Cancer Society[14] indicated that most adults do not receive mammography or stool guaiac examinations as recommended.

We used claims data from the RAND Health Insurance Study to estimate the frequency of preventive care and to determine whether cost-sharing was an important determinant of compliance with preventive care recommendations.

Methods

The Health Insurance Experiment

The Health Insurance Experiment (HIE) was a randomized trial of cost sharing on the demand for health services and the health status of individuals. The HIE enrolled families for either three or five years in six sites: Dayton, Ohio; Seattle, Washington; Fitchburg, Massachusetts; Franklin County, Massachusetts; Charleston, South Carolina; and Georgetown County, South Carolina. The experiment ran from 1974 to 1982.

Participants in the HIE were a random sample of the general population at each site with the following exclusions: (1) those 62 years of age and older when the experiment began; (2) those with incomes in excess of $25,000 in 1973 dollars ($58,000 in 1984 dollars); (3) those eligible for the Medicare disability program; (4) those in the military and their dependents; (5) those in jail or

institutionalized in long-term hospitals; (6) those with military service-related disabilities. The populations sample included was considered to be generally representative of the United States population under age 65.[15,16]

Families participating in the experiment were randomly assigned to one of 14 different insurance plans with different levels of cost sharing. In each plan, there was an upper limit of, at most, $1,000 on out-of-pocket expenses per family. The plans were grouped into five basic categories: free care, 25 percent coinsurance rate, 50 percent coinsurance rate, 95 percent coinsurance rate, and an Individual Deductible Plan (95 percent coinsurance for outpatient care with a maximum out-of-pocket expenditure of $150 per person or $450 per family and free inpatient care). Plans covered ambulatory and hospital care, mental health care, dental services, and drugs. Coverage for preventive services was the same as for other medical services. Physicians of study participants were not notified of plan assignment.

These analyses use data from the first four sites and from the first three years of experiment. Data from South Carolina were excluded because the claims data at that site were incomplete at the time our analysis was done. However, there is no reason to suspect that compliance with preventive care recommendations was better in South Carolina than in other sites. With the exception of children born into the study, we considered only individuals enrolled for the entire three years. After the exclusion guidelines were applied, 3,823 individuals were eligible for inclusion in the study. These included 819 adult males aged 17–44, 248 males aged 45–65, 878 females aged 17–44, and 331 females aged 45–65, 647 children aged 0–6, and 803 children aged 7–16. We also included the 97 newborns were both born into the study and remained in the study for at least 18 months.

Classification of Visits

The focus of this analysis was all claims for face-to-face, outpatient visits in which "preventive services" were provided. Data on the completeness of claims data for visits have been previously reported. [17] For children, we defined preventive visits as all those associated with the diagnosis or procedure codes for well care examinations, immunizations, or tuberculosis tests. For adults, we defined such visits as all those associated with claims for the following diagnoses and procedures: immunizations, annual physical examinations, administrative examinations, general medical examinations, multiphasic screening examinations, routine gynecologic examinations, and office visits listed only as well care visits.

Pap smears, mammography, and sigmoidoscopy were considered to be "preventive services" only if the diagnoses (other than well care) listed on the claim form associated with the visit could not conceivably have been the reason for the laboratory test.

Each laboratory test was linked with the visit at which it was requested using a set of rules based on provider and dates of service. [18]

Visits were classified as "preventive," or "nonpreventive" according to the type of services that were delivered. Visits were classified as both "preventive" and "nonpreventive" if a preventive service was given during a nonprevetive visit. Charges were allocated according to the proportion of diagnoses and procedures that were preventive or nonpreventive.

Because physicians rarely bill separately for counseling about health habits, we could not examine the amount or nature of this activity with HIE claims

data. We also did not examine prenatal, maternity, dental, or mental health care.

Standards for Comparison

We used recommendations of the Canadian Task Force, the American Cancer Society, the American College of Physicians, and the American Academy of Pediatrics to derive standards with which to compare the frequency of preventive care seen in the HIE sample. For children these were: diptheria-pertussis-tetanus (DPT) and polio immunization at 2, 4, 6, and 18 months; measles-mumps-rubella (MMR) vaccination at 12–18 months; and tuberculosis (TB) skin testing at 12–18 months. For adults these included: tetanus immunization every 10 years; influenza vaccine yearly for high-risk adults; Pap smears every three years for women 17–65; mammography every one to three years for women over age 45; sigmoidoscopy every three years for men and women over age 45.

Data Analysis

We calculated proportions of participants receiving a given procedure using analysis of variance methods. Except for the individual deductible plans, all cost sharing plans were grouped together for analysis. We used two-tailed t-tests to contrast proportions for free and cost-sharing plans and corrected all inferences for intrafamily and intertemporal correlation.

Charges for Increasing Preventive Care

We estimated the charge for increasing preventive care from the level seen in the HIE to a level that would comply with recommended standards using the following assumptions:

• All procedures are done in a physician's office.

• The charge for a person with no physician visit during the HIE equals the charge for an intermediate visit plus the charge for the procedure(s) in question because a physician visit would be required for the enrollee to undergo the procedure. If a person with no visits needed multiple procedures, there was a charge for only one visit.

• The charge for a person with a previous physician visit equals the charge for the procedure in question or the charge for the procedure in question plus the charge for upgrading a visit (e.g., from "intermediate" to "extended") because a longer visit would be required for the enrollee to undergo the procedure. This did not apply to childhood immunizations.

• The figures are given are in 1984 dollars.

The charges for visits and procedures used in these calculations are the mean charges for such services appearing in claims during the HIE. These figures were: newborns—intermediate visit, $23; males age 17–44—intermediate visit, $29; extended visit, $41; males age 45–65—intermediate visit, $26; extended visit, $36; females age 17–44—intermediate visit, $30; extended visit, $33. For procedures, charges were: DPT vaccine—$7, polio vaccine—$6, Pap smear—$13, mammogram—$87.

This analysis did not take into account the costs of the following: investigation of false positive tests, hours of work lost in obtaining the procedure, any unnecessary or nonrecommended tests performed during an additional visit, any worry or concern associated with undergoing a procedure, and any complications that arose as a result of the procedure.

Results

Newborns

During the first 18 months of life, most recommended preventive care consists of immunizations and well-care examinations. We report three, rather than four, doses of DPT and polio vaccines for several reasons. First, an infant is considered to have adequate immunity against DPT or polio after he has received at least three doses of vaccine. Second, vaccine administration may be delayed because of an intercurrent viral illness. Finally, some infants do not receive vaccines exactly on schedule. Even with one delayed vaccine, nearly 100 percent of the sample would ideally have received three doses of vaccine. Only 44 percent of the 97 newborns in our sample received three doses of DPT vaccine by the time they were 18 months old; 45 percent received three doses of polio vaccine; 60 percent received an MMR; and 55 percent received tuberculosis skin testing. Finally, 7 percent of newborns had no well care in the first 18 months of life (Table 1).

Adults

Based on the recommendations that adults receive tetanus immunizations every 10 years; 30 percent of the adult sample should have received a tetanus vaccination during the three-year study. Yet, only 1 percent of the study sample received tetanus immunizations for preventive purposes, i.e., unrelated to trauma. When we included all accident-related immunization in our analysis, only 4 percent met the standard. Eight percent of the sample aged 45–65 had chronic obstructive pulmonary disease and thus should have received influenza vaccine. Only 3 percent of adults received this vaccine during the first three years of the HIE and only two participants had annual vaccinations.

Pap smears were the most frequently performed cancer screening procedure. About 66 percent of women aged 17–44, and 57 percent aged 45–65 received at least one Pap smear in the three years of the study. In contrast, only 2 percent of women aged 45–65 received mammography as a preventive measure at least once in three years. If mammograms performed for reasons other than prevention are included, this figure rises to 8 percent. No women had yearly mammography.

Three percent of adults aged 45–65 had sigmoidoscopies during the three-year period; less than 1 percent were considered preventive measures.

Effects of Cost-Sharing

Table 2 presents data on the effect of cost sharing on immunizations and pap smears. Higher levels of cost sharing were associated with fewer immunizations for children under age seven; adults on the free plan received more immunizations than those in cost-sharing plans; women in both age groups enrolled in the free care plan received

TABLE 1—Compliance with Preventive Care Recommendations

Procedure	Population	% Complying with Standard	% That Should Have Complied with Standard
Immunization	newborns		
DPT 3+ doses		44	100
Polio 3+ doses		45	100
Measles-Mumps-Rubella		60	100
Tuberculosis Skin Testing	newborns	55	100
Well Care Examination one or more visit(s)	newborns	93	100
Vaccinations	adults aged 17–65		
Tetanus		1[a]	30
Influenza		3	8
Pap Smears	women aged 17–44	66	100
	women aged 45–65	57	100
Mammography	women aged 45–65	2[b]	100
Sigmoidoscopy		<1[c]	100

[a]4% if accident-related vaccines are included
[b]8% if nonpreventive tests are included
[c]3% if nonpreventive tests are included

TABLE 2—Effect of Cost Sharing on Immunizations and Pap Smears: Per Cent with Any in Three Years

| Procedure | Population/ Age Group | Levels | | Difference | |
		Free Plan	Cost Sharing Plans	Free Minus Cost Sharing	95% Confidence Interval
Any Immunizations					
	Children 0–6	58.9	49.1	9.8	.9, 18.7
	Adults 17–44	6.4	4.7	1.7	−.8, 4.2
	Adults 45–65	15.7	7.7	8.0	1.6, 14.4
Pap Smears					
	Women 17–44	72.2	62.6	9.6	3.0, 16.2
	Women 45–65	65.0	51.9	13.1	2.2, 24.0

more Pap smears than those on cost-sharing plans.

Charges for Attaining Standards

Although we could not estimate the extent to which life expectancy might be extended by preventive practices, we did estimate the monetary charges involved in bringing the HIE sample up to compliance with recommendations for childhood immunization, Pap smears, and mammography. The charge, averaged over all children less than 18 months, would be $22 per child more than is now spent to ensure that every child had a complete set of immunizations. The average additional charge would be about $9 per woman aged 17–65 for at least one well care visit with a Pap smear every three years. If mammography were performed once every three years for women aged 45–65, the additional charge for this age group would rise to $97.

Discussion

Unlike previous studies, this study provides data on preventive procedures based on actual claims data from representative population samples at five sites. Thus it does not suffer from the limitations of self-reported data or from a focus on university-based practices. As in other studies, use of all preventive procedures in the HIE population was far below that recommended. While participants on free care plans did receive significantly more Pap smears and immunizations, use of these services remained quite low.

Cost sharing was clearly not the only obstacle to receipt of preventive care. Other reasons for the low use of preventive services need to be explored and may relate both to physician and patient factors. Some physicians may not have been aware of the Canadian Task Force and the American Cancer Society recommendations, which were introduced during the time of the HIE. Romm[10] and Dietrich[19] indicate that physicians are more likely to perform preventive procedures when they judge their importance to be high. McPhee et al.[13] point out that some physicians do not perform cancer screening tests because of forgetfulness, dislike of performing the procedure, and lack of time. Yankauer recommends that physicians make use of nonpreventive visits to provide preventive care.[20] Hopefully, use of preventive services will increase as mechanisms to encourage physicians to provide preventive care during office visits become more prevalent and effective. Factors influencing patient demand for preventive services may include sociodemographic characteristics, public awareness of the benefits of preventive care, fear of receiving a given procedure, and discomfort and inconvenience associated with cancer screening tests.

The charges for increasing compliance appear high, particularly since they do not include costs of educating both physicians and the public about preventive care. It is also possible that these charges may be unrealistically low because of changes in physicians' pricing practices. It may be possible to lower these charges by use of mass screening techniques, public health services, and more efficient use of nonpreventive visits.

Several limitations of these data deserve mention. First, this data set recognizes only those procedures which generate a separate bill. Although this could have resulted in underestimating frequencies of preventive procedures, the fact that our reported frequencies of Pap smears and immunizations are similar to those reported by the national Center for Health Statistics[6] and the CDC[5] suggests that these claims data are fairly complete. Secondly, we may have missed some preventive procedures performed during visits for reasons other than prevention, thereby underestimating the frequency with which they were performed. However, this seems unlikely because inclusion of tetanus vaccinations, mammograms, and sigmoidoscopy for nonpreventive reasons did little to change our estimates of compliance. Finally, classification of visits as preventive or nonpreventive is based on the diagnosis listed on the claim form. We do not have data on the accuracy of such diagnoses and thus cannot assess how often our classification of visits may have been wrong.

Regardless of these limitations, it is clear that despite numerous recommendations, preventive procedures are underused. Free care may increase the prevalence of some preventive practices, but free care alone is an insufficient incentive to provide adequate levels of preventive care. Future research should address the nonmonetary issues affecting both physicians' decisions to provide, and patients' decisions to seek, preventive care.

The past decade has seen increased public demand for, and attention to, health promotion, of which specific preventive care procedures are a part. At the same time, pressures to reduce health care costs are creating incentives to reduce the amount of preventive care. The conflicts between increased public demand, the pressures of cost containment, and the otherwise low provision of preventive services by physicians must be reconciled.

We are indebted to Robert H. Brook, Katherine Kahn, Joseph P. Newhouse, Alvin Schultz, Martin F. Shapiro, and Robert B. Valdez for their helpful comments and reviews. Prepared under a Grant from the Health Care Financing Administration 318–P–97777/9–03. The views expressed in this paper are those of the authors and do not necessary reflect those of the Health Care Financing Administration or the RAND Corporation. Presented in part at Society for Research and Education in Primary Care Internal Medicine, May 1986.

Notes

1. Canadian Task Force on the Periodic Health Examination: Task Force Report, Can Med Assoc J 1977: 121:1193–1254.
2. Eddy D: Guidelines for the Cancer Related Checkup. CA-A Cancer Journal for Clinicians 1980: 30:194–237.
3. Medical Practice Committee, American College of Physicians: Ann Intern Med 1981: 95:729–732.
4. American Academy of Pediatrics: State of Continuity of Pediatric Care, Committee on Standards of Child Health Care, 1978.
5. Center for Disease Control, United States Immunization Survey: 1979, U.S. Dept. of Health, Education, and Welfare.
6. National Center for Health Statistics: Use of Selected Medical Procedures Associated with Preventive Care, United States, 1973. Vital and Health Statistics, Series 110, No. 11. DHEW Pub. No. (HRA) 77–1538. Rockville, MD, March 1977.
7. Kosecoff, J. et al: General medical care and education of internists in university hospitals. Ann Intern Med 1985: 102:250–257.
8. Woo B, Woo B, Cook EF, et al: Screening Procedures in the Asymptomatic Adult, Comparison of Physicians' Recommendations, Patients' Decisions, Published Guidelines, and Actual Practices. JAMA 1985; 254:1480–84.
9. Cohen DI, Littenberg B, Wetzel C, et al: Improving physician compliance with preventive medical guidelines. Med Care 1982; 20:1040–1045.
10. Romm FJ, Fletcher SW, Hulka BS: The Periodic Health Examination: Comparison of Recommendations and Internists' Performance. South Med J 1981; 74:265–276.
11. Battista RN: Adult cancer prevention in primary care: Patterns of practice in Quebec. Am J Public Health 1983; 73:1036–49.
13. McPhee SJ, Richard RJ, Solkowitz SN: Performance of cancer screening in a university general internal medicine practice: Comparison with the 1980 American Cancer Society guidelines. J Gen Intern Med 1986; 1:275–281.
14. Gallup Organization: A survey concerning cigarette smoking, health check-ups, cancer detection tests. Conducted for the American Cancer Society, January 1977.
15. Brook RH, Ware JE Jr, Rogers WH, et al: The effect of coinsurance on the health of adults. Santa Monica: RAND Corporation, R–3055–HHS, December 1984.
16. Morris CN: Sample selection in the health insurance experiment: Comparing the enrolled and nonenrolled populations. Santa Monica: RAND Corporation, N–2354–HHS, October 1985.
17. Rogers WH, Newhouse JP: Measuring unfiled claims in the health insurance experiment. *In*: Burstein L, Freeman HE, Rossi PH: Collecting Evaluation Data. New York: Sage Publications, 1985.
18. Lillard LA, Manning WG, Peterson CE, Lurie N, Goldberg G, Phelps CE: Preventive Medical Care: Standards, Usage, and Efficacy. Santa Monica: RAND Corporation, forthcoming.
19. Dietrich AJ, Goldberg H: Preventive content of adult primary care: Do generalists and subspecialists differ? Am J Public Health 1984; 74:223–27.
20. Yankauer A: Public and Private Prevention. Am J Public Health 1983; 73:1032.

15

The Uninsured: From Dilemma to Crisis

Emily Friedman

Some health policy issues are like bad pennies; despite repeated efforts to resolve them, they keep coming back. Probably no health policy issue of this century (with the possible exception of insuring and structuring long-term care, which affects far fewer people) has proven as intractable as access to acute care for Americans who lack coverage for the cost of that care. It was a problem for most Americans at one time; after the introduction of private insurance early in the twentieth century, it became a problem more of specific groups, notably the elderly and the poor. Coverage of those who were uninsured was a policy centerpiece (largely unrealized) of President Harry S. Truman's administration. With the passage of Medicaid and Medicare in 1965, it was thought the issue was largely resolved.

The uninsured, however, like the proverbial poor, seem always to be with us. In fact, their numbers have grown significantly in the past 15 years. Proposals for solutions are rife, but consensus on how to attack the problem has proven, to say the least, elusive. Nevertheless, the dilemma of the uninsured has become a crisis, affecting all aspects of the health care system and many aspects of society.

Who Is Uninsured?

Most estimates place the number of Americans lacking public or private coverage between 31 and 36 million.[1-4] The 1987 National Medical Expenditure Survey found that 47.8 million people lacked insurance for all or part of 1987, with between 34 and 36 million uninsured on any given day and 24.5 million uninsured throughout that year.[1,2]

The U.S. Bureau of the Census found that, from the first quarter of 1986 to the last quarter of 1988, 63.6 million people lacked coverage for at least 1 month and 31.5 million lacked it in the final quarter of 1988.[3] The Employee Benefit Research Institute reported that, in 1988, 33.3 million Americans had no private insurance and were ineligible for public coverage.[4] Even the more conservative figures represent a significant increase over the 26.6 million uninsured reported in the 1977 National Health Care Expenditures Study.[5]

When examined further, the statistics provide a troubling picture. Although most figures discussed herein are from the 1987 National Medical Expenditure Survey, virtually all other studies have found substantially the same patterns.

In terms of age, those who are 19 to 24 years old are most likely to be uninsured; 20.3 percent of this group were uninsured for all of 1987, and another 18.2 percent were uninsured for part of the year.[1,2] Children younger than 18 years were the next most likely to lack coverage, with nearly one in four uninsured either all or part of the year. The National Center for Health Statistics reports that, in 1988, 17 percent of children under 18 years had neither private insurance nor Medicaid coverage.[6] Given the importance of preventive and early intervention care to the health of the young, these rates are a cause of concern.

Of those aged 25 to 54 years, 19.8 percent were uninsured all or part of the year, as were 13.6 percent of those aged 55 to 64 years.[1,2] (Medicare covers virtually all Americans 65 years or older.) The fact that more than one in eight Americans who are 55 to 64 years old lack coverage at least part of the year is disturbing, in that this group faces a much higher risk of serious health problems than do younger Americans.

Racial and ethnic differences affect rates of coverage. Of non-Hispanic whites, 18.6 percent were uninsured for all or part of 1987, as were 29.8 percent of black Americans and 41.4 percent of Hispanic Americans.[1,2] Studies using differing methodologies going back as far as 1978 have shown that Hispanic Americans are the most likely to be uninsured of any ethnic group.[7] As Hispanics represent the fastest-growing ethnic population group in the nation, their consistently low rate of coverage is a potential warning of worse yet to come.

Men are slightly more likely to be uninsured than women; 23.8 percent of men were uninsured for at least part of 1987 as opposed to 21 percent of women.[1,2] This undoubtedly reflects the fact that virtually all men, regardless of their income, are excluded from eligibility for Medicaid. Also, Medicaid now covers low-income pregnant women with incomes up to 185 percent of the poverty line, as well as many mothers with dependent children. Furthermore, women are disproportionately represented in the poverty population, so, to the extent that Medicaid covers that

Reprinted with permission from *JAMA, The Journal of the American Medical Association* 265, no. 19 (May 15, 1991): 2491–95. Copyright © 1991 American Medical Association.

population, more women than men are likely to be protected.

Income level is also associated with lack of coverage. The uninsured represented 47.5 percent of those with incomes below the poverty line in 1987, 45 percent of those with incomes between poverty and 125 percent of poverty, 36.7 percent of those with incomes from 125 percent to 200 percent of poverty, 17.8 percent of those with incomes 200 percent to 400 percent of poverty, and 8.8 percent of those with incomes above 400 percent of poverty.

The proportion of uninsured varies by state, depending on several factors, including the level of Medicaid coverage in the state, the demographics of the population, insurance practices, overall income, the nature of employment, and state health policy. The National Medical Expenditure Survey found lack of insurance highest in the South (27.4 percent of the population were uninsured at least part of the year) and West (27.2 percent) and lowest in the Midwest (16.7 percent) and Northeast (15.7 percent).[1,2] The Employee Benefit Research Institute found that lack of coverage ranged from less than 10 percent in Massachusetts, Pennsylvania, Michigan, Wisconsin, and Iowa to more than 25 percent in Louisiana, Texas, and New Mexico.[4] However, with so much coverage tied to employment and with states changing Medicaid and other health policies constantly, these figures are volatile.

Many Underinsured as Well

If the policy debate is to be framed accurately in terms of issues of coverage and access, a second group, the underinsured, must also be mentioned. This population is more difficult to define, because it faces risks that are more specific. That is, a patient's diagnosis can determine whether coverage is sufficient or not, and surveys of whether a person has coverage at all are unlikely to reveal such gaps in protection. Where a person receives care, how long the person is a patient, what types of treatment are required, and whether there is a dollar or time limit to coverage all affect the sufficiency of insurance. Nevertheless, a 1985 estimate, based on data

projected from the 1977 National Health Care Expenditures Study, was that 26 percent of the nonelderly population, or approximately 56 million people in 1984, were "inadequately protected against the possibility of large medical bills."[8]

To this population, whose major problem is insufficient overall coverage, could be added those whose insurance precludes coverage of a given condition or imposes a waiting period before such coverage becomes operative (which is often the case with pregnancy). Also included are those who are covered by Medicaid but lack access to physician care because of physician reluctance to treat Medicaid clients and those who, insured or not, face difficulty in obtaining obstetric care because of the decreasing number of obstetricians willing to accept new patients (American College of Obstetrics and Gynecology, news release, May 3, 1988).[9–12]

Physician resistance to treating such patients has been ascribed to many causes, including low and delayed Medicaid payments, fears of malpractice litigation, paperwork, cultural or language problems, noncompliance, and other factors, including racial discrimination.[13] Certainly, the prospect of low or nonexistent payment is a disincentive to most providers.

The total number of uninsured and underinsured, even if the latter group has not been sufficiently identified, could easily represent one in every four Americans on any given day.

Erosion of Medicaid

How such a large number of Americans came to be at risk, through lack of coverage or lack of access or both, is a challenging question. Theoretically, coverage of health care costs is available to virtually all Americans through one of four routes: Medicare for the elderly and disabled, Medicaid for low-income women and children (and some men) and those with certain disabilities, employer-subsidized coverage at the workplace, or self-purchased coverage for those ineligible for the previous three. However, as many as 10 million more Americans were uninsured at least part of the year in 1987 than in 1977. What happened?

Of the four routes to coverage, Medicare has aged best. A universal enfranchisement that is neither means tested nor related to the workplace, Medicare each year covers more Americans for most acute care. Beneficiaries' out-of-pocket costs remain high, however, and coverage for long-term care remains skimpy, especially with the repeal of Medicare catastrophic care coverage.

Medicaid, however, has suffered a more equivocal fate. Although passed by Congress, Medicaid is a state-level program, with each state defining income levels and other standards of eligibility and the federal government subsidizing a certain portion of expenses, depending on the state's overall wealth. Thus, coverage has always varied from state to state, with Northern states and some Western states offering more generous benefits than Southern and other states.

In the early 1980s, both the federal and state governments sought to control or reduce Medicaid expenditures in the face of tax cuts, growing costs, and reduced federal funds for the program. This led to freezes and reductions in both eligibility and provider payments. The result was a basically stable number of beneficiaries despite an increase in the poverty population. Because of Medicaid's categorical approach to eligibility, certain groups—most low-income men and childless couples, for example— do not qualify. However, there was little growth between 1980 and 1985 even among potentially eligible populations.

Medicaid's fortunes began to change in the late 1980s, as Congress mandated Medicaid coverage of pregnant women (at least for pregnancy-related services) and young children with incomes as high as 185 percent of the poverty line. These mandates were resisted by many states because they required substantial increases in spending; by 1990, the governors of 49 states had asked Congress to refrain from further mandates— a request Congress did not heed as it increased child eligibility that year.

Medicaid faces another vexing problem: Although families receiving Aid to Dependent Children constitute between 70 percent and 75 percent of the Medicaid population, three fourths of Medicaid expenses go to the costs of care for the aged, blind, and disabled, especially patients in nursing homes. Indeed, Medicaid has, perhaps in violation of the intent of Congress, become a form of long-term care reinsurance for the Medicare population. In the absence of either major growth in affordable private long-term care insurance or inclusion under Medicare of more extensive long-term care coverage, the stress on the Medicaid program is likely to continue.

As a result of the rather tangled path it has traveled, Medicaid never covered the entire poverty population and was estimated to cover only 38.7 percent of that group in 1983. [14] By 1989, it was estimated that only 40 percent of the poverty population was covered by the program. [15] Although congressional mandates may boost that figure somewhat, the majority of the poor remain unprotected by the program that was designed to cover them.

The Workplace Connection

The third route to coverage—employer-subsidized insurance for workers and often for dependents—has also seen serious erosion in recent years. This was the cornerstone of health insurance in the past—appropriate for a nation steeped in the Puritan work ethic and even more appropriate in an age in which labor shortages of many types are looming. The unspoken agreement was that, if a person was employed, he or she would receive health insurance benefits, subsidized to some degree by the employer or at least priced lower than individual coverage to reflect the fact that the subscriber belonged to an employee group.

However, the workplace is no longer a guarantor of coverage, if it ever was. The National Medical Expenditure Survey found that, in 1987, of the uninsured population, 46.4 percent were working adults, 6.8 percent were nonworking spouses of working adults, and 23.6 percent were children of working adults. [1,2] In other words, 76.8 percent of the uninsured either were employed or were nuclear-family dependents of the employed. [1,2] The Employee Benefits Research Institute found that, in 1988,

85 percent of the uninsured were either workers or family members of workers. [4]

The employed uninsured are unevenly distributed. The National Medical Expenditure Survey found that they were more likely to work part time or to be self-employed and to work in settings with fewer than 100 workers, especially in settings with fewer than 25 workers. In settings with fewer than 10 employees, 26.3 percent of workers were uninsured. [1,2]

Service industries, as opposed to manufacturing industries, were more likely to employ uninsured workers, reflecting both the lack of a tradition of employment-based coverage in the service sector and a much lower level of unionization, which is usually associated with generous health benefits. [1,2] The Employee Benefit Research Institute, using March 1989 data from the Bureau of the Census, found similar patterns. [4]

Thus, the majority of the uninsured are tied, directly or through family relationships, to a workplace that is no longer an automatic source of insurance. In some cases the employer does not offer coverage. In others the coverage is offered but is not affordable or is not purchased by the employee. In still others the employee acquires coverage for himself or herself but not for a dependent spouse or children. All of these possibilities are more likely in small business settings.

Employers are not necessarily the villains. Insurance products for small business are both limited and expensive. According to the General Accounting Office, small businesses have little ability to spread risk over a large number of employees, which results in higher premiums, should an employee incur large costs. [16]

Small businesses also face a far greater likelihood of premiums being based on experience rating rather than on community rating. Small employee groups are also seen by insurers as a higher risk, which means that, compared with larger employee groups, they are subject to more exclusions, medical testing of applicants, and denials of coverage because of health status and are less able to absorb the significant increases in premium prices that

have been the pattern of the past two decades. [16]

Indeed, a major element in the crisis of the uninsured is the simple fact that health care costs a great deal more than it once did. The U.S. Department of Health and Human Services reported in 1990 that, for 1989 (the last year for which final data were available), national health care spending increased 11.1 percent, to $604.1 billion (U.S. Dept of Health and Human Services, press release, December 20, 1990). This meant that U.S. spending on health care from 1980 through 1989 increased 128 percent. Insurance premiums reflect those costs plus insurers' own expenses and margins, leading to average increases in premiums that reached 18 percent in 1989. [17] In addition to increasingly selective attitudes toward risk on the part of insurers, insurance is becoming less affordable simply because the cost of the services it covers is doubling every few years.

If small businesses face problems in offering and retaining coverage, the individual insurance market faces collapse. This is the population that insurers characterize as the highest risk, requiring disproportionate administrative costs and usually proving unprofitable.

Medical underwriting, experience rating, refusal to cover those deemed "uninsurable," cancellation of policies on short notice, and high premiums are common if not almost universal barriers for those seeking individual coverage. As a result, for an individual unable to qualify for group or public coverage, obtaining affordable insurance is dependent on having a sufficiently high income and very good health status. This, needless to say, eliminates many of those who are most likely to need coverage, that is, those who are poor, sick, and/or unable to acquire workplace-based insurance.

The working uninsured are a complex population, and even data-based generalities are dangerous. Despite the small-business focus, many of the uninsured work for large firms, as is the case with agricultural and seasonal workers. Some of the uninsured simply choose not to acquire coverage, although they represent a small minority of this population. Some are eligible for either public or private coverage but are unaware of this and thus have never sought it. Although most of the uninsured are poor or near poor, some are middle-class people denied coverage by virtue of poor health status or "risky" jobs. It is a highly heterogeneous population, with multiple reasons for being at risk. Nevertheless, it is safe to say that the original notion of tying coverage to employment is working less well with each passing day. In times of economic downturn, when higher unemployment produces more medical indigence and lower tax revenues to fund public programs such as Medicaid, the fragility of the entire concept of linking coverage to employment becomes painfully clear.

Why a Crisis Now?

Most crises are born of a series of small events that one day reach critical mass. So it has been with the uninsured. The framers of Public Law No. 89–97, which brought Medicare and Medicaid into being in 1985, believed that universal health insurance was just around the corner, yet it failed to materialize.[18] When it was reported in 1980 that 26.6 million Americans lacked coverage, a response might have been expected but was not forthcoming. A large number of efforts—expansion of Medicaid; coverage of children by Blue Cross and Blue Shield plans; state insurance pools for the "uninsurable"; and coverage experiments funded by states, localities, and private sources—have attempted to address at least part of the problem, yet it continues unabated.

Has the issue reached critical mass? If not, it is well on the way to doing so, for at least five reasons.

1. Although coverage is not the sole determinant of health status, it is a key factor in improved health, as Medicaid data have demonstrated.[19] Although availability of care does not guarantee it will be used,[20,21] the uninsured have been shown to receive less care, even if they are able to gain entry to the system.[22] It is thus not unreasonable to assume that medical indigence is associated with lack of care and poorer health status. In other words, coverage does make a difference.

2. The health care system is suffering damage as a result of being asked (implicitly) to provide care for the uninsured who cannot pay. Because the uninsured often do not have access to physicians in private offices, health maintenance organizations, or other settings, they disproportionately seek care at hospitals. As an anonymous physician once observed, "They do not go to the doctor; they go to the institution."

Nevertheless, it was estimated in 1985 that physicians provided $9.2 billion in bad debt and charity care in 1982.[23] A 1988 survey by the American Medical Association found that physicians reported $6.3 billion in uncollected revenues that year (Socioeconomic Monitoring Service data, American Medical Association, 1988).

According to the American Hospital Association, hospitals in 1989 provided $11.1 billion in uncompensated care, an increase of $7.2 billion over 1980.[24] Although not all of this can be attributed to care of the medically indigent, most of it does represent such services. However, not all hospitals are equally affected, because the uninsured are not equally distributed. Teaching hospitals, Veterans Affairs hospitals, public hospitals, children's hospitals, and inner-city hospitals are harder hit, and the load among even these facilities is unequal.[25] Staggering under the pressure of the acquired immunodeficiency syndrome epidemic, drug abuse, increased trauma, problem pregnancies, and other results of social change and social neglect, most municipal and some private hospitals are barely coping with emergency care and are hardly able to provide timely—let alone elective—services to the uninsured. Rural hospitals face problem of their own, because of chronic low occupancy; one or two long stays by uninsured patients can doom a facility.

Care is often theoretically available through public or private clinics and other settings, both funded and voluntary. However, these are often so overloaded that access is illusory. In Chicago, Ill, for example, as of November 1990, pregnant women had to wait 125 days for an appointment with a physician at a public clinic (*Chicago Tribune*, November 25, 1990: 4, p 1).

Thus, a minority of U.S. hospitals carry the majority of the burden of the uninsured, and that burden is growing. As a result, there is quarreling among hospitals, between hospitals and physicians, and between hospitals and governments as the cost of treating the uninsured increases while subsidies (especially philanthropy) decline. With emergency departments in some cities (including New York, NY) now the most common source of inpatient admissions, and with nearly 100 hospitals closing each year,[26] more and more hospitals are facing a horrendous choice: caring for all the uninsured and failing, or turning at least some of them away and surviving.

As a result, serious questions are being asked about the level of charity care that hospitals, clinics, physicians, and other providers should be expected to provide. Certainly, those entities holding charitable tax exemptions should be expected to provide some indigent care, although the requirement for such care was removed from the federal tax code in 1969.

Should some hospitals have case loads that are 10 percent or 20 percent uninsured while others have virtually no uninsured patients? Should indigent care provided by hospitals be subsidized largely by a haphazard patchwork of subsidies, tax levies, adjustments in Medicare and Medicaid payments, and other partial measures that are neither reliable nor well organized?

3. Another factor contributing to calls for action on the uninsured is the increasingly uncomfortable situation of employers. The number of employers who do offer coverage is dropping (*Business Week*, November 26, 1990:187), which is not surprising in view of the increasing cost of insurance and the voluntary nature of the arrangement.

The playing field is becoming more unequal: Some employers offer coverage, some do not. Some offer a lavish benefit package, other offer a lean one. Some are self-insured and, because of a federal statutory prohibition, cannot be required by states to offer mandated benefits; others must provide a wide range of benefits that raise the cost of coverage considerably. Whether one has coverage no longer depends on *whether* one is employed but rather on *where* and by *whom*.

Employer discomfiture is being exacerbated by calls for mandated employer coverage of all workers and even of dependents. Only the state of Hawaii has succeeded in legally requiring that most people working more than 19 hours per week be covered by employer-subsidized insurance.

The state of Massachusetts has passed legislation requiring most employers to provide a certain level of coverage to workers or else pay an assessment; it is scheduled to go into effect in 1992. However, the law is being challenged in court, and the newly elected governor of the state has proposed repeal of the employer mandate.[27] Other states are interested in some form of employer mandate, but the federal prohibition on state regulation of self-insured employers under the Employee Retirement Income and Security Act makes it extremely difficult to require these firms to participate (Hawaii has a federal waiver). Employers, anxious about being forced to subsidize expensive benefits but concerned about uninsured workers and unequal benefits, are also seeking a solution.

The uninsured have become a workplace issue in another way. The youngest baby boomer is now 26 years old; nearly 20 years of large numbers of entry-level workers have given way to a much leaner supply. If health insurance benefits are not offered by employers, what will lure new workers? Asking women, for example, to give up Medicaid coverage to become uninsured workers seems questionable in terms of incentives. In a labor-short era, the role of workplace benefits is critical.

4. Another force for a solution is the interrelationship of the uninsured and health care costs. On the one hand, it can be argued that, if health care for the more than 200 million Americans who have at least some coverage is so expensive, we cannot afford to cover the 31 to 37 million who have no coverage. On the other hand, it can be argued that the uninsured represent significant hidden costs. After all, most of them do receive care, at least when their lives are at stake or when they are having babies. Given their compromised or nonexistent ac-

cess to primary and preventive care, however, their point of entry into the system is too often a hospital emergency department. The timing of their seeking care is also often a case of too little, too late.

As a result, conditions that could have been prevented or treated in a cost-effective manner—from measles to carcinoma of the breast to diabetes—become emergencies, with both higher costs and worse outcomes. This, in turn, distorts staffing and practice in emergency services, leading, in the words of a health policy analyst many years ago, to primary care in the emergency setting, equivalent to tending a rose garden with a bulldozer. It is hardly a cost-effective use of health care resources.

The larger economic issue is the most of us pay the hidden costs of medical indigence, one way or another. Every insurance premium includes some of the costs of care of the uninsured. Even self-insured employers pay part of that cost. Paying patients subsidize nonpaying patients. The society as a whole pays the price of prenatal care that is not given, immunizations that are not provided, cancers that are not detected, diabetes that is not monitored, mental illness that is not discovered. The uninsured can be very expensive.

5. The last factor driving the need for action may appear secondary in a health care economy that has become hard edged. Nevertheless, issues of ethics and equity are as important and powerful as the economic or logistical issues. Foremost among these is whether a democracy that thinks of itself as the moral hope of the world can justify grave inequalities in access to health care, which in most countries is considered an essential human need.

It is often pointed out that, among developed nations, only the United States and South Africa have not implemented universal access to care. This is overstated; there are holes in every safety net. However, the holes in our net are more numerous and yawn deeper and wider than in many less-wealthy nations.

We claim that other nations ration care because the insured must wait sometimes; however, in our nation, the

uninsured can wait forever. We claim that ours is the best health care system in the world; however, if tens of millions of Americans have little or no access to care, the claim rings hollow.

In addition, a health care system that has become too selective in terms of whom it treats carries with it the seeds of its own destruction. Our system has been built—properly, in my opinion—on a tradition of pluralism, public guarantees and private largesse, and both institutionalized and voluntary giving; a tradition of faith, hope, and charity.

Should the public lose faith in that arrangement (and in recent years we have seen evidence of such a loss of confidence),[28,29] the very basis of the health care system is in jeopardy. Health care providers can hold themselves out as morally superior, but if they are not seen as such by the populace, voluntarism and autonomy can easily be replaced by fiat.

Many of our health status indicators are lagging or beginning to lag behind those in the rest of the developed world—and, indeed, in some of the Third World. Pressure is building to give up on our current system and develop another, based on the Canadian or some other centralized model.[28,29] The moral standing of American health care is on the line. We must produce a workable answer to the crisis of the uninsured, or all of us—health care providers and the society alike—could suffer the terrible and long-term consequences of inaction.

[The author] acknowledges the assistance provided in the preparation and revision of this article by William H. Dendle III, MPH, Irene Fraser, Ph.D., and Alan Sager, Ph.D.

Notes

1. Short PF, Monheit A, Beauregard K, *National Medical Expenditure Survey: A Profile of Uninsured Americans: Research Findings 1*. Rockville, Md: National Center for Health Services Research and Health Care Technology Assessment; 1989.

2. Short PF. *National Medical Expenditure Survey: Estimates of the Uninsured Population, Calendar Year 1987: Data Summary 2*. Rockville, Md: National Center for Health Services Research and Health Care Technology Assessment; 1990.

3. Nelson C, Short K. *Health Insurance Coverage, 1986–88*. Washington, DC: US Dept of the Census; 1990. Current Population Reports, Household Economic Studies, Series P–70, No. 17.

4. Chollet D, Foley J, Mages C. *Uninsured in the United States: The Nonelderly Population Without Health Insurance, 1988*. Washington, DC: Employee Benefit Research Institute; 1990.

5. Kasper JA, Walden DC, Wilensky GR. *Who Are the Uninsured?* Hyattsville, Md: National Center for Health Services Research; 1980. National Health Care Expenditures Study, Data Preview 1.

6. Bloom B. *Health Insurance and Medical Care: Health of Our Nation's Children, United States, 1988*. Hyattsville, Md: National Center for Health Statistics; 1990. Advance Data From Vital and Health Statistics of the National Center for Health Statistics, No. 188.

7. Trevino FM, Moyer ME, Valdez RB, Stroup-Benham CA. Health insurance coverage and utilization of health services by Mexican Americans, mainland Puerto Ricans, and Cuban Americans. *JAMA*. 1991;265:233–237.

8. Farley P. Who are the underinsured? *Milbank Mem Fund Q*. 1985;63:476–503.

9. Friedman E. Doctors, doctors everywhere: and patients who can't get care. *Health Business*. January 4, 1991;6: 1T–2T.

10. Medicaid participation declines. *SMS Rep*. September 1989;3:1–3.

11. Yudkowsky BK, Cartland JDC, Flint SS. Pediatrician participation in Medicaid: 1978 to 1989. *Pediatrics*. 1990;85:567–577.

12. Access to normal obstetrical care: a disturbing trend. *SMS Rep*. January 1989;3:3.

13. Fossett JW, Perloff JD, Kletke PR, Peterson JA. Medicaid patients' access to office based obstetricians. Presented at the 118th Annual Meeting of the American Public Health Association; October 3, 1990; New York, NY.

14. Gornick M, Greenberg JN, Eggers P, Dobson A. Twenty years of Medicare and Medicaid: covered populations, use of benefits, and program expenditures. *Health Care Financ Rev*. 1985;7(annual suppl):13–59.

15. Swartz K, Lipson D. *Strategies for Assisting the Medically Uninsured*. Washington, DC: Urban Institute and the Intergovernmental Health Policy Project; 1989.

16. *Health Insurance: Availability and Adequacy for Small Businesses*. Hearings before the Subcommittee on Antitrust, Monopolies, and Business Rights of the Senate Committee on the Judiciary, 101st Cong, 2nd Sess (1990) (testimony of Mark V. Nadel, associate director for national and public health issues, Human Resources Division, General Accounting Office).

17. Cerne F. Rate decreases unlikely despite health insurers' healthy profits. *Am Hosp Assoc News*. November 5, 1990;26:8.

18. Friedman E. *The Problems and Promises of Medicaid*. Chicago, Ill: American Hospital Association; 1977.

19. Friedman E. Medicare and Medicaid at 25. *Hospitals*. August 5, 1990;64:38–54.

20. Aday LA. Access to what? for whom? *Health Manage Q*. Fourth quarter 1990; 12:18–22.

21. Piper JM, Ray WA, Griffin MR. Effects of Medicaid eligibility expansion on prenatal care and pregnancy outcome in Tennessee. *JAMA*. 1990;264:221–2223.

22. Hadley J, Steinberg EP, Feder J. Comparison of uninsured and privately insured hospital patients: condition on admission, resource use, and outcome. *JAMA*. 1991;265:374–379.

23. Ohsfeldt R. Uncompensated medical services provided by physicians and hospitals. *Med Care*. 1985;23:1338–1344.

24. *Medicaid Underpayments and Hospital Care for the Poor: A Fact Sheet*. Chicago, Ill: American Hospital Association; 1991.

25. Friedman E. Hospital uncompensated care: crisis? *JAMA*. 1989;262:2975–2977.

26. Friedman E. Analysts differ over implications of more hospital closings than openings since 1987. *JAMA*. 1990; 264: 310–314.

27. Massachusetts health care law threatened. *Med Health*. February 11, 1991;45:2.

28. Blendon R. Three systems: a comparative survey. *Health Manage Q*. 1989;11:2–10.

29. Blendon R, Leitman R, Morrison I, Donelan K. Satisfaction with health systems in 10 nations. *Health Aff*. Summer 1990; 9:185–192.

16

Rationing Health Care: The Choice Before Us

Henry Aaron and William B. Schwartz

Rising sales cause joy in most industries, but increasing outlays for health care are causing distress not only among those who must pay the bills but among health care providers themselves. After adjusting for inflation, total and per capita personal health care expenditures have risen at annual rates of 5.5 and 4.1 percent since 1950.[1] The proportion of gross national product devoted to personal health care nearly tripled. Official forecasts project that the United States will be devoting 15 percent of total production to health care by the year 2000.[2] Successive administrations have proposed a variety of measures intended to contain medical costs, but the results have been so unsuccessful that some observers speculate that the United States may be forced to ration health care.[3,4]

The term "rationing" is used in two distinct senses. First, market economies persistently deny goods to those who cannot afford them. All goods, including health care, are rationed in this sense, especially for the poor and some others who face large expenses and lack insurance. Such price rationing of medical care has a long and, in our view, ignoble history in the United States. This problem affects about 15 percent of all Americans. Second, the term "rationing" is used to refer to the denial of commodities to those who have the money to buy them. In this sense sugar, gasoline, and meat were rationed during World War II. The question now being raised is whether health care should be rationed in this sense, whether its availability should be limited, even to those who can pay for it. This kind of rationing would affect the 85 percent of all Americans who currently have health insurance and any others who may later be added to their ranks. While the first question is urgently important, we shall be focusing on rationing in the second sense.

In this article, we address key questions surrounding rising health costs. Why have recent efforts at cost containment failed? Can the United States afford unlimited, high-quality care for everyone? If not, is rationing unavoidable? If so, how will it be carried out and what will be its effect on the health and lives of most Americans?

The Economic Basis of Rising Outlays on Health Care

Standard economic theory suggests that spending on health care is excessive. According to this doctrine, when people pay less than the full cost of what they buy, they will consume more than is socially optimal unless their consumption benefits not only themselves but others. This line of argument suggests that insurance induces excessive health expenditures because people pay for only part of the cost of care.

Patients in 1987 paid, on the average, only about 10 cents of each dollar devoted to hospital care, a share that has changed negligibly for two decades. And they pay about 26 cents of each dollar paid to physicians, a share that has fallen steadily. Although these averages conceal large differences among patients, the fully insured (or those who have exceeded ceilings on patient outlays) and physicians acting in the patients' interests have the incentive to seek any service, however costly, that provides any benefits at all. Because of insurance, these decisions impose large costs on others.

The Unavoidable Dilemma

The intersection of this payment system and three distinct features of the health care system lead inevitably to rising costs. The first and most important is technology. Diagnostic procedures and therapies that are now routine were unknown when most physicians now in practice began their training. Computed tomography, magnetic resonance imaging, nuclear medicine, organ transplants, many of the drugs for control of ulcers and of the symptoms of coronary artery disease, open heart surgery, total parenteral nutrition, and a host of other diagnostic and therapeutic procedures have been introduced or become standard in the past two decades. Other technologies, described later, indicate that the rate of innovation is not abating. Nearly all of these innovations promise to increase the number and cost of beneficial interventions.

A second factor driving up costs is the tendency for the price of services characterized by low growth in productivity to rise relative to the price of commodities.[5] Although a day in the hospital today differs in many ways from a day in the hospital in, say, 1960, the hotel services of feeding and space rental and most services of nurses and orderlies are produced with little more efficiency than in the past.

The final factor is the aging of the population. Although the average annual cost of health care rises sharply with age, this factor accounts for only a minor proportion of the 651 percent growth of real personal health care outlays between 1950 and 1987. [6]

Each of these inflationary forces shows every sign of continuing for decades.

Many observers deny any imminent need to consider rationing. They argue instead that we can continue to provide whatever beneficial services are available if we eliminate inefficiencies and wasteful practices. But, as we shall show, such reforms, although potentially important in absolute size, promise one-shot savings and can only briefly defer the need to consider whether and how to ration medical care.

Why One-Time Savings Cannot Solve the Cost Problem

Various methods have been proposed for cutting costs and improving efficiency—elimination of redundant medical capacity, cessation of useless medical procedures, increased competition, better management, and reduced fees for certain physicians. Unless they are used to reduce the availability of beneficial services—in short, unless they are used to compel nonprice rationing—all promise to arrest or slow the growth of medical costs only temporarily.

The potential savings from eliminating chronically empty beds, now numbering some 300,000, are surprisingly small because the same number of patients will presumably be cared for whether or not the duplicated facilities are closed and because the marginal costs of alternative care is high relative to the marginal savings from closing excess facilities. [7]

The potential savings from eliminating useless medical procedures, by contrast, could run into many billions of dollars. Health maintenance organizations (HMOs) claim that through superior efficiency and elimination of useless services (mostly excess hospital days) they deliver high-quality service at costs well below those of other providers. One study supported these claims, [8] in that it was found that one HMO provided comprehensive care for approximately 25 percent less than did providers reimbursed on a fee-for-service basis for fully insured patients. However, the HMO was no less costly than fee-for-service care for patients who faced an annual deductible of $450 per family or 95 percent cost-sharing. [8] If costs of all fee-for-service hospital and physician care were reduced by 15 percent, an estimate based on the difference between costs of HMOs and the mixture of other insurance plans, there would have been a once-and-for-all reduction in expenditures of approximately $20 billion. [8,9]

Additional savings that entail no rationing will become possible as evaluation of established medical procedures identifies classes of patients in which selected procedures now in use produce no medical benefits. [10] Even a small percentage saving in an industry currently absorbing more than $500 billion per year is a high-stakes effort that should be vigorously pursued, but continuation of annual growth of real personal health care expenditures of 4.1 percent per capita would quickly dwarf the savings from increased efficiencies. [1]

For a variety of reasons, not all providers could become as efficient as the best run HMOs, and economies would be realized over many years. As a result, savings would be achieved gradually and, therefore, would be hard to detect against the strongly rising trend in medical outlays. In short, the United States faces a choice between letting medical outlays claim an ever rising share of output, while recognizing that some will go for services producing small but positive benefits, and trying to devise socially acceptable arrangements under which some patients who have the means to pay, directly or through insurance, are denied some beneficial care.

Policy Attempts to Control Spending on Health Care

The past two decades have seen repeated and highly touted efforts fail to slow the growth of spending on medical care.

Regulation

Starting in 1974 Congress sought to curtail growth of investment in medical structures and equipment by requiring advance authorization (a certificate of need or CON). Although potential penalties for noncompliance were severe, evaluations found that they were seldom invoked and that many hospitals allocated to other activities the resources not used in disapproved investments. [11]

Former President Richard M. Nixon's price control program, begun in 1971, temporarily lowered the growth of spending on hospital services. The controls were so complex that they could not be sustained. When controls were removed, real hospital spending rose at an average annual rate of 6.9 percent in 1975 and 1976. President Jimmy Carter responded in 1977 by proposing a cap on growth of revenues per patient day. Hospitals promised to slow spending growth voluntarily but, after brief success, the effort wilted following congressional rejection of President Carter's proposal.

In 1984 the Health Care Financing Administration (HCFA) began to reimburse hospitals fixed sums for Medicare patients based on primary and secondary diagnoses at the time of admission (the "diagnosis-related group" or DRG, system). Under the prior system, HCFA had paid hospitals the audited cost of services covered by the Medicare program. Under the DRG system, hospitals receive the same amount whatever they spend, except in relatively rare outlier cases. Preliminary evidence suggests that the program has slowed growth of hospital spending under Medicare. [12] However, it is not clear how much of this slowdown is simply the realization in the Medicare program of economies being achieved throughout the health care system, how much entails shifting of costs outside the hospital setting, and how much represents the rationing of beneficial services.

Competition

Some analysts have claimed that competition among health care providers can greatly reduce growth of spending on health care without any loss in the quality of care or the imposition of rationing. In pursuit of this goal, some have supported a cap on the exclusion from the personal income tax of employer-financed health insurance premiums, development and dissemination of statistics on the quality of care rendered by various hospitals and physicians, solicitation of competitive bids by employers from various groups of providers, and a host of other measures to promote efficient provision of medical care and to narrow margins earned by hospitals and physicians.[13] Increased cost consciousness, it is claimed, would encourage insurance plans in which patients directly pay for an increased share of the cost of their own health care. If, in addition, patients had reliable data on medical outcomes of various providers, patients and their employers would be able to avoid high-cost hospitals and physicians who do not provide demonstrably superior care. Supporters claim such measures will not only improve the quality of care, but will also save enough money to forestall the need to ration medical care.

Even if increased competition achieves all that its advocates claim, the elimination of inefficiencies promises a one-time saving unless it slows the introduction of new medical technologies. If new technologies are introduced at an unchanged rate, the main underlying force that has driven up outlays for four decades would remain intact. In that event, the respite from rising outlays, however welcome, would be transitory.

Costs in Other Developed Countries

Many developed nations other than the United States provide seemingly high-quality care on a basis many regard as more equitable than our own and for much lower overall costs (Table 1). Only Great Britain among advanced societies avowedly rations medical care. Since medical techniques disseminate rapidly, yet spending varies widely, a puzzle emerges. How can countries with per capita incomes approximating our own spend so much less on medical care than we do and yet avoid rationing?

Demography is not the answer. European countries, with per capita incomes comparable to our own, have older populations yet spend less on health care than we do. Alternative explanations are that the relative price of health care has risen faster in the United States than elsewhere or that growth of gross domestic product has been slower. In fact, economic growth in the United States in the past 15 years has been about average among major industrial countries. Furthermore, reliable information from which to measure health care spending in constant prices is unavailable.

A contributory factor to higher outlays in the United States seems to be that we spend more on billing and such other administrative costs as marketing than do other countries. Some estimates place the cost of administration at as much as 22 percent of national health care spending, perhaps two-fifths larger than would be necessary with a single payer.[14]

Indices such as life expectancy and infant mortality in other industrialized countries typically match or exceed our own.[15] This fact is often taken to mean that significant denial of services cannot be occurring in these countries. But rationing of such health services as measures to prevent blindness, relief of severe skin disorders, replacement of a damaged hip, and relief of the pain of coronary artery disease, which serve

primarily to improve the quality of life, rather than to extend it, would not show up in mortality statistics. Furthermore, mortality rates are heavily dependent on lifestyle, diet, and income distribution, factors generally regarded as far more important than medical care as influences on mortality rates.[16]

What Rationing Entails

Americans are unfamiliar with nonprice rationing or its consequences. They have not thought about whether or not to implement it. Should we turn to rationing, which services will be denied to which patients, and how will the decisions be made?

The clearest answers to these questions come from Great Britain. Per capita spending on health care, about one-third in Britain of that in the United States, requires a degree of rationing there far beyond any that is conceivable here. But Britain and the United States share many important features—language, democratic values, and similar patterns of medical education and physician competence—as well as important political and social similarities. For this reason, British experience shows the kinds, if not the severity, of choices we shall face.

One of the most remarkable aspects of rationing in Britain is that some decisions that appear medically irrational are socially acceptable. For example,

Table 1. Health care outlays as a percentage of gross domestic product, 1960–1986 (*29*).

Country	Year		
	1965	1980	1986
Australia	4.9	6.6	7.2
Canada	6.1	7.4	8.5
Denmark	4.8	6.8	6.1
France	5.2	7.4	8.5
Germany (West)	5.1	7.9	8.1
Italy	4.0	6.8	6.7
Japan	4.5	6.6	6.7
The Netherlands	4.4	8.2	8.3
New Zealand	4.3	7.2	6.9
Norway	3.9	6.6	6.8
Sweden	5.6	9.5	9.1
Switzerland	3.8	7.2	8.0
United Kingdom	4.1	5.8	6.2
United States	6.0	9.2	11.1

per capita spending on total parenteral nutrition or TPN (an expensive form of intravenous feeding often of marginal value) was nearly as high in Britain as in the United States. At the same time, many tertiary-care university hospitals lacked a CT scanner.

Nonmedical values and circumstances appear to explain such situations. For example, services depending on specialized capital equipment are easier to ration than are those that rely on multi-use inputs. Thus, CT scanning, which requires specialized equipment and staff, is tightly controlled. TPN, in contrast, is difficult to control without directly infringing on each physician's clinical freedom.

Age and cost interact to influence allocation decisions. Until the early 1980s, most patients over the age of 55 or 60 with chronic kidney failure were allowed to die without hemodialysis, a costly procedure dependent on specialized equipment and dedicated clinic space. After continous ambulatory peritoneal dialysis, a relatively low cost procedure, became routine, the number of older dialyzed patients nearly doubled.[17] In contrast, the British have made full-scale treatment of hemophilia generally available through special clinics. Although per capita costs are high, aggregate costs are low because only about 75 new cases of hemophilia appear each year. Furthermore, the symptoms are highly visible—severe bleeding and swollen joints. British physicians and administrators generally acknowledged that equally generous treatment would not be provided if there were 7,500 new cases annually instead of 75.[3]

Still other considerations influence allocations to other diseases. A dread disease such as cancer elicits disproportionate support. The high costs of failure to treat patients with severe arthritis of the hip help explain the relatively generous allowances made for hip replacement. In contrast, funding for surgical treatment of coronary artery disease is meager because treatment with drugs is relatively inexpensive. These factors influence the availability of resources in a fashion independent of the expected medical benefits.

The Physician as Gatekeeper

The denial of useful life-saving care is hard on both providers and patients. In Britain, primary care physicians, who are forced to act as gatekeepers for the system, bear this unpleasant responsibility. Physicians make the denial of potentially beneficial care seem routine, or even optimal, by recasting a problem of medical scarcity in economic terms.

Some British physicians understand clearly that they are not providing all care that could be beneficial. As one doctor put it,[3] (p. 102),

The sense that I have is that there are many situations where resources are sufficiently short so that there must be decisions made as to who is treated. Given that circumstance, the physician, in order to live with himself and to sleep well at night, has to look at the arguments for not treating a patient. And there are always some—social, medical, whatever. In many instances he heightens, sharpens or brings into focus the negative component in order to make himself and the patient comfortable about not going forward.

Although rationing has been most dramatic in the treatment of chronic kidney failure, many senior British health officials and physicians long denied that any age cutoff existed. The explanation for this puzzling disparity lies in the referral patterns of primary care physicians. Recognizing that dialysis capacity was limited, these doctors routinely favored younger over older patients whenever some complicating illness such as diabetes was present. Even older patients without other medical problems were usually viewed as unsuitable for referral because, as one doctor put it, without trying to be arch, "everyone over the age of 55 is a bit crumbly."

Such rationalization is understandable. Continued referrals of "inappropriate" candidates would be pointless, forcing the nephrologist either to tell patients that care is unavailable or to contradict the clinical judgment of the referring doctor. The local physician responds by telling the patient that, given the overall medical picture, dialysis is not appropriate. In short, rationalization serves the function performed in ordinary markets by price—it equates

the amounts demanded with the amounts supplied.

Acknowledging Appropriateness of Limits

Some British physicians acknowledge resource constraints but justify them because their country is just not wealthy enough to do all that might be medically beneficial. In the words of the head of the intensive care unit at one of London's major teaching hospitals,[3] (p. 102),

[The number of intensive care beds has] to be appropriate to the surroundings. Now what we have by your standards is way short of the mark. It would be too small in America, but if you took this unit and put it down in Sri Lanka or India, it would stick out like a sore thumb. It would be an obscene waste of money.

Against this background, a leading oncologist described his thoughts about the problems that might be caused by development of a costly cure for a common form of cancer, metastatic carcinoma of the colon,[3] (p. 94)

It is something I wake up screaming about. I suspect that not everybody who might benefit from [therapy] would get it in practice. If you could cure every patient who has cancer of the colon, most of whom are going to be over 65, over 55 anyway, I think we might find ourselves making value judgments about which to treat and which not to.

Safety Valves for the Disaffected

The professional and managerial classes in Britain are less willing to accept "no" for an answer than are other social classes. Many routinely seek such elective care as hip replacement, elective abortions, or hernia repair outside the National Health Service (NHS) by paying for such care either directly or with private insurance, which about 10 percent of the British now have.[18]

Although blatant corruption is apparently rare, aggressive or influential patients can often secure referrals from general practitioners for a second opinion at specialized centers or by going directly to emergency rooms for services that local doctors deem "unsuitable." As a result, per capita expenditures by the National Health Services were reported to be 41 percent higher for members of the upper two socioeconomic groups (professionals, employers, and managers) than for members of the "lowest" two classes. [19] Such safety valves help explain the continued popularity of the NHS.

Rationing in the United States

Health care rationing in the United States has moved from the realm of academic speculation to practical reality during the 1980s. Its role is likely to grow in the future. The introduction of DRGs signaled that government would not reimburse hospitals for any and all costs they might incur for Medicare patients. While initial DRG reimbursements were generous and imposed onerous choices on few hospitals, annual adjustments have been insufficient to cover both inflation and the added costs of new technology. As a result, the margin between hospital income and expenditures has narrowed. [20] In addition, many private insurance companies have begun to require prior approval for reimbursement for various diagnostic and therapeutic procedures.

In perhaps the most dramatic instance of avowed rationing, the legislature of the state of Oregon announced in February 1988 that it would not pay for organ transplants for patients under the Medicaid program because, in the view of the legislature, the same funds would provide greater benefits if devoted to prenatal services and because the legislature was unprepared to pay for both. Following this announcement, the Oregon legislature sought the opinions of various groups on the relative priorities that should be attached to different medical interventions and of the cost of providing all care with priority scores above specified levels. With this information in hand, the legislature plans to decide how much it can spend per capita under the Medicaid program. It will then solicit bids at that cost from providers prepared to provide care under the Medicaid program for all eligible patients. The per capita allowance will require providers to limit services to those that fit within the predetermined spending level—in short, to ration care. The Oregon procedure underscores the

fact that every other state already limits the range of services provided to Medicaid patients and denies reimbursement for all services to low-income households who are ineligible for Medicaid. The strongest evidence that the United States will have to ration care if it wishes to slow growth of health care spending on a sustained basis comes from the creativity of medical scientists, who continue to develop new services that promise both significant benefits for large numbers of people and large added costs for public and private budgets. Indeed, the flow of technological innovation shows little sign of abating and may be accelerating. Some permit previously impossible interventions. Others reduce the discomfort or risk associated with previous procedures. Even if a given diagnostic service is less costly per patient, total outlays may rise because the noninvasive nature of such technologies frees the physician from the need to balance pain or risk to the patient against the value of information to be gained. Still other advances improve previously available therapies, sometimes at great cost. The following advances illustrate both the potential value and cost of emerging medical technologies.

Magnetic resonance imaging is the latest addition to the list of diagnostic devices that provide useful information noninvasively. But other expensive technologies, such as positron emission tomography and magnetic resonance spectroscopy are already in limited use and can be expected to be applied with increasing frequency.

Other costly emerging technologies include erythropoietin, a hormone that stimulates production of red blood cells. This drug has become available for treatment of severe anemia associated with chronic renal failure. Given that roughly 80,000 of the 106,000 patients undergoing chronic dialysis are suitable for this treatment, [21,22] and that the estimated cost is $10,000 per patient year, [23] the annual cost from this new drug will approach three-quarters of $1 billion. Because it is also likely to be valuable in the treatment of anemia associated with AIDS and cancer, the total cost will eventually be much larger.

A second example is the automatic implantable cardiac defibrillator, a device that is activated when the heart develops life-threatening arrhythmia. Expert opinion suggests that given the likely diffusion of the technology, there will be about 20,000 potential candidates for this therapy annually. At a total cost per patient of about $46,000 ($16,000 for the device and $30,000 for the hospitalization and surgical implantation), the annual cost would be about $1 billion. [24]

The recent finding that AZT can delay the onset of AIDS in patients who test positive for human immunodeficiency virus opens up a new use for this drug. The estimated cost for this therapy is $5 billion annually. [25]

Some advances bring demonstrable improvements in traditional procedures, but at great cost. Radiopaque contrast media are used in about 10 million x-ray examinations per year. [26] Fatal reactions to this material are rare, but perhaps 300 deaths per year could be prevented by the use of a new low-osmolar agent that is ten times as expensive as those now in use. [26] The cost of this switch would be about $1 billion, or more than $3 million per life saved. [26]

The successful development of an artificial heart promises to have an equally large impact. Some 30,000 potential recipients per year would add $3 billion to $4 billion to expenditures, and follow-up care would increase this estimate substantially. [27]

Other therapies, at an earlier stage of development than those just listed, also promise to boost costs. Such treatments include gene therapy, proton beam accelerators, tissue growth factors, and monoclonal antibodies. It is apparent that the advances now coming on stream, together with those now in development, will quickly overwhelm any one-time savings that can be achieved by eliminating useless care.

In addition to higher costs that advancing technology will imply for the large majority of the U.S. population with insurance, measures to extend health insurance to the roughly 15 percent of the population currently without it would also add to the growth of total health spending. The increase in costs would be less than proportional, however, for two reasons. First, about 22.8 percent of the uninsured had incomes of at least $30,000 per year in 1986.[28] Such households no doubt directly pay for many health services already. Second, even those who are too poor to pay anything themselves now receive some care. The cost of this care is now covered in a variety of ways—through taxes, charitable contributions in cash or in kind, and through premiums for the insured that are inflated to cover the costs of uncompensated care.

Although nonprice rationing seems inevitable if the growth of health care spending is to be slowed, it is unlikely that the United States ever would impose limits as severe as those common in Britain. Patients and physicians in the United States enjoy a well-merited reputation for demanding and supplying aggressive, high-quality treatment. Furthermore, cost containment is likely to increase the frequency of malpractice claims by discouraging physicians from providing some services that would otherwise be deemed appropriate. U.S. courts have explicitly stated that although cost consciousness has become an important feature of the U.S. health care system, both insurers and providers can be held responsible "when medically inappropriate decisions result from defects in the design or implementation of cost containment mechanisms. . . ."[29] In the conflict between cost containment and standards of care, the mandate for cost containment is likely to prevail, but not without turmoil.

Concluding Remarks

Growth of medical costs will be contained on a sustained basis only if we are prepared to ration care to those who are insured and are able and willing to pay for services. If we choose this road, we shall have to face many of the issues with which the British have grappled.

Concern for fundamental values such as age, visibility of an illness, and aggregate costs of treatment will inevitably shape our decisions on resource allocation. Physicians and other providers will increasingly experience tension between their historic commitment to doing all that is medically beneficial and

the limitations imposed on them by increasingly stringent cost limits. And we can almost certainly expect a substantial fraction of our society, much larger than in Britain, to use whatever means are available to get care that is in short supply. Whether we allow a separate hospital sector to develop outside the constrained system will be a key policy issue and a difficult political decision.

We see the British experience not as a frightening deterrent to serious consideration of rationing. Rather the British experience with rationing, particularly stark because of its severity, sharply delineates the kinds of choices we shall have to make. Understanding how the British made these decisions can help us find ways to make our less extreme but still painful choices acceptable. The current cost of excessive spending on services providing only small benefits is enormous and is certain to grow. The stakes in evolving politically and socially acceptable methods of curtailing such outlays are enormous.

Notes

1. S. W. Letsch, K. R. Levit, D. R. Waldo, *Health Care Fin. Rev.* 10, 109 (1988); P. Feldstein, *Health Care Economics* (Wiley, New York, ed. 3, 1988).
2. *Health Care Fin. Rev.* 8, 1 (1987).
3. H. J. Aaron and W. B. Schwartz, *The Painful Prescription: Rationing Hospital Care* (Brookings, Washington, DC, 1984).
4. D. Callahan, *Setting Limits: Medical Goals in an Aging Society* (Simon and Schuster, New York, 1987); R. H. Blank, *Rationing Medicine* (Columbia Univ. Press, New York, 1988).
5. W. J. Baumol, *Am. Econ. Rev.* 57, 415 (1967); W. J. Baumol and W. G. Bowen, *Performing Arts: The Economic Dilemma* (Twentieth Century Fund, New York, 1966).
6. C. R. Fisher, *Health Care Fin. Rev.* 1, 65 (1980).
7. W. B. Schwartz and P. L. Joskow, *N. Engl. J. Med.* 303, 1449(1980).
8. W. G. Manning, et al., ibid. 310, 1505 (1984).
9. J. P. Newhouse et al., ibid. 305, 1501 (1981); W. B. Schwartz, *J. Am. Med. Assoc.* 257, 220 (1987); W. P. Welch, *J. Health Econ.* 4, 293 (1985).
10. C. M. Winslow et al., *J. Am. Med. Assoc.* 260, 505 (1988); *N. Engl. J. Med.* 318, 721 (1988); *J. Am. Med. Assoc.* 260, 505 (1988).
11. W. B. Schwartz, *N. Eng. J. Med.* 305, 1249 (1981).
12. L. B. Russell, *Medicare's New Payment System: Is it Working?* (Brookings, Washington, DC, 1989).
13. A. C. Enthoven, *Health Care Fin. Rev.* (1986), annual suppl., p. 105; W. McClure, *Business Health* 2, 41 (1985).
14. D. U. Himmelstein and S. Woolhandler [*N. Engl. J. Med.* 314, 441 (1986)] estimate that the United States could have saved $29.2 billion to $38.4 billion of the $77.7 billion spent on health care administration in 1983.
15. Organization for Economic Cooperation and Development, *Financing and Delivering Health Care: A Comparative Analysis of OECD Countries* (Paris, 1987).
16. V. Fuchs, *Who Shall Live* (Basic Books, New York, 1983).
17. I. T. Wood, N. P. Mallick, A. J. Wing, *Brit. Med. J.* 294, 1467 (1987).
18. *Britain 1989: An Official Handbook* (Her Majesty's Stationery Office, London, 1989).
19. J. LeGrand, *Economica* 45, 125 (1978).
20. Committee on Ways and Means, U.S. House of Representatives, "Background material and data on programs within the jurisdiction of the committee on ways and means" (Government Printing Office, Washington, DC, 1989), p. 289.
21. Health Care Finance Administration, "The end stage renal disease program and medical information system" (Washington, DC, 1988), facility survey tables as of 31 December 1988.
22. Ad Hoc Committee for the National Kidney Foundation, Am. *J. Kidney Disease* 14, 163 (1989).
23. J. W. Eschbach and J. W. Adamson, *J. Blood Purif.*, in press.
24. G. C. Larsen et al., *Med. Decision Making* 9, 324 (1989).
25. P. S. Arno, D. Shenson, N. F. Siegel, P. Franks, P. R. Lee, *J. Am. Med. Assoc.* 262, 1493 (1989).
26. P. D. Jacobson and C. J. Rosenquist, ibid. 260, 1586 (1988).
27. R. W. Evans, *Issues Sci. Technol.* (Spring 1986), p. 91.
28. D. Chollet, *Uninsured in the United States: The Nonelderly Population Without Health Insurance, 1986* (Employee Benefit Research Institute, Washington, DC, 1988).
29. *Wickline v. State of California*, Calif. Rep. 228, 661 (1986).
30. G. J. Schieber and J. Poullier, *Health Affairs* 7, 105 (1988).
31. Several of the studies cited in this article were supported by grants from the Robert Wood Johnson Foundation and the Commonwealth Fund.

II
The Issues

A Changing Patterns of Morbidity
and Efficacy

B Financing Strategies and Incentives

C Rationing, Access to Health Care
Services, and the Uninsured

D The Delivery System and System
Administration

17

A Controlled Trial of the Effect of a Prepaid Group Practice on Use of Services

Willard G. Manning, Arleen Leibowitz, George A. Goldberg, William H. Rogers, and Joseph P. Newhouse

Health-maintenance organizations have been advocated for many years as an important innovation in medical-care delivery; indeed, for a decade, federal legislation and subsidies have encouraged their formation. Previous studies played a large part in persuading the Congress and the executive branch to promote enrollment in HMOs. They indicated that the prepaid-group-practice variant of HMOs has ambulatory-visit rates similar to those in fee-for-service medicine but has hospital admission rates that are as much as 40 percent lower[1-4]—a prospect with wide appeal.

However, a cloud of doubt has lingered concerning the ability of HMOs to keep the promise of reduced cost. Virtually all studies comparing HMOs with fee-for-service medicine have used a self-selected sample—that is, they compared persons who had voluntarily chosen an HMO with those who either had opted for fee-for-service medicine or had had no choice. If persons choosing an HMO were healthier than those choosing the fee-for-service system, the observed reduced use of HMOs could simply have been an artifact. Indeed, the single previous randomized study

found that one prepaid group practice did lower hospital use but had sufficiently higher use of ambulatory care to make it significantly more expensive overall.[5] This finding, however, has not dimmed enthusiasm for prepaid group practices, perhaps because the particular plan studied was small and just beginning.

To isolate the relation between prepayment and use of services, we have conducted a controlled trial in one well-established prepaid group practice. Specifically, we sought to answer two questions. First, when persons previously receiving care from fee-for-service physicians are randomly assigned to receive care at a prepaid group practice, how does their use differ from that of persons who remain with fee-for-service physicians? Second, when persons previously receiving care from fee-for-service providers are randomly assigned to receive care at a prepaid group practice, how does their use differ from the use of persons who are already enrolled in the prepaid plan?

The prepaid group practice that we studied, Group Health Cooperative of Puget Sound (GHC), is located in Seattle, Washington. It was established in 1947 and currently has an enrollment of 324,000 people—about 15 percent of the Seattle-area population. Its history has been described elsewhere.[6] In 1976, at the beginning of our study, GHC owned its own hospital; in 1977 it opened a second hospital.

Methods

Design of the Trial

We compared four groups. The first three were samples of the Seattle-area population who were not enrolled in GHC in 1976 but who were otherwise eligible for the trial. Ineligible persons included those over 62 years of age at the time of enrollment, Seattle-area families with incomes of more than $56,000 in 1983 dollars (this excluded 1 percent of the families contacted), those who were institutionalized, members of the military and their dependents, veterans with service-connected disabilities, and those eligible for Medicare disability or the end-stage renal-dialysis programs.

Participants in the first two groups were assigned to plans that covered virtually all health services from fee-for-service physicians and ancillary personnel, such as speech therapists. In the first group the services were provided at no cost to the participant; this plan is referred to as the "free fee-for-service plan." In the second sample, participants had to share the costs of their medical care. They paid 25 or 95 percent of their medical bills, subject in most cases to a limit on out-of-pocket expenditure of up to $1,000 per family (less for the poor). In the individual-deductible plan, however, participants paid 95 percent of outpatient bills, up to $150 per person or $450 per family per year; all inpatient services were free. Partici-

Reprinted with permission from *The New England Journal of Medicine* 310, no. 23 (June 7, 1984), pp. 1505–10. Copyright © 1984 by the Massachusetts Medical Society.

pants in these first two groups formed part of the sample we had studied previously to assess the effects of cost sharing on use of services and health outcomes.[7,8]

Participants in the third group, the GHC experimental group, received free services at GHC. If the Cooperative did not provide a service (e.g., chiropractic), the plan offered full coverage for provision of the service outside GHC. If participants, on their own, sought outside care for a service that GHC provided, they were reimbursed only 5 percent of the cost. However, referrals that GHC made to fee-for-service providers, as well as emergency out-of-area care, were fully covered. Except for the restriction to GHC providers and facilities, the benefits received by the GHC experimental group were identical to those received by the free fee-for-service group.

Although there was an element of randomization in the assignment of families to the fee-for-service and GHC experimental groups, a statistical method analogous to stratification was used to obtain greater comparability among the three groups than would be expected if simple random assignment were used.[9]

The fourth group used in our analysis was a random sample of GHC members in 1976 who otherwise met the eligibility requirements described above and had been enrolled in the Cooperative for at least one year. Hereafter, we refer to this group as the GHC controls. Participants in this group remained in whatever benefit plan they were enrolled in at the start of the experiment. Although control participants received most services free of charge, some involved moderate cost sharing.

At enrollment the free fee-for-service group consisted of 431 persons (162 families), the cost-sharing fee-for-service group consisted of 782 persons (319 families), the GHC experimental group consisted of 1149 persons (448 families), and the GHC control group consisted of 733 persons (301 families). Refusals to participate and sample loss after enrollment, although differing by group, did not appear to affect any of our qualitative conclusions.

The GHC control group was enrolled in the study for five years; half the GHC experimental group was enrolled for five years, and the remainder for three years; and 25 percent of the fee-for-service sample was enrolled for five years, and the remainder for three years. Assignment to three- or five-year participation was made at random. In analyses not shown in this paper we have found that use rates did not differ significantly between the three- and five-year groups, so we have combined them in the analyses presented here.[10] The sample used in our analyses consisted of originally enrolled participants while they remained in the experiment and in the Seattle area.

Measurement of Use

Data on use at GHC are from abstracted GHC records.[11] Data on out-of-plan use, in the case of the GHC groups, as well as all data on use by the fee-for-service participants, come from claim forms filed with the experiment, which functioned as the participants' insurance company.

We compared the number of visits and the number of admissions, but such a partial comparison does not detect any differential intensity of service per visit or per admission between GHC and fee-for-service participants. Therefore, we constructed a measure of intensity, which we call "imputed expenditure." Our method for calculating imputed expenditure differed for hospital services and physician services. For admissions at the GHC hospitals, we used the dollar figure that GHC would have charged, had it billed the services to a payer outside the Cooperative. (GHC does bill for some admissions; two common instances are emergency admissions of nonenrollees and Workman's Compensation cases.) For admissions at fee-for-service hospitals, we used the hospital's actual billed charges.

In the case of physician services, we compared the number of California Relative Value Studies units that GHC and fee-for-service physicians delivered.[12] To arrive at an imputed-expenditure figure, we valued units in both systems at the same dollar figure.

In addition to comparing the rates at which the participants saw physicians, we compared the rates of preventive-care visits in the various plans. Preventive care included any "well-care" service other than vision, hearing, and prenatal care. Well-care services were defined by the physician's diagnosis, by the use of certain procedures (e.g., immunizations), or by a preventive-treatment-history code, in conjunction with the patient's indication that the reason for the visit was preventive care. We used the patient's reason for the visit because we feared that some fee-for-service physicians might fail to label some visits as preventive (because many standard health-insurance plans, although not ours, do not reimburse for preventive services). Any such failure in labeling would bias a comparison of the amount of preventive care the various groups received.

Analytical Methods

We generally calculated sample means (analysis of variance) for each of the four groups. Work reported elsewhere shows that adjustment for participant characteristics did not qualitatively affect any of our conclusions.[10]

In the estimation of imputed expenditure, however, we have obtained a worthwhile gain in precision by including age and sex as covariates. The values for imputed expenditure in Table 1, however, are not corrected for any age and sex differences among the four groups. In particular, any effects from the control group's slightly higher mean age and number of female subjects are reflected in the values in Table 1. We have corrected all standard errors for intertemporal and intrafamilial correlation.[10]

Results

Although the GHC experimental and control groups differed little with respect to imputed expenditure on medical services, they both differed markedly from the free fee-for-service group (Table 1). Imputed expenditures were 28 percent lower in the GHC experimental group than in the free fee-for-service group ($P<0.01$) and about 23 percent lower in the GHC control group ($P<0.05$).

The magnitude of the expenditure reduction at GHC was comparable to that achieved by 95 percent coinsurance in the fee-for-service system, although the means by which expenditure was reduced were considerably different. The percentage of GHC enrollees seeking care was comparable to or even exceeded the percentage in the free fee-for-service plan; GHC had a lower expenditure than the free fee-for-service plan because fewer GHC enrollees were admitted to the hospital. With 95 percent coinsurance, the percentage of enrollees seeking care, as well as the percentage admitted to the hospital, was notably lower than the percentage of participants in the free fee-for-service plan. The reduction in use appears to have been largest in the individual-deductible plan, even though inpatient services were free in this plan. However, the difference in expenditure between the individual-deductible plan and the other two cost-sharing plans was not significant and could well have reflected random variation; if data from three other sites are combined with these data, enrollees in the individual-deductible plan spent more (but not significantly more) than those enrolled in the 95 percent coinsurance plan. [7]

The differences between GHC and the fee-for-service plans come even more sharply into focus when we examine admissions, hospital days, and visit rates (Table 2). There were 40 percent fewer admissions (P<0.01) and hospital days in the two GHC groups than in the free fee-for-service plan, but face-to-face visits occurred at the same rate in all three plans. In contrast, all the cost-sharing plans had both lower admission rates and lower visit rates than the free fee-for-service plan. The differences in total expenditure and admission rates between the 95 percent coinsurance plan and the two GHC groups were not significant at the 5 percent level, but the differences in the rate of face-to-face visits were significant at this level.

Although the overall rates of face-to-face visits were similar for the two GHC groups and the free fee-for-service plan, the number of preventive visits was significantly higher in the two GHC groups; cost sharing further reduced preventive visits, to a level below the values in the free fee-for-service plan (Table 2).

Use of non-GHC services by the two GHC groups was relatively limited (Table 3). Not surprisingly, participants in the experimental group were more

Table 1. Comparison of Likelihood of Using any Service, Likelihood of Hospitalization, and Imputed Annual Expenditure among the Group Health Cooperative (GHC) and Fee-for-Service Plans.*

PLAN	USE OF INPATIENT OR OUTPATIENT SERVICE IN YEAR	ONE OR MORE HOSPITALIZATIONS IN YEAR	IMPUTED ANNUAL EXPENDITURE PER PARTICIPANT (1983 DOLLARS) [†]
	% of participants		
GHC experimental	86.8	7.1	439
	(1.0)	(0.50)	(25)
GHC control	91.0	6.4	469
	(0.8)	(0.55)	(44)
Fee-for-service			
Free	85.3	11.1	609
	(1.6)	(1.17)	(66)
25%	76.1	8.8	620
	(2.7)	(1.37)	(103)
95%	68.4	8.5	459
	(3.4)	(1.18)	(72)
Individual deductible	73.9	7.9	413
	(2.4)	(0.96)	(51)

*The sample consists of all participants present at enrollment, while they remained in the Seattle area. Except for decedents, observations on partial years of participation have been deleted. Standard errors are in parentheses.

†Values include both in-plan and out-of-plan use by GHC participants. The method of imputing expenditure is described in the text and in the Appendix. The t statistics for the difference in expenditure between the GHC experimental group and the five groups listed below it are 0.87, 3.22, 2.22, 0.30, and −0.56, respectively. Because of the inclusion of age and sex as covariates, these t statistics are larger than those that would be calculated from the standard errors shown in the table.

likely than controls to seek care outside GHC. About 2 percent of the experimental group sought care each year exclusively from ancillary providers, such as speech therapists, chiropractors, Christian Science practitioners, and podiatrists. Half the out-of-plan admissions were related to accidents or to psychiatric diagnoses.

Discussion

The Literature on Prepaid Group Practice

Our results show minor and generally insignificant differences between the two GHC groups, suggesting that results from noncontrolled studies may not be seriously contaminated by selection effects. In particular, imputed expenditures were 6 percent lower in the experimental group than in the control group. In view of the standard errors for these expenditure figures, which were between 5 and 10 percent of the mean, it is unlikely that there was a large difference between the groups.

The validity of our results is strengthened by their general consistency with the results in the literature regarding

prepaid group practices. Luft's review of several noncontrolled studies found that such practices had 10 to 40 percent fewer hospitalizations than fee-for-service practices. [3,4] In our study, GHC controls were 40 percent less likely to go into the hospital than those in the free fee-for-service group and about 5 to 20 percent less likely to be admitted than those in the cost-sharing groups.

It is plausible that the difference in admission rates between the GHC control group and the free fee-for-service group should be as large as differences observed in the literature. The free fee-for-service plan had better ambulatory benefits than virtually all fee-for-service plans described in the literature, and more extensive coverage of ambulatory services leads to more hospitalization among those using fee-for-service physicians. [7] For the same reason, the difference between the admission rates in the GHC control group and in the cost-sharing plans should be near the low end of Luft's range.

Outpatient-visit rates among GHC controls were not significantly higher than rates in the free fee-for-service plan but were significantly higher than those in the cost-sharing plans (P<0.01). Luft found roughly similar results among a

Table 2. Annual Rates of Admission and Face-to-Face Visits.*

PLAN	ADMISSION RATE †	HOSPITAL DAYS	FACE-TO-FACE VISITS ‡	PREVENTIVE VISITS §
	per 100 persons		*per person*	
GHC experimental	8.4	49	4.3	0.55
	(0.67)	(9.6)	(0.14)	(0.02)
GHC control	8.3	38	4.7	0.60
	(1.01)	(9.0)	(0.17)	(0.02)
Fee-for-service				
Free	13.8	83	4.2	0.41
	(1.51)	(26)	(0.25)	(0.03)
25%	10.0	87	3.5	0.32
	(1.43)	(28)	(0.35)	(0.03)
95%	10.5	46	2.9	0.29
	(1.68)	(9.9)	(0.34)	(0.04)
Individual deductible	8.8	28	3.3	0.27
	(1.20)	(5.1)	(0.33)	(0.03)

*The sample includes all participants present at enrollment, while they remained in the Seattle area. For GHC control and experimental groups the data include both in- and out-of-plan use. Standard errors are in parentheses.

†A count of all continuous periods of inpatient treatment.

‡Includes all visits involving face-to-face contact with health providers for which a separate charge would have been made in the fee-for-service system. Excludes radiology, pathology, prenatal and postnatal care, speech therapy, psychotherapy, dental care, chiropractic, podiatry, Christian Science healing, and telephone contacts.

§Includes well-child care, immunizations, screening examinations, routine physical and gynecologic examinations, and visits involving Pap smears (other than for an established diagnosis of cancer). Excludes visits for prenatal care, vision, and hearing. In the case of GHC, includes in-plan and out-of-plan visits.

Table 3. Annual Use of Services Outside GHC.*

TYPE OF USE	GHC EXPERIMENTAL GROUP	GHC CONTROL GROUP
Hospital admissions (per 100 persons) †	0.74 (0.26)	0.21 (0.09)
Hospital-days (per 100 persons)	15 ¶ (9)	1.4 (0.8)
Ambulatory face-to-face visits (per person) ‡	0.14 (0.02)	0.08 (0.02)
Visits to chiropractors, podiatrists, Christian Science practitioners (per person)	0.72 (0.12)	0.12 (0.06)
Visits to speech therapists (per person) §	0.0002 (0.0002)	0.007 (0.006)
Expenditures per person (1983 dollars) §	63 (13)	15 (5)

*The sample includes all participants present at enrollment, while they remained in the Seattle area. Standard errors are in parentheses.

†Comparison significant at P<0.05.

‡A face-to-face visit was one for which a separate charge would have been made in the fee-for-service system. Excludes radiology and pathology and visits involving pregnancy, speech therapy, psychotherapy, chiropractic, podiatry, and Christian Science healing. Comparison significant at P<0.05.

§Comparison significant at P<0.01.

¶One case accounts for two thirds of this mean; inpatient psychiatric cases account for one sixth of it.

variety of studies he reviewed.[3] Thus, the comparison of use in the GHC control group with use in the fee-for-service groups resembles comparisons in the literature and lends support to the validity of the findings for the GHC experimental group.

The Lower Hospitalization Rate at GHC

Services delivered in the hospital account for about half of all U.S. expenditures on personal health services.[13] That GHC could lower the hospitalization

rate so markedly relative to the free fee-for-service group invites closer scrutiny. What could be the explanation? In order to achieve sharply lower hospitalization rates, GHC may have been providing more preventive care or treating more cases on an outpatient basis and avoiding hospitalization. The data examined to date do not provide any clear explanation for the lower hospitalization rate at GHC. Although preventive visits were more numerous at GHC than in the fee-for-service plans, the hospitalization rates were not significantly different from those in the fee-for-service cost-sharing plans, which had only about half as many preventive visits as the GHC groups. Moreover, about two thirds of the preventive visits were for well-child care or gynecologic examinations. Because gynecologic and pediatric admissions represent a minority of hospitalizations, it seems unlikely that preventive care accounted for much of the large difference in hospitalization rates. Indeed, despite the concentration of preventive care among children, the percentage reduction in admission rates among children was similar to the percentage reduction among adults $X^2_5 = 3.83$, P>0.50, Table 4).

Outpatient-visit rates in the two GHC groups were similar to those in the free fee-for-service group; if some problems for which fee-for-service participants were hospitalized were being managed on an outpatient basis at GHC, one might expect such rates to be higher. Of course, the similar outpatient-visit rates at GHC could have been the result of more intensive outpatient treatment of those whom fee-for-service physicians would have hospitalized, combined with less intensive treatment of those who would not have been admitted in any event. Further investigation will be required to address this possibility.

How Many Dollars Would Be Saved if HMO Enrollment Increased?

The 28 percent difference in imputed expenditure between the GHC experimental plan and the free fee-for-service plan is striking (Table 1). However, one can ask how much error the imputation process might have introduced. Although a more detailed analysis could yield a more precise figure, it seems unlikely that the true difference could have been much less than 25 percent. Both admissions and total hospital days were 40 percent lower at GHC than in the free fee-for-service plan (Table 2), and ambulatory-visit rates were similar. How many dollars might such a reduction in use save? First of all, suppose the reduction in admissions was random. In that case inpatient expenditure, which accounted for somewhat over half the total expenditure,[7] would fall by 40 percent. If ambulatory expenditure in the two systems was similar, the total expenditure would fall by about a quarter, as our imputed figures indicate.

But suppose the 40 percent reduction in admissions was not random but rather was disproportionately made up of short-stay admissions. This would suggest that GHC also reduced the length of stay among patients it admitted. Otherwise, the reduction in hospital days would have been less than 40 percent. A combination of reduced admissions and reduced length of stay that together yielded a 40 percent reduction in hospital days could certainly have caused a true reduction in expenditure by approximately 25 percent.

Moreover, our method does not account for any efficiencies GHC may have enjoyed in the delivery of physician services, such as greater substitution of paramedical personnel. To estimate the magnitude of such efficiencies, if there are any, would require a study of costs within each system—something we did not attempt. Nonetheless, it is difficult to escape the conclusion that the true expenditure was substantially lower in the two GHC groups than in the free fee-for-service group.

One might question whether the free fee-for-service plan is a relevant reference group. Few individuals in the population who use fee-for-service physicians do so without sharing the cost; therefore, one might adopt the cost-sharing plans as a standard of comparison. In the case of the 95 percent coinsurance plans, the differences between GHC and the fee-for-service system narrow sharply.

Table 4. Likelihood of One or More Admissions per Year among Children and Adults.*

PLAN	CHILDREN (<18 YR)	ADULTS (≥18 YR)
	per cent	
GHC experimental	3.5 (0.56)	9.2 (0.68)
GHC control	3.6 (0.70)	7.8 (0.73)
Fee-for-service		
Free	6.2 (1.13)	13.7 (1.71)
25%	5.8 (1.92)	10.6 (1.62)
95%	3.2 (1.08)	11.6 (1.62)
Individual deductible	6.0 (1.64)	8.7 (1.26)

*The sample consists of all participants present at enrollment, while they remained in the Seattle area. Except for decedents, observations on partial years of participation have been deleted. A chi-squared value for comparability of response is 3.8 with 5 df, P>0.50. Standard errors are in parentheses.

Does this mean that if the current proportion of the population enrolled in prepaid group practices (5 percent) were to increase markedly, use of the hospital would not change much? In fact, one might expect considerably less hospitalization as the HMO market share grows, because the national hospitalization rate is not far from the free-plan value. In a previous analysis of fee-for-service data from four sites (including Seattle), we found that the annual likelihood of one or more hospitalizations among average Americans under age 65 was 9.5 percent, which is close to the free-plan value of 10.2 percent, whereas the values in the cost-sharing plans ranged from 7.2 to 9.0 percent.[7] Because the national average appears to be close to the free-plan rate, our data suggest the potential for a substantial drop in use of inpatient services.

On the other hand, the reduced cost of prepaid group practices that is due to lower use of inpatient services will be partially offset by the increased use of ambulatory services, as compared with current levels of use in fee-for-service cost-sharing plans. National ambulatory-visit rates fall between the rates observed in the 25 percent and 95 percent fee-for-service plans.[7] On balance, the net effect from increased enrollment in prepaid group practices would still be a saving, unless cost sharing in the fee-for-service system were to increase above present levels.

Policy Implications

Plainly, there was much less hospitalization among study participants receiving care at GHC than among those with similar benefits (i.e., no cost sharing) who received care from fee-for-service physicians. Because of our experimental design, we can virtually rule out population characteristics as an explanation of the lower hospitalization rate at GHC. We conclude that GHC physicians were simply practicing a different style of medicine from that of fee-for-service physicians. Although our study was limited to a single, not necessarily typical prepaid group practice, the general consistency between our results and those in the literature indicates that a less "hospital-intensive" style of medicine than that practiced by the average physician is possible.[3,14]

But is such a style desirable? The results presented above shed little light on this question. We have obtained extensive measures of the health status of our participants,[8,15-18] and future analysis of these data should detect any pronounced effects of the different style of medical treatment on health status. Nonetheless, prepaid group practices have existed for decades, and it seems unlikely that there can be large deleterious health effects from their style of medicine.

In contrast, the different style could well affect patient satisfaction. Indeed, because many persons choose not to enroll in a prepaid group practice, it seems almost certain that th!eir expected level of satisfaction, were they to join, would be lower than in fee-for-service medicine. To be sure, some may decline the option to join because they receive no cost advantage (e.g., the employer pays the entire health-insurance premium). However, others pay more to receive their care from the fee-for-service system, and one can surmise that they believe they receive something in return.

Whatever the motivation of those choosing the fee-for-service system, many observers argue that such persons ought to pay all the additional costs. [19,20] For this to occur, employers (or the government) would have to pay an equal sum for each available health-plan option instead of paying more for a fee-for-service plan than an HMO plan, as many do now. If employers did pay an equal sum, price competition between HMOs and fee-for-service insurance plans could well increase.

Some fear that increased price competition without regulation of benefit packages will bring risk selection—that is, better risks in one plan than in another. [19] We found no appreciable difference in use between the GHC experimental and control groups, suggesting that there was no risk selection in this case. Nonetheless, this result may not be generalizable. Economic theory suggests that risk selection can occur if individuals know more about their future health demands than do insuring organizations or HMOs, [21–23] and other studies have found evidence of risk selection. [3,24]

In sum, GHC delivered a different, less-expensive style of medicine than did fee-for-service practitioners in the Seattle area when both treated comparable groups receiving free care. Adding cost sharing to the fee-for-service insurance plans brought expenditures more closely into line with those of GHC but appeared to result in yet another style of care, one with markedly fewer ambulatory contacts. How the GHC style fares on dimensions other then expense remains an open question, but the lower

expense at GHC cannot be explained by differences in the population that it treats.

We are indebted to our Rand colleagues Rae Archibald, Robert Brook, Marie Brown, Maureen Carney, Allyson Davies, Naihua Duan, Emmett Keeler, and Ken Krug, to our former colleagues Carl Morris and Marshall Rockwell, Jr., to William Schwartz of Tufts University, and to our past and present DHHS project officers Larry Orr and James Schuttinga for helpful advice and comments over the years and for assistance in implementing the project; to Glen Slaughter, Cliff Wingo, Marilyn Hecox, Lauron Lindstrom, Judi Wilson, Tom Weston, and their colleagues at Glen Slaughter and Associates for processing claims and maintaining the status of the sample during the experiment; to Bernadette Benjamin and Jack Seinfeld for their meticulous programming and data management; and to the Group Health Cooperative of Puget Sound for agreeing to participate in the study and especially to Richard Handschin, its director of research during the study period, for assistance in the trial's implementation and comments on this manuscript. Neither the Cooperative nor any of the above individuals necessarily agrees with or endorses the findings reported here.

Supported by the Health Insurance Study grant (016B80) from the Department of Health and Human Services.

*See NAPS document no. 04193 for 10 pages of supplementary material. Order from NAPS c/o Microfiche Publications, P.O. Box 3513, Grand Central Station, New York, NY 10163. This material is presented in more detail in a report by Rand. [10]

Notes

1. Gaus CR, Cooper BS, Hirschman CG. Contrasts in HMO and fee-for-service performance. Soc Secur Bull 1976; 39(5):3–14.

2. Luft HS. Assessing the evidence on HMO performance. Milbank Mem Fund Q 1980; 58:501–36.

3. Idem. Health maintenance organizations: dimensions of performance. New York: John Wiley, 1981.

4. Idem. How do health-maintenance organizations achieve their "savings"?: rhetoric and evidence. N Engl J Med 1978; 298:1336–43.

5. Perkoff GT, Kahn L, Haas PJ. The effects of an experimental prepaid group practice on medical care utilization and cost. Med Care 1976; 14:432–49.

6. MacColl WA. Group practice and pre-

payment of medical care. Washington, D.C.: Public Affairs Press, 1966.

7. Newhouse JP, Manning WG, Morris CN, et al. Some interim results from a controlled trial of cost sharing in health insurance. N Engl J Med 1981; 305:1501–7.

8. Brook RH, Ware JE Jr, Rogers WH, et al. Does free care improve adults' health? Results from a randomized controlled trial. N Engl J Med 1983; 309:1426–34.

9. Morris CN. A finite selection model for experimental design of the health insurance study. J Econometrics 1979; 11:43–61.

10. Manning WG, Leibowitz A, Goldberg GA, Rogers WH, Newhouse JP. A controlled trial of the effect of a prepaid group practice on utilization. Santa Monica, Calif.: Rand Corporation 1984)).

11. Goldberg GA. The health insurance experiment's guidelines for abstracting health services rendered by Group Health Cooperative of Puget Sound. Santa Monica, Calif.: Rand Corporation, 1983. (Rand publication no. N–1948–HHS).

12. Committee on Relative Value Studies, California Medical Association. 1974 Revision of the 1969 California relative value studies. San Francisco: California Medical Association, Sutter Publications, 1975.

13. Waldo DR, Gibson RM. National health expenditures, 1981. Health Care Financ Rev 1982; 4(1):1–35.

14. Nobrega FT, Krishan I, Smoldt RK, et al. Hospital use in a fee-for-service system. JAMA 1982; 247:806–10.

15. Brook RH, Ware JE Jr, Davies-Avery A, et al. Overview of adult health status measures fielded in Rand's Health Insurance Study. Med Care 1979; 17(7): Suppl:1–131.

16. Eisen M, Donald CA, Ware JE, Brook RH. Conceptualization and measurement of health for children in the health insurance study. Santa Monica, Calif.: Rand Corporation, 1980. (Rand publication no. R–2313–HEW).

17. Conceptualization and measurement of physiologic health for adults. Santa Monica, Calif.: Rand Corporation. (Rand publication no. R–2262–HHS).

18. Measurement of physiologic health for children. Santa Monica, Calif.: Rand Corporation. (Rand publication no. R–2898–HHS).

19. Enthoven A. Health plan: the only practical solution to the soaring cost of medical care. Reading, Mass.: Addison-Wesley, 1980:70–92.

20. McClure W. Implementing a competitive medical care system through public policy. J Health Polit Policy Law 1982; 7:2–44.

21. Arnott R, Stiglitz J. Equilibrium in competitive insurance markets—the welfare economics of moral hazard. I. Basic analytics. Kingston, Ontario: Queens University, 1982. (Discussion paper 465)

22. Cave JAK. Equilibrium in insurance markets with incomplete information: adverse selection under asymmetric information. Santa Monica, California: Rand Corporation, April 1984. (Rand publication no. R–3015–HHS).

23. Rothschild M, Stiglitz J. Equilibrium in competitive insurance markets: an essay on the economics of imperfect information. Q J Econ 1976; 90:629–50.

24. Eggers P, Prihoda R. Pre-enrollment reimbursement patterns of Medicare beneficiaries enrolled in 'at-risk' HMOs. Health Care Financ Rev 1982; 4(1): 55–73.

18

Frequency and Costs of Diagnostic Imaging in Office Practice: A Comparison of Self-Referring and Radiologist-Referring Physicians

Bruce J. Hillman, Catherine A. Joseph, Michael R. Mabry,
Jonathan H. Sunshine, Stephen D. Kennedy,
and Monica Noether

The potential for conflicts of interest and higher costs for health care arising from the ownership by physicians of the diagnostic facilities to which they refer patients has attracted considerable attention recently in the medical literature[1-5] and lay press[6,7] and has been the subject of government study and legislation.[8-10] The ownership of imaging centers by physicians has received much of the media attention. However, most self-referral for medical imaging—in which physicians perform and interpret diagnostic imaging examinations of their own patients rather than refer them to imaging specialists—takes place in the physician's office.

The few previous studies investigating the effect of self-referral on the use and costs of imaging have been limited by methodologic flaws, small study populations, and lack of controls. To overcome these limitations, we analyzed a large data base of private insurance claims and evaluated the imaging done in physicians' offices during episodes of outpatient medical care. After controlling for differences in patients'

Reprinted with permission from *The New England Journal of Medicine* 323, no. 23 (December 6, 1990), pp. 1604–8. Copyright © 1990 by the Massachusetts Medical Society.

clinical presentations and physicians' specialties, we compared the frequencies with which the patients underwent imaging examinations during episodes of medical care for acute conditions, according to whether their physicians could perform those imaging examinations themselves. We also compared the resultant charges for the imaging examinations.

Methods

Selection of Data Base and Clinical Presentations

We purchased access to a data base (Medstat Systems, Ann Arbor, Michigan) comprising all the health insurance claims of 403,458 employees and dependents of several large American corporations. The insurance programs provided comprehensive coverage, including outpatient imaging services, with no copayments required. The data base was selected for its uniformity and completeness. Seventy-nine percent of the study population lived in the north central United States, 6 percent in the Northeast, 11 percent in the South, and 4 percent in the West. Fifty-one percent were female, and 49 percent male. Fifty-five percent were 0 to 34 years old, 33

percent were 35 to 54 years old, and 12 percent were 55 or older. Ninety-three percent of the physicians making claims for care provided to these patients practiced in metropolitan areas.

Using this data base, we compared the frequency of imaging and the charges for imaging among self-referring physicians and among physicians who instead referred patients to radiologists (radiologist-referring physicians) for four clinical presentations, selected for their variety and the volume of associated imaging procedures. The presentations, with the associated diagnostic inquiry, were as follows: acute upper respiratory symptoms (Was chest radiography performed?), pregnancy (Was obstetrical ultrasonography performed to assess fetal size and gestational age?), low back pain (Was radiography of the lumbar spine performed?), and (in men) difficulty urinating (Was excretory urography, cystography, or ultrasonography performed?).

Definition and Initiation of Episodes

We surveyed the *International Classification of Diseases, 9th Revision, Clinical Modification* (ICD-9-CM),[11] selecting all codes that might reasonably represent diagnoses that would be entered by physicians whose patients presented with symptoms related to any of the four clinical presentations. A detailed tabulation of the codes is available elsewhere.*

We developed and applied to the claims data base a computer algorithm, modeled on previous methods, for defining episodes of outpatient medical care occurring in physicians' offices. [12] The date of a claim for an index ICD-9-CM code in an office setting was used to define the starting date of an episode. Episodes were considered to have ended after specified periods—four weeks for upper respiratory infection, nine months for pregnancy, six weeks for low back pain, and six weeks for difficulty urinating. Claims made between the initiation and termination dates of an episode were eligible for inclusion in that episode. Depending on the clinical presentation, a lag period of two to eight weeks followed the termination of each episode, so that follow-up visits for the original episode would not be counted as new episodes of care. The length of the episodes and lag periods was initially proposed on the basis of medical experience. We ensured that these durations were appropriate by evaluating the completeness of 600 randomly selected episodes and determining that the use of alternate durations for the episodes of up to two-thirds longer affected the number of episodes by only 1 to 6 percent in the case of the clinical presentations studied.

To be included in the study, episodes of care had to begin after January 1, 1986, and end before June 1, 1988. Episodes were excluded if the only physician involved in the episode was a radiologist or if the specialty of any physician involved was unknown. Within valid episodes, we deleted any claims for which no charge or payment was made, any claims for supplemental payments, and any claims for which the age or sex of the patient or the physician's identification number was unknown. We also excluded claims that were unrelated in terms of ICD-9-CM coding to the clinical presentations under investigation and claims made by physicians whose specialty codes indicated practices unrelated to the clinical presentations under study. A list of the specialties of the physicians included in the analysis is available elsewhere.*

Categorization of Physicians and Classification of Episodes

The physicians who filed the claims included in the episodes studied were distinguished by their physician identification numbers; these numbers were coded to protect confidentiality. With regard to each clinical presentation, the physicians were grouped, according to their involvement in episodes for which they were the only nonradiologist physician to file a claim (one-physician episodes), into the following categories: self-referring physicians, who charged at least once for an index imaging examination; radiologist-referring physicians, who never charged for an index imaging examination and who were involved in at least one one-physician episode in which a radiologist performed such an examination; and physicians whose patients had no imaging in any one-physician episodes. One-physician episodes comprised 92 percent of all valid episodes.

We considered the possibility that some physicians categorized as radiologist-referring might actually be self-referring physicians who happened not to have performed any imaging in the episodes in our sample. We performed a correction to account for this possibility.* Since this correction did not alter the results, we report only our unadjusted data here.

The categorization of the physicians who participated in the one-physician episodes was used to develop six categories of similar and dissimilar pairs of physicians for the 7 percent of valid episodes in which two different physicians, neither a radiologist, cared for the patient (two-physician episodes). The 471 valid episodes (0.7 percent) in which more than two nonradiologist physicians were involved were not included in the analysis. We performed separate classifications of the one-physician and two-physician episodes on the basis of the categorization of the physicians and whether a claim for a related imaging examination was filed during the episode, as evidenced by the encountering of an appropriate diagnostic-imaging-procedure code.*

Estimation of the Frequency of Imaging

For the one-physician episodes, our estimates of the frequency of imaging by the self-referring physicians and the radiologist-referring physicians were based on the observed frequencies for these two categories of physicians. Applying maximum-likelihood methods to the information we derived from our data about the imaging practices of self-referring and radiologist-referring physicians, we adjusted these observed frequencies to account for the episodes attributable to the physicians who had performed no imaging. This adjustment was based on the assumption that the imaging practices of the physicians within each category were homogeneous. However, this was almost certainly not the case. As a result, the correct adjustment of the observed frequencies is uncertain. For this reason, we report here the most likely estimates of the imaging frequencies for the self-referring and the radiologist-referring physicians. In addition, to account for heterogeneity in the physicians' imaging practices, we developed estimates biased upward and downward that show that our results are not affected qualitatively by the choice of the adjustment for the episodes involving the physicians who performed no imaging over the entire range of possible adjustments. The methods we employed, the initial categorization of the physicians and classification of episodes, and the upward- and downward-biased estimations of imaging frequencies are available elsewhere.*

Statistical Analysis

For the analyses of both the one-physician and the two-physician episodes, we assessed the differences between self-referring and radiologist-referring physicians in terms of the proportion of episodes that involved imaging, the charges for imaging performed, and the average imaging charges per episode. To calculate the results for the group, we weighted the results for individual physicians according to the number of episodes in which they were involved. The significance of the differences between self-referring and radiologist-referring physicians was determined by the usual t-statistic for the difference in means between the two groups. We conducted a similar analysis based on the specialties of the physicians involved in the episodes, to compare differences within specialties. The null hypothesis of no difference was rejected at a P level of <0.05.

Complexity of Imaging Procedures

For each clinical presentation, we compared the complexity of the imaging examinations performed by the self-referring physicians with that of the examinations performed by the radiologists by calculating the mean (+/- SD) relative values of their procedures (i.e., a measure of the complexity of the procedure).[13]

Results

One-Physician Episodes

The data base generated 62,880 one-physician episodes for the four study groups. After exclusions (see Methods), there were 60,829 valid episodes involving 6,419 physicians. One-physician epi-sodes represented 92 percent of all valid episodes. These were distributed as follows: upper respiratory symptoms, 47,794 episodes involving 3,452 physicians; normal pregnancy, 1,377 episodes involving 468 physicians; back pain, 9,634 episodes involving 2,001 physicians; men with difficulty urinating, 2,024 episodes involving 498 physicians.

Table 1 shows the frequencies with which imaging was used during the episodes, the charges for imaging, and the charges for imaging per episode for self-referring and radiologist-referring physicians. The mean imaging charges of the self-referring physicians were significantly higher (P for all comparisons, <0.0001) than those of the radiologists for all clinical presentations except difficulty urinating. Depending on the

clinical presentation, the episodes involving self-referring physicians resulted in imaging 4.0 to 4.5 times as frequently, with average imaging charges per episode 4.4 to 7.5 times higher than those for the episodes involving radiologist-referring physicians (P<0.0001 for each clinical presentation, for both frequency of imaging and average imaging charges per episode).

Two-Physician Episodes

There were 4,688 valid two-physician episodes, or 7 percent of all episodes. The results for these episodes support the findings in the one-physician episodes. Depending on the clinical presentation, the episodes involving two self-referring physicians were 1.7 to 3.7 times as likely to result in imaging as episodes involving two radiologist-referring physicians (P<0.01 for each presentation). Complete results for all six categories of physician pairs are available elsewhere.*

Differences among Specialties

For each specialty and each clinical presentation, the self-referring physicians performed imaging 2.4 to 11.1 times as often as the radiologist-referring physicians, and at a cost per episode for imaging that was 3.0 to 17.1 times higher, depending on the specialty and clinical presentation (Table 2) (P<0.01 for each specialty studied with regard to each clinical presentation).

Complexity of Imaging Examinations

The mean (+/- SD) complexity score for chest films was 3.02 +/- 0.14 for self-referring physicians, and 3.00 +/- 0.20 for radiologist-referring physicians. For obstetrical ultrasonography, the comparison was 11.24 +/-1.14 versus 11.35 +/- 0.96; for lumbar spine films, 3.98 +/- 0.63 versus 4.14 +/- 0.52; and for the combination of urography, cystography, and ultrasonography, 8.46 +/- 0.70 versus 8.35 +/- 0.43. Thus, the differ-

Table 1. Categories of Physicians and Episodes, Frequencies of Imaging, and Imaging Costs in One-Physician Episodes.*

VARIABLE	SELF-REFERRAL	RADIOLOGIST-REFERRAL	SELF/RADIOLOGIST REFERRAL RATIO	P VALUE†
Upper respiratory symptoms				
Physicians (%)	38	62	0.6	—
Episodes (%)	57	43	1.3	—
Episodes with imaging (%)	46	11	4.2	0.0001
Mean charges ($)	54	40	1.4	0.0001
Mean charges per episode ($)	25	4	6.2	0.0001
Pregnancy				
Physicians (%)	48	52	0.9	—
Episodes (%)	56	44	1.3	—
Episodes with imaging (%)	59	13	4.5	0.0001
Mean charges ($)	304	185	1.6	0.0001
Mean charges per episode ($)	180	24	7.5	0.0001
Low back pain				
Physicians (%)	49	51	1.0	—
Episodes (%)	66	34	1.9	—
Episodes with imaging (%)	54	12	4.5	0.0001
Mean charges ($)	70	63	1.1	0.0001
Mean charges per episode ($)	38	8	4.8	0.0001
Difficulty urinating (men)				
Physicians (%)	38	62	0.6	—
Episodes (%)	46	54	0.8	—
Episodes with imaging (%)	32	8	4.0	0.0001
Mean charges ($)	264	241	1.1	0.14
Mean charges per episode ($)	84	19	4.4	0.0001

*Mean charges shown are for episodes with imaging. Mean charges per episode were calculated as the fraction of episodes with imaging times the mean imaging charges in episodes with imaging.

†P values are for the difference in values between self-referring and radiologist-referring physicians.

Table 2. Frequency of Imaging and Costs per Episode in One-Physician Episodes, According to the Specialty of the Physician.*

VARIABLE	UPPER RESPIRATORY SYMPTOMS		PREGNANCY		LOW BACK PAIN		DIFFICULTY URINATING (MEN)	
	SELF-REFERRAL	RADIOLOGIST-REFERRAL	SELF-REFERRAL	RADIOLOGIST-REFERRAL	SELF-REFERRAL	RADIOLOGIST-REFERRAL	SELF-REFERRAL	RADIOLOGIST-REFERRAL
General and family practice								
No. of episodes	14,913	5104	30	113	2919	1251	95	258
% with imaging	47	14	92	11	58	11	83	7
Mean charge ($)	26	5	260	16	40	6	217	16
Internal medicine								
No. of episodes	5,351	3464	NA	NA	1533	1043	57	155
% with imaging	58	24	NA	NA	50	13	89	8
Mean charge ($)	30	10	NA	NA	38	9	239	14
General surgery								
No. of episodes	2,335	340	NA	NA	353	84	NA	NA
% with imaging	44	15	NA	NA	67	13	NA	NA
Mean charge ($)	22	4	NA	NA	50	8	NA	NA
Pediatrics								
No. of episodes	3,660	8458	NA	NA	NA	NA	NA	NA
% with imaging	18	2	NA	NA	NA	NA	NA	NA
Mean charge ($)	10	1	NA	NA	NA	NA	NA	NA
Obstetrics/gynecology								
No. of episodes	NA	NA	724	475	NA	NA	NA	NA
% with imaging	NA	NA	58	14	NA	NA	NA	NA
Mean charge ($)	NA	NA	178	25	NA	NA	NA	NA
Orthopedics								
No. of episodes	NA	NA	NA	NA	1024	124	NA	NA
% with imaging	NA	NA	NA	NA	46	15	NA	NA
Mean charge ($)	NA	NA	NA	NA	30	10	NA	NA
Urology								
No. of episodes	NA	NA	NA	NA	NA	NA	709	683
% with imaging	NA	NA	NA	NA	NA	NA	25	8
Mean charge ($)	NA	NA	NA	NA	NA	NA	65	19

*P<0.01 for all differences between self-referring and radiologist-referring physicians. NA denotes insufficient number of episodes for analysis.

ences in complexity ranged from 1 to 4 percent and do not account for the differences identified in the charges for imaging.

Discussion

For the clinical presentations we studied, patients with similar sets of symptoms were at least four times as likely to have diagnostic imaging performed as part of their evaluation if they sought care from a physician who performed imaging examinations in the office rather than from one who referred patients to a radiologist. Because self-referring physicians performed imaging studies more frequently and generally charged more than radiologists for similar imaging procedures, patients seeking care from self-referring physicians incurred considerably higher charges for diagnostic imaging than patients whose physicians referred them to radiologists. These effects cannot be attributed to differ-

ences in the mix of patients, the specialties of the physicians, or the complexity of the imaging examinations performed.

Previously, Childs and Hunter[14] found that physicians other than radiologists who provided imaging services used imaging more frequently than their peers in caring for elderly patients in Northern California. In a 1978 survey of 5,447 physicians, Radecki and Steele[15] determined that nonradiologist physicians with imaging facilities either in their offices or at the same site have higher rates of use than physicians without such facilities. A similar study of the effect of the site of imaging facilities used by family practitioners produced a similar result.[16]

The differences between our study and those performed previously include the relatively large number of patients and physicians we studied and the emphasis on specific clinical situations and episodes of medical care. Analyzing episodes of care permitted us to focus

directly on the issue that seemed most pertinent—whether individual patients with specific symptoms were more likely to receive imaging examinations when their physicians operated imaging equipment. As compared with the global measures used in previous studies, this method controls better for other variables—physicians' specialization, the complexity of examinations, differences in the types of patients seen by physicians, and the number of patient-physician encounters that might occur during the course of a patient's medical care. Finally, the focus on episodes as the unit of analysis allows a more accurate assessment of the activities and costs of medical care, the chief focus of our study.[12]

We have attempted to account for what we perceive to be the major possible biases of our study. After assessing the effect of correcting our results to account for the small percentage of physicians who had probably been miscategorized, and evaluating alternative probabilistic models for assigning the episodes involving physicians whom we could not categorize definitively, we found that these considerations did not affect the results qualitatively.* Our population of patients did not represent the American population, geographically or according to age. However, the geographic concentration tended to lessen the effects of regional differences in practice patterns, and it seems implausible that the large differences we identified in the use of imaging would be related to age. Although there is no assurance that the clinical presentations we studied represent the imaging practices of physicians in other clinical settings, the dimensions and consistency of our findings with regard to four very different clinical presentations and types of imaging examinations suggest that this practice pattern may be widespread.

We based our methods on those used by previous investigators,[12,17,18] but with adaptations to account for the large number of physicians and patients in our data base. Doubtless, the initial visits to physicians that triggered episodes of outpatient care occurred in an undefined context of patients' seeing their personal physicians, being referred by one physician to another, and seeking the specialist they believed to be appropriate. Although the manner in which the patients ended up seeing the physicians they did might potentially have affected the results, it is important to note that the results were uniformly sustained in our analysis of individual specialties. Also, with regard to our means of defining the index symptoms, determining the start of episodes, and including claims in episodes, there is nothing to suggest that our choices unequally biased the probability of imaging or the imaging charges in favor of either self-referring or radiologist-referring physicians. We believe that the dif-ferences between these two groups of physicians are so considerable that such issues have little relevance to the results.

Our findings of increased use of imaging and increased costs attributable to nonradiologist physicians who operate their own imaging equipment should

be of interest to regulatory and reimbursement agencies. It is impossible to determine from our results whether the imaging practices of the self-referring physicians or those of the radiologist-referring physicians represent the more appropriate care. Nor is it possible to determine the extent to which financial incentives are responsible for the higher levels of use and charges among the self-referring physicians. These physicians may perform imaging more frequently because they have financial incentives to do so, because imaging is more convenient when performed in a physician's office, or because physicians who perform imaging more often are more likely to acquire imaging equipment. Nonetheless, the differences between the self-referring and radiologist-referring physicians in the use of imaging are so large that some concern over the role of financial incentives must be invoked. Schroeder and Showstack[19] have detailed the potent financial incentives for a physician to incorporate imaging into an office practice. More recently, Hemenway et al.[20] validated this concern by showing an increase in the use of imaging when a group of ambulatory clinics changed to a method of compensation that used the frequency with which physicians ordered imaging examinations as the basis for paying them.

The American Medical Association has stated that the referral of patients to facilities in which physicians have an ownership interest is permissible, provided that patients are apprised of this relation and have other choices, and provided that physicians always act in their patients' best interests.[21] With respect to diagnostic imaging, however, it is unlikely that patients, even if so apprised, will be able to assess the appropriateness of such referrals accurately or seek imaging elsewhere. Particularly in the office setting, patients cannot be said to have a meaningful choice when their physicians advise them to undergo imaging. The potential to self-refer patients for imaging must surely complicate physicians' decisions and perhaps jeopardize their obligation to place their patients' interests above their own.

We are indebted to Medstat Systems, Inc., for assistance in providing access to the insurance-claims data base and help in developing the algorithm used to identify episodes of outpatient care; to Dr. Barbara J. McNeil for reviewing the penultimate version of the manuscript and making suggestions for its improvement; and to Ms. Janet Wallace for her help and patience during numerous revisions of the manuscript.

*See NAPS document no. 04816 for 16 pages of supplementary material. Order from NAPS c/o Microfiche Publications, P.O. Box 3513, Grand Central Station, New York, NY 10163-3513.

Notes

1. Relman AS. Dealing with conflicts of interest. N Engl J Med 1985; 313:749–51.

2. Dobson R, Todd JS, Manuel B, et al. Conflicts of interest and the physician entrepreneur. N Engl J Med 1986; 314:250–3.

3. ECRI Technology Management Assessment. Meeting the challenge of free-standing imaging centers. J Health Care Technol 1985; 1:257–78.

4. Morreim EH. Conflicts of interest: profits and problems in physician referrals. JAMA 1989; 262:390–4.

5. Stark FH. Physicians' conflicts in patient referrals. JAMA 1989; 262:397.

6. Waldholz M, Bogdanich W. Warm bodies: doctor-owned labs earn lavish profits in a captive market. Wall Street Journal. March 1, 1989:A1, A6.

7. Koizumi LS, ed. Referrals for sale. Medicine and Health Perspectives. October 3, 1988:1–4.

8. Kusserow RP. Report to Congress of the U.S. Inspector General: financial arrangements between physicians and health care businesses. May 1989. (Publication no. OAI–12–88–01410).

9. Hyman DA, Williamson JV. Fraud and abuse: setting the limits on physicians' entrepreneurship. N Engl J Med 1988; 320:1275–8.

10. Iglehart JK. Congress moves to regulate self-referral and physicians' ownership of clinical laboratories. N Engl J Med 1990; 322:1682–7.

11. The international classification of diseases, 9th revision, clinical modification (ICD-9-CM). 2nd ed. Vol. 1. Diseases: tabular list. Washington, D.C.: Government Printing Office, 1980. (DHHS publication no. (PHS) 80–1260).

12. Hornbrook MC, Hurtado AV, Johnson RE. Health care episodes: definition, measurement, and use. Med Care Rev 1985; 42:163–218.

13. Medicare Program: fee schedules for radiologist services. Fed Regist 1989; 54:8894–9023.

14. Childs AW, Hunter ED. Non-medical factors influencing use of diagnostic x-ray by physicians. Med Care 1972; 10:323–35.

15. Radecki SE, Steele JP. Effect of on-site facilities on use of diagnostic radiology by non-radiologists. Invest Radiol 1990; 25:190–3.

16. Strasser RP, Bass MJ, Brennan M. The effect of an on-site radiology facility on radiologic utilization in family practice. J Fam Pract 1987; 24:619–23.

17. Keeler EB, Rolph JE. The demand for episodes of medical treatment: interim results from the Health Insurance Experiment. Santa Monica, Calif.: Rand Corporation, 1982:1–5. (Publication no. R–2829–HHS).

18. Keeler EB, Rolph JE. The demand for episodes of treatment in the Health Insurance Experiment. J Health Econ 1988; 7:337–67.

19. Schroeder SA, Showstack JA. Financial incentives to perform medical procedures and laboratory tests: illustrative models of office practice. Med Care 1978; 16:289–98.

20. Hemenway D, Killen A, Cashman SB, Parks CL, Bicknell WJ. Physicians' responses to financial incentives: evidence from a for-profit ambulatory care center. N Engl J Med 1990; 322:1059–63.

21. Todd JS, Horan JK. Physician referral—the AMA view. JAMA 1989; 262:395–6.

19

The Hassle Factor Defined

American Society of Internal Medicine

What has become known as "the hassle factor" in modern medical practice and in the provision of health care in America . . . has been defined by the American Society of Internal Medicine (ASIM) as:

The increasingly intrusive and often irrational administrative, regulatory review and paperwork burdens being placed on patients and physicians by the Medicare program and other insurers.

Such hassles can have direct consequences on patients as medical students are discouraged from certain fields of medicine, as patients find physicians less accessible or willing to add to their patient caseloads, as administrative costs increase—leading to higher premiums and physicians' fees, as patients are denied insurance benefits for necessary and appropriate services, and as physicians find their roles changing from patient advocate to cost-containment watchdog for the insurance company.

ASIM, representing physicians nationwide who are specialists in adult medical care, believes the reduction of the hassle factor should be a top public policy issue. Judging from the letters, phone calls and resolutions from ASIM members, the administrative burdens—or hassles—associated with the Medicare program and other payers are now the biggest concern of internists. Physicians are tired of review programs that require them to justify every decision they make on behalf of their patients but

seem incapable of disciplining those physicians who are truly abusing the program. The federal government spends more than $300 million a year to oversee the quality of care given to Medicare patients, yet it found "confirmed quality problems" in only a little more than 2 percent of the cases it reviewed during 1988–1989. Of these cases, most problems involved lack of documentation rather than actual harm to patients.[5] Physicians are tired of going through multiple appeals in order to get paid for their services. One visit by a patient to a physician's office has been estimated to generate on average 10 pieces of paper.[6] Physicians are concerned with Medicare's seeming indifference or hostility to professional input. And they are angry about a never-ending deluge of new requirements—some well-intentioned, many not—that have no relationship to the way medicine is really practiced, or are extremely costly or difficult to comply with. As a pediatrician in San Diego said to The New York Times, "I enjoy seeing patients and I think I would go into medicine again, but I've had to be very strong to endure the headaches and the hassles."[7]

This paper outlines many of the regulations and paperwork burdens introduced recently into modern medical practice and some of the major reasons for these circumstances. It also will illustrate some of the effects on the physician's ability to care for his or her patients according to his or her best medical judgment. Finally, it presents a series of ASIM recommendations for improving the environment of medical practice while assuring that high quality health care and appropriate medical

services are delivered to patients. A glossary of terms used throughout this paper is contained in Appendix A.

The 1980s: The Regulation of Health Care

Although one of the basic tenets of the "Reagan Revolution" was the deregulation of almost all major industries in the United States, the treatment of health care during the last decade was exactly the opposite of that philosophy. Over the course of the decade, physicians and other health care providers were faced with a growing list of administrative responsibilities, regulatory requirements and other management duties that forced them to cut back on the amount of time they devote to patient care, to hire additional office staff to contend with the paperwork and telephone calls, and to respond increasingly to third-party inquiries about the necessity and appropriateness of the care they provide.

In 1983, the federal government instituted the Prospective Payment System (PPS) for Medicare whereby payments for hospital services were limited to certain amounts. Hospitals able to treat patients for less than the Medicare payment kept the surplus. When treatment costs exceeded the Medicare payment, the facility would absorb the loss. On the one hand, hospital administrators pressured physicians to release patients from the hospital earlier. On the other hand, peer review organizations pressured physicians to keep patients out of the hospital entirely and to treat them on an outpatient basis.

In 1985, Medicare began to "flag" certain claims for services for further review and to require additional documentation from physicians before paying those claims. In 1987 and 1988, physicians were required to refund to patients any amounts collected on services deemed by the Medicare insurance carrier and peer review organization to be "unnecessary." To avoid this, physicians had to inform the patient in writing prior to provision of the service that Medicare might not pay for that particular procedure. Also in 1987, a fee freeze from the previous year was replaced by the maximum allowable actual charge (MAAC) system for nonparticipating physicians—i.e., those physicians who do not agree to accept Medicare fees as payment-in-full for all services. These MAACs (see Glossary for definition) involve a complicated formula to determine the limits placed on total charges a physician can bill a Medicare beneficiary. Diagnosis codes, procedure codes (which number more than 7,000) and physician identification numbers on all claims have been required in the last five years—without them payment will not be made by Medicare. The list of diagnosis categories from which physicians must choose contains more than 11,000 three- to five-digit codes. Providing many of these codes imposes an enormous burden on physicians' staffs while producing information that is of questionable benefit to the Medicare program.

Clerical staff accounts for 47 percent of nonphysician employees in doctors' offices. Most of their time is spent on billing and other administrative tasks. [8] Physicians must fill out and sign lengthy questionnaires in order for their patients to receive home care services and medical equipment and to admit patients into nursing homes. For example, Health Care Financing Administration (HCFA) Form 484 must be filled out by the physician to certify a Medicare patient's need for home oxygen therapy. On the form itself, there is a notation that the form takes approximately 25 minutes to complete. If the physician has the information called for on the form readily available, it may not take as long to fill out—perhaps no more than 5 to 10 minutes. However, if the physician must contact the laboratory or hospital for data, such as blood gas measurements for the patient, this process can take longer. One internist re-

ceived 15 such forms in a two-week period. Depending on the availability of data, the physician will spend two to six hours preparing paperwork—time that could have been devoted to additional study on treatment of complex illnesses or to seeing patients.

Beginning in September 1990, physicians will be required to submit all Medicare Part B claims on behalf of their patients. A 1986 study found that internists already spend almost one-fifth (18 percent) of their time on administrative tasks. [9] Considering that approximately 400 million Medicare claims are filed each year, this time spent on paperwork will undoubtedly increase. [10] (A list of some of these administrative responsibilities imposed on physicians in the last 10 years is included in Appendix B.)

Medicare is not alone in the extent and complexity of rules required of those who participate in the system. A procedure manual of instructions for filling out a one-page billing form for the New York Medicaid program was 135 pages long and was followed by 260 pages of procedural codes. [11]

These governmental requirements do not include the proliferation of rules promulgated by private firms engaged by employers around the country to manage utilization of health benefits by their employees. Today, between 200 and 300 utilization review (UR) firms operate in the U.S., each with its own distinct medical necessity rules and preauthorization requirements that obligate physicians to confer with a "reviewer" before undertaking dozens of treatments or procedures. A story in *The Washingtonian* magazine told of an Arlington, Virginia, internist dealing with a utilization review firm hired by the employer of his patient to manage hospitalizations of employees. Twice within the first week of what was expected to be a lengthy hospital stay for this seriously ill patient, the physician was called by the UR firm. When he complained to the reviewer, he was told, "If you don't deal with me, you don't get paid." Said the physician, "They implied that my major concern was that I wouldn't get paid. My concern was that the guy wouldn't die if he left the hospital. He'll be dead whether I get paid or not." [12]

Why More Regulations?

Why have health care regulations increased? To put it simply—money. In 1988, the nation spent $540 billion on health care. More than one third of that money, $158 billion, is spent by the federal government in Medicare and Medicaid outlays. Health care spending increased by approximately 10 percent a year during the 1980s. [13] This has been driven not only by increases in physician and hospital bills but also by a growing senior population that needs more care, the development and use of sophisticated medical technology, increases in drug costs, higher wages to attract health support personnel and cost-shifting by hospitals and other health facilities to pay for indigent care. As the government has watched its health costs mount, it has attempted to stem the dollar outflow through budget reductions, changes in reimbursement policy and increasingly intrusive review requirements. In the private sector, businesses and health insurers have turned to managed health care systems and utilization review as means to control their own expenditures on health care.

ASIM recognizes the need on the part of government and the private sector to restrain health care costs. However, mounting evidence suggests that many of the cost-control methods employed are ineffective and have, in some instances, added to expenditures. Adding more administrative burdens will not be a solution until an honest effort has been made to determine those existing controls and regulations that have had a positive impact on costs without sacrificing quality of care and those rules that have proven counterproductive. To the extent that some containment measures deny needed health care and services, cost control is being bought at a very high price.

Who Cares If Physicians Are Unhappy?

There are many who believe, and often say, that physicians make enough money to put up with a few rules. For most physicians, however, the primary concern is that the rules imposed on them are affecting their ability to provide the best possible care to their patients. As an internist in South Dakota said in a letter to ASIM, "I have tried to put up with the increasing administrative burdens, keeping in mind that the reason I went into medicine was to take care of patients." There is growing unease among physicians that if current trends continue, it is the patients who will lose the most.

Few would disagree that when factory workers, teachers, government officials, nurses, office workers or business people become frustrated, angry and disillusioned with their jobs, their productivity and commitment declines. The same is true, of course, for physicians. Although most physicians' commitment to their patients and to providing high quality care remains strong, there is growing evidence that the cumulative effect of paperwork duties, third-party rules and uncooperative administering agencies is sapping the enthusiasm of many physicians for the practice of medicine. Earlier this year, in a survey of physicians conducted by the American Medical Association (AMA) and the Gallup Organization, almost 40 percent said they would definitely or probably not go into medicine if they had it to do all over again. [14]

Will this frustration and disillusionment among physicians have a direct impact on patient care? ASIM believes the negative effects of the hassle factor can already be seen in a variety of developments that are affecting adversely the quality and availability of care.

Reduced Benefits to Patients

One of the major reasons for the hassle factor is the increasing amount of cost-containment rules imposed by insurance companies to reduce their own financial outlays. These frequently impede the delivery of necessary medical care. Gerald Grumet, MD, writing in *The New England Journal of Medicine,* has characterized this trend as "rationing by inconvenience." In that article, he notes, "In managed care's arsenal of cost-control weaponry, probably none is more potent—except for restricting hospital admissions—than superseding the physician's autonomy by a managerial review process in which armies of claims

clerks, administrators, auditors, form processors, peer reviewers, functionaries and technocrats of every description insinuate themselves into a complex system that authorizes, delivers and pays for medical care." [15]

"Paradoxically, the savings that ordinarily accrue to an efficiently managed business are reversed in the case of insurance carriers, whose bungling, confusion and delay impede the outflow of funds. For carriers, inefficiency is profitable. The result is a mounting number of dysfunctional bureaucracies with eyecatching logos and slick marketing techniques that contrast sharply with the difficulties encountered each time medical services are used." [16]

For example, one manner in which patients are denied insurance benefits for appropriate medical care is through the use of medical necessity screens by Medicare and other third-party insurers. Medicare carriers and private insurers use numerical screens to flag certain claims to determine if the services rendered are medically necessary. For example, a Medicare carrier will establish a numerical screen for lengthy, or "intermediate," hospital visits. If a physician submits a claim for an intermediate hospital visit which exceeds the number of such visits determined "medically necessary" by the carrier, then that claim will be pulled for further review by a carrier employee to see if, in fact, a longer visit with the patient was required. Ostensibly, the purpose of medical review screens is to modify physician behavior so that unnecessary services are not provided to patients— a very legitimate public purpose. However, carriers often reject outright any "screened" claims that are in fact for services that should be covered by Medicare. In many cases, when the physician appeals the denial and the denial is reversed, the carrier soon thereafter denies a similar claim for a similar service for the same patient. In effect, the Medicare carrier will have denied beneficiaries the insurance benefits to which they are legally entitled.

Even so, a recent HCFA-funded study conducted by several University of Minnesota researchers and published by the Blue Cross and Blue Shield Association questioned the success of

carrier screens in changing physician behavior. The authors found that "screens are only marginally effective (at best) in reducing the rate at which medically unnecessary claims are submitted." The authors attributed the ineffectiveness of such screens, at least in part, to the fact "that physicians generally view the carriers and their medical staffs as antagonists. Physicians often complained that most of the decisions about medical necessity were made by lay employees who lacked the professional expertise to make informed, much less authoritative decisions on medical necessity. Knowing physicians held this attitude . . . we were not surprised to find little evidence of behavioral change." [17]

Private insurers use similar methods to deny patients reimbursement for medically appropriate services that, under the terms of the insurance policy, should be covered. Privately insured patients frequently experience their own version of "sticker shock" when they discover how little of the care provided by the physician is actually covered by insurance. Insurers spend billions of dollars marketing their benefits of "comprehensive coverage"—and billions more making sure that, when claims for services come in, the true level of coverage is anything but comprehensive.

In the worst cases, insurance company cost-containment policies designed to impede the use of medical services could result in the delivery of poor quality care or no care at all. However, physicians' continued commitment to their role as patient's advocate—even if it means taking on the patient's insurer—has protected most patients from direct harm as a result of these cost-control practices.

Two recent examples illustrate the potentially adverse impact third-party payer policies can have on patients. In the first case, an Oklahoma oncologist was treating a patient who was undergoing chemotherapy for cancer. This patient came to his office one day with a slightly elevated temperature. Such a patient, as a result of the chemotherapy, does not have sufficient white blood cells to fight off an infection that a higher temperature indicates. The physician admitted the patient to the hospital knowing that the insurance company would refuse to pay for the admission because the patient's temperature wasn't high enough to meet the insurer's screens. After battling with the insurer, the physician was able to get the payer's decision reversed. Reflecting on that episode, the physician said, "I could have sent the patient home and waited for her temperature to rise some more. But that would not be proper, high-quality medical care. As long as we keep fighting, we can get good medical care for these people, but why do we have to continually go through these hassles?"

In the second instance, an Arizona internist had a patient in a skilled nursing facility learning how to use a prosthesis (artificial limb). Ordinarily, the patient, whose condition was stable at time of admission, would not require anything more than one visit during the month. However, this diabetic patient developed heart irregularities, depression and anorexia and needed changes in his insulin, all of which required the physician to monitor the patient on a more frequent basis. The carrier nevertheless denied the physician's claim for service on the grounds that Medicare usually pays for only one nursing home visit per month.

Prior authorization of services is another way in which Medicare, private insurers and managed care systems screen for medical necessity. Although such precertification requirements can be a useful method for determining if a procedure is medically warranted, they can, if used too broadly or improperly, have life-threatening consequences. Warning patients to obtain approval before they use an emergency room or ambulance unless their condition is critical, as has been done by some health maintenance organizations (HMOs), puts people "in the predicament of having to decide whether or not they are dying."[18]

Another approach recently employed by the utilization management program of the "Big Three" automakers places the physician and hospital at financial risk if preadmission authorization is not obtained from the insurer.[19] Failure to comply with these requirements, even for emergency admissions for which authorization must be ob-

tained within 24 hours, will result in fines or 20 percent cuts in payments from the insurer or both. As a result, physicians will have to make sure each patient they admit to the hospital has obtained this authorization, or get the approval themselves.

Legal rules are another way in which certain approaches to care are mandated that can have an adverse impact on the physician's ability to offer the care he or she believes is best for the patient. Illustrative of this is the experience of a San Diego internist whose elderly patient needed a short nursing home stay to recuperate from a fall. The physician wanted to bypass admitting the patient into a hospital because of the hospital-based infections that might hurt the patient's chronic lung condition. Unfortunately, Medicare law required a hospital stay of three days prior to a nursing home admission in order for the admission to be reimbursed.

After the patient was admitted to the hospital, she died from a hospital-acquired lung infection. The physician said, "How do we protect ourselves so that we don't grieve when we recognize a needless death, which is against all that we stand for? I suppose we could build a wall around our emotions and render our medical care as coldly as the bureaucracy administers its laws."[20]

The cases cited above are examples of third-party payer policies in which the physician must argue with the insurer to ensure the delivery of appropriate medical care to his or her patient. Sometimes the physician is successful in contesting the insurer and other times the "rules and regulations" win. Had the physician been unwilling to take on the insurer, the patient might have been denied insurance benefits for necessary care. At worst, the patient might have received no care or poor care. Sometimes, despite the best efforts of the physician, the "system" not only impedes delivery of care that is best for the patient but also causes that patient irreparable harm.

Fortunately, for most patients, physicians do prevail in countering unreasonable or arbitrary decisions on the part of insurers and Medicare carriers. However, it makes no sense for public policy to set up a system in which

physicians must fight constantly to provide appropriate care and for patients and physicians to be reimbursed for that care. A better way would be to assure that third-party review and payment criteria are valid in the first place.

Too Few Primary Care Physicians

Medical schools have witnessed a decline in applicants from a high in 1974 of three persons for each slot to a low in 1988 of 1.6 applicants for every medical school opening.[21] In addition, the number and percentage of those graduating from U.S. medical schools choosing internal medicine resident programs—in other words choosing to go into one of the major fields of primary care—decreased by 6 percent from 1985 to 1987.[22] Between 1981 and 1988, medical school graduates choosing any of the primary care specialties (internal medicine, family practice, pediatrics) declined, whereas those selecting other subspecialties increased during that time period.[23] Among the factors contributing to this decrease are the extensive mental and emotional involvement with patients required of internists; the low fees relative to other specialties; the office overhead, which can consume 60 percent or more of fees received; and the debts in excess of $50,000 that many students have when they graduate from medical school.[24] As the elderly population grows, this trend in fewer medical students choosing primary care as a concentration will have a serious impact on patients' access to physicians in the future. This is already apparent in the inability of many rural areas to attract and keep family physicians and internists. Nationally, there is an average 1,300 people per physician in urban areas compared with 2,275 people per physician in rural communities.[25]

Primary care increasingly is viewed by practicing physicians, as well, as a less desirable field of medicine than other specialties. For example, a 1989 survey of internists in New York state found that paperwork, regulations and financial reimbursement were among the most frequently cited sources of dissatisfaction among the respondents. Over one-third of those surveyed indicated they would consider leaving practice. As the authors of an article about this survey said, "If withdrawal from practice combines with the inability to attract medical students into the field, it is not difficult to construct a scenario in which physicians in practice will become difficult to find."[26]

Erosion of the Physician-Patient Relationship

As the frustration grows, changes are taking place in the way Medicare beneficiaries view physicians—and how physicians view patients. Instead of thinking about the individual who comes through the office door, physicians are beginning to think: "Will I be able to justify this visit to the carrier? How many times will I or the patient be denied payment? Will I be cited by the peer review organization (PRO) for something I do?" When patients begin to be viewed pejoratively as "Medicare patients," the reaction among physicians may come to be as extreme as that expressed by a New York internist who wrote, "My answer to the hassle factor is to stay out of Medicare. I do not see nursing home patients nor do I see any new patients over age 64." This deep-seated dissatisfaction with the program is evident in other parts of the country as well. At a recent congressional hearing investigating problems with the administration of Medicare in Georgia, the HCFA regional administrator observed that 150 physicians in the state have stopped seeing Medicare patients out of irritation with the program."[27]

For most physicians, however, the effects of the hassle factor on the doctor-patient relationship are far more subtle. A loss of patient confidence—and satisfaction—is a consequence of insurers constantly questioning physicians' medical judgments, and of policies designed to coerce physicians into saving money in direct conflict with what patients want and expect.

On one hand, an informed public has increasingly demanded that physicians make patient satisfaction the primary goal and that this same patient satisfaction be included in reimbursement criteria. On the other hand, what may satisfy patients also may increase costs and is, therefore, in direct conflict

with the expectations of third-party payers. No one is suggesting that third-party payers reimburse every type of service patients want or expect. However, it must be recognized that, as physicians are increasingly called on to control costs, some loss of patient satisfaction is bound to occur.

Commenting on this dichotomy, C. Burns Roehrig, M.D., editor of *The Internist: Health Policy in Practice*, observed, "If patient satisfaction is to be a primary goal and a basis for financial reward, there can be no push for the physician to discharge a patient from the hospital when it may be safe but not comfortable and convenient. Nor can the doctor be expected to prescribe a generic drug when a patient asks for a brandname product, to become more 'efficient' by spending less time with patients or using physician extenders, or to decline a dermatology consultation requested by a patient for the treatment of rather ordinary acne. But health economists generally consider all these to be essential to control costs."[28]

However, it is not only physicians who are beginning to see damage to the doctor-patient relationship. Eva Skinner, a Board member of the American Association of Retired Persons, has written that patients' confusion about Medicare is "compounded when physicians, traditionally viewed as protectors, as well as healers, give up in frustration and cite Medicare rules and regulations' as the reasons for changes contrary to patients' expectations."[29]

Writing in his column, "The Patient's Advocate," *Washington Post* staff writer Victor Cohn noted, "Some authorities consider concerns like Roehrig's overstated; some do not. But if he is right— and I believe he is right to no small extent—doctors should be more concerned than ever about satisfying their patients, if only to gain allies in the struggle to maintain a healthy degree of free choice and independence for both patients and physicians."[30]

ASIM believes that the medical profession has a responsibility to do everything it can to continue to provide high-quality, affordable care for all patients, regardless of the rules set up by insurers. It would be a tragedy for the medical profession and the public if physi-

cians determine that they have no choice but to turn away from certain patients. Physicians may decide that they can no longer in good conscience go along with such restrictions if they conclude that Medicare and other insurers are: demanding more and more paperwork as a prerequisite to getting appropriate services reimbursed; arbitrarily denying more and more medically necessary services; and financially penalizing physicians and their patients for providing the care that patients need and expect. Rather than being accomplices to policies that they find to be wrong, primary care physicians may instead decide that going into another specialty, type of practice, or career is the least objectionable course of action. Alternatively, those who remain increasingly will find that the rules imposed by insurers place them on a collision course with what their ethics and sense of commitment tell them is best for their patients.

Higher Costs

In 1986, a study of health care administrative costs using 1983 data revealed that the costs of program administration, private insurance, and hospital, nursing home and physician office administration totalled more than $77 billion—or 22 percent of all health care spending at that time. Of that amount, $18.5 billion represented the net costs of Medicare, Medicaid, and private insurance administration and overhead.[31] More recent studies show these administrative expenses as growing more. For example, an analysis of 1988 national health care spending trends revealed that, of the $540 billion spent on all health care in the U.S. that year, $26 billion was used by the federal and state governments and private insurers for claims processing and program administration.[32] Finally, AMA figures show that program administration and the net cost of private health insurance grew by 182 percent from 1980 to 1987, providing further evidence of the rapid escalation of health administration costs.[33] These more recent studies do not address the additional administrative costs incurred by physicians, hospitals and nursing homes. However, it is likely that the overall cost of health care bureaucracy—

public and private program administration coupled with the costs incurred by physicians and other providers—is even greater than it was in 1983. As these costs of program administration and claims processing grow, they result directly in higher premium costs to the insured and greater tax expenditures to fund the public programs.

As administrative requirements increase, physicians must hire additional staff to handle the paperwork. The same study that illustrated such dramatic health administration increases also revealed that approximately 45 percent of physicians' gross income nationally was devoted to their office overhead costs. [34] Of insurance company overhead, hospital administrative costs, nursing home administration and physicians' overhead, the latter ($31 billion) represented the largest category of expenditure for health care administration. Clerical staff, most of whose time is spent on billing and claims submission tasks, now constitute almost 50 percent of the nonphysicians employed in physicians' offices. [35] According to an AMA study, this office staff spends approximately 47 hours per month dealing with Medicare claims and more than 33 hours per month processing private insurance claims. [36] Physicians themselves estimated they spend almost 10 hours a month on administrative tasks related to Medicare and private insurance. [37] As patients pay their doctor bills, they should realize that a significant portion goes to physicians' overhead costs.

Notes

1. Platt, Frederick W., MD, "What Do Internists Think?" *Archives of Internal Medicine*, Vol. 149, No. 8, August 1989.
2. "Are People Listening to Doctors Today?—The Media Respond," *The Internist: Health Policy in Practice*, April 1989.
3. Lee, Philip, MD and Lynn Etheredge, "Clinical Freedom: Two Lessons for the U.K. from U.S. Experience with Privatization of Health Care" *Lancet*, Vol. 1, No. 8632, Feb. 4, 1989.
4. "Changes in Medicare Bring Pain to Healing Profession," *The New York Times*, Feb. 18, 1990.
5. *PRO Performance Statistics*, Health Care Financing Administration (HCFA), 1988–89.
6. Wohl, S., *The Medical Industrial Complex*, Harmony Books: New York, 1984
7. "Changes in Medicare Bring Pain to Healing Profession," *The New York Times*, Feb. 18, 1990.
8. Reynolds, R.A., and R.L. Ohsfeldt, eds., *Socioeconomic Characteristics of Medical Practice*, American Medical Association, Chicago, 1984.
9. Himmelstein, D.U., MD, and S. Woolhandler, MD, "Cost Without Benefit: Administrative Waste in U.S. Health Care," *New England Journal of Medicine*, Vol. 314, No. 7, Feb. 13, 1986.
10. U.S. General Accounting Office (GAO), *HCFA Can Reduce Medicare Paperwork Burden for Physicians and Their Patients*, June 1990.
11. Computer Sciences Corporation, Medical Management Information System Provider Manual—Physicians, Albany, NY, 1988.
12. "That's Not Covered," *The Washingtonian*, Diane Granat, March 1990.
13. Levit, K., M. Freeland, and D. Waldo, "National Health Care Spending Trends: 1988," *Health Affairs*, Summer 1990.
14. "Changes in Medicine Bring Pain to Healing Profession," *The New York Times*, Feb. 18, 1990.
15. Grumet, Gerald W., "Health Care Rationing Through Inconvenience: The Third Party's Secret Weapon," *New England Journal of Medicine*, Vol. 321, No. 9, Aug. 31, 1989.
16. *Ibid.*
17. Nyman, John A., *et al.*, "Changing Physician Behavior: Does Medical Review of Part B Claims Make a Difference?" *Inquiry*, Vol. 27, No. 2, Summer 1990.
18. Grumet, "Health Care Rationing Through Inconvenience."
19. Memorandum to providers from Blue Cross and Blue Shield of Missouri, August 1989.
20. Everett, Lidia, MD, "San Diego County Opinion," *Los Angeles Times*, Feb. 4, 1990.
21. Knox, Richard A., "What's Ailing Doctors?" *Boston Globe Magazine*, March 18, 1990.
22. Graettinger, John S., MD, *Annals of Internal Medicine*, Vol. 108, January 1988.
23. American Association of Medical Colleges, Graduation Questionnaire, 1988.
24. McCarty, Daniel J., MD, *New England Journal of Medicine*, Vol. 317, No. 9, Aug. 27, 1987.
25. McIlrath, Sharon, "Town Suffers Care Crisis as Medicare Rates Force MDs Out," *American Medical News*, May 11, 1990.
26. Hershey, Charles O., MD, *et al.*, *Archives of Internal Medicine*, Vol. 149, No. 8, August 1989.
27. HCFA Regional Administrator. House Energy and Commerce Subcommittee on Health, March 5, 1990.
28. Roehrig, C. Burns, MD, "Patients Are Out of Control!" *The Internist: Health Policy in Practice*, March 1988.
29. American Medical Association, QA Review, Consumers' View, Vol. 2, No. 5, June 1990.
30. Cohn, Victor, "The Question Your Doctor Doesn't Ask: Are You Satisfied?" *The Washington Post* Health Section, Feb. 20, 1990.
31. Himmelstein, "Cost Without Benefit: Administrative Waste in U.S. Health Care."
32. Levit, K., "National Health Care Spending Trends: 1988."
33. American Medical Association, Council on Long Range Planning and Development, Environment of Medicine, 1989.
34. Himmelstein, "Cost Without Benefit: Administrative Waste in U.S. Health Care."
35. *Ibid.*
36. *AMA Socioeconomic Monitoring System Report*, 1989.
37. *Ibid.*
38. Rep. J. Roy Rowland (D-Ga.), *Congressional Record*, April 4, 1990.
39. Nyman, "Changing Physician Behavior."
40. GAO, *HCFA Can Reduce Medicare Paperwork Burden for Physicians and Their Patients*.
41. *Ibid.*
42. *Ibid.*
43. *Ibid.*
44. Agency for Health Care Policy and Research, Public Health Service, Department of Health and Human Services, "Guideline Attributes," March 1990.
45. American Medical Association/Specialty Society Practice Parameters Partnership, "Attributes to Guide the Development of Practice Parameters," April 1990.
46. Nyman, "Changing Physician Behavior."
47. Lohr, Kathleen, PhD, and Steven Schroeder, MD, "Special Report: A Strategy for Quality Assurance in Medicare," *New England Journal of Medicine*, Vol. 322, No. 10, March 8, 1990.
48. *Medicare: A Strategy for Quality Assurance*, Institute of Medicine, National Academy Press, March 1990.
49. Leberto, Tony, "AMA to Clamp Down on UR," *Managed HealthCare*, Jan. 8, 1990.
50. Ruffenbach, Glenn, "Denials of Medical Claims Provoke a Legal Backlash," *The Wall Street Journal*, Feb. 13, 1989.
51. *Ibid.*
52. Dundas, Richard G., MD, Letters to the Editor, *The Bennington (Vt.) Banner*, May 22, 1990.

20

The Deteriorating Administrative Efficiency of the U.S. Health Care System

Steffie Woolhandler and David U. Himmelstein

Medicine is increasingly a spectator sport. Doctors, patients, and nurses perform before an enlarging audience of utilization reviewers, efficiency experts, and cost managers (Figure 1). A cynic viewing the uninflected curve of rising health care spending might wonder whether the cost-containment experts cost more than they contain; one is reminded of the Chinese proverb "There is no use going to bed early to save candles if the result is twins."

In 1983 the proportion of health care spending consumed by administrative costs in the United States was 60 percent higher than in Canada and 97 percent higher than in Britain.[2] Recent U.S. health policies have increased bureaucratic burdens and curtailed access to care. Yet they have failed to contain overall costs. This study updates and expands estimates of the costs of health administration in North America through 1987.[2] The results demonstrate that the bureaucratic profligacy of the U.S. health care system has increased sharply, while in Canada the proportion of spending on health care consumed by administration has declined.

Methods

We examined four components of administrative costs in the United States and Canada: insurance overhead, hos-

pital administration, nursing home administration, and physicians' overhead and billing expenses. All estimates are for fiscal year 1987, the most recent year for which complete data were available. Costs are reported in 1987 U.S. dollars, based on the 1987 exchange rate of $1.33 (Canadian) = $1 (U.S.); calculations of per capita spending were based on populations of 243,934,000 in the United States and 25,652,000 in Canada.

Figures on insurance overhead in the United States were obtained from the Health Care Financing Administration.[3] Although nationwide data on the costs of hospital and nursing home administration were not available, the California Health Facilities Commission regularly compiles detailed cost data, based on Medicare cost reports, on that state's hospitals and nursing homes. Four years ago we confirmed that administrative costs in California's health facilities were similar to those in at least two other states.[2] Since then, trends in hospital and nursing home financing and organization in California have paralleled developments in the nation as a whole.[4,5] We computed total hospital administrative costs by summing costs in the following categories: general accounting, patient accounting, credit and collection, admitting, other fiscal services, hospital administration, public relations, personnel department, auxiliary groups, data processing, communications, purchasing, medical library, medical records, medical-staff administration, nursing administration, in-service education, and other administrative services. We excluded costs attributed to research administration,

administration of educational programs, printing and duplicating, depreciation, amortization, leases and rentals, insurance, licenses, taxes, central services and supply, other ancillary services, and unassigned costs. We assumed that administration represented the same proportion of total hospital costs in California as nationwide. We derived estimates of nationwide administrative costs for nursing homes from the California data in a similar manner.

Although Canada's 10 provincial health programs differ in some details, they share common structural features that tend to streamline bureaucracy. Each program provides comprehensive coverage for virtually all provincial residents under a single publicly administered plan. Private insurance may cover additional services, but duplication of the public coverage is proscribed; hospitals are paid a lump-sum (global) amount to cover operating expenses, and physicians bill the program directly for all fees.

The Health Statistics Branch of Health and Welfare Canada and Statistics Canada's Canadian Center for Health Information provided unpublished data on nationwide spending for insurance, hospitals, and nursing homes. These data were derived from the provincial governments' reports of their expenditures for insurance administration and from detailed cost reports submitted by hospitals and nursing homes. We computed total hospital administrative costs by summing costs in the following categories: hospital administration ("other"), advertising, association-membership fees, business machines, collec-

Reprinted with permission from *The New England Journal of Medicine* 324, no. 18 (May 2, 1991), pp. 1253–58. Copyright © 1991 by the Massachusetts Medical Society.

tion fees, postage, auditing and accounting fees, other professional fees (such as legal fees but excluding medical fees), service-bureau fees, telephone and telegraph, indemnity to board members, travel and convention expenses, medical records and hospital library, and nursing administration. We excluded administrative and support services for educational and research programs, insurance, interest, printing, stationery and office supplies, materiel management, and central supply. Statistics Canada tabulates administrative costs for nursing homes as a single category. These data are less reliable than the hospital figures, since cost reporting by nursing homes is voluntary, and the number of facilities reporting varies substantially from year to year.

We confirmed the accuracy of the Canadian federal data, using more detailed but incomplete data from British Columbia, the Maritimes, Ontario, Quebec, and Saskatchewan[6-10] (and personal communications: D. Cunningham, British Columbia Ministry of Health; P. Lim, Continuing Care Employee Relations Association of British Columbia; and J. Davis, Ontario Ministry of Health). Because these data generally matched the national figures, we have not reported them separately.

Only indirect or incomplete information is available on the billing costs of Canadian and U.S. physicians. We therefore used two different methods to estimate these costs, one based on physicians' reports of their professional expenses and the other on the numbers of employees in physicians' offices. The expense-based method (Method 1) probably overestimates the actual difference in billing costs between the two nations, whereas the personnel-based approach (Method 2) may underestimate the difference.

Our first approach, Method 1, rests on the assumption that the entire difference in physicians' billing and overhead expenses (excluding malpractice premiums)[11,12] between the United States and Canada is attributable to the excess administrative costs borne by American doctors. The American Medical Association (AMA) estimates U.S. physicians' incomes and practice expenses on

the basis of the results of a survey of a representative sample of nonfederal, practicing physicians (excluding interns and residents).[12] Revenue Canada tabulates physicians' professional expenses on the basis of tax returns (L. Rehmer, Health Information Division, Health and Welfare Canada: personal communication). Because these figures are "distorted, primarily because of the way group practice physicians tend to report expenses" (L. Rehmer, Health Information Division, Health and Welfare Canada: personal communication), we used Revenue Canada's corrected tabulation, which included only the 91 percent of physicians who reported professional expenses amounting to between 5 percent and 300 percent of their net incomes. We added to both the U.S. and Canadian figures an estimate of the value of the physicians' time devoted to billing[13] (and D. Peachey: personal communication); we assumed that this time was valued at the same rate as other professional activity.

Using Method 2, we also estimated physicians' billing costs on the basis of data on the number of clerical and managerial personnel employed in their offices, as well as the costs of outside billing services. For the United States, we obtained information on physicians' office personnel from data tapes from the Census Bureau's March 1988 Current Population Survey (CPS).[14] Since comparable survey data were unavailable for Canada, we used information from a detailed study of office staffing patterns in the province of Quebec in 1977.[15] These earlier figures were slightly higher than informal current estimates provided by the Ontario Medical Association (D. Peachey: personal communication). For both the United States and Canada, we assumed that the total annual cost per employee averaged $35,000 (including wages, benefits, taxes, work space, equipment, telephone, supplies, and other costs attributable to the employee) and that the ratio of clerical workers to physicians (excluding residents) was identical in offices and other settings. We added to both the U.S. and Canadian figures estimates of the value of physicians' personal time spent on billing, calculated as described above. For the United States we added the cost

of outside billing services as determined by a recent survey by the AMA.[13]

Finally, to evaluate trends over time, we recalculated the 1987 figures to maintain strict comparability with the less detailed and less complete data for 1983.[2] As in our earlier paper,[2] we estimated physicians' billing and overhead costs by the expense-based method (Method 1). However, we excluded the cost of physicians' time spent on billing because comparable data were unavailable for 1983. In keeping with our earlier method, we included malpractice costs in physicians' overhead expenses but corrected for increases over time in these costs.[11,12,16] For each country we took average total professional expenses in 1987, subtracted the average 1987 malpractice premium, then added the average 1983 malpractice premium (all expressed as a percentage of gross income). The 1983 figures were converted to 1987 dollars with use of the gross-domestic-product price index for each country.[17]

Results

Insurance Overhead

In 1987 private insurance firms in the United States retained $18.7 billion for administration and profits out of total premium revenues of $157.8 billion.[3] Their average overhead costs (11.9 percent of premiums) were considerably higher than the 3.2 percent administrative costs of government health programs such as Medicare and Medicaid ($6.6 billion out of total expenditures of $207.3 billion).[3] Together, administration of private and public insurance programs consumed 5.1 percent of the $500.3 billion spent for health care, or $106 per capita.

The overhead costs for Canada's provincial insurance plans amounted to $235 million (0.9 percent) of the $26.57 billion spent by the plans[17] (and Health Information Division, Health and Welfare Canada: personal communication). The administrative costs of Canadian private insurers averaged 10.9 percent of premiums ($200 million of the $1.83 billion spent for such coverage) (Health Information Division, Health and Welfare Canada: personal communication).

Total administrative costs for Canadian health insurance consumed 1.2 percent of health care spending, or $17 per capita.

Hospital Administration

Hospital administration represented 20.2 percent of hospital costs in California in 1987–1988.[18] Extrapolating this figure to the total U.S. hospital expenditures of $194.7 billion in 1987[2] yielded an estimate of $39.3 billion, or $162 per capita, consumed by hospital administration. In Canada, hospital administration cost $1.27 billion, amounting to 9.0 percent of total hospital expenditures of $14.14 billion (Health Information Division, Health and Welfare Canada: personal communication), or $50 per capita.

Nursing Home Administration

The administrative costs in California's nursing homes accounted for 15.8 percent of total revenues in 1987–1988.[19] On the basis of this figure, we estimate that administration cost $6.4 billion of the $40.6 billion spent nationally for nursing home care,[3] or $26 per capita. Canadian nursing homes spent $231 million on administration in 1987–1988, amounting to 13.7 percent of the total expenditures of $1.69 billion (Statistics Canada, Canadian Center for Health Information: personal communication), or $9 per capita.

Physicians' Billing Expense

Method 1

When calculated according to Method 1, U.S. physicians' overhead and billing expenses, excluding malpractice premiums, made up 43.7 percent of their gross professional income[12]—$44.9 billion of the $102.7 billion spent for physicians' services.[3] In addition, physicians spent an average of six minutes on each Medicare and Blue Shield claim.[13] Assuming that the time required to bill other insurers was similar, the average physician spent about 134.4 hours per year (4.4 percent of his or her total professional activity) on billing; this time had a total value of $4.5 billion. Thus, the total value of U.S. physicians' billing

and overhead was $49.4 billion, or $203 per capita.

Canadian physicians' professional expenses, excluding malpractice premiums, amounted to $1.99 billion, or 34.4 percent of their gross income (L. Rehmer: personal communication). According to the director of professional affairs of the Ontario Medical Association, "The commitment of time to billing . . . is trivial and can be measured in seconds [per claim]" (D. Peachey: personal communication). Assuming that the average physician spends 1 percent of his or her professional time on billing, with a total value of $58 million annually, the total cost of physicians' billing and overhead was $2.04 billion, or $80 per capita.

Method 2

The average office-based physician in the United States employed 1.47 clerical and managerial workers (D. U. Himmelstein, S. Woolhandler: unpublished data), at an annual cost of $51,564 per physician, for a total of $20.0 billion. As calculated above (Method 1), the time physicians spent on billing was valued at $4.5 billion. In addition, 13.9 percent of physicians contracted with outside billing firms, at an average annual cost of $23,196 each,[13] for a total of $1.3 billion. Physicians' total billing and clerical expenses amounted to $25.8 billion, or $106 per capita.

The average office-based general practitioner in Quebec employed 0.733 receptionists and secretaries[15] at an annual cost of $25,655 per physician, for a total of $1.0 billion for Canadian physicians. In addition, the time physicians spent on billing was valued at $58 million. Physicians' total billing and clerical expenses were thus $1.06 billion, or $41 per capita.

Total Costs of Administration

Table 1 summarizes the per capita costs of health care administration in the United States and Canada, including physicians' billing and overhead costs as calculated by the two different methods. Overall expenditures for health care administration in the United States totaled $96.8 billion to $120.4 billion ($400 to $497 per capita), accounting for 19.3 to 24.1 percent of the $500.3 billion spent for health care. Canadians spent $3.00 billion to $3.98 billion for health care administration ($117 to $156 per capita), amounting to 8.4 to 11.1 percent of the $35.9 billion spent for health care. The difference of $283 to $341 in the per capita cost of health care administration and billing accounted for 43.5 to 52.5 percent of the total difference in health spending between the two nations. If U.S. health care administration had been as efficient as Canada's, $69.0 to $83.2 billion (13.8 to 16.6 percent of total spending on

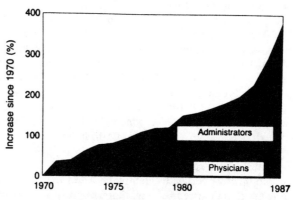

Figure 1. Growth in the Numbers of Physicians and Health Care Administrators from 1970 to 1987.

The data are from *Statistical Abstract of the United States* for these years (Table 64-2, 109th edition).[1] Because of a modification in the Bureau of the Census' definition of "health administrators," the change between 1982 and 1983 is interpolated rather than actual.

health care) would have been saved in 1987.

The difference between the United States and Canada in billing and administrative costs has markedly increased since 1983.[2] Insurance overhead in the United States has risen from 4.4 percent to 5.1 percent of total health care spending, whereas insurance overhead in Canada has declined from 2.5 percent to 1.2 percent.[2] Hospital administrative costs have risen from 18.3 percent to 20.2 percent of total hospital spending in the United States, whereas in Canada these costs have climbed slightly from 8.0 percent to 9.0 percent.[2] Administrative expenses in U.S. nursing homes rose from 14.4 percent to 15.8 percent of costs, whereas administration's share of total costs rose from 10.5 to 13.7 percent in Canada.[2] Physicians' professional expenses (excluding malpractice premiums) have increased from 41.4 percent to 43.8 percent of gross income in the United States, whereas the Canadian figure declined from 35.5 percent to 34.4 percent.[2]

When we recalculated the 1987 figures to maintain comparability with the less complete 1983 data, we found that U.S. administrative costs rose from 21.9 percent to 23.9 percent of health care spending between 1983 and 1987, whereas in Canada administrative costs declined from 13.7 percent to 11.0 percent.[2] After adjustment for inflation, the divergence was even more striking. The costs of the health care bureaucracy in the United States rose by $32.2 billion (37 percent) between 1983 and 1987, an increase of $118 per capita. Administrative costs in the Canadian health care system fell by $161 million during this period, a decrease of $6 per capita.

Discussion

Most of our analysis is based on well-substantiated data, although in some areas reliable figures are sparse. The comparability of the data on hospital administrative costs in Canada and the United States is uncertain. However, we relied on detailed budgetary categories that appeared closely matched in the two nations. Although data on the administrative costs of health maintenance organizations are limited, they

do not appear to differ substantially from those in the U.S. fee-for-service sector.[20-22]

Both of our methods for estimating physicians' billing costs are imprecise. The expense-based method (Method 1) may overstate the difference between the United States and Canada, since it assumes that the entire discrepancy in the proportion of income devoted to professional expenses was accounted for by malpractice premiums, billing, and administration. The personnel-based method (Method 2) may understate the difference because it assumes that aides and other clinical personnel employed in physicians' offices performed no activities related to billing, that the total annual cost per clerical worker was no less in Canada than in the United States, and that Canadian billing operations have not been streamlined since 1977 despite computerization. An official of the Ontario Medical Association estimates that electronic claims sub-mission and reconciliation takes about one sixth as much staff time as paper-based billing (D. Peachey: personal communication).

In the United States, clerical and managerial staff accounted for 59.5 percent of the nonphysician employees in doctors' offices in 1988, and 74,700 more were added over the ensuing two years (D. U. Himmelstein, S. Woolhandler: unpublished data). In contrast, technicians and technologists accounted for only 7.3 percent of nonphysician office workers in 1988 and for only 5.7 percent in 1990 (D. U. Himmelstein, S. Woolhandler: unpublished data). In 1988, the staff in a typical U.S. physician's office spent about one hour on each Blue Shield or Medicare claim,[13] at least 20 times more than in Ontario (D. Peachey: personal communication; D. Weinkauf: personal communication). In a typical practice in Canada, "One person does all the billing, bookkeeping and typing . . . for 8 physicians."[23]

Our estimates omit the administrative costs of union and employer health-benefit programs and the administrative work done by hospital nurses and other nonphysician clinical personnel—all probably greater in the United States than in Canada. Moreover, patients in the United States spend far more time

(and anguish) on insurance paperwork than do Canadians; these costs are not reflected in our figures. On the other hand, some argue that funding health services through taxes, as in Canada, erodes productivity throughout the economy by discouraging work and investment—the so-called dead-weight loss.[24] Within the range of tax rates in North America, however, the magnitude, and even existence, of this dead-weight loss is controversial.[25]

The United States spent 37 percent more in real dollars on health administration in 1987 than in 1983.[2] The recent quest for efficiency has apparently amplified inefficiency. Cost-containment programs predicated on stringent scrutiny of the clinical encounter have required an army of bureaucrats to eliminate modest amounts of unnecessary care. Each piece of medical terrain is meticulously inspected except that beneath the inspectors' feet. Paradoxically, the cost-management industry is among the fastest-growing segments of the health care economy and is expected to generate $7 billion in revenues by 1993.[26] The focus on micromanagement has obscured the fundamentally inefficient structure required to implement such policies. In contrast, Canada has evolved simple mechanisms to enforce an overall budget, but it allows doctors and patients wide latitude in deciding how the funds are spent. Reducing our administrative costs to Canadian levels would save enough money to fund coverage for all uninsured and underin-

Table 1. Cost of Health Care Administration in the United States and Canada, 1987.

Cost Category	Spending per Capita*	
	U.S.	Canada
Insurance administration	106	17
Hospital administration	162	50
Nursing home administration	26	9
Physicians' overhead and billing expenses		
Expense-based estimate	203	80
Personnel-based estimate	106	41
Total costs of health care administration†		
High estimate	497	156
Low estimate	400	117

*All costs are expressed in U.S. dollars.

†The high estimate incorporates physicians' administrative costs derived by the expense-based method, and the low estimate costs derived by the personnel-based method.

sured Americans.[27] Universal comprehensive coverage under a single, publicly administered insurance program is the sine qua non of such administrative simplification.

The fragmented and complex payment structure of the U.S. health care system is inherently less efficient than the Canadian single-payer system. The existence of numerous insurers necessitates determinations of eligibility that would be superfluous if everyone were covered under a single, comprehensive program. Rather than a single claims-processing apparatus in each region, there are hundreds. Fragmentation also reduces the size of the insured group, limiting savings from economies of scale. Insurance overhead for U.S. employee groups with fewer than 5 members is 40 percent of premiums but falls to 5.5 percent for groups of more than 10,000.[28] Competition among insurers leads to marketing and cost shifting, which benefit the individual insurance firm but raise systemwide costs.

A lack of comprehensiveness in coverage also drives up administrative costs. Copayments, deductibles, and exclusions are expensive to enforce and lead many enrollees to purchase secondary "Medigap" policies. The secondary insurers maintain redundant and expensive bureaucracies.[29]

The efficiency of U.S. health care is further compromised by the extensive participation of private insurance firms whose overhead consumes 11.9 percent of premiums, as compared with 3.2 percent in U.S. public programs.[3] Even the "public" figure reflects the inefficiency of the private firms that process claims for Medicare for an average of $2.74 per claim,[30] whereas Ontario's Ministry of Health processes claims for $0.41 each (J. Davis: personal communication). Moreover, the inefficiency of private insurers is not unique to the United States. The small private-insurance sectors of Canada, the United Kingdom, and Germany have overheads of 10.9 percent, 16 percent, and 15.7 percent, respectively.[31,32] A major advantage of public programs in terms of efficiency is their use of existing tax-collection structures, obviating the need for a redundant bureaucracy to collect money for health services. Thus, the overhead in Germany's premium-based, quasi-public sickness funds is between 4.6 percent[33] and 4.8 percent (H. Kuhn: personal communication)—considerably higher than the overhead in tax-funded systems.

The scale of waste among private carriers is illustrated by Blue Cross/Blue Shield of Massachusetts, which covers 2.7 million subscribers and employs 6,682 workers[34]—more than work for all of Canada's provincial health plans, which together cover more than 25 million people[7-10] (and J. Davis: personal communication; D. Cunningham: personal communication); 435 provincial employees administer the coverage for more than 3 million people in British Columbia (D. Cunningham: personal communication).

The existence of multiple payers in the United States also imposes bureaucratic costs on health care providers. Hospitals must bill several insurance programs with varying and voluminous regulations on coverage, eligibility, and documentation. Moreover, billing on a per-patient basis requires an extensive internal accounting apparatus for attributing costs and charges to individual patients and insurers. In contrast, Canada's single-payer system funds hospitals through global budgets, eliminating almost all hospital billing. The striking administrative efficiency of the Shriners' hospitals in the United States, which bill neither patients nor third parties and devote only 2 percent of their revenues to administration,[35] suggests that payment mechanisms rather than cultural or political milieus determine administrative costs. Here, too, the European experience parallels North America's. British hospitals that are assigned global budgets devote 6.9 percent of spending to administration,[36] but those paid on a per-patient basis (such as Humana's Wellington Hospital in London) spend 18 percent.[37] The synchronous growth of bureaucratic profligacy and unmet health needs is reminiscent of Dickens' somber tale of six poor travelers who were relegated to outbuildings when the hostel built for them was fully occupied by its charitable administrators.

I found, too, that about a thirtieth part of the annual revenue was now expended on the purposes commemorated in the inscription over the door; the rest being handsomely laid out in Chancery, law expenses, collectorship, receivership, poundage, and other appendages of management, highly complimentary to the importance of the six Poor Travellers.[38]

The house of medicine is host to a growing array of specialists in fields unconnected to healing. At its present rate of growth, administration will consume a third of spending on health care 12 years hence, and half of the health care budget in the year 2020.

We are indebted to Mr. Lothar Rehmer, Ms. Judith Dowler, Dr. Jane Fulton, and Mr. Gilles Fortin for providing much of the raw data on Canadian health spending and to Dr. David H. Bor for his invaluable advice.

Notes

1. Bureau of the Census. Statistical abstract of the United States. 102nd–109th eds. Washington, D.C.: Government Printing Office, 1981–1989.
2. Himmelstein DU, Woolhandler S. Cost without benefit: administrative waste in U.S. health care. N Engl J Med 1986; 314:441–5.
3. Letsch SW, Levit KR, Waldo DR. National health expenditures, 1987. Health Care Financ Rev 1988; 10(2):109–22.
4. American Hospital Association. Hospital statistics: 1984 ed. Chicago: American Hospital Association, 1984.
5. American Hospital Association. Hospital statistics: 1988 ed. Chicago: American Hospital Association, 1988.
6. Hospital statistics 1986–1987. Toronto: Queen's Printer, 1987.
7. Ontario Ministry of Health. Annual report 1988–89. Kingston: Ontario Ministry of Health, 1989.
8. Regie de L'assurance-maladie du Quebec. Rapport Annuel 1986–1987. Quebec: Government of Quebec, 1987:30.
9. Saskatchewan Medical Care Insurance Commission. Annual report 1985–86. Regina: Government of Saskatchewan. 1986.
10. Nova Scotia Medical Services Insurance. Annual statistical tables: fiscal year 1985–86. Halifax: Government of Nova Scotia, 1986:3.
11. Canadian Medical Protective Association (CMPA) membership fees, 1971–1990. Toronto: Canadian Medical Association, 1989.
12. Gonzalez ML, Emmons DW, eds. Socioeconomic characteristics of medical practice 1989. Chicago: American Medical Association, 1989.

13. AMA Center for Health Policy Research. The administrative burden of health insurance on physicians. SMS Report 1989; 3(2):2–4.

14. Bureau of the Census. Current population survey, March 1988: technical documentation. Washington, D.C.: Department of Commerce, 1988.

15. Berry C, Brewster JA, Held PJ, Kehrer BH, Manheim LM, Reinhardt U. A study of the responses of Canadian physicians to the introduction of universal medical care insurance: the first five years in Quebec. Princeton, N.J.: Mathematica Policy Research, 1978.

16. Reynolds RA, Abram JB, eds. Socioeconomic characteristics of medical practice 1983. Chicago: American Medical Association, 1983.

17. Poullier J-P. Compendium: health care expenditure and other data. Health Care Financ Rev 1989; 11:Suppl:111–94.

18. Aggregate hospital financial data for California: report periods ending June 30, 1987–June 29, 1988. Sacramento: California Health Facilities Commission, 1989.

19. Aggregate long-term care facility financial data: report periods ending December 31, 1987–December 30, 1988. Sacramento: California Health Facilities Commission, 1989.

20. PHS will be challenged to maintain unbroken streak of profitability. Mod Healthcare 1989; 19(31):32–4.

21. Kenkel PJ. Improving managed care's management. Mod Healthcare 1990; 20 (19):27–34.

22. Kenkel PJ. Medicaid HMOs struggle for viability: federal plan aims to ease the burden. Mod Healthcare 1990; 20(16): 32.

23. Gerber PC. What your life would be like under a Canadian-type NHI. Physician's Manage 1990; 30(5):32–9.

24. Ballad CA, Shoven JB, Wholley J. The total welfare costs of the U.S. tax system: a general equilibrium approach. Natl Tax J 1985; 38:125–40.

25. MacEwan A, Campen J. Crisis, contradiction, and conservative controversies in contemporary U.S. capitalism. Rev Radical Polit Econ 1982; 14(3):1–22.

26. Cost-management industry grew in 1988. Mod Healthcare 1989; 19(33):64.

27. Woolhandler S, Himmelstein DU. Free care: a quantitative analysis of health and cost effects of a national health program for the United States. Int J Health Serv 1988; 18:393–9.

28. Congressional Research Service, Library of Congress. Cost and effects of extending health insurance coverage. Washington, D.C.: Government Printing Office, 1988. (Education and Labor serial number 100–EE).

29. Statement of Janet L. Shikles, Director, Health Financing and Policy Issues, Human Resources Division, General Accounting Office, before the Subcommittee of Health, Committee on Ways and Means, U.S. House of Representatives, March 13, 1990. Washington, D.C.: Government Printing Office, 1990. (SUDOC no. GAO/T–HRD–90–16).

30. Statement of Janet L. Shikles, Director, Health Financing and Policy Issues, Human Resources Division, General Accounting Office, before the Subcommittee on Health, Committee on Ways and Means, U.S. House of Representatives, June 14, 1990. Washington, D.C.: Government Printing Office, 1990. (SUDOC no. GAO/T–HRD–90–42).

31. Vayda E. Private practice in the United Kingdom: a growing concern. J Public Health Policy 1989; 10:359–76.

32. Verband der privaten Krankenversicherung e.V. Die private Krankenversicherung, Zahlenbericht 1988/1989.

33. Die gesetzliche Krankenversicherung in der Bundesrepublik Deutschland im Jahre 1988. Bonn, Germany: Bundesministerium für Arbeit und Sozialordnung, 1989.

34. Blue Cross/Blue Shield corporate report. Boston: Blue Cross/Blue Shield of Massachusetts, May 1990.

35. Guest DB. Health care policies in the United States: can the "American Way" succeed? Lancet 1985; 2:997–1000.

36. Compendium of health statistics. London: Office of Health Economics, 1984.

37. Parker P. A free market in health care. Lancet 1988, 1:1210–4.

38. Dickens C. Seven poor travellers. In: Dickens the Younger C, ed. Stories from the Christmas numbers of "Household Words" and "All the Year Round" 1852–1867. New York: Macmillan, 1896.

III

Universal Health Programs Abroad

Introduction

Robert B. Sullivan

Looking abroad for solutions to problems of access and cost is not a recent development in the United States. By the late nineteenth century, American scholars and researchers were beginning to investigate the delivery and financing of health care in Europe. Several publications on workers' insurance in Germany appeared in this country in the 1890s. A decade later the Russell Sage Foundation funded a trip by two Americans, Lee Frankel and Miles Dawson, to Europe to look at the state-sponsored insurance plans there. Other investigators made similarly motivated journeys, particularly after the British enacted a compulsory health plan in 1911. [1] A century after those early publications, a flourishing literature, from which come the four articles in this section, attests to continuing interest in developments abroad. [2]

But as previous sections in this volume suggest, Americans have been ambivalent about following the example of other countries in designing and adopting a universal health program for the U.S. Ironically, as the last industrialized country (besides South Africa) without universal or near-universal medical coverage, the United States may be especially well-positioned to benefit from the experiences of countries whose health plans have been in place for decades. [3] A working knowledge of the principal foreign systems helps delineate what is—and what might be—feasible, notions integral to any thorough grounding in universal health programs.

In the quest to press attractive features from vari-ous foreign programs into service in American health program proposals, cultural perceptions and traditions, perhaps because not readily measurable, have sometimes received short shrift. Yet foreign financing and organizational structures are reflections of collective values that did not take root overnight and that differ considerably from one country to another. Canadian health economist Robert Evans ("'We'll Take Care of It for You': Health Care in the Canadian Community") illustrates the importance of cultural subtleties by looking at two cultures with a number of similarities—Canada and the United States. Evans asks how financing arrangements have affected the behavior of medical care providers in the two countries, and what factors have influenced the divergent evolution of medical care organization. His articulation of Canadian cultural premises, often

overlooked by Americans, yields some refreshingly candid perspectives. "Canadians consider getting sick in the United States," Evans writes, "as the equivalent of a rather severe mugging." The monolithic Canadian "system" that Americans are wont to speak of, he reminds us, is actually ten different provincial systems that share financing with the federal government in Ottawa. Evans also compares Canada with Britain and continental Europe, noting the general absence outside the United States of competition among funding sources and providers, whether for patients or for profits. [4]

Some American policymakers, for whom familiarity has bred disenchantment with the limitations of the British and Canadian systems, have turned their attention once more to countries outside the British Commonwealth. As John K. Iglehart reports in the two-part article "Germany's Health Care System," the German system holds particular appeal for those who view private-sector pluralism and autonomy as a sine qua non of American medical care organization. In that system, not-for-profit organizations reconcile the demands of private interests with the public welfare in order to maintain broad access to medical care while checking the tendency for increases in costs to outstrip growth in national productivity. The German government, which finances the system through contributions by employers and employees, rarely intervenes. The German medical profession, moreover, plays a formal role in policymaking. American health insurers, eager for a system that steers clear of Canadian monopsony but assailed for the costly duplication of overhead that 1,500 separate companies generate, can point to nearly 1,200 sickness funds in the less-costly German system. But in Germany, as well, cultural values undergird the system's effectiveness. Iglehart, for example, cites "social solidarity" and a predisposition to compromise. And in a few areas—such as access to long-term and preventive care, continuity between ambulatory and hospital care, physician supply, and the performance of health services research—the German system fares worse than the American. [5]

Few discussions of medical care organization abroad fail to elicit references to the dysfunctions of "socialized medicine." And to the American mind, no Western democracy (with the possible exception of Britain) has a more socialized system than Sweden. In "The Effects of Sweden's Corporatist Structure on Health Policy and Outcomes," Diane Duffy shows the Swedish system to defy the stereotypes that attend such classification. After acknowledging that the Swedes fund over 90 percent of their health care budget from tax revenues, she points out that much tax revenue is collected and allocated by 26 county organizations, thus permitting a high degree of local decision making. Broad social agreement on health care issues, according to Duffy, limits the national government's role largely to the provision of information. Swedish policy, in fact, emphasizes decentralization and consensual coordination among associations and governmental bodies. Policy decisions that animate sharp political debates in the U.S. are less controversial among Swedes, who seldom dispute the importance of preventive care, the need for an equitable geographic allocation of resources, or the benefits of worker involvement in the management of facilities. Duffy believes that, as a result, health status in Sweden (as measured by infant mortality and life expectancy at birth) is the best in the world. But many researchers question whether medical care is as important a determinant of health status as socioeconomic status, nutrition, and public health measures, dimensions that Duffy excludes from her analysis. The ouster late in 1991 of Sweden's social democrats, whose half-century of political power saw the creation and establishment of today's health care system, also suggests rising popular dissatisfaction and political tensions that Duffy, writing less than three years earlier, apparently did not detect.

Although Americans have traditionally looked to European countries like Sweden, Germany, and Britain for system models, the impressive economic growth of the Pacific Rim is drawing attention to Asian health care systems as well. Japan's medical care objectives, according to John Iglehart ("Japan's Medical Care System"), resemble those of other developed countries: access, quality, and control of costs. Japan boasts health status indicators to rival Sweden's, more CAT scanners per capita than in the U.S., and three times as many physician visits and hospital beds per person as in America—all at less than half America's per capita health care expenditures. Health insurance provisions include cost-sharing and copayments (which, interestingly, appear to have had little impact on utilization of physician services). Iglehart contrasts surprising weaknesses in management sophistication, quality control, and consumer involvement in Japan's health care sector with the world-class organization that characterizes Japanese business. Although not stressed in the article, Japan, like Sweden, is an ethnically homogeneous society with fewer social cleavages than immigrant nations like the U.S. and Canada often display. Some researchers believe such cultural unity may promote the high social consensus necessary to create and sustain universal entitlement to medical care—in contradistinction to wide divergences of opinion among Americans. [6]

Many groups with vested interests in perpetuating the status quo in American health care organization caution that foreign systems—usually those with features inimical to their interests—cannot be "transplanted" to the United States. To our knowledge, however, no country has yet adopted another country's plan without first modifying it extensively to fit its own political and social contours. Just as travellers consult maps to find the most direct routes, familiarity with experiences abroad may reduce the experimentation required to achieve American health policy objectives. No map, of course, can guarantee good weather or the absence of detours on the way.

Notes

1. Odin W. Anderson, "Health Insurance in the United States, 1910–1920," *Journal of the History of Medicine and Allied Sciences* 5 (1950): 366, 366n10, 372.
2. Readers with particular interests in cross-national comparisons might find the following works helpful: "Comparative Health Systems: The Future of National Health Care Systems and Economic Analysis," *Advances in Health Economics and Health Services Research: A Research Annual*, ed. Jean-Jacques Rosa, Suppl. 1 (Greenwich, CT: JAI Press, 1990); Mark G. Field, ed., *Success and Crisis in National Health Systems: A Comparative Approach* (New York: Routledge, 1989); Milton I. Roemer, *National Strategies for Health Care Organization: A World Overview* (Ann Arbor: Health Administration Press, 1985); Marshall W. Raffel, ed., *Comparative Health Systems: Descriptive Analyses of Fourteen National Health Systems* (University Park, PA: The Pennsylvania State University Press, 1984); Milton I. Roemer, *Comparative National Policies on Health Care* (New York: Marcel Dekker, 1977).
3. Cf. Carol Sakala, "The Development of National Medical Care Programs in the United Kingdom and Canada: Applicability to Current Conditions in the United States" *Journal of Health Politics, Policy, and Law* 15, no. 4 (Winter 1990): 12.
4. For counterpoint to some aspects of Evans's portrait, see John K. Iglehart, "Canada's Health Care System Faces Its Problems," *New England Journal of Medicine* 22, no. 8 (February 22, 1990): 562–68. The importance of the Canadian system to government policymakers in the U.S. is evident from the favorable assessment published by the U.S. Congress (House), Committee on Government Operations, *Canadian Health Insurance: Lessons For the United States*, Report to the Chairman (Washington: United States General Accounting Office, June 1991). Readers seeking further analysis of the social and political conditions under which national programs have developed should see Carol Sakala's "The Development of National Medical Care Programs in the United Kingdom and Canada: Applicability to Current Conditions in the United States," *Journal of Health Politics, Policy, and Law* 15, no. 4 (Winter 1990): 709–53. In an attempt to distill implications for the American situation, as well as to counter the "pervasive sense [among Americans] that the United States is unique," Sakala describes the effects of two world wars, the Depression, and political dissent and includes concise chronologies of "key events" in the establishment of the British National Health Service and the Canadian hospital and medical insurance programs. Britain and Canada, however, acted when their systems were far

less complex, and thus more tractable, than is the U.S. system in the 1990s. Sakala nevertheless concludes that mounting pressures from many quarters in the United States may be fostering the beginnings of consensus among politicians, providers, and business. For comparisons of, and misconceptions about, the British and American systems, see J. Lister, "The Politics of Medicine in Britain and the United States," *New England Journal of Medicine* 315, no. 3: 168–75, and Christopher Potter and Janet Porter, "American Perceptions of the British National Health Service: Five Myths," *Journal of Health Politics, Policy, and Law* 14, no. 2 (Summer 1989): 341–65.

5. Two illuminating articles comparing systems in the Netherlands and the U.S. with the preunification German system, both by Bradford Kirkman-Liff, are "Health Insurance Values and Implementation in the Netherlands and the Federal Republic of Germany: An Alternative Path to Universal Coverage," Journal of the American Medical Association 265, no. 19 (May 15, 1991): 2496–2502; and "Physician Payment and Cost-Containment Strategies in West Germany: Suggestions for Medicare Reform," *Journal of Health Politics, Policy, and Law* 15, no. 1 (Spring 1990): 69–99. A more general summary is available by Fritz Beske, "The Federal Republic of Germany" in *International Handbook of Health Care Systems*, ed. R. B. Saltman (Westport, CT: Greenwood Press, 1988).

6. For the sociological, political economy, and historical dimensions of medical care system evolution, see J. Rogers Hollingsworth, Jerald Hage, and Robert Hanneman, *State Intervention in Medical Care: Consequences for Britain, France, Sweden, and the United States: 1890–1970* (Ithaca: Cornell University Press, 1990); *idem, A Political Economy of Medicine: Great Britain and the United States* (Baltimore: Johns Hopkins University Press, 1986); and *idem* and Robert Hanneman, *Centralization and Power in Social Service Delivery Systems: The Cases of England, Wales, and the United States* (Boston: Kluwer-Nijhoff Publishing, 1984). For references to discussions of American attitudes towards the health care system, see Robert J. Blendon and Karen Donelan, "The Public and the Emerging Debate Over National Health Insurance" (Chapter 25 in this volume).

21

"We'll Take Care of It for You"
Health Care in the Canadian Community

Robert G. Evans

The "scientific" understanding of human health and illness, the collection of life sciences and associated technologies that generate the intellectual basis for clinical activity, is an international cultural enterprise. Differences among nations are at most different accents in a common language. Patterns of medical practice, "who does what and with which and to whom," may vary internationally depending on where a new drug, technique, or piece of equipment happens to have been developed first. But diffusion, like treason, is largely a matter of dates.

The provision of health services, the application of this common intellectual property, is carried out by trained individuals and within organizations that are also quite similar, throughout the developed world at least. Physicians, hospitals, nurses, pharmacists, dentists are virtually universal features of the international health care landscape, although their definitions and competencies may vary in detail. But their patterns of work and their interrelationships are more diverse, being powerfully influenced by the specifics of each national reimbursement system—the set of institutions and processes whereby financial resources are assembled from the general population and then distributed among the providers of care. This health care "industry"

Reprinted by permission of *Daedalus*, Journal of the American Academy of Arts and Sciences, from the issue entitled, "In Search of Canada," Fall 1988, vol. 117/4.

accounts for a very large proportion of economic activity in all modern societies—between 8 and 12 percent of national income.[1] Each country has evolved a distinctive way of organizing, and especially of paying for, its provision of health services. Through these systems societies show their individuality. Thus, the Canadian health care system, as distinct from the Swedish, or the American, or the British, is a particular style of organization and payment rather than a type of medical knowledge or practice.

To suggest that each country has chosen a distinctive form of health care financing, however, is to create an incomplete and misleading picture. While policy analysts of various persuasions treat organizational structures, on paper at least, as readily adjustable mechanisms or as means to general social ends, the reality appears to be more organic and evolutionary. Each nation is both legatee and prisoner of its own history and its enduring cultural values and symbols.

Students of comparative health care systems emphasize the fundamental continuity of institutions, despite occasional announcement of radical reform and the continuing background rhetoric of rapid change. When "revolutions" occur—the creation of the National Health Service in the United Kingdom, for example, and of the universal public health-insurance plans in Canada—they turn out on close examination to have deep historical roots and to represent the continuation of old traditions under new names.[2]

This underlying stability reflects the fact that a nation's health care system is a massive and complex social undertaking, not to be tampered with lightly. The system in place at any moment balances a multitude of conflicting interests and objectives, both overt and covert. But it also serves as a symbol of the fundamental shared values of the society.

Health care is perceived (not always accurately) as a matter of life and death. Access to care may determine the very continuation or termination of the individual, a matter in which the community as a whole is deeply concerned. More generally, the health of an individual is regarded in most societies as a precondition of full participation in the life of the community, like legal or political status, and not merely a "commodity" of purely private interest.

The financing of health care thus serves as a mirror or a lens in which those dominant cultural values can be viewed and compared from one society to another. The comparison between Canada and the United States is particularly instructive, for they have done a sort of natural experiment in health care financing. These very similar societies with very similar systems of medical care have developed radically different funding systems. The behavior and subsequently the organization and performance of the two systems have increasingly diverged in response to markedly different financial opportunities and constraints.[3]

For the student of health care systems, the interesting question is how various financing systems have influenced system behavior and organization. The deeper and more difficult question is why the two societies have evolved such radically different ways of funding health care. The first is a generic question about the behavior of health care systems; the second is a specific question about Canadian, and American, society.

For the differences *did* evolve. They were not, like the parliamentary and presidential systems of government, matters of inheritance. Modern systems of health care finance are a response to technical and social pressures that developed in the twentieth century, and it is within the last forty years that the Canadian and American roads have diverged so sharply. The public systems of hospital insurance were put in place in each of the Canadian provinces between 1946 and 1961, and the medical insurance systems between 1962 and 1971, with supporting federal legislation and cost sharing in 1957 and 1966 (effective 1968) respectively. The American system took on its modern form in 1965.[4]

Thus, English-speaking Canadians who seize on their health care system as one outstanding illustration of a rather elusive cultural identity ("Are we *really* different from the Americans?" they ask) have got it right. The Canadian approach to funding health care may be markedly superior to the American on various objective and widely held criteria—many students of health care, including this one, believe that it is—and if so, the Canadian system is an important and rather rare collective achievement.[5] Like beating the Russians at hockey, beating the Americans at anything is a source of considerable satisfaction.

The more basic point is simply that the Canadian health care system, precisely because it is different, responds to and reflects significant, if perhaps subtle, features of "Canadianness." It is one of the most convincing forms of evidence, perhaps *the* most convincing, that we are not Americans after all. (It may be difficult for non-Canadians, whether Americans or others, to appreciate what a relief that is.) But our approach differs from the various European health care

systems as well, although we are closer to Europe than to the United States, and again the differences are indicative of underlying cultural values.

To fully describe the health care funding and delivery system of each Canadian province would be a mammoth undertaking interesting only to the most dedicated specialist. Each province is different, and the picture is constantly changing in detail. Nor are the details unimportant. There are significant differences in system behavior from one province to another and over time. Analysts who insist that "the Canadian system" is not one but ten (twelve, if one counts the territories) are right.[6]

But those who perceive a well-defined common pattern within the diversity are not wrong either. From the point of view of the ordinary Canadian citizen, playing the various roles of potential or actual patient, of taxpayer, and of voter, the form of organization and payment is essentially similar across all the provinces. Moreover, from the user's perspective, the system has remained more or less stable for about twenty years. The major conflicts and changes of this period have deeply concerned providers and governments at both the federal and the provincial level[7] but, with few exceptions, have not directly affected the ordinary citizen as he, or more often she, has used and paid for health care.

That Canadian-in-the-street, confronted with what she believes to be a health problem, may decide to consult a physician. She will normally go to a general practitioner in independent private practice (though she may approach any physician she chooses), and the physician may or may not accept her as a patient. Free choice of physician—and patient—is an established principle, subject only to the qualification that if no practitioner were willing to take a particular patient, the medical community as a whole would have some obligation to offer service. Exactly how that responsibility would be discharged and by whom is, however, somewhat obscure; the problem rarely arises.

When the patient arrives, the physician will do the sorts of things physicians do—taking a history and noting

the symptoms; performing, prescribing, or recommending various diagnostic and therapeutic maneuvers, drugs, or further consultations; and if the condition warrants, sending the patient to a hospital at which the doctor has admitting privileges. Almost any specialist consulted will also be a private practitioner, having a close association with one or more hospitals but not usually being a hospital employee. At no point will there be any charges to the patient for the services of the physician or the hospital, although obviously there are both monetary and nonmonetary costs involved in seeking and receiving care.[8]

The physicians will be reimbursed for their services by an agency of the provincial ministry of health, according to a uniform schedule of fees negotiated at periodic intervals by that agency and the provincial medical association. With minor exceptions, however, the decisions about which services to provide or recommend are entirely up to each physician and subject to the compliance of the patient.

Claims for reimbursement are checked for correspondence with the rules for payment, included as part of the negotiated fee schedule in force, and "practitioner profiles" are screened to identify patterns of practice that are extraordinarily unusual relative to norms defined by the behavior of a physician's peer group, but these are very wide bounds. In general, the clinical autonomy of the physician is maintained.

The hospital, however, will not be reimbursed directly for the particular services provided to this patient. Hospitals are supported through global budgets negotiated annually with the ministry of health. Salaries of physicians employed by the hospital—residents and interns, salaried chiefs of service, emergency-room staff—are paid from the global budget. Diagnostic services and prescription drugs provided to inpatients are likewise included, but diagnostic services provided to ambulatory patients, by either hospitals or freestanding facilities, may be paid for through fees for individual services.

The hospital and medical services are thus almost entirely (between 90 and 95 percent) reimbursed from government budgets. The overall share of public funding for health care is substantially lower, about 75 percent, because expenditures for dental care and nonprescription drugs, and a significant share of those for prescription drugs, are met through direct patient payment or private insurance.

There is also substantial direct payment for long-term institutional care, although the public/private split here is largely a matter of bookkeeping. Patients in extended-care hospital beds and publicly supported residents in other long-term care facilities are charged a per diem fee, calculated not on the basis of the actual charges but as a share of the minimum public pension. The logic of this charge is that the few patients who are in such care (and who now account for a large, and growing, share of hospital days) are in effect being provided with room and board by the hospital. Since the public pension is also intended to provide a minimum standard of living, there is no obvious justification for the state to pay twice. But insofar as this component of private payment represents absorption of another form of public support, its privateness is more form than substance.

From general taxation and federal grants, provincial ministries of health raise the revenue to support the health system, which is their largest single activity. In the beginning, these grants were proportionate to the provincial outlays on medical and hospital care, but since 1977 they have been set by formulas unrelated to actual outlays. Accordingly, while a high proportion of health expenditures is actually funded through federal taxation, provincial governments are entirely at risk for any increases in costs (and are the fiscal beneficiaries of cost containment).

Three provinces retain a system of "health insurance premiums," but these are insurance premiums in name only. They are uniform charges unrelated to the risk faced by the person covered or to the overall cost of services. They are de facto compulsory for most of the population, and most importantly, no one can be denied services for failure to pay. The uninsured resident who uses services may be billed for back premiums but not for the cost of the services.

(In the same way, the property owner who has not paid municipal taxes will be billed for back taxes but will not be denied the services of the fire or police departments upon need and will not be billed for the actual costs of the services received.) Accordingly, these premiums are treated by all analysts as part of the general tax system, not as a separate "insurance" system. [9]

Stripped of a vast array of fascinating detail, the Canadian health care system is a fully linked triangular relationship. Members of the public receive care "free" as patients and pay for it through the general tax system. Professional providers determine the appropriate care to be provided to patients, unencumbered by any considerations of what the patient is able or willing to pay for, and are reimbursed in forms and at rates determined in negotiation with provincial governments. Those governments, in turn, raise the necessary revenues through taxation and distribute them to providers.

This picture is incomplete, however, in that it presupposes a health care system with fixed capacity, a given stock of manpower and facilities such as hospital beds and equipment. But physicians cannot admit patients to beds that do not exist, or refer for diagnostic or treatment services that are not available. Nor can patients be seen by physicians who have not been trained. The reimbursement system thus must cover not only the cost of current operations but also the costs of reproducing, expanding, and upgrading the existing system. These capital costs, in the broadest sense, include new technology—equipment and techniques and the financing to support them—as well as the construction of new hospital capacity and the training of additional professionals to direct its use.

The flow of capital into the health care sector and the determination of the amount and type of service it will offer is also negotiated by the professional community and the provincial governments, partly directly and partly through political pressure. Some hospitals also make direct appeals to the general public for charitable funding, but this source, while of increasing interest to hospital managements, is

significant only for a very few high-profile hospitals.

This negotiation of system capacity is a natural extension of the professionals' role in negotiating their own reimbursement. The billing opportunities, the incomes, of professionals who are reimbursed by fees for services depend heavily on the extent of their access to the "free" capital equipment and supporting staff provided through the hospital system. New technologies and expanded facilities thus permit physicians to provide more services, to raise their "productivity," and to capture this increase in the form of higher incomes at any given level of fees.

Negotiation of capacity also reflects the overlap between two different bases for public decision making, both generally accepted as legitimate and thus a source of conflict. The professional community is believed to have special expertise in deciding what services are required to meet the needs of the population served. In each medical case, the provider determines what is medically necessary, what clinical interventions are appropriate in the care of the patient. Clinical autonomy at the level of the individual, then, logically extends to questions of what types and amounts of facilities and personnel should be available to meet the needs of patients collectively.

The provincial government has an equally legitimate role, however, in deciding what to pay for, where, and when, so long as it acts (and in this field it does) with broadly based public support. This right to make legitimate choices among medical and nonmedical priorities on the community's behalf is further strengthened by the fact that, as a matter of common observation, the skills and knowledge acquired and deployed in the clinical setting with individual patients do not in general carry over to the epidemiological or planning context. The whole is not simply the sum of the parts.

Nor, as I have indicated, is the practitioner a disinterested interpreter of the community's needs. New facilities translate into expanded practitioner incomes and professional opportunities. Negotiations over access to new capital inevitably respond to provider as well as patient interests. Furthermore, the interests of patients, individually or collectively, are not coterminous with those of the community as a whole: the average patient and the average citizen are different people. The tension among competing sources of legitimacy in decision making is a theme to which we shall return.

These formal and informal negotiations, over both current reimbursement and expansion of system capacity, take place almost entirely between providers of care and governments. The public is involved in the negotiations as voters, appealed to by providers as potential patients—to support campaigns for more services—or by governments as taxpayers interested in containing overall outlays. But the system of funding does not allow for separate financial arrangements between providers and individual patients with respect to services covered by the public plans.

Physicians cannot "extra-bill" their patients by demanding additional payments above the negotiated fee schedule payable by the provincial government in return for covered services. (Services deemed not medically necessary, on the other hand, are to be charged to the patient in full, at any amount the physician chooses, in principle. In practice, these turn out to be rather rare.) Looked at from the other side of the coin, patients cannot offer physicians side payments for more favorable consideration.[10] The economic link between use of care and contribution to its cost has been disconnected through the public programs. The surrounding regulatory structure makes attempts by either providers or patients to reconnect that linkage difficult or impossible—and is intended to do so.

This balance of rights and responsibilities among individuals, the community, and providers of care reflects the attitudes and values of the Canadian population. It would be naive to imagine that many Canadians had actually thought through in any coherent way the system of values of which their health care system is the concrete expression, let alone that they would all agree. But the level of public support for the present system is extremely high. The system has successfully withstood

challenges to its basic principles from several quarters—from medical associations, some provincial governments, the private insurance industry—and continues to hold off such challenges because most members of the population approve of it. They believe it works and that it is "right."

At the most basic level, the public funding system embodies a view of the relationship between the individual and the environment. Nature is, at best, rather hostile and difficult to control. With no regard for virtue or vice, illness or injury can strike anyone. There is no moral reason why the victim should be exposed to financial insult on top of physical injury. Health care in Canada is free, because to charge the patient is to tax the sick.

Indeed, even if the victim *did* contribute to his or her own misfortune—as the smoker with lung cancer or the teenage motorist has—risk taking is not a calculated, voluntary act. Stupidity is as much a natural force as an unanticipated blizzard, and foolish behavior arises in a social context. There may be good reasons for taxing cigarettes and for identifying and penalizing dangerous driving, but charging health care costs to the estate of the lung cancer victim or denying him care if he cannot afford to pay is inherently offensive and serves no useful social purpose.

A person holding an alternative view might say that the natural environment provides ample opportunity to look out for oneself. Illness and injury are indicative of avoidable carelessness, correctable incompetence, or even punishable moral turpitude. ("Bad luck" may be evidence of divine displeasure.) People who get into difficulty should therefore bear at least part of the financial consequences, as well as the physical ones. Such a distribution of burdens is fair (why should others bear the cost of an individual's decisions?) and also tends to encourage "better" behavior. Being responsible for one's own acts is a mark of maturity and morally uplifting. It signifies that one takes care and tries to be competent.

The Canadian funding system implicitly rejects the latter view and treats illness as primarily the result of natural or social malevolence rather than per-

sonal default. This view in turn is consistent with a deep sense of the powers of the individual in relation to the environment. The system implies a further judgment about the relationship between individual choice and professional authority. When the patient recognizes a problem, he takes it to a professional, who diagnoses it and determines what treatment is medically necessary.

The legislation governing the public plans explicitly identifies medical necessity as the ground for reimbursement. The individual is not expected to manage the care episode himself but to draw upon professional services as he sees fit. Furthermore, the professional provider is assumed to be equipped with both a base of knowledge sufficient to determine what ought to be done and an ethical imperative to ensure that he will do it without undue regard for his own interest—that is, he will act "professionally."

In this context, there is no particular point in involving the patient economically. The typical patient follows the orders of authority, and that authority acts responsibly in giving orders.

Still another alternative is to take a more activist view and to see the patient, in choosing among providers and the forms of advice given, as manager of his or her own care. This perspective may also include the concern that providers tend to slant their advice in the direction most profitable to themselves unless monitored by vigilant patients protecting their own economic interests. There may be no unambiguously right response to the patient's problem—it is a matter for individual choice—and even if there is, the professional cannot be trusted to recommend it.

This third view underlies the line of argument that has always been of most interest to economists, particularly those who have limited familiarity with the health care field. Patients, they say, should be exposed to some part of the costs of their own health care, whether or not they are wholly or partly responsible for their illnesses (the ethical case gets a little fuzzy here), so that they will either be more careful shoppers for care and/or keep the professional ambitions or the greed of providers in check. Free care leads to abuse and overuse through inappropriate behavior on the part of patients, providers, or both.

To some extent, these three views are amenable to empirical testing. One can bring certain sorts of evidence to bear, although the long-continued debate and deep disagreement of academic specialists in this field indicate the difficulty of unambiguous resolution.[11] While these debates go on and provide entertainment and employment for academics, health care consultants, and public relations specialists, however, the Canadian health care system puts a particular judgment of the issue into practice, as it has done for decades.

In a very real sense, the manipulation of evidence has been irrelevant. The Canadian public has accepted, and continues overwhelmingly to support, a system of health care and health care finance whose basic structure implies that, in this domain, the individual is not responsible for his own misfortunes (or at least no useful purpose is served by treating him as if he were). Further, the proper response to such misfortune is to seek and rely on duly accredited professional authority. Such authority can in general be relied upon. Presumably, that is what most Canadians believe. And presumably, citizens of the nations that have evolved reimbursement systems that place direct economic burdens on the users of care implicitly take, on balance, a different view.

But that is only the beginning of the story. The collective funding structure implies that the community accepts responsibility for ensuring that the individual will have access to needed care. In itself this is not unusual; the collective provision of the preponderance of, if not all, funding for hospital and medical care is universal in the developed world.[12] A society that expressed indifference, in principle, to the potential and preventable extinction of some of its members could hardly claim to be called a society at all. What is less common is the degree to which, in Canada, this collective responsibility is placed on the shoulders of government and then interpreted as requiring not only ensurance of access but access on equal terms and conditions.

"Equal terms and conditions" lies behind both the removal of all direct financial barriers to the public system and the discouragement or suppression of private arrangements, so that everyone has access to the same system. "Equality before the health care system" has been established as a political principle similar to "equality before the law."

The contrast with the United States is obvious, but in this case comparison with the United Kingdom is perhaps more instructive. There the National Health Service (NHS) is a public program, funded from tax revenue, accessible to all. But individuals can, if they choose, seek care in a private system, which is generally perceived to be more convenient and to provide a better quality of service.

U.K. citizens continue to pay into, and have the right of access to, the public system, and they generally use that system if severe illness or emergency strikes. But for "cold surgery," minor illness, and the non-life-threatening problems of the basically healthy, the private system provides an attractive alternative for those who can afford it. Employee groups can also buy private insurance for private care, coverage whose cost can be kept down because it is to a limited degree subsidized through the income tax system and because it is understood—sometimes explicitly—that any major, expensive illness will be cared for by the NHS. Moreover, employee groups are a self-selected population with low risks and adequate economic resources—precisely the people and rational insurers look for.

In most of the Canadian provinces, patients' private payment for medical or hospital care is not directly prohibited. What is not permitted, however, is for physicians or hospitals to be both in and out of the public system, as they are in Britain. This is a critical constraint. The British private consultant can use his dual role to select and steer patients according to their resources and the nature of their problems. He can even use his position within the NHS to manipulate waiting lists and other aspects of access so as to ensure that private care will be preferable to those who can afford it. The Canadian physi-

cian who chooses to "go private" must go all the way. He cannot use a strategic position within the public system to cream off only the profitable patients for his private services.

The hostility toward "multiclass medicine" in Canada is thus partly based on straightforward grounds of prudence. The private alternative is not simply an expansion of the choices and opportunities available to patients—a form of rhetoric to which it would be difficult to object. It may also represent a constraint on the services available to users of the public system insofar as their access becomes limited or other aspects of their care degraded through the strategic behavior of providers with an economic interest in the private sector.

Developments in the United Kingdom in 1987 and 1988 illustrate a still more extreme form of this risk. Strategic behavior may not be limited to providers. An ideologically hostile government may seek, and certainly is suspected of seeking, to undermine a popular public program that it does not dare to attack directly. A policy of restricting funding in the public sector is much more acceptable politically if several of one's most influential supporters are already users of the private sector. The maintenance of a constituency in support of a public program is much easier, on the other hand, if everyone has to use that program. Concerns over quality and access find louder voices in support.

Such interactions between the presence of a private alternative and the quality or even viability of a public system are of considerable interest to students of health care systems. They are important questions, and they weigh with some who are in a position to shape policy. But it is doubtful whether these questions are really fundamental to the differences in public attitude between the United Kingdom and Canada. Is the average citizen even aware of these issues? It seems more likely, at least to this observer, that private medicine in the United Kingdom is simply a continuation of the good old British tradition of snobbery and class privilege, which many an earlier generation of immigrants to Canada was glad to leave behind.

In the United Kingdom most citizens find it right and proper that the "better" class of people should receive their care under more genteel surroundings and pay for the privilege. Yet most Canadians find this opinion offensive. Health care touches the individual so closely—again the perception of life and death--that it is difficult to separate class-specific medicine from the implication that some people's lives are worth more than others'.

Indeed, Canada has a deep-rooted suspicion of class-based systems of any kind. Private schools are a minor part of the educational picture, private universities are nonexistent, and public transportation is all single-class, with the exception of the airlines (why?). Canada may not be a classless society, but Canadians are strongly attached to the belief that it is.

Several of the European health care systems also seem to have a class component in their funding, perhaps a remnant of Bismarck's influence. When health insurance was originally provided for the German workingman, it was provided by a government under the control of other interests, attempting *inter alia* to undermine the appeal of socialism. Given this objective, there was no obvious reason to include other classes in the program. Furthermore, the European reliance on various forms of payroll tax draws on labor income alone. By relying on general (primarily income and sales) tax revenues, the Canadian system spreads the burden over all income earners.

As the technology of health care has evolved and its potential costs have grown beyond the reach of almost anyone's budget, more and more groups in the European populations have gained some form of insurance. But coverage in many countries remains linked in one way or another to status. The German sickness funds are defined by occupations, with regional funds for those without an occupational base and private coverage for those with the highest incomes. The Dutch compulsory coverage, again, applies only up to a certain income limit. The Belgian funds recruit on a religious basis.

In general, competition for enrollees is limited. Rather, each fund tends to serve a distinct and separate population. Moreover, above some income level, individuals are expected to pay for their own care and/or purchase private insurance, which may be publicly subsidized. All forms of coverage may be regulated and supplemented to ensure universal coverage but not all in the same system or fund.

That both physicians and patients seem to prefer this approach suggests the symbolic importance of special treatment for the upper classes and of direct access to the patient's own resources for the physician. The right to charge some patients directly, even if only a small fraction of them, rather than having to deal with a bureaucracy (whether public or private) seems very important to physicians in all countries.

The bitter battles over extra billing, culminating in the Ontario physicians' strike of 1986, made clear how important such a right is to physicians in Canada. These struggles, which went on for a number of years before and after the enactment of the Canada Health Act of 1984, made equally clear the extent and the depth of the popular opposition to this practice.[13] This conflict drew sharp lines of battle between the majority of physicians in the country and the majority of the population. The population won.

Thus, while Canadian health care shares with European systems the underlying judgment that illness is an unavoidable misfortune, to be remedied by seeking and following professional advice with funding provided entirely or almost entirely through collective mechanisms, it differs in its powerful commitment to the principle that the provision of care and the pattern of funding should be the same for everyone. We are all equal when faced with disease or death, and our institutions reflect that sense of equality.

It is no coincidence that the historical origins of the Canadian health care funding system were in the province of Saskatchewan at a time when its population was almost entirely made up of small farmers and people who supported and depended on the farming industry. Weather and world markets, both beyond any control, dictated everyone's fortunes, and everyone went up and down together. The sense of equality before shared adversity that was natural in this environment also seems to have struck a resonant chord in the rest of the country.

The reliance on collective funding through government was a natural response to a communitywide problem. It was also the usual Canadian response to the country's predicament of how to deal with a small population thinly distributed over a large landmass. In the European countries, highly differentiated and concentrated populations made it natural to begin with aggregations intermediate between the individual and the state—with workers' friendly societies or religious organizations. In an earlier and simpler state of medical and administrative technology, such groups were large enough to pool the expenditure risks of their members, and, most important, linked by an affinity that makes people willing to share their misfortunes and their care.

In Canada, however, the natural focus for collective activity has always been government. As residents of a small country heavily dependent on world markets, flanked on the north by a large and hostile wilderness and on the south by a large—and, well, large—neighbor, Canadians have instinctively turned to the state as the instrument of collective purposes. A multiplicity of competing organizations is a luxury we cannot afford.

Nor is private organization and competition accorded the intrinsic value in and for itself that it receives in the United States. In the rhetoric of the business and economic community, which so strongly influences U.S. policy, even a badly functioning private marketplace often appears to be definitionally superior to a well-functioning public agency. Americans seem to accept the form of economic organization as an end in itself, independent of any external performance criteria. This ideology has never put down deep roots in Canada, where both public initiatives and semiprivate regulated monopolies that pursue some version of public purpose (along with private profit) are a tradition older than the country itself.[14]

Accordingly, the collective funding of health care costs takes place through the monopoly suppliers of hospital and medical insurance in their respective regions—the provincial governments. The Canadian system is socialized insurance, not socialized medicine. But the provinces are also the predominant buyers of hospital and medical services from private physicians and hospitals. This kind of monopsony has become central to the control of health expenditures, and through them, to the management of health care delivery.

The recognition of this power, a counterweight to their professional authority and a threat to their economic position, lay behind the opposition of physicians to the creation of the universal public plans. Indeed, the subsequent political struggles over extra billing have served to define more clearly the limits of "physician autonomy."

Medical associations have always attempted, in Canada and elsewhere, to extend their claim of special expertise in the clinical setting to include control over the broader questions of how the delivery of medical care should be organized, how physicians should be reimbursed, and how much. [15] In the debates surrounding Medicare, the passage of the Canada Health Act, and the physician strikes in Saskatchewan (1962) and Ontario (1986), these claims to wider political authority were put very explicitly, in direct confrontation with the power of elected governments. The majority of the population decisively rejected these claims. Whether their rejection will have consequences for the authority of the medical profession in other spheres or for the doctor-patient relationship is difficult to calculate.

Yet, at the time the public plans were set up, there was no general public sentiment in favor of limiting physician autonomy. Indeed, the report of the Royal Commission on Health Services (the Hall Commission) expresses the opposite intention, that the public funding system should not interfere with professional independence. [16] What was perhaps not appreciated was the extent to which organized medicine interpreted that independence as depending upon, and therefore conferring, special authority over the whole field of health policy.

The advocates of public insurance emphasized instead the manifest inability of private insurers—privately organized competitive forms of collective financing for health care—to cover the entire population. The laws of the marketplace dictate that competitive for-profit insurers, responsible to their shareholders and competing for subscribers, must inevitably exclude those in greatest need and those least able to pay for either insurance or care. [17] In the majority of cases such persons would, then, go without or become a charge on the public purse. (European systems built up from several or many funds can maintain universality because the funds are not in competition for enrollees or organized for profit.)

The real options in Canada, or anywhere else, are not public-versus-private forms of collective funding. Private insurance for the whole population is impossible in a competitive marketplace because insurers cannot cover the poor and the ill, and remain competitive. Still less likely is a real choice between individual and collective funding; the patterns of distribution of needs and of economic resources rule out self-payment for the bulk of health care. The only choices, unless a society is prepared simply to accept the exclusion of a significant proportion of its population from the health care system, are universal public coverage or a mixed public and private system, with the public system covering those with the greatest needs and the least resources.

But this mixed approach, so the Hall Commission argued, would be both administratively much more expensive than the other approach and incapable of providing coverage to much of the population, noy only on equal terms and conditions but at all. The history of the United States system, with the world's highest and most rapidly escalating health care costs, the highest proportion of funds going to administrative cost, and nearly 20 percent of its population uninsured (and perhaps another 10 percent grossly underinsured), bears out the Hall Commission's predictions rather well.

In summary, then, the Canadian health care system reflects a strong commitment to egalitarianism combined with a strong respect for, and substantial confidence in, duly constituted authority. [18] This authority includes both the politically legitimate authority of the state and the professionally legitimate authority of the providers of care. These attitudes stand in sharp contrast to those lying behind the American approach, where the health care funding system, like many other institutions, responds to a combination of individualism and suspicion of authority. But the emphasis on egalitarianism also distinguishes the Canadian approach from those in a number of the European countries, where remnants of class- and status-based funding and care persist.

The reliance on government raises one of the most fundamental questions in Canadian political organization: Which government? The longest and most carefully defended border in the world is between the government of Canada and the governments of each of the provinces. Canadians have a fascination with federal-provincial relations that most other nations reserve for religion or sex.

It is inevitable that the health care funding system as the expression of many of our national symbols and values should provide a setting for playing out federal-provincial conflicts. These, in turn, reflect the extraordinary ambiguity of Canadians' feelings of nationality: Are we really citizens of one country or of ten provinces in a loose association of convenience? Well, it depends. In the particular case of health care, it depends on either creative federalism or constitutional subterfuge, according to one's point of view.

The British North America Act of 1867, the act of the British parliament that until 1982 provided the constitutional basis for the government of Canada, specified that matters pertaining to health care were under the jurisdiction of the provincial governments. Such matters were at that time seen as local problems, of no great interest to the national government. The federal government has, accordingly, no constitutional authority to run a health service or a health insurance plan for the general population, and it does neither. Strictly speaking, Canada has no health care system, only a collection of provincial plans.

The federal government does have constitutional authority to raise revenues by direct or indirect taxes and to make grants or other distributions of those revenues. It can make conditional grants to provinces, which can establish and administer public heath insurance programs conforming to federally established standards. These standards form the core of Canadian health insurance—public administration, comprehensiveness of benefits, portability between provinces, universality of coverage on equal terms and conditions, and accessibility.

The essential similarity of the provincial plans thus derives from the requirements imposed at the outset as conditions for federal support. That support was initially in the form of cost sharing; the federal government returned to the provinces roughly 50 percent of all outlays on "allowable" health services. An offer of finance on that scale was obviously one that no province could refuse. In 1977 the federal contribution was changed to, in effect, a block grant unrelated to actual health care outlays. The contribution remained conditional, but in the new environment the conditions were much more tenuous. In 1984 the federal Canada Health Act made the conditions more explicit and provided for penalties—cash withholding—for provinces whose plans were in default of the federal standards.

This form of organization, provincial administration under broad federal guidelines and with major federal funding support, has worked out rather well in practice. But it has provided a continuing focus for conflict—sometimes just grandstanding but sometimes real—between the federal and the provincial governments. Political profile and large amounts of money are available and at risk in these arrangements. Underlying the conflicts, moreover, are both political and constitutional ambiguities or contradictions that go to the heart of Canadian political life.

Before passage of the Constitution Act in 1982, those ambiguities were solely political. The principle of absolute parliamentary sovereignty was as clearly established in Canada as it was in Westminister, with the minor qualification that it might not be clear, for any given issue, in which parliament—federal or provincial—that sovereignty re-

sided. Hence, the long and endlessly fascinating history of federal-provincial diplomacy, negotiations between what, from some perspectives, are sovereign powers with overlapping and competing jurisdictions.

Both derive their legitimacy from representing the same population. If they disagree, which is the true representative? Provincial governments have from the beginning of the health insurance plans argued, with considerable justification, that the imposition of federal standards on health insurance, clearly a matter of provincial jurisdiction, was illegitimate federal incursion into their political territory.

No provincial government, however, has ever directly challenged the validity of the basic principles of Medicare—public administration, comprehensiveness, universality, portability, and accessibility. This acceptance reflects their support by a large majority of the populations in each of the provinces. Provincial governments have argued, rather, that they should have the right to interpret these general principles on their own initiative. The role of the federal government should be limited to sending checks.

On the other hand, it is quite clear that from time to time provincial administrations have been elected with broad support within the provinces but do not share (or in some cases even understand) these basic principles. Between the shift to federal block funding in 1977 and the reassertion of federal standards in 1984 were several provincial initiatives that were very hard to reconcile with these principles. At the same time, public opinion in those provinces remained strongly supportive of Medicare.

In moving to clarify and provide ways of encouraging conformity with national standards, the federal government was both asserting a national interest in this field and acting according to the clearly expressed wishes of its electorate. The federal Parliament passed the Canada Health Act unanimously, despite the opposition of a number of provincial governments. All federal parties were acutely aware of the level of public support; to be against Medicare would be political suicide.

But the opposing provincial governments were also duly elected and explicitly sovereign in the field of health care and health policy. They had every right to claim to be speaking for the people of their provinces. An outside observer, listening to the tone of their comments and watching their maneuvers, might well conclude that on this issue they were not, that some at least intended to proclaim the letter and kill the spirit. But no one elects outside observers.

Who speaks for Canadians? We do not know. On this issue, partly because public opinion was so clear-cut but also in large part because of the particular personalities involved and the federal political balance at the time, the federal government overrode the provincial objections.[19] It did not, constitutionally could not, impose regulatory constraints on provincial behavior in this sphere. But it could and did use its spending power to create incentives for provincial governments to conform.

The ambiguity, however, remains. We do seem to have a habit of electing governments with conflicting principles and objectives and of hoping that, between them, they will thrash out an acceptable compromise in areas of competing jurisdiction.

The political ambiguity is now taking on a legal and constitutional dimension. Since 1982, the role of the courts in resolving conflicts of sovereignty between Canadian governments has dramatically expanded. And with the proclamation of the Charter of Rights and Freedoms, we have been moved into a world in which parliamentary sovereignty is itself abridged by the recognition of the fundamental rights of the individual (fundamental, that is, unless the government in question chooses to invoke the "notwithstanding" clause and abridge them anyway).

Does the new Constitution limit the federal spending power insofar as that spending may intrude into areas of provincial jurisdiction? Or does the answer depend on the relation between the extent of the intrusion and the objectives of the measure? Will the courts take a narrow view of their own role, leaving political questions to the politicians, or will they expand their legislative activities? To take one example central to the structure of the Canadian health care system, does the virtual elimination of the economic relationship between provider and patient violate some fundamental economic right of either provider or patient, or both?

The United States Constitution, for example, is interpreted by the courts as entrenching certain fundamental *economic* rights. The rights to "life, liberty, and the pursuit of happiness" seem for Americans to refer, self-evidently, to the pursuit of money. On the other hand, as Canadians are fond of pointing out, the corresponding fundamental constitutional principle in Canada is the preservation of "peace, order, and good government." The new Charter rights refer to "the security of the person," which the courts have so far interpreted as meaning physical security rather than constitutionally protected rights to engage in economic activities.

It would be premature to suggest that the jurisprudence has even begun to settle down in this area. We are probably in for years, if not decades, of extensive public and private support of the legal profession, some of whose members refer to the new legislation as their pension plan. A constitutional challenge to the federal Income Tax Act, for example, has been rejected in the Alberta Supreme Court but has yet to reach the Supreme Court of Canada. Courts of appeal in Ontario and British Columbia have just given contradictory rulings on the constitutionality of mandatory retirement. In due course that too will go up to the Supreme Court. And so on.

It is no exaggeration, then, to say that we do not know what our fundamental law is on the allocation of authority between federal and provincial governments or between government and the individual. On the first allocation, of course, we never really did know with any great assurance. The boundaries of jurisdiction were negotiated politically and have shifted over time. The second interface is quite new. The whole situation is new in that we may be facing a major shift in the processes of conflict resolution, from the political to the legal. Or we may not,

for the courts may throw these issues back to the politicians.

The impact of these broad constitutional changes on the medical care funding system could be profound. Indeed, constitutional challenges to specific pieces of health legislation are among the judicial vehicles through which these questions may be resolved. The Canada Health Act is under challenge as intruding on provincial jurisdiction; the Ontario legislation making extra billing a punishable offense and the British Columbia legislation restricting the numbers of physicians entitled to bill the provincial plan are both being challenged as violations of individual rights under the Charter.[20]

All these challenges are coming from medical associations, even the dispute of the Canada Health Act—in part because medical associations tend to be wealthy and combative and in part because physicians believe that the political process surrounding Medicare has not adequately reflected their views and interests. In the courts they hope to win back what they have lost in the legislatures.

In this field the political system seems to have responded quite well to the wishes of the general population. The constitutional challenges thus underline the extent to which the views and the interests of the medical profession have diverged from those of the rest of the Canadian community. It will be more than a little ironic if the legal system overrides the political process so as to enable the medical profession to enforce its preferred forms of health care organization and financing on a reluctant public—all in the name of the Charter of Rights and Freedoms!

Conflicts between providers and governments are, however, inherent in the structure of the Canadian health care funding system and have been from the beginning. They are traceable to yet another ambiguity. It is easy enough to say that the Canadian system reflects a combination of egalitarianism and respect for authority—but which authority?

The patient brings his problem to the professionals, who decide what is to be done. The sum of their decisions defines the level of activity of the health

care system. But independently of these decisions, provincial governments decide, with minor exceptions, what the level of spending on medical and hospital care will be. Hence the chronic and occasionally strident complaint of the medical profession that the system is globally "underfunded."

No government, no society, seems willing to make available sufficient funds to support all the activities that health care providers would like to offer their patients or to supply the incomes that the providers would like to receive. The continuing conflict is partly about who should have the authority to determine the size and shape of the health care system and partly a struggle over income shares, over how much doctors, nurses, and other providers should earn relative to the rest of the population.

The conflict, like that between the federal and the provincial governments, is a genuine one between legitimate forms of authority. No politically responsible government can give a private group the key to the public treasury, particularly a group whose priorities include not only making health policy but writing their own income checks. The electorate has given the Canadian governments a clear mandate to manage the overall level of health care expenditure.

On the other hand, governments have never been given a mandate to determine the content of medical practice. Canadians trust their physicians a good deal more than they trust their politicians on such technical matters, and both groups know it. The Canadian system gives governments control over the reimbursement function, not the delivery of care; it is a public health insurance system, not a public health service.

When the two sources of legitimacy collide and professionals' demands exceed public allocations, how should the issue be resolved? Physicians, or at least their organizations, have consistently argued for resolution through a third principle of legitimacy—consumer sovereignty. If the recommendations of professionals exceed what the legitimately elected and supported government wishes to provide, let individuals register their choices in "the marketplace"—let a private system of payment emerge to pick up the difference. Provincial governments, tired of the constant struggle to limit the growth of health outlays on behalf of a rarely grateful public, often find the same concept tempting.

Yet opponents are quick to point out that the consumer sovereignty principle, the individual's "right" to spend her own resources as she sees fit, has minimal relevance in a marketplace that self-regulating providers control. A genuinely *free* market in health care, with no public or private regulation over who may provide services and how, has never been observed anywhere in the modern world. Such a market has no political support from any serious participant in or student of health policy (or from the general public), in Canada or elsewhere, and interests only the economic lunatic fringe.

In a professionally controlled and publicly regulated market, which is the only form we have or are ever likely to see, consumer sovereignty as an ethical principle loses much of its attraction. [21] It becomes merely a justification for mechanisms whereby professionally determined priorities can override those determined through the public political system, which is exactly why professionals favor it. But the determination of who gets what on the basis of the principle of consumer sovereignty yields results that are inconsistent with the other basic values expressed through the health care system—egalitarianism, collective responsibility, and reliance on professional judgment of medical necessity instead of patients' ability to pay (or to buy private insurance).

Canadians have therefore chosen to leave the resolution of the contradiction between professional priorities and political constraints to negotiation between the two parties and have thus far not permitted them to mitigate their mutual conflict by agreeing to reopen channels to the patient's resources. Legitimate sources of authority should be able to work out their differences somehow, without necessarily requiring any clearly defined means of resolving the dispute (such as the courts or gunfire). They should be able to discover, and be guided by, the broader public interest—it is the Canadian way.

A nation's health care financing system is not merely a complicated mechanism for displaying its predominant moral and cultural values. It must also do its basic job, raising the resources necessary to support the provision of an acceptable standard and distribution of health care and contributing to, or at least not getting in the way of, the effective management of that care. A system that was grossly underfunded, whose political system was incapable of reflecting the priorities of its citizens, or whose citizens were unwilling or unable to respond to the fiscal needs of the health care system, could be putting its population's health in jeopardy. So could a system constantly wracked by conflicts, strikes, slowdowns, and general demoralization.

On the other hand, devotees of rather simple-minded economic views of human behavior constantly insist that free care leads to overuse, abuse, waste, and exploding costs. This would appear on the surface to be a testable empirical issue. But a fascination with "the price system," or "the market," which in some systems of thought plays a role very similar to that of God for the eighteenth-century Deists, [22] leads to the conviction that "free" anything is profoundly immoral as well as fattening and therefore ought to be illegal regardless of its consequences.

If we stick to what is truly consequential, we may return to the point made at the outset, that medical technology is an international enterprise. Furthermore, the job of organizing, applying, and paying for that technology has very similar objectives in all countries, even if the criteria for evaluation may differ somewhat. This similarity suggests that comparisons of systems' performance around the world should provide a reasonable basis for evaluation. In particular, it enables us to contemplate the consistency (or otherwise) between the symbolic and the functional roles played by a health care funding system. Do different symbolic expressions of values make it easier or more difficult to do the job?

Such a discussion must include a clear sense of context. All health care systems are in perpetual crisis. Cycles of media attention rise and fall, but the same issues come up over and over

again in each system. Crises may play an important role in the normal operation of health care systems. Perhaps the prolonged absence of a crisis would indicate a serious problem.

The Canadian approach to funding was declared unworkable by its opponents—physicians and private insurers—in the early 1960s, and the same interest groups have continued to detect imminent collapse right up to the present. The American health care system is well into the third decade of the longest-running cost explosion since the great inflation of the sixteenth century. The British National Health Service is presently gripped by what appears to be the most bitter of its periodic crises. All over Europe, governments are struggling to contain costs in the face of aging populations, advancing technology, and growing professional numbers and ambitions. (Their academic advisers, particularly economists, sometimes suggest that they look to the United States for solutions, which makes about as much sense as looking to the U.S.S.R. for advice on organizing grain production or to the U.K. for ski-jumping coaches.)

Still, individuals often regard their own health care systems as the best in the world. [23] Like confidence in one's own physician, confidence in one's own national way of organizing health care seems to be a natural, and perhaps quite functional, response to uncertainty and incomplete information. It may also reflect the adaptation (and perhaps the contribution) of each system to underlying cultural values.

Thus, Canadians consider getting sick in the United States as the equivalent of a rather severe mugging. It has similar economic and physical consequences, and provincial governments have sent medical evaluation flights to rescue their citizens from the U.S. hospital system. In contrast to humane and civilized Canada, Americans are left to die in the streets after their money runs out. Nevertheless, Americans continue to refer to their health care system, whatever its problems may be, as the world's best and, to the astonishment of Canadians, appear to be serious (the poor, benighted devils)! And Americans would be equally astonished, perhaps with as good reason, to see the attachment of the British to their National Health Service, which in the United States is called a nightmare.

Popular acceptance, therefore, is no basis for discrimination among national systems. What can be compared most readily (though comparing them is by no means easy either) is relative overall costs and the stability of those costs over time. Though it might seem the least important aspect of a health care system—compared with, for example, what that system does to and for its patients—comparative cost performance does interact with issues of equity and access and perhaps of effectiveness.

The connection arises because although there are no clear, or at least operational, criteria for deciding how much is enough for any country to spend on health care, it is clear that continuing escalation of costs relative to national resources is not a sustainable situation. All developed countries have in the last decade come to place a high priority on stabilizing the growth of health care costs in their national systems. A system that fails to do so will be changed—it is simply a question of when—and will go on being changed, in increasingly radical ways, until some degree of stability can be attained.

For nearly two decades, the Canadian health care system has achieved a remarkably good record in both preserving universal access to comprehensive coverage and moderating the growth of health care costs. This performance has been outstanding in comparison with that of the United States system, which displays accelerating cost escalation, increasingly radical institutional change, and deteriorating equity.[24] The Canadian performance also looks good in comparison with that of the other OECD countries—a more demanding comparison.[25] On the whole, the European countries have been much more successful in stabilizing their systems than has the United States but less so than Canada; and concerns about equity and access are starting to emerge in those systems that have never had the same firm foundation of egalitarianism.

A more detailed analysis, however, brings out the falsity of the often-asserted conflict between the overall control of the size of the health care sector and the preservation of access and quality of care. A comparison of the Cana-

dian and the United States experience, for which detailed data are readily available, shows that the greatest differences in cost—contained in Canada and exploding in the United States—are in the administration of the payment system and in the inflation of physicians' fees.[26] Canada gets an outstanding bargain on the first, and reasonably good performance on the second. In the United States, both are escalating at an accelerating rate. Neither of these components of health expenditures translates into clinical services for patients. The first is simply system overhead—in the United States, pure waste motion—and the second is the result of a struggle over income shares.[27]

There is also a marked difference in the technical intensity of servicing within hospitals, the number and cost of diagnostic and therapeutic maneuvers that the average patient undergoes.[28] But since many observers of North American hospital care have long expressed concern about overtreatment in hospitals, and since reduced use of hospitals is a major thrust of U.S. health policy, the difference in treatment intensity cannot be taken as an a priori indicator of reduced access to effective care in the Canadian system.[29]

The Canadian system is by no means a model of efficiency in any absolute sense. As in every other system, there are wide variations in servicing patterns and costs that have no apparent connection to the underlying needs of the populations served. Much of what is done is ineffective, unnecessary, or unnecessarily costly. But these are not problems peculiar to Canada. While it is true that the funding system provides few, if any, rewards or incentives to providers for efficient performance, the same could be said (and has been) for all other national systems. The organizational problems health care poses are devilishly difficult, and Canada has not found a solution that has escaped everyone else.

We have, however, succeeded in removing the economic barriers to access to high-quality health care for the whole population. At the same time, we have stabilized the overall share of our national income taken up to pay for care, and we have shifted the economic burdens from those who happen to be ill

to those who can afford to pay. While people in every country may profess to believe that their own health systems are the best ones, the level of satisfaction of Canadians with their arrangements must be among the highest in the world. To a certain extent, our satisfaction reflects our tendency to be smug about our own decency and moral rectitude, but we do get some reinforcement from external observers.

On the other hand, there is also evidence that the compromise between professional autonomy and public fiscal responsibility, which has been central to the operation of the Canadian system, is starting to fray. Provincial governments are finding that moderating expenditure growth is requiring increasing attention to "utilization control"—service patterns and volumes—rather than simply restraint of fees and of hospitals' global budgets. Even moderate increases in health care costs absorb virtually all the governments' fiscal maneuvering room, simply because health is such a large proportion of provincial budgets.

The provincial governments are trying to put explicit caps on overall outlays, and while these may not directly impinge on the clinical activity of the providers, the caps' indirect effects are becoming stronger. As each funding system moves toward overt recognition that it steers health care practice, the system's managers may have to negotiate with providers more explicit objectives and criteria for system performance.[30]

Explicit attention to the outcomes of health care, however, exposes what may be the most puzzling feature of the Canadian, and perhaps any other, health care system. What is it trying to do? What is the enormous commitment of resources expected to buy? The easy answer—improved health—is indeed what most citizens, patients, and taxpayers think they are getting, and they may be right. But like the Zen archer, the Canadian health care system hits its target (if it does) by not looking at it. The clinician worries about the impact of his interventions on his patients. The managers of the whole health care system, however—clinical as well as financial—pay little attention to explicit measures of the population's health.

We know, of course, that in a general way our various morbidity and mortality rates are improving. But we have little idea how, if at all, this improvement links up with the enormous effort we devote to providing health care. When physicians complain about underfunding, they are arguing that more expenditure would improve their patients' health; when governments restrain budgets or manpower, they are implicitly arguing the reverse. The evidentiary base for either position is rudimentary or nonexistent.

Moreover, such evidence as there is raises more questions than it answers. Various not very satisfactory measures show improvement in both Canada and the United States, and at almost the same rates.[31] There is no evidence that the massive additional expenditures in the United States buy any better outcomes. Americans now spend about 30 percent more, in relative terms, than we do, and the gap is widening. Conversely, the better access for the whole population that universality implies yields no clear-cut Canadian advantage.

When we look at the distribution of outcomes through the population, we find marked correlations of socioeconomic status with health. The rich live longer and better. But these gradients are observed in the United Kingdom with the National Health Service, in the United States with a highly unequal and for some, inaccessible system, and in Canada with its egalitarian insurance system. We know that the public insurance plans did redistribute care down the income spectrum, and cost burdens in the reverse direction; but it is not clear that there was any corresponding equalization of health. The health of individuals and of populations depends on much more than their health care, and how a society organizes and pays for its health care system may not greatly affect this pattern of dependence.[32]

Thus far, the general population has been left out of the discussion of such complex issues and has not had to deal with the disturbing questions they entail. When one takes a problem to a physician, one does not want to consider in detail whether his interventions have any scientific (or other) basis or are doing more good than harm. Let the authorities worry about that. And acceptance of the idea that poor health and early death—for some—are built into the structure of our society and are beyond the reach of health care, implies that we either consider more radical interventions (against poverty, for example, or unemployment) or simply admit that we do not care much.

Even more stark dilemmas lurk in the care of the elderly, which is absorbing an increasing proportion of total health spending.[33] To a considerable degree, present medical technologies prolong, not living, but dying. As one author puts it, declining mortality is the principal source of increasing morbidity.[34] The very comforting fiction, or at best part-truth, of an increasingly powerful "life-saving" health care system is preferable to the realities of salvage, and very partial and temporary salvage at that. "Humankind cannot bear very much reality," T. S. Eliot has pointed out.

Or perhaps we can, but why should we? Unpleasant prospects that we cannot do very much about do not deserve extensive contemplation. So long as the interaction between the political and the professional authorities results in compromises that are financially bearable, and apparently satisfactory in terms of health outcomes (at least we have no information to the contrary), then why should the general public get involved?

It should only if the combined impact of demographic change and the deployment of health technology seems to be leading to a shift in the terms of those compromises. Politicians and bureaucrats do not dare to be seen taking decisions with life-and-death implications. Providers of care seem to be becoming more reluctant to set limits on their own, to let the deformed infant or the elderly stroke victim go quietly. The "spare parts" society, whether dream or nightmare, is coming closer.

Nor are the penalties for faulty decisions merely financial. It is our own future that is in question: we as individuals will have to forego or undergo the interventions our health care system provides. The "stroked out" ninety-year-old in the nursing home or the intensive care unit may be me. Is that where I want to be? Nunc dimittis. On the other hand, a new pair of knees so that I can play golf may be just the ticket. (I could never play golf before.)

Of course, there is more to the well-lived life than simple survival, and more to health than health care, as we in Canada and everyone else can see. If we focus more on health than on health care, we will have to recognize the inherent limits of medicine. But our health care system is controlled by the providers of and the payers for health *care*, not health.[35] Can we continue to rely on our professional and government agents to thrash out these decisions on our behalf? Or will they perpetuate a care system that meets *their* needs rather than ours—a compromise between esoteric medical intervention and fiscal controllability that we find less and less relevant to us?

The challenge for the future may be to find ways to discover and express our collective values with respect to the definition of health itself. What sort of outcomes as opposed to services do we as a community think worth buying? And through what institutional channels, present or projected, do we give effect to those views?

If history is any guide, we will be able to watch these issues debated in an open free-for-all in the United States, thoroughly entangled in a web of competing economic interests. The debate will produce analyses of extraordinary competence and clarity, which will not, however, be decisive for actual policy.

Meanwhile, in Canada we will rely on the responsible authorities to come up with some sort of solution or at least a response. As agents, they are very far from perfect, but they may be the best we've got. In the final analysis, defects and all, the system we have seems to be a remarkably good compromise of quality, affordability, equity, and humanity. Not bad, eh?

Notes

1. G. J. Schieber and J.-P. Poullier, "Trends in International Health Care Spending," *Health Affairs* 6 (3) (1987):105; Organization for Economic Cooperation and Development (OECD), *Financing and Delivering Health Care*, OECD Social Policy Studies no. 4 (Paris: OECD, 1987); A. J. Culyer, *Health Expenditures in Canada:*

Myth and Reality, Past and Future (Toronto: Canadian Tax Foundation, 1988).

2. T. R. Marmor, "Doctors, Politics and Pay Disputes: Pressure Group Politics Revisited," in T. R. Marmor, ed., *Political Analysis and American Medical Care: Essays* (Cambridge: Cambridge University Press, 1983); W. A. Glaser, *Paying the Doctor* (Baltimore: Johns Hopkins University, 1970).

3. T. R. Marmor, "Comparative Politics and Health Policies: Notes on Benefits, Costs, Limits," in Marmor, *Political Analysis*.

4. M. G. Taylor, *Health Insurance and Canadian Public Policy* (Montreal: McGill Queen's University Press, 1978); M. G. Taylor, "The Canadian Health Care System 1974–1984," in R. G. Evans and G. L Stoddart, eds., *Medicare at Maturity: Achievements, Lessons & Challenges* (Calgary: University of Calgary Press for the Banff Centre, 1986); R. Fein, *Medical Care, Medical Costs: The Search for a Health Insurance Policy* (Cambridge: Harvard University Press, 1986).

5. R. G. Evans, "Health Care in Canada: Patterns of Funding and Regulation," in G. McLachlan and A. Maynard, eds., *The Public/Private Mix for Health: The Relevance and Effects of Change* (London: Nuffield Provincial Hospitals Trust, 1982); R. G. Evans, "Finding the Levers, Finding the Courage: Lessons from Cost Containment in North America," *Journal of Health Politics, Policy and Law* 11 (4) (1987):585.

6. M. L. Barer and R G. Evans, "Riding North on a South-Bound Horse? Expenditures, Prices, Utilization and Incomes in the Canadian Health Care System," in Evans and Stoddart, eds. *Medicare at Maturity*; M. L. Barer, R. G. Evans, and R. J. Labelle, "Fee Controls as Cost Control: Tales from the Frozen North," The *Milbank Quarterly* 66 (1) (1988).

7. Taylor, "The Canadian Health Care System."

8. All generalizations, including all those in this paper, are false. There will be charges for services that are judged "medically unnecessary"; in some provinces such charges include self-referral to a specialist. Private hospital accommodation that is not in the physician's opinion required by the patient's condition may be had on payment of a "preferred accommodation differential." Elective cosmetic surgery is likewise chargeable to the patient. Finally, prescription drugs outside the hospital and dentistry are not covered under the universal hospital and medical insurance plans. Individual provinces have prescription drug and dental insurance plans, but these usually cover only part

9. of the population and/or part of the outlay.

The general population, however, does not appear to realize this. If the retired population, whose premiums are not deducted at source, simply stopped paying their premiums en masse, not much could be done about it. The "tax" is in effect voluntary!

10. In some provinces a physician has the option of simply not participating in the public plan, in which case neither he nor his patient is reimbursed. He may then charge whatever he likes for his services. But he cannot work both sides of the street, seeing some patients and/or conditions privately and setting his own fees, and yet also seeing others under the public plan. Furthermore, no private insurer can sell coverage for services already covered under the public plans, so the nonparticipating physician must make his entire practice from uninsured, selfpaying patients. Not surprisingly, few practitioners make this choice.

11. M. L. Barer, R. G. Evans, and G. L. Stoddart, *Controlling Health Care Costs by Direct Charges to Patients: Snare or Delusion?* Ontario Economic Council Occasional Paper no. 10 (Toronto: Ontario Economic Council, 1979); J. P. Newhouse, "The Demand for Medical Care Services: A Retrospect and Prospect," in J. Van der Gaag and M. Perlman, eds., *Health, Economics, and Health Economics* (Amsterdam: North-Holland, 1981); R. G. Evans, *Strained Mercy: The Economics of Canadian Health Care* (Toronto: Butterworth's, 1984); W. G. Manning et al., "Health Insurance and the Demand for Medical Care: Evidence from a Randomized Experiment," *American Economic Review* 77 (3) (1987): 251.

12. Schieber and Poullier, "Trends"; OECD, *Financing and Delivering*.

13. S. Heiber and R. Deber, "Banning Extra-Billing in Canada: Just What the Doctor Didn't Order," *Canadian Public Policy* 13 (1) (1987): 62.

14. It is not so long ago that most of the land area of what is now Canada was controlled by the Hudson's Bay Company ("Here Before Christ"), a private company whose history is substantially longer than that of the Canadian Confederation.

15. R. G. Evans, "The Political Economy of Health Care," in J. N. Clarke et al., eds. *Health Care in Canada: Looking Ahead* (Ottawa: Canadian Public Health Association, 1987).

16. Royal Commission on Health Services (Hall Commission), *Report*, vol. 1 (Ot-

tawa: The Queen's Printer, 1964), especially chap. 1.

17. Royal Commission on Health Services, *Report*, especially chap. 18; R. Fein, *Medical Care, Medical Costs*, especially chaps. 2, 3.

18. In practice, of course, the American health care system is predominantly collectively funded. The realities of modern health care do not permit any other approach. But the collective instruments created for this purpose are a bewildering variety of private organizations. The state steps in only as the insurer of absolute last resort for groups—the elderly and the poor—who cannot by the most extreme stretch of the ideological imagination meet their own needs through some private coalition.

19. A most unpopular federal government, reaching the end of its mandate and its life, hoped to trap the Opposition into being "against Medicare," on the assumption (probably inaccurate) that this was the only issue significant enough in the public mind to turn the tide. The Opposition avoided the trap and in 1984 came to power with an overwhelming majority.

20. M. L. Barer, "Regulating Physician Supply: The Evolution of British Columbia's Bill 41," *Journal of Health Politics, Policy and Law* 13 (1) (1988): 1.

21. What self-governing professions offer the consumer is not a competitive market but "guild-free choice," a sophisticated form of restraint of trade. Alain Enthoven draws this distinction particularly clearly in "Managed Competition in Health Care and the Unfinished Agenda," *Health Care Financing Review*, Annual Supplement (1986): 105. He also emphasizes the impossibility, indeed the absurdity, of a "competitive marketplace" in specific health services for individual consumers. If genuine competition in health care is possible at all, it can be only among integrated organizations contracting to provide a combination of insurance and care on a capitated basis, as American HMOs do, for example. See his *Health Plan: The Only Practical Solution to the Soaring Cost of Medical Care* (Reading, Mass.: Addison-Wesley, 1980).

22. A. J. Cuyler, "The Quest for Efficiency in the Public Sector: Economists versus Dr. Pangloss (or, Why Conservative Economists Are Not Nearly Conservative Enough)," in H. Hanusch, ed., *Public Finance and the Quest for Efficiency* (Detroit: Wayne State University Press, 1984).

23. J.-P. Poullier, personal communication subsequent to the OECD study of inter-

national health care financing and delivery systems.

24. Evans, "Finding the Levers."

25. Cuyler, *Health Expenditures*.

26. Barer, Evans, and Labelle, "Fee Controls as Cost Control."

27. U. E. Reinhardt, "Resource Allocation in Health Care: The Allocation of Lifestyles to Providers," *The Milbank Quarterly* 65 (2) (1987):153.

28. A. S. Detsky et al., "The Effectiveness of a Regulatory Strategy in Containing Hospital Costs: The Ontario Experience, 1967–1981," *New England Journal of Medicine* 309 (3) (1983):151; Barer and Evans, "Riding North."

29. D. Feeny, G. Guyatt, and P. Tugwell, *Health Care Technology: Effectiveness, Efficiency, and Public Policy* (Montreal: Institute for Research on Public Policy, 1986).

30. R. G. Evans et al., "Boundaries to Experience, Barriers to Understanding: The Reality of Health Care Cost Control in Canada," *New England Journal of Medicine* (forthcoming).

31. R. N. Battista, R. A. Spasoff, and W. O. Spitzer, "Choice of Technique: Patterns of Medical Practices," in Evans and Stoddart, *Medicare at Maturity*.

32. D. Black et al., *Inequalities in Health: the Black Report* (Harmondsworth, Middlesex: Penguin Books, 1982); D. B. Dutton, "Social Class, Health, and Illness," in L. Aiken and D. Mechanic, eds., *Applications of Social Science to Clinical Medicine and Health Policy* (New Brunswick, N.J.: Rutgers University Press, 1986); R. Wilkins and O. Adams, *Healthfulness of Life* (Montreal: Institute for Research on Public Policy, 1983).

33. Though not, despite popular wisdom, because of the increased numbers of elderly persons. The average per capita use of care by the elderly, the things done to and for them by the health care system, is rising much more rapidly than their numbers alone. See M. L. Barer et al., "Aging and Health Care Utilization: New Evidence on Old Fallacies," *Social Science and Medicine* 24 (10) (1987):851.

34. L. M. Verbrugge, "Longer Life But Worsening Health? Trends in Health and Mortality of Middle-aged and Older Persons," *Milbank Memorial Fund Quarterly, Health and Society* 62 (3) (1984):475; L. M. Verbrugge, "Recent, Present, and Future Health of American Adults" in L. Breslow, J. E. Fielding, and L. B. Lave, eds., *Annual Review of Public Health*, vol. 10 (Palo Alto, Calif: Annual Reviews Inc., 1989).

35. Accordingly, we spend more and more to "save" lighter and lighter neonates with ever more severe problems, but we make very little effort to prevent low birth weight in the first place.

22

Germany's Health Care System: Part One

John K. Iglehart

With every important advance in medical care, the challenge of providing a country's population with comprehensive health services has become more formidable, because increases in the cost of such services continue to outstrip the rate of economic growth in all major Western nations, patients resist reductions in insured care, and physicians maintain their expensive pursuit of clinical excellence. Among industrialized countries, West Germany's health insurance system came closest during the 1980s to limiting increases in spending to a rate that equaled the growth of its national income; the disparity between these two measures was greatest in the United States.[1]

The essence of Germany's successful scheme is a blend of government-mandated financing by employers and employees, combined with the private provision of care by physicians, controlled hospital expenditures, and administration by not-for-profit insurance organizations. These insurance organizations, known as sickness funds, establish and collect the contributions of employers and employees. The sickness funds turn this revenue over to regional associations of ambulatory care physicians that reimburse doctors for their services on the basis of a negotiated fee schedule. The sickness funds that operate in a given geographic area also negotiate a per diem rate with local hospitals.[2] All payers in an area pay the same negotiated per diem rate to a hospital, whatever the patient's diagno-

Reprinted with permission from *The New England Journal of Medicine* 324, no. 7 (February 14, 1991), pp. 503–8. Copyright © 1991 by the Massachusetts Medical Society.

sis. All of Germany's citizens have access to a comprehensive set of medical benefits and a free choice of physicians, regardless of their ability to pay, and practitioners enjoy a substantial degree of clinical autonomy.

Germany operates a century-old system of social insurance that represents a middle ground in the spectrum of approaches Western countries have adopted to protect their populations from the economic consequences of illness. Although it is difficult to pin precise labels on health care systems because of their diversity, the key differentiating feature is the degree to which they rely on government or private mechanisms to finance and provide care. On the basis of this feature, the four general approaches are a predominantly private-sector model (as in Switzerland and the United States); a national-health-service model (as in the United Kingdom); a provincial-government health insurance model (Canada); and a social-insurance model (France, the Netherlands, and what was West Germany). One of the more formidable challenges facing Germany as a consequence of its recent unification is the transformation of East Germany's national health service into a social-insurance plan modeled on that of West Germany.

West Germany's ability in the 1980s to hold its increase in spending for personal health services to a level that approximated the growth of its gross national product[1] is important, because in all countries the size of the disparity between these measures usually indicates whether a health system is operating in a socially acceptable fashion or whether its payers and providers face

strong pressure to moderate the growth of expenditures. The U.S. system clearly faces such pressure. It is unstable and subject to calls for reform[3] because it is inaccessible to millions of uninsured people and because the rate of growth of its expenditures is high—on average, 33 percent higher every year than the rate of growth of its national economy during the 1980s, as compared with 3 percent higher in West Germany. Beyond these measurable indicators, the U.S. system lacks an overall policy framework that links together its disparate parts, and this provokes anxiety among providers concerned about increased second-guessing of medical decisions by third parties and about the uncertain nature of reforms that now appear inevitable. Although Germany's third parties and its providers of care certainly have their differences, there is a remarkable degree of consensus between them, stemming from a cultural preference that favors reaching compromises before deadlock occurs—a preference that is quite evident throughout German life. An overarching policy framework that establishes by law important roles for private payers and organized medicine also lends credibility and stability to their ongoing discussions. The government generally accepts the results of these discussions, but in the 1980s it enacted a series of cost-containment laws that reflected its belief that stronger discipline was needed than those holding a private stake were prepared to impose on themselves.

In this report, I discuss the German health care system—its evolution, its method of financing, and its administration by not-for-profit sickness funds and associations of physicians treating about 88 percent of the people. Most (5.5 million) of the rest of the population purchases comprehensive coverage through 42 private commercial companies. Governments finance the bulk of care for civil servants directly, and the employees usually purchase private insurance to supplement this coverage. I conducted research for this report during six weeks I spent in West Germany during the spring and summer of 1990. During that period I interviewed a variety of federal and state officials, economists, physicians, and hospital directors, and I visited ambulatory medical clinics and hospitals, a large private clinical laboratory, and a rehabilitation center. It was a period of particularly intense activity for the federal Ministry of Labor and Social Affairs, the principal government influence in the social-insurance scheme, because of the rapid movement toward unification on October 3.

U.S. interest in the German health care system is not in viewing it as a model for replication, but in examining how selected issues are addressed, in particular how physicians are paid, how the government regulates the sickness funds, how costs are constrained, and how care for the poor is financed. This more limited focus was evident when the Physician Payment Review Commission engaged in a discussion of the West German system on September 13. The discussion followed a recent visit to Germany by two commissioners, Dr. Thomas R. Reardon, a trustee of the American Medical Association, and Uwe E. Reinhardt, an economist who believes that the United States should examine the German experience closely, and the commission's executive director, Paul B. Ginsburg. Stuart H. Altman, chairman of the Prospective Payment Assessment Commission, three officials of the General Accounting Office, an investigative arm of Congress, and I accompanied them. As Philip R. Lee, chairman of the Physician Payment Review Commission, said at the end of the discussion:

It seems that Germany is Germany, and there are really substantial organizational, social, and cultural differences that make any broad application of some of those lessons really rather a limited one. But I think there are areas

that Paul [Ginsburg] has identified that merit our further investigation.

The areas Lee referred to are how physicians' practice costs are incorporated into the German relative-value scale; how Germany ties changes in the level of fees in a locality to changes in the volume of services billed; how local negotiations on fee levels coordinate with national policy; and how Germany profiles the practices of individual physicians as a tool to constrain costs and ensure quality.

The greater attention being paid to Germany in U.S. public-policy circles obviously extends well beyond the German system of social insurance. As a country in the throes of a fundamental transformation after a 45-year separation, Germany faces the challenge of putting back together its monetary, political, and social systems. The task of transforming East Germany's state-run health care system into an enterprise modeled on West Germany's social-insurance plan will require substantial changes in the approach of formerly East German physicians to medical practice. East Germany's network of large public clinics and hospitals, many of which are in grim condition and lack modern forms of technology, were staffed by state-salaried physicians who worked for paltry sums ($600 a month on average) and owned none of the sources of production of care. To become private practitioners, these physicians must lease or purchase equipment, hire staff, and rent office space, things they never did as employees of the East German state. In addition, the German Hospital Association estimates that it will cost at least $20 billion to bring the hospitals in the east up to the standards of those in the west.

The Evolution of Social Insurance

Before the recent collapse of Communism, nowhere were the political differences between East and West more clearly delineated than in Germany. In the years after World War II, West Germany evolved into a major industrial and trading power with worldwide economic ties and a population of 61 million. During the same period, East Germany's 17 million people lived un-

der a repressive Communist regime that held its citizens captive behind an imposing wall and that failed to develop an agricultural and industrial capacity comparable with that of the West. At the time of unification, East German workers earned $660 a month on average, less than a third of the $2,100 in West Germany, although the Communist government provided a broader array of subsidized benefits, such as housing.

For the sake of simplicity, the evolution of Germany's health insurance system in the twentieth century can be broken into four periods. I cite the system's history because, although the scheme is more than a century old, one of its most remarkable features is the extent to which its fundamental structure has remained unchanged. Actually, Prussia enacted statutory health insurance for several industries and occupations in 1845, before the creation of the German state. Another important feature that undergirds the current system is the belief that nations are obliged to provide a strong network of social benefits to all their citizens. This "principle of social solidarity" has helped to rationalize the income-related nature of health care financing in Germany. The four periods of evolution are the period from expansion of social insurance in the 1880s under Otto von Bismarck, the first chancellor of the German state, to 1914; World War I and the Weimar Republic (from 1915 to 1932); the Third Reich (1933 to 1945); and the period from World War II to the present.

Moving to quell social unrest among workers who were flocking into Germany's cities during the Industrial Revolution and to tame the growing influence of labor unions, Bismarck proposed social-insurance coverage as a way to buy political support from the workers in exchange for economic protection and material benefits. Laws enacted in 1883, 1884, and 1889 established several types of social insurance—accident, disability, health, old age, and unemployment—that are still provided to workers and, where applicable, their dependents. In the early years, cash payments in lieu of pay for workers injured on the job or out of work because of sickness were the most important benefit. Medical insurance was considered a secondary matter. [4,5]

Bismarck's initiative "opened a new realm of domestic policy," wrote Peter Rosenberg, a student of the German system and an official in the Ministry of Labor and Social Affairs, several years ago. [6]

The idea of this policy started by Bismarck was that the welfare of people does not result automatically out of economic growth in a free-market economy; the distribution has to be regulated, and the state should not limit itself to providing economic freedom. . . . Since World War II, this idea has been elaborated in the FRG [Federal Republic of Germany] under the title social market economy. This means that social and economic policy should be one unit to avoid an unjust distribution of income and property and to avoid poverty due to sickness, age, and unemployment. Social policy has to minimize the negative distributive effects of a liberal market economy, but it also has to respect the necessity of economic growth and accept, insofar as possible, the market economy. During the 19th Century the preeminent question was whether the state should influence social conditions at all, but the discussion since then has centered around the extent of state intervention.

In the early years of Germany's experience with social insurance, the sickness funds dominated relations with physicians. Indeed, the original 1883 law gave sickness funds the responsibility of providing medical care and did not create a separate role for physicians or their organizations. At first, the funds hired physicians as employees. This arrangement provoked a long series of conflicts between the funds and their physician employees. In the 1920s, some sickness funds turned over the money allocated for fees to the entire panel of physicians with whom they were affiliated and let the doctors divide it up. This trend spread with the encouragement of the Weimar Republic (governed at first by Socialists who were connected with the sickness funds and who wanted to buy peace), and gradually, the panel of physicians in each city became a collective-bargaining entity that also funneled payments to members on behalf of the sickness funds. The panels were officially designated as regional associations of ambulatory care doctors in 1931, when the social-insurance law was expanded to recognize them. To-

day, these associations are Germany's most powerful physicians' organizations; they negotiate physicians' fees with the sickness funds and serve as paymasters for ambulatory care doctors, who must belong to them in order to treat members of the sickness fund.

Bismarck envisioned health insurance as a way to promote political stability and encourage the development of civic spirit without the loss of individuality in workers. The vision of Adolf Hitler's National Socialism in this regard was far broader and more perverse. It favored the development of a "German people's community," a strategy characterized in 1939 by its minister of labor, Seldte, in the following fashion: "The whole social security system serves only one aim today: the healthy, enthusiastic, productive, militarily fit, racially valuable German man of the future." [6]

The National Socialists' drive to raise a racially and militarily fit elite led to the transformation of German social insurance from a scheme administered by sickness funds free of government domination to a system that could be reordered by arbitrary, authoritarian measures at any time. Another important change dictated by the National Socialists prohibited "non-Aryan" physicians from treating sickness-fund patients and required that "Aryan" physicians not only demonstrate clinical competence, but also possess a knowledge of eugenic racial theory and political reliability. Although countless books have been written about World War II and Germany under Hitler, less attention has been paid by English-speaking authors to the history of physicians under the Nazi regime. But five recent books have documented the important role of physicians in the evolution of Nazism and some of its most sordid dimensions. [7-11]

After the defeat of the Third Reich and the end of World War II, West Germany was rebuilt with a new constitutional structure of basic freedoms that Western democracies had long guaranteed, and its system of social insurance was also restored. In the process, the medical profession won a dominant role for solo office-based physicians in the provision of ambulatory care, prohibit-

ing industrial or public health doctors from treating patients and discouraging the use of physician's assistants and the creation of group practices. [12]

The Sickness Funds

Unlike many other European countries, which increased their dependence on centralized government planning and regulation to constrain health expenditures during the 1980s, Germany depended more heavily on sickness funds and regional associations of physicians to allocate health care resources. These not-for-profit organizations have two distinguishing characteristics. First, they are compulsory-membership organizations that serve as intermediaries between individuals and the government; membership in both is based primarily on occupational status. Second, the organizations are empowered by law to control work-related aspects of their members' behavior and to administer government programs relating to their members. The organizations reflect Germany's belief that political stability can be achieved by cementing individual loyalties to social groups. [13] This structure of funds and regional associations serves as an administrative umbrella and the financial conduit through which 88 percent of West Germany's citizens receive care and physicians are reimbursed for their services.

Through amounts deducted from their paychecks, all workers who earn less than $36,580 must by law contribute to the sickness fund that finances their medical care; employers currently contribute a like amount. Before 1950, workers paid two thirds and employers one third of the contribution to the sickness fund. An employee's contribution is a fixed percentage of gross income; it is calculated independent of the health risk presented by the employee and the employee's dependents. The contribution thus has a redistributive dimension.

Each year the funds calculate the amount of money they will need for self-sustained operation. To collect that amount, the funds are empowered to set the rate at which employees and employers contribute. Ultimately, the sickness funds turn the money over to the regional associations of physicians, which disburse it to doctors on the basis of the negotiated fee schedule. Currently, the combined contribution of employees and employers varies from 8 to 16 percent of a worker's gross salary; in 1989 the average was 12.8 percent. The amount of this contribution is the most sensitive political issue enlivening the debate over Germany's social-insurance plan, and I shall discuss it at greater length in a subsequent report. Workers whose earnings exceed $3,048 per month can remain in a sickness fund or opt for private insurance and thus not contribute to a fund. The majority of workers in this category remain with their sickness fund.

The legal requirement that all employers and employees contribute financially eliminates the possibility that workers and their dependents will face the economic consequences of illness without coverage or that providers will be denied remuneration after rendering a service. Among those insured by the 1,147 sickness funds are about 1.8 million formerly employed people (7.4 percent of the work force as of June 1990) and their dependents, who continue to be covered through their fund despite their loss of work. The premiums of about two thirds of the unemployed are paid by the Federal Labor Administration. The premiums of the remaining one third are covered by local welfare agencies. Federal law stipulates that unemployed people and their dependents must receive the same benefits through the sickness funds as those who work.

The premiums of retired persons are paid by their pension funds in the form of a flat percentage of the pension; that percentage is equal to the average national payroll contribution paid by workers—12.8 percent. Premiums paid by the elderly covered only about 40 percent of the cost of their care in 1989. The sickness funds of which they remain members subsidize the rest of their health care expenditures by increasing the contributions demanded of active workers. Sickness funds with a disproportionate number of retired members receive compensatory contributions from a national reserve fund created for the purpose.

There are many different sickness funds, and people usually join one or another fund because of where they live, what they do, or what company employs them. Although switching is common, most people belong to a single sickness fund throughout their lives. The large number of funds (1,147) makes for an unwieldy administrative structure, but it is a function of how the funds have evolved over the past century. The German government has not sought to consolidate sickness funds to reach a more manageable number, because it lacks the authority to do so and such an effort would provoke serious controversy; many workers hold an allegiance to their sickness funds that would make any attempt to consolidate them politically risky.

Local sickness funds, whose members come from a single geographic area, provide health insurance to about 40 percent of Germany's workers, the overwhelming number of whom hold blue-collar jobs. So-called "substitute funds" are national in scope, and they insure 27 percent of insured workers, most of whom hold white-collar jobs. Some 700 companies with more than 450 employees have created their own funds. These funds finance the care of the company's workers exclusively—about 12 percent of the work force. Sickness funds that insure employees affiliated with crafts provide protection for another 12 percent of the work force. About 8 percent of the population—all with incomes that exceed $36,580—is privately insured.

The funds finance a comprehensive set of dental and medical benefits for their insured members, who make liberal use of these services. On average, Germans visit their ambulatory care physicians 10.8 times a year.[14] The major benefits in 1989 were hospitalization (31.5 percent of the total health expenditures of the sickness funds), ambulatory care (17.5 percent), the purchase of prescription drugs (15.6 percent), cash benefits to offset the loss of income during illness (6.6 percent), the purchase of medical appliances (6 percent), dental care (5.9 percent), administration (5 percent), the purchase of dental prostheses (3.8 percent), preventive measures, including visits to spas (3.8 per-

cent), maternity benefits (2.1 percent), and funeral benefits (1 percent).

Among the more intriguing benefits, reflecting Germany's capacity to accommodate both high-technology medicine and homeopathy, are visits to spas, of which there are several types. In one type of visit, insured people (who pay $10 per day) can visit a spa once every three years for a period of several weeks if a physician believes it will improve their health. In another type of visit, a person in a stressful occupation (e.g., a middle-aged police officer who works the night shift) can spend four weeks at a sanitarium if a physician supports it as preventive care. A patient recovering from a serious operation also can spend four weeks recuperating at a spa if an attending physician considers it useful. In these last two examples, medical costs (minus some copayments) are covered by the sickness fund; the cost of housing, food, and transportation is borne largely by the patient. Most physicians seem to have adopted a very relaxed attitude about prescribing spa treatment. Although they recognize that such treatment may not always be clinically necessary, doctors believe it certainly can do no harm, and they know that patients favor it and the sickness funds finance most of its cost. Another reason for spa visits is competition for subscribers among the sickness funds.

Some 6.3 million Germans—affluent people and many childless couples—purchase comprehensive private insurance. Such patients may choose among a number of plans, with various degrees of cost sharing and premiums that vary commensurately. The premiums charged by private insurers reflect the actuarial risk according to age, in five-year cohorts. A person who signs a private insurance contract pays the existing premium for the appropriate five-year cohort. Thereafter, the premium is never increased as a function of the insured's age. It can be raised only to reflect general increases in health care costs that affect all age groups. A private German health insurance policy overcharges young people relative to their short-term actuarial risk, but their premiums do not change as they age; a reserve is thus created that helps cover their higher health costs later in life.

In contrast, sickness funds subsidize the cost of family care by calculating workers' premiums on the basis of their gross income, not their age or the number of dependents who are covered. The scope of benefits with private insurance is similar to that of the sickness funds with the exception of some amenities (a private room, a television, or a telephone for hospitalized patients, for example) and the suggestion (not well documented in the literature) that privately insured patients get more prompt appointments, receive better attention from ambulatory care physicians, and are usually cared for by department chiefs in university hospitals or their designates.

Some people purchase supplemental private insurance. Many of them are civil servants, the bulk of whose care (50 to 80 percent, depending on family size) is financed directly by the federal or state government; they purchase supplemental coverage to insure against paying the remaining costs out of pocket. Private insurance reimburses physicians and hospitals at fee levels more than twice those negotiated by the sickness funds; privately insured patients are thus a welcome sight in any practitioner's office or hospital-admissions department.

Payment of Physicians

For the most part, however, the incomes of ambulatory care physicians derive from the care they provide to the 88 percent of the population that depends on the sickness funds to cover the cost of medical treatment. To be eligible to bill for such services, doctors must be members of a regional association of physicians. Some 73,000 ambulatory care physicians belong to the regional associations, which pay doctors for the care they provide, monitor their patterns of service to patients, and guarantee the availability of ambulatory care to people insured by the funds. The money that the regional associations pay doctors comes from the sickness funds, which turn over in a regular lump sum the bulk of the revenue they collect from employees and employers. Beyond the regional associations, which are sponsored and operated by doctors, the interests of

German physicians also are supported by private, voluntary professional groups, although organizations representing medical specialties do not seem to be as dominant as in the United States.

Regional associations represent only the ambulatory care physicians. Another organization—the Marburgerbund—represents hospital-based doctors. These different organizations are a reflection of one of the key features that distinguish German medical care—the sharp demarcation that separates ambulatory care physicians and hospital-based doctors. The vast majority (more than 90 percent) of ambulatory care physicians are prohibited from treating patients in hospitals. In turn, most hospital-based physicians are barred from treating patients on an ambulatory care basis. Ambulatory care physicians are reimbursed on a fee-for-service basis, and the rates are established through a schedule negotiated prospectively with the sickness funds. Hospital-based physicians are paid a salary by the hospital at a level based on specialty and seniority. Chiefs of service negotiate with the hospital for special supplements. Money for salaries comes from the per diem operating costs that hospitals negotiate every year with the sickness funds.

The operating and capital costs of German hospitals flow from different funding streams. Although hospitals receive their operating money from sickness funds, their capital comes mostly from state and some local-government contributions. As a funding source, private philanthropy accounts for very little of total hospital capital. Capital funds sought by all hospitals are reviewed and approved through a state planning process. For-profit hospitals, which make up 15.8 percent of all hospitals and have 3.8 percent of all beds, also receive their capital from public sources and are subject to the same planning process. On the average, German hospitals have fewer pieces of high-technology equipment than most big urban hospitals in the United States, but they have more such equipment than Canadian hospitals.[15] Canada and Germany concentrate their most expensive forms of medical technology in teaching hospitals to a much

greater extent than does the United States.

Patients in Germany are free to select any ambulatory care physician. When they visit the offices of such doctors, 58 percent of whom are medical specialists and most of whom are solo practitioners, they hand the receptionist or secretary a treatment voucher on which the doctor notes the services provided. Since 1984, patients have by law been able to claim only one treatment voucher per quarter, usually held by a patient's general practitioner, but there is no restriction on how many times a voucher can be used. Patients must obtain a referral certificate for visits to a specialist. This restriction, imposed recently to discourage unnecessary use, does not always prevent patients from seeking an appointment with a specialist directly. Some specialists serve as their patients' primary physicians and thus hold the patients' vouchers.

To be reimbursed, generalists and specialists who provide ambulatory care submit a list of all the treatments they have rendered during a quarter to their regional association. The association in turn calculates the amount owed to each practitioner and reimburses its members on a regular, lump-sum basis. No money passes between the patients covered by the sickness funds and their physicians. In most instances, patients therefore have no idea how much their treatment costs, except for the very small (by U.S. standards) cost-sharing amounts paid for some services, such as hospitalization, prescription drugs, dental treatments, and spa visits.

Germany's social-insurance plan has successfully achieved its overriding objective: to provide all citizens with ready access to medical care at a cost the country considers socially acceptable. To do so, the country has struck a number of balances between the conflicting imperatives that face all health care systems regardless of how they are structured. Since 1977 the German government has enacted a series of cost-containment laws that have stabilized spending and imposed higher requirements for cost sharing, which now represents about 7.5 percent of all revenues collected to finance care through the sickness funds. Dental prostheses, for which patients must now pay half the cost, have thus become far more expensive for consumers. On the basis of a 1988 cost-containment law, scrutiny of physicians' patterns of use will intensify in the future, as I shall explain in a subsequent report. Germany has barely scratched the surface in examining the outcomes of clinical decision making, an activity that has become a new priority for organized medicine, government, and private third-party payers in the United States.

Although Germany's medical profession has not always agreed with the more restrictive new policies, it has had an important influence in shaping them because of its role, guaranteed by law, in health policy making. Despite misgivings about its new directions, the medical profession remains in general very supportive of the German health care system. From 1977 to 1989 the number of ambulatory care physicians increased 31 percent to 73,381, during a period of little or no population growth. In part because of the growing number of physicians in a system that has essentially capped expenditures and has a record of greater success in constraining costs for ambulatory care than hospital costs, but mainly because German workers have prospered generally, the average income of ambulatory care doctors ($100,000 after the deduction of professional expenses but before income taxes in 1986) fell from 6 to about 3 1/2 times the average wage of an industrial worker between 1970 and 1986.[15] The average income of dentists is higher than that of physicians, in part because German dental schools produce proportionally far fewer new practitioners than do medical schools and because dental care is a well-insured service of the sickness funds.

In a subsequent report I shall elaborate on other operational details of the system and discuss Germany's abundant supply of physicians and its successful quest to constrain the growth of health spending in the 1980s.

Notes

1. Schieber GJ. Health care financing trends: health expenditures in major industrialized countries, 1960–1987. Health Care Financ Rev 1990; 11(4):159–67.
2. Glaser WA. Paying the hospital: the organization, dynamics, and effects of differing financial arrangements. San Francisco: Jossey-Bass, 1987.
3. Blendon RJ, Leitman R, Morrison I, Donelan K. Satisfaction with health systems in ten nations. Health Aff (Millwood) 1990; 9(2):185–92.
4. Blanpain J, Delesie L, Nys H. National health insurance and health resources: the European experience. Cambridge, Mass.: Harvard University Press, 1978.
5. Raffel MW, ed. Comparative health systems: descriptive analyses of fourteen national health systems. University Park: Pennsylvania State University Press, 1984.
6. Rosenberg P. The origin and the development of compulsory health insurance in Germany. In: Light DW, Schuller A, eds. Political values and health care: the German experience. Cambridge, Mass.: MIT Press, 1986:105–26.
7. Gallagher HG. By trust betrayed: patients, physicians, and the license to kill in the Third Reich. New York: Henry Holt, 1990.
8. Kater MH. Doctors under Hitler. Chapel Hill: University of North Carolina Press, 1989.
9. Proctor R. Racial hygiene: medicine under the Nazis. Cambridge, Mass.: Harvard University Press, 1988.
10. Weiss SF. Race hygiene and national efficiency: the eugenics of Wilhelm Schallmayer. Berkeley: University of California Press, 1987.
11. Lifton RJ. The Nazi doctors: medical killing and the psychology of genocide. New York: Basic Books, 1986.
12. Light DW. Introduction: state, profession, and political values. In: Light DW, Schuller A, eds. Political values and health care: the German experience. Cambridge, Mass.: MIT Press, 1986:1–23.
13. Stone DA. The limits of professional power: national health care in the Federal Republic of Germany. Chicago: University of Chicago Press, 1980.
14. Sandier S. Health services utilization and physician income trends. Health Care Financ Rev 1989; 10:Suppl:33–48.
15. Rublee DA. Medical technology in Canada, Germany, and the United States. Health Aff (Millwood) 1989; 8(3):178–81.

Germany's Health Care System: Part Two

Germany's universal health insurance plan is grounded in a social contract that places a strong emphasis on the provision of medical care to all citizens by private ambulatory care physicians who largely have clinical autonomy but who

Reprinted with permission from *The New England Journal of Medicine* 324, no. 24 (June 13, 1991), pp. 1750–56. Copyright © 1991 by the Massachusetts Medical Society.

have relinquished their economic freedom to the professional associations that negotiate on their behalf with insurance organizations known as sickness funds. Hospital-based physicians, who are employees of the institutions for which they work, are paid by salary. Germany's health system is administered by private not-for-profit organizations, authorized by law to wield power on behalf of payers and providers. The federal government intervenes only when it concludes that the broader interests of society are being neglected.

Thus, the private organizations that have the legal authority to administer Germany's health insurance plan—1,128 sickness funds and 18 regional associations of physicians—operate within a strict framework of federal and state regulation, but not government domination. This system will be extended in a similar form to what was East Germany. To the United States, which values collaboration between the private and public sectors and favors a limited role for government, Germany's century-old experience is an impressive demonstration of the accommodation of private interests to the broader public good to achieve what is in the United States an elusive but oft-stated goal: providing all citizens with access to an adequate level of medical care at a socially acceptable cost.

Germany's ability to reconcile these conflicts reflects the "principle of social solidarity" that I underscored in the first part of this article[1] as the glue that has long helped to hold the system together. A series of cost-containment laws enacted in the 1980s represented action deemed necessary by Parliament because Germany's health insurance plan had failed to achieve an overriding policy goal set in 1977—the establishment of a so-called "income-oriented expenditure policy." This policy held that the average rate at which employers and employees pay premiums to the sickness funds (to cover the medical costs of insured persons) should not rise more rapidly than workers' wages and salaries. By embracing such a policy, Germany in essence declared that it had reached the limit in the proportion of the gross national product it was prepared to allocate to medical care. And that spending limit was tied directly to the growth of the salaries and wages of workers.

The message Parliament conveyed by seeking to stabilize the relation between the growth of health spending and workers' incomes was very popular with the electorate, but it was greeted less enthusiastically by providers of care. Government would strive to protect employers and employees from further increases in heath insurance premiums, but it would not do so by reducing benefits more than very moderately, nor by increasing patient cost-sharing requirements. This point was cited in a new analysis by Schneider: "The crucial point of the Cost-Containment Acts . . . is the fact that, with very few exceptions, services have not been limited. Members of the sickness funds

have unlimited access to the whole range of medical and dental care."[2] The cost-containment burden has thus been imposed largely on providers through tighter controls on physicians' fees and hospital budgets and on pharmaceutical manufacturers by forcing them in essence to reduce the prices of their brand-name drugs. Reflecting the effect of this policy, the average combined rate of the equal contributions employers and employees make to the sickness funds (a measure closely monitored by politicians) dropped marginally in 1990 to 12.8 percent of a worker's gross salary. It had increased from 11.4 percent in 1984 to 12.9 percent in 1989. As a consequence, the share of the gross domestic product consumed by the sickness funds decreased from a high of 5.52 percent in 1988 to 5 percent in 1989.

Whether the contribution rates, which are calculated annually by every sickness fund, increase is influenced but not dictated by the Concerted Action Conference for Health, a body of 64 representatives of the major organizations that participate in the health insurance program, including dentists, employers, hospitals, labor unions, pharmaceutical manufacturers, pharmacists, physicians, sickness funds, and state governments. The conference, which is convened twice a year by the federal minister of labor and social affairs, was created as a consensus-building instrument by the 1977 law that established the income-oriented expenditure policy. The conference does not have governmental powers as such, but the pressure it applies through its well-publicized activities has helped Germany to make the growth of medical spending and that of the general economy virtually equal.

After assimilating the latest data on costs and income trends, which are provided by ministry officials each spring, the conference's representatives recommend global increases in the compensation of dentists and ambulatory care physicians and percentage cost increases for pharmaceutical products and hospital expenditures. These recommendations are used as guidelines by negotiators who subsequently strike agreements on behalf of the system's payers, pro-

viders, and suppliers. Since 1986, the conference has been influenced by a series of annual reports produced by a seven-member advisory committee on a variety of issues that face the system: alleviating a shortage of nurses, reducing the number of hospital beds, granting primary care physicians a gatekeeper role in the system, and introducing capitation as a form of payment to physicians. The advisory body also raises other questions about the health care system and how it could operate more efficiently, which are not always welcomed by interests comfortable with the status quo.

In this second of two reports on the German health care system, I describe some of its important features, including the binding relation between the remuneration physicians receive for ambulatory care services and the volume of services they provide. Another issue I discuss is the high rate at which Germany is educating new physicians. The rapid growth in the number of physicians is making it increasingly difficult for new doctors to secure positions in hospitals, where many of them have traditionally begun their practices. I begin by reporting the latest spending trends among the 24 member countries of the Organization for Economic Cooperation and Development and how Germany compares.

International Trends in Medical Spending

The overriding reason the health care systems of other Western countries have attracted increased attention in the United States is that they provide universal coverage to their populations and spend considerably less than the United States, which is still struggling to provide access for all its citizens. The most impressive economic indicator of the performance of (West) Germany's health care system as compared with that of other Western countries is the degree to which it has been able to restrain the growth in its medical spending in the 1980s to a rate that approximates the growth rate of its economy. In 1988, German health spending rose to 8.9 percent of the gross domestic product, but in 1989, according to data from the German government, that figure dropped to 8.2 percent, reflecting the country's strong economy and the effect of its cost-containment laws. [3]

The new spending data showed the maintenance of a trend that emerged during the 1980s: the gap in health spending between the United States and other major industrialized countries continues to widen. In 1989 the United States spent $2,354 per capita for personal health services—11.8 percent of its gross domestic product, or $604.1 billion. The 1989 spending levels in other major Western countries were as follows: Canada, $1,683 (8.7 percent of the gross domestic product); Sweden, $1,361 (8.8 percent); France, $1,274 (8.7 percent); Germany, $1,232 (8.2 percent); Japan, $1,035 (6.7 percent); and the United Kingdom, $842 (5.8 percent).

A New Era of Cost Constraint

Through the mid-1970s, Germany's health insurance program was expanding, adding protection for previously underinsured groups such as farmers and students, broadening the benefits that all sickness funds must offer by law, and modernizing the country's hospitals. But with the enactment of the 1977 law, which introduced the principle of an income-oriented expenditure policy and created the Concerted Action Conference, a new era of cost containment dawned. Over the next 12 years, Parliament enacted a variety of measures that did not represent structural reform but were incremental steps intended to moderate the growth of health spending by squeezing reimbursements to ambulatory care providers and, most recently, forcing down the prices of brand-name pharmaceutical products to the levels of their generic equivalents.

In health spending, the chief priority of Germany's elected politicians was to stabilize the rate at which employers and employees contribute to the sickness funds. Every spring, after the Concerted Action Conference has recommended the annual aggregate increases in providers' fees and suppliers' prices, negotiations begin at the state and local levels to set remuneration rates and hospital budgets that reflect the conference's guidelines. I failed to un-

cover a satisfactory explanation of the effect of these constraints on individual encounters between physicians and patients or on the general provision (or withholding) of medical care and its quality. Indeed, other analysts who have published English-language accounts of the German system do not discuss the clinical consequences of cost constraints. In 1989 there was actually a reduction in medical expenditures by the sickness funds. [2,4]

One of the more heated struggles over how resources are allocated pits acute inpatient care against ambulatory care, without a great deal of regard for what might best suit the patient. The sharp division between hospital-based and ambulatory care physicians has led to "lengthy referral chains, duplication of equipment, and repetition of diagnostic tests by different doctors," Hurst reported. [4] One current reflection of this tension is the slowness with which ambulatory surgery has developed in Germany. In general, hospitals and their employed physicians have resisted this innovation because it would reallocate some of their resources to doctors who treat patients in an outpatient setting. Hospitals are generally barred from operating outpatient clinics, because by law that is the province of solo practitioners and other physicians in ambulatory settings. On the other hand, ambulatory care physicians have sought to expand their technological reach, to offer their patients services previously provided in hospitals. Patients also feel safer and better cared for in hospitals, and outpatient surgery is a concept foreign to most of them.

Another important influence in the continuing debate over how resources are allocated is the part states play in overseeing performance and in preserving Germany's heavy use of inpatient care. Germany delegates the principal authority over hospitals to its states. Capital funds sought by hospitals are subject to state review and approval. To some extent this process limits the diffusion of medical technology to hospitals more than in the United States, [5] but it is complicated by politicians who frequently interfere on behalf of their community hospitals. But the states are not responsible for negotiating hospital per diems, which are established through

bargaining with the sickness funds. A general criticism of this divided decision-making process is that states are less sensitive to the implications of new capital expenditures on operating costs, because they are not responsible for total hospital spending. States protect their prerogatives in relation to hospitals virtually whenever the federal government seeks to intervene. All federal laws must be approved by the Bundesrat, a chamber of 45 representatives of the 11 state governments that is part of Germany's parliamentary apparatus.

The political limits of hospital cost containment have been shaped in large part by the divided nature of policy making. In 1982, when the conservative coalition government of Helmut Kohl was at "the zenith of its influence" and "anti-welfare state rhetoric" was running strong, as Dohler wrote, [6] the administration's effort to reduce the number of German hospital beds bore very little fruit. The 1982 law introduced incentives to encourage hospitals to eliminate inpatient beds, which at the time numbered 11.5 per 1,000 population. Today, there are 11 beds per 1,000. In Germany, the average length of a hospital stay in 1988 was longer (16.6 days, down from 20.8 days in 1977), the density of acute care beds was higher, and the number of staff per bed was lower than in most Western countries. The 1990 report of the Concerted Action Conference's advisory committee said:

The unwarranted occupation of hospital beds remains an unsolved problem. A study commissioned by the Federal Ministry of Labor and Social Affairs showed that 40 percent of the patients under age 60 and 38 percent of the patients over 60 could be discharged earlier. This means that 18 percent of all hospital days—which corresponds to 85,000 beds—were unwarranted from a medical point of view.

Controls on Ambulatory Care Physicians

Ambulatory care physicians have been subject to tighter controls than German hospitals. An expenditure cap has been imposed on reimbursements for the services they provide to patients. The cap links the reimbursement that ambulatory care doctors receive for each service to the number of services rendered by each practitioner, and it works as follows. Every year, the sickness funds and the regional associations of physicians negotiate a global budget, arrived at in essence by multiplying the number of insured persons by an agreed amount per covered person. The sickness funds turn over the bulk of the revenues they collect from employers and employees to the regional associations of doctors. These associations reimburse their members for the ambulatory services they provide, on the basis of a fee schedule negotiated with the funds. The role of the physicians' associations as payers is unique to Germany.

The funds and the regional associations agree in their annual negotiations on a monetary conversion factor that, when multiplied by the point values in the fee schedule and the probable number of claims, will approximate the budgeted amount of money. Physicians draw from this regional pool, which is also used for the administrative costs of the associations and other special purposes, such as a program of disability and survivors' insurance for physicians and subsidies to doctors who agree to practice in underserved areas. If physicians' bills in the aggregate exceed the negotiated global budget in any given quarter, the conver-sion factor for all claims is reduced slightly, to keep the final annual tally within the fixed budget. In other words, there is an explicit trade-off between the use of services and the amount of individual reimbursements—the higher the volume, the lower the payment per claim; the lower the volume, the higher the payment per claim. As a consequence, physicians do not know exactly how much they will be reimbursed for each claim.

The expenditure cap has been an effective way to control the growth of physicians' fees and hence their clinical incomes, which fell in real (inflation adjusted) terms in the 1980s, but it has had less influence on the volume of services provided by doctors. [7] On average, expenditures for ambulatory care increased at an annual rate of 5.4 percent from 1977 to 1989, but physicians' fees increased at an annual rate of only 1 percent. Fee increases have thus been much lower than the average inflation rate of 3 percent for consumer prices. [2]

At an international conference in Bonn in 1988, Gerhard Brenner, an economist at the central research institute affiliated with the regional associations of physicians, said in a paper:

The research institutes maintained by insurers and physicians have jointly been analyzing the effects of fee policies on the [cost containment] goal since 1977. Published results of this joint investigation are available for the period 1980–1986, which clearly show that insured persons' wages and salaries subject to [payroll] deductions increased 27.5 percent during the period and the total volume of fees for ambulatory medical services charged the insurers rose 27.3 percent. . . . The 27.3 percent rise in expenditures . . . was generally caused by an increase in the number of ambulatory services of 19.1 percent, i.e., considerably more ambulatory services were performed per member and illness.

Nevertheless, German doctors are still well compensated as compared with their counterparts in other European countries. [8] In 1988 the average net income of ambulatory care physicians (after office expenses but before taxes) derived from services provided to privately insured patients and through the sickness funds was $98,624, according to the central research institute of the regional associations of physicians. (On average, general practitioners earned $80,979 and medical specialists earned $111,378 in 1988.) In 1987 a revised fee schedule for physicians was implemented to reduce the income disparities between primary care physicians and those who practice in the more highly paid specialties. On average, Brenner and Rublee report, increases in income from the fourth quarter of 1986 to the fourth quarter of 1987 were recorded in pediatrics (20 percent), laboratory medicine (12.1 percent), gynecology (8.1 percent), otolaryngology (2.5 percent), and general practice (2.1 percent). Radiology had the largest average loss (9.7 percent). Orthopedics, dermatology, and neurology recorded losses of 5 to 6 percent. [9]

Collective Incentive to Monitor Physicians' Services

One of the consequences of the link between the cap on expenditures and the volume of service is that all members of a regional association of physicians draw their revenues from the same zero-sum pool, which is negotiated every year with the sickness funds. This dynamic gives the regional associations a powerful incentive to monitor the patterns of use of their members. All reviews are retrospective. Physicians are not required to seek third-party approval before performing any procedure, except some forms of psychotherapy. Because the regional associations of physicians both receive and pay physicians' claims, which include a breakdown of the services provided, they know in "extraordinary detail" the nature of the clinical practices of their members, according to Dr. Ullrich Oesingmann, chairman of the board of the federal association of regional physicians' organizations, in a discussion with an American delegation last July.

For every 10 physician members, the regional associations employ one person to review and pay claims and perform other administrative tasks. In these respects, they resemble American health insurers, and ironically, German physicians often feel an antipathy toward their regional associations that is similar to the attitude many American doctors have toward third-party payers. The administrative costs of the regional associations of physicians constitute about 2.5 percent of their expenditures; the administrative expenses of the sickness funds, most of which have smaller budgets and smaller staffs, average about 6.5 percent of their expenses, Oesingmann said. For many years the regional associations of physicians have engaged in what is characterized as "economic monitoring," to review service use and set utilization standards. Doctors whose service patterns differ substantially from the norm are invited to discuss their practices privately with the appropriate physicians' committees or are sent letters of notice.

An estimated 7 to 10 percent of the physician members of a regional association are contacted every quarter, but most inquiries involve clarification of a claim or further documentation, according to Oesingmann. He said that fully half the physicians who are contacted have been contacted repeatedly. If problems persist, claims can be denied, and this occurs about 2 percent of the time, he said. But once bills are deemed valid, they are reimbursed. There are no bad debts. There is an elaborate appeals process for physicians who disagree with a complaint lodged against them by the regional association. Only the most egregious cases against physicians are publicized, and usually only after the appeals process has been exhausted.

The 1989 law stipulated that regional physicians' associations, in collaboration with sickness funds, develop a more pervasive approach to monitoring the patterns of use of its members. Every quarter the clinical practices of a random sample of 2 percent of the ambulatory care physicians are to be examined, including patterns of drug prescription and hospital referral and other use of services. The associations are moving to implement the directive, although the law does not stipulate how it should be done, other than noting that payers and providers should be involved in its design.

Of the seven cost-containment laws enacted by Parliament in the 1980s, the Health Care Reform Act that took effect in January 1989 seems to have achieved the most striking short-term results in stemming the previous trends in health spending. Schneider characterized the 1989 law as "the most important statute since the law of 1911 on which the basic foundations of the social sickness fund system were constituted."[2] The 1989 law increased patient cost-sharing requirements for hospital visits (although only from $3.50 to $7 a day, with a maximum of 14 days in any calendar year), spa treatments, dental prostheses (which increased to 50 percent of the cost of the service), and pharmaceutical products, and curtailed death and dental benefits and the reimbursement of transportation costs. In addition, the 1989 law authorized sickness funds to terminate contracts with "inefficient" hospitals, directed hospitals to publish price lists for their services, and ordered the creation of medical-equipment committees to reduce unnecessary duplication of equipment in hospitals and assess emerging forms of technology in a more organized fashion. Limited improvements in benefits were also enacted, including the introduction of new screening tests for disease and some financial support for families caring for a chronically ill patient at home.

Controls on the Price of Drugs

The most controversial provisions of the 1989 law imposed a new system of reference prices on pharmaceutical products over the strong opposition of the industry. The measure was promoted most aggressively by Norbert Blum, minister of labor and social affairs, as a way to moderate the growth of spending on prescription drugs by an estimated $1.2 billion a year by 1992, or about 12 percent of current expenditures. The sickness funds cover the cost of all approved pharmaceutical products prescribed by physicians, except for a trivial copayment for outpatients. All drug products prescribed by physicians are dispensed through free-standing pharmacies. Physicians may dispense drugs only in emergency situations. Blum explained the rationale for reference pricing in this way:

One medicine costs DM [Deutsche Mark] 30 and another, equally good with the same active substance costs DM 90. Why should the health insurance system pay for the most expensive, why shouldn't it buy the DM 30 product? The health insurance system has always been based on the principle that the services financed must represent value for money.[10]

Until this law was enacted, the German government had not intervened directly in the setting of pharmaceutical prices, which were among the highest in Europe.[11] During the 1980s, the government and the sickness funds did demonstrate their growing concern over price trends by developing a list of drugs for which sickness funds would not reimburse pharmacists, publishing prices of comparable drugs, encouraging the prescribing of generic products, and exhorting physicians to prescribe drugs "economically." Only 4 of Germany's 26 medical faculties had departments of clinical pharmacology in 1988.[12]

Under the new pricing system, three classes of drugs are to be established according to different criteria for the purpose of determining the sickness funds' maximal reimbursement levels for pharmaceutical products. A committee composed of physicians and sickness-fund managers is establishing the classes, and the funds themselves—which reimburse pharmacists for drugs—are setting the reference prices. In the first phase, reference prices were set at the level of the generic product in a group of drugs. The practical consequence of the new policy was to force pharmaceutical companies to lower their prices or face the loss of market share. Reference prices established in the first phase were 30 to 66 percent below the market prices of the original products. The share of the entire outpatient drug market claimed by generic products has increased from 7 to 22 percent since 1981. When original and generic products are in competition, the generic drugs are prescribed by physicians more than half the time. The second and third phases, which the government is now implementing, will group drugs on the basis of pharmacologically and therapeutically comparable active ingredients and pharmacologically comparable principles of action (i.e., products that act on a disease according to similar principles). A reference price will then be set for each group.

Physicians maintained their discretion to prescribe any drug under the new law, but responded in most instances in the first phase by prescribing products that cost the same or less than the reference price, rather than face questions from patients concerned about paying out of pocket to obtain a higher-priced brand-name product. Brenner, the economist, said in an interview that:

most doctors accepted generic products without reservations because when physicians, most of whom prescribe 50 to 70 drugs a day, have to explain to patients that drugs costing more than the reference price require a copayment, the time that takes affects their income much more than prescribing a drug sold at the reference price.

Before long, this issue became moot because the pharmaceutical companies all reduced the prices of their brand-name products to the level of the generic equivalents rather than risk the loss of their market share, and they did so more rapidly than anyone had anticipated. The companies are now seeking to recoup their lost revenues by raising the prices of drugs not yet part of the reference-price system.

In a recent position paper, the Association of the German Pharmaceutical Industry said that:

there is a risk that in view of the [creation of a] single European market [in] 1993 other European countries will take similar measures to contain costs in the health sector primarily through the prices of pharmaceutical products. First signs have become apparent in the Netherlands, Denmark and France.

U.S. pharmaceutical manufacturers have another concern—that Germany is seeking to obtain a "free ride" for its consumers, primarily at the expense of American consumers. A 1988 report prepared by a Washington law firm for the U.S. Pharmaceutical Manufacturers Association but never publicly distributed said:

To the extent that pharmaceutical prices are forced down in Germany through the reference price system, the funds to support research, development and promotion will have to come from somewhere else. The closing of the German market in this respect is a particularly serious problem because Germany has traditionally been one of the largest and most open markets for the sale of pharmaceutical products. Only in another large and open market, such as the United States, could pharmaceutical manufacturers hope to recoup at least a portion of the funds that will be needed for self-sustaining future innovation.

Supply of Physicians

One of the dimensions of the German system with serious future implications for physicians' incomes, practice styles, and aggregate costs is the rate at which new doctors are being educated. In 1990 the 26 (West) German medical faculties bestowed degrees on some 12,000 students, about 40 percent of whom were women. With a population of 61 million, West Germany was educating far more new physicians per capita than the United States, which has four times the population and 126 medical schools that graduate 16,000 students a year. Between 1970 and 1989, while the total population of West Germany was declining, the number of practicing physicians grew at an annual rate of about 3.2 percent. The density of physicians in East Germany was a bit lower than that in the West (2.3 vs. 2.8 doctors per 1000

population in 1985); more of them were employed in administrative positions, and several thousand departed for West Germany after the opening of the Berlin Wall. All German universities with medical faculties are public institutions, and most of the students' costs other than books and incidental expenses are paid by the government. The admissions process, the structure of the training programs, and the testing of the students' performance are all prescribed by law. Although it has a bountiful supply of physicians, Germany has a serious shortage of nurses, a situation that has sometimes led to the temporary closing of hospital operating suites. Most German nurses are trained in three-year, hospital-based programs. Once employed, they lodge many of the same complaints voiced by their counterparts in the United States and other countries, particularly about their low pay and their low status in relation to that of physicians. University-based training in nursing is virtually nonexistent in Germany.

The German constitution guarantees all qualified students the opportunity to pursue the occupation of their choice if they pass the necessary qualifying examinations. That guarantee has made it difficult for Germany to reduce the number of new doctors who graduate from its universities, because all qualified students must be placed. In the past year, however, as a consequence of policies promulgated by the ministry of health, medical schools have begun to limit the size of their classes, with the rationale that unless schools can guarantee the quality of teaching, they must make their classes smaller. One influence on this question was a recent report produced by a study group affiliated with Germany's Science Council, an elite group of scientists and government officials. The report concluded that German medical schools are good at teaching students clinical theory, but that their capacity to provide practical experience in actual clinical settings is inadequate. The report recommended that the teacher:student ratio be one teacher for every two students. The ratio currently ranges from 1:12 to 1:30 in preclinical training and from 1:5 to

1:15 in clinical training.[13] In accepting this recommendation, medical schools have begun trimming their production of new physicians to some 10,000 a year, still proportionately far more than are being trained in the United States and most other Western countries. Once students complete their medical training and have gone through the formality of joining a regional medical association of physicians, they have a legal right to treat sickness-fund patients and bill for their services accordingly.

Future Challenges

Germany's century-old health insurance scheme provides comprehensive protection for all its citizens, but like the social systems of all industrialized nations, it faces innumerable challenges. Currently, the overriding issue is unifying the economic, political, and social systems of what were once East and West Germany, a herculean task that will postpone other efforts to improve Germany's health insurance program. Bringing hospitals in the east up to the standards of the west will alone cost around $20 billion, but easing the transition of physicians from state employees to private practitioners will also be difficult. Initially, physicians in the east will be paid at a rate that is 45 percent of that doctors in the west receive.

On other fronts, Germany faces an important issue regarding how to structure an expansion of long-term care in nursing homes and home settings. Should long-term care be provided mainly through private insurance, or should the scope of the sickness funds extend to more comprehensive long-term care? Schneider reported that current expenditures for long-term care are "the fastest growing health-care expenses,"[2] but services are not adequate to meet the estimated future demand. In another sphere, activities aimed at health promotion and disease prevention are not well developed in Germany, particularly as they apply to diet, nutrition, and smoking. Labeling foods for calorie and salt content is not required, and the warning labels on cigarette packages are mild, although stronger warnings are being prepared. The water is not fluoridated, nor are there any national programs for the primary prevention of cardiovascular disease. Germany has virtually no disease-specific patient registries or reporting systems, largely because of people's reluctance to have their names placed on lists, an attitude formed by the Nazi experience. Efforts are nonetheless under way to develop such mechanisms. Research in health services, health economics, and epidemiology is also underdeveloped as compared with research in the United States.

Like all health care systems, Germany's has features arrived at through historical accident, cultural preference, and political compromise that make little sense today, such as the unwieldy number of sickness funds, the sharp demarcation between ambulatory care settings and hospitals, and the reluctance of solo practitioners to organize beyond their specialties. But Germany has learned to live with these features and the additional expense they create by moderating spending in other ways, particularly by limiting the fees of ambulatory care physicians and imposing much higher cost-sharing requirements on dental patients. Still, the forces for higher spending are stronger than the forces for restraint. [14,15]

For Americans in search of a formula for reforming their own pluralistic system and protecting all citizens against the financial consequences of disease, Germany does offer some lessons. The society-wide framework within which Germany makes policy, monitors costs, and ensures access is an interesting approach, as is the strict relation between workers' salaries and the rate at which employers and employees pay premiums (and thus the rate of growth in health spending). Maintaining this relation will become increasingly difficult as the supply of physicians grows

more rapidly than the population and as the ratio between workers and retirees continues to deteriorate. But perhaps the most important lesson for American physicians is that in Germany, the associations that represent doctors have assumed a legally vested role as active participants in all dimensions of policy making, from cost containment to ensuring access. Because they are part of the system's legal framework, these associations are compelled to be more socially accountable than medical organizations in most countries. American medical organizations have no such legal mandate, and they therefore wield less influence in policy making and with individual physicians. When I asked Dr. James S. Todd, executive vice-president of the American Medical Association, for his view of this feature of the German system, he responded that:

One of the main strengths of the German system, which we are currently studying, is the presence of formalized medical input. In particular, the medical profession in Germany has formal negotiating roles with government and other participants on a variety of issues. Such formal roles for medicine in the decision-making process in this country are badly needed, particularly in areas such as reimbursement, appropriateness of fees, and the review of the quality and appropriateness of services. However, the role organized medicine has been able to play in these activities has been strictly circumscribed and in major instances prohibited by the Federal Trade Commission and the Justice Department.

Notes

1. Iglehart JK. Germany's health care system. N Engl J Med 1991; 324:503–8.
2. Schneider M. Cost containment in health care in Federal Republic of Germany. Health Care Financ Rev 1991; 12(3):87–97.
3. Schieber GJ, Poullier J-P. International health spending: issues and trends. Health Aff (Millwood) 1991; 10(1):106–16.
4. Hurst JW. Reform of health care in Germany. Health Care Financ Rev 1991; 12(3):75–86.
5. Rublee DA. Medical technology in Canada, Germany, and the United States. Health Aff (Millwood) 1989; 8(3):178–81.
6. Dohler M. Policy networks, opportunity structures and neoconservative reform strategies in health policy. Presented at the International Sociological Association World Congress of Sociology, Madrid, 1990.
7. Kirkman-Liff BL. Physician payment and cost-containment strategies in West Germany: suggestions for Medicare reform. J Health Polit Policy Law 1990; 15(1):69–99.
8. Sandier S. Health services utilization and physician income trends. Health Care Financ Rev 1989; 10:Suppl:33–48.
9. Brenner G, Rublee DA. The 1987 revision of fees in Germany: impact on physician income. Health Aff (Millwood) (in press).
10. Reher R, Reichelt H. Drug reference prices in West Germany: the practical solution. Surrey, England: PJB Publications, 1989. 11. Sermeus G, Adriaenssens G. Drug prices and drug legislation in Europe: an analysis of the situation in the twelve member states of the European countries. Brussels, Belgium: Bureau of European Unions of Consumers, 1989. (BEUC112/89)
12. Orme M, Sjoqvist F, Bircher J, et al. The teaching and organisation of clinical pharmacology in European medical schools. Eur J Clin Pharmacol 1990; 38:101–5.
13. Arnold M, Brauer H-P, Deneke JFV, Fiedler E. The medical profession in the Federal Republic of Germany. Cologne, Germany: Deutscher Arzte Verlag, 1982.
14. Glaser WA. Lessons from Germany: some reflections occasioned by Schulenburg's "report." J Health Polit Policy Law 1983; 8(2):352–65.
15. *Idem.* Health insurance in practice. San Francisco: Jossey-Bass (in press).

23

The Effect of Sweden's Corporatist Structure on Health Policy and Outcomes

Diane M. Duffy

Introduction

In 1985 Sweden and Norway outperformed all other countries with respect to health outcomes. These two countries are consistently first or second on indicators ranging from longevity to infant mortality (see Table 1). In terms of resource supply, however, Sweden initially had no greater potential than any of the other Western industrial countries. For example, prior to 1950, Sweden, the United Kingdom, and the United States all had comparable expenditures for health services. As a percentage of gross national product, all spent under 5 percent. Over the years the disparity between these countries has grown. In recent years expenditures have climbed to 6 percent in England, just over 8 percent for the United States, and nearly 10 percent for Sweden (Heidenheimer and Elvander 1980, 228). Additionally, in 1959 Sweden lagged behind other countries in number of physicians available for care (1,120 inhabitants per physician compared to 940 in France and 710 in Switzerland) (Immergut 1986, 27). Even more recently (1974), the ratio of physicians to population in Sweden (16.2 physicians per 10,000) was lower than in Canada (16.6), Italy (19.9), the United States (16.5), and West Germany (19.4) (Culyer 1981, 141).

What makes Sweden so successful in health outcomes? Why is it outperforming other countries in the health arena? Robert Alford believes the policy

outcomes are constrained by historically developed structures of institutions and interests and are shaped by resource availability, stability of institutional arrangements, and degree of national consensus (Alford and Friedland 1985, 409). Politics is what mediates between the institutional contradictions in the state and human interests and, in turn, influences the outcomes. Politics therefore becomes an important theoretic factor for policy performance. However, the political process may be perceived in varied ways, depending on one's interpretation of central actors and events. To Alford, these perspectives include the pluralist, managerial, and class.

Within Alford's framework, the pluralist sees Sweden as having a highly consensual political climate and a considerable amount of political participation, leading to a state which is governable and orderly. Group demands and public interest are achieved by a combination of party politics and bureaucratic maneuvering (Alford and Friedland 1985, 52). In this respect, the Social Democratic party has dominated party politics since the 1930s. With its working-class support, it has been able to shape the direction of social programs in the face of an entrenched and well-developed state bureaucratic apparatus.

To advocates of the managerial perspective, the capitalist aspect of the state is subordinated to the bureaucratic (Alford and Friedland 1985, 223). Sweden resolves the constant tension between the tendencies to centralize and

those to fragment by following a route to interest aggregation, in which organizational elites play a central role in resolving economic dilemmas. The state (commonly called a "legacy of feudalism") is an accepted presence; therefore, during the relatively late transition (early Twentieth century) from an agricultural to industrial nation, the state maintained a role in coordinating interests between large-scale business and banking and emerging political parties and unions.

Finally, the class perspective views the tension between capital accumulation and working-class struggle as an integral element. The former is a constraint on what the state can do, while the latter becomes subordinated to crisis and the fiscal management of the state (Alford and Friedland 1985, 9). Advocates of this view see the state as providing protection and funds in the form of public investment to capitalists who seek to concentrate their wealth and power.[1]

This paper continues the exploration of political, institutional, and behavioral configurations. More specifically, it will be argued that it is the particular style of corporatism in Sweden—which emphasizes decentralized processes and reflects a consensual culture and structure—that is facilitative of favorable health outcomes.

Overview of the Swedish Health Care System

Sweden's health system is a predominantly socialized one, backed by public

Reprinted with permission from *Scandinavian Studies* 61, no. 2–3 (April 1, 1989), pp. 128–45.

TABLE 1

HEALTH OUTCOME INDICATORS

Country	Infant mortality rate/1,000 live births		Life expectancy at birth (years)		Perinatal mortality/1,000 births		Maternal mortality/100,000 births	
	Rate	Rank	Rate	Rank	Rate	Rank	Rate	Rank
Canada	9.1	4	75	4	17.7	3	10.8	3
France	9.0	3	75	4	18.8	4	24.0	6
Norway	7.8	2	76	1	16.8	2	3.3	2
Sweden	7.0	1	76	1	14.1	1	2.7	1
United Kingdom	10.1	5	73	7	23.3	6	17.2	5
United States	10.5	7	75	4	24.8	7	15.2	4
West Germany	10.1	5	74	6	23.2	5	45.9	7

Source: Culyer et al. 1981, 141.

financing. Essentially, Sweden provides free health services and benefits for all citizens, runs government-owned hospitals, and has developed standardized remuneration schemes for health providers. In Sweden, responsibility for health care is split between the central government and twenty-six county bodies. National coordination is accomplished through the state's National Board of Health and Welfare in order to ensure equal access to services and quality of care. The central government has responsibility for overall health manpower and resources, including salary negotiations; control over health professional schools; and the number and distribution of medical posts and facilities across the country. City councils have regional monopoly over health resources, planning, and taxation (Stahl 1981, 173). City and county councils administer health services, operate most hospitals, employ over three-fourths of Sweden's physicians, and finance around 60 percent of health care costs through local tax receipts (Andrain 1985, 122–23).

Thus, health care and its delivery are shaped by local input; control over decision making is decentralized. Care is provided not only through hospital outpatient departments, for which county councils provide the major direction, but also, recently, through plant occupational health services and community centers, where workers sit on the board.

Corporatist Elements in the Health Arena

Scholars of corporatism have focused almost exclusively on income and economic policy, obscuring the pervading effects of corporatism on other sectors of public policy. A careful review of corporatism and policy structures can reveal how it shapes the form of health care being delivered in Sweden and can, more importantly, point out the effects of these corporatist arrangements on health itself.

Lehmbruch's definition of corporatism will be used as a reference in examining the effect of a corporatist structure on health policy:

Corporatism is more than a peculiar pattern of articulation of interests. Rather, it is an institutionalized pattern of policy-formation in which large interest organizations cooperate with each other and with public authorities not only in articulation (or even 'intermediation') of interests, but—in its developed form—in the authoritative allocation of values and in the implementation of such policies. [Lembruch 1979, 150]

This definition reflects a more cooperative relationship than other definitions. It conveys a sense of group interaction and is one in which actions are rooted in a societal orientation toward the government and the government's responsibilities toward the people it represents (an important point for regime legitimacy and democratic theory).

The form this cooperation takes (i.e., state initiated and directed versus state facilitated) can be examined using Lehmbruch's three distinguishing features of corporatism: (a) degree of institutionalization, (b) autonomy of the cartel of organizations with regard to the government, and (c) degree of centralization of the associational subsystem (Lehmbruch 1979, 164).

Degree of Institutionalization

Compared to the Netherlands and Austria, the degree of institutionalization of corporatism in Sweden is low.[2] No formal structures have been instituted in which actors are required to participate. The state plays a secondary role of information provision, while a highly centralized process of collective bargaining takes place among associational participants. This role of government is distinctively different from that in other "corporatist countries," where the government plays either a more active participatory role—as in Austria—or an explicitly leading role—as in Germany (Lehmbruch 1979, 158–64).

Lehmbruch attributes this relative lack of formal interference of the state to the "high degree of centralization and concentration of the associational arrangements" (Lehmbruch 1979, 165). However, there may be other reasons as well. For one, decision making is bifurcated into those issues handled at the

% of GDP

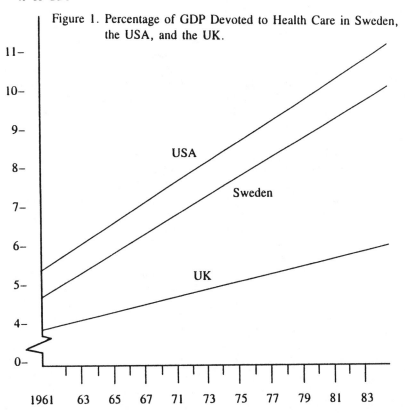

Figure 1. Percentage of GDP Devoted to Health Care in Sweden, the USA, and the UK.

Source: OECD 1985, 12; adapted from Heidenheimer and Elvander 1980, 229.

increasingly more responsibility being handed over to the county councils (Twaddle and Hessler 1986) and to worker committees at the shop level (Navarro 1984). This transfer of responsibility has meant a lesser role for centralized bureaucracy in health care and a proportionately greater reliance on collective bargaining as a means for decision making at the central level. [3]

Autonomy of the Cartel of Organizations in Relation to the Government

Sweden has a strong tradition of interest group participation that goes beyond mere communication among the groups. The power structure is such that the state exerts minimum formal interference. However, it does act by providing information on economic constraints and desirable outcomes, which are considered in the collective bargaining process among the peak associations (Lehmbruch 1979, 164). This state action is in distinct contrast to the more informational role played in West Germany by *interest associations*. The Konzertierte Aktion (KA) acts more as an instrument of the government than anything else, and negotiations center only around parameters set forth by the government.[4] Similarly, in France, unions have played an even lesser role, and therefore interaction is predominantly between business and the government (Lehmbruch 1979, 168).

In Sweden, consensus building and stronger egalitarian policies seem to be facilitated by what Lehmbruch calls a "subordination to national goals." Voluntary peak associations see themselves not only as active participants and partners in the process but also as representatives of particular interests that must be integrated into a national plan. Twaddle and Hessler refer to such a general orientation toward health care in their review of the work of the Swedish Commission of Inquiry on Health and Sickness Care (formed in 1975 to propose new laws governing health care):

> With the broad range of interest groups represented on the commission, ideological differences existed, but party loyalties and other differences did not preclude compro-

central level and those decentralized. There is, further, an elaborate system for input into central decision making through commission review (committees of interest group representatives and government officials) and the *remiss* process (written input from interested parties). What this system allows is (a) the circumscription of the discussion to those issues that are of a national interest and important to the coordination of scarce resources, (b) preservation of local decision making, (c) provision of ample time for the actors in the process to assess and react to proposals, and (d) creation of a conduit for subsystem interests to be articulated through the associational structure to the central level.

Thus, while the process seems centralized, only selective issues are handled at that level, and, further, there is a mechanism to link grass-roots' concerns to centralized negotiations. The participatory means used for handling major

policy questions (such as income policy or health resource coordination) diminishes the need for more formalized institutional structures and reflects participatory mores that stress civic responsibility and input.

In health policy this participation means that the salaries of health care workers and the number and distribution of health facilities and professional posts, health professional educational facilities, and fees for health services are considered at the central level. They are also subject to the collective bargaining processes with input and recommendations provided from such bureaucratic arms as the National Board of Health and Welfare (which itself is composed of a representation of interested parties). Other decisions related to health planning and financing are handled at the county level.

Since 1970, this division between centrally determined and locally determined issues has been accentuated with mise. This was more true in medical care than in other areas, because health had evoked ideological consensus to a remarkable degree. Reflecting larger societal values, the commission of inquiry defined "health" as a basic human right of all citizens. There was no political debate or disagreement on this fundamental tenet, nor was there any debate concerning eliminating financial and geographic barriers to medical care, having a national health insurance system, and establishing medical facilities close to the largest number of people possible. [Twaddle and Hessler 1986, 23]

What *was* debated were the special interests of the associational participants: role of the physician specialist as gatekeeper and head of a clinic (versus an administrator); transfer of control from the hospital sector to community-based or ambulatory services; decentralization of health and welfare budget process to the counties; refocus from acute care to long term care; and reduction of specialist positions and power, while increasing autonomy of nonphysician workers in the system. It is over such issues that one can observe the autonomous roles of interest groups.

During the commission hearings, representatives of the county councils, labor unions, and physician groups faced off in negotiation over their own interests, with the Ministry of Health playing a participatory role. The process was one in which sectoral interests vied for power, and consensus was reached through deliberations and compromise among participating groups.

Centralization of the Associational Subsystem

At the top of the interest groups are the so-called "peak associations," which have negotiating power. Hierarchical organization and negotiating power are the primary measures of the degree of centralization of special interests.[5]

In Sweden, central negotiations focus around four major groups: Svenska Arbetsgivarföreningen (SAF, the Employers' Association) Sveriges Akademikers Centralorganisation (SACO, the Union of University Graduates), Landsorganisationen (LO, the Trade Union Federation), and Tjänstemännens Centralorganisation (TCO, the white-collar unions). These are the four major actors with respect to income policy. However, when the effects of negotiations "spill over" beyond income—as in health policy—other actors are drawn into the process. In health care, these include such groups as the Landstingsförbundet (CCF, the Federation of County Councils) and the health professional school faculties.

Within the health sector, one is able to examine the centralization feature on the salary issue clearly, since workers of varied educational and status levels compete for limited salary resources. On one end of the spectrum, there are physicians, psychologists, and other professionals with doctoral degrees, independent practice rights, and a (comparatively) higher societal status; on the other, unskilled labor with lower educational levels and roles that are administratively subordinate. Worker groups are split into different union membership (e.g., physicians join SACO; nursing personnel the LO, TCO, or SACO, depending on their occupational status), but even within any one unit there are also competing interests and differences of opinion with respect to terms of negotiation over income and/or working conditions. For example, junior and senior physicians both belong to the Swedish Medical Association (SMA). However, because of the hierarchical structures, junior physicians may be concurrent members of the Swedish Association of Junior Physicians (SYLF), the SMA, and SACO—with SACO being the peak association. Junior physicians and the senior physician specialists may differ over salary and working conditions (as they did during the 1960s, leading up to the Seven Crowns Reform).[6]

Similarly, the nurses' union and the LO differ in outlook on certain issues:

. . . the director of the nurses' union described the struggle she had with the LO, the confederation of blue-collar unions, over the nurses' demand for a 40 percent wage increase (they received only 15 percent): "But you see LO doesn't like us to have very much pay. We have to struggle against LO. We cooperate about working conditions but *not* about the salaries." [Twaddle and Hessler 1986, 29–30]

Sweden's corporatist system has a mechanism to mediate these differences before negotiations occur at a centralized level. According to Katzenstein (1985, 33), when disagreements exist at lower levels, they are worked out among the concerned interests *before* a position is taken centrally. Three outcomes result from this lower level activity: (a) there is a reduction in the number of decisions that must be handled centrally, (b) the preference toward decentralized decision making is again reinforced, and (c) the negotiating power of the peak associations is preserved. It appears that with the resolution of each subsystem, differences may follow two potentially different paths: (a) peak associations are able to command sufficient discipline within their member associations to force a (re)alignment of the position of the dissident member to conform with the position(s) of the majority of the member associations; or (b) a member association persisting in a deviant position loses credibility and thus negotiating power at the centralized level, since it is not underpinned by peak association support and therefore the norm of compromise and consensus-building. Thus, its claims lose legitimacy and may be dismissed as self-interested concerns.

This loss of peak association support is exemplified in the case of the physicians during the Swedish Seven Crowns Reforms. Disagreements between physician factions were resolved when SACO sided with the SYLF over the salary issue, and senior physicians were forced to relent. This outcome contrasts with that in France in 1960, when physician interests were similarly split into factions. However, none of the factions was even partially backed by a strong peak association, such as Sweden's SACO. Instead, in France, physicians contracted individually with primary (sickness) funds, weakening the physician union's position as sole negotiator. Such individual contracts consistently placed organized physicians in a defensive posture and were the cause of major setbacks initiated by the state. In both Sweden and France, physician groups lost power and privileges. However, the dynamics were considerably different. In Sweden, physicians were limited by other interest groups within SACO; however, the power of the peak association was preserved. In France, physicians were limited by the state; no peak association played a major role.

Historically, then, the Swedish peak associations have been able to dominate negotiations because the centralized power structure within the interest group system has been preserved. Coordination is easier to accomplish and more efficient.

Merits of Corporatism for Health Policy

Consensus and Legitimacy

The fact that people are less able to function optimally without good health has massive implications for human suffering and economic well-being, and it creates fiscal and moral burdens for society. The opportunity to maintain good health and to obtain adequate care in times of illness are basic human needs recognized as rights by many societies. They grow out of a combined sense of personal responsibility and social concern. However, society's role in health rights is not perceived from country to country in the same way. In particular, the extent to which a society views the government to be a guarantor of these rights varies. That is, the comprehensiveness and diligence of government's role in assuring "good health" will range from a "safety net," minimum level approach (frequently associated with the United States), to an all-encompassing program of social and medical programs, ensuring not only the equality of services but the equality of opportunity to attain *optimal* health status. This latter, more inclusive perspective seems to be the orientation in the Scandinavian countries (Culyer 1981). In Sweden, the goal of comprehensiveness is reflected in the extent to which health care is funded by the government through tax financing—91.6 percent in Sweden versus 42.7 percent in the United States, 76.0 percent in France, 77.1 percent in West Germany (Heidenheimer et al. 1983, 58) and the low percentage of out-of-pocket costs paid by consumers for health care—10 percent (Stahl 1981, 174).

There is evidence, however, that such collective ends in Sweden are achieved at a cost: restrictions on individual behaviors and privileges. Individual freedom of choice is subordinated to the collective interests of society. For example, there have been restrictions placed on physicians' salaries and limitations on number, kind, and location of medical posts available for practice, forcing some physicians into areas that they would not have ordinarily chosen. Such policies have been established after considerable deliberation. At the base of such policies seems to be a rule for decision making similar to that outlined by Stokey and Zeckhauser (1978): policies that will benefit some groups only by imposing significant costs on others should not be undertaken unless (a) they yield positive net results and (b) the redistributional effects of the change are beneficial. (The presumption is, however, that there is general agreement that such redistribution is desirable and achievable.) Or better yet, one might say that, in the case of Sweden, benefits are *distributed* to the collectivity by members of the collectivity itself and not *redistributed* from one group to another.

Sweden, it may be argued, has been more successful in attainment of its goals of comprehensiveness and access because the Swedish political system has the necessary prerequisites: clear policy preferences, agreed-upon policy priorities, a strong will to realize objectives, and the organizational means to reach policy goals (Andrain 1985, 201). Thus, Andrain feels that in Sweden there is not only the needed general consensus to support health goals and programs, but also the structure to carry them out.

Addressing the question of consensus on health issues in Sweden, Immergut (1986, 12–13) argues that the successes of the Social Democrats over the years can be interpreted as an indication of electoral support for Swedish social programs. First, she points out, there is the perception that resumption of control of the government in 1945 was predicated on an "electoral mandate to establish a Swedish welfare state." Second, the Liberal party defeat (and Social Democratic victory) in 1959 was attributed to its position on the superannuated pensions and proposals for rolling back the welfare state. Third, the 1968 landslide victory by the Social Democrats was understood by political observers to be reaffirmation of support for the party's stand on social programs, of which the Seven Crowns Reform package was a primary goal.

Process and Democracy

A general consensus, however, has little value unless it is underpinned by, and articulated through, basic democratic principles. Anderson (1979, 278) outlines three criteria for interest representation to be compatible with democratic theory. The process must be: (a) capable of generating policies that are in the public interest, (b) impartial to varied interests' positions, and (c) supplemental to the process of direct popular representation.

Health policy in Sweden meets these criteria because of the particular style of corporatism. Collective bargaining and *remiss* procedures are placed within the context of a basic conception of public good; national goals and commission mandates originate through parliamentary processes; and outcomes of deliberation and interest bargaining are often reconfirmed through parliamentary enactment of findings into law (Heidenheimer and Elvander 1980, 76).

Thus, collective bargaining has been the basis of policy formation. It not only includes a process of interchange, consensus, and compromise among functional groups, but it has also been predicated on explicitly stated criteria of public purpose. Twaddle and Hessler provide an example of this in their review of the 1975 Commission of Inquiry proceedings:

. . . [members] were instructed to specify overall goals for health and sickness care; to assume that everyone living in the country should have an equal right to health and sickness care; to include other social services, with special attention to coordination between medical care and general sickness insurance; and to include all of health and sickness care: private practice, school health, and occupational health (all administered outside the Department of Health) as well as public medical care services. [Twaddle and Hessler 1986, 22]

It is the justification of policies according to a concept of public good that Anderson (1979, 26-27) believes to be the cornerstone upon which the corporatist structure in Sweden rests its legitimacy; and it is around what Stokey and Zeckhauser (1978, 281) refer to as "proximate" or "intermediate" objectives that agreement, deliberation, and compromise occur and in which alternative policy choices are considered.

Swedish Health Outcomes: Effects of Structure-process

It can be argued that decisions over how much to spend and where to target the expenditure reflect basic values and orientations fundamental to the society. In the case of health, these values give rise to the very structure of the system itself. That is, societal values shape not only fiscal policy but also the very nature and form health delivery takes (e.g., cure-oriented or preventative, private or public, acute care based versus community worker based, centralized versus decentralized, professional monopoly in a decentralized market versus consensus reaching among functional groups).

The need to look beyond monetary allocation as a reflection of values is underscored when one compares Table 1 with Figure 1. The latter reflects the similarity between the United States and Sweden and their dissimilarity to the United Kingdom, considering GDP devoted to health care. Table 1, however, indicates that the U.S. is more like the UK than like Sweden in health outcomes. This is curious since the UK and Sweden both have forms of national health services, while the U.S. is a predominantly privatized system. Neither the pattern of money expended nor the form used to deliver care matches outcomes. The explanation of this apparent anomaly rests in value orientations that are reflected in particular political, institutional, and behavioral configurations. These configurations, in turn, create conditions for the development of policies that are conducive to positive outcomes.

Three ways can be cited in which Swedish health policy has been shaped to facilitate such positive outcomes. They include (1) an increased preference for a balance between preventive care and curative care; (2) geographic redis-

tribution of health resources, including human resources; (3) decentralized health decision making, including mechanisms both for community and worker control of health facilities and for enforcement of standards. All three strategies have been implemented to increase equality in quality and access to health services. The law that grew out of the 1975 Commission of Inquiry is a specific example of legislation formulated along these lines. Its provisions handed over medical care, previously administered at the central level, to the counties. The counties (specifically the County Boards, comprised of a broad representation of community interests) became increasingly responsible for health promotion as well as for comprehensive medical services for their own residents. Planning and administration of services was also broadened to include nonphysician professionals in the process (Twaddle and Hessler 1986, 30–31).

A second example of efforts to increase health care equality and access is Sweden's 1978 Work Environment Act. According to Navarro, Sweden has developed substantially greater protective health norms and standards (than has the United States, for example) that extend to (a) the labor process; (b) occupational scientific competence, knowledge, and information; and (c) occupational health services. This development is reflected in more comprehensive work-related benefits, which include longer paternity and maternity leaves, higher pension benefits, and better sickness and accident compensation than in the United States (Navarro 1984, 141) Additionally, safety delegates have been trained to improve their ability to recognize and act on potential health and safety problems, and their power to act at the shop level in response to problems has been strengthened. (This includes the authority to close down production in the interest of worker health and safety).

Further, building on the concept that an individual's care should be delivered in the individual's immediate environment, workers pushed for and won concessions that placed primary health facilities at or near the place of employment and under worker-controlled safety committees rather than under county council management.

Workers were determined to allocate proportionately greater resources to preventive health rather than to curative medicine, as had been the counties' tendency. By placing the clinics under their own control they could assure their preference for an even greater emphasis on preventive care (Navarro 1984, 151). Given that the Board of Health and Welfare and the Federation of County Councils preferred consolidation of services with existing county facilities, union support and corporatist style negotiations become central to assuring worker participation and the nurturance of greater support for preventive care and ease of access.

A final example of efforts toward designing equality in access to health services is the actual geographic distribution of resources. Here specifically, the distribution of physicians will be discussed (although conceptually the argument can be extended to other health professionals, services, and facilities as well). As in other countries, geographic distribution of physicians has been historically skewed to urban areas and away from rural, peripheral regions (Berg in Heidenheimer and Elvander 1980). There has been, in like manner, a disproportionate number of specialists, compared to general practitioners, exceeding the overall needs of the country. While some effort had been undertaken prior to 1940 to remediate problems of shortages and maldistribution, more aggressive effort was needed. Sweden and Norway both tackled those problems by increasing the number of medical schools in the 1950s and 1960s (from three to six in Sweden's case) over the protests of certain groups of physicians. Sweden also began to assign physicians to certain geographic areas, to funnel resources to educate students as general practitioners rather than as specialists, and to increase emphasis on preventive and outpatient care in preference to acute, hospital-based care.

While other countries have attempted to use such strategies, they have not been as successful in passing enabling legislation due to strong opposition from special interests (most notably physicians). Sweden has been more successful because of the power of bureaucrats at the local and county levels and the lobbying of peak associations of other (nonphysician) occupational interests. Further, the power of the physicians' block was diffused as splits occurred among junior and senior physicians (represented by the SYLF and the SMA, respectively) and medical school faculties. Physician professional power, which was key to blocking legislation in other countries (e.g., in the United Kingdom), became muted in Sweden in the presence of the corporatist structure's inclusion of other interest groups. Thus physicians' groups had no exclusive access to bureaucracy and had to compete with the interests of other very powerful groups. Immergut (1986, 6) describes the physicians' dilemma this way:

. . . physicians were ultimately forced into a moderate position. Issues were never discussed solely in terms of the profession, but tended to be considered in more general terms particularly in terms of the rights of employees versus the willingness of the employers to finance the system.

Over the years, physicians lost other key battles, which resulted in the demise of fee for service, the loss of professional self-government as Health Boards took over specialty licensing and certification and allocation of manpower, and "insulation" of private practitioners from hospital practice (Heidenheimer and Elvander 1980, 119-41). Further, affordable access and treatment seem to have been achieved in part through restrictions on physician salaries and through limitations of medical posts in those areas overpopulated with medical practitioners (thereby forcing some physicians into the underserved areas and alleviating problems of maldistribution).

Outcomes

The relevance of this discussion to health outcomes can be demonstrated in the case of infant mortality rates. If health decisions were based solely on efficiency criteria (and egalitarian interests and/or varying priorities of interests were not taken into consideration), distribution of health resources would be more "effectively" achieved by concentration of expenditures and equipment in urban areas where a greater percentage of the population resides. This efficiency, however, would be achieved at the expense of resources allocated to

rural areas. We would then see a higher standard of health in urban areas and a lower one in the rural. Urban areas that had better health care (and therefore better performance on infant mortality statistics) would then develop to a greater degree than the less fortunate rural areas. Since such maldistributions can lead to higher infant mortality rates in the less advantaged areas, the result would be a higher *overall* infant mortality rate in the country that based decisions on efficiency criteria alone. In contrast, those countries that (a) have made a concerted effort to distribute both expenditures and resources (including manpower) in an egalitarian manner and (b) have the structural means to achieve these goals would have lower overall infant mortality rates.

Sweden (and Norway) fall into this latter group; Sweden seems to have acted upon an overall commitment to egalitarian goals. These goals are realized through (a) corporatist arrangements to consider varying perspectives and priorities in policy formation; (b) a particular brand of corporatism that stresses a decentralized approach to planning, implementation, evaluation, and feedback; and (c) retention of selected powers within the central bureaucracy to serve as coordinating mechanisms. Such a configural arrangement of powers and responsibilities has been built upon a general consensus and commitment to goals and implemented through institutional structures and behavioral patterns. These configurations have resulted in an environment exceptionally conducive to favorable health outcomes.

Such a view of Sweden's health policy and outcomes is consistent with Alford's belief in an alliance between politics and power. It reflects a situation in which the autonomy of existing institutions is preserved, strategic coalitions are made, and contingent actions formulated. This confluence of events and actions is grounded in the struggle for superiority under unique historical circumstances. It goes beyond perspectives of the state and their inherent contradictions to conjoin actions, structures, and functions in a coherent approach to policy analysis that addresses situational, structural, and systemic power. It is, at the same time, a useful

and parsimonious way to view and evaluate public policy.

Notes

1. This paper will not, however, explore the role of class configuration in shaping health policy and outcomes. For a critique of corporatism using a class perspective, see Panitch (1977).
2. The Netherlands has the most institutionalized corporate structures: Stichting van den Arbeid (the Foundation of Labour), Sociaal-Economische Raad (the Social-Economic Council), and College van Rijksbemiddelaars (the Board of Government Conciliators). In Austria, Paritätische Kommission Für Preis- und Lohnfragen (the Joint Commission on Prices and Wages) is the formal institution created to represent business, labor, and agricultural interests (Lehmbruch 1979, 158-59, 164-66).
3. This may be particularly true since the remaining centrally based issues are occupationally based ones and subject to conflicting claims by health workers. Since increased claims by one group means reduced opportunity for another, there may be intense bargaining over these issues. One caution needs to be presented here, however. There have been recent suggestions (Stjernquist 1986; Kvavik 1987) that the bureaucracy may be assuming more responsibility for central decision making in recent years. Whether this is a transitory phenomenon or a more sustained pattern is yet to be seen. There is no clear evidence, additionally, that this pattern has extended to the health policy arena. Nor is the cause clear. Kvavik, for instance, hypothesizes that the trend may be associated with recent coalition governments. The nature of this development has yet to be outlined. It may indicate that the outcomes of interest group deliberations have been consistent with governmental (i.e., bureaucratic) actions and therefore constitute an endorsement of policy. Alternately, it may be an initial sign of a breakdown in the form of corporatist structure being discussed here.
4. According to Lehmbruch (1979, 161), the KA is a regular meeting of economic interest associations convened several times a year by the Federal Minister of Economy and is composed of more than fifty interest group participants.
5. Katzenstein (1985, 33) discusses another feature, inclusiveness, which he believes is a measure of concentration of interests. For example, since the 1930s over 90 percent of the Swedish medical professionals have been enrolled in the national

medical associations. In contrast, only 60 percent of the French physicians have been similarly enrolled in their national associations (Immergut 1986, 27). The Swedish associations are generally considered to be more centralized and to have a greater concentration of interests because of this.

6. The Seven Crowns Reform "stipulated a uniform flat-rate fee for outpatient care, removed physicians from financial transactions, abolished fee-for-service compensation for outpatient care and physicians' reception of private patients at public facilities, sought to equalize incomes within the medical profession, increased inpatient fees by 100 percent, and increased insurance coverage for some patients" (Heidenheimer and Elvander 1980, 143–44).

References

Alford, Robert, and R. Friedland. 1985. *Powers of Theory: Capitalism, the State and Democracy.* Cambridge: Cambridge UP.

Andrain, Charles. 1985. *Social Policies in Western Industrial Societies.* Berkeley: California UP.

Anderson, Charles. 1979. "Political Design and the Representation of Interest." *Trends Toward Corporatist Intermediation.* Ed. Phillippe Schmitter and Gerhard Lehmbruch. Beverly Hills: Sage. 270–97.

Carnoy, Michael. 1984. *The State and Political Theory.* Princeton: Princeton UP.

Culyer, A. J., Alan Maryland, and Alan William. 1981. "Alternative Systems of Health Provision: An Essay on Motes and Beams." *A New Approach to the Economics of Health Care.* Ed. Mancur Olson. Washington, DC: American Enterprise Institute. 131–50.

Heidenheimer, Arnold, and Nils Elvander. 1980. *The Shaping of The Swedish Health System.* London: Croom Helm.

Heidenheimer, Arnold, Hugh Heclo, and Carolyn Adams. 1983. *Comparative Public Policy.* 2nd ed. New York: St. Martin's.

Immergut, Ellen. Aug. 1986. "The Political Economy of Private Medical Practice: The Swedish, French and Swiss Cases." American Political Science Association Meeting, Washington, DC.

Katzenstein, Peter. 1985. *Small States in World Markets.* Ithaca, New York: Cornell UP.

Kvavik, Robert. Jan. 1987. Personal Interview.

Lehmbruch, Gerhard. 1979 "Liberal Corporatism and Party Government." *Trends Toward Corporatism Intermediation.* Ed. Phillippe Schmitter and Gerhard Lembruch. Beverly Hills: Sage. 150–72.

Navarro, Vincente. 1984. "The Determinants of Health Policy, A Case Study: Regulating Safety and Health at the Workplace in Sweden." *Journal of Health Politics, Policy and Law* 9.1: 137–56.

OECD. 1985. *Measuring Health Care 1960-83.* Social Policy Studies 2. Paris: Organization for Economic Cooperation and Development.

Panitch, Leo. 1977. "The Development of Corporatism in Liberal Democracies." *Comparative Political Studies* 10.1: 61-90.

Population Reference Bureau. 1985. *World Population Data Sheet.* Washington, DC.

Stahl, I. 1981. "Can Equality and Efficiency Be Combined? The Experience of the Planned Swedish Health Care System." *A New Approach to the Economics of Health Care.* Ed. Mancur Olson. Washington, DC: American Enterprise Institute. 172–95.

Stjernquist, N. Nov. 1986. "The Changing Role of Parliament in a Corporatist Society: The Case of Sweden." Talk given at U. of Minnesota.

Stokey, Edith, and Richard Zeckhauser. 1978. *A Primer for Public Policy Analysis.* Toronto: W. W. Norton.

Twaddle, Andrew, and Richard Hessler. 1986. "Power and Change: The Case of the Swedish Commission of Inquiry on Health and Sickness Care." *Journal of Health Politics, Policy and Law.* 11.1: 14–40.

24

Japan's Medical Care System: Part One

John K. Iglehart

Japan's medical care system, like those of most Western industrialized nations, is based on three essential objectives: ready access, high quality, and reasonable cost. Within that framework, however, every culture influences the provision of medical care in countless ways. For example, Japan's medical care system reflects in some respects the entrepreneurial, market-driven nature of its economy, yet it also expresses a policy that hospitals should be organized on a nonprofit basis, that all citizens should have access to care regardless of their capacity to pay, and that physicians should place the patient's welfare above material gain.

Although Japan shares with other Western nations the task of allocating limited resources for medical services that are in heavy demand, its per capita health expenditure ($831) in 1986 was significantly less than those of the United States ($1,926), Canada ($1,370), Sweden ($1,195), France ($1,039), and West Germany ($1,031). Indeed, how Japan provided its citizens universal access to comprehensive medical care rendered by private physicians, selected by patients without restrictions, and still spent only 6.7 percent (1986) of the country's gross domestic product (GDP) in doing so, is one of the more fascinating questions about the system. The estimate was calculated by the Organization for Economic Cooperation and Development on the basis of data provided by Japan's Ministry of International Trade

and Industry.[1] Japan's Ministry of Health and Welfare estimates that spending totaled only 6.4 percent of the country's GDP in 1986. The difference is one of definition. Although this percentage is low by comparison with that of other nations, the real annual rate of growth in health expenditures per capita (9.1 percent) during the period 1960 to 1984 was more rapid in Japan than in any other Western country, according to the Organization for Economic Cooperation and Development.

Japan's ability to finance a substantial increase in its per capita expenditures for medical care during the 1970s without major political or public complaint derived from the rapid growth of its economy. In more recent years, the government, as the chief overseer of Japan's largely privately financed health insurance plans, has grown restive over the increasing portion of the GDP that is allocated to medical care, particularly for the elderly. Persons 65 years and older constituted 10.3 percent (12.5 million) of Japan's population in 1985. By the year 2010, it is expected that the number will more than double, to 27.1 million or 20 percent. Over the same period, the ratio of active to retired workers will drop from 5.9:1 to an estimated 2.8:1. By the year 2020, Japan's population will be among the oldest in the world.

This report will discuss the current status of Japanese medical care, a fee-for-service system cherished by its citizens because they believe steadfastly in the medical model and the physicians who symbolize it and because they place a high value on their personal health. I collected the information on which this essay and a subsequent re-

port are based during two recent two-week trips to Japan, in which I interviewed a variety of physicians, government officials, and other persons with a stake in Japanese medical care. I also searched the English-language literature on the system.[2-10]

The Evolution of Japanese Medical Care

Japan's health care system has evolved over centuries to serve its 122 million citizens, who live on four major islands (and 3,900 adjacent smaller islands) that stretch over an area of 377,435 km^2—slightly smaller than the state of California. Japan's capital, Tokyo, a vast metropolis with a population in 1985 of 8.4 million, lies almost at the latitudinal center of the Northern Hemisphere. More than two thirds of Japan's land mass is covered by mountains and forests and is thus uninhabitable. As a consequence, most of its people live on only a tiny fraction of the land, making Japan (behind Bangladesh and South Korea) the third most densely populated country in the world, with 318 people per square kilometer in 1984. The comparable world average is 35 people, and the United States average, 25.

Situated on the border of East and West, Japan has demonstrated a capacity over the centuries to learn foreign cultures and ideas and then adapt them to its own milieu. Within this context, two major paradigmatic shifts marked the evolution of Japanese medical care. The first was the introduction of traditional Chinese medicine in the sixth century A.D., a period in Japanese history when acupuncture and herbal medications were the favored treatments for

Reprinted with permission from *The New England Journal of Medicine* 319, no. 12 (September 22, 1988), pp. 807–12. Copyright © 1988 by the Massachusetts Medical Society.

a wide variety of ailments. Almost a thousand years later, Western medicine was introduced into Japan, largely through the influence of Portuguese Catholic missionaries. Later, between 1600 and 1867, a policy of isolationism dominated the country. Foreigners were forbidden to enter the country, with the exception of Dutch and Chinese traders, who were allowed to enter at only one location—the Nagasaki harbor. But through this entry point, Dutch medicine made its way into Japan, with notable influence on the provision of care.

Western influence on Japanese medical care accelerated after the Meiji Restoration, a reform era that followed a civil war in 1867. The war pitted an alliance of powerful landowners, young samurai, and mercantile capitalists in a successful struggle against the existing feudal system. The Meiji era (1868 to 1912) represents one of the more remarkable chapters in Japanese history. [11] Again, Japan's new leaders sought to replicate the institutions and practices of other countries that seemed best suited to the modernization of their own. For example, Japan adopted the methods of the British Navy and Merchant Marine, the Prussian Army, American business (in part), and German medicine, which at the time was considered the most advanced in Europe. The embrace of biomedicine by Meiji leaders was bolstered in large part by their attraction to Western technology in general. [12]

Although the present structure of social insurance is based largely on the Health Insurance Law of 1922, public and private actions dealing with citizens' welfare and the protection of workers date to the late 1800s. In imitation of the German experience, large corporations created mutual aid associations in the early 1900s, which financed care for some employees, and communities supported private clinics at which salaried physicians saw patients. The Relief Regulations of 1874, regarded as the forerunner of the modern Japanese social security system, were followed by other laws—the Factory Law of 1911, the Popular Life Insurance Law of 1916, and the Military Relief Law of 1917. The history is too rich to relate here, but

suffice it to say that the Health Insurance Law of 1922 was not a radical departure in social policy, but rather a continuation and extension of existing programs in response to the needs of the times. [7]

More than 100 national laws govern health and medical affairs in Japan today. The Ministry of Health and Welfare is responsible for implementing most of these laws. Its activities span the range of public and environmental health, social welfare, medical care financing, pharmaceutical regulations, and pensions. Japan's 47 prefectures (jurisdictions similar to the states of the United States) and its local governments also have roles in the financing, administration, and delivery of public health and social services.

The government has never wavered in its view that physicians trained in biomedical science should be the dominant providers of medical care in Japan. This conviction is reflected in laws that make other health care workers subservient and a requirement that hospital administrators must be physicians, regardless of who owns the institution. One reflection of the continued, if slight, influence of Chinese medicine is that health insurance schemes cover selected herbal medicines and that some pharmaceutical companies sell them to physicians. But herbal medicines represent only 1 to 2 percent of all drugs prescribed by physicians.

Health Status

Obviously, factors other than medical care and its availability enter into the complex equation that determines any society's health status. [13] For example, Japan's low-fat diet is considered a prominent ingredient in maintaining the health of its people. And certainly, the high rate at which Japanese men use tobacco products (63 percent smoke) places their well-being at greater risk. Other cultural factors that influence Japan's health status include its strong commitment to cleanliness and a resistance to invasive medical procedures. Whenever possible, Japanese people prefer bed rest and prescription drugs to surgery. As a consequence, Japan spends

more on prescription drugs than any other Western nation, but its surgical rates are lower than those in the United States.

These cultural characteristics and a variety of other factors combine to make the Japanese population, according to several important indicators, the healthiest in the world. To appreciate the magnitude of this achievement fully, one must contrast it with the dire conditions that prevailed in Japan four decades ago, after World War II. In 1947, the estimated life expectancy at birth for Japanese male infants was 50 years and for female infants 53.9 years; in 1950, it was 59.6 years and 63 years, respectively, for male and female infants. One account of the conditions prevailing in Japan after the war was rendered by officials of the Section of Public Health and Welfare of the General Headquarters, Supreme Commander for the Allied Powers.

During the war increased industrialization and urbanization on the four main islands of Japan, plus the dominance of military aims over all social welfare activities, had a pronounced influence on public health and welfare administration. Pressure of militarism brought greater emphasis on such emergency requirements as a rapid turnout of medical students, nurses and dentists. It also resulted in the cessation of many public health activities of benefit to the civilian population. The conversion of many factories, engaged in the manufacture of medical and sanitary supplies and equipment, to war material production, plus the lack of adequate professional people to serve the civilian population, resulted in a complete breakdown of all public health and welfare function. [14]

The Section of Public Health and Welfare of the Allied Powers, headed by Dr. Crawford F. Sams, ordered immediate measures to control the epidemic of infectious diseases, but it also sought to institute Western-style reforms dealing with medical education, public health administration, and health information systems. After Japan recovered its autonomy in 1952, many of these reforms, based on Western values, were eventually abandoned, such as the medical internship system, which students had strongly resisted. One of the reforms, the development of a vital-statistics system, became an important permanent fixture of Japan's medical care system. [15]

By 1986 the life expectancy at birth of the average Japanese was 75.2 years for men and 80.9 years for women—the highest in the world. In 1987 Japan's infant mortality rate was the lowest among all countries—5.2 deaths per 1,000 births. By comparison, life expectancy in the United States last year was 71 years for men and 78.1 years for women, and the U.S. infant mortality rate in 1986 was 10.6 per 1,000 live births. Factors that influence Japan's low infant mortality rate include universal access to medical care, a literate society eager for medical advice, the availability of a handbook on maternal and child health that has been issued routinely to every pregnant woman since World War II, and one of the world's highest registered-abortion rates (23.9 per 1,000 women of childbearing age). The relation between Japan's abortion rate and its low infant mortality rate is not entirely clear, because almost all the induced abortions are sought for economic reasons rather than to eliminate high-risk pregnancies, according to the Ministry of Health and Welfare.

The country's intense drive to industrialize has led to dramatic improvements in living standards, but its narrow concentration on economic growth and material prosperity has also generated new social, cultural, and mental strains.[16] Japan's current rate of suicide is about twice that of the United States. Pollution and drug-induced disorders have been major problems since the 1960s, and lack of proper housing, inadequate sewage and garbage-disposal systems, and increased traffic congestion and accidents have also exacted a toll on Japan's health status. Industrialization has led to a range of occupational hazards much like those faced by workers in Europe and North America[17] and a changing pattern of disease in Japan.

Although Japan's life expectancy and infant mortality rates continue to improve, its citizens report more sickness every year, perhaps as a consequence of the ready availability of medical care financed largely by third parties, the average citizen's close attention to his or her health, and the country's aging population. In 1985, 145.2 of every 1,000 persons—1 in 7—reported in a national survey that they were sick. A

similar increase in morbidity among Americans was reported recently in the *Journal*.[18] The morbidity rates from the annual survey by the Japanese Ministry of Health and Welfare were based on responses to questions about whether the respondent was experiencing any "abnormality in physical or mental condition" at the time of the survey.

Physicians' Services

One of Japan's responses to its rapid urbanization and other social phenomena has been the embrace of sophisticated, high-technology medical services delivered by physicians. Japan has more CAT scanners per capita than the United States. On average, a Japanese citizen visits his or her physician 15 times a year, as compared with about 5 times in the United States. Physicians are revered figures in Japanese society, although their stature has eroded a bit in recent years. Patients' waiting times are long (patients are generally seen without an appointment on a first-come-first-served basis, and waiting one hour or more seems to be the norm), and the average encounter itself is very short, but physicians do not seem to be disparaged for this practice. Emiko Ohnuki-Tierney, a professor of anthropology at the University of Wisconsin who studied elements of her native country's medical care system, has discussed the physician-patient encounter.[19]

At most private offices, clinics and hospitals, doctors see large numbers of patients. For example, at hospital X [described as a 226-bed, private hospital in suburban Kobe] during three morning hours on May 19, 1979, two doctors at the internal medicine clinic saw 100 outpatients who were there for the first time, in addition to 102 patients who had been seen there at least once before. During the same period, the one doctor on duty at the eye clinic saw 48 patients, and the doctor at the ear, nose, and throat clinic saw 45 patients. The obstetric-gynecology clinic, where I conducted most of my fieldwork, usually had one doctor on duty who was occasionally joined by a resident, and the average number of patients each morning was between 40 and 50. . . . Many Japanese blame the insurance system for people making frequent but virtually free visits to doctors and for doctors accommodating and often encouraging these visits. . . . There is, however, another factor that is responsible for the phenomenon—the relative readiness with which

the Japanese both recognize departures from health and consult doctors about them.

The part played by private practitioners has always been important in Japanese medicine. Private doctors have remained the focal point of the system even though Japan's network of health insurance plans has led to a form of socialization of medical care. Care is rendered for the most part in two settings—private clinics and hospitals. There are some 9,400 hospitals in Japan and about 27,000 clinics with fewer than 19 beds. Any facility with 20 or more beds is considered a hospital. Most hospitals are owned by physicians, and virtually all the clinics are physician-owned and -operated. I will discuss in greater detail in a subsequent report how physicians practice and are paid. I will also describe the intense rivalry that pits most hospitals against clinics that operate nearby.

Japanese Health Insurance

The vast bulk of medical care in Japan is financed through a health insurance system that currently accounts for more than 90 percent of total medical expenditures when patients' cost-sharing amounts are included. The insurance system has evolved incrementally since 1922, resulting in a gradual expansion of coverage, which became universal in 1961. The Japanese Constitution, adopted in 1947, buttressed the importance attached to personal well-being by guaranteeing all citizens "the right to maintain the minimum standards of wholesome and cultured living." Article 25 declares: "In all spheres of life, the state shall use its endeavors for the promotion and extension of social welfare and security, and of public health."

The health financing programs that implement Japan's commitment to universal access to care can be divided into two broad categories: employee health insurance, under which 75 million people (employees of private corporations and of national and local governments and their dependents) are covered, and community health insurance (alternatively referred to as national health insurance), which extends financial protection to 45 million additional citizens. The latter fall into a variety of categories:

all unemployed adults (including the elderly), employees of small businesses, the self-employed, and farmers. As a rule, people covered under community-based plans are at higher medical risk and have fewer financial resources than those protected by employee health insurance. All employers must sponsor and partially finance a plan or contribute financially to a scheme that is publicly administered. The government pays the administrative expenses of all of Japan's health insurance plans, none of which are organized on a for-profit basis.

Employee plans are further divided into programs managed by private health insurance societies (large corporations) and those managed by the government (primarily plans for employees of medium and small businesses). In this role, government performs an administrative function as a fiscal intermediary. It does not underwrite the coverage, the cost of which is shared by employers and employees. As a rule, a health insurance society is the fiscal intermediary for a single company (generally, a firm with 700 or more employees). The health insurance societies, or kenpo kumiai, as they are called, that perform the intermediary function for large corporations are regulated by Japan's Ministry of Health and Welfare. But their place in Japanese corporate life extends well beyond the intermediary function, as Wolfson and Levin have explained.[20]

One of the mottos of Japanese companies—kigyo wa hito nari, or the company is people—recognizes the value of each employee as a company asset. A healthy, well-informed employee is seen as the most important investment a company can have. The kenpos are the principal social and economic vehicles for helping to make this happen. At the end of fiscal 1984, there were 1711 kenpos providing coverage to about 28 million people. Of these, 12 million were employees and more than 16 million were dependents.

In addition, under the category of employee health insurance, there is seamen's insurance and mutual aid associations, whose beneficiaries include seamen, civil servants employed by the national and local governments, and teachers. The variety of categories reflects the evolutionary nature of Japan's

health insurance system. Because the plans emerged incrementally, patients' cost-sharing arrangements and benefits are not all the same, producing some problems of equity among them.

Employee health insurance plans are financed by premiums based on earnings and cost sharing by patients. Under society-managed health insurance and mutual-aid-association insurance, premium rates range from 6 to 9.6 percent (of the monthly remuneration of the insured person, divided between employer and employee); each entity has the discretion to establish the contribution rate within this range. On average, the employer pays 4.6 percent and the employee 3.5 percent. An employee's contribution is deducted from his or her paycheck. The contribution rate of government-managed health insurance is 8.9 percent (of the monthly remuneration of the insured person, equally divided between employer and employee).

Under all the employee health insurance plans, an insured person must, in addition to contributing to the cost of the premium, pay 10 percent of the cost of the medical care he or she uses, with a limit of 54,000 yen ($400) per month. An employee's dependents face a cost-sharing requirement of 20 percent for inpatient care and 30 percent for outpatient care. These cost-sharing amounts are usually paid in cash by a patient before he or she leaves the physician's clinic or hospital. Although there are few or no available data, these cost-sharing requirements (combined with Japan's rising standard of living) have done little to diminish the average citizen's proclivity to visit the physician often.

Medical care benefits covered under employee health insurance include virtually every treatment a physician might render in both the inpatient and outpatient setting. The scope of covered medical benefits is established by law. Exceptions to the liberal coverage offered include preventive examinations (similar to physical examinations in the United States) and the normal delivery of a baby. Because giving birth is not an expense prompted by the onset of disease, health insurance plans do not pay for deliveries, but if complications lead,

for example, to a cesarean section, that procedure is covered. Like many other surgical operations, cesarean sections are performed far less frequently in Japan than in the United States.[21]

The standard hospital accommodation that employee health insurance covers is a semiprivate room with four to six beds. Wards of 8 to 12 hospital beds are not uncommon in Japan, particularly in older facilities. In one Tokyo facility that I visited, Shitaya Hospital, a private room with bath, telephone, and television set cost 16,000 yen extra a day. As a rule, the Japanese attach less importance to privacy in the hospital and physician's office than do Americans. As Ohnuki-Tierney explained in her book,

In a private practitioner's office, the examination room is barely separated from the waiting room. Furthermore, while the examination goes on, nurses and other personnel may pass by, and the patient's family members often stay throughout the examination. In contrast to this open atmosphere, the examination process in the United States clearly expresses the cherished cultural values of privacy and the sacredness of the body. During an American examination, the doctor and the patient are alone in a room behind a closed door, with a thick wall guaranteeing absolute privacy.[18]

Beyond coverage of medical expenses, employee health insurance plans offer additional benefits not required by statute. These include cash benefits to cover normal deliveries and injury and sickness allowances, maternity allowances during absence from work, a nursing allowance (when an insured woman nurses her children, she receives 2,000 yen per child in a lump sum), and partial coverage of patient cost-sharing requirements. Some employee health insurance plans are more generous than others in covering these items.

Community health insurance, a conglomeration of plans administered by cities, towns, villages, and private bodies representing specific trades or professions, provides coverage to an additional 45 million people. The medical benefits covered are essentially the same as those provided by employee health insurance, but additional cash benefits for sickness, injury, maternity, and the death of the insured person are considerably less generous under community-sponsored schemes. Community health insurance is financed by premiums paid by covered persons (the maximum per year in a household is 370,000 yen [$2,740]), a patient cost-sharing requirement of 30 percent, which can be lower depending on individual economic circumstances, and government subsidies. The premiums are calculated on the basis of a person's income and the actuarial value of the benefit. In addition to the premiums and patient cost-sharing amounts, which cover less than half the average cost of care to a patient, financing derives from national and local government support.

Although Japan's various health insurance plans impose different levels of cost-sharing on their beneficiaries, raising questions of equity that have long concerned the government but that remain nevertheless, all the plans protect their beneficiaries against the prospect of financial devastation by a serious illness. All plans include a ceiling (54,000 yen a month per illness, or $400) on the amount of out-of-pocket expenditures a patient can incur before all additional expenses are covered. For example, if an employee covered under employee health insurance incurred a hospital bill of 600,000 yen, 90 percent would be covered by the plan. Of the remaining 60,000 yen owed, the beneficiary would be required to cover 54,000 yen; the insured would be reimbursed by the health insurance plan for the remaining 6,000 yen.

Medical care for the elderly (defined as persons over 70 years of age and bedridden people between the ages of 65 and 70 years) is also a component of Japan's universal network of health insurance. Medical benefits for the elderly are financed through national government contributions (20 percent), local government bodies (10 percent, divided between prefectural and city, town, or village governments), and contributions from employee health insurance and community health insurance plans. Before the Health and Medical Services for the Aged law was enacted in August 1982, the national government was responsible for financing more of the medical care of the elderly. Because older people consume a great deal

of care, community-based plans that paid for the bulk of their care were plagued with financial problems, often requiring assistance from the national government.

The 1982 law placed more of the burden of new medical spending for the elderly on employee health insurance plans paid by employers. Its enactment also demonstrated that Japan is more willing than the United States to impose policies on employers that are deemed to reflect their legitimate social obligation—in Japan's case, requiring employers and employees to shoulder a greater proportion of the cost of care for the elderly. The financial impact of the 1982 law is apparent in trends in the growth of Japan's medical care expenditures between 1983 and 1986. During that period, national government expenditures for medical care (and the percentage of total expenditures they represented) rose only slightly, from 4.45 trillion yen (30.6 percent) to 4.46 trillion yen (26.1 percent), while employers' payments for their employee health insurance increased from 7.64 trillion yen (52.5 percent) to 9.32 trillion yen (54.6 percent). Employees' contributions represent the bulk of the remaining costs.

The 1982 law also imposed small cost-sharing requirements on the elderly—a controversial policy step designed to curb that population's increasing use of medical care. For every day in the hospital, an elderly patient must pay 400 yen ($3). The cost-sharing requirement for outpatient care is 800 yen a month ($6). Many elderly people who are taking a drug for an ailment visit a physician weekly to have their prescriptions refilled. The 1982 law also sought to reduce hospitals' current economic incentive for keeping elderly patients in the hospital for months (and sometimes years because of a very limited number of nursing home beds) by reimbursing facilities on a diminishing scale—the longer the stay, the lower the rate—and sought to encourage the use of more home care for the elderly to avoid hospital stays.

Despite the government's efforts to moderate the growth of medical care spending on behalf of the elderly, such spending has continued to rise more

rapidly than that for the nonelderly, mostly because the rates at which the elderly use services have increased more sharply. In 1986, health-care expenditures on behalf of the elderly reached 30.1 percent (523,300 yen per capita versus 140,300 yen per capita for the population as a whole), although the elderly represent only 10.3 percent of the total population.

That they have comprehensive insurance is not the only reason that the elderly are using more medical care. Perhaps equally important is a cultural change taking place in Japanese society. The reverence in which Japan holds its elderly seems to be diminishing in the face of their increasing numbers, lack of space to care for elderly family members at home, and the increasing employment of women, the traditional care givers, outside the home. One consequence of these multiple developments is that elderly people are paying more visits to their physicians. Ohnuki-Tierney discussed this phenomenon:

Because of rapid changes in attitude toward the aged and changes in family structure, which now emphasizes the nuclear family, these older people often feel lonely and uncomfortable, even when they are living with their offspring. Some of the waiting rooms at neighborhood doctors' offices have become local gathering places for the elderly. Some older people prefer to be hospitalized, even when their illnesses are not grave, and are unwilling to be discharged after recovery. Some doctors accommodate this behavior, either in their waiting rooms or in the hospitals, since their services to the elderly are reimbursed by the government. Others discourage the practice, pointing out that clinics and hospitals are not homes for the elderly.[19]

Japan's medical care system offers all its citizens an impressive array of services for a moderate price. Nevertheless, the government and providers of care are currently discussing many issues. Some of these include the long hospital stays in Japan (the average for all patients, including both short-term and long-term care, is 39 days), the heavy use of pharmaceutical products, and the number of new physicians being trained in the country's medical schools. I will discuss these and other issues in a subsequent report.

Notes

1. Schieber GJ, Poullier JP. International health spending and utilization trends. Health Aff (Millwood) 1988; 7(4):105–12.

2. Ikegami N. Health technology development in Japan. Int J Technol Assess 1988; 4:239–54.

3. Fujii M, Reich MR. Rising medical costs and the reform of Japan's health insurance system. Health Policy 1988; 9:9–24.

4. Levin PJ, Wolfson J, Akiyama H. The role of management in Japanese hospitals. Hosp Health Serv Adm 1987; 32:249–61.

5. Gelb A. Lessons from the Japanese. Am J Gastroenterol 1985; 80:738–42.

6. Abe MA. Hospital reimbursement schemes: Japan's point system and the United States' diagnostic-related groups. Med Care 1985; 23:1055–66.

7. Steslicke WE. Development of health insurance policy in Japan. Health Polit Policy Law 1982; 7:197–226. .

8. *Idem.* Medical care in Japan: the political context. J Ambulatory Care Manage 1982; 5(4):65–77.

9. Lock MM. East Asian medicine in urban Japan: varieties of medical experience. Berkeley, Calif.: University of California Press, 1980.

10. Steslicke WE. Doctors in politics: the political life of the Japan medical association. New York: Praeger, 1973.

11. Hashimoto M. Health services in Japan. In: Raffel MW, ed. Comparative health systems: descriptive analyses of fourteen national health systems. University Park, Pa.: Pennsylvania State University Press, 1984:335–70.

12. Long SO. Health care providers: technology, policy and professional dominance. In: Norbeck E, Lock M, eds. Health, illness, and medical care in Japan: cultural and social dimensions. Honolulu: University of Hawaii Press, 1987:66–88.

13. Payer L. Medicine and culture: varieties of treatment in the United States, England, West Germany, and France. New York: Henry Holt, 1988.

14. Steslicke WE. The Japanese state of health: a political-economic perspective. In: Norbeck E, Lock M, eds. Health, illness, and medical care in Japan: cultural and social dimensions. Honolulu: University of Hawaii Press, 1987:24–65.

15. Marui E. Japan's experience with public health reform in the early occupation days: foreigner's plans and indigenous systems. In: Reich MR, Marui E, eds. International cooperation for health: problems, prospects, priorities. Dover, Mass.: Auburn House Publishing (in press).

16. Sonodo K. Health and illness in changing Japanese society. Tokyo: University of Tokyo Press, 1988.

17. Reich MR, Frumkin H. An overview of Japanese occupational health. Am J Public Health 1988; 78:809-16.

18. Barsky AJ. The paradox of health. N Engl J Med 1988; 318:414-8.

19. Ohnuki-Tierney E. Illness and culture in contemporary Japan: an anthropological view. Cambridge, Mass.: Cambridge University Press, 1984.

20. Wolfson J, Levin PJ. Health insurance, Japanese style. Bus Health 1986; 3(6):38-40.

21. Notzon FC, Placek PJ, Taffel SM. Comparisons of national cesarean-section rates. N Engl J Med 1987; 316:386-9.

Japan's Medical Care System: Part Two

Japan's medical care system, remarkably inexpensive by American standards, has nevertheless entered an era of economic stress and incremental change as a consequence of efforts to address its most serious challenges. These challenges include medical expenditures that are rising more rapidly than the cost of other goods and services; a growing number of new practicing physicians, which the government is seeking to reduce; a hospital length of stay that averages 39 days (including both acute and chronic care); and heavy prescription of pharmaceuticals by physicians who order and dispense drugs far more frequently than do doctors in most other countries.

Another pressure compelling Japan to examine the adequacy of its traditional medical care system is its rapidly aging population. Because Japan's population is aging more rapidly than that of virtually any other industrialized nation, it will soon face far greater demands for medical and social services. Reporting an expression of government's concern over this problem under a headline entitled, "Health Care for Elderly Pushes Medical Costs to Record High," The *Japan Times* on June 12 said:

Medical expenditures by people in Japan hit another record high of 17.07 trillion yen [$100 billion] during fiscal 1986, the Health and Welfare Ministry said Saturday [June 11]. The total represented a 6.6 percent increase from the previous record of 16.2 trillion yen set in fiscal 1985. The ministry said that the 6.6

percent growth means that the nation has failed to achieve a policy goal of holding down the growth in medical expenses to or below the growth in national income, which was 4.1 percent in fiscal 1986.

It is not simply the rising costs of health care for the elderly that concern the government. It is also the problem of finding a way to move elderly patients with chronic ailments, who need both social services and medical care, from hospital beds to more appropriate settings. Japan currently lacks the necessary alternatives—nursing homes and other geriatric facilities built according to a social model. In addition, many families lack the space to house and care for their elderly members, and women, the traditional care givers, increasingly work outside the home. Japan has begun to experiment with intermediate care facilities that can better accommo-

Reprinted with permission from *The New England Journal of Medicine* 319, no. 17 (October 27, 1988), pp. 1166–72. Copyright © 1988 by the Massachusetts Medical Society.

date the social needs of its infirm elderly citizens.

Any attempt to expand Japan's capacity for long-term care and address other social needs must compete with other priorities—lower taxes and higher pensions, to mention two. Following other governments (Canada and the United Kingdom, for example) along the path taken by the Reagan administration in 1981, the ruling Liberal Democratic Party of Japan in July adopted direct tax cuts of 5.6 trillion yen ($44.6 billion) on an annual basis, effective April 1, 1989, as part of a major tax-reform package. The package also included a new national sales tax of 3 percent, with some medical, educational, and welfare services exempt and a slight reduction in the generous tax deductions that Japan's clinic-based physicians have long enjoyed. The new sales tax would generate approximately 5.4 trillion yen a year, far below the estimated amount of revenue (9 trillion yen) that would be lost as a consequence of the proposed tax reductions. In 1988, Japan's national government faced a budget deficit of 159 trillion yen ($1.2 trillion). Japan's public expenditures for social security benefits and medical care, as a fraction of its national income, are lower than those of all of the major Western countries.

Government expressions of concern over rising costs are intensifying the economic struggle that pits Japan's physicians against third-party payers, private and public. But, reflecting the pluralistic nature of the society, physicians do not cite rising medical costs as the main issue when asked about the serious problems affecting the provision of care in their country. Instead, they offer a variety of answers. Medical school deans worry that too many of their students are more interested in research, technology, surgical procedures, and material gain than in patient care. Senior academic faculty members, dominant in the teaching hospital like their German role models, are concerned with maintaining their powerful positions. Younger, hospital-based physicians, whose careers often depend on their head professor's opinion of them and whose numbers have increased substantially in the past decade, worry

about finding established clinical positions at a time when very few posts are available.

Physicians in clinics and small hospitals are concerned about the growing competition from the larger public hospitals, which maintain outpatient clinics that have increasingly attracted patients, and whether they (the doctors) will be able to maintain their income levels. Physicians who own clinics make substantially more money than do salaried doctors. The Japan Medical Association (JMA), which has aggressively promoted the interests of the private clinic and small-hospital-based practitioner for many years and to which about 50 percent of Japan's 191,346 physicians (in 1986) belong, has placed a priority on the development of a continuing medical education program to help the solo doctors who constitute their principal constituency maintain their skills at a higher level. There are no formal mechanisms for reviewing the quality of medical care in any setting.

In this, the second of two reports on the Japanese medical care system,[1] I will discuss the economic incentives that influence medical care, the schism that separates physicians who practice in clinics from those who practice in hospitals, the long hospital stays in Japan, and physicians' heavy prescription of drugs. Although every country's medical care system is different, one way to compare Japan's scheme with those of other industrialized nations is through data on spending. I will begin by citing the latest available international spending data as reported by the Organization for Economic Cooperation and Development (OECD)[2] and by noting Japan's increasingly important role in international medical circles.

International Trends in Medical Spending

Among the 24 OECD countries, Japan ranked in the lower half in the share of its gross domestic product (GDP) that was allocated to medical care in 1986. The countries that spent more than 8 percent of their GDP on medical care were the higher-cost nations: the United States was highest of all, at 11.1 percent. Japan was clustered with the lower-cost

nations, spending an estimated 6.7 percent of its GDP on medical care. Its standing among nations in this regard has remained low—even though its medical spending has increased rapidly—because of the rapid growth of its general economy. In 1986, Japan's medical expenditures totaled 17.07 trillion yen, a fiftyfold increase over the figure for 1956.

At a time when Japan has arrived as an economic power among nations, it has also begun to assert leadership on the world health stage. The clearest reflection of its determination in this regard has been the campaign it waged recently to elect Dr. Hiroshi Nakajima to the director generalship of the World Health Organization (WHO). Nakajima, a physician, had been regional director of WHO's Western Pacific region for a decade. In late April, the World Health Assembly ratified the nomination of Nakajima to succeed Dr. Halfdan Mahler. Three months earlier, WHO's Executive Board had voted, on a third ballot, 17 to 14 in favor of Nakajima over Dr. Carlyle Guerra de Macedo, a Brazilian who heads the Pan American Health Organization and who was supported by the United States. The *New York Times* reported that before the balloting, Japan—playing politics as it is usually played by major nations in international agencies—"pressed third-world governments to support Dr. Nakajima, in some cases offering foreign aid projects as inducements."[3]

Economic Incentives in Japanese Medicine

Japan's medical care system reflects clinical and cultural influences, including tradition and a continuing dialogue involving government, the medical profession, and private purchasers of care. Increasingly, though, the power to make decisions affecting the financing and delivery of medical care seems to be gravitating toward the elaborate governmental machinery constructed to implement economic and social policies since World War II.[4] The Ministry of Health and Welfare (like all Cabinet departments) is able to attract a larger number of qualified persons, including physicians, to its bureaucratic ranks than does its U.S. counterpart, because the posts offer considerably more prestige and higher pay than comparable posts in American government.

Japanese practicing physicians are paid on a fee-for-service basis, with all prices fixed by a nationally uniform, itemized, and minutely defined schedule, known as the point-fee system. The ministry sets the fees in consultation with the Central Social Insurance Medical Council, a 20-member advisory body representing the public, payers, and providers. The ministry provides the council's staff support. Each medical service is assigned a certain number of points, and each point is worth 10 yen. The points assigned are based on the degree of technical skill required to provide a particular service or consultation and the cost of materials, such as drugs, laboratory tests, and injections.

The fees established for a particular service or procedure are common throughout the system. No matter how skilled a physician is at rendering a particular service or how prestigious the

hospital in which it is performed, the same fee is paid to all providers for the same service. In Japan, unlike the United States, physicians' fees and hospital costs are not separated for purposes of reimbursement; whether the charge is for an inpatient procedure or for ambulatory care provided at a hospital-based clinic, it is only the medical facility that is reimbursed. Hospital-based physicians are full-time, salaried practitioners.

The Ministry of Health and Welfare, in consultation with the advisory body, has structured the fee schedule for physicians in a way that constrains most fees. As Table 1 shows, physicians' visits and most diagnostic and laboratory tests cost less in Japan than in the United States and Europe. The fees are expressed in local currencies and in U.S. dollars, adjusted for purchasing-power parities (exchange rates that correct for price-level differences among countries). George J. Schieber, an American economist who analyzed physicians' fees in various countries while

assigned to the OECD, urged that these data be "interpreted with caution, since procedures may not be defined exactly the same across countries and fees may vary by specialty of the physician or place of service (e.g., lab or physician's office)."[5]

Whether Japanese physicians provide a medical service depends on fee levels, clinical need, and cultural factors. The fee schedule is influential in the allocation of medical resources, because virtually all care is financed through health insurance plans that base their reimbursement of providers on the schedule. However, the fee schedule does not always predict physicians' behavior accurately, as Dr. Naoki Ikegami, chairman of the Department of Hospital and Medical Administration at Keio University School of Medicine, recently explained.[6]

There are 53,107 patients receiving renal dialysis in Japan which makes it the highest ratio in the world (443.7 per million population, end of 1983 figures). Although pressure from the patient's organization to provide public assis-

Table 1. Medical Service Fees, 1984, in Local Currency and U.S. Dollars at Purchasing-Power Parities.[*]

	BELGIUM		GERMANY		FRANCE		LUXEMBOURG		NETHERLANDS†		DENMARK		SWITZERLAND‡		EUROPEAN MEAN	EUROPEAN HIGH/LOW	UNITED STATES‡	JAPAN	
	BF	$	DM	$	FF	$	FL	$	Fl	$	K	$	SF	$	$		$	YEN	$
1. GP home visit	430	12	29	14	81	13	680¶	18	—	—	89¶	11	52	24	15	2.2	31	2,000¶	10
2. First consultation of internal medicine with major examination	659	18	21	10	95	15	1135	31	52	22	337	41	73	34	25	4.1	72	1,350	7
3. Normal delivery by GP	5084	139	97	45	950	154	4055	109	604	258	446	54	449	207	138	5.7	—	—	—
4. Cholecystectomy	8317	227	293	136	920	149	7385	199	328	140	—	—	930	429	213	3.2	1754	80,000	394
5. Total hysterectomy	8911	243	325	151	1150	187	8025	216	423	181	—	—	940	433	235	2.9	1754	61,000	300
6. Appendectomy	4752	130	174	81	575	93	3805	103	188	80	—	—	560	258	124	3.2	1135	37,500	185
7. Examination of urine	83	2	—	—	119	19	111	3	—	—	22	3	14	6	7	9.5	5	2,450	12
8. Prothrombin-time test	131	4	—	—	26	4	111	3	—	—	44	5	27	12	6	4.0	7	400	2
9. Total cholesterol	136	4	—	—	17	3	134	4	—	—	68	8	42	19	8	6.3	9	600	3
10. Thorax radiography	664	18	53	25	122	20	595	16	22	9	411	50	125	57	28	6.3	41	—	—
11. Colon radiography	3318	91	95	44	446	72	1355	37	58	25	454	55	397	183	72	7.3	155	—	—
12. Radiography of lumbo-sacral column	1611	44	90	42	180	29	360	10	31	13	363	44	270	124	44	12.4	93	—	—
13. Electroencephalography	2043	56	69	32	805	131	1055	28	86	37	219	26	245	113	60	4.3	125	5,000	25
14. Electrocardiography	530	14	30	14	92	15	525	14	—	—	88	11	84	39	18	3.5	45	1,500	7
15. Bronchoscopy	1792	49	70	33	345	56	2425	65	153	65	398	48	212	97	59	2.9	413	3,200	16
16. Rectosigmoidoscopy	754	21	106	49	115	19	850	23	117	50	398	48	235	108	45	5.7	72	900	4
17. Extraction of one lower molar	298	8	16	7	92	15	295	8	11	5	104	13	18	8	9	3.0	—	2,400	12
18. Filling: one face	529	14	26	12	74	12	495	13	19	8	—	—	—	—	12	1.8	—	—	—

[*]Adapted from Schieber,[5] with the permission of the publisher. BF denotes Belgian franc, DM deutsche mark, FF French franc, FL Luxembourg franc, Fl guilder, K krone, SF Swiss franc, and GP general practitioner.

†The data for the Netherlands, depending on the procedure, refer to the year 1981, 1982, 1983, or 1984.

‡Where a choice among plans or a range of fees is presented, the maximal fee is chosen (e.g., the electroencephalography fee for France). In the case of Switzerland, the differences between minimal and maximal fees are on the order of 2:1.

§The U.S. data are for New York City, New York, where fees are the highest in the United States, almost double the U.S. average.

¶Additional mileage charges for general practitioner home visits are paid in Luxembourg, Denmark, and Japan. Fees may refer to different specialties; definitions of procedures may not be exactly comparable; and there may be some noncomparability in terms of technical (e.g., laboratory) and professional (physician interpretation) components of various procedures.

tance may have contributed, the main reason for the rapid diffusion of renal dialysis has been ascribed to the fact that the tariff for this procedure was initially set high to induce its rapid utilization. When the required level was attained, the tariff was reduced by nearly half. However, in other areas, evidence of the successful inducement by the tariff is not available. For example, although the tariff for physicians' home visits has been greatly increased, there has been a consistent decrease in the number of visits. At the same time, the number of the elderly over 65 in hospitals has increased from 0.3 percent of the total inpatients in 1955 to 4.4 percent in 1984.

The ministry has also influenced surgical rates through the fee schedule. By constraining fees for surgical services—and reinforcing the cultural aversion to invasive procedures—the schedule has kept surgical rates low and thus kept medical costs contained. I found no published information comparing Japanese and U.S. surgical rates. I have based my conclusion that Japanese surgical rates are low on three factors: the belief of ministry officials that that is the case, the unpublished calculations of one such official who took graduate medical training in the United States, and the effective ban on organ transplantation (with the exception of kidneys donated by living persons) that results from Japan's not recognizing brain death as a valid definition of death.

In a celebrated case 20 years ago, a Japanese physician was accused of murder, but never convicted, after declaring a teenage boy who drowned brain dead and transplanting his heart into another youth. The case has inhibited the profession from performing this procedure. Earlier this year, the JMA approved a report from its Life Ethics Council recommending that Japan officially recognize brain death as a form of death. [7] In June, Dr. Taro Nakayama, a Diet member, led members of the ruling Liberal Democratic Party on an "organ transplant survey mission" to several European countries and the United States in an effort to promote more transplantation in Japan. A similar JMA mission to the United States had been organized for the same purpose several weeks earlier. The Japanese legal community remains skeptical about accepting the concept of brain death.

Physicians must accept as payment in full the fees that are allowed by the ministry's schedule. But there is another important dimension to physician remuneration that is largely unknown in the United States and other Western countries. Physicians often receive small or large sums of money and other gifts from patients as expressions of gratitude. This is a longstanding and accepted practice, but there is no documentation of how much these presumably tax-free gifts add to physicians' incomes. No one includes them in estimates of Japanese medical expenditures. Another medical expense that the ministry characterizes as a "hidden charge" is a hospital surcharge for patients who have private rooms and private-duty nurses.

In general, the physician fee schedule tends to favor the ambulatory services provided by physicians in clinics over inpatient hospital care. This bias has a long history, dating back to the powerful reign (1957 to 1982) of Taro Takemi as president of the JMA. During Takemi's era, in the early years of which the government needed the association's support for universal health insurance coverage, the JMA was a forceful advocate for Japan's clinic-based physicians. The forms of the association's advocacy varied, but certainly bolstering incomes was a priority—from influencing changes in the fee schedule to maintaining physicians' ability to prescribe and dispense drugs, to winning preferential tax status for clinic-based doctors (72 percent of their professional income had previously been exempt from taxation; now the exemption rate varies between 52 and 72 percent, depending on a practitioner's income). The association has always maintained very close ties to the ruling Liberal Democratic Party.

In 1986, there were 79,369 medical clinics, more than 90 percent of which were owned and operated by physicians. A clinic is similar in many respects to the private office of an American physician, with several major differences: many Japanese clinics maintain beds for patients, and doctors who practice in them do not have hospital admitting privileges. By law, clinics can operate up to 19 beds; a patient can fill a clinic bed for only 48 hours, but that

stricture is not enforced. There were 283,390 beds in medical clinics in 1985. In that same year, there were 9,608 hospitals—a hospital is a facility with 20 or more beds—7,688 of which were private institutions. These private hospitals, most of them owned by physicians, had 961,277 beds. The larger hospitals in Japan are, generally speaking, public institutions; they are the facilities that most often have affiliations with Japan's 80 medical schools, which graduate some 8,000 students a year. Public hospitals, which include the prestigious National Cancer Center and institutions that serve patients with tuberculosis and mental disorders, number 1,486 and have some 370,000 beds. The ratio of the total number of hospital and clinic beds to the population is 1,461:100,000, one of the highest among OECD countries.

The JMA's strong advocacy of clinic-based physicians over the years has alienated some hospital-based doctors, who make less money and whose incomes are taxed far more heavily. When clinic-based physicians were in the majority, this antipathy was less important to the JMA than it has become in recent years. Thirty years ago, 47 percent of Japan's physicians owned and operated their own clinics and hospitals. Of the remainder, 45 percent were full-time, salaried hospital-based physicians. Today, approximately 36 percent of Japan's physicians own and operate clinics and hospitals, and about 56 percent are hospital-based. The average age of the clinic-based doctor is about 58; fewer physicians are attracted to clinic practice because of its emphasis on primary care, the uneven quality of its care, and the increased amount of capital required to maintain it. Increasingly, new physicians are opting for hospital-based practice because hospital salaries are rising, the prestige is greater, there are more posts available, and hospitals present the opportunity to work in a teaching environment. The changing nature of Japanese medical practice and the retirement of Takemi in 1982 have diluted the influence of the JMA, but as Ikegami has pointed out, hospital-based physicians have not yet harnessed the potential power of their greater numbers to achieve political ends.

Numerically the physicians in the clinics have formed, until recently, the majority and, moreover, have been relatively united in their interests. In contrast, physicians in hospitals have been divided between the public hospitals, in which high technology has tended to be concentrated, and the private hospitals in which more basic care is provided. Moreover, the specialty societies' power has not been strong due to their divisions into medical school rivalries and the lack of development in specialty certifications.[6]

The competition between clinics and hospitals to attract patients is intense, because clinic physicians are not allowed to follow their patients into the hospital once patients are referred there. Hospital medical staffs are composed of full-time physicians who are employees of the institution. As a consequence, clinic-based physicians are reluctant to refer their patients to hospitals unless absolutely necessary, because to do so means essentially relinquishing them, at least for the illness in question. Without an organized referral system, clinics and hospitals often offer similar services, purchase duplicate equipment, and maintain excess capacity. In an effort to constrain the development of more hospital capacity, the Diet mandated prefectural governments in 1985 to establish local health plans. These plans, which the JMA views skeptically, are currently being drafted.

Although private clinics and hospitals are organized as nonprofit institutions—in the sense that they do not have stockholders to whom they are accountable financially—the physicians who own and operate these facilities do have a proprietary interest in their viability. Legal restrictions have prevented the emergence of investor-owned healthcare organizations. Depending on the size of the clinic, a physician owner generally oversees the entire operation. Often family members assist in its operation, either as health personnel or as part of the administrative structure. It is not unusual for a medical clinic to be owned and operated by a family over many generations. In all instances, though, a physician must by law serve as director of a clinic. Reflecting this pattern, about one third of Japan's medical students are sons or, increasingly, daughters of physicians.

Physicians who operate clinics with beds were estimated in 1987 to have earned the highest incomes of all Japanese doctors—7.3 times the wage of the average worker (3,359,000 yen a month, or $2,488). Physicians who operate clinics without beds earned approximately 6.5 times the income of the average worker. Salaried physicians, the vast majority of them hospital-based, earned about 3.4 times the average worker's wage. Levin and colleagues have described the relation between Japanese physicians and their health care facilities.[8]

Actually, most Japanese health care providers and hospitals are small entrepreneurial units with no connection to the corporatized world of Japanese management. The overwhelming majority of Japanese hospitals are owned by . . . physician[s] who ha[ve] no formal training in administration. These individuals are called "incho" or medical director. Japanese law requires that the incho has total responsibility for the management and medical care provided in a hospital. . . . In those hospitals owned by the incho through inheritance or purchase, he is incho for life. . . . As the medical director, he selects the physicians to staff the hospital. . . . The incho decides what types of services to offer in his hospital, which of these services should expand or contract, and what major equipment should be purchased. He also arranges for the recruitment of physicians from his medical school.

Long Hospital Stays

to physicians that are virtually required do not appear in official accounts. Another factor in long hospitalizations according to Ohnuki-Tierney is the way workers' roles are defined in Japanese organizations.[9]

A worker's job does not consist of tasks assigned exclusively to that particular individual. Instead, "diffuse job definitions" or "a lack of sharp jurisdictional definitions of job duties" results in extensive job rotation. This practice enables coworkers to cover the tasks of the sick person with relative ease.

Although hospital stays are long, they are less expensive than those of any other OECD country, according to Schieber.[5] Examining the latest available comparable data (1982) from the 24 member countries, Schieber found a range of 2.5 to 1 in hospital expenditures per person,

of 6.4 to 1 in expenditures per bed, of 6 to 1 in expenditures per day of hospital use, and of 3.6 to 1 in expenditures per admission.

Per capita expenditures ranged from under $300 per person in Japan ($230), Finland ($280), and Ireland ($260) to more than $500 per person in Iceland ($510), the Netherlands ($540), and the United States ($580). . . . Expenditures per bed in 1982 varied from $19,000 in Japan to $122,000 in the United States with an OECD average of $50,000. . . . Expenditures per hospital day varied from less than $100 per day in Finland ($70) and Japan ($60), to $360 per day in the United States with an OECD average of $170. . . . Expenditures per admission varied from $1,600 or less per admission in Finland ($1,300), Australia ($1,460), and Ireland ($1,600) to more than $3,400 in the Netherlands ($4,640) and the United States ($3,450). [Japan's comparable figure was $3,190, excluding clinic-based hospital beds.]

Drug Prescribing and Dispensing

Since World War II, one of the issues that has subjected Japanese medical practice to continuing question has been physicians' prescribing and dispensing of drugs. The appropriateness of the practice was questioned by General Crawford F. Sams, an American physician who was chief of the Section of Public Health and Welfare of the allied powers. Sams is reported to have said that "there are two things in Japan which surprise most Americans. One is that doctors prepare and sell medicine. The other is that dentists sell gold."[10]

Sams asserted at the time that if physicians continued this practice they would lose respect and be regarded as mere tradesmen. He further argued that Japan should adopt the American practice whereby physicians prescribe drugs and pharmacists dispense them. Several years later, legislation was introduced in the Japanese Diet and enacted in 1951 that called for the separation of the functions of prescribing and dispensing, effective in 1955. The Ministry of Health and Welfare, the Federation of Health Insurance Societies, and the Japan Pharmacists Association supported the legislation. After a sustained campaign by the JMA against separation of the functions, amendments to the statute were adopted in 1955 that, according to Steslicke, "provided for so many exceptions that the intent of the law was completely subverted."[10]

In the ensuing years, the issue has remained alive because virtually all clinic-based physicians continue to prescribe and dispense drugs. Hospital-based physicians prescribe, and the hospital pharmacy dispenses the drugs. Although the Ministry of Health and Welfare remains committed to separating the functions, a course the JMA is on record as supporting, the government agency has emphasized another policy that reflects its efforts to constrain the growth of medical spending: reducing the percentage of national medical expenditures that is accounted for by pharmaceuticals by cutting drug reimbursements. In 1981, reimbursements for drugs by health insurance plans represented 38.7 percent of all health expenditures. By 1987, the total had dropped to 28 percent. (In the United States, pharmaceutical expenditures represented 8 percent of total medical spending, although there are substantial differences in definitions that make an exact comparison difficult). Reducing drug prices has been a controversial policy within the ministry and the industry because of its potential effects on physician behavior, companies' research-and-development budgets, product sales, and overall pharmaceutical consumption patterns, according to an unpublished manuscript by Professor Michael R. Reich, who directs the Takemi Program in International Health at the Harvard School of Public Health. The ratio to sales of expenditures for research and development—including government research grants employed to promote Japanese companies—is higher in pharmaceuticals than in any other industry in Japan.

A pharmaceutical product is generally not sold in Japan unless it is on the national health insurance reimbursement list. The ministry is responsible for maintaining the list (which totals some 13,650 drugs), regulating the approval of new drugs (new drugs are approved an average of 8 to 10 months faster than in the United States), and also establishing drug prices, which are used by all health insurance plans. In the past decade, the agency has reduced the prices it will pay for pharmaceuticals seven times. In four instances, the reductions involved all drugs; on three other occasions only some drugs were affected. During the 1980s, drug prices have been reduced an average of 61.4 percent. Whether clinic-based doctors, hospitals, or drug manufacturers have borne the brunt of these cuts remains in question, but some observers believe that companies absorbed most of them to maintain their physician customers. A recent industry publication explained the process:

Under the public health insurance system, products on the NHI Reimbursement List are reimbursed by the health insurance schemes. [Drug] wholesalers work from the NHI reimbursement price, offering discounts which vary according to customer, product and size of order—doctors [as opposed to hospitals] tend to receive the largest discounts. The dispenser keeps the difference between the buying price and the NHI reimbursement price. Traditionally, doctors have held a near-monopoly over the dispensing of pharmaceuticals, although this is gradually changing. There is a tendency for them to dispense those pharmaceuticals which give the largest profit. Since 1981 [actually, the first revision of the drug price list dates to the early 1950s], the Ministry of Health and Welfare has been reducing the prices of pharmaceuticals on the NHI reimbursement list, based on the actual marketplace prices to retailers. There is a tendency for doctors to dispense more, and more expensive, pharmaceuticals to replace lost income.[11]

There is a relation between reimbursement levels for particular drugs and physicians' prescribing patterns, particularly with respect to antibiotics, the most prescribed type of drug in Japan. Another industry analysis discussed this phenomenon:[12]

An unusual feature of the Japanese market is the dominant, though declining, share held by antibiotics. The vagaries of the reimbursement price system have meant that antibiotic prices have been exceptionally high, [wholesalers'] discounts deep and the doctor eager to prescribe. The development, production and marketing of antibiotics have been a major preoccupation of many of the leading companies and the doctor has cooperated by choosing antibiotics as a fairly safe and innocuous way of increasing his prescribing levels. . . . The tendency for the doctor to maintain his income through heavy prescribing is endemic and it is not surprising that the Japanese have the highest per capita drug consumption in the world. The use of high priced powerful antibiotics is particularly notable. In 1984, antibiotics accounted for 18.4 percent of drug production . . . and of that 84.2 percent was broad spectrum gram positive and gram negative products leaving only 15.8 percent for narrow spectrum. This heavy consumption of powerful broad spectrum antibiotics introduces problems of side-effects and microbial resistance as regards public health policy.

The ethics of drug prescribing practices in Japan does not seem to have been thoroughly explored by the profession or the industry; the dominant industry position is to maintain the status quo, but an occasional voice can be heard questioning it. An American who recently addressed the subject was P. Reed Maurer, Japan representative of the U.S. Pharmaceutical Manufacturers Association. In a speech this spring to Japanese journalists who cover the Ministry of Health and Welfare, Maurer said current practice

focuses attention on the economic rationale for prescribing drugs versus their medical benefits and risks. The selection of drugs should be made on the basis of what is good for the patient, not what is economically good for physicians and hospitals.

There are important dimensions of contemporary medical care that have been neglected in Japan as compared with the West: graduate medical education, quality assurance, and disciplines that analyze the cost of care and the nature of disease. Graduate medical education is an uncertain experience for young physicians because there is no established process for training and certifying medical specialists; as a consequence, medical specialization is underdeveloped, and many young doctors languish in teaching hospitals for years without the ability to chart their careers. This situation was the root cause of the student riots at Tokyo University that rocked Japan in the 1960s, but the disturbances provoked very little change in the system of graduate medical education. There are no formal mechanisms to ensure quality of care in either the hospital or the clinic, and there are few sound clinical trials. The decisions of physicians are rarely, though increasingly, questioned by patients, payers, or other physicians. As a consequence, medical malpractice claims by patients are rare; the small number of lawyers in Japan undoubtedly has a role, too. The disciplines of biostatistics, economics, epidemiology, health services research, management, and policy in relation to medical care are also neglected in Japan, owing perhaps to the failure of government to support their development and to the traditional dominance of physicians. However, there are about 150 members of the Japanese Society of Medical Decisionmaking, which indicates growing interest in examining the efficacy of clinical practice there.

Japan's private corporations have demonstrated an awesome capacity to market their automobiles, electronic gadgets, motorcycles, and television sets in world markets. In the process, Americans have become enchanted with the achievements of Japanese management. Its medical care system, however, stands

in rather sharp contrast. It operates without a similar emphasis on management, quality control, and consumer sovereignty, although it does provide care to all citizens and at a reasonable cost and contributes to Japan's impressive health status. As physicians and patients continue to lay greater claim to available resources, it seems inevitable that the profession will face increasing demands to rationalize a system that evolved over the course of the twentieth century to address growing problems, but that is an anachronism in Japan today.

Notes

1. Iglehart JK. Japan's medical care system. N Engl J Med 1988; 319:807–12.
2. Schieber GJ, Poullier JP. International health spending and utilization trends. Health Aff (Millwood) 1988; 7(4):105–12.
3. Lewis P. Divided World Health Organization braces for leadership change. New York Times. May 1, 1988:20.
4. Steslicke WE. Medical care in Japan: the political context. J Ambulatory Care Manage 1982; 5(4):65–77.
5. Schieber GJ. Financing and delivering health care: a comparative analysis of OECD countries. OECD social policy studies no. 4. Paris: Organization for Economic Co-operation and Development, 1987.
6. Ikegami N. Health technology in Japan. Int Technol Assess 1988; 4:239–54.
7. Haberman C. Japan ruling on death opens way for transplants. New York Times. January 14, 1988:B7.
8. Levin PJ, Wolfson J, Akiyama H. The role of management in Japanese hospitals. Hosp Health Serv Adm 1987; 32:249–61.
9. Ohnuki-Tierney E. Illness and culture in contemporary Japan: an anthropological view. New York: Cambridge University Press, 1984.
10. Steslicke WE. Doctors in politics: the political life of the Japan medical association. New York: Praeger, 1973.
11. World drug market manual. Vol. 2. Asia, Africa and Australasia. London: IM-SWORLD Publications, 1987.
12. Japan pharmaceuticals industry briefing paper. London: Wood Mackenzie, 1986.

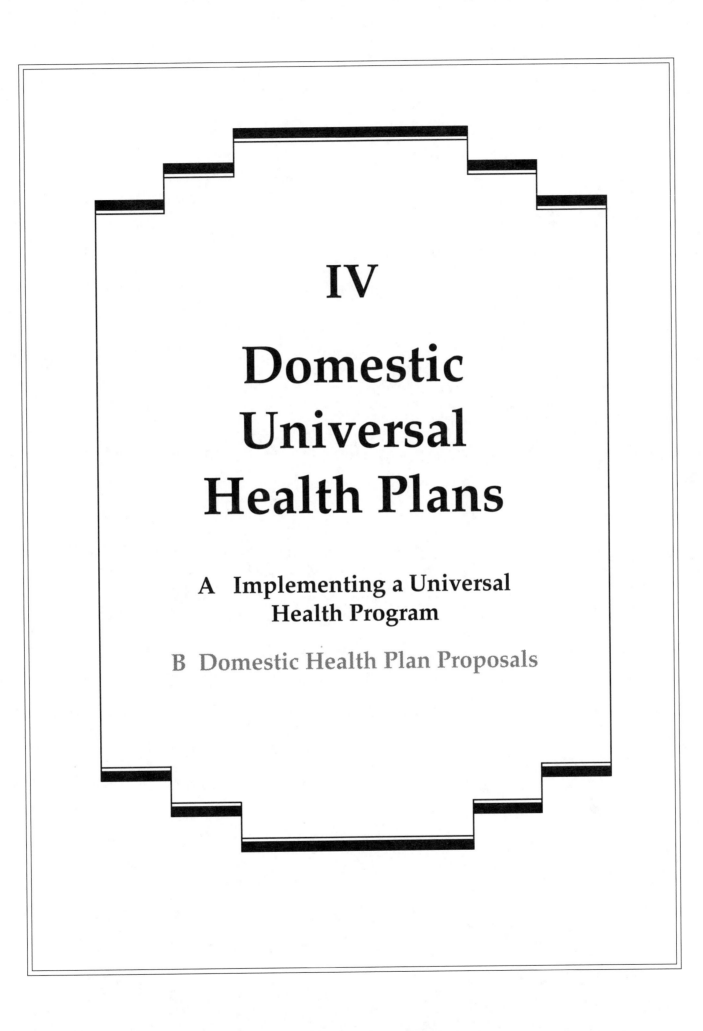

IV

Domestic Universal Health Plans

A   Implementing a Universal Health Program

B   Domestic Health Plan Proposals

Introduction

Linda Reivitz

It is the essence of a constitutional system that its people should think straight, maintain a consistent purpose, look before and after, and make their lives the image of their thoughts.

Woodrow Wilson, 1908[1]

Discussions on the subject of program implementation usually begin with an analysis of the passage of legislation. But they can end years or even decades later as groups affected by that legislation interact with a bureaucracy setting standards or promulgating rules and regulations. Since there is much good literature on this latter phase of the process elsewhere, the articles in this section discuss instead what must occur first—the passage of some form of legislation itself.[2]

Readers should understand that the current difficulty in getting Congress to enact new programs is neither new nor unique to health care. Political scientists have long understood, for example, that "the making of government decisions is not a majestic march of great majorities," in part because great majorities are not interested in the goings-on in Washington. Decision making instead takes place "by endless bargaining" and "the steady appeasement of relatively small groups. . . ."[3] Moreover, Congress, by its very nature, is conservative and slow to act—regardless of the direction—a trait well-suited to minorities interested in no change at all.[4] It is perhaps not surprising, then, that many of the articles in this section treat the effects of legislative inertia.

Robert Blendon and Karen Donelan in "The Public and the Emerging Debate over National Health Insurance," for example, explain succinctly just why implementing a national system will be difficult. They find that while three of four Americans support some form of national health plan, they do not agree on what that plan should look like or how it should be financed. Nor are they willing to pay any substantial increases in taxes to bring such a plan about. Using the welfare system to bring health care services to the poor often evokes ambivalence, if not hostility. The authors believe that as long as public ambivalence remains, "the political influence of those who do not want to change our current system will be strengthened." They suggest five

principles for national health plan proposals. A plan, they say, should contain elements of both private and public financing; rely on taxes other than the income tax; be funded in part from funds reallocated from other programs; transfer the Medicaid program outside the welfare system; and be phased in over a period of time.

Echoing Blendon and Donelan, James Morone ("Beyond the Words: The Politics of Health Care Reform") attempts to "map the political terrain in which health system reformers operate" and observes that policy options available to deal with needed changes in our health system flow from the American dislike of government. He illustrates the tinkering, gimmicks, and implicit policies that have been attempted in the past—all, he says, with remarkable nonsuccess. He enumerates contemporary solutions: an expansion of the medical assistance program; the use of DRGs for all payers, as was done in New Jersey—an example of what he calls a "covert" government program; pluralism, or the use of many different market-based solutions, in different states or localities; and a national health system. American health policy, Morone predicts, will "progress through each of these solutions, one at a time, slowly 'slouching' toward national health insurance."

By contrast, Robert Evans, "Tension, Compression, and Shear: Directions, Stresses, and Outcomes of Health Care Cost Control," relies on economic analysis to explain just why health care reform is so difficult. Different players in the system—insurers, providers, taxpayers and others—have different economic interests that they act to protect. Health care providers especially find it in their interest to drive costs up; others resist such growth; and still others are ambivalent about cost increases, as long as they are shifted to someone else. Evans rejects arguments that a health system with strict expenditure controls simply will not work or will require the rationing of services. He does not minimize the conflict that strict cost controls generate or the difficulty in achieving them. The real question for policymakers, he says, is whether a society can or will "create organizational structures in which those responsible for exerting compressive forces [to reduce health care expenditures] not only have the ability and motivation to do the task but cannot escape it."

While Stephen Shortell and Walter McNerney ("Criteria and Guidelines for Reforming the U.S. Health Care System") concede that wholesale change in our health care delivery and financing system is not likely soon, they provide a thoughtful set of guidelines for the interim on which to judge reform proposals and then outline the elements of a U.S. system based on those guidelines. Theirs is a system financed from a variety of sources, where resources meet patient needs, payment is based on outcome measures, and costs are controlled with an expenditure cap rather than regulations on physician behavior.

Whereas the Shortell and McNerney criteria help assess the merits of specific reform proposals, Richard Merritt and Linda Demkovich ("Exhausting Alternatives") give us numerous examples of many ongoing state initiatives, which some believe "may just turn out to be the basis of a universal health plan for the country." Merritt and Demkovich take it as a given that no national health plan will be passed at the federal level in the foreseeable future. They describe the three main strategies states have used to provide health coverage for those without it: (1) gap fillers, or programs that target one or more group within the uninsured, most notably children; (2) insurance reforms and employer-based programs, often in the form of laws to "crack the small group market" and financial incentives to subsidize employee health insurance; and (3) single payer systems under which governments pay and otherwise provide for comprehensive health care coverage. Merritt and Demkovich rebut those who argue that this state action—"by masking the underlying rot in the system"—is actually delaying the time when major change will provide access to all. "State-level initiatives aren't necessarily incompatible with a federal plan," they conclude, "if one's vision is broad enough to allow for the notion of a national program that provides for universal access and uniform benefits but that is based on a decentralized administrative system."

For those who want to see a national health program soon, these articles may be disappointing—not because the authors oppose a national health plan, but because they tell us repeatedly why that has not yet happened and why incremental change is far more likely. [5] But unalloyed pessimism is probably not warranted either. As Morone points out, it is often easier to thwart political action than to undertake it. And as students of government and veterans of efforts to achieve policy change know, achieving reform requires a fortuitous coming together of events, including a proper public climate and a window of opportunity, as well as a set of carefully considered solutions, before it can go

forward. [6] As long as health care reform is on the political "front burner," which it is, the possibility for major and beneficial change exists. Moreover, as one author recently pointed out, in spite of a lack of presidential leadership, Congress has enacted significant changes in our health care system in the last decade, from benefit expansions in Medicare and Medicaid to physician payment reform, and engaged in vigorous consensus-building efforts that have brought together diverse and historically acrimonious groups. [7]

We *are* making changes for the better and providing help to those who need and deserve it. We can, of course, do better still. Each author in this section shares perspectives from personal experience on what is possible and acceptable, politically, ethically, historically and programmatically. In short, they give us a prescription, not for a perfect system, but a system that is better than the one we have now.

Notes

1. *Constitutional Government in the United States* (New York: Columbia University Press, 1961), p. 23.
2. See, for example, Jeffrey Pressman and Aaron Wildavsky, *Implementation* (Berkeley: University of California Press, 1973); Judith Feder, "Medicare Implementation and the Policy Process," *Journal of Health Politics, Policy and Law* 2 (Summer 1977): 173–89; and Frank J. Thompson, "The Enduring Challenge of Health Policy Implementation," in *Health Politics and Policy*, 2nd ed., by Theodore J. Litman and Leonard S. Robins, 2nd ed. (Albany, NY: Delmar Publishers, 1991).
3. Robert A. Dahl, *A Preface to Democratic Theory* (Chicago: University of Chicago Press, 1956), pp. 146, 150.
4. See Barbara Hinckley, *Stability and Change in Congress*, 3rd ed. (New York: Harper and Row, 1983).
5. In fact, had space permitted, many more articles on this theme could been added to this volume. See Samuel Levey and James Hill, "National Health Insurance—The Triumph of Equivocation," *New England Journal of Medicine* 321, no. 25 (December 21, 1989): 1750–54; and David Blumenthal, "The Timing and Course of Health Care Reform," *New England Journal of Medicine* 325 no. 3, (July 18, 1991): 198–200; and Drew E. Altman, "Two Views of a Changing Health Care System," in *Applications of Social Science to Clinical Medicine and Health Policy*, ed. Linda H. Aiken and David Mechanic (New Brunswick, NJ: Rutgers University Press, 1986), pp. 100–112.
6. See, for example, Karen Davis, "Research and Policy Formulation," in *Applications of Social Science to Clinical Medicine and Health Policy*, ed. Linda H. Aiken and David Mechanic (New Brunswick, NJ: Rutgers University Press, 1986), pp. 113–25; and John Kingdon, *Agendas, Alternatives, and Public Policies* (Glenview, IL: Scott, Foresman and Company, 1984).
7. Lynn Etheredge, "Negotiating National Health Insurance," *Journal of Health Politics, Policy and Law* 16, no. 1 (Spring 1991): 157–67.

25

The Public and the Emerging Debate Over National Health Insurance

Robert J. Blendon and Karen Donelan

Opinion surveys conducted this year indicate that nearly three of four Americans (72 to 73 percent) favor some form of a national health care program. [1,2] In fact, as Figure 1 shows, support for one type of proposal—a plan financed entirely by government—is now at the highest point since World War II. [3–10] The public's enthusiasm for such a program now approximates the level of support for Medicare in the year before its enactment. [11] Nevertheless, a closer examination of the survey results reveals that the public holds a number of apparently conflicting views about the preferred design of a national health care program. The purpose of this review is to highlight the conflicts as well as the points of consensus and to identify key principles particular to American culture that should be incorporated in any new universal health care program if it is to achieve widespread popular support.

Our findings draw on survey data related to national health insurance and its financing that were collected primarily in the periods from 1971 to 1977 and from 1986 to 1990. The first period was selected because of its similarity to the current one. [12] As shown in Figure 1, during the 1970s as at no other time, the majority of Americans (54 to 60 percent) reported in surveys that they favored a government-financed plan of national health care. [6–8] During the same decade,

more than a dozen initiatives for national health insurance were introduced in Congress, including one sponsored by a Republican president. [13,14] Yet no program was enacted. The reasons behind the rejection of the proposals have clear implications for the current debate about national health care. Careful attention to the realities of public opinion on the part of policy makers and others concerned with enacting a national health plan can prevent the failure of similar proposals, as well as the type of backlash that ultimately led to the recent repeal of the Medicare Catastrophic Coverage Act.

Data and Methods

Our conclusions are based on a review of data drawn from several hundred opinion surveys on health care issues that were conducted by 25 survey organizations between 1938 and 1990, using various methods and instruments. Only a limited number of the findings are reported here. Those presented were selected for inclusion on the basis of the following five criteria.

First, to be included, they had to relate directly to key policy issues that have been identified in various congressional reports as important to past and present debates about the adoption of a national health care plan and its financing. [15,16] For example, a review of surveys conducted in 1989 and 1990 shows that the public is more likely to say that it favors a national health plan if the wording of the question is not specific about the role of government (72 to 73 percent), [1,2] and indicates less support in

response to questions that specify a government program financed through taxes (67 percent). [10] Because the wording of questions in surveys about national health insurance can have pronounced effects on the responses, the trends reported here focus primarily on two major types of plans under consideration—one that covers all Americans and is completely financed through taxes or Social Security, and another in which a federal mandate requires that all employers provide insurance for their employees and in addition government programs are set up to aid the unemployed and the poor. We excluded a number of survey questions from this analysis because of their lack of specificity about either the type of plan proposed or its financing.

Second, we required that multiple surveys addressing the same issue within a given period show consistent results. For example, we reviewed five questions from four surveys conducted from 1988 through 1990 that indicated that 61 to 73 percent of Americans favor some form of national health care plan. [1,2,10,17] Three of these surveys met our criteria for describing a plan financed entirely by government. They indicated that the level of support for such a plan was 61 percent in 1988, 67 percent in 1989, and 66 percent in 1990. The question asked in 1989[10] was identical to that asked in two previous surveys (1980 and 1982) [8,9] and was therefore chosen for presentation in Figure 1. Our third criterion required that if data are presented as part of a time trend, the wording of the question must be consistent over the period. If, for the purposes of brevity

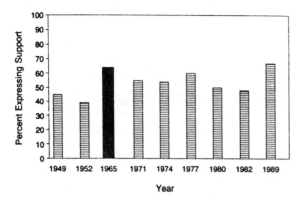

Figure 1. Support Expressed in U.S. Public-Opinion Surveys for a National Health Care Program Financed Totally by Government. Shaded bars denote national health program, and the solid bar Medicare. Sample sizes for the surveys shown are as follows: 1949, 1500 participants; 1952, 1500; 1965, not available; 1971, 1600; 1974, 1503; 1977, 1447; 1980, 1536; 1982, 1530; and 1989, 2019. P<0.0001 for the differences between 1989 and each of the other years; χ^2 with 2 df, all >55.

and timeliness, only one measure of a given issue is to be presented, the most recently available data in reply to questions asked in multiple years are reported. For example, surveys in both 1989 and 1990 found Americans unwilling to support a national health plan if it limited their choice of physician (35 and 30 percent, respectively).[1,10] Only the 1990 figure is included in these results. Fourth, in most cases, we excluded results from surveys with fewer than 1,000 randomly selected participants. The sole exception involved an international study in which samples of fewer than 1,000 persons were used for two countries.[18] Finally, we excluded all questions that were obviously biased or confusing in wording or design, as compared with other related surveys or published literature.

In all, of the several hundred surveys we reviewed, only 41 met these five criteria. For the data presented in each figure, sample sizes, survey dates, and statistical comparisons are noted in the corresponding legend.

In interpreting the findings of opinion surveys, one should recognize that they are subject to sampling error. This may result in the collection of somewhat different data than would have been obtained if the entire population had been interviewed, even though such data are generally weighted according to the age, sex, and racial distribution of the population. The size of sampling errors decreases as the number of people

surveyed increases. For a telephone survey of 1000, the magnitude of error for each question was estimated to be +/-4 percent. In addition, response rates for these surveys are not generally reported by the organizations conducting them. Thus, the views of some members of the population may be underrepresented in the findings.

Statistical Analysis

We compared the frequency distributions of Americans' responses for 1989 with those for previous years (Figure 1) and the distribution of responses for the United States with that for European countries (Figure 2), using chi-square analysis with appropriate degrees of freedom. The statistical package used was Epi Info.[19]

Findings

What lessons can be learned from an examination of the public's views on these issues? First, Americans see universal access to health care as an important concern, but it is not as important to them as other issues are, or as it is to citizens of several European nations. For many years, public-opinion surveys have indicated that a majority of Americans (75 to 82 percent) believe government should provide the resources necessary for medical care to be available to everyone who needs it.[20,21] However, as Figure 2 shows, they do not feel as

strongly about this issue as do citizens of some European countries.[18,22]

Evidence of the American public's level of concern about health care can be seen in a recent survey. Although in 1990 72 percent of Americans said they favored some form of national program, only 14 percent considered health care one of the two most important problems facing the country, as compared with 64 percent who said the drug problem was such an issue.[1,23] The public's lack of strong concern for universal access makes it difficult to generate the strong support necessary to enact a national health program that would entail a major restructuring of the American health care system. In a 1990 survey in which 73 percent of Americans reported supporting a national health plan in some form, only 30 percent said they would favor such a program if it limited their choice of physician, and only 36 percent if it led to their waiting longer to receive care.[2]

Second, the surveys show that Americans remain unsure whether the United States should have a system of financing universal health care that is predominantly public or private. Although 89 percent report that they want major reform of our health care system,[17] surveys indicate that the public is uncertain whether this effort should result in an insurance system that is primarily private or public. Because Americans are dissatisfied with our current system, when they are given a single choice for change—i.e., a health plan financed entirely by government—they will support it in opinion surveys.[1,2,10] During the 1970s, however, surveys conducted on this issue showed that when Americans who favored a national health program were given two choices, their preferences were divided between a universal system of public insurance (22 to 27 percent) and a mixed system of compulsory private health insurance provided through employers and combined with government insurance for those without jobs (38 to 40 percent).[24,25] When the survey was repeated in 1990, the results revealed the same uncertainty, but more support was expressed for a plan financed entirely by government. With questions worded similarly to those used in the 1970s, the survey showed that 46 percent preferred a universal public plan

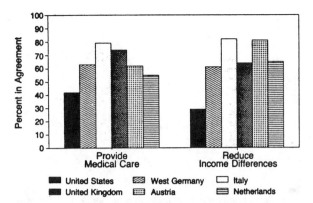

Figure 2. Comparison of Public Opinion in Six Nations about the Responsibility of Government to Provide Medical Care and Reduce Differences in Income.

The surveys on the responsibility to provide medical care were conducted in 1985. Sample sizes in each country were as follows: United States, 677 participants; United Kingdom, 1530; West Germany, 1048; Austria, 987; Italy, 1580; and the Netherlands, 1600. $P<0.01\times10^{-6}$ for differences between the United States and each European country; χ^2 with 5 df, all >120. The surveys on reducing income differences between the rich and the poor were conducted in 1987, with sample sizes as follows: United States, 1564; United Kingdom, 1212; West Germany, 1397; Austria, 972; Italy, 1027; and the Netherlands, 1638. $P<0.01\times10^{-6}$ for differences between the United States and each nation; χ^2 with 1 df with Yates' correction, all >537.

and 33 percent supported a mixed private-and-public plan. [26] When these data are viewed in the context of data from earlier years, it appears that Americans remain divided over this choice. The force of public opinion behind the enactment of a national health care program was weakened in the 1970s because of such indecision. As long as public ambivalence remains and those who support a universal system continue to debate its structure, the political influence of those who do not want to change our current system will be strengthened.

Third, according to the surveys Americans are unwilling to pay more than a modest tax increase to make a universal health plan a reality. Three surveys undertaken from 1988 through 1990 show that the level of public support for a national health plan declines in proportion to the increase in taxes proposed to fund it. [1,27,28] Americans express support for such a program as long as it entails only a small increase in their tax burden. For example, a 1990 survey reports that 72 percent support the adoption of a comprehensive national health insurance program even if it requires a tax increase. Only 22 percent, however, indicate a willingness to

pay more than $200 per year to see this happen, and a third (33 percent) remain undecided. Similar responses have been reported in other surveys over the past decade. [29] In fact, they were reported as early as 1938, when nearly half the Americans who said they favored a tax-funded program of free health care for the nation's poor retracted their support after being asked to pay for it through increased taxes. [30]

Why is the American public so resistant to paying the increased taxes needed to translate its beliefs into action? The answer appears to be embedded in our culture. As Figure 2 shows, Americans are less committed than citizens of European industrialized countries to the idea that it is the government's responsibility to even out differences in wealth between people of high and low incomes. [18,22] In both 1988 and 1989, the progressive federal income tax was considered the least popular of the federal and state taxes. Relatively flat taxes such as state sales taxes, the burden of which often falls disproportionately on the poor, are more widely favored by the public. [31] These views are somewhat surprising, given that the United States currently has one of the lowest levels of taxation among the 18 wealthiest indus-

trialized countries. Only Japan raises less tax revenue. [32] Even so, Americans still perceive themselves as overly taxed by government. Nearly 6 of 10 Americans describe their federal income taxes as too high; other studies have documented similar public concern about excessive taxation. [33,34]

The effect of these beliefs about taxes can be seen in the recent repeal of the Medicare Catastrophic Coverage Act of 1988, which was the first major increase in insurance entitlement since the implementation of Medicare. The original proposal by Otis R. Bowen, secretary of Health and Human Services, had overwhelming support (79 to 89 percent) among all segments of American society. [35,36] After the legislation was implemented, however, it was recognized more widely that the bulk of the cost of the new program would be paid for by a surcharge on the income taxes of elderly persons with middle incomes and above. Surveys conducted before the repeal of the act indicated that among elderly Americans familiar with the content of the legislation, 53 percent opposed it, and 39 percent opposed it strongly. The principal reason they gave was that they thought the new program was not worth the increase in individual taxes. [37]

Finally, Americans are deeply ambivalent about using the welfare system to provide adequate medical care to the nation's poor. Medicaid, the program that pays for health services for the poor, is financed and administered through the welfare system. It is caught in the conflict Americans feel about health and welfare programs that aid the poor. Opinion surveys indicate that Medicaid's health care aspects are popular. [20] As Figure 3 shows, since 1973 only 25 to 30 percent of Americans surveyed have reported that the United States was spending too little on welfare, which encompasses Medicaid—making it the lowest-ranked item in the domestic-spending budget on a scale that includes health, the environment, and education, as well as highways, parks and recreation, and mass transport, among others. These findings contrast sharply with Americans' views on increasing spending to improve the nation's health: more than two thirds believe the nation spends too little, and only 3 percent say we spend too much. [3]

Surveys conducted in 1989 suggest that if the Medicaid program were not seen as part of an unpopular welfare system, public support for expanding the coverage provided for low-income Americans would be stronger. In these surveys, 51 percent strongly endorsed the idea of increasing government spending to ensure that everyone below the poverty line has access to adequate medical care. [38] At the same time, however, only 31 percent reported strongly favoring a substantial increase in the Medicaid program to accomplish this. [39]

Implications for the Future

Our review suggests that despite the high level of public interest in a national health care plan, Americans may be unable to agree on a specific proposal, as they were in the 1970s. To build a consensus around a single program that takes into account the attitudes we have described, we propose that five principles be incorporated into proposals for a national health plan.

Principle 1: Any new proposal for universal health care should not try to resolve the dispute over whether the system of financing health care adopted should be predominantly public or predominantly private. Rather, it should contain elements of both. The current surge of public interest in national health insurance will falter as it did in the 1970s if the two major proponents of change find themselves in conflict over the nature of the future health care system. There are a number of creative compromises available that incorporate the various perspectives. In one initiative that involves programs in both the private and public sectors, the federal government would require all employers to provide their employees with private health insurance (excluding children but including spouses), and would enact a universal public insurance program for children. The latter program would extend the principle that Social Security financing should be available to persons in age groups outside those that ordinarily participate in the labor force. This proposal would increase the nation's public investment in its children while strengthening and enlarging the system

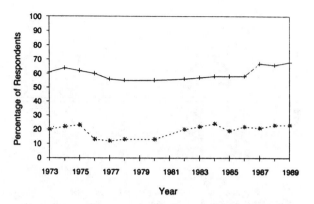

Figure 3. Percentage of Americans Surveyed from 1973 through 1989 Who Reported That the United States Spends Too Little on Health (Solid Line) and Welfare (Dashed Line).
The General Social Survey of the National Opinion Research Center is conducted annually with a national full-probability sample ranging in size from 972 (in 1975) to 2084 (in 1978).

of private health insurance provided through the workplace. In another option, people under the age of 65 would be allowed to purchase Medicare as an alternative to private health insurance. This would provide a unique opportunity to test the efficiency of an all-government plan as compared with those provided by private insurers.

Any new initiative should provide universal coverage and not focus exclusively on the needs of poor or unemployed persons. Previous surveys have shown that nearly two thirds of Americans prefer that a new governmental health plan include everyone, not just those who earn low incomes. [40] This opinion is likely to be held more widely today, since 6 of 10 persons who are currently uninsured are members of families with at least one working member and a household income above the poverty line. [41]

Principle 2: Any new program of universal health care should rely on taxes other than the progressive income tax for its chief financing. According to specific surveys that have elicited respondents' preferences for methods of financing such a program, the most popular taxes to raise are cigarette and liquor taxes (favored by 79 percent), Social Security taxes paid by employers for their employees (66 percent), insurance premiums paid by the individual (59 percent), and income taxes (52 percent). Other poll results indicate support for a sales tax earmarked for health-related purposes. [35]

Principle 3: Some of the resources for a program of universal health care should come from the reallocation of funds already being spent within the health sector or in other (non-health-related) government programs. Many Americans see such other sources of financing as possible alternatives to the raising of new taxes. Reallocating funds within the health sector would require finding a way to control the administrative costs of our current health insurance system, which now makes outlays of more than $35 billion per year. [42] Perhaps because most Americans (86 percent) view this system as poorly organized and inefficient, 69 percent believe that its costs can be reduced without affecting the quality of care. [1,43] Consequently, a logical target for savings might be found among administrative expenditures for activities that do not involve the rationing of medical care. Rationing is a policy that only one in five Americans would support. [43]

The second possibility—identifying funds outside the health sector—concerns the potential for reaping a large peace dividend as a result of the apparent end of the Cold War. The magnitude of this dividend could have profound implications for a national health care program by making available new sources of funds. Six of 10 people now say that the peace dividend should be used for domestic social priorities and not to reduce the deficit or taxes. [44]

Principle 4: So that low-income groups not covered by other universal insurance proposals will be best served, the administration of Medicaid should be transferred to a locus outside the welfare system. Although this step may seem cosmetic, years of opinion surveys suggest that being identified as a health program is important symbolically in garnering support.[45] Like the popular Head Start program for children of low-income families, Medicaid should be completely separate from public assistance.

Principle 5: Any new program should be phased in over a period of years. To avoid a major political backlash over sharply rising taxes, any new plan should be implemented gradually over an extended period. The plan should cover first the populations that are provided for most easily and at the lowest cost— i.e., children and employees of large and medium-sized businesses. Over time, the coverage should be extended until the plan achieves universal access.

We are indebted to Humphrey Taylor of Louis Harris and Associates, Gretchen Straw of the American Association of Retired Persons, and John Benson of the Roper Center for Public Opinion Research for providing data essential to this analysis.

Notes

1. Health care in the United States. Los Angeles Times. March 20, 1990. Storrs, CT: Roper Center for Public Opinion Research.

2. Gallup Poll. February 19, 1990. Storrs, CT: Roper Center for Public Opinion Research.

3. Gallup Organization. November 4, 1949. American Institute of Public Opinion 49–449. Storrs, CT: Roper Center for Public Opinion Research.

4. Gallup Organization. October 2, 1952. American Institute of Public Opinion 52–503. Storrs, CT: Roper Center for Public Opinion Research.

5. Louis Harris and Associates. Harris survey, January 1971. Storrs, CT: Roper Center for Public Opinion Research.

6. Louis Harris and Associates. Harris survey, June 10, 1974. Storrs, CT: Roper Center for Public Opinion Research.

7. CBS News/New York Times. July 1977. Storrs, CT: Roper Center for Public Opinion Research.

8. CBS News/New York Times. February 19, 1990. Storrs, CT: Roper Center for Public Opinion Research.

9. New York Times national health care survey. New York Times. March, 1982. Storrs, CT: Roper Center for Public Opinion Research.

10. NBC News. June 9, 1989. Storrs, CT: Roper Center for Public Opinion Research.

11. Erskine H. The polls: health insurance. Public Opin Q 1975; 39:128–43.

12. Etheredge L. Universal health insurance: lessons of the 1970s, prospects for the 1990s. Front Health Serv Manage 1990; 6(4):3–35.

13. Waldman S. National health insurance proposals. Washington, DC: Social Security Administration, 1974:21–44. (SSA 74–11920.)

14. Feder J, Holahan J, Marmor T, eds. National health insurance: conflicting goals and policy choices. Washington, DC: Urban Institute, 1980.

15. Insuring the uninsured: options and analysis. Special Committee on Aging serial 100-0. Washington, DC: Congressional Research Service, 1988.

16. Committee on Ways and Means. National health insurance resource book. Washington, DC: Government Printing Office, 1974.

17. Blendon RJ, Taylor H. Views on health care: public opinion in three nations. Health Aff (Millwood) 1989; 8(1):149–57.

18. Smith TW. The welfare state in cross-national perspective. Public Opin Q 1987; 51(3):404–21.

19. Dean JA, Dean AG, Burton A, Dicker K. Epi Info, version 3. Stone Mountain, Ga.: United Service Organization, 1988.

20. Melville K, Doble J. The public's perspective on social welfare reform. New York: Public Agenda Foundation, 1988.

21. Fortune Magazine survey, July 1942. In: Cantril H, ed. Public opinion, 1935-1946. Westport, CT: Greenwood Press, 1978:440.

22. America: a unique outlook? The Public Perspective. March/April 1990: 113.

23. Blendon RJ, Donelan K. The 1988 election: how important was health? Health Aff (Millwood) 1989; 8(3):6–15.

24. Watts W, Free LA. State of the nation. New York: Universe, 1973:288.

25. Opinion Research Corporation. Public opinion index. December 31, 1976. Storrs, CT: Roper Center for Public Opinion Research.

26. Louis Harris and Associates. March 1990. Storrs, CT: Roper Center for Public Opinion Research.

27. Pokorny G. Report card on health care.

Health Manage Q 1988; 10:4-5.

28. Employee Benefit Research Institute. Public attitudes on health insurance. Med Benefits 1989; 6(18):3–4.

29. Goodman LJ, Steiber SR. Public support for National Health Insurance. Am J Public Health 1981; 71:1105–8.

30. American Institute of Public Opinion. May 20, 1938. In: Cantril H, ed. Public opinion, 1935–1946. Westport, CT: Greenwood Press, 1978:400.

31. Opinion roundup: what Americans are saying about taxes. Public Opin Q 1989; 11(6):21–6.

32. Bureau of the Census. Statistical abstract of the United States: 1989. Washington, DC: Government Printing Office, 1989.

33. National Opinion Research Center. General social survey 1989. Storrs, CT: Roper Center for Public Opinion Research.

34. Gallup Poll. March 28, 1990. Storrs, CT: Roper Center for Public Opinion Research.

35. 1987 Health care outlook annual report. New York: Louis Harris and Associates, September 1987:151–4.

36. AARP Research and Data Resources. Opinions of Americans age 45 and over of the Medicare Catastrophic Act. Washington, DC: American Association of Retired Persons, 1989. 37. Medicare Catastrophic Coverage Act survey for the Coalition for Affordable Health Care. Richmond, Va.: Wirthlin Group, May 15, 1989.

38. Harvey LK, Shubat SC. AMA surveys of physician and public opinion on health care issues 1989. Chicago: American Medical Association, 1988.

39. ABC News/Washington Post. August 1989. Storrs, CT: Roper Center for Public Opinion Research.

40. Yankelovich, Skelly and White. Monitoring attitudes of the public, 1979. June 1979. Storrs, CT: Roper Center for Public Opinion Research.

41. Health insurance and the uninsured: background data and analysis. Special Committee on Aging serial 100–1. Washington, DC: Congressional Research Service, 1988:101–92.

42. Division of National Cost Estimates. National health expenditures, 1986–2000. Health Care Financ Rev 1987; 8(4):1–36.

43. Blendon RJ. The public's view of the future of health care. JAMA 1988; 259:3587–93.

44. CBS News/New York Times. January 13, 1990. Storrs, CT: Roper Center for Public Opinion Research.

45. Smith TW. That which we call welfare by any other name would smell sweeter. Public Opin Q 1987; 51:75–83.

26

Beyond The Words: The Politics of Health Care Reform

James A. Morone

How do we introduce reforms in America? The common-sense answer at which political scientists have been hooting for years imagines a rational search for solutions to contemporary problems: a problem arises, policy makers seek solutions, they choose the one that seems best.

Political scientists generally take a different view. Political organizations, they argue, rarely operate so sensibly. For example, instead of searching for solutions to problems, a public official is just as likely to be searching for problems that permit him to employ a favored solution. American public policy is said to be forged in a barely organized anarchy where an almost random amalgam of problems, solutions, institutions, and players drift in and out of the process in no particular order. As a result, the political consequences—our public policies—are erratic and difficult to predict.[1]

This paper aims at a middle ground. My purpose is to map the political terrain in which health system reformers operate. While acknowledging the political flux, I analyze current policy choices within the recurring and predictable dimensions of American reform.

First, I lay out the major problems on the health care agenda, emphasizing the political past and potential future of our troubles. The next section turns to solutions; I argue that American reformers constantly return to the same types of answers and consistently shun others. Section three focuses on what we have done to the institutions that link problems and solutions—private markets and government regulators. Finally, I examine four broad policy alternatives for the l990s: Pluralism, the code word for advocates of competition; an expansion of Medicaid; what might be described as implicit or covert government programs; and national health insurance—the N words which should not be uttered by liberal proponents. Generally speaking, I expect American health policy to progress through each of these solutions, one at a time, slowly "slouching" toward national health insurance.

Problems

Political scientists have long contended that the issues on the political agenda are, in themselves, a political matter. Different interests compete to turn their concerns into national priorities. Naturally, objective conditions (say rising health care costs) set the boundaries of the debate, but the political key is how those conditions are interpreted.[2]

Today the American health policy agenda is especially crowded with dilemmas competing for attention. Perhaps the most important are rising costs, uninsured citizens and account-ability for the medical system as a whole. Consider each in turn.

Rising health costs have been a fixture in American health policy for more than two decades. The usual perception is that when Medicare was implemented in 1966, costs began to soar. In fact, costs were already rising. In the five years preceding Medicare health care costs rose 13 percent as a proportion of Gross National Product while in the five "cost crisis" years that followed they rose 20 percent.[3] However, before Medicare, policy makers simply interpreted rising costs within the framework of the dominant issue; inflation was one more barrier to access. After Medicare, inflation was suddenly being financed partially through tax revenue, and costs swiftly became the major health policy concern.

Twenty years later costs continue to rise. In 1965 health spending consumed 6 percent of GNP, in 1975 8.4 percent, in 1980 9.1 percent, in 1986, 10.9 percent. Despite a steady tattoo of cost-containment efforts, the overall rate of growth has not even been slowed. In 1986, for example, costs rose 0.3 percent of GNP, exactly the average since 1980; the hospital and physician sectors grew at annual rates of 10.2 percent and 11.9 percent while general inflation rose just 1.1 percent. Moreover, the health sector consumes a larger portion of the economy in the United States than in any other member of the Organization for Economic Cooperation and Development (OECD). The nearest competitor is France, 13 percent lower at 9.4 percent of Gross Domestic Product (GDP). Be-

Reprinted by permission of the author from the *Bulletin of the New York Academy of Medicine* 66, no. 4 (July–August 1990), pp. 344–65. asfdf

Presented as part of the National Health Policy Seminar *Toward a Health Care Financing Strategy for the Nation* held by the Committee on Medicine in Society of the New York Academy of Medicine from October 1986 to August 1988.

tween 1982 and 1986 the health sector grew more rapidly in the United States than it did in all but three OECD nations (Finland, Iceland, and Switzerland). In fact, during the past four years most industrialized nations saw a decline in the health sector's portion of their GDP. [4] Such figures suggest the unambiguous failure of American cost control policy. Nevertheless, the entire matter—still a "problem" by any objective measure—has diminished somewhat as a policy issue. Although the United States is spending more and 73 percent of its citizens label medical fees "unreasonable," cost control has lost its monopoly at the top of the American health care agenda.[5]

The new policy dilemma is the roughly 38 million Americans who have no health insurance. Many of the poor and low wage earners cannot pay for their health care. Their sheer number places enormous pressure on medical providers who treat them. The problem has become visible largely because of programs designed to deal with rising costs.

Until recently Americans dealt with indigent care in two ways. Medicaid paid directly for many poor and near poor patients. Perhaps more important, loose private funding arrangements (partially subsidized by the tax code) permitted providers to treat indigent patients and to shift the costs to their properly insured patients. Public welfare programs were, in effect, backed by an elaborate private network of cross subsidies. In response to the cost problem, however, both public and private payers began restricting reimbursements to providers. States began to cut back their Medicaid programs until, by the mid-1980s, they covered less than 40 percent of the population under the official poverty line. Worse, such private payers as commercial insurers began to cut back their own payments, jeopardizing traditional cross subsidies for the poor.

For a long time the United States could have it both ways—limited government programs and relatively widespread access to care. For reasons explored in the next section, Americans have always preferred implicit solutions

(such as private cross subsidies) to public relief programs (such as Medicaid). The unravelling of the former now places an enormous access problem squarely on the public agenda. Demands for reform come not just from the poor, who often find it difficult to control the policy agenda, but from the more politically weighty medical institutions, which are being pushed into deficit by patients who cannot pay. Solutions to the new problem are complicated by failure to resolve the old one by steadily rising medical costs.

Finally, while the related problems of inflation and indigents dominate contemporary discourse, a host of secondary issues compete for attention: long-term care in an aging society, medical education, prenatal care, the AIDS epidemic, and malpractice suits to name a few. A large array of changes—mostly designed as cost control devices—have been set into place with little concern for their cumulative effect or their impact on medicine. It is not clear what the American stew of regulatory controls, financial incentives, and reimbursement innovations is adding up to. However, it raises a profound underlying question: who is accountable for American medicine?

Various models of accountability are, of course, available. We can look to government, to citizen planning boards, to large corporate capitalists, to individual consumers or—as is the case in most nations—to the profession itself. However, the United States is trying all the models at once, diffusing responsibility and driving the medical sector in unpredictable, perhaps dangerous, directions. Whatever the cumulative effect, one clear upshot is an enormous encroachment on physician autonomy. The entire range of innovations ultimately share a common ideal: reshaping provider behavior to some murky standard of efficiency. As a result, a vague sense of gloom has developed among many physicians, especially younger ones. The general public seems to concur. Three quarters of them believe that the "health care system requires fundamental change" while only a fifth agree that "it works pretty well." [6] The matter of accountability—which raises such

fundamental questions as what kind of medical system we are to have, and the nature of the physicians' role within it—constitutes perhaps the most significant and intensely felt problem lurking just off the contemporary policy agenda. Though it complicates almost all our policy debates, it is a difficult problem to articulate, much less address. And, like the issue of indigent care, it is the kind of problem which the American political system is especially maladroit at reforming. The following section explains why.

Solutions

Solutions available to American policy makers are comparatively limited and tend to repeat a set of distinctive patterns. These limits flow from a familiar ideology: Americans do not like government. Perhaps because, in Tocqueville's celebrated phrase, Americans "were born free without having to become so," they have traditionally distrusted governmental activity, socialist enterprises, and welfare policies.[7] Each is viewed more as a threat to individual liberty than as a mechanism for the public good. Infused by this wariness of their state, Americans designed a government with relatively weak powers and studded it with checks and balances designed to thwart unwanted actions far more easily than to undertake desired ones. Fragmented political authority—attenuated parties, the separation of political branches, federalism—create barriers to any reform. More generally, there are at least three interrelated consequences for political reformers.

First, since Americans distrust both politics and politicians, they tend to seek solutions that rely on neither. Rather than empower leaders to make political choices (say bargaining over medical prices), they restlessly seek out mechanistic, self-enforcing, automatic solutions that can be set in place without further politics or even self-conscious deliberation. For more than a century, reformers have sought permanent policy fixes. The benign, invisible hand of a properly functioning market is the paradigmatic case. However, markets are only the most often repeated expression of an ideal deeply imbedded in American political culture.

The same ideal animates a broad range of contemporary health care reforms. Whether HMOs, DRGs, capitation, regional health planning, or medical vouchers, all share the progressive aspiration that with a bit of tinkering and a few new incentives the problems of the health care system can be solved without politics. The health care system will, it is imagined, run itself without the intrusion of government regulators making choices sullied by politics. Each policy proposal promises some kind of magic fix.

Second, and relatedly, emphasis on policy gimmicks leads to devaluation of good public administration. If hard choices are to be automatic ones, there is no need to find public officials capable of difficult judgments. The recruitment patterns, social standing, and reward structures of public service all reflect this low priority. The result is both less effective administration and a reliance on implicit or covert solutions.

For example, public administrators are, in effect, empowered to negotiate with hospitals under the technical cover of DRGs. Effective administrators might actually employ the device to make thoughtful choices about which medical services to reward or restrain—essentially setting social values on different services.[8] More often, those values are set by default. In either case, the reality of administrators setting hospital prices is obscured by the politically useful illusion that DRGs are "scientifically" derived. The search for a magic fix results both in less concern about effective administrators and reliance on implicit policy choices. The two consequences are analytically distinct. Competent administrators can expand their scope of authority by making conscious but hidden choices. Nevertheless, burying their deliberations retards development of an effective public service.

Third, distaste for government action is articulated most forcefully in the well known reaction against welfare programs. The United States is, as Rodwin puts it, "commonly regarded as a welfare laggard." European leaders such as Bismark or Lloyd George offered welfare benefits in a bid for working class support; Americans worry more about prompting laziness than promoting loyalty.[9] Despite their relatively large numbers, poor people are unpopular clients for public programs. Social welfare programs that have flourished have been those that mix the less needy into the clientele, for example, social security, disability insurance, Medicare.

Reformers searching for solutions to contemporary American dilemmas are bound by these aspects of American reform: faith in gimmicks, an ascetic's stance toward public administration, a penchant for implicit solutions, and a marked preference for respectable clients. These tendencies shaped past programs, constrain current possibilities, and are likely to characterize the fate of future policies. The next sections trace the evolution of American institutions within this broad ideological rubric. I focus on the popular, admittedly sketchy, distinction between markets and government—settings that respectively elicit the most enthusiasm and the most skepticism in the United States.

Institutions: Politics and Markets

Solutions must be set in institutions. In the broadest general terms, Americans value private sector competition and are wary of governmental intervention. However, the health care politics of the past two decades have significantly altered both the symbols and the realities associated with these categories. This section examines some of the changes and speculates on the implications for contemporary health care reform.

Markets

Free market competition offers a powerful image and a politically effective solution. Over time, different political interests have infused it with entirely different meanings and advanced it as an answer to all kinds of troubles. I shall argue that the recent difficulties of the market approach changes the politics of health system reform—essentially shifting the action into the government sector.

Originally, free medical markets meant deferring to providers. In effect, the market was a circumlocution for professional autonomy and power. The profession claimed control over both medical practice and health care policy. The frequent invocation of market capitalism did not rule out government action. Rather, a broad range of policy programs which ceded public authority to professional judgments were enacted with the enthusiastic support of provider groups. (Licensure regulations, The Hospital Construction Act, popularly known as Hill Burton, and the National Institutes of Health all illustrate the pattern.) On the other hand, reforms that were perceived as threats to professional autonomy (national health insurance, for instance) were loudly decried as tyrannical, usurpatious, and socialistic. Physicians warned against destruction of free markets as a way to muster political allies against government incursions onto their political and professional turf. In effect, they mobilized precisely the political biases described in the preceding section.

As long as the issue on the political agenda was insuring access to care, deferring to providers was a plausible policy. After all, Americans thought their medicine was the envy of the world—the only problem was seeing to it that everybody shared its benefits. Professionals could claim to know how best to do so. However, the politics of deference ended when Medicare authorized massive public funding with minimal public control. The effort to fit a new kind of program into the old institutional forms swiftly changed the dominant health policy problem from access to cost control.

The new problem promoted revision of the old solution. Deferring to providers was an unlikely way to cut costs. The same free market symbol that the profession had long used in its struggle for autonomy was now turned against it. The free market ideal had a new meaning. Now it was a way to discipline providers, to force them to behave more efficiently. The task, argued the new market advocates, was to tinker with the incentives in the medical system until each actor was responding to the proper cues. Consumers would get incentives to shop for high quality at a low price; payers would also shop for the best deal. Providers would race to win customers. Either they would become more efficient or lose their customers and go broke.[11]

There were many variations of the free market argument. Almost by definition, they evinced the classic characteristics of policy solutions in the United States: they avoided government (and the dead hand of regulatory administration) and instead promised a set of automatic, mechanistic answers that, once set in place, would operate more or less permanently.

Ironically, setting the solution into place was complicated by the same ideology that promoted the solution in the first place. Much of its appeal stemmed from reliance on private initiative rather than public intervention; yet introducing a comprehensive market system required carefully coordinating a wide array of government actions (including HMO regulations, adjustments in the tax law, changes in antitrust policy, and so on). After the Nixon, Ford, and Carter administrations tinkered with these changes on the political margins, the Reagan administration finally appeared to give full head to what was soon known as the competition revolution. Crucially, it did not introduce the many regulatory innovations required to launch a comprehensive competitive effort. Instead, the administration encouraged each health care actor to harness competition in whatever manner it saw fit. A wide range of devices—competitive, quasicompetitive, even noncompetitive—were unleashed on the health care system in the name of free markets and efficiency.

The result was a fierce effort among health care payers to constrain their own costs. Although each took a different fiscal tack, all introduced their efforts with the rhetoric of competition and efficiency. Corporations offered their employees the option of enrolling in HMOs. Many left traditional insurance carriers and self insured; some negotiated special deals with health care providers through Preferred Provider Organizations (PPOs). Blue Cross tried to restrain its own premiums with its highly touted "managed care," then hedged its bets by sponsoring HMOs. Commercial insurers responded with their own cost controlling schemes, in many cases promising lower premiums in exchange for higher patient cost sharing. Medicare introduced its complex DRG price setting scheme as a form of competition. Medicaid and Medicare (Part B) simply froze fees.

Perhaps what is most remarkable about all this activity is the extent to which it failed. Indeed, the competition revolution has exacerbated the major dilemmas of contemporary health care policy.

In the first place, managerial innovations have not controlled costs. As noted above, health care inflation quickened relative to GNP during the Reagan years. Moreover, competition among payers may have contributed to the problem. It has forced enormous administrative costs on health providers. Worse, the very notion of multiple payers may have an inflationary bias. After all, many of their cost control strategies from DRGs to PPOs are simply institutional devices through which payers negotiate with providers—one of the keys to Western European cost control strategies as well. However, Americans undermine the bargaining strategy by establishing a multitude of bargainers in the name of competition and choice. Providers seek to maintain their incomes by shifting costs from the payers most effective at controlling their own costs (notably, Medicare and Medicaid) to those least effective (business corporations have proved notoriously ineffective).[12] In effect, providers are offered a multiplicity of safety valves through which to escape tough cost control programs. Ultimately, many payers, each competing to keep its own costs down, facilitate continued inflationary pressure on everybody's costs.

A second distressing consequence is the rise of the uninsured. This follows logically from the competition among payers whose incentives are to pay as little as possible for their own clients and nothing at all for anybody else. Increased patient cost sharing and declining health care insurance coverage are partially responsible. However, the still more fundamental problem, noted above, is that an elaborate system of cross subsidies is coming to an end. The problem is complicated by increasing fragmentation of the risk pool.

Since a relatively small number of patients consume a large portion of medical resources, the most effective way to reduce payments is not through tough negotiating or efficient managerial devices but, rather, avoiding poorer risks. Incentives for competing payers are clear: pay as little as possible for your own clients, insure the healthiest possible market segment, and, above all, do not bear anybody else's costs. Providers in turn face a corresponding set of incentives: find patients whose payers pay relatively more, shift costs from the payers who pay less to those who pay more, seek less sick patients (who are less costly to treat), and, above all else, avoid nonpayers, who will demolish your reputation for efficiency. Thus, everyone's market incentives are similar: seek the healthy and shun the sick. The result is fast erosion of the medical commons, a destruction of the very notion of community.

What is not yet fully recognized is the enormity of the policy task that confronts us as a result. Americans have traditionally had political trouble converting previously implicit solutions—solved behind the political scene with limited government action and funding—into explicit programs. Now that the old system of hidden cross subsidies has ended, we face the problem of designing programs that will extend some sort of medical coverage to 38 million people. The sheer numbers of the uninsured are staggering. To put them in perspective, the number of Americans without health insurance today is more than twice the size of Medicare's constituency when that program was first implemented.

Throughout the 1970s policy makers looked hopefully to the promises of competition. Here was an efficient, apparently painless solution to the problem of health care costs which fit traditional American ideologies as well as the increasingly conservative temper of the time. By the middle of the 1980s, a raft of new policies had been (not completely honestly) introduced and celebrated as forms of competition. As the troubles of the health care sector worsened and multiplied, the image of an efficient, painless, competitive solution began to vanish. It is becoming clear that Americans will have to solve their medical sector dilemmas without the hidden, automatic, nongovernment gimmick implicit in the magic of competitive markets.

Government

The difference between health politics in the United States and those in other industrialized nations is usually taken to be a question of financing—Americans don't have national health insurance. There is another, often overlooked difference every bit as important for the politics of reform: the comparative incapacity of American government.

The general reluctance to develop competent public administration has been particularly disabling for health care policies. Negotiating with a well organized, highly interested, highly trained profession requires skill and competence. Relying instead on pluralism, gimmicks, and implicit solutions (honored as choice, competition, and proper incentives) may conform to the American spirit of reform but offers little opportunity to control the medical sector or to manage its problems.

However, as the market solution has declined, American government has slowly developed its capacity for sustained administrative action within the health arena. The progress has been slow, hesitant, obscure, and often contradictory. Nevertheless, what appears, at first blush, to be a random succession of programs can also be interpreted as the government's slow progress from deference to control.[13]

To illustrate the point, consider the evolving political and administrative realities that underlay the major postwar health policies. The Hill Burton Act, for example, included elaborate legislative precautions designed to proscribe any administrative meddling in medicine; the federal government promised financing without controls. Almost 20 years later, Medicare appeared to carry

on in the same tradition—the legislation opens with stern prohibitions against any governmental "supervision or control over the practice of medicine." (Social Security Act, 1965, Section 101) However, in this case, Congress protested so loudly precisely because it had broken with a half century of deference and passed the entitlement over the bitter objection of organized medicine. When funding without "supervision or control" proved inflationary, the federal government inched further into the medical sphere. The Peer Review program (PSROs, passed in 1972) appeared to be a timid capitulation to organized medicine in the face of the cost crisis. Although it created local boards mandated to constrain physician practice, the boards were not permitted to use national standards, to collect national data, or to place nonphysicians in decision making roles. On the political surface, the federal government appeared to avoid the prospect of building up its administrative authority or competence. However, the reality was a new albeit timidly asserted mission; for the first time, public agencies were seeking to reverse the practice patterns of the profession, to encourage physicians to do less.[14]

The National Health Planning Act, signed in January 1975, turned the attention of health policy analysts to local boards mandated to write health plans and to oversee capital expenses in medical facilities. The local boards, Health Systems Agencies (HSAs), derived their authority largely from state "Certificate of Need" Laws and they sought legitimacy, not by deferring to physicians but by turning to the public. The policies of these health agencies revolved, in large measure, on the apparently bizarre effort to get citizens "broadly representative" of their communities to constrain capital expenditures. The entire episode still baffles most observers. What was the purpose of asking lay people to face aroused hospital administrators in packed meeting halls and vote whether to grant exceptions to incomprehensible bureaucratic standards that ostensibly forbad more beds or machines? Once again, the federally designed effort seemed to go out of its way to avoid competent national administration.

However, something important was happening.

Most observers look at the long, late night HSA meetings and ask the apparently sensible questions: Did the HSAs stick to their tasks and say "no" to providers? Did doing so reduce health care costs? The answers are occasionally and no. But they are the wrong questions. What is important about those late night meetings is not that the providers usually won but that they had to argue their case before lay people in the first place. Those arguments took place in communities across the country. They broke the long tradition of deferring medical matters to medical providers. In many communities, new constituents—community leaders, businessmen, public officials—continued to play active roles in medical politics even though the health agencies soon faded from the scene. It is no coincidence that the first American laymen to cross the boundaries of professional dominance and cast judgments about medical matters were not public administrators. They were citizens "broadly representative" of the people. New kinds of controversial government action are often introduced by the latter, rarely by the former. In short, reformers nervous about the legitimacy of their reforms have often made progress against American skepticism about the role of government with a call to "the people."[15]

While the Health Agencies did not transform American health politics, they were a critical step in the progress from the deference of Hill Burton to the development of an independent public capacity to shape health policy, even to the point of significantly altering the practice patterns of the profession. To note just a few examples of the programs which soon followed: in a handful of states, public officials set the prices for all hospital services, regardless of payer. In states such as New Jersey and Massachusetts, broad government programs approximate the publicly mandated health insurance schemes that have long been decried as "socialistic." Medicare's hospital reimbursement method (DRGs) was designed to effect the way physicians practice medicine. By the late 1980s federal officials were proposing changes in Medicare physician payment as a mechanism to promote some medical specialties over others.

This is not to deny that governmental health policies remain inchoate and contradictory. Reforms such as those just noted are rarely administered in a fashion to inspire confidence in the American public sector. However, in the larger historical perspective, they are the latest steps in a steady progress away from the deferential politics that once typified American health policy. Governmental capacity has grown on both the state and the national level; so has the range of interventions that the public sector can legitimately attempt (when it finds the political will—no small caveat, of course).[16]

The upshot for reformers, I think is clear, Americans are most comfortable with their market cure; however, a decade of complication has harmed, perhaps ruined, the appealing market image of a simple, painless, democratic solution that can reduce inflation while making providers more responsive without the meddling of government. Even under the Reagan presidency (indeed, especially under Reagan), the government continued a long trend toward assuming a central role in medical policy. The host of new problems created by old policies is likely to continue the trend. Unfortunately, there is a problematic tension between the politically simple and the politically sensible: more gimmicks, hidden solutions, middle class clients, and weak administrators are likely to win approval. Simple, carefully designed administrative programs might be more effective, but they remain politically difficult to win. Tension between the politically possible and programmatically sensible remains the central conflict for political reformers as what Victor Fuchs calls the counterrevolution—the backlash against payer reforms—gets under way.[17]

Into the 1990S: Contemporary Reform Proposals

The following section considers four types of reform proposals in the context of the problems, solutions, and changing institutional frameworks described above. On the surface at least, the

reforming task is complicated by shifts in each one of these dimensions.

Health system problems have become interrelated: continuing inflation is now linked to an enormous access problem and relatively widespread anxiety about the rapidly changing nature of the medical sector. Proposals that seek to address one trouble while exacerbating another are apt to be politically unstable and relatively short lived. Moreover, the most facile solution is gone, at least for the moment. Calling for free market competition in health care no longer evokes the same clear, easy, political resonance. At the same time, the role and capacity of the government has continued to evolve. However, the underlying political instincts that led Americans to celebrate the former and doubt the latter remain. Reform proposals continue to embody the faith in automatic solutions, implicit rather than explicit policies, and hostility toward the "undeserving" poor.

Pluralism

A host of different perspectives march under the amorphous banner of pluralism. Essentially, pluralists argue that Americans should keep their options open. Since no obviously correct solutions have emerged, Americans should encourage diversity and experimentation. States can each pursue reforms that fit the local political and medical cultures, thus restoring an old ideal of American states as laboratories, where many different experiments can be tried before policies are thrust on the nation as a whole. At the same time, private payers and entrepreneurs can continue their own efforts to promote efficiency and to cut costs. The key to the pluralist argument is simple: the federal government should avoid any bold new departures; it should avoid constraining future choices; indeed, it would do best by doing nothing at all.

The pluralist view rests on a mix of perceptions and prejudices. It begins with the perception that a systematic effort to introduce market principles has fallen from political favor—tainted by current public and private programs sold as competition. Consequently, current reforms are likely to involve active

government. Related prejudices are familiar and reflect all the usual patterns in the American reforming mindset. The pluralists feel a deep and hostile skepticism toward the government, particularly national government. They believe that private sector solutions derived, somehow, from business principles will ultimately work. They constantly refer to the better management and improved efficiency that emanate from corporate benefits officers or for-profit medical enterprises. And they place their faith in the scattershot of largely payer efforts to induce efficiency through such mechanisms as managed care, capitation, or "a new generation of insurance products."[18]

Clearly, the political image of health care competition has been reconstructed once again, and now appears in the call for national government restraint along with private and local initiatives. Many old market images are present: avoid government coercion, maximize free choice and flexibility, seek incentives for efficiency, be pragmatic, trust in business principles. And in deference to the academic proponents of this view, a new argument has attached itself to the list: study the consequences of the many options.

Like the original proponents of free market medicine, this new generation takes comfort in the usual reluctance to press big new government programs when there is no major crisis at hand. And, as the pluralists see it, there is no major crisis in medicine. On balance, they view the pastiche of public and private forces that are currently transforming medicine as a reasonably good thing. Pluralists point out that the length of stay in the nation's hospitals is falling. New medical care settings (even sectors) are proliferating. Ultimately, this perspective is rooted in what might be called a business school faith—all this activity, all this innovation, all these new forms of private sector administration and management must be on balance a good thing.

In fact, I believe that the pluralist view is exactly wrong. Furthermore, it is precisely the mindset that created the current problems in the medical system. First, a multiplicity of public and private regulators are less likely to constrain costs, regardless of their many innovative gimmicks. These devices amount to a host of different ways of negotiating with providers. By opting for a large number of them, Americans invite medical providers to shift costs from more effective regulators to the less effective and from more effectively regulated health care settings to those less carefully constrained. The image of choice is powerful. But the choice in this context is illusory. It is choice among many inefficient efforts to control costs—indeed, they are inefficient precisely because there are so many. As Eli Ginzberg puts it, an "open ended" third party payment system is invariably an inflationary one.[19]

Secondly, the pluralist mode is hard on the poor. In theory, relatively healthy groups that work their way out of the general risk pool stand to profit: the corporations that self insure, the new closed panel medical plans that select a healthier than average population, the insurance company that effectively manages its beneficiaries. However, this leaves a weaker, sicker pool less protected by classic insurance principles. The pluralistic ideal—let each payer worry about its own costs—gives each the same incentive: avoid the weak, the sick, and the poor. Harvey Sapolsky terms it a race to "beggar thy neighbor."[20] These are not unfortunate side effects. They are the direct incentives structured into a health care system which sets aside ideals of community—of a single communal insurance pool—for notions of individualistic competition.

The problem of the poor is made far more complicated by the American view of welfare. Fragmenting the communal pool and exposing the poor creates a situation that is conceptually uncomplicated but politically almost impossible. It requires large public expenditures toward groups who are very unpopular program clients in an era of large budget deficits. The next solution takes up the question directly.

Finally, the pluralist ideal of multiple payers each pursuing efficiency in its own way is apt to make life increasingly miserable in the medical sector itself. Foreign observers are already astonished at the diminished autonomy of American physicians. A wide multiplicity of gimmicks and incentives are now designed to reshape their behavior. Taken individually, most are not yet particularly powerful, but their cumulative effect is another matter. As Vladeck points out, the lack of public financing creates more rather than less invasive regulations, from both public and private sources.[21]

Fixing Medicaid: The Rationalist Perspective

On the face of it, the sensible solution to the problem of indigent care is expansion of Medicaid. Of course, we could fiddle with many of the details, even change the name, but now that the system of hidden private subsidies has come apart, many thoughtful observers are calling for the public sector to pick up the slack. Indeed, proponents range from liberals horrified at the size of the indigent population to pluralist corporate executives frustrated by inability to avoid the indigent costs shifted to them.

However, in politics the most direct route between two points is often not a straight line. A new national effort in welfare medicine may be good logic but it is poor politics. Before considering how to fix Medicaid, consider why it is broken.

Welfare medicine is difficult to legislate in the United States. And, unlike most other areas—where winning the legislation poses the most political difficulty—welfare medicine is even more difficult to maintain. The poor, as noted above, make a politically unpopular clientele. Their unpopularity is only partially offset by the indirect beneficiaries, the medical profession. When health care costs rise more quickly than general inflation, government officials face a difficult choice. They can spend relatively more on Medicaid, perhaps at the expense of a more popular constituency, or they can cut the program back. The record of the past two decades is unambiguous—officials chose the latter.[22]

These are predictable political consequences as long as medical inflation runs faster than general inflation. In effect, public officials are asked steadily to increase the size of a program aimed at an unpopular constituency. The pressure of deficits, intermittent tax revolts, and competing priorities exacerbates the problem. And Medicaid (even along with Medicare) does not permit public policy makers a large enough lever to control health system costs. The predictable result is a succession of freezes, cuts, and cost control devices that restrict growth of Medicaid programs in the face of medical inflation. Over time, government officials seek to control their own costs and, as a consequence, induce either cost shifting or bad debt.

In short, restoring Medicaid—making it as it should have been made from the start—is an important task and an appealing reform. However, if attempted without a simultaneous and successful assault on general medical inflation, advocates should be prepared for the same painful political treadmill of the past two decades—steady erosion of benefits and beneficiaries in an effort to control program costs.

The political lesson is not a new one. Programs for the poor tend to be poor programs in the United States. The problem is especially exacerbated in an area with a high rate of inflation. Protecting the health care of the poor requires containing the health care costs of everyone else. Public programs aimed only at the poor do not have the leverage with which to do so. Instead, they leave public officials with incentives to cut back the programs to control their own costs—effectively shifting the problems of the poor to providers and private payers. If pluralists think too much about the costs to private payers, many rationalist liberals do not worry about them enough. Reformers will need to think in global health system terms if the reforms they manage to win are to be maintained.

The New Jersey Model: Semi-implicit, Semi-global

The conundrum for reformers is clear: how to address both costs and access in a political system skeptical of government intervention and welfare programs? A third category of contemporary proposals seeks to do so, essentially by tailoring programmatic details to political necessity. One example is the New

Jersey model, although all sorts of variations are possible.[23] The key is to focus equally on both the proposed program and its political effects.

In New Jersey public officials used DRGs to set prices for all payers. At the same time they established an uncompensated care pool, essentially taxing each payer (public and private) to assist the hospitals that served the uninsured. Thus, one program addressed both the problems of inflation and indigents.

The crux of the cost containment effort was not DRGs but the introduction of a single negotiator empowered to set prices throughout the system. In effect, this limits cost shifting and provides state officials a reasonably powerful lever against rising costs. Of course, the extent to which they actually use their negotiating leverage is a function of both the will and the skill of state health officials. The related problem of indigent care was addressed, essentially, by taking each hospital's uncompensated care load and dividing it among the major payers very roughly according to their proportion of the total hospital bill. There is plenty of dispute about the merits of the New Jersey system; opponents claim that it stifles innovation, retards new forms of health service delivery, and rewards inefficient management. However, no one doubts its role in assisting, perhaps saving, inner city hospitals that serve the poor.

The details, however, are less important than the political effects. Here is a program that appears incremental, obscure, pragmatic, and technocratic; at the same time, it seems to avoid welfare, administrative interventions, and new taxes. Although none of these impressions is entirely accurate, they are nevertheless crucial. They substantially reduce the political barriers to the reform. Consider the political pieces one at a time.

First, "extending DRGs from Medicare to all payers and factoring the costs of uncompensated care into the prices" is incremental. American policy makers are always wary of bold new policy ventures. American institutions are designed to deflect them. Extending DRGs is an incremental step. It takes a price-setting mechanism in place for one payer and extends it to others.

Second, it sits easily in American reforming traditions. Rather than explicitly empowering public officials to jawbone prices with providers, it offers an apparently scientific, self-equilibrating mechanism designed to force efficiency on the medical sector. Here is a gimmick that "objectively" sets a price; efficient providers do the work for less and make money, the inefficient won't and don't. As noted above, this can be seen as a somewhat devious way to introduce the centrally negotiated prices that characterize many European systems. However, it does so in a thoroughly American fashion. It relies on an efficiency gimmick while avoiding the appearance of active intervention by public administrators.

Third, it does not look like welfare. "Factoring the costs of uncompensated care into DRG prices" hardly sounds like a liberal effort to sneak a free lunch to the poor. On the contrary, the direct beneficiaries are not poor people but the hospitals that serve them. In short, the program establishes a thoroughly respectable institutional client, entitling the poor only in an indirect—and politically obscure—fashion.

Fourth, the program buries much of the tax hike for covering indigents in the premiums of the private sector. Each payer carries a portion of the burden. Although economists are often critical of such "hidden taxes," poor economics often make good politics. No doubt the program's budget projections will annoy economists still further when cost increases in Medicare and Medicaid are offset by projected savings resulting from the all payer system, thus rendering the whole enterprise budget neutral in "the long run."

Finally, the politics of this proposal are obscure. They are difficult to explain, hard to turn into a cause, unlikely to harm a legislative career. Reforms that stay out of the political limelight are more likely to win. This is especially true of reforms directed (albeit indirectly) at the poor. By avoiding broad symbols, the proposal reduces the likelihood of bureaucrat or welfare bashing. Such relative obscurity is a significant political advantage for a program designed to address the twin health sector dilemmas of inflation and poverty.

The model presented here, patterned on the New Jersey case, is just one possibility. The policy proposal does need not turn on DRGs—any other mechanism will do, so long as it is technical, apparently automatic, seems to provide incentives for efficiency, and is reasonably obscure. And while there may be other ways to treat the health care problems of the poor, the trick is to keep it from looking too much like a welfare program. Nor do I mean to propose this as an ideal model; on the contrary, it is full of problems. For example, it focuses only on acute care hospitals, ignoring ambulatory, chronic, and long-term-care settings. Moreover, the complexity of the system may be a political advantage, but it is likely to pose difficulties for both patients and providers.

Still, in the end, I believe that something like this will emerge. The problems of medical inflation and indigents are too pressing to ignore over the long run. Action, when it comes, is likely to be designed for political ease as much as programmatic logic. The key for political reformers and medical leaders is to help to see that these imperatives are balanced. Too much emphasis on political factors results in poorly designed programs; too little emphasis results in irrelevance.

Beyond the N words: The Changing Politics of National Health Insurance

Finally, there is national health insurance. Reformers have tried to win this policy, off and on, for 70 years. Their failure is one of the most distinctive features of the American welfare state. Note, however, that the reform itself has evolved, changing to fit new problems and achieve entirely different ends.

Twenty years ago national health insurance was about an egalitarian health care system, "a right to health care." Today, the old reform is infused with a new content. The new national health insurance is about cost control. The medical system, we are told, will remain inflationary until a single, unitary, mechanism is set in place to control the level of resources that we allocate to health care. Now the key to this policy proposal turns on providing American government the institutional capacity to set a global medical budget. Egalitarian outcomes are merely happy side effects.

Advocates make the argument today, not by referring to conceptions of justice, but by comparing American medical inflation to that of other nations. The Canadian health care experience has become a fixture in debates over American health care financing. As Robert Evans has argued, American and Canadian health expenditures were almost identical (as percentage of GNP) until Canada implemented its national health insurance program, known as Medicare. In the 15 intervening years our costs have continued to rise while theirs are more or less level. By 1987 Americans were spending 2 percent more of their GNP on health care than the Canadians.[24]

The key point is not that the comparative data are beyond dispute. They are not. Rather, it that the dispute over national health insurance now turns on how to control costs effectively. American medicine has no global budgeting mechanism and by far the highest rate of inflation. The new policy question is whether those two matters are related. Does the absence of political mechanisms implicit in national health insurance programs contribute to our continuing inflation? Uwe Reinhardt was answering precisely this question when he told the New York Academy of Medicine: "Americans spend 2 percent of their gross national product for nothing more than the privilege of making the following statement: we have no national health insurance."[26]

If the foreign comparisons are instructive, then rising costs may eventually drive us in the direction of a government centered health system. Significantly, the usual retort is not that the American system is superior for the additional expenditure. The braggadocio with which Americans once made international comparisons has melted before the enormous number of uninsured and the pervasive sense of gloom that permeates American health care. Rather, national comparisons are now set aside as misleading in unpredictable

ways. After all, argue the skeptics, American institutions, political culture, and regulatory mores are different, even peculiar. Bargaining arrangements that work well in a nation that respects public administration (not to mention polite queues) might be a mess in a nation of bureaucrat bashers (and queue jumpers).

If foreign comparisons are only partially instructive, we need a comparable American industry. Harvey Sapolsky argues that there is an obvious case: the American defense industry.[25] Here is another highly technical industry performing services simultaneously vital and baffling to the laymen. In both cases, we must often rely on the same providers: a few high tech-defense firms, the local hospital. Moreover, we set impossibly conflicting values before producers in both sectors. Health providers are asked to square the circle between high quality, broad access, and low costs; likewise, defense contractors are asked for timeliness, high performance objectives, and low cost. In each case, other values are important enough that costs are apt to spin out of control. However, the two industries are funded differently. Health care relies on "open ended" funding from a variety of public and private sources. Defense is funded—like classic national health insurance schemes—by the government.

The differences in cost experiences are remarkable. Health care, as a percentage of GNP, has continued its steady upward spiral, stopping only for a very occasional year such as 1984. In contrast, defense has been kept under political control. Despite occasional rises (1965–1967, 1974–1975), it consumed a steadily diminishing portion of the American economy until the Reagan administration. The Reagan defense build-up illustrates the syndrome of government controlled expenditures: a popular politician articulates a new demand for spending; a large increase in funds is allocated; spending rises relative to other national priorities occur; however, the growth soon runs up against competing national goals, programs, and tax resistance; before long, the growth ends. After the growth of the early and mid-1980s, defense spend-

ing flattened out and began to decline as a percentage of GNP.

No comparison "proves" anything, but mounting evidence suggests that global budgets are the most likely way to take control of rising sectorial costs. What is most significant in political terms is the growing discussion of just this point. It is not often that Americans look abroad for a policy fix for anything.

Despite these intimations of cost control, few policy entrepreneurs are interested in pushing a proposal defeated as often as this one. Still, at least two political constituencies are apt to fare somewhat better in a Canadian style system—one is obvious, the other not.

First, obviously, are the poor. As I have argued above, current incentives are to avoid sick and poor people. The old national health insurance logic was based on a desire to even out the medical differences among classes. That logic has not changed as class differences have grown. Only the blindest hostility to the public sector would lead to the conclusion that poor Americans would be made worse off by a national health care system. Enfolding the poor into a national Social Security style system is likely to give them better health care and set into place political coalitions to protect their gains. Modeling the American system on that of Canada might very well reduce inflation as it assists the poor.

Second, physicians themselves might find relief in a national system. To be sure, it would likely end the steady transfer of national resources to the medical sector, but it would also end the steady diet of new bureaucratic and economic techniques designed to push and pull American physicians into practicing more "efficiently." Most nations with a fixed medical budget defer to providers as to how to allocate those funds. They do not need to change the practice of medicine because they control total costs more directly. In contrast, Americans abjure budgetary limits and try instead their array of gimmicks—PROs, DRGs, PPOs, and on and on. Ironically, nationally financed medicine is likely to mean more professional autonomy over medical matters. It is, of course, an unlikely political deal. However, American physicians could do far worse than to support a national health plan in exchange for increased autonomy, that is, in exchange for an end to the long series of manipulative policies designed to change the way they practice medicine.

A national health plan might be both popular and effective. It might substantially ameliorate the problems of the health care system described above. However, it is radically at odds with the kinds of solutions which have typified American politics. In the short run, all three of the policies noted above are more likely than this one.

And yet, liberals ought to take heart. If we are still a long way from Harry Truman's ideal, we are nevertheless far closer than we were a decade ago. This is so for two reasons: first, the decline of competition and deregulation as the American panacea. And second, the reconstruction of national health insurance from an avowedly liberal device aiming at equity to a strategy for promoting cost control. Cost control is more politically respectable since its clients are the middle class. Politically savvy liberals will emphasize the evolution. The imperatives of cost control may eventually prove harder to resist than the ideal of equity.

I thank Marvin Lieberman, Leonard Robbins, and Theodor J. Litman for their many contributions to this paper.

Notes

1. For a fresh approach to these classic themes see Kingdon, J.: *Agendas and Public Policies*. Boston, Little, Brown, 1984.

2. For an extended analysis of the tension between "objective conditions" and political interpretations see Stone, D.A.: *Policy Paradox and Political Reason*. Boston, Little, Brown, 1988.

3. Computed from Wattenberg, B.J.: *The Statistical History of the United States*. New York, Basic Books, 1976, p. 74.

4. American figures from Anderson G. and Erickson, J.E.: National medical care spending. *Health Affairs* 6:96–101, 1987.

5. OECD figures from Schieber. G.: Trends in international health care spending. *Health Affairs* 6:105–12, 1987.

5. Blendon, R. and Drew Altman, D.: Public Opinion and Health Care Costs. In: *Health Care and its Costs* Schram, C., editor. New York, Norton, 1987. On the other hand, 71% of those who had been treated recently responded that the fees they had been charged were "reasonable."

6. Ibid.

7. De Tocqueville, A.: *Democracy in America*, Lawrence, G., translator. Garden City, N.Y., Doubleday, p. 9. The classic analysis of the American view of government is Hartz, L.: *The Liberal Tradition in America*. New York, Harcourt, Brace and World, 1955. For a recent application to comparative health politics, see Rodwin, V.: American exceptionalism in health politics: the advantages of backwardness. *Med. Care Rev.* 44:119–53, 1987.

8. For a discussion of the implicit value choices in DRG payments see Veatch, R.M.V.: The Implicit Ethics of DRGS. *Seton Hall Conference on the New Jersey All Payer System*, June, 1985. See also Morone, J.A. and Dunham, A.: Slouching to national health insurance, *Yale J. Reg.* 64:101–15, 1988.

9. Rodwin, op. cit., pp. 120–21. On the European uses of welfare benefits, see Starr, P.: *The Social Transformation of American Medicine*. New York. Basic Books, 1982, 237 ff.

10. This was a standard political routine. Real estate interests (against housing legislation), capital (resisting labor), white Southern Democrats (resisting civil rights), the Catholic Church (resisting federal administration reorganization), and the opponents of water fluoridation are among the interests that used similar arguments. Morone, J.A.: *The Democratic Wish*. New York, Basic Books, 1990, ch. 1.

11. Enthoven, A.: Consumer choice health plan. *N. Engl. J. Med.* 298:650–658. 1978. (part 1) and 709–720, 1978 (part 2). In my opinion, the clearest exposition of the market logic remains McClure, W: The medical system under national health insurance: four models. *J. Health Politics Policy Law* 1:22–68, Spring, 1976.

12. Etheredge, L.: Ethics and the new insurance market. *Inquiry* 23:311, 1986.

13. For an elaboration of the themes in this section, see Morone, *op. cit.*, chapter 8.

14. On Hill-Burton, see Thompson, F.: *Health Politics and the Bureaucracy*. Cambridge, MA, MIT Press, 1981, chap. 2. On Medicare see Marmor, T.R.: *The Politics of Medicare*. New York, Aldine, 1973.

15. Morone. op. cit., chap. 8.

16. The point is deftly illustrated for Congressional Politics in Brown, L.: The new activism: Federal health politics revisited. *Bull. N. Y. Acad. Med.* 66:294–317, 1990.

17. Fuchs, V.: The counterrevolution in health care financing. *N. Engl. J. Med.* 316:18, 1987, 1154 ff.

18. The press is full of rather double-edged reports which explain why the latest "products" will succeed where the previous efforts failed. See, for example, Honeywell: Push to track doctors. *New York Times*, February 23, 1988, p. D2. See also Boland: Trends in second generation PPOs. *Health Affairs* 6:75–81, 1987.

19. Ginzberg, E., A hard look at cost containment. *N. Engl. J. Med.* 316:1151–54, 1987.

20. The process is nicely described by Harvey Sapolsky (who dubbed the strategy "a race to beggar thy neighbor." An evaluation of the New Jersey DRG Hospital Payment System," *N. J. Med.* 85, 32–37, 1988.

21. Vladeck, B.: America's hospitals: What's right and what could be better? *Health Affairs* 5:100–07, 1986.

22. Etheredge, op. cit., p. 310.

23. The argument here follows Morone, J.A. and Dunham, A.: Slouching to National Health Insurance. For more detail on the New Jersey case, see Dunham, A. and Morone, J.A., *The Politics of Innovation*. Princeton, N.J., HRET Press, 1983; Sapolsky, H.: *An Evaluation of the New Jersey DRG System;* Windman, M. and Light, P.: *Regulating Perspective Payment*. Ann Arbor, MI, Health Administration Press Perspectives, 1988.

24. Evans, R.: *Strained Mercy*. Toronto, Butterworths, 1984; Finding the levers, finding the courage: lessons from cost containment in North America. *J. Health Politics Policy Law* 11:585–615, 1986. Evans et al. Controlling health expenditure the Canadian reality. *N. Engl. J. Med.* 320:571–77, 1989.

25. Sapolsky, H.: Prospective payment in perspective. *J. Health Politics Policy Law* 11:640–42, 1986.

26. Evans, R. et al.: Controlling health expenditures—the Canadian reality. *N. Engl. J. Med.* 320:571–77, 1989.

27

Tension, Compression, and Shear: Directions, Stresses, and Outcomes of Health Care Cost Control

Robert C. Evans

Health "Costs": Paid, Passed On, or Pocketed?

The public rhetoric surrounding the costs of health care invests them with an almost elemental quality, like gravity or the tides. Vast impersonal forces drive them upward, and the task of health care policy, in every developed society, is to find ways of "controlling" those costs. *Controlling*, almost self-evidently, refers to slowing their growth and limiting their share of overall national income and wealth.

Yet the meaning of *control is* by no means restricted to the placing of limits. The controls of an automobile include the accelerator and the steering wheel, as well as the brakes. *Controlling health care costs* can refer equally well to efforts *to increase* such costs, or to reallocate them across the members of a society.

But would anyone wish to do so? Obviously, yes. The dominant rhetorical tone, and the thrust of explicit policy, may equate control and limitation. But the total outlays which any community makes on health care are simultaneously and by definition the total incomes of the persons who work in, or otherwise provide resources to, the health care industries. Health care "costs" are the "sales" of these industries, the sources of both their personal

Reprinted with permission from *Journal of Health Politics, Policy, and Law* 15, no. 1 (Spring 1990), pp. 101–28. Copyright © 1990 by Duke University Press.

incomes and their professional self-expression.

The providers of health care, in every society, have a powerful economic, but also professional and psychological, interest in "controlling" the costs of health care—driving them upward—in the process of drawing more resources into their sector, to respond to their priorities (Evans 1985; Marmor et al. 1976; Reinhardt 1987). And in every society, they possess a number of powerful forms of influence enabling them to do so.

Providers may participate in the conventionally acceptable expressions of concern about the burden of rising costs. To do otherwise might jeopardize their political credibility. But it is doubtful that they are so naive as to share these concerns. Health care cost escalation is for providers not a "crisis" but an expansion of opportunity, so long as it does not become so rapid or so severe as to lead to truly radical and potentially threatening readjustments of the overall organization.

The organizations and individuals responsible for reimbursing the costs of health care have a somewhat different view of those costs, and correspondingly a more complex form of interest in control. It is useful to distinguish between organizations which simply administer the payments process—social and private insurers—and those which ultimately bear the costs—firms, governments, workers and their unions, and individual patients or insurance

subscribers. The latter have a clear interest in limiting the extent of their own outlays. But the objectives of the administering organizations are more ambiguous.

Insurers, public or private, derive the resources available for their own purposes from the spread between total premiums and other contributions, and total outlays. They may therefore have an interest in controlling their own outlays *for given levels of receipts.* But increases in total costs of health care also increase the demand/need for insurance and the volume of funds under administration. Moreover, aggressive attempts to limit the growth of costs may alienate providers and threaten other institutional objectives. Correspondingly, insurers have tended over the years to make rhetorical rather than effective responses to escalation.

The concern of reimbursers, however, whether they are the ultimate payers or simply administrators of others' payments, is for their own fiscal situation. Transferring the burden of costs to some other individual or group is equivalent to reducing it, as far as the institution is concerned, and may be a great deal less stressful managerially and politically. The consequences of such "cost pass-through" for overall, systemwide, performance (and for the incomes of providers) are of course very different from those of actual reduction and are quite apparent in the aggregate data. But collective consequences do not show up on the bottom line of the individual transactor, at least not directly and in an identifiable form.

Conflicting Interests: Sources and Directions of Stress

These alternative objectives for the control of health care costs, up, down, and sideways, suggest an analogy with concepts from engineering. The stresses generated in a society by the application of forces to control health care costs can be analyzed as tension, compression, and shear.

The attempts by some organized groups to keep overall costs rising create tension stresses as the resources of the rest of society are stretched to provide a combination of larger incomes and wider professional opportunities for the providers (and would-be providers) of health care. These include not only individual doctors, nurses, druggists, and dentists, but also the large and powerful organizations and associations in which they are combined—hospitals, health science centers, professional associations, and private corporations. Added to them are the whole range of suppliers of pharmaceuticals, equipment, insurance and consulting services, and, more generally, all those whose incomes are generated in the health industry.

Against these forces are arrayed those who have an interest in compressing the industry, in resisting its growth dynamic. Their concerns may be simply over relative income shares—higher incomes for health care providers imply lower for everyone else, ceteris paribus—or, more generally, they may be concerned that the expansion of the health care sector represents a distortion of a society's priorities such that too few resources are left available for other more important objectives.

But for most individuals and paying organizations, the shifting of costs to someone else can be a strategy as effective as, and perhaps less costly than, the actual control of costs. Such sideways shifts build up shear stresses as the "target" groups attempt to resist the cost transfer. In this environment, attention shifts from the levels and trends in overall costs to the distributional issues of who shall carry the principal

burdens of paying for them, whatever those burdens turn out to be.

To push the analogy with materials analysis slightly farther, much of the rhetorical conflict over cost control, its possibility and consequences, is implicitly a debate over the properties of the "material" of which the health care system is composed. Providers argue that the system is like a strut, which responds to compression by catastrophic failure—buckling. A strut made of high tensile-strength steel, however, can bear very high tensile stresses. Advocates of limitations see a system made of masonry—very strong in compression, but easily fractured or "tipped over" in tension. Similarly, shear stresses may lead to adjustment by bending and reshaping, like metals, or fracture, like glass.

The buildup of stresses within the health care systems of all countries, the long-perpetuated sense of crisis, is thus a reflection of the influences of these three types of forces. The tensions created by the expansionary dynamic of the health care system itself lead either to offsetting compressive forces or to shear stresses as individual components of the system try to relieve themselves of the tension by transferring the stress to other participants, who in turn resist.

A very basic question within this framework, however, is whether the forces at work are internally or externally generated. Secondly, and not wholly unrelated, is the question of whether the material of the health care system is "elastic"—do the levels and patterns of health care expenditure respond to such forces?—or whether the forces applied merely determine the level of stress in a system whose basic shape is beyond the control of policy.

Thirdly, if policy measures can be shown to have an effect on health care costs and patterns, which ones work, and how? The different interest groups in any society have very different objectives for the control of health care costs. Which policies link with which objectives? Correspondingly, whose objectives will be brought forward by the balance of political power in a particular society?

Finally, assuming that we can gain some understanding of the effects of different policy approaches, what criteria should be applied in their selection? Policy analysts and economists typically try (not always successfully) to look at such issues from the perspective of some representative citizen, who might be behind the Rawlsian "veil of ignorance." This person would be thinking about health policy as citizen, as taxpayer, as potential (not actual!) patient, choosing before knowing which role or roles he or she will occupy. What policies might such a person prefer, what forces might he or she want to have controlling health costs, and how might we find out?

Health Care Spending and Health: The Links are Missing

On the first point, we noted at the outset that much of the public rhetoric about health care costs portrays the principal forces bearing on them as external to the health care system itself. The changing demographic structure of populations, the extension of the reach of medical technology, the growing expectations and wealth of the citizenry all represent developments outside the health care system to which that system can only react. From this perspective, the external environment generates a discrepancy between actual and attainable health states. The health care system translates those needs into medically appropriate workloads, or "needs for care," and determines the resources required to provide that care. Optimum health policy, then, consists of raising and delivering the necessary resources when asked and otherwise staying out of the way so that providers can get on with the job.

This "naive medicotechnical" conception of the functioning of the health care system has, in its most simplified expression, been out of favor among policy analysts for a long time (Evans 1984). But it still carries great political and symbolic significance. In a more sophisticated form (and entangled with economic concepts of dubious relevance), it is the basis for the "painful prescription" school of advocacy in the U.S.

(Aaron and Schwartz 1984; Schwartz et al. 1988). Their argument is that efforts to constrain the growth of health care costs must inevitably lead to the imposition of "rationing," i.e., the denial of effective services to those who could benefit from them (cf. Marmor and Klein 1986).

When clothed in economic rhetoric, the argument confuses the desideratum of medical effectiveness with that of consumer sovereignty. Rationing may be "bad" either because people are denied services which would improve their health—"needs"—or because they are denied services for which they would be willing to pay—"demands." There is, of course, no necessary connection between the two; but any stick will do to beat a dog.

If any efforts to restrain expenditures must lead to the horrors of rationing—unmet needs or frustrated preferences—it follows that current levels of funding, in particular in the United States, must be at or near the levels required to meet the needs/demands of the population, and furthermore that their steady uptrend is simply a response to growing needs/demands. Whatever is actual is rational, and whatever is rational is actual. Leave us alone, just send money. This appears to summarize the views of the American Medical Association, among others.

Yet efforts to relate the rate of cost expansion to changes in demographic structure have conclusively demonstrated that this has not been a major source of escalation in the past and (less conclusively) is unlikely to be so in the future. Much of the conventional rhetoric on the "costs of aging" is simply factually wrong, and the sources of error are now well known, if not well attended to.[1] Furthermore, the "inevitable" cost impact of technology turns out to be dependent not so much on the characteristics of the technology itself, but on the way in which practitioners in different systems choose to use it— choices which are extraordinarily arbitrary. The demands of the populations served are determined primarily by what they are told about what is available and what it will do for them, claims which have a very flexible relationship with

the scientific evidence. The expansionary dynamic in health care is within the health care system itself; external forces are not irrelevant, but they cannot explain the steady upward pressure (Evans 1985, 1987; Barer et al. 1987).

At the same time, students of medical care utilization have consistently found very wide variations in patterns of medical practice, in every jurisdiction studied. Furthermore, attempts to evaluate the appropriateness of the care provided show high rates of servicing which cannot be justified on any professional criterion. This extensive evidence for the absence of any firm connection between what is done and what can be shown to be "needed" further undermines the argument that the latter is tightly linked to the former (Wennberg and Gittelsohn 1973, 1982; Wennberg 1984; Roos and Roos 1981; Roos 1983; Chassin et al. 1986; Paul-Shaheen et al. 1987; Ham 1988).

Utilization patterns within health care appear to be determined neither by the objective needs of the patient nor by the characteristics of the available technology, but by a very subjective process of interpretation by individual practitioners. This leads to widely varying patterns of care (and costs) from place to place, time to time, and practitioner to practitioner, without any evidence of corresponding variations in health outcomes. This heterogeneity lies behind Maynard's (1981) flat statement: "It is foolish to believe that increases in health care inputs and throughputs lead to increases in health care outcomes." The broad literature on "technology assessment" makes the same point from a different perspective (e.g., Bunker et al. 1977; Banta et al. 1981; Feeny et al. 1986). Since so much of what is done in health care is ineffective, questionable, or simply unevaluated, it is hardly surprising that wide variations in use and cost of services are unconnected with observable differences in outcomes.

But it is not at all foolish to *claim* the existence of such a tight linkage between inputs and outputs, if one is trying to convince individuals or communities to contribute more resources to the health care sector. The naive medicotechnical model and its more

recent variant, the "painful prescription," are an important part of the political rhetoric with which advocates of the expansion of health expenditures advance their campaign.

"Shroud waving," or threatening the noncompliant patient or society with dire consequences ("You don't want your baby to die, do you?") is an ancient strategy. The modern allegation that attempts to restrain cost escalation must lead to rationing and unnecessary pain, suffering, and perhaps death is simply "your money or your life" in more roundabout language.

Indeed, even if utilization patterns were externally determined by the objective needs of patients, this would still not imply that *expenditures* were beyond the control of public policy. It would leave open the question of the levels of income—fees, wages, and profits—to be paid to those who provide them (Reinhardt 1987). If the provision of health care were carried out under circumstances which in any way approximated those of the "perfectly competitive market" of the economic textbooks, such income levels would be externally determined by those markets. But it isn't, and they aren't (Culyer 1982; Evans 1984). Prices of medical services, in particular, show extreme variation between countries, and (where permitted) within countries, which bear no relation to market forces (Reinhardt 1989). Such price variations have a powerful influence on provider incomes.

Relative incomes in the health care sector are, at least in the short run, largely influenced by political and policy choices (Marmor 1983). Indeed, it is quite conceivable that much of the rhetoric about the externally determined nature of health expenditures is motivated precisely by the desire to deflect attention from incomes, particularly in those countries (the United States, West Germany, and Canada) where professional incomes are relatively high.

Different Countries, Different Costs, Different Policies

While the sources of expansionary pressure are largely internal to health care systems themselves, the compressive stresses arise from the action of external forces of various kinds operating principally through the systems of reimbursement, and from the overall public regulatory process. The strength of these forces, and their mode of application, vary considerably from country to country.

All developed nations participate in the common cultural enterprise represented by the development of clinical capabilities and their underlying bases in science and medical technology. Furthermore, the institutions and personnel—doctors, hospitals, nurses, pharmacists, dentists—seem to be similar across national boundaries. But the organization of and payment for the delivery of health services vary much more from one jurisdiction to another. In a sense, different countries have "experimented" with alternative institutional arrangements for applying a common technology to common health problems (Marmor et al. 1978).

The result of this uncontrolled experimentation has turned out to be a wide variation in levels of and trends in health expenditures, both per capita and as a share of national income. Trends in spending also vary markedly from country to country in the short term, although in the 1980s there has been a significant convergence of trends in the OECD countries—except in the United States (see below). Just as the variety in patterns of clinical practice under similar conditions undercuts the argument that objectively identifiable needs determine the utilization of services, so the variety of international experience establishes that different policy choices significantly affect overall cost outcomes. Some forms of application of compressive forces "work" in limiting the growth of overall spending; others do not.

But all such compressive forces must be applied in opposition to strongly motivated expansionary forces emanating from the health care system itself. Since these forces seem to be rooted in the aspects of health care delivery which are common across international boundaries, international differences in cost outcomes must then be traceable to the way in which specific institutions re-

solve this inevitable conflict of forces. Furthermore, to the extent that compressive forces are successfully applied, they will tend to build up strains within the system and the society as a whole which must somehow be contained and/or relieved.

It is important to emphasize, however, that there *are* significant differences in the relative success of cost containment in different countries, because there is a line of argument, going back over a decade, which implies that such differences are either nonexistent or unimportant (Kleiman 1974; Newhouse 1977). In this view, the proportion of a nation's income which is spent on health care rises over time, in a systematic fashion, as the overall (per capita) income of the country rises. The analogy is drawn with "luxury" goods, on which people spend (relatively) more as their incomes rise. This argument has been supported by correlations of health spending (in percentage of national income) on measures of per capita income, using individual countries as observations, which have been remarkably close, which might suggest that little or no residual variation, one way or another, was left to be explained by the influence of policy.

Statistical analyses can at best show consistency with some causal hypothesis. On the other hand, a small number of examples, or even one, in which identifiable policies in particular countries have had identifiable and substantial impacts on patterns of health spending suffice to prove that policy *is* possible, and that there is no "iron law" that links health spending to economic growth. For that matter, even significant differences in spending patterns between one country and another, if they persist over time, are evidence of systematic rather than random effects. Such persistent differences are suitable material for further analysis, explanation, and evaluation.

The most recent compilation of international data on health spending by the OECD (Schieber and Poullier 1989) shows substantial intercountry variation. There is indeed a tendency for the proportion of national income spent on health care to be larger in wealthier

countries. But there is also considerable variation in experience across countries and within countries over time, reflecting the impact of alternative policy approaches (see Table 1).

In each country there has been a period of rapid expansion in health spending (as a share of total income), followed (except in the United States) by stabilization. But both the timing of the growth and stabilization and the levels at which stabilization occurs are quite variable. West Germany, for example, went through a period of rapid escalation in the early 1970s, which was followed by explicit and relatively successful measures to limit cost growth. In France, by contrast, the period of escalation started later and continued into the early 1980s. Between 1975 and 1985, therefore, health spending increased its share of French national income by over 25 percent; in Germany, the increase was only 5 percent. In the mid-1980s, the ratio has stabilized in both countries.

In Sweden, the period of escalation persisted throughout the 1970s, leaving that country at the top of the table by 1980. Subsequently, the share of health spending has undergone a sustained and substantial fall, moving Sweden from 35.7 percent above the OECD average in 1980 to 20 percent above in 1987. A similar pattern of sustained decline occurred in Denmark, although that country has been consistently below average in its spending share. These experiences are in clear contradiction to the suggestion, based on cross-sectional correlations, that rising incomes necessarily lead to a rising share of income spent on health care. The Japanese data provide an additional counter-example, as the rapid increase in Japanese incomes in the mid-1980s (particularly if measured in U.S. dollars!) have been associated with virtual stability in the health care cost share.

The data from the OECD countries, presented in more detail by Schieber and Poullier, display a number of other interesting and suggestive patterns. For our purposes, however, they suggest two significant conclusions. First, the comparative international experience clearly reflects the varying timing and

Table 1.   Health Care Expenditures as a Percentage of Gross Domestic Product: Selected Countries, 1960–1987

	1960	1965	1970	1975	1980	1985	1986	1987
Canada	5.5	6.1	7.2	7.3	7.4	8.4	8.7	8.6
Denmark	3.6	4.8	6.1	6.5	6.8	6.2	6.0	6.0
France	4.2	5.2	5.8	6.8	7.6	8.6	8.7	8.6
West Germany	4.7	5.1	5.5	7.8	7.9	8.2	8.1	8.2
Italy	3.3	4.0	4.8	5.8	6.8	6.7	6.6	6.9
Japan	2.9	4.3	4.4	5.5	6.4	6.6	6.7	6.8
Sweden	4.7	5.6	7.2	8.0	9.5	9.4	9.1	9.0
United Kingdom	3.9	4.1	4.5	5.5	5.8	6.0	6.1	6.1
United States	5.2	6.0	7.4	8.4	9.2	10.6	10.9	11.2
OECD average	3.8	4.5	5.3	6.5	7.0	7.4	7.4	7.5

Source: Schieber and Poullier (1989).

impact of public policies to influence health care costs—first expansion and then compression. The details and effects of the different countries' compressive policies are beyond the scope of this paper, and can probably only be assessed with extensive local knowledge. But the aggregate data quite clearly reflect the success of such policies, when they can be mobilized. Second, as one might anticipate from the more detailed studies of health care use and effectiveness, the substantial international variations in levels of health care spending do not appear to be associated with any corresponding differences in either health outcomes or public satisfaction. Increasing perceptions of "crisis" are emerging in a number of countries, but this appears to be a consequence of efforts at cost control (whether or not successful—*vide* the United States) rather than the level of spending per se. On the other hand, the development of comparable data sets across such a wide range of countries and differing national systems of organization and finance is a major task. Comparisons cannot be drawn too precisely in the data themselves, let alone in the even more difficult task of analyzing the forces and policies behind the divergent trends.

The North American "Experiment" with Alternative Reimbursement Policies

One pair of countries, however, stands out in sharp relief because of their remarkable degree of overall similarity—cultural, linguistic, and geographic. Canada and the United States are by no means scale models of each other, but their differences are rather subtle and not always apparent to the external observer. Moreover, their systems of organization of health services delivery are, or were until quite recently, also very similar. And finally, and very importantly, the health expenditure statisticians of the two countries maintain contact with each other, to try to reconcile their data concepts and categories and to preserve, if not identify, at least effective comparability.

But starting in the 1950s, their ways of *reimbursing* health care began to diverge sharply. By 1971, Canada had universal coverage of hospital and medical care for all of its citizens, within provincially based, government-run plans financed from tax revenue, and with no parallel private system of either insurance or delivery. The United States, in contrast, chose to rely on a patchwork of public and private plans, with a level of direct patient payment which is easily the highest in the developed world.

The experience of these two countries is thus the closest we are ever likely to come to a "quasi-controlled experiment," conducted in real time with real bullets. It is not perfect—one can certainly point to potential perturbing factors which are not fully controlled—but it is the best we are ever likely to get. And it has the overwhelming advantage that it is the experience of systems actually "in the field"; the issue of generalizability which haunts the randomized controlled trial does not arise. Accordingly, a number of studies have exploited this quasi-experiment, including the collections of papers in Andreopoulos (1975) and Evans and Stoddart (1986). Whether the conclusion from such a comparison is transferable to other systems or countries is certainly open to question. But the possibility of such divergent behavior is not.

Figures 1 and 2 summarize the experience to date, with preliminary data for 1987 and (in Canada) 1986. (The denominators here are GNP; OECD comparisons use GDR.) The argument that the share of health care costs in national income must rise with incomes is decisively refuted. Furthermore, the differing Canadian and U.S. experiences are traceable to their differences in the subsectors of hospital and medical spending—precisely those which are covered by the Canadian public plans—and they date from 1971, the year in which coverage became universal across Canada. By now, the cost differential has grown to about 2.5 percentage points of GNP, a massive savings on the Canadian side. Moreover, after some suggestion in the early 1980s of convergence, the gap is now widening again.

While this expenditure gap has grown, the universality of coverage in Canada has been maintained and strengthened. On the other hand, efforts to control costs in the United States have led to an estimated 37 million people with no insurance coverage at all, and to perhaps an even larger number whose coverage is grossly inadequate for any major illness (Library of Congress 1988). (A number of U.S. plans work backwards: they place a limit on the insurer's liability, and thus fail to cover the very large losses for which insurance is most needed.)

The United States is itself an outlier relative to the more general OECD pattern of health care funding (Schieber and Poullier 1989; Abel-Smith 1985). It shows both the highest (relative) costs and the lowest level of public coverage, along with a number of other peculiar characteristics in organization and ideology. But the Canadian expenditure

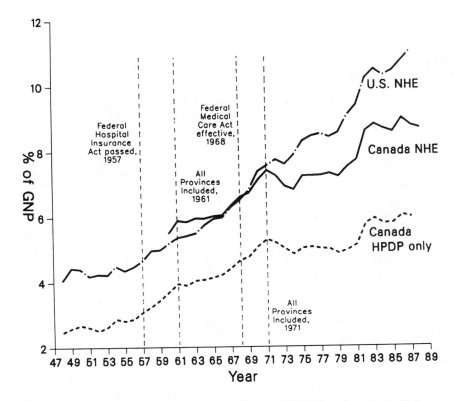

Figure 1. Total Health Expenditures as a Share of GNP, Canada and the U.S., 1948–1987

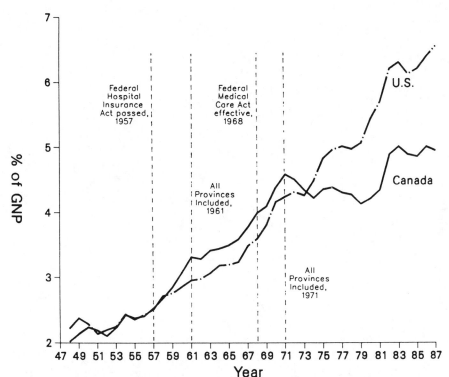

Figure 2. Hospital and Physician Expenditure as a Share of GNP, Canada and the U.S., 1948–1987

trends are also notable relative to the overall pattern of the OECD countries, as Culyer (1988) has shown.

Prior to 1971, health spending in Canada took up a larger share of income in Canada (after adjusting for relative income levels) than in most other OECD countries. Canada looked rather like the United States, relative to the rest of the group (Figures 1 and 2). This should not be surprising, since the delivery and payment systems of the two nations were quite similar. After 1971, however, the Canadian ratio drifted steadily down through the OECD pack, until by the mid-1980s it was distinctly on the low side. The great recession of 1982 put a major dent in Canada's national income, which was not felt by the providers of health services (in Canada *or* in the United States, interestingly). Before and since that date, however, health spending has moved closely in line with the national economy. The application of compressive forces to health spending, which has increasingly characterized health policy throughout the OECD world since the late 1970s, began earlier in Canada and has thus far been among the most successful there.

The Components of Control

A full and detailed account of the process of control in Canada is far beyond the ambitions or capacities of this paper (see, e.g., Tuchy 1986; Glaser 1987). It is possible, however, to identify quite briefly the results of this process, as reflected in the major cost components which differ most sharply between the two countries. These can then be related to specific institutional characteristics of the two systems. The major discrepancies are in the costs of administering the payment system itself, the rate of escalation of physicians' fees, and the intensity of servicing per patient and per patient day in the hospital system.

Controlling Overhead Costs: The "Bureaucracy"

The most dramatic proportional differences between a universal public insurance program and a multiple-source, predominantly private system are in the costs of the insurance process itself.

Figure 3, which displays the trends since 1960, shows that these "overhead costs" of managing and paying for, as opposed to providing, health care are accounting for a rapidly, though irregularly, increasing share of the United States GNP. Moreover, this explicit measure of administrative costs greatly understates their true magnitude. A substantial and apparently growing portion of the budget of American hospitals is allocated to administrative and billing functions, although in the aggregate statistics these are included as hospital costs rather than as costs of prepayment and administration. Similar costs are incurred, although on a smaller scale, in physicians' private practices and in nursing homes (Himmelstein and Woolhandler 1983).

No system can run itself; there must be some outlays for administration, management, and reimbursement. But in the Canadian system, in which all residents are automatically eligible for coverage, physicians are reimbursed according to a uniform fee schedule, and hospitals are allocated a prospectively negotiated budget for their activities, these costs are kept to a minimum. The design and marketing of complex contracts, and the marketing of facilities and services themselves, the determination of coverage status, the allocation of accounts, the settling of subsequent conflicts—all these are avoided.

Thus the multiplicity of insurers and the competitive environment are adding increasing amounts to American health care costs but not to care, yet again emphasizing the fallacy of the automatic linkage between expenditures, services, and outcomes. A large and growing share of the American total is spent, not on doctors and nurses, but on accountants, management consultants, and public relations specialists. Their contribution to the health of the American public is difficult to discern (unless one is trained in neoclassical economics and able to see with the eye of faith).

Moreover, the expansion of these expenditure categories creates, simultaneously, another large group of beneficiaries from, and advocates of, *rising* health care costs. The increasing emphasis on competition and managed care has, in Reinhardt's (1982) graphic

analogy, set many new places at the health care feast. These administrative overheads, which, from the Canadian perspective, are just so much waste motion, add $50–100 billion to American costs. But the firms and individuals who earn these sums as their incomes can be expected to fight very hard to protect and expand their profits and livelihoods, however useless their activities may be from an overall social perspective.

This is not to suggest that any other national system is ever likely to engage in administrative waste on the American scale. (All such waste motion, it should be recalled, is duly recorded in the national accounts as national income and output, of course, even though it is no more productive than digging holes in the ground and filling them in again, but that is another story.) The general message, however, is that the more diverse and complex the funding system, the more expensive it is likely to be. Sophisticated systems of "managed care," like competitive markets, are not free. In the economics textbooks, we take no account of the overhead costs of running a market system; they are assumed away, like friction. But the Ameri-

can example shows that the "frictional" costs of multisourced funding systems can become very large indeed.

And the word *become* is significant. Figure 3 indicates that the American system was not always so expensive to administer. Thirty years ago, when it was still dominated by not-for-profit insurers reimbursing private medical practitioners and not-for-profit hospitals, with an organizational structure as simple and traditional as Canada's still is, the overhead costs were proportionally much lower—not much different from Canada's, in fact. Since then, American administrative costs have been on a rapidly rising trend, yet the result has been *less* coverage, not more, and the extra effort has not even achieved its alleged primary goal of cost containment.

Controlling Physician Fees

Even after allowing for the differing growth of overhead costs, however, the expenditures on actually providing care are significantly lower in Canada, for both physicians' services and hospital costs. (Physicians' services include, as in the United States, both general prac-

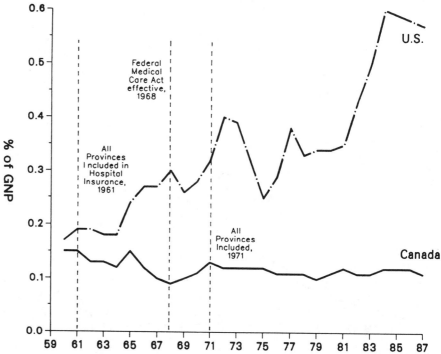

Figure 3. Costs of Insurance and Administration as a Share of GNP, Canada and the U.S., 1960–1987

titioners and specialists, who are reimbursed by fees for service even if they work in hospitals.) In the case of physicians' services, however, we find that there is remarkably little difference, over the last twenty years (or even longer), in the numbers or rates of growth of physician supply per capita in Canada and the United States. Nor is there much difference in the growth of productivity per physician (measured by gross billings divided by an index of fees), although the Canadian rate of increase is somewhat higher. Since 1971, the growth in services per capita has been remarkably similar in both countries (Barer et al. 1988). [2] The major difference is in trends in fees. In the United States, physicians' fees have risen faster than the general rate of inflation in almost every year of the last forty. Prior to 1971, a similar, though less pronounced, pattern of sector-specific inflation was seen in Canada as well. But after 1971, physicians' fees in Canada *dropped* sharply in real terms—running well behind inflation until the mid-1970s—and since then have on average risen at about the same level as prices generally.

The American environment, regulated, competitive, or whatever, has thus permitted physicians to push their fees steadily upward, in the face of rapid and sustained increases in their numbers and output. Indeed the increase in real fees in 1986 was the highest in the historical record. In Canada, the introduction of universal public insurance coverage coincided with the introduction of periodically bargained uniform fee schedules in each province that were binding on all practitioners. Under this fee-setting process, fee levels have roughly stabilized in real terms. [3]

Essentially, the public system is able to act as a monopoly in confronting physicians; Canada does not have socialized medicine but socialized insurance. Using this monopoly power, the reimburser can offset the still very significant political and organization-al power of physicians. [4] The fragmented, multiple-source payment system in the United States has, up till now, completely failed to develop any alternative method of containing medical fee inflation.

There is, of course, a great deal of evidence suggesting that particular American institutions, in particular settings, have been quite effective in cost control: HMOs, PPOs, IPAs, and various other organizations. All of this may be true. But such findings have been available, and valid, for at least thirty years. The key question is whether such political successes can be shown to have had any effect on overall expenditure patterns, for the nation or even for those regions in which they are most prevalent. To date the answer is unambiguously negative (Luft et al. 1986; Johnson and Aquilina 1986; Gabel et al. 1988).

There has been a great deal of speculation in the United States as to how competitive pressures might be created, in a multiple-payer environment and/or when patients are paying most of their own bills, so as to exert effective downward pressure on fees—or just keep them from rising. But evidence of such effects is conspicuous by its absence. The speculation has, however, been able to survive the uncooperative behavior of the real world. It is surprisingly often presented to external observers as if it were a factual description of American experience, rather than a collection of hypotheses.

Controlling Hospital Use and Technology

The third area of major difference in costs, hospitals, is somewhat more complex than the other two. Costs are lower, per capita, in Canada, but utilization rates are higher. To some extent this is a result of Canadian hospitals providing care in long-term care units to patients who in the United States would be in nursing homes. But even when one focuses on acute beds alone, the Canadian use rates are substantially higher. Moreover, Canadian hospitals have average occupancy rates of 85–95 percent in metropolitan centers, compared with about 60 percent in the United States. Clearly our population is not being denied access to hospital beds.

But the procedural intensity is much lower, and has been growing less rapidly, for at least two decades (Barer and Evans 1983, 1986; Detsky et al. 1983). To some extent this reflects the increased administrative, financial, and marketing activity which must all be carried in the budget of an American hospital, and which, when deflated by an index of the prices and wages paid by hospitals, shows up as "increased servicing." More services are indeed being paid for, per patient or patient day, but they are not patient care.

After allowing for that component, however, it seems likely (no one has yet checked in detail, and the study would not be simple) that there is a real and substantial difference in the rate of increase of clinical procedural performance. More, and more expensive, things are done, on average, to patients in American hospitals, for any particular diagnosis or problem; this probably accounts for a large part of the difference in hospital costs between the two systems (Newhouse et al. 1988; Evans 1988).

Again, the reasons for the difference are traceable to the differences in reimbursement systems. Canadian hospitals receive their operating budgets from a single source, the provincial reimbursement agency. Capital budgets come largely from the same source but are controlled and allocated separately. Thus the amounts and locations of expensive diagnostic and therapeutic equipment can be directly controlled, subject to all the usual political pressures from within and outside the health care system, by the reimbursing agency: the provincial government.

The typical American hospital has multiple sources of revenue, which pay for items of service or episodes of care, but at rates which include an allocation for capital costs. It has thus much greater flexibility in the acquisition of new equipment, and since it is generally reimbursed on a form of fee-for-service rather than a global prospective budget, new capacity becomes a profit center, as well as a cost center. (At least it does if the hospital can attract physicians who can attract patients.) Not surprisingly, both facilities and servicing have proliferated much more rapidly in this environment. Whether the additional activity can be shown to have had any positive effect on the health of patients is another matter.

Concentrating and Motivating the Controllers

The comparison of the Canadian and American experiences in health care funding has numerous fascinating aspects and is particularly gratifying for a Canadian. But the more important point for a wider audience is that it underscores the importance of a unified, single-source funding system as a way of concentrating the interests in cost containment—in applying compressive forces.

The forces of expansion are by no means absent from the Canadian environment; our providers of care can think of ways to use any amount of resources, if they could get them. Nor are they uninterested in higher fees and/or salaries. And the private insurance industry, while it does not have great hopes of getting back into health care coverage, certainly has not changed its preference for a partially privatized system. Private insurers would be very pleased to sell insurance to the majority of the population, which is basically healthy, as in the United States, or even to a minority with minimal needs, as in the United Kingdom.

But the critical feature of the Canadian system is that provincial governments cannot slide away from their financial responsibility for virtually all hospital and medical care funding. They have no option but to engage in the difficult and politically dangerous process of compression. If they do not, they must satisfy the ambitions of the health care system by cutting other forms of public spending—whose advocates also sit in Cabinet—or by raising taxes or public debt. All are unattractive. The true costs of health spending are thus brought to confront its advocates.

This is not to say that they *enjoy* the process. Indeed, several provincial governments of more-conservative beliefs would be only too pleased to escape from the pressures involved, by transferring part of the burden back to patients or through private insurance back to employers, employees, and private buyers. But the present statutory framework created by the federal government makes such cost transferring financially unrewarding, and there would be se-

vere political consequences for any Canadian government which was perceived by its electorate as threatening the basic principles of Medicare.[5]

Again a more general principle emerges, which is illustrated by the American contrast but has wider applicability in the European or OECD context (and perhaps further): The success of cost-containment policies depends on the extent to which shear forces can be contained.

Evading the Conflict with Providers: A Recipe for Failure

The natural and least demanding form of behavior for any organization or individual confronted with the upward pressure of health costs is to try to move them sideways—to government, to the patient, to the employer, anywhere but here. Furthermore, this shifting behavior is strongly supported and encouraged by providers, precisely because it undermines the containment process. From the providers' point of view, the logical strategy is to try to convert compressive forces into shear forces, so that overall outlays can be kept rising. The time and energy of payers is then fully absorbed in struggling with each other over who will pay the bill, rather than concentrated on struggling with providers over how big the bill shall be.

Thus we find that the strongest, indeed almost the only, advocates in Canada of reintroducing direct charges to patients are medical associations and their spokesmen, and private insurance companies. The former see such extra billing as the way in which they can escape from the relatively tight negotiating process which has constrained their fee growth; the latter see the opportunity for new markets—new costs—in the provision of private insurance against private payments, for those who can afford it.

Both groups are quite open and explicit, most of the time, that their objectives are to *increase* total outlays on health care, which they claim to be underfunded. They are less explicit that this would, by definition, also increase total incomes earned in its provision, more specifically their own. Even less discussed is the connection between the

health of the Canadian population and either higher incomes for physicians or an increased proportion of total outlays spent on actuaries and insurance salesmen.

There is an occasional nod in the direction of the conventional rhetoric of economics, that charging "consumers" of health care will result in reduced utilization and costs, but it is quite obvious that no one really believes this. If medical associations thought that there was any risk of a reduction in their members' workloads and incomes, they would not be such staunch advocates of charging patients. In fact, however, medical associations are quite familiar with the American experience, showing that utilization rates continue to climb even at very high rates of direct patient payment.

Provincial treasurers, even of right-wing governments, do not appear to believe in price elasticity either. At present, a province which imposed user charges would have its federal grant reduced by the amount of the charges; but it would still retain all savings from reduced utilization. No province now has user charges.

The argument which medical associations *do* press, and which is calculated to appeal to provincial governments in difficult fiscal circumstances, is a cost-shifting argument. Provincial governments can relieve the pressure of health care costs on their own budgets by allowing physicians to charge patients directly. Overall costs may rise—providers' objectives—but the public share will fall. To the extent that provincial governments can be persuaded to focus only on their own liabilities, not on total costs, both parties can be satisfied—at the patient's expense. Compressive forces will be relieved and converted into shear forces. The increases in health care costs will be funded, not just by taxes on the general population, but also by additional taxes on the sick themselves.

This turns out to be identical to the argument presented to employers by advocates of direct charges in the United States. If the burden of private insurance premiums is becoming unacceptable, two options present themselves. Employers can organize as buyers of care, to negotiate more effectively with providers over prices and utilization patterns—compressive forces. Or they can try to shift the costs of care back to their employees through increased "cost sharing."

The former approach, as expressed through "business groups on health," preferred provider organizations, and the work of such advocates as Joseph Califano, Lee Iacocca, and Alain Enthoven, has been greatly expanded during the last decade, or even half decade. But the persistent refusal of overall cost trends to respond (Gabel et al. 1988) has inevitably led to a certain response of *sauve qui peut* among the American business community, and an increased interest in cost shifting as a response with a shorter time horizon, lower administrative costs, and a more reliable impact on the firm's bottom line. Nor is there any shortage of economic analysts available to assure employers that they are doing the right thing, that shifting the burden to patients will actually lead to lower costs overall (Manning et al. 1987). If the aggregate data on costs show rather that cost escalation is proceeding as rapidly as before, well, it would have been even *more* rapid in the absence of increased cost sharing! A Canadian, living and working in an environment in which relative cost stability is not only consistent with but, as far as we can tell, a direct result of universal and comprehensive coverage, finds this state of mind difficult to penetrate.

Facing and Managing the Inevitable

The North American experience therefore shows that *if* one's objective is really cost control, the only demonstrably successful approach is through monopsonistic control of the payment process. This may be through a single payer, or through multiple payers whose behavior is strictly coordinated by regulation, to create a de facto unity, as in West Germany. In this environment, and assuming that there is a political will to do so, cost escalation can be contained. The experience of Western European countries in the 1980s has confirmed the significance of this "sole-source funding," which students

of North American health care have emphasized for a decade or more.

Successful cost control, however, must inevitably thwart, to a greater or lesser degree, the professional and economic ambitions of providers, both clinical and administrative/financial. Powerful offsetting forces generate severe strains. One must expect, therefore, continuing proposals from providers to modify, "make more flexible," the payment environment. "More consumer choice" is a common form of this rhetoric: Let the public, or the monopsony, payment system provide some basic minimum or safety net form of coverage, and let "consumers" make their own decisions about the form of coverage or payment they would like above this level.

It is striking, however, that such proposals seem to come only from provider groups, or from payers looking for a way to ease the financial pressure on themselves.[6] They are rarely if ever initiated by the "consumer" patients they are supposed to benefit. The intellectual framework of consumer choice is of course almost totally irrelevant to the circumstances in which the bulk of medical care is provided. The average patient is very different from the average citizen; activity and expense is heavily concentrated on a relatively small part of the population, and the concentration is increasing. (One renal failure patient, or liver transplant, will pay for a lot of office visits, and, at least in Canada, the proportion of hospital care used in the care of the very elderly and dying both is large and has dramatically increased in the last fifteen years; see Evans et al. 1988; Roos et al. 1987.)

For this and other reasons, the pressures of the marketplace transmitted by individual patients have been totally ineffective, and no civilized country relies on them in any serious way. Market pressures transmitted by organizations acting on the consumer/patient's behalf have much more appeal in theory, but as yet no record of success. Pressures exerted by a government, or quasi-governmental agency backed up by regulation, actually do work, because they mobilize and strongly motivate those with the capacity to do the job.

But the stresses of this activity will inevitably result in periodic efforts, encouraged by providers, to shift the burden. Cost containment is a "public good": a large part of society benefits from its success, but no one really wants the misery of having to do it. The problem for public policy, then, is to create organizational structures in which those responsible for exerting compressive forces not only have the ability and motivation to do the task but cannot escape it. This is the position in which our provincial governments, through luck or good management, now find themselves.

Conversely, the policy objectives of providers are best served by an environment in which no organization has effective responsibility for or control over total costs, but in which funds flow through numerous and complex channels and the opportunities for shifting are legion. This creates a form of prisoner's dilemma for payers. The optimal individual strategy is to spend one's energy on efforts to shift costs, thereby increasing them in total because individual efforts to constrain the total have almost no chance of being effective. It is hard to imagine a more satisfactory environment for providers.[7]

Satisfactory from a financial perspective, at least. The principal focus of this paper has been financial issues, a focus justified by their intrinsic importance, and by the argument at the outset that one can to a large extent divorce financial from "real" considerations, at least over a fairly broad range. The claim that financial outlays are rigidly linked either to the amounts and types of services provided by a health care system or, even more importantly, to its impact on the health of a population turns out to be without foundation. It is simply part of the political rhetoric surrounding the struggle over resource shares.

. . . And Moving On

But ultimately, the really important questions have to do with the impact of health care on health, and the appropriate amount and mix of resources to be devoted to this task.[8] This raises questions both about the allocation within the health sector itself and about the balance or resources between health care and other things. Since there is extensive evidence that the health of both individuals and populations depends on much more than health care alone, one cannot exclude the possibility that excessive health spending can actually threaten health, by diverting resources from other more effective activities. This is the other end of the spectrum from the argument, which seems at least plausible, that there must be some irreducible minimum below which containment of health spending results in a threat to the health of patients.

At this level we may identify three classes of objectives, those defined over health spending per se, those defined over the level and pattern of health care activities, and those defined over health outcomes. The degree of parallelism and of conflict over these objectives varies across groups in the society.

The objective which appeals to the policy analyst, and presumably to the Rawlsian representative citizen, is served by a combination of improved outcomes and reduced outlays—more for less. To the representative citizen, such outlays refer to *all* outlays, regardless of whose budget they flow through. Since all the citizens of a country must pay all its health care costs, through whichever channel they flow, costs transferred are not costs saved. (Indeed, they are usually costs increased.) Procedural activity is not a good in itself; most rational individuals would rather forego interventions. The level of activity is thus either a neutral element or a "bad," a form of cost.[9]

To the providers, however, expenditures are a good in themselves, regardless of their effects on outcomes. Since health expenditures are their incomes, a successful preventive program which required no medical input and greatly reduced (perceived) needs for care would be an economic disaster. Similarly, activity levels are part of their objectives, insofar as such activities provide professional self-expression and satisfaction—saving lives, celebrating cures, but not wiping noses or witnessing inevitable death. Providers are do-

ers by nature; the act is, at least in part, its own reward (like the publication). Outcomes also matter, but outcomes achieved by specific clinical interventions matter more than those achieved through nonmedical means.[10]

Finally, payers qua payers have an interest in controlling their own outlays, by either compression or shear. Payers who are also politically responsible to an electorate seem to have an interest paralleling that of providers in the provision of services. New hospitals, new high-technology equipment, increasing levels of activity have a political payoff in themselves. The difference is that payers would like more activity at lower cost; providers want more activity at higher cost.

As for outcomes, the extent of payer interest is variable and hard to document. This is perhaps not surprising, given the variable and hard-to-document relationship between health care itself and health outcomes. For most of the past fifty years or so, payers have been primarily concerned with facilities, services, and costs. In earlier years they placed more emphasis on expanding the former, working together with providers. More recently they have placed more emphasis on the latter, in increasing confrontation with providers. But the interest in outcomes per se is relatively recent, weak, and by no means universal.

A generation of experience with international health care funding, however, has produced a good deal of information about the process of cost containment; what works and what does not. Failure is apparently a result of institutional frameworks which prevent compressive forces from being mobilized and concentrated, and which divert them into shear forces while permitting the inherent tensile forces in all health care systems to proceed unchecked. Success comes from containing the shear forces.

But what forms of organization, funding, and other incentives actually increase the effectiveness of the health care system itself, in addressing its alleged primary goal of improving health status? Even more difficult, how can the health care system, with its insatiable

appetite for resources, be harnessed into a more broadly based effort to improve health status through a range of interventions which go well beyond health care itself? Such a pattern of interventions may be more effective than further increases in health budgets, but it will most assuredly be counter to the interests of health care providers—even if we knew with any assurance what exactly we ought to be doing.

These issues, however, point beyond this paper. They address the aims and objectives of the whole of health policy, not merely those of cost control. On the latter alone, much more evidence is now available.

This research ws supported by National Health Scientist Award no. 6610-1440-48 from the National Health Research and Development Program of Health and Welfare Canada, and by a fellowship from the Canadian Institute for Advanced Research.

Notes

1. The share of health care costs accounted for by elderly people has indeed been rising, but the common attribution of this increase to the growing numbers of elderly people, as life expectancies are extended, is incorrect. What has happened is that the average number and cost of services per elderly person *at each age* has been rising, and rising significantly more rapidly than for the rest of the population. This increase in the intensity of servicing per person, age-adjusted, reflects changes in medical practice patterns and ways of treating the elderly patient, which have had an impact on the costs of their care far greater than the effect of demographic factors (Barer et al. 1987; Barer et al. 1989; Evans et al. 1989). The latter are like a glacier; they can reshape the entire landscape over a period of fifty years, but have little impact in the short term. (Canadian estimates place the effects of changes in population age structure on health care costs in the neighborhood of 1 percent per capita per year; Woods, Gordon 1984.) Demographic factors do, however, provide a convenient cover or rhetorical diversion to distract policy attention from the real forces at work by alleging a superficially plausible external explanation for changes taking place within the health care system itself.

2. The steady growth in such services is often obscured in the United States by the tendency to measure output trends by visit rates, rather than by total services provided. The situation is further confused by studies of only the noninstitutionalized population and sometimes only the nonelderly noninstitutionalized population. But the total expenditure data, taken together with data on fee increases, make it clear that the volume of physicians' services is rising much faster than the visit rate. This could reflect an increased rate of related servicing, during or ancillary to the visit, or an increased concentration of servicing and billings for the institutionalized population. Whatever the reason, however, it is clear that in the United States visit data are wholly inappropriate as a measure of the increase in physician activity.

3. For most of the post-1971 period, some physicians in some provinces were able to bill patients in amounts above the negotiated schedule. But such extra billing was never a significant part of total expenditures. Since 1984 it has been eliminated all over Canada, over great physician opposition but with even greater popular support.

4. It is sometimes argued that fee controls will either drive physicians out of the market—migration or change of employment—or cause them to change their billing practices so as to maintain their overall incomes. The first has definitely not happened in Canada; concerns are with physician oversupply, not undersupply. The second effect definitely does appear in the Canadian utilization data. But the fee negotiation process is broad enough to include the aspects of the fee schedule which create the opportunities for such expansions of billings, and the utilization response, while not eliminated, has been kept within acceptable bounds. At present, however, there is an increasing interest in more explicit management of utilization as part of the fee negotiations (Lomas et al. 1989). An unanswered question, however, has to do with physician incomes. If fees have grown so much more slowly in Canada, and utilization per physician has not grown much faster, then should not American physicians' incomes be pulling rapidly away from those in Canada? Such data as are available do not show this. Are overheads in physician offices rising faster in the United States? Are changes in the organization of practice in the United States, and the growth of various organizations employing physicians,

leading to reduction in the proportion of billings actually retained by each physician? This area might repay further study. But the aggregate data are what they are.

5. The federal government transfers substantial sums of money to the provinces to share the costs of the health insurance programs. These sums are reduced, dollar for dollar, by any amount of direct charges to provincial residents which may be imposed or permitted, in respect of insured services. Thus a provincial government which either imposes charges or permits physicians or hospitals to extra bill its residents loses an amount from its own revenues equal to the (estimated) amount paid out of pocket by patients.

6. There is one exception to this generalization. A certain school of economists, alone among academic students of health care, continues to propose cost shifting. They appear genuinely to believe, despite the international evidence, that such shifting can reduce overall costs, unlike the provider advocates who hope, more plausibly, to raise costs. The sources of this conviction, in ideology and interest, deserve some analysis.

   No doubt economists, just like clinicians, have an economic as well as a personal interest in applying and promoting their own "human capital"—the particular analytical tools which they know best—regardless of their inappropriateness to the situation at hand. Faced with a clinical problem, a surgeon is more likely to propose surgery, and an economist to propose a private market. But it may also be that economics training programs tend to recruit and retain differentially people with a particular ideology or set of views about what a society's objectives ought to be, which are a distinctly biased subset of the wider society. Faced with the international data on comparative costs, some economists have simply responded that cost, or for that matter health, outcomes are irrelevant, and that competitive, market systems are an end in themselves, rather than a means to other ends. It is doubtful that this statement of personal values would find general assent.

7. Satisfactory, that is, for providers as a whole. The remarkably favorable environment in the United States has drawn in large numbers of individuals and firms, and indeed created whole new industries, to share the rich financial feast of health care costs. Traditional banqueters—physicians in private prac-

tice—complain of being increasingly jostled away from the table by the new crowd. It may be that the process of "rent dissipation" is well underway in the new competitive environment, and in the end no one will win. Per capita incomes fall even as total costs rise.

8. Such an assignment of objectives is itself a statement of values and cannot be derived from either evidence or analysis. It contrasts sharply with the usual formulation in economics, that the objective should be to maximize "utility," as reflected in the indirect evidence of individuals' responses to price signals. That too is a value judgment, a preanalytical choice. But it is one, for health costs, which has been rejected almost all over the world, as reflected in the political choices which citizens have made. Policy recommendations based on value foundations inconsistent with those held by the community to which the recommendations are made seem difficult to justify, but interesting to try to explain.

9. Economists in particular have grown far too accustomed to referring to health care as a "good." But it is not the *care* which is a good, only its presumed and expected effects. The process of care brings about a distinct reduction in utility, ceteris paribus—consider dental visits, or time spent in the hospital. The individual who undergoes care is by no means a "beneficiary," to be envied by his fellow citizens, but an unfortunate who, given the option, would gladly forego both the care and the accompanying episode of illness or injury. Two weeks in the hospital costs much more than a two-week tropical vacation, but the individual who enjoys the former is not better off, on any measure, than the one who undergoes the latter. Given that he or she was ill, the hospital patient may have been made better off by the care. But the possibility of this gain is conditional on the prior, and greater, loss of utility from becoming ill. (Greater, that is, for the ordinary, rational individual. There is a form of mental illness, Munchausen's syndrome, whose sufferers derive positive satisfaction from undergoing health care interventions and counterfeit illness to get care. Presumably this behavior is well modeled by the standard neoclassical approach to the demand for health care.)

10. Although dentists support fluoridation of community water supplies, and physicians support compulsory use of automobile seat belts and campaign against smoking. All generalizations, after all, are false.

References

Aaron, H. J., and W. B. Schwartz. 1984. *The Painful Prescription: Rationing Hospital Care.* Washington, DC: The Brookings Institution.

Abel-Smith, B. 1985. Who Is the Odd Man Out? The Experience of Western Europe in Containing the Cost of Health Care. *Milbank Memorial Fund Quarterly* 63 (1): 1–17.

Andreopoulos, S., ed. 1975. *National Health Insurance: Can We Learn from Canada?* New York: John Wiley.

Banta, H. D., C. Behney, and J. S. Willems. 1981. *Toward Rational Technology in Medicine: Considerations for Health Policy.* New York: Springer.

Barer, M. L., and R. G. Evans. 1983. Prices, Proxies and Productivity: An Historical Analysis of Hospital and Medical Care in Canada. In *Price Level Measurement: Proceedings from a Conference Sponsored by Statistics Canada,* ed. E. Diewert and C. Montmarquette. Ottawa: Minister of Supply and Services Canada.

———. 1986. "Riding North on a Southbound Horse? Expenditures, Prices, Utilization and Incomes in the Canadian Health Care System. In *Medicare at Maturity: Achievements, Lessons and Challenges,* ed. R. G. Evans and G. L. Stoddart. Calgary: University of Calgary Press.

Barer, M. L., R. G. Evans, C. Hertzman, and J. Lomas. 1987. Aging and Health Care Utilization: New Evidence on Old Fallacies. *Social Science and Medicine* 24 (10): 851–62.

Barer, M. L., R. G. Evans, and R. I. Labelle. 1988. Fee Controls as Cost Control: Tales from the Frozen North. *Milbank Quarterly* 66 (1): 1–64.

Barer, M. L., I. R. Pulcins, R. G. Evans, C. Hertzman, J. Lomas, and G. M. Anderson. 1989. Trends in Use of Medical Services by the Elderly in British Columbia. *Canadian Medical Association Journal* 14 (1): 39–45.

Bunker, J. P., B. A. Barnes, and F. Mosteller. 1977. *Costs, Risks, and Benefits of Surgery.* New York: Oxford University Press.

Chassin, M. R., R. H. Brook, R. E. Park, J. Keesey, A. Fink, J. Kosecoff, K. Kahn, N. Merrick, and D. H. Solomon. 1986. Variations in the Use of Medical and Surgical Services by the Medicare Population. *New England Journal of Medicine* 314 (5): 285–90.

Culyer, A. J. 1982. The NHS and the Market: Images and Realities. In *The Public/Private Mix for Health: The Relevance and Effects of Change,* ed. G. McLachlan and A. Maynard. London: Nuffield Provincial Hospitals Trust.

———. 1988. *Health Expenditures in Canada: Myth and Reality, Past and Future.* Toronto: Canadian Tax Foundation.

Detsky, A. S., S. R. Stacey, and C. Bombardier. 1983. The Effectiveness of a Regulatory Strategy in Containing Hospital Costs: The Ontario Experience, 1967–1981. *New England Journal of Medicine* 309: 151–59.

Evans, R. G. 1984. *Strained Mercy: The Economics of Canadian Health Care.* Toronto: Butterworths.

———. 1985. Illusions of Necessity: Evading Responsibility for Choice in Health Care. *Journal of Health Politics, Policy and Law* 10 (3): 439–67.

———. 1987. Hang Together or Hang Separately: The Viability of a Universal Health Care System in an Aging Society. *Canadian Public Policy* 13 (2): 165–80.

———. 1988. Split Vision: Interpreting Cross-Border Differences in Health Spending. *Health Affairs* 7 (5): 17–24.

Evans, R. G., M. L. Barer, C. Hertzman, G. M. Anderson, I. R. Pulcins, and J. Lomas. 1989. The Long Goodbye: The Great Transformation of the British Columbia Hospital System. *Health Services Research* 24 (4): 435–59.

Evans, R. G., and G. L. Stoddart, eds. 1986. *Medicare at Maturity: Achievements, Lessons and Challenges.* Calgary: University of Calgary Press.

Feeny, D., G. Guyatt, and P. Tugwell. 1986. *Health Care Technology Effectiveness, Efficiency, and Public Policy.* Montreal: Institute for Research on Public Policy.

Gabel, J., C. Jajich-Toth, G. de Lissovoy, T. Rice, and H. Cohen. 1988. The Changing World of Group Health Insurance. *Health Affairs* 7 (3): 48–65.

Glaser, W. A. 1987. *Paying the Hospital.* San Francisco: Jossey-Bass.

Ham, C., ed. 1988. *Health Care Variations: Assessing the Evidence.* London: The King's Fund Institute.

Himmelstein, D. U., and S. Woolhandler. 1983. Cost Without Benefit: Administrative Waste in U.S. Health Care. *New England Journal of Medicine* 314: 441–45.

Johnson, A. N., and D. Aquilina. 1986. The Competitive Impact of Health Maintenance Organizations and Competition in Minneapolis/St. Paul. *Journal of Health Politics, Policy and Law* 10 (4): 659–75.

Kleiman, E. 1974. The Determinants of National Outlay on Health. In *The Economics of Health and Medical Care,* ed. M. Perlman. London: Macmillan.

Library of Congress, Congressional Research Service. 1988. *Health Insurance and the Uninsured: Background Data and Analysis.* Washington, DC: U.S. GPO.

Lomas, J., C. Fooks, T. Rice, and R. J. Labelle. 1989. Paying Physicians in Canada: Minding Our Ps and Qs. *Health Affairs* 8 (1): 80–102.

Luft, H. S., S. C. Maerki, and J. N. Trauner. 1986. The Competitive Effects of Health Maintenance Organizations: Another Look at the Evidence from Hawaii, Rochester, and Minneapolis/St. Paul. *Journal of Health Politics, Policy and Law* 10 (4): 625–58.

Manning, W. G., J. P. Newhouse, N. Duan, E. B. Keeler, A. Leibowitz, and M. S. Marquis. 1987. Health Insurance and the Demand for Medical Care: Evidence from a Randomized Experiment. *American Economic Review* 77 (3): 251–77.

Marmor, T. R., A. Bridges, and W. L. Hoffman. 1983. Comparative Politics and Health Policies: Notes on Benefits, Costs, Limits. In *Comparing Public Policies: New Concepts and Methods,* ed. D. E. Ashford. Beverly Hills, CA: Sage.

Marmor, T. R. and R. Klein. 1986. America's Health Care Dilemma Wrongly Considered. *Health Matrix* 4 (1): 19–24.

Marmor, T. R., and David Thomas. 1983. Doctors, Politics and Pay Disputes: "Pressure Group Politics" Revisited. In *Political Analysis and American Medical Care: Essays,* ed. T. R. Marmor. Cambridge University Press.

Maynard, A. 1981. The Inefficiency and Inequalities of the Health Care Systems of Western Europe. *Social Policy and Administration* 15 (2): 145–63.

Newhouse, J. P. 1977. Medical-Care Expenditure: A Cross-National Survey. *Journal of Human Resources* 12: 115.

Newhouse, J. P., G. M. Anderson, and L. L. Roos. 1989. Hospital Spending Between the United States and Canada: A Comparison. *Health Affairs* 7 (5): 6–16.

Paul-Shaheen, P., J. D. Clark, and D. Williams. 1987. Small Area Analysis: A Review and Analysis of the North American Literature. *Journal of Health Politics, Policy and Law* 12 (4): 741–809.

Reinhardt, U. E. 1982. Table Manners at the Health Care Feast. In *Financing Health Care: Competition vs. Regulation,* ed. D. Yaggy and W. G. Anlyan. Cambridge, MA: Ballinger.

———. 1987. Resource Allocation in Health Care: The Allocation of Lifestyles to Providers. *Milbank Quarterly* 65: 153–76.

Roos, L. L. 1983. Supply, Workload and Utilization: A Population-Based Analysis of Surgery in Rural Manitoba. *American Journal of Public Health* 73 (4): 414–21.

Roos, N. P., P. Montgomery, and L. L. Roos. 1989. Health Care Utilization in the Years Prior to Death. *The Milbank Quarterly* 65 (2): 231–54.

Roos, N. P., and L. L. Roos. 1981. High and Low Surgical Rates: Risk Factors for Area Residents. *American Journal of Public Health* 71 (6): 591–600.

Schieber, G. J., and J. P. Poullier. 1989. Trends in International Health Care Expenditure Trends: 1987. *Health Affairs* 8 (3): 169–77.

Schwartz, W. B., F. A. Sloan, and D. N. Mendelson. 1988. Why There Will Be Little or No Physician Surplus Between Now and the Year 2000. *New England Journal of Medicine* 318 (14): 892–97.

Tuohy, C. J. 1986. Conflict and Accommodation in the Canadian Health Care System. In *Medicare at Maturity: Achievements, Lessons, and Challenges*, ed. R. G. Evans and G. L. Stoddart. Calgary: University of Calgary Press.

Wennberg, J. E. 1984. Dealing with Medical Practice Variations: A Proposal for Action. *Health Affairs* 3 (2): 6–32.

Wennberg, J. E., and A. Gittelsohn. 1973. Small Area Variations in Health Care Delivery. *Science* 182: 1102–108.

———. 1982. Variations in Medical Care Among Small Areas. *Scientific American* 246 (April): 120–34.

Woods, Gordon Management Consultants. 1984. *Investigation of the Impact of Demographic Change on the Health Care System in Canada: Final Report*. Study Prepared for the Task Force on the Allocation of Health Care Resources, Canadian Medical Association, August.

28

Criteria and Guidelines for Reforming the U.S. Health Care System

Stephen M. Shortell and Walter J. McNerney

It would be tempting to suggest that the U.S. health care system is now in disarray were it not for the fact that it has never really been otherwise. There is increasing anger and frustration among employers, consumers, uninsured people, payers, and providers, all of whom are struggling with what are perceived to be competing demands to contain costs while trying to improve productivity, increase quality, and expand access to services. Clearly, our health care system needs more comprehensive strategies to address the multiple needs of different groups.

We do not lack for new ideas or alternative models. In the past few years there has been increased interest in the British system and particularly the Canadian one.[1] Enthoven and Kronick[2] have refined Enthoven's earlier consumer-choice health plan. We have also seen innovations in the delivery of care, ranging from Kaiser staff-model health maintenance organizations (HMOs) and Humana's efforts to integrate group insurance with hospital services in defined markets to communitywide experiments in cost-effective care delivery, such as the Rochester Area Hospital Corporation.[3] What we appear to lack, however, is the ability to put the concepts, ideas, and models together into a package that appeals to a suitably broad cross section of the American public.[4] We are up against ourselves and our deeply held respect

Reprinted with permission from *The New England Journal of Medicine* 322, no. 7 (February 15, 1990), pp. 463–66. Copyright © 1990 by the Massachusetts Medical Society.

for autonomy and pluralism, which take on added importance in view of the great diversity of our culture. Whatever we might like to believe about ourselves, we do not have as high a sense of responsibility for each other as do our British and Canadian neighbors. For these reasons, any change in our health care system is likely to be incremental rather than radical. We are beginning to recognize the need for a deeper structural response to a world that is qualitatively different from what it was a decade ago. Yet we continue to respond in a quantitatively cyclical fashion, making increases here and cuts there, as we probe the margins of political feasibility that are tied to our dominant values of autonomy and pluralism. As Stevens writes, "American national health policy is made through negotiated consensus among shifting coalitions."[5] In short, in health care we are not yet ready to bite the bullet.

There are different degrees of incrementalism, however, and the pace is increasing rapidly. The Medicare Prospective Payment Act of 1983 has been followed by recent congressional approval of a payment schedule for physicians that is based on relative values and is to be implemented over the next two years. This development, coupled with many private-sector initiatives and the fundamental restructuring of American health care organizations (through new systems, alliances, consolidations, mergers, and the like),[6] suggests that an infrastructure is being built that may accommodate a wider variety of interest groups. Building blocks are being assembled that may permit an accelera-

tion of incremental steps that, taken together, may contain the seeds of fundamental reform. In creeping up on the challenge in our characteristic piecemeal fashion, we may well ask whether we shall recognize the possibilities when we see them. If nothing else, it should be clear that an open-ended, market-driven system alone is not the answer to the interrelated challenges of containing costs, enhancing quality, and increasing access.

The debate over comprehensive national health insurance will continue, but for various reasons such a scheme is unlikely to gain wide support in the near future. Under the circumstances, public policy should focus on improving the options for informed choices among methods of financing and delivery (some with caps on expenditure), improving the productivity and effectiveness of care, and providing universal access to care. To these ends several approaches are possible, and many will undoubtedly be espoused. Rather than advocate one plan over another, however, we believe it helpful to offer criteria and guidelines that can be used as reference points for all emerging proposals. We believe these criteria can strengthen our ability to address key issues and thus help focus the public-policy debate, which now lacks cohesiveness and—in the full sense of the word—integrity.

Criteria and Guidelines

There are two interwoven themes to our suggestions—responsibility and accountability. Any proposal for reform of the U.S. health care system must recognize the responsibility to provide care to the more than 30 million uninsured people and those otherwise unable to obtain needed medical care. At the same time, such a proposal must recognize the need for both clinical and fiscal accountability. The challenge is to structure a system in which people receive medical services of demonstrated efficacy and quality, provided in accordance with established standards of efficiency and productivity. Relman has referred to this increased emphasis on assessment and accountability as the "third revolution in medical care."[7] The revolution, however, must also incorporate a judicious measure of our long-cherished autonomy and pluralism.

Our themes of assessment and accountability are reflected in five criteria: the establishment of a set of benefits mandated for all; the allocation of resources on the basis of defined needs; the payment of providers on the basis of performance; the establishment of clinical and fiscal accountability at the level closest to that of care delivery (to preserve autonomy and pluralism); and the establishment of a global cap on expenditures based on the needs of the population and the capabilities of providers in the area. The main features of these guidelines are shown in Figure 1.

Mandated Benefits

Any proposal for reform must address the need to reduce the number of disparities in access to care that currently exist. The issue is not whether we have two or more levels of health care in this country or whether we are now rationing health care services. To both questions, the answer is obviously yes. The real question is how we can provide everyone with access at least to minimal basic services of acceptable quality.[8] To be viewed as a responsible nation—not altruistic, charitable, or loving, but responsible—we must include the disenfranchised.

Over the years, various proposals for basic benefits have been made, the most recent being Senator Edward M. Kennedy's (D–Mass.) Basic Health Benefits for All Americans Act (S. 768 and H.R. 1845). These proposals generally include coverage for physicians' ser-

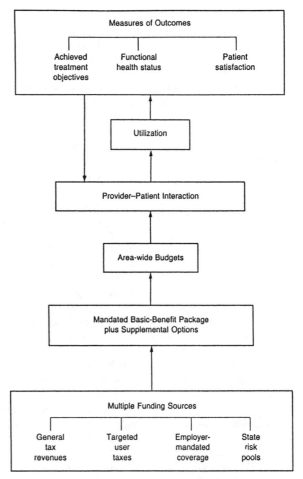

Figure 1. Elements of the U.S. Health Care System as Configured According to the Proposed Criteria.
According to this proposal, funds would be allocated on the basis of the health needs of the population served and used according to the informed judgment of the provider and the patient, in the light of clinical guidelines for practice. Payment to providers would be ba⌄ed on the outcomes achieved in the light of the defined area-wide budgets.

vices, hospital care, emergency care, prescription drugs, and prenatal and well-baby care, some mental health coverage, and catastrophic-illness coverage over a fixed deductible such as $3,000. Some proposals also include limited coverage for dental and vision care. Some states, such as Oregon, have used focus groups of professionals and laypersons with consultation from ethicists to help determine a basic set of Medicaid benefits.[9] In addition, there is a growing body of data, knowledge, and experience in the delivery of health services to the poor associated with a number of pilot programs over the past decade. These data can be analyzed and the

knowledge pooled to obtain workable estimates of utilization and costs with various possible mandated benefit packages. Given the diversity of opinion on the financing of a nationally established minimal-benefit package such as this, the most workable guiding principle would be to ensure multiple sources of financing, so that an undue burden does not fall on a single source. Thus, increases in the general tax revenues, the imposition of specially targeted "sin" taxes (on alcohol and cigarettes, for example), and a requirement that employers pay at least some of the premium for their employees should all be considered. To make the last proposition more accessible, the formation of trusts including a number of employers should be encouraged.

For such benefits to be effective, several conditions must be met. The benefits must be mandated for all public and private payers; they must be stated and defined specifically enough to keep payers from selecting only the better risks; the enrollment periods must be at least 12 to 18 months long to avoid excessive, unproductive shopping and higher administrative costs; the prices should reflect the risks, to minimize selection that disfavors needy or disadvantaged persons; data on the performance of providers must be improved and made more widely available; and incentives to reward managed care must be continued and improved. Various subsidy programs will be needed, as suggested by Enthoven and Kronick,[2] to help small employers and persons above or below the poverty line who are ineligible for other assistance, and supplemental programs such as state risk pools must be implemented in all states.

Matching Resources with Needs

After a set of benefits is defined, the next step is to ensure that resources are available to meet consumer needs. It has been difficult to assess needs thus far, because adequate measures have been lacking and there has been no way of collecting information in a data base that could be used to guide the allocation of resources. As a result, reliance has often been placed on data collected for other purposes (such as claims data) or on statistical norms that fail to take into account the vagaries of clinical practice and thus lack professional credibility.

Advances in the measurement of functional health status,[10-12] treatment outcomes,[13,14] and patient satisfaction have made it increasingly possible to define the health care needs of a given geographic population. On the basis of such assessments, expected levels of use can be determined, together with the resources needed to deliver the defined level of care. Data such as those derived from the National Health Interview Survey, the National Ambulatory Medical Care Survey, the Health Care Expenditure Survey, and the ongoing

collection of data by the Health Care Financing Administration on the use of health services by Medicare beneficiaries can be drawn on and supplemented by the growing research on health status and patient outcomes to provide even more refined estimates for purposes of resource allocation. These efforts should be further augmented by initiatives in the private sector such as those undertaken by the Pennsylvania Health Care Cost Containment Council that involve employers, nongovernmental payers, and foundations.[15] From such data the costs of various benefit packages (including those that exceed the basic benefits) can be determined, with their associated resource requirements. When resources fall short of the estimated requirements, these data will provide an informed context in which to set priorities and make trade-off decisions that take into account the health needs of the population. This approach permits health plans to "risk rate" specific geographic segments of the population, as proposed by Enthoven and Kronick,[2] and to charge higher prices to cover the higher costs of providing care to groups with greater needs.

Performance-Based Payment

Any plan must specify how providers will be held responsible for the quality and effectiveness of the care they provide. With the growing emphasis on outcomes management,[16] assessment of the effectiveness of specific medical procedures,[17] and interest in the development of guidelines for practice,[18] it is increasingly possible to pay providers on the basis of outcome measures. Until such measures are developed to apply to a wider set of conditions and procedures, providers should be held accountable for the features of their care involving structure and process that are thought to be most strongly associated with positive patient outcomes. By means of practice guidelines and other measures of appropriate use, payers should provide incentives for higher-performing institutions by channeling more patients to them through selective purchasing, exclusive contracting on the basis of performance, and related means. Incentives might also be developed for

providers that address special needs in prevention, primary care, rehabilitation, mental health, home health, and hospice care. Incentives should also be designed to reward superior performance in providing low-income groups with prenatal care and treatment for chronic disease. In brief, we need to move away from the current preoccupation with general acute inpatient care to provide services that meet the needs of segments of the population across a broad continuum of care.

Local Initiative and Collaboration

As the health field has evolved, it has become apparent that the most effective groupings are local or regional ones. Thus, clinical and fiscal accountability should be established at the level closest to the delivery of patient care. At this level, providers should be encouraged to pursue their strategic initiatives, innovate, and learn from their mistakes.

The care provided in local communities may be organized in a variety of ways—in health care systems similar to the corporations envisioned by the American Hospital Association's Ameriplan proposal,[19] Kaiser staff-model HMOs, large groups of physicians with different specialties, organizations combining hospitals and physicians, or related configurations. Highly specialized services should be offered in collaboration to minimize needless overlap. If necessary, antitrust regulations should be reassessed to promote cost-effective care.

In addition, collaboration among public and private payers, third-party carriers, providers, and consumers should be fostered in order to avoid, as much as possible, the practice of defensive medicine and excessive selection that disfavors the needy and to encourage stronger, more open dialogue on communitywide health issues and problems. Such collaboration will help to eliminate retroactive cost shifting and the abdication of responsibility to provide care to defined groups. It will help to overcome the weakness of the health care market, while leaving room for providers to exercise strategic choice in the delivery of health services. The

Rochester Area Hospital Corporation is an example of such collaboration.[3]

Expenditure Caps

The above criteria for our health care system are necessary but not sufficient. Ultimately, what is needed to make such a plan succeed is the presence of various forms of caps on expenditures that will overcome market weaknesses and bring increases in health care outlays more in line with increases in the consumer price index or with an index of the gross national product specially developed for service industries. The only sure way to control health care costs is to cap them. Caps on expenditures are needed to instill fiscal accountability. The alternative—more prescriptive regulation of the behavior of individual providers—would lead to severe problems of implementation and restrict necessary innovation.

Various options should be pursued, including the capitation of managed care systems and the use of targets for expenditures based on geographic area. As previously noted, rates should be set on the basis of age, sex, health status, and related demographic factors. New forms of technology and the effect of inflation should also be taken into account and consideration given to the establishment of separate capital budgets based not only on the need in an area but also on the performance of the provider in using the new technology. The provider's ability to provide care within the targets set for expenditures should be assessed from the data on practice outcome and patient satisfaction. Thus, clinical and fiscal accountability would be linked and based on an epidemiologic assessment of the health needs of the population.

Conclusion

The lack of focus in the debates on health policy and the proposals for reform is untenable. In the near future a variety of proposals for reform are likely to come from both public and private sources, and there is a legitimate basis for disagreement on the wisdom and probable efficacy of any one course of action. But the lessons of the past suggest a few of the necessary next steps. The medically disenfranchised must be included in basic health care. The criteria for both fiscal and clinical accountability must be met. Care must be linked to the defined needs of the population and made reasonably affordable through a number of sources of revenue. And there must be room for creativity and innovation in regard to specific delivery approaches. The criteria and guidelines proposed here meet these needs. Their aim is to produce a better-informed consumer and a more accountable provider, working with new ground rules within preestablished revenue limits based on defined needs. Federal and state governments and the private sector should be encouraged to undertake experiments in the local and regional delivery of health care that can be evaluated against these criteria.[20] Having a framework within which to assess various reforms and pilot projects makes it possible to accumulate knowledge about the merits of specific proposals. These proposals can then be refined and generalized to other segments of the population as they are deemed workable.

Notes

1. Blendon RJ. Three systems: a comparative survey. Health Manage Q 1989; 11(1):2–10.
2. Enthoven A, Kronick R. A consumer-choice health plan for the 1990s: universal health insurance in a system designed to promote quality and economy. N Engl J Med 1989; 320:29–37.
3. Hartman SE, Mukamel DB. "How might a low cost hospital system look?" Lessons from the Rochester experience. Med Care 1989; 27:234–43.
4. Levey S, Hill J. National health insurance: the triumph of equivocation. N Engl J Med 1989; 321:1750–4.
5. Stevens R. In sickness and in wealth. New York: Basic Books, 1989:355.
6. Shortell SM, Morrison EM, Friedman B. Strategic choices for America's hospitals: managing change in turbulent times. San Francisco: Jossey-Bass, 1990.
7. Relman AS. Assessment and accountability: the third revolution in medical care. N Engl J Med 1988; 319:1220–2
8. Welch HG. Health tickets for the uninsured: first class, coach, or standby? N Engl J Med 1989; 321:1261–4.
9. Lund DS. Oregon considers rationing Medicaid health benefits. American Medical News. March 17, 1989:54.
10. Lohr KN, ed. Advances in health status: conference proceedings. Med Care 1989; 27:Suppl 3:S2–S294.
11. Ware JE Jr, Brook RH, Rogers WH, et al. Health outcomes for adults in prepaid and fee-for-service systems of care: results from the health insurance experiment. Santa Monica, CA: Rand, 1987.
12. Brook RH, Kamberg CJ. General health status measures and outcome measurement: a commentary on measuring functional status. J Chronic Dis 1987; 40:Suppl:1315–54.
13. Wennberg JE, Mulley AG Jr, Hanley D, et al. An assessment of prostatectomy for benign urinary tract obstruction: geographic variations and the evaluation of medical care outcomes. JAMA 1988; 259:3027–30.
14. Greenfield S. The state of outcome research: are we on target? N Engl J Med 1989; 320:1142–3.
15. Gamm LD, Hurley RE, Eisele FR, Gage BJ. The Pennsylvania health care cost containment council: a pro-competition information strategy. College Park, PA: Department of Health Policy and Administration, Pennsylvania State University, 1989.
16. Ellwood PM. Outcomes management: a technology of patient experience. N Engl J Med 1988; 318:1549–56.
17. Roper WL, Winkenwerder W, Hackbarth GM, Krakauer H. Effectiveness in health care: an initiative to evaluate and improve medical practice. N Engl J Med 1988; 319:1197–202.
18. Chassin MR. Standards of care in medicine. Inquiry 1988; 25:437–53.
19. AMERIPLAN: a proposal for the delivery and financing of health services in the United States: report of a Special Committee on the Provision of Health Services. Chicago: American Hospital Association, 1970.
20. Shortell SM. Strategic choices. Health Manage Q 1989; 11(4):26–7.

29

Exhausting Alternatives

Richard E. Merritt and Linda Demkovich

"You can always rely on [Americans] to do the right thing, but only after they have exhausted all the other alternatives." That quote, attributed to Winston Churchill, has become popular on the health-policy circuit as a reminder that if "the right thing" is ensuring all citizens access to basic health care, the United States still has a long way to go.

Even as debate over universal access sputters and stalls at the federal level, the 50 states, individually, have been busy exploring and experimenting with a range of alternatives for strengthening—or, in some cases, scrapping—the existing system. Some day, advocates of state action say, one of those experiments may just turn out to be the basis of a universal health plan for the country.

There are, of course, disadvantages to relying on the states. On a practical level, for example, 50 (or even 10 or 12) separate state plans could spell chaos for interstate businesses. Skeptics also worry that focusing attention on the states could ease the pressure for a uniform national solution.

On the plus side, mistakes made at the state level can be more easily pinpointed and corrected. Also, once the bugs have been worked out, a national program can profit from what's taken place in the state "laboratories." (Remember that DRGs were pioneered at the state level before being incorporated into Medicare.) Finally, because health costs are a more visible—and more vulnerable—part of state budgets, any

state reforms are more apt to reflect concerns about both access and cost containment.

New York State Sen. Tarky J. Lombardi, a Republican, offered a blunt assessment of the federal track record since 1965, when Medicare and Medicaid began: "It's been an abomination. They're not providing health care; they're just paying the bill. And if you think the federal government is going to do something other than shift costs, think again. State health budgets are so large that we're all but going bankrupt."

While some will dispute Lombardi's view, few will disagree that the federal government—beset by the monster deficit—will not be in a position in the foreseeable future to act on a universal access plan. So it will be left to the states, most of which face overwhelming deficits of their own, to fill the policy void—a challenge that many already have taken steps to meet.

Over the last six years, more than 30 states have formed task forces or commissions to investigate the demographics of their uninsured populations, identify barriers in the insurance market and recommend remedies. Out of those activities three main strategies have emerged: gap-fillers, or incremental approaches that target one or more subsets of the uninsured; employer-based programs and insurance reforms, aimed mainly at small businesses; and single-payer systems that rely on government (or a government-designated entity) to provide—and raise revenues for—comprehensive health care coverage.

An important caveat: few of the plans that fall under the generic rubrics identified above have been in place long enough to draw conclusions beyond

short-term successes or failings. With competition for funds intensifying, plans already off the drawing board may be scaled back or terminated, while others may be stymied in the blueprint stage. Still, several trends bear watching.

Gap-Fillers

One of the most popular "gap groups" has been children—not surprising, given the fact that one in three children under age 17 is uninsured. Through a series of mandates, Congress has expanded eligibility under Medicaid so that all poor children aged 18 and under will be covered by the turn of the century. Despite complaints about costs, state officials have generally welcomed the mandates as opportunities to beef up Medicaid by forcing often-reluctant legislatures to increase appropriations and by drawing down a larger share of matching funds from the federal government.

On their own, several states have reached beyond the mandates in efforts to insure poor children who are ineligible for Medicaid. Minnesota in 1987 and Colorado and New York in 1990 enacted basic but comprehensive insurance programs for children in low-income households. By dropping prenatal services, Minnesota has been able to expand its Children's Health Plan from age 6 to 8 and, in 1989, to 18. Colorado's program covers children to age 9, New York's to age 12. Although the three programs are structured, administered, and financed somewhat differently, all require participants to pay a modest enrollment fee and all specify the basic package of services to be provided.

Reprinted with permission from *Health Management Quarterly* 13, no. 1 (1991): 11–15. *Health Management Quarterly* is a publication of The Baxter Foundation.

While the concept is appealing, the price tag ($2.3 million in Minnesota, $1.3 million in Colorado and $20 million in New York) may dissuade further expansions and may also discourage other states from following suit until the extent of the recession has been better gauged.

The real pioneer of the incremental approach has been Washington state, which has taken several steps to move closer to the goal of universal access. The linchpin is the Health Care Access Act of 1987, encompassing a Basic Health Plan for uninsured residents below 200 percent of poverty who are ineligible for Medicare or Medicaid, a risk pool for people who have been denied insurance because of a preexisting medical condition, enhanced Medicaid coverage, and financial assistance to hospitals and community health clinics that serve disproportionate numbers of poor and uninsured patients. The Omnibus AIDS Act of 1988 and the Maternity Care Access Act of 1989 round out the package.

Of particular interest to watchful policymakers around the country has been Washington's Basic Health Plan, which gives participants a choice of competing, prepaid managed-care programs in which to enroll. Implementation of a pilot program, limiting enrollment to 30,000 in the first three years, began in January 1989 but has been slower than expected. Enrollment stood at 13,500 at the end of 1990. This is partly because of an initial hesitancy by insurers to take part, partly because of problems in making a scattered constituency aware of the plan's existence.

Budget problems will probably prevent the legislature from expanding the plan statewide, but officials still hope the enrollment target of 25,000 by June 30, 1991, can be met. "I see no sentiment to get rid of it," Robert Crittenden, an adviser to Washington Gov. Booth Gardner, said of the Basic Health Plan, "It's shown us what voluntary efforts can do, as well as the limitations of voluntary efforts."

Employer-Based Plans

Aware of their own shaky financial underpinnings and knowing that the vast majority of the uninsured have ties to the work force (an estimated 14.8 million are employed, while 2.6 million are unemployed), a growing number of states are offering employers—especially smaller employers—a "carrot" in the form of financial incentives to subsidize employee health insurance. On average, the Small Business Administration has reported, small firms pay 40 percent more for group insurance than their larger counterparts because there is a smaller pool across which insurers can spread the risk.

In the closest thing to an identifiable trend, nine states—Oregon in 1989 and Florida, Illinois, Kansas, Kentucky, Missouri, Rhode Island, Virginia, and Washington in 1990—have authorized creation of basic benefits plans. Aimed at small employers, the plans allow companies to offer workers a basic package, stripped of the mandated benefits, including mental health, that employers say are prohibitively expensive. The plans can cost as little as $60 per person per month. A December 9 *New York Times* article quoted an official of the Blue Cross/Blue Shield Association as saying that "virtually every state" will look at this approach in 1991. A drawback to the basic benefits strategy is that "contingent" (part-time) employees, who constitute a growing part of the work force, will probably not be eligible or able to afford to buy in.

Using another kind of carrot, the Oklahoma, and Oregon legislatures have authorized tax credits to firms that provide insurance, although the carrot turns into a stick in 1994 for Oregon firms that do not comply. After that date, employers that elect not to play will pay a surtax, which will be used to finance coverage for uninsured workers.

Another fertile field that more states are expected to plow in 1991 is reform of the insurance industry, with special emphasis on the small-group market. The leader in this effort was Connecticut, which last year adopted a law that prohibits medical underwriting, creates a reinsurance mechanism to allow companies insuring high-risk individuals to offer group premiums priced at no more than 150 percent of standard-risk premiums, thereby spreading losses across all insurers in the state, and requires development of special transition policies for small firms that have not previously offered insurance. The law authorized subsidized group insurance for low-income pregnant women and for children who are ineligible for Medicaid. It also made a number of expansions of the Medicaid program itself.

W. David Helms, director of the Robert Wood Johnson Foundation's Health Care for the Uninsured program, which has spent more than $6 million since 1986 on a study of barriers to the small-employer insurance market in 10 states, says insurance reforms such as eliminating underwriting are "essential" to cracking the small-group market, as are state subsidies for low-income workers. But, Helms warned, "if it's still a voluntary market, the industry will simply price the product higher." Short of a mandate, Helms said, "you won't get universal coverage. You are going to be left with less than a perfect solution."

Only two states have found the political will to mandate universal, employer-based coverage. The first—Hawaii—enacted its Prepaid Health Care Act in 1974 and, after a long legal battle with the business community, was granted a congressional waiver in 1982 from the federal, pension law (ERISA) that exempts self-insured firms from insurance regulation by the states. Although the waiver was welcomed by state officials, it essentially froze Hawaii's law as it was written in 1974; efforts to expand it to include new benefits, such as mental health and substance abuse, have been stymied. Moreover, Congress has shown no inclination to make similar concessions to other states by loosening the terms of ERISA.

In 1988, Massachusetts moved toward universal coverage with passage of the Health Security Act. Though it has several components, including a health-insurance plan for students and a fund for the unemployed uninsured, its core is a "play or pay" program that requires all firms employing six or more workers to pay a 12 percent surtax on the first $14,000 of earnings for each eligible employee, or up to $1,680 per employee per year.

Not surprisingly, businesses in Massachusetts immediately challenged the surtax and last year succeeded in convincing the legislature to delay its effective date for two years, until 1994. The provision was vetoed by outgoing

Gov. Michael S. Dukakis, who had made the landmark law a central theme of his unsuccessful 1988 presidential bid. This year, however, with Dukakis no longer in office and with the collapse of the "Massachusetts Miracle" of economic resurgence, opponents of the surtax stand a good chance of winning not just a delay but perhaps even a repeal.

New York Assemblyman James R. Tallon, a Democrat and majority leader, said he views the Hawaii and Massachusetts successes in mandating universal insurance as unique—the former because of its geographic insulation, the latter because of its insulated economic situation at the time the law was enacted. "Absent that, I don't know how you get universality of coverage," Tallon observed, since "the substantial share of the burden [of financing mandated coverage] will be borne by general taxes or businesses." In both cases, he said, states that have mandated coverage will be subject to interstate competition and will be at an economic disadvantage vis-a-vis their neighbors that do not.

"It's very easy for states to make major changes targeted at individual sectors of the system or to achieve reforms of the insurance market," Tallon said. "We'll also see states grapple with another round—maybe even an accelerated round—of attempts to change Medicaid," he predicted. But achieving a major restructuring of the system is another matter, "I'm less optimistic about states doing that, individually or together."

Single-Payer Systems

Frustrated by federal inaction, a growing group of state legislators have major restructuring very much on their minds. Though still mostly in the concept stage, bills proposing to replace the existing "patchwork" insurance system with a single-payer system are expected to be on the agenda in several states, including California, Colorado, Ohio, and Wisconsin, in the coming year. In addition, the Robert Wood Johnson Foundation is supporting a small pilot project in New York State to test the feasibility of a centralized claims-processing system, a core component of the universal insurance plan advanced by New York's health commissioner in September 1989.

A prototype of the single-payer system is the Universal Health Insurance for Ohio (UHIO) plan. Introduced initially in 1989, the plan calls for issuing a single card to all Ohio residents to cover the full cost of physician, hospital, and clinic services, prescription drugs, dental and vision care, and mental-health and substance-abuse treatment. Cosmetic surgery and routine long-term care in nursing homes would be excluded. The plan would be run by a board appointed by the governor and approved by the state senate. Benefits would be financed by: a payroll tax on both employers and employees, to replace private health insurance premiums, copayments, and deductibles; a tax on the gross earning of the self-employed; and an increase in excise taxes on tobacco and alcohol products.

The bill's sponsor, Ohio State Rep. Robert F. Hagan, a Democrat, said that, like Canada, which sold its national health plan province-to-province, "we have to go state to state until we convince [the federal government] of the need for a national plan." Congress could help, he said, by giving at least one state a waiver "to implement a single-payer approach and work it out over a period of five to 10 years."

To remove some of the barriers to state-level experiments, the federal government could also ease up on ERISA, offer more flexibility on Medicaid waivers and offer planning and research grants in support of state-based health plans.

In Hagan's view, it has become increasingly apparent that the federal government "cannot do it." Problems ranging from the collapse of the savings and loan industry to the Persian Gulf war to the deficit will keep federal policymakers from focusing attention on the "crisis" in the health system, he asserted.

New York's Tallon said the recession could actually help efforts to forge a national plan. "When the economy is tough," he noted, "a broader base of people feel the risk, and the risk becomes more immediate." What's needed, he added, is a presidential candidate in 1992 who will make universal insurance a priority issue. The challenge to the federal government is to design a general framework and spell out basic criteria, giving the states "lots of room" in the plan's design and administration.

Some see the various state initiatives as merely "fingers in the dike"—a dike that has too many holes already. State "solutions" are doing a disservice to the ultimate goal of universal access by masking the underlying rot in the system—rot that must be exposed, discarded, and replaced with a new structure, these critics say.

The counterargument, of course, is that intensified state activities are helping to keep the public's attention focused on a problem that shows no signs of going away and may indeed yield the basis for real and more fundamental reform.

As Tallon's reasoning suggests, state-level initiatives aren't necessarily incompatible with a federal plan, if one's vision is broad enough to allow for the notion of a national program that provides for universal access and uniform benefits but that is based on a decentralized administrative system. This would give the states control over key elements such as reimbursement and regulation of providers, revenue sources, quality assurance, and organization of the delivery system.

In the final analysis, the solution to the crisis in health care is not likely to be exclusively federal or state but rather a partnership involving all levels of government. Achieving that partnership will be the challenge of the 1990s.

IV

Domestic Universal Health Plans

A   Implementing a Universal
Health Program

B   Domestic Health Plan Proposals

Introduction

Pamela Spohn

The final section of the anthology focuses on domestic health policy and a number of the more prominent proposals for financing and system reform. Many of these proposals are strikingly similar in substance to those put forth more than a decade ago. The major difference between then and now is that the severity of the problem—decreased access to care coupled with unabated cost escalation—has significantly deepened during the 1980s.

For example, Congressman Ronald Dellums's 1974 proposal for a comprehensive, community-based health care system is philosophically and conceptually aligned with the Physicians for a National Health Plan (PNHP) proposal presented in this section. Likewise, the Carter Administration's National Health Plan, introduced in 1979, included an employer mandate and reform of the Medicaid program—assumptions and structural elements found in the more recent Davis proposal.[1] A final example—the managed competition proposal of Enthoven and Kronick—is a revisitation and refinement of a 1978 Enthoven proposal known as the Consumer-Choice Health Plan.[1]

Some historians and political pundits have suggested that among the major reasons for earlier failures to enact national health insurance in the U.S. was the belief, widely held until the mid-1980s, that most people had insurance coverage. Coverage under Medicare and Medicaid, in conjunction with employer-based private health insurance, presumably assured access to care for the vast majority of Americans. During the latter half of the 1980s, however, this belief retreated behind the harsh reality that millions of Americans, including large numbers among the employed, were not covered either under public or private health insurance plans.

Although recent studies have largely dispelled the myth about the adequacy of the health care financing system, a reluctance to address these problems at the federal level remains. Numerous bills have been introduced in just the past few years: from employer mandates—Universal Health Coverage Act of 1990 (Representative D. Obey/D–WI) and the Basic Health Benefits for All Americans Act of 1989 ([S.B. 768 and H.R. 1845] Senator E. Kennedy/D–MA and Representative H. Waxman/D–CA)—to mixed public and market reform—the Comprehensive American Health Care Act ([S. 2535] Senator McConnell/R–KY)—to national health insurance plans such as USHealth ([H.R. 2930] Representative E. Roybal/D–CA)—only to be stalled or killed in legislative committees.

Inaction at the federal level has been attributed to a lack of consensus about the appropriate policy course to pursue. Powerful nongovernmental groups with vested interests—physicians, hospitals, business, labor, and the insurance industry—have succeeded in stifling broad reforms.

Adding yet further complexity and intrigue to the health care financing debate are professional and trade organizations that have developed their own national health plan proposals.[3] The relative distribution of power across these various political cleavages has shifted as new coalitions form and old ones are consumed or die. Recently, however, signs of consensus have begun emerging as special interest groups, to greater or lesser degrees, have felt mounting pressure to act in the face of a system out of control.

In lieu of federal action, some health policy experts argue that solutions will occur first at the state level (see Rashi Fein, "The Health Security Partnership: A Federal-State Universal Insurance Cost-Containment Program").[4] In fact, an increasing number of states are responding to access-related problems by enacting legislation to fill specific gaps in health insurance coverage. State strategies range from employer mandates (Hawaii and Massachusetts) and Medicaid expansions (all states were required in OBRA 90 to extend coverage to poor mothers and children up to the age of 6), to establishing high risk pools for the medically uninsurable (26 states as of December 1990) to the development and promotion of "bare bones" private-market policies (17 states as of June 1991).[5]

The states though have also experienced formidable barriers in their attempts to enact meaningful reforms. This is evidenced in the case of Massachusetts where the much-heralded Health Security Act of 1988 "is faltering under the weight of a soured economy, a hostile new Governor and the fierce opposition of small business owners" (New York Times, April 1991).

Comparing Proposals

The proposals before the public present a disconcertingly complex array of benefits and coverage, not to mention provisions for financing and administration. One way to compare the various proposals is to establish criteria by which each may be evaluated. The choice of criteria entails a number of considerations. Should criteria be rank-ordered (that is, are some dimensions of a health care plan more important than others)? For example, are equity considerations more important than efficiency measures? Further elaboration of these core issues involves asking more specific questions. Just how equitable is the financing scheme? Does the plan promote efficiency? Does it include effective cost controls? Does it address the nonfinancial barriers to care (provider willingness to care for the poor, geographic and specialty maldistribution of physicians and other health care personnel, cultural insensitivities of health care providers and institutions)?

The reader may find the six dimensions suggested below helpful for categorizing and evaluating the plans in this section. Each of these dimensions should be viewed as a continuum with the extreme scenarios at either end. While there is nothing absolute about the dimensions presented here, using such a schematic might assist the reader in judging the adequacy of the proposal from one's own hierarchically established value base.

Financing Mechanisms

Public ——————————————— Private
[broad-based taxes] [mixed public/private] [employment-
                                      based, user fees]
Grumbach (PNHP)   *Davis*   *Enthoven/Kronick*
Harrington et al.

Cost Control Feature

Highly Regulated ——————— **Market-based Controls**
[all payer prospective payment, [cost-sharing, competition]
caps on annual budgets, etc.]
Grumbach (PNHP)   *Davis*   *Enthoven/Kronick*
Harrington et al.

Integration of Acute and Chronic Care Benefits

High Integration ——————— **No Integration**
[integrated budgets and   [separately financed systems]
delivery system]
Grumbach et al.   *Davis*
Harrington et al.   *Enthoven/Kronick*

Comprehensiveness of Benefits

Comprehensive Benefits ——————— **Basic Benefit Plan**
[preventive, acute, and   [e.g., catastrophic only,
chronic care coverage]   bare bones, limited coverage]
Grumbach et al.   *Enthoven/Kronick*
Harrington et al.   *Davis*

Organization and Delivery of Care

Organized Systems ——————— **Fee-for-Service**
Enthoven/Kronick   *Davis*
    Harrington et al.
                        Grumbach et al.

Administration

Federal ——————— **States** ——————— **Private**
Davis   *Harrington et al.*   *Enthoven/Kronick*
                     Grumbach et al.

Summarizing the Proposals

1. *Reform Strategy.* One way to summarize the proposals in this section is to group them according to the level of the political/economic system targeted. For example, the Enthoven/Kronick plan proposes to initiate a "comprehensive reform of the economic incentives that drive the system." As Kronick notes elsewhere, there are "two potential strategies for achieving health care cost control: (1) industrywide price controls and (2) creation of a cost-conscious, consumer-choice environment with managed competition among health plans on the dimensions of efficiency and quality."[6] Clearly the Enthoven/Kronick plan relies on the competitive market and informed consumers to achieve both cost control and the provision of quality health care services.

There are a number of questions that derive from this approach. Should health care be considered a commodity to be brokered in the marketplace? Is competition in the health care marketplace an achievable goal: that is, is it possible to achieve a level playing field between providers and consumers? Can equity of access and quality be achieved for all segments of the health-services–consuming public? Little evidence indicates that efficient, quality health plans will willingly compete for patients in blighted urban areas or sparsely populated rural communities. The further issue is of un-even distribution of group practices throughout the country and how groups will form in states that have historically supported a fee-for-service delivery system. In its current form, the managed competition model fails to adequately address these implementation issues.

Alternatively, Karen Davis's plan proposes a significant expansion of Medicare and employer-based insurance because herein lie "the strongest elements of the current U.S. health financing system." Consonant with this level of reform are the HIAA (Schramm), Pepper Commission (Rockefeller), and AMA (Todd) plans,[1] which argue for the maintenance or expansion of a private insurance market in tandem with a sizable public plan (Medicare, Medicaid, or a hybrid of the two) that assumes responsibility for providing "primary and preventive care for the [poor] and near poor" (Schramm[1]) for "all persons with incomes below the poverty level" (Todd[1]).

In this approach, government intervention is seen as an integral component of the system, responsible for assuring access and quality and for controlling costs. Unlike the Enthoven/Kronick plan, which relies on the private market-place, the onus of fiscal and programmatic responsibility falls on the shoulders of government, and to a lesser extent on the business community in its role as prudent purchaser. In these variously described mixed public-private models, the role assumed by the private insurance industry varies significantly. Davis notes that her plan "differs from the plan advanced by the Pepper Commission and other mixed public–private plans in that it does not stress reform of the private health insurance market" but "rather, the proposal gives all employers and nonworking individuals the option of coverage under Medicare, with its administrative efficiency and strong cost-containment provisions." In contrast, other private–public proposals under discussion call for a significant level of insurance reform.

Although laudable for the practicality of their approach, i.e., preserving major elements of the present system, these mixed plans also propagate the known shortcomings inherent in the system. For example, there are no safeguards against the high administrative costs associated with the private insurance industry. Further, although Davis notes the possibility of adverse selection, she does not persuade the reader that Medicare (or its equivalent in the other proposals) will do other than enroll disproportionate numbers of high-risk beneficiaries, thus ultimately becoming a less competitive plan than the private offerings.

At an extreme end of the reform continuum are the Physicians for a National Health Plan (PNHP) proposals (Grumbach et al. and Harrington et al.). [7] These plans call for a fundamental restructuring of the current system of financing, each of which creates a single public payer to, as Grumbach et al. state, "replace the present array of more than 1,500 private insurers, Medicaid and Medicare." Although extremely attractive for their comprehensiveness of coverage and equity functions, the plans ultimately appear doomed because of the breadth and simplicity of design they propose.

Criticisms raised about PNHP include disenfranchisement (i.e., major opposition from organized medicine); cost controls without market competition; and the loss of the private health insurance industry from the economy. The vested interests alluded to earlier, particularly the American Medical Association and the private insurance industry, have waged a full-court press against such sweeping reforms. Each, with their own chosen rhetorical arguments, has discredited such an approach as not politically feasible in the U.S. system—a political economy characterized by pluralism and market competition.

2. *Nonfinancial Barriers as Implementation Issues* . There are many "details" of health care delivery that have not been addressed in the proposals in this section, such as the maldistribution of health care providers (both geographically and by specialty) and an inappropriate emphasis on financing acute care at the expense of chronic care services. One could argue that these implementation issues are best dealt with after the overall financing scheme and administrative arrangements have been agreed to by the relevant actors. In the alternative, it could be persuasively argued that these systems' design issues must be integral components of any serious reform proposal.

In most public policy arenas where universality and entitlement programs are being crafted, the tendency of policy solutions has been to aim toward the middle—the average American family with a working adult. Unfortunately, this focus has left tens of millions of Americans unprotected against catastrophic illness and chronic disease. Thus, when considering a proposal that assumes, as do Kronick and Enthoven, "a relatively few managed care organizations competing to serve competent sponsors and cost-conscious consumers.á . á . á," the reader should remember that terms such as "competent sponsors" and

"cost-conscious consumers" are not value-free. They carry meanings and implications for the most vulnerable of health care consumers—for the poor, disabled and otherwise disenfranchised citizens (for example, persons with AIDS, undocumented workers) as well as for the most secure. Is it likely that individuals who historically have been excluded from mainstream medicine, as well as health care consumers who have become accustomed to the most sophisticated technological interventions, will automatically become prudent purchasers—"cost-conscious consumers"?

The admonition of Blendon and Edwards (as paraphrased from Ginzberg and Ostow) that opens this section is worth restating as the reader considers the various health system reform proposals offered here and elsewhere. "Even if we do enact a universal health care plan, we will need additional solutions to 'the range of [nonfinancial] factors that will continue to impede access to effective care for a significant segment of the population.'"

In conclusion, a considerable amount of work has taken place in the past several years to address the problem of health access in the U.S. Numerous proposals for reform and change have been put forth—some have made it into federal and state legislative arenas in the form of legislation, while others are still being debated as conceptual. We have reviewed a number of the conceptual pieces in this section, but it would be misleading to suggest that the proposals included herein represent the full range or the most well-designed options. We encourage the reader to look both to the states—in particular to California, New York, Washington, Connecticut, Ohio, Oregon, and Wisconsin—and to the proposals put forth by such diverse groups as the National Association of Social Workers, the Heritage Foundation, the National Leadership Commission and the National Association for Public Health Policy. In each proposal the range of benefits and coverage and the financing mechanisms are differently configured, and yet somewhere we can confidently expect a compromise solution to emerge.

Notes

1. Three other proposals that have been widely discussed, which are variations on the public–private theme, are the Health Insurance Association of America's (HIAA) plan [Carl Schramm, "Health Care Financing for all Americans," *Journal of the American Medical Society* 265, no. 24 (*June 26, 1991*): 3296–99]; the American Medical Association's (AMA) proposal [James S. Todd, *et al.* "Health Access America—Strengthening the US Health Care System" *Journal of the American Medical Society* 265, no. 19 (*May 15, 1991*)]: 2503–6]; and the Pepper Commission's proposal [John D. Rockefeller, "A Call for Action: The Pepper Commission's Blueprint for Health Care Reform" *Journal of the American Medical Society*, 265, no. 19 (*May 15, 1991*): 2507–10].

2. For a discussion of these earlier proposals, see: S. Cyphert and J. Rohrer, "A National Medical Care Program: Review and Synthesis of Past Proposals," *Journal of Public Health Policy* (Winter 1988); L. Etheredge, "Universal Health Insurance: Lessons of the

1970s, Prospects for the 1990s," *Frontiers of Health Services Management* 6, no. 4 (1990); L. S. Rodberg, "Anatomy of a National Health Plan: Reconsidering the Dellums Bill After 10 Years," *Health/PAC Bulletin* 17 (1987); Alain Enthoven, "Consumer-Choice Health Plan: A National Health Insurance Proposal Based on Regulated Competition in the Private Sector," *New England Journal of Medicine* 298 (1978); J. Feder, J. Holohan, and T. Marmor, *National Health Insurance: Conflicting Goals and Policy Choices* (Washington: The Urban Institute, 1980).

3. Professional and trade organizations that have developed their own national health plan proposals include the National Association of Social Workers, the AFL-CIO; the American Nurses Association, and the American Public Health Association.

4. Rashi Fein, "The Health Security Partnership: A Federal-State Unviersal Insurance Cost-Containment Program," *Journal of the American Medical Society* 265, no. 19 (May 15, 1991).

5. The state inventory of "bare-bones" coverage can be found in *Barebones Coverage: Health Insurance That Doesn't Insure*, Families USA Foundation Report (Washington, DC). States with high-risk insurance pools were extracted from the HIAA Fact Sheet, December 1990.

6. Lynn Etheredge, "Commentary," *Frontiers of Health Services Management* 6, no. 4 (Summer 1990), p. 36.

7. The Grumbach and Harrington proposals should be viewed as two parts of a whole. The long-term care proposal (Harrington) is meant to complement the acute medical care provisions of the PNHP proposal (Grumbach).

30

Caring for the Uninsured: Choices for Reform

Robert J. Blendon and Jennifer N. Edwards

These recent events provide the impetus for this theme issue of *The Journal*: (1) Government reports show a 24 percent increase in the last decade in the total number of uninsured people and a 40 percent increase in the number of uninsured children.[1-4] Most uninsured children are part of a family with a working adult. (2) Recent studies have found that, despite considerable amounts of uncompensated care provided by hospitals and physicians, Americans without health insurance face major barriers to the receipt of needed health services. Although they suffer from higher rates of ill health than the insured population, the uninsured report fewer hospitalizations and fewer visits to a physician, shorter hospital stays, and fewer discretionary inpatient hospital treatments and tests, at higher cost. The uninsured also experience higher mortality rates when hospitalized than persons with health insurance coverage who have similar medical diagnoses.[5-11] (3) There is evidence of growing public dissatisfaction with our inability to resolve this serious problem, and there are signs of a broad consensus that some type of major reform is now required.

On one hand, current opinion survey findings show that Americans are relatively well satisfied with the medical care they receive personally compared, for example, with citizens of Canada, Great Britain, or (West) Germany. However, growing public concern over access to care for the unin-

sured and sharply rising costs have led Americans to be much less satisfied with the overall workings of our health care system (Table 1).[12,13]

In addition, as shown in the figure, increased awareness of and experience with these problems have led the public, corporate executives, and labor union leaders to support some form of universal insurance coverage, even if it means an increase in taxes.[14,15]

These factors led the editors of *The Journal* to ask readers last August to propose major options to resolve this problem.[16] Eighty authors or groups of authors from a variety of professional backgrounds submitted proposals for needed reforms. This issue of *The Journal* is an attempt to include in one place most of the major approaches to this problem at the national level. (Additional national proposals have appeared

Reprinted with permission from *JAMA, The Journal of the American Medical Association* 265, no. 19 (May 15, 1991), pp. 2563–65. Copyright © 1991 American Medical Association.

Table 1.—Public Satisfaction With Health Care System and With Own Medical Care in Four Nations*

Country	Very Satisfied With Own and Family's Care, %	Satisfied With Current Health Care System,† %
United States	55	10
Canada	60	56
Great Britain	39	27
(West) Germany	45	41

*From the Harvard Community Health Plan and Louis Harris & Associates.[13]
†Believed that only minor changes were needed.

Support for universal health insurance coverage, even if it means an increase in taxes, among the general public, corporate executives, and labor union leaders. Asterisk indicates that there were minor wording differences in the question asked of the general public (from public opinion polls conducted by the Metropolitan Life Insurance Company and Louis Harris & Associates[14] and by the Los Angeles Times[15]).

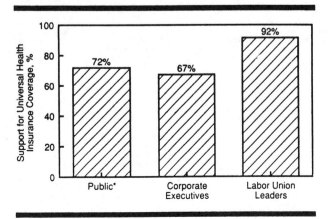

Table 2.—Proposals for Reform in This Issue of The Journal*

Author of Proposal	Coverage	Administration	Financing	Cost Containment/ Provider Reimbursement	Other Distinctive Features
TYPE I: COMPULSORY PRIVATE INSURANCE THROUGH EMPLOYERS, WITH GOVERNMENT INSURING NONWORKERS AND THE POOR					
Kirkman-Liff	Universal	Private: insurers offer community-rated plans Government: Medicare/Medicaid enrollees get vouchers to buy private insurance	Employer/employee premium sharing; federal government pays employer share of premium for nonworkers	Copayments/cost sharing; managed care optional; reimbursement negotiated between provider and payer representatives	Copies some features of German and Dutch systems; LTC benefits unmentioned
Todd et al (American Medical Association)	Nearly universal; excludes nonpoor nonworkers	Private: insurers offer private plans or state risk pool for uninsurable and others Government: unchanged	No change	Changes tax treatment of employee benefits; health promotion; repeals state-mandated benefits; seeks reduction in administrative costs; improves Medicaid reimbursement levels; private insurance unchanged	Adds private LTC benefits and expands Medicaid; catastrophic coverage; reforms Medicare trust fund
Rockefeller (Pepper Commission)	Universal	Private: insurers offer private plans Government: replaces Medicaid with new program for poor nonworkers, and self-employed, with buy-in option for employed	Employer/employee premium sharing; existing government sources plus new taxes	Encourages use of managed care; cost sharing; improves consumers' knowledge; malpractice reform; public program pays Medicare rates; private insurance unchanged	Insurance reform; universal coverage of LTC
Bronow et al (Physicians Who Care)	Nearly universal; excludes nonpoor nonworkers	Private: community-rated insurance plans with high deductibles Government: expanded Medicaid coverage	Employer/employee premium sharing plus individual medical savings accounts; government unchanged	High cost sharing; reimbursement unchanged	Adds public-private LTC coverage and catastrophic coverage
Nutter et al (Medical Schools Section, American Medical Association)	Nearly universal; excludes nonpoor nonworkers	Private: insurance plus insurance risk pools Government: expanded Medicaid coverage	Employer/employee premium sharing; employment-based tax to cover new Medicaid costs; elderly pay for Medicare expansion	All-payer, prospective payment for hospital and professional services	Eliminates deductibility of employer contributions; adds LTC and catastrophic coverage to Medicare
TYPE II: LAW REQUIRING EMPLOYERS TO PROVIDE PRIVATE INSURANCE TO EMPLOYEES OR PAY EQUIVALENT TAX, WITH GOVERNMENT INSURING NONWORKERS AND THE POOR					
Davis	Universal	Private: insurers offer private plans Government: Medicare coverage for all others	Employer/employee premium sharing or employer payroll tax; income tax; general revenues	All payers adopt Medicare rates and volume performance standards for hospitals and physicians	Allows states to buy Medicaid enrollees into Medicare; LTC expansion optional for states
Schwartz (Kansas Employer Coalition on Health)	Universal	Private: insurers offer private plans Government: regional public sponsors and Medicare	Employer/employee premium sharing; tax on individuals in pool; general revenue	Malpractice reform; increased cost sharing; health promotion; insurance price increases tied to Consumer Price Index, with government adjustments; mandatory community rating of insurance	Insurers join reinsurance pools
Enthoven and Kronick	Universal	Private insurance, Medicare, and public sponsors for all others	Employer/employee premium sharing; other sources unchanged	Increased cost sharing; market forces growing from competing managed care plans; changes the tax deductibility of employer health benefits	Emphasizes managed care delivery systems; no change in LTC benefits
Holahan et al	Universal	New federal-state program for anyone not covered by an employer or Medicare	Employer/employee premium sharing or tax; existing and new state and federal tax revenue	Federal share of health expenditures tied to growth in GNP; states have strong cost-containment incentives; tax deductibility of benefits limited to standard benefit package; reimbursement unchanged	Federalizes LTC benefits; cost containment left to the states; eliminates Medicaid

		TYPE III: TAX CREDIT FOR PURCHASE OF PRIVATE INSURANCE			
Butler (Heritage Foundation)	Universal	Individuals purchase private coverage from competing insurers independent of employers; Medicare/Medicaid beneficiaries get vouchers	Individual payment for all premiums or care; government pays for poor	Changes in tax treatment of health benefits to discourage overinsuring and overuse; reimbursement unchanged	Purchase of LTC coverage at discretion of individuals
		TYPE IV: ALL-GOVERNMENT INSURANCE SYSTEM			
Roybal (USHealth Act)	Universal	Single insurance system run by new agency; role for private insurers	Same sources of revenue to be paid into single account	Prospective payment, with total budget cap of 12% to 13% of GNP; all reimbursement based on Medicare rules	Adds broad range of health and LTC benefits
Grumbach et al (Physicians for a National Health Program)	Universal	Public administrator replaces Medicare, Medicaid, and private insurance	Payroll tax; existing government revenue sources; new taxes	Annual hospital budget negotiated with state plan based on past expenditures, performance, and cost and use projections; physicians paid on negotiated fee schedule	Each state determines who runs the plan; no copayments and deductibles; LTC fully covered
Fein (Committee for National Health Insurance)	Universal	States have much flexibility with federally specified benefits and budget oversight	Federal and state taxes and premiums paid into single state agency; agency pays insurers or providers on capitated basis; federal contribution increases based on growth in GNP	State and national health care budgets; negotiated payments to insitutional providers; negotiated physician fee schedule; expansion of capitated systems; consolidated administration; government review of technology and treatment effectiveness; administrative savings	Encourages state experimentation; LTC benefits unchanged

*LTC indicates long-term care; GNP, gross national product.

in recent issues,[17-20] and state proposals will appear in subsequent issues.) After rigorous peer review, 13 definitive proposals were selected from among the many thoughtful ones submitted. These proposals follow one of four approaches: (1) a compulsory, employer-based private insurance program, with the government insuring nonworkers and the poor; (2) a plan that requires employers to provide their employees with health insurance or pay a tax, with the government insuring nonworkers and the poor; (3) a program of income-related tax credits for individuals, independent of their employers, for the purchase of private insurance; and (4) an all-government insurance system.

Table 2 displays the proposals grouped into these four categories in a way that facilitates comparison. Although this summary masks some innovative features of individual proposals, it highlights the broad similarities. Each proposal shares the goal of achieving near-universal access to care through improved insurance coverage of the population; it is the *means* to achieve this that separate them.

We expect this framework to promote a better understanding of the choices available to us as a nation to address the problem of access to care, and ultimately to aid in finding a consensus on some acceptable, uniquely American approach to reform. Before the publication of this issue of *The Journal*, a series of national opinion surveys asked a random sample of the general public, corporate executives, and labor union leaders about their preference for two of the four types of proposals presented herein (Table 3).[14,21] The findings indicate that, although most people favored some type of universal plan, there was no majority supporting either approach. This lack of agreement on any specific plan is simi-

lar to the dilemma faced in the 1970s. During the early part of that decade, more than a dozen initiatives for universal health coverage were introduced in Congress. However, leaders of key groups and the public were unable to reach agreement on any single approach to reform.[22-24] Because the problem of adequately caring for the uninsured has been worsening, we hope that the discussion generated by this theme issue will make it easier to reach a national consensus.

When considering the various proposals, it is important to keep in mind the caveat raised by Ginzberg and Ostow[25] in their article in this issue. Even if we do enact a universal health care plan, we will need additional solutions

Table 3.—Preferences for Universal Health Insurance Systems*

System Option	Corporate Executives, %	Labor Union Leaders, %	Public, %
Favor an all-government national health plan	27	58	46
Favor a compulsory private insurance plan, with government providing for the unemployed	35	28	33
Favor no change in the present system	35	10	19

*From Louis Harris & Associates Inc.[17,21]

to "the range of [nonfinancial] factors that will continue to impede access to effective care for a significant segment of the population."

Notes

1. Walden D. Wilensky G, Kasper J. *Changes in Health Insurance Status: Full Year and Part Year Coverage: Data Preview 21*. Rockville, MD: National Center for Health Services Research; 1985. US Dept of Health and Human Services publication PHS 85–3377.

2. Short P. *Estimates of the Uninsured Population, Calendar Year 1987*. Rockville, MD: Public Health Service; 1990, US Dept of Health and Human Services publication PHS 90–3469. National Medical Expenditure Survey Data Summary 2.

3. Cunningham P, Monheit A. Insuring the children: a decade of change. *Health Aff*. Winter 1990;9:76–90.

4. Congressional Research Service. *Health Insurance and the Uninsured: Background*

sion, resource use, and outcome. *JAMA*. 1991;265:374–379.

12. Blendon R, Leitman R, Morrison I, Donelan K. Satisfaction with health systems in 10 nations. *Health Aff*. Summer 1990; 9:185–192.

13. *Comparing Health Systems: Health Service Satisfaction in Six Countries*. Boston, Mass: Harvard Community Health Plan and Louis Harris & Associates; 1990.

14. Taylor H, Leitman R. *Trade-offs and Choices: Health Policy Options for the 1990s*. New York, NY: Metropolitan Life Insurance Company and Louis Harris & Associates; 1990. Study 902026.

15. *Health Care in the United States*. Storrs, Conn: Roper Center for Public Opinion Research and the Los Angeles Times; 1990. Poll 212.

16. Lundberg GD, Blendon RJ. A special *JAMA* issue on caring for the uninsured and the underinsured. *JAMA*. 1990;264: 739.

17. Kleinman LC. Health care in crisis: a proposed role for the individual physician as advocate. *JAMA*. 1991;265:1991–1992.

18. Moore GT. Let's provide primary care to all uninsured Americans—now! *JAMA*. 1991;265:2108–2109.

19. Daniels N. Is the Oregon rationing plan fair? *JAMA*. 1991;265:2232–2235.

20. Gleicher N. Expression of health care to the uninsured and underinsured has to be cost-neutral. *JAMA*. 1991;265:2388–2390.

21. *Health Care Poll*. Storrs, Conn: Roper Center for Public Opinion Research and Louis Harris P Associates; 1990.

22. Blendon R, Donelan K. The public and the emerging debate over national health insurance. *N Engl J Med*. 1990;323:208–212.

23. Etheredge L. Universal health insurance: Lessons of the 1970's, prospects for the 1990's. *Front Health Serv Manage*. Winter 1990;6:3–35.

24. Waldman S. *National Health Insurance Proposals*. Washington, DC: Social Security Administration; 1974:21–44. Publication SSA7–11902.

25. Ginzberg E, Ostow M. Beyond universal health insurance to effective health care. *JAMA*. 1991;265:2559–2562.

31

Expanding Medicare and Employer Plans to Achieve Universal Health Insurance

Karen Davis

The United States has a mixed public-private system of financing health care. In 1988, of 244 million Americans, 13 percent were covered by Medicare, 6 percent by Medicaid, 57 percent by employer health plans, 9 percent by individual insurance or other sources, and 15 percent were uninsured.[1] This patchwork approach to health insurance coverage, while it serves some Americans well, contributes to a complex, costly health care system. The United States spends 12 percent of its gross national product on health care—far more than any other industrialized nation. Of greatest concern, an estimated 37 million uninsured people are vulnerable to receiving inadequate health care in the event of illness or injury and are exposed to the risk of severe financial hardship from health care bills.[2-4]

This article presents a plan to cover the entire U.S. population by building on the two strongest elements of the current system—employer-provided health insurance and the Medicare program, which currently covers elderly and disabled persons—while instituting a new universal provider payment system to control rising costs. This plan would achieve greater efficiency and simplicity by establishing a common basic benefit package under both Medicare and employer plans, and establishing common provider payment meth-

ods applicable to both Medicare and employer plans. It would be financed through a combination of employer and individual premium contributions, payroll taxes, personal income taxes, and other general tax revenues.

Rationale

The strongest elements of the current U.S. health financing system are the Medicare program and health insurance provided through large employer-based plans. Both are popular with beneficiaries and have a proven record of administrative efficiency with a low ratio of administrative expenses to benefits. Medicare has adopted new methods of paying hospitals and physicians that provide incentives for provider efficiency, simplify administration for both the program and providers, improve the equity of payment among providers, and give the federal government an enhanced ability to moderate the historical rates of spending growth.[5,6] Many large employer plans have been innovative in the establishment of incentives for employees to join lower-cost health maintenance organizations and other managed care plans.[6]

The Medicaid program is an important source of health financing for the poor and has been instrumental in improving access to health care for many of the nation's poor.[7-9] It is the only significant source of financing for long-term care—with over 40 percent of Medicaid expenditures devoted to nursing home care. However, the program

has a number of limitations. Medicaid provider payment rates are clearly substandard. The program is administratively complex, causing many eligible people to fail to participate.

The most unsatisfactory sources of insurance coverage are individual insurance plans and small group insurance. Such plans have high administrative costs, charge high premiums, exclude individuals who are major health risks, and exclude coverage for preexisting conditions.[9,10]

Building on the strongest parts of the current U.S. health financing system would have several advantages. With an existing administrative structure, expanded coverage could be implemented relatively quickly with minimal disruption of current coverage. Further, by building on current programs rather than replacing them, current revenue sources would be maintained. Any new taxes or other revenues could be targeted for care of the uninsured, rather than, for example, requiring major tax increases to replace existing private coverage.

Basic Structure

All employers would be required to provide basic health insurance coverage to full-time and part-time workers and dependents, or pay a payroll tax contribution toward the cost of their coverage under Medicare. Required employer financial obligations under either private insurance or Medicare would be limited to 6 percent of workers' wages. This

Reprinted with permission from *JAMA, The Journal of the American Medical Association* 265, no. 19 (May 15, 1991), pp. 2525–28. Copyright © 1991 American Medical Association.

would expand coverage to two thirds of the uninsured who are members of working families. States would be given the option of buying all current Medicaid beneficiaries and others below the poverty income level into Medicare, shifting most of the cost of basic hospital and physician benefits to the federal government. The remaining uninsured would be covered under Medicare, and would be assessed an income-related premium through the income tax system.

Benefits

The current Medicare benefit package would be expanded to include preventive care for pregnant women and children, in addition to the current benefit package of hospital services, physician services, limited home care and nursing home care, limited mental health services, and limited adult preventive services. The cost-sharing structure of Medicare would be revised to include a maximum $250 per person, or $500 per family deductible—rather than separate deductibles for hospital and physician services. A coinsurance of 20 percent would apply to all services other than hospital care. Cost sharing would be limited to $1,500 for an individual, or $3,000 for a family annually.

Employer Responsibilities

Employers would be required to contribute toward the health insurance coverage of full-time and part-time (defined as at least 10 hours per week) workers and dependents. Since all employers would be subject to this requirement, working spouses would be covered under their own employer's plan.

Employer coverage under private plans would be required to cover benefits at least as comprehensive as the Medicare benefit package. Employers could choose to provide benefits beyond this benefit package, without penalty to employers or workers.

Employers would be required to contribute at least 6 percent of employee earnings on average toward private plan coverage, not to exceed the cost of the basic benefit plan. Employees would be responsible for the remainder of the

premium, but could negotiate with employers to cover a higher percentage. Alternatively, employers could meet this obligation by paying a 6 percent payroll tax to Medicare, resulting in coverage of workers and dependents under Medicare. Families bought into coverage under Medicare by employers would also contribute 2 percent of their family income toward coverage. Contributions to health coverage under either private plans or Medicare for low-income families would be offset by an increase in the earned income tax credit to ensure that such coverage would be affordable for low-wage workers.

State Medicaid Plans

States would be given the option of buying all Medicaid beneficiaries and other individuals below the federal poverty income level into Medicare. Currently, states are required to buy Medicare coverage for all elderly, and disabled Medicare beneficiaries with incomes below the federal poverty level, and recent legislation will require Medicaid programs to pay the Medicare premiums for those with incomes up to 120 percent of the federal poverty level. In addition, under recent legislation states will be required to provide Medicaid coverage to all children up to age 18 years in families with incomes below the federal poverty level.

Under the proposal, states would be given the option of enrolling all Medicaid beneficiaries in Medicare. However, states electing this option would be required to extend this option to all uninsured poor adults as well as children. States would be responsible for sharing with the federal government the cost of the Medicare Part B premium (currently $32 monthly), deductibles, and coinsurance on covered services. The effect of this provision is to shift most of the cost of hospital and physician services for Medicaid beneficiaries to the federal government, and nearly all states could be expected to do so. In addition, states could elect to supplement the Medicare benefit package, covering prescription drugs, dental care, and other optional services with full state funding.

The federal government would continue to share in the cost of long-term care services for Medicaid beneficiaries according to the current federal-state matching rate. Reform of long-term care financing is also an important issue for the national health policy agenda, but is not addressed herein. It adds significantly to the cost of any health insurance reform proposal, and is, in my view, best addressed separately on its own merits.

The Medicare provider payment rates for hospitals, physicians, and other providers would apply to services provided to low-income beneficiaries bought into Medicare coverage by the states. Physicians would not be permitted to charge low-income beneficiaries fees in excess of the Medicare allowable fees.

Remaining Uninsured

An estimated 5 to 8 million nonpoor individuals would remain uninsured after expansion of employer coverage to all working families and Medicaid buy-in to Medicare of all poor individuals. Some of these individuals are early retirees who do not have retiree health benefits; some are disabled individuals who have not met the two-year waiting period for Medicare coverage.[11]

All remaining uninsured individuals would be automatically covered under Medicare. They would be assessed a tax equal to 2 percent of their income, prorated over the year for any portion of the year during which the individual was not covered by private insurance. This would guarantee that all individuals who fail to be covered under an employer plan, an individual health insurance plan, or a state Medicare buy-in plan would be protected from the risk of financial catastrophe in the event of a serious illness or injury.

Medicare Beneficiaries

Medicare beneficiaries would experience some changes under the plan. The cost-sharing structure would be modified to include a single deductible of $250 per person for all services, rather than separate hospital and physician deductibles. A ceiling on out-of-pocket expenses of $1,500 per person would be established. On average, beneficiary cost-sharing burdens could be expected to decline, especially for those who have catastrophic illnesses or injuries.

Financing

The current Medicare Trust Funds would be replaced with two new trust funds: the Medicare Elderly and Disabled Beneficiaries Trust Fund and the Medicare Employed Families and Individuals Trust Fund. Current Medicare beneficiaries services would be financed by revenue flows into the Medicare Elderly and Disabled Beneficiaries Trust Fund. Newly covered Medicare beneficiaries, including those bought in by employer contributions and by state Medicaid plans, would be covered under the Medicare Employed Families and Individuals Trust Fund.

The current financing of care for the elderly and disabled would be modified somewhat. Payroll tax contributions of 1.45 percent of earnings up to $125,000 for employers and employees would continue to be assessed and would flow into the Medicare Elderly and Disabled Beneficiaries Trust Fund. The current Medicare Part B flat premium would be replaced by a premium set at 2 percent of family income, not to exceed the full actuarial value of Medicare. Revenues from this income-related premium would be approximately equal to current Part B premium receipts, although the distribution of the financial burden of the premium would clearly be shifted to higher-income Medicare beneficiaries. The premium would be collected through the income tax system, and forgiven for anyone with no net tax liability.[12] The premium would no longer be voluntary, but required of all Medicare beneficiaries. General tax revenues would continue to subsidize care for elderly and disabled beneficiaries, at a rate equivalent to the current general tax revenue contribution to Part B of Medicare.

Financing of the Medicare Employed Families and Individuals Trust Fund would be based on the 6 percent of payroll contributions by employers and 2 percent of income contributions of families and individuals newly covered under Medicare. States would contribute the state share of Medicare Part B premiums and cost sharing for Medicaid and other poor beneficiaries based on the current state matching rate under Medicaid. Federal general tax revenues would be used to provide any additional subsidies required to cover the remaining cost of employed families and non-working individuals.

Provider Payment and System Reform

Employer plans would incorporate Medicare's provider payment methods. Specifically, physicians would be paid according to the Medicare Fee Schedule for all services, and a maximum limit on balance billing would be set on all services similar to that in the Medicare program. Employers electing to pay the balance bills for workers and dependents would be permitted to do so.

The Medicare Fee Schedule would result in lower physician payments than is currently the case in some private employer plans. Physicians would receive higher payments for Medicaid and uninsured patients. This would provide greater equity to physicians who currently provide a disproportionate share of care to low-income patients, and expand availability of care to such patients.

The Medicare Volume Performance Standard that now establishes a target for growth in expenditures for physician services under Medicare would be modified to include employer plans. This economic incentive to control unnecessary growth in the volume of services would be supplemented by the development of appropriateness guidelines and expanded research on effectiveness of medical procedures and treatment.

Hospitals would be paid a flat rate for the care of inpatients covered under employer plans based on the diagnosis related group prospective payment system. Hospitals would not be permitted to charge patients over and above the allowed rate. Again, while Medicare rates are lower than in some employer plans, bad debts for care of the uninsured and low payments by Medicaid would be eliminated under the plan.

Beneficiaries enrolled in both Medicare and employer plans would be given the option of enrolling in health maintenance organizations or other managed care plans. Employers would be permitted to pay a higher percentage of the premium, reduce cost sharing, or otherwise provide financial incentives to workers and dependents to enroll in more cost-effective managed care plans. However, the current practice by which larger employers obtain favorable price discounts through preferred provider organizations would no longer be permitted. Instead preferred provider organizations would be required to compete on the basis of the effectiveness of their utilization review and other managed care techniques.

Cost

While careful cost analysis would be required to estimate the fiscal impact of the proposal, a rough estimate can be obtained by drawing on the work of the Pepper Commission.[13] The benefits and coverage of the proposal are quite similar to the Pepper proposal, although the sources of financing, cost-containment methods including universal provider payment, role of private insurance, and administrative mechanisms differ. Like the Pepper plan, it can be expected that the incremental federal governmental outlays will be on the order of $25 billion annually (my estimate). These costs would be somewhat lower given the expansions of Medicaid that have occurred since the cost of the Pepper proposal was estimated. The cost-containment mechanisms set forth may also result in lower costs over time.

The new federal budgetary costs would be met through a combination of employer payroll tax contributions set at 6 percent of earnings for those newly covered under Medicare and individual contributions set at 2 percent of earnings for those covered under Medicare. Any remaining revenues could be met either through a 2 percent income tax surcharge on all tax-paying households or the establishment of a new upper income tax bracket of 38 percent.

Comment

The principal advantage of the plan is that it is a feasible approach that draws on the strengths of the current system while simplifying the benefit and provider payment structure and instituting innovations to promote efficiency. It minimizes the need for additional federal outlays, spreads the financial burden of health spending more equitably among employers and states, and makes health insurance more affordable to small businesses, self-employed, and nonworking individuals.

The plan achieves greater equity within the health care system by reducing the fiscal burden of hospitals, physicians, and primary care centers providing charity care to the uninsured and contributes to their financial survival. It protects all Americans from the financial hardship of health care bills, and it helps get all children off to a healthy start in life through comprehensive coverage of maternal and infant health care.

It builds on the existing administrative system for employer-provided health insurance and Medicare and, most important, realizes savings from lower administrative costs of these plans.

The combination of a universal provider payment system, coupled with expenditure constraints and incentives for managed care, should greatly improve the ability of government and employers to constrain rising health care costs. It preserves pluralism in the health system, while permitting effective cost containment through a unified payer approach to setting physician and hospital payment rates similar to those of other industrialized nations.

This approach has a minimal disruptive economic impact and is likely to have a negligible impact on employment in small firms, with some expansion of jobs in the health sector. Its design minimizes any inflationary impact on the health sector, while making American products more competitive in international markets through effective cost controls and more equitable sharing of costs among employers.

The plan differs from the plan advanced by the Pepper Commission[13] and other mixed public-private plans in that it does not stress reform of the private health insurance market—such as requiring community-rating, prohibiting the exclusion of preexisting conditions,

or establishing risk-sharing pools. While these measures are commendable and perhaps worthy of trial, they are working against the economic incentives insurers have to avoid bad risks and are likely to be circumvented through imaginative marketing practices.

Rather, the proposal gives all employers and nonworking individuals the option of coverage under Medicare, with its administrative efficiency and strong cost-containment provisions. This should provide an incentive to private insurers to offer plans with good benefits at competitive premiums to avoid loss of enrollees to Medicare. However, it can be expected that the Medicare alternative will be relatively more attractive to low-wage employers, groups with greater than average health risk, and small firms that do not wish to search for a less costly private plan.

The tendency of low-wage employers to seek Medicare coverage, however, can be viewed as an advantage. It should help increase the stability of coverage of low-income individuals as they gain employment and leave welfare. Their coverage under state purchase of Medicare will continue as employer purchase of Medicare.

The option of purchasing Medicare should also reduce the extent of variation in experience-rated premiums among employer private insurance plans, by permitting high-risk groups to choose Medicare coverage. Dumping individuals identified as poor risks on Medicare should be mitigated by the requirement that an employer make an all-or-nothing decision to cover employees under Medicare. Persons deemed bad risks could not be singled out for public plan coverage. Medicare coverage, however, could be expected to be attractive to early retirees with health problems who do not have employer retiree health benefits or who cannot purchase private insurance individually at an attractive premium. Medicare becomes, in effect, the mechanism for pooling the cost of many high-risk persons, with necessary subsidies provided by general tax revenues.

The United States cannot afford to continue on its present course with a

costly health system that subjects many of its most vulnerable citizens to inadequate health care. It is hoped that this article will contribute to shaping a consensus for change.

Notes

1. *Overview of Entitlement Programs: 1990 Green Book*. Washington, DC: US House of Representatives, Committee on Ways and Means; 1990.
2. Davis K. Availability of medical care and its financing. In: Rogers DE, ed. *Doctoring America*. Baltimore, Md: The Johns Hopkins School of Medicine; 1990.
3. Freeman HE, Blendon RJ, Aiken L, Sudman S, Mullimix C, Corey C. Americans report on their access to health care. *Health Aff*. 1987;6:6–18.
4. Blendon RJ. What should be done about the uninsured poor? *JAMA*. 1988;260:3176–77.
5. Ginsburg PB, LeRoy LB, Hammons GT. Medicare physician payment reform. *Health Aff*. 1990;9:178–88.
6. Davis K, Anderson GF, Rowland D, Steinberg EP. *Health Care Cost Containment*. Baltimore, MD: The Johns Hopkins Press; 1990.
7. Davis K, Rowland R. Financing health care for the poor: contribution of health services research. In: Eli Ginzberg, ed. *Health Services Research: Key to Health Policy*. Cambridge, MA: Harvard University Press; 1991:93–125.
8. Rogers DE, Blendon RJ, Moloney TW. Who needs Medicaid? *N Engl J Med*. 1982;307:13–18.
9. Davis K. *National Health Insurance: Benefits, Costs, and Consequences*. Washington, DC: The Brookings Institution; 1975.
10. Davis K. National health insurance: a proposal. *Am Econ Rev*. 1989;79:349–52.
11. Davis K. Uninsured older adults: the need for a Medicare buy-in option. In: *Health Insurance Options: Expanding Coverage Under Medicare and Other Public Health Insurance Programs*. Washington, DC: US House of Representatives, Committee on Ways and Means; 1990.
12. Davis K, Rowland D. *Medicare Policy: New Directions for Health and Long-term Care*. Baltimore, Md: The Johns Hopkins Press; 1986.
13. U.S. Bipartisan Commission on Comprehensive Health Care. *A Call for Action*. Washington, DC: The Pepper Commission on Comprehensive Health Care; 1990.

32

Universal Health Insurance
Through Incentives Reform

Alain C. Enthoven and Richard Kronick

American national health expenditures are now about 13 percent of the gross national product, up from 9.1 percent in 1980, and they are projected to reach 15 percent by 2000, far more than in any other country.[1-3] These expenditures are straining public finances at all levels of government. At the same time, roughly 35 million Americans have no health care coverage at all, public or private, and the number appears to be rising.[4-7] Millions more have inadequate insurance that leaves them vulnerable to large expenses, that excludes care of preexisting conditions, or that may be lost if they become seriously ill. The American health care financing and delivery system is becoming increasingly unsatisfactory and cannot be sustained. Comprehensive reform is urgently needed.

Diagnosis

The etiology of this worsening paradox is extremely complex; many factors enter in. Some factors we would not change if we could (e.g., advancing medical technology, people living longer). We emphasize factors that are important and correctable.

First, our health care financing and delivery system contains more incentives to spend than to not spend. It is based on *cost-unconscious demand* . Key decision makers have little or no incen-

tive to seek value for money in health care purchases. The dominant open-ended fee-for-service (FFS) system pays providers more for doing more, whether or not more is appropriate. ("Open ended" means that no budget is set in advance within which the job must be done.) Once insured, consumers are not cost conscious. Deductibles and coinsurance at the point of service have little or no effect on most spending, which is on sick people who have exceeded their out-of-pocket spending limits. "Free choice of provider insurance" blocks cost consciousness on the demand side by depriving the insurer of bargaining power. This approach is rapidly yielding in the marketplace to preferred provider insurance. In its present forms, preferred provider insurance helps to regulate price but is not yet very effective in controlling the volume of services. Medicare, Medicaid, and the subsidies to employer-provided health care coverage built into the income and payroll tax laws are all open ended and encourage decisions in favor of more costly care. These incentives are reinforced by a medical culture that esteems use of the most advanced technology, high patient expectations, and the threat of malpractice litigation if these expectations are not met.

Contrary to a widespread impression, America has not yet tried *competition* of alternative health care financing and delivery plans, using the term in the normal economic sense, i.e., *price* competition to serve cost-conscious purchasers. When there is price competition, the purchaser who chooses the

more expensive product pays the full difference in price and is thus motivated to seek value for money. However, in offering health care coverage to employees, most employers provide a larger subsidy to the FFS system than to health maintenance organizations (HMOs), thereby destroying the incentive for consumers and providers to choose the economical alternative. Many employers offer no choice but FFS coverage.[8,9] Others offer choices but pay the whole premium, whichever choice the employee makes. In such a case, the HMO has no incentive to hold down its premium; it is better off to charge more and use the money to improve service. In many other cases, employers offer a choice of plan, but the employer pays 80 percent or 90 percent of the premium or all but some fixed amount, whichever plan the employee chooses. In all these cases, the effect is that the employer pays more on behalf of the more costly system and deprives the efficient alternatives of the opportunity to attract more customers by cutting cost and price.

The rational policy from an economic point of view would be for employers to structure health plan offerings to employees so that those who choose the less costly plans get to keep the full savings. Several factors discourage them from doing this. Employers became committed to paying the price of the FFS plan in the 1960s and 1970s, when costs were much lower and HMOs were few. Now this commitment is hard to break. When an employment group considers more costly and less

Reprinted with permission from *JAMA, The Journal of the American Medical Association* 265, no. 19 (May 15, 1991), pp. 2532–36. Copyright © 1991 American Medical Association.

costly health plans, it knows that government will pay about one third of the extra cost of the more costly plan through tax remission. Labor unions see management commitment to full payment of costs of the open-ended system as a precious bargaining prize. There is a need for collective action. If one employer attempts to convert to cost-conscious employee choice while other employers remain with the employer-pay-all system, the employer will get disgruntled employees in the short run but no reformed, cost-effective health care system in the long run. For the latter to happen, most employers in a geographic area must convert to cost-conscious choice.

The second major problem is that our present health care financing and delivery system is not organized for quality and economy. One of the main drives in the present system is for each specialist to exercise his or her specialty, not to produce desired outcomes at reasonable cost. In a system designed for quality and economy, managed care organizations would attract the responsible participation of physicians who would understand that, ultimately, their patients bear the costs of care, and they would accept the need for an economical practice style. Data would be gathered on outcomes, treatments, and resource use, and providers would base clinical decisions on such data. We have few outcome data today. The FFS system often pays more to poor performers who have high rates of complications than to good performers who solve patients' medical problems quickly and economically. High-quality performers are not rewarded, because of the payment system and because employers and consumers do not have the data to identify them.

There are too many beds and too many specialists in relation to the number of primary care physicians. A high-quality cost-effective system would carefully match the numbers and types of physicians retained and other resources to the needs of the population served so that each specialist and subspecialist would be busy seeing just the type of patient she or he was trained to treat. We have a proliferation of costly specialized services that are underutilized. For example, in 1986, more than one third of the hospitals in California doing open-heart surgery performed fewer than 150 operations, the minimum annual volume recommended by the American College of Surgeons (*Los Angeles Times*, December 27, 1988:3).

The third major problem area is "market failure." The market for health insurance does not naturally produce results that are fair or efficient. It is plagued by problems of biased risk selection, market segmentation, inadequate information, "free riders," and the like.[10] Insurers profit most by avoiding coverage of those who need it most. The insurance market for small employment groups is breaking down as small employers find insurance unavailable or unaffordable, especially if a group member has a costly medical condition. Most employment groups are too small for risk spreading or economical purchase of health insurance. Systematic action by large collective purchasers is needed to manage competition to reward providers of high-quality economical care and to make affordable coverage available to individuals and small groups.

Fourth, public funds are not distributed equitably or effectively to motivate widespread coverage. The unlimited exclusion of employer health benefit contributions from the taxable incomes of employees is the second-largest federal government health care "expenditure," trailing only expenditures for the Medicare program. While providing incentives for the well-covered well-to-do to choose even more generous coverage, this provision does little or nothing for those (mainly lower-income) people without employer-provided coverage. Most of the $46 billion the federal budget lost to this tax break in 1990 went to households with above-average incomes, many of whom would have bought at least catastrophic expense protection without the tax subsidy, while little went to households with below-average incomes, people whose decisions to insure could be substantially affected by such subsidies. The system works backwards: the most powerful incentives to insure go to those in the highest income tax brackets. From a tax effectiveness point of view, it should be the reverse. Government-provided subsidies should give everyone strong incentives to purchase coverage and to choose economically.

In brief, powerful *incentives* that shape behavior in the health care system and that influence the distribution of services point the system in the wrong direction: services too costly for those who are covered, and the exclusion of millions from any coverage at all.

Our Proposal

We propose a set of public policies and institutions designed to give everyone access to a subsidized but responsible choice of efficient, managed care (HMO, preferred provider insurance plans, etc).[11,12] We propose *comprehensive reform of the economic incentives* that drive the system. We propose cost-conscious informed consumer and employer (or other sponsor) choice of managed care so that plans competing to serve such purchasers will have strong incentives to give value for money. We also propose a strategy of *managed competition* to be executed by large employers and public sponsors (explained below), designed to reward with more subscribers those health care financing and delivery plans that offer high-quality care at relatively low cost. The goal of these policies would be the gradual transformation of the health care financing and delivery system, through voluntary private action, into an array of managed care plans, each competing to attract providers and subscribers by finding ways to improve the quality of care and service while cutting costs. We propose restructuring the tax subsidies to create incentives to cover the uninsured and to encourage the insured to be cost conscious in their choice of plan. We propose the creation of public institutions to broker and market subsidized coverage for all who do not obtain it through large employers. We favor substantial public investments in outcomes and effectiveness research to improve the information base for medical practice and consumer/employer choice.

Public Sponsor Agencies

The Public Sponsor, a quasi-public agency (like the Federal Reserve) in each state, would contract with a number of private-sector health care financing and delivery plans typical of those offered to the employed population and would offer subsidized enrollment to all those who do not have employment-based coverage. Except in the case of the poor, the Public Sponsor would contribute a fixed amount equal to 80 percent of the cost of the average plan that just meets federal standards. The enrollee would pay the rest. (The 80 percent level was chosen to balance two incentives. First, we wanted the subsidy level to be low enough so that there would be room for efficient plans to compete by lowering prices and taking subscribers away from inefficient plans. Second, we wanted the subsidy to be high enough so that the purchase of health insurance would appear very attractive even to those who expect to have no medical expenses.) To the enrollee, the Public Sponsor would look like the employee benefits office.

In the case of the poor, we propose additional subsidies. People at or below the poverty line would be able to choose any health plan with a premium at or below the average and have it fully paid. For people with incomes between 100 percent and 150 percent of the poverty line, we propose public sharing of the premium contribution on a sliding scale related to income.

Public Sponsors would also act as collective purchasing agents for small employers who wished to take advantage of economies of scale and of the ability of Public Sponsors to spread and manage risk. Small employers could obtain coverage for their groups by payment of a maximum of 8 percent of their payroll.

Today, a substantial part of the money required to pay for care of the uninsured comes from more or less broadly based state and local sources, including employers' payments to private hospitals for bad debt or free care and direct appropriations from state and local governments to acute-care hospitals. In our proposal, federal funds (the sources of which are described below) would be the main source of support for the Public Sponsors. These funds would be supplemented by funds from state and local sources.

Mandated Employer-Provided Health Insurance

For better or worse, we have an employment-based system of health insurance for most people under age 65 years. It can be modified gradually but not replaced overnight. Most employers and employees agree that health care will be included in the compensation package. This is responsible behavior; if one of the group gets sick, the group pays the cost. Some employers and employees do not include health care in the package. The effect is irresponsible behavior; if an employee becomes seriously ill, these employers and employees count on someone else to pay. They are taking a "free ride." It is hard to justify raising taxes on the insured to pay for coverage for the employed uninsured unless those uninsured are required to contribute their fair share.

The existence of Public Sponsors would give all employers access to large-scale efficient health care coverage arrangements. However, in the absence of corrective action, the availability of subsidized coverage for uninsured individuals would create an incentive for employers to drop coverage of their employees. This would create additional expense for the Public Sponsor without compensating revenue. To prevent this, our proposal requires employers to cover their full-time employees (employers would make a defined contribution equal to 80 percent of the cost of an average plan meeting federal standards and would offer a choice of health plans meeting federal standards).

Premium Contributions from All Employers and Employees

Many people who are self-employed, who have part-time or seasonal work, or who are retired and under age 65 years do not have enough attachment to one employer to justify requiring the employer to provide coverage. Thus, an employer mandate for full-time employees would leave out millions of people. Moreover, in the absence of corrective action, a requirement that employers cover full-time employees creates a powerful incentive to use part-time employees.

We propose that employers be required to pay an 8 percent payroll tax on the first $22,500 of the wages and salaries of part-time and seasonal employees, unless the employer covered the employee with a health insurance plan meeting federal standards. Self-employed persons, early retirees, and everyone else not covered through employment would be required to contribute through the income tax system. An 8 percent tax would apply to adjusted gross income up to an income ceiling related to the size of the household. The ceiling would be calculated to ensure that households with sufficient income paid for approximately the total subsidy that would be made available to them through the Public Sponsor.

The proceeds of these taxes would be paid by the federal government to the states, on a per-person-covered basis, for use by Public Sponsors in offering subsidized coverage to persons without employment-based coverage.

This tax would be at the federal level because individual states might be deterred from levying such a tax by employer threats to move to a state without the tax.

Limit on Tax-Free Employer Contributions

We propose that Congress change the income and payroll tax laws to limit the tax-free employer contribution to 80 percent of the average price of a comprehensive plan meeting federal standards. The average price of a qualified health plan in 1991 might be roughly $290 per family per month. As a condition of tax exemption, employer health plans would be required to use fixed-dollar defined contributions, independent of employee choice of plan, not to exceed the limit, so that people who choose more costly health care plans must do so with their *own* money, not with that of the taxpayer or employer.

The purposes of this measure are twofold. First, it would save the federal budget some $11.2 billion in 1988 dollars. This money could be used to help finance subsidies for the uninsured comparable to those received by the employed insured. Second, making people cost conscious would help enlist all employed Americans in a search for value for money in health care, would stimulate the development of cost-effective care, and would create a market for cost-effective managed care. Thus, this tax reform is defensible on grounds of both equity and efficiency.

Budget Neutrality

The Congressional Budget Office has estimated the effects of our proposal on coverage, costs, and the federal budget and has found that our proposed new revenues would equal the added outlays.[13] We have not done a state-by-state analysis, but, in the aggregate, required state and local contributions appear to approximately equal outlays for care of the uninsured.

Managed Competition

The market for health insurance does not naturally produce results that are fair or efficient. It is plagued by problems of biased risk selection, market segmentation, inadequate information, etc. In fact, the market for health insurance cannot work at the individual level. To counteract these problems, large employers and Public Sponsors must structure and manage the demand side of this market.[10] They must act as intelligent, active, collective purchasing agents and manage a process of informed cost-conscious consumer choice of "managed care" plans to reward providers of high-quality economical care. Tools of effectively managed competition include the annual open-enrollment process; full employee consciousness of premium differences; a standardized benefit package within each sponsored group; risk-adjusted sponsor contributions, so that a plan that attracts predictably sicker people is compensated; monitoring disenrollments; surveillance; ongoing quality measurement; and improved consumer information.

Outcomes Management and Effectiveness Research

As Ellwood[14] and Roper et al.[15] have pointed out, there is a poverty of relevant data linking outcomes, treatments, and resource use. Although such data

are costly to gather, they constitute a public good, and their production ought to be publicly mandated and supported. Combined with the incentives built into our proposal, such data could be of great value to providers and patients seeking more effective and less costly treatments. Without incentives for efficiency, such data are likely to have little impact on health care costs.

Mutually Supportive Components

Some components of our proposal have been proposed individually. However, they would be much more effective as parts of an integrated, comprehensive reform program than they would be alone. Consider, for example, a law that employers must cover their full-time employees. Alone, this law would leave out people who are not employed on a full-time basis and their dependents— 12 million people. Without a payroll tax on uninsured employees, employers would have a strong incentive to escape the mandate by using part-time employees. Without Public Sponsors, the law would not address the problem of availability of affordable coverage for small employers. Without the limit on tax-free employer contributions, the law would not address the need for cost-containment strategy.

We recognize the propensity of the American political system to seek minimal, incremental change. Some components of our proposal would be viable and helpful on their own. However, we believe that effective solution of the problems of access and cost requires a comprehensive stretegy, and the merits of the combined package exceed the merits of the individual components.

Will It Work?

Our confidence that a reasonably well-managed comprehensive reform plan along these lines can be made to work rests on two propositions.

First, efficiently managed care does exist. It is possible to improve economic performance substantially over the non-selective FFS, solo practice, third-party intermediary model. The best documented example was a randomized comparison of per capita resource use be-

tween Group Health Cooperative of Puget Sound and traditional third-party insurance and FFS providers in Seattle, Wash., in the Health Insurance Experiment of the RAND Corp.[16] Group Health Cooperative of Puget Sound cared for its assigned patients at a cost about 28 percent lower than that in the FFS sector, resulting essentially equal health outcomes and overall patient satisfaction about 95 percent as high. Satisfaction with interpersonal aspects of care and technical quality was 98 percent as high as in the FFS sector.[17,18] Group Health Cooperative of Puget Sound accomplished this without much cost-conscious demand and without any significant competing organized system. One wonders how much better they might have done if there had been several such organizations competing to serve cost-conscious consumers. Other nonrandomized studies have produced similar results.[19]

Many physicians and patients may prefer practice styles other than prepaid group practice. We do not have similar experimental evidence on the economic performance of independent practice associations and preferred provider insurance plans. However, we have observed wide variation in the performance of providers. For example, in Los Angeles, California, in 1986, one hospital performed 44 coronary artery bypass grafts with an 11.4 percent death rate and median charges of $59,000, while another hospital performed 770 coronary artery bypass grafts with a 3.8 percent death rate and median charges of $16,000 (*Los Angeles Times*, July 24, 1988:3). Some managed care plans would find ways of selecting economical providers of high quality and would channel business to them, improving quality and cutting costs substantially.

Second, people do choose value for money. Our limited experience with even attenuated price competition in employment groups such as federal employees, California state employees, and Stanford University suggests that, over time, people do migrate to cost-effective systems. A recent study of health plan choice in the Twin Cities, Minnesota, area found that employees' decisions are quite sensitive to health plan prices.[20,21] This accords with generally accepted principles of economic behavior.

We have been asked, "Why, if nonprofit HMOs are so much more efficient and desirable, have they failed to grow except very modestly?" In times past, legal and professional barriers were important, including illegal restraints of trade.[22] In recent years, the main inhibitor of the growth of HMOs has been the employer contribution policies we have discussed; that is, most employers do not structure their health plan offerings in such a way that the employee who chooses the most economical plan gets to keep the savings. Nevertheless, some nonprofit HMOs have been growing rapidly; through the 1980s, Harvard Community Health Plan averaged membership growth of more than 11 percent per year, and the Kaiser-Permanente Medical Care Program averaged 5.2 percent growth on a much larger base. However, the success of our proposal does not depend only on nonprofit HMOs. Other forms of cost-effective managed care may do the job. What we propose is a restructured market system in which the efficient prosper and the inefficient must improve or fail.

Comprehensive Reform that Relies on Incentives is Preferable to Direct Government Controls

One alternative to the system we have proposed is a system like Canada's, in which the government is the sole payer for physician and hospital services. While Canada's system has evident strengths, there would be major difficulties in successfully adopting or implementing it in the United States. First, it would require a political sea change to adopt such a system here. A tax increase of approximately $250 billion per year would be required, the intense opposition of insurers and many provider groups would need to be overcome, and the concerns of many employers and citizens about the effects of such a system on access and quality would need to be allayed. In the era in which the Berlin wall has been torn down, one must be cautious about branding any proposal as politically infeasible, but it is difficult to imagine a politician winning election on a platform including an extremely

large tax increase. Second, government regulatory processes tend to freeze industries and often penalize efficiency. The Canadian system is not as frozen as it might be because proximity to the United States exposes Canadians to our innovations. If American medical care were also entirely financed and regulated by the government, the negative effects of regulation would likely loom larger.

A second alternative would be to leave the financing of health insurance for the employed population in the private sector but to have the government regulate physician and hospital prices for all payers. It is possible to imagine a political compromise in which such a system could be adopted—in the midst of a recession, providers might agree to accept all payer price controls in exchange for an employer mandate, and employers might acquiesce to a mandate in exchange for price controls—but it is hard to imagine that such a regulatory structure could be effective over time in promoting quality or economy. Such price controls would be met by continuing provider efforts to circumvent and modify them. Providers would lobby for adjustments and exceptions deemed to enhance equity, increasing the complexity of the regulations and the incentives for those who were not favored to seek favor. Congress would have created a rich new barrel of pork to reward electoral supporters and contributors—an especially attractive source, because price increases for private sector rates could be granted without requiring a tax increase.

Furthermore, such a system does not contain incentives to shift medical care resources from less productive to more productive uses. The current mantra in cost containment is the development of practice guidelines and the application of these guidelines to eliminate the ineffective practices that exist in our medical care system today. While we strongly support the development of better outcomes data and practice guidelines, in the absence of change in the financial incentives created by the FFS system, such guidelines will do little either to control costs or to lead to improvements in efficiency. For guideline development to succeed, medical

care would have to be much more of a science and much less of an art than it is likely to be at any time in the foreseeable future.

Finally, administrative costs in the present system are high and increasing.[23] These costs arise from many causes: the multiplicity of payers, each with its own forms, processes, and data requirements; the high marketing costs associated with the coverage of individuals and small groups; the costs of determining eligibility for coverage in a system in which millions have no coverage; the costs of billing patients for covered services; the costs of payers attempting to determine whether services were actually provided and were appropriate; and others. We believe administrative costs would be greatly reduced under our proposal. After a competitive shakedown, there would be relatively few managed care organizations in each geographic area. Everyone would get coverage through large group arrangements. Eligibility determination would be simple in a system of universal coverage. Today, the best managed care organizations do not bill patients for services. Providers are paid by health plans in simplified ways using prospective payments for global units of care. In a system with relatively few managed care organizations competing to serve competent sponsors and cost-conscious consumers, payers would not have to attempt to micromanage the delivery of care because providers would be at risk. Administrative costs and the "hassle factor" would be much lower than they are today. However, the most important economies would be in the effective organization of the process of care itself.

Over time, we would expect slowed growth in the price of the average health plan and continuing improvements in efficiency comparable to those in other competitive industries.

The authors gratefully acknowledge support from the Robert Wood Johnson Foundation, Princeton, New Jersey, and the Henry J. Kaiser Family Foundation, Menlo Park, California.

Notes

1. Office of the Actuary, Health Care Financing Administration. National health expenditures, 1986–2000. *Health Care Finance Rev.* Summer 1987;8:1–36.

2. Schieber GJ, Poullier JP. Recent trends in international health care spending. *Health Aff.* Fall 1987;6:105–112.

3. *1991 US Industrial Outlook.* Washington, DC: US Dept of Commerce; 1991.

4. Kronick R. *The Slippery Slope of Health Care Finance: Business, Hospitals, and Health Care for the Poor in Massachusetts.* Rochester, NY: University of Rochester; 1990. Thesis.

5. Wilensky GR. Filling the gaps in health insurance: impact on competition. *Health Aff.* Summer 1988;7:133–149.

6. Ries P. Health care coverage by age, sex, race, and family income: United States, 1986. In: *Advance Data From Vital and Health Statistics of the National Center for Health Statistics: No. 139.* Hyattsville, Md: Public Health Service; 1987. US Dept of Health and Human Services publication PHS 87–1250.

7. *Health Insurance and the Uninsured: Background Data and Analysis.* Washington, DC: Congressional Research Service, Library of Congress; 1988.

8. Jensen GA, Morrisey MA, Marcus JW. Cost sharing and the changing pattern of employer-sponsored health benefits. *Milbank Q.* 1987;65:521–542.

9. Foster Higgins Health Care Benefits Survey. *Managed Care Plans.* New York, NY: Foster Higgins; 1989.

10. Enthoven A. *Theory and Practice of Managed Competition in Health Care Finance.* Amsterdam, the Netherlands: Elsevier Science Publishers; 1988.

11. Enthoven A, Kronick R. A consumer choice health plan for the 1990s: universal health insurance in a system designed to promote quality and economy, I. *N Engl J Med.* 1989;320:29–27.

12. Enthoven A, Kronick R. A consumer choice health plan for the 1990s: universal health insurance in a system designed to promote quality and economy, II. *N Engl J Med.* 1989;320:94–101.

13. Long S, Rodgers J. *Enthoven-Kronick Plan for Universal Health Insurance.* Washington, DC: Congressional Budget Office; 1988.

14. Ellwood PM. Outcomes management: a technology of patient experience. *N Engl J Med.* 1988;318:1549–1556.

15. Roper WL, Winkenwerder W, Hackbarth GM, Krakauer H. Effectiveness in health care. *N Engl J Med.* 1988;319:1197–1202.

16. Manning WG, Leibowitz A, Goldberg GA, Rogers WH, Newhouse JP. A controlled trial of the effect of a prepaid group practice on use of services. *N Engl J Med.* 1984;310:1505–1510.

17. Davies AR, Ware JE, Brook RH, Peterson JR, Newhouse JP. Consumer acceptance of prepaid and fee-for-service medical care: results from a randomized controlled trial. *Health Serv Res.* 1986;23:429–452.

18. Sloss EM, Keeler EB, Brooke RH, Operskalski BH, Goldberg GA, Newhouse JP. Effect of a health maintenance organization on physiologic health. *Ann Intern Med.* 1987;106:130–138.

19. Luft HS. How do health-maintenance organizations achieve their 'savings?' rhetoric and evidence. *N Engl J Med.* 1978;298:1336–1343.

20. Feldman R, Dowd B, Finch M, Cassou S. *Employee-Based Health Insurance.* Rockville, MD: National Center for Health Services Research; 1989. US Dept of Health and Human Services publication PHS 89–3434.

21. Feldman R, Finch M, Dowd B, Cassou S. The demand for employment-based health insurance plans. *J Hum Res.* 1989;24:115–142.

22. Weller CD. 'Free choice' as a restraint of trade in American health care delivery and insurance. *Iowa Law Rev.* 1984;69:1351–1392.

23. Himmelstein DU, Woolhandler S. Cost without benefit: administrative waste in US health care. *N Engl J Med.* 1986;314:441–445.

33

Liberal Benefits, Conservative Spending:
The Physicians for a National
Health Program Proposal

Kevin Grumbach, Thomas Bodenheimer, David U. Himmelstein,
and Steffie Woolhandler

The American approach to financing health care has gone awry. From physicians to patients, from The Heritage Foundation to the AFL-CIO, there is agreement that the system needs reform. But what kind of reform? Although all concur that the system is ailing, proposals diverge in their therapeutic approach. Many advocate adjustments of familiar regiments: larger doses of employment-based insurance and greater infusions of public funds to expand Medicaid or to subsidize risk pools for the uninsured. [1-4] Because such measures do not confront the interdependent problems of rising costs and declining access, they cannot ensure health services to all at a cost the nation can afford. A lasting remedy requires basic restructuring of the way we pay for care. [5,6]

The Physicians for a National Health Program plan would cover all Americans under a publicly administered, tax-financed national health program (NHP). A single public payer would replace the present array of more than 1,500 private insurers, Medicaid, and Medicare. A unitary program could initially pay for expanded care out of administrative savings without adding new costs to the overall health care budget and would

establish effective mechanisms for long-term cost control. Although consolidation of purchasing power in a public agency may cause apprehension among some physicians, the program could free them from the myriad administrative intrusions that currently plague the practice of medicine.

Structure of the NHP

We have previously described the design of the NHP in some detail. [7,8] It would create a single insurer in each state, locally controlled but subject to stringent national standards. States could experiment with the precise structure of the single insurer. Some may place it within a government agency, while others may choose a commission elected by the citizens or appointed by provider and consumer interests.

Everyone would be fully insured for all medically necessary services including prescription drugs and long-term care. Private insurance duplicating NHP coverage would be proscribed, as would patient copayments and deductibles. Physicians and hospitals would not bill patients directly for covered services. Hospitals, nursing homes, and clinics would receive a global budget to cover operating expenses, annually negotiated with the state health plan—based on past expenditures, previous financial and clinical performance, projected changes in cost and use, and proposed new and innovative programs.

Itemized patient-specific hospital bills would become an extinct species. No part of the operating budget could be diverted for hospital expansion, profit, marketing, or major capital acquisitions. Capital expenditures approved by a local planning process would be funded through appropriations distinct from operating budgets.

Fee-for-service practitioners would submit all claims to the state health plan. Physician representatives (probably state medical societies) and state plans would negotiate a fee schedule for physician services. The effort and expense of billing would be trivial: stamp the patient's NHP card on a billing form, check a diagnosis and procedure code, send in all bills once a week, and receive full payment for vitually all services—with an extra payment for any bill not paid within 30 days. Gone would be the massive accounts receivables and the elaborate billing apparatus that now beleaguer private physicians. Alternatively, physicians could elect to work on a salaried basis for globally budgeted hospitals or clinics, or in health maintenance organization capitated for all nonhospital services.

Costs of the NHP

To estimate total costs, we start by using the Health Care Financing Administration's projection of 1991 costs under current policies as our "baseline" figure. The Health Care Financing Administra-

Reprinted with permission from *JAMA, The Journal of the American Medical Association* 265, no. 19 (May 15, 1991), pp. 2549–54. Copyright © 1991 American Medical Association.

tion estimates that $567 billion will be spent on personal health care services and products in 1991, excluding nursing home costs and insurance overhead and profits (Table 1).[9] (Although long-term care is covered by the NHP, we have omitted these costs to permit comparison with other acute care proposals.)

Universal coverage should increase the use of health services by the uninsured. According to the Lewin/ICF Health Benefits Simulation Model, approximately $36 billion of the $567 billion in 1991 spending projected under current policies will be accounted for by care for the uninsured, including free care at public hospitals, uncompensated care at private facilities cross-subsidized by insurance revenues, and services purchased out-of-pocket. The Lewin/ICF model estimates that an additional $12.2 billion would be required to increase the utilization by the uninsured to levels commensurate with those of the insured (Needleman et al.[10] and J. Sheils, oral communication, October 1990).

The NHP will not only assist the uninsured, but will also cover services (e.g., preventive) and payments (e.g., deductibles) that many insurers currently exclude. Would this more extensive coverage "induce" a surge of utilization among those currently insured? The RAND Health Insurance Experiment found that costs for persons assigned to a plan with no cost sharing were approximately 15 percent higher than the age-adjusted, per capita health care expenditures for the United States as a whole.[11] However, a more natural experiment, a study before and after the implementation of an NHP in Quebec, failed to detect the overall utilization surge predicted by the RAND experiment.[12,13] Although the use of physician services in Quebec rose among those with lower incomes, the increase was counterbalanced by a decrease in utilization among the affluent. The net effect was convergence of utilization rates (adjusted for health status) among income groups, with no change in the overall rate.

Would an across-the-board increase in utilization be desirable? In the RAND experiment, lower-income patients with medical problems who received free

Table 1.—Personal Health Care Costs for 1991, Excluding Nursing Home Care, With and Without a National Health Program (NHP), in Billions of Dollars*

	NHP	Current Policies
"Baseline" conditions	567	567
New costs for previously uninsured	12	...
Discount for 11.2% hospital administrative savings	(31)	...
Discount for 6.25% physician administrative savings	(9)	...
Subtotal: Personal Health Care	539	567
Insurance administration and profits	8†	35‡
Total Personal Health Care Plus Insurance Overhead	547	602

*This assumes Canadian-level administrative efficiency and changes in utilization only among the previously uninsured.
†1.4% of personal health care expenditures.
‡This is the amount estimated by the Health Care Financing Administration.*

care had better outcomes than those in cost-sharing plans.[14] At the same time, many medical services currently provided are of no or of extremely marginal benefit,[15–17] and it is not the intent of the NHP to inject an additional bolus of such unnecessary care into the health care system.

All these factors make it difficult to predict the level of overall utilization that would result from the NHP. For this analysis, we have added on the full $12.2 billion cost of bringing utilization rates of the uninsured up to those of the insured. We will discuss in the "Budgeting Under the NHP" section below how the NHP budget could also accommodate increases in utilization among the currently insured.

Savings of the NHP

The administrative efficiencies of a single-payer NHP offer the opportunity for large savings during the implementation of the program.[18] Providers would be relieved of much of the expense of screening for eligibility, preparing detailed bills for multiple payers, responding to cumbersome utilization review procedures, and marketing their services. In 1987, California hospitals devoted 20.2 percent of revenues to administrative functions,[19] in contrast to 9.0 percent spent by Canadian hospitals (L. Raymer, Health and Welfare Canada, written communication, April 1990). (These figures exclude malpractice premium costs and administrative person-

nel in clinical departments such as nursing.) The 11.2 percent difference is attributable to Canada's simplified hospital payment method, a method we propose for the United States.

Determining the potential administrative savings in physician expenditures is more difficult. Although practice expenses are 49 percent of physician gross income in the United States and only 36 percent in Canada,[20,21] it is uncertain how much of this difference is due to billing costs. Malpractice costs for U.S. physicians, for example, are higher than those in Canada. We therefore extrapolated billing cost data from a recent American Medical Association survey to project minimum expected administrative savings in physician expenditures.[22] The average physician spent approximately $14,500 in 1988 billing Medicare and Blue Shield alone, representing 5.5 percent of gross physician income. In addition, physicians spent approximately 2.75 percent of their own professional time on billing-related activities for these claims. (The survey did not measure the costs of billing other third parties or patients and therefore yields a low estimate of physician billing costs.) We liberally estimate that physician billing expenses in Canada are 1 percent of physician costs and that Canadian physicians spend at the most 1 percent of their time on billing (D. Peachey, M.D., Ontario Medical Association, written communication, June 1990). In sum, U.S. billing costs for physician time and practice expenses are at least 8.25 percent of total physician expenditures in contrast to at most 2 percent of Canadian physician costs. An NHP functioning at Canadian-level administrative efficiency could save at least 6.25 percent of physician costs. Most of these savings can be realized rapidly. In the private practice of one of the authors (T.B.), for example, the change to a single payer would allow an immediate reduction in office payroll of 18 percent.

Administrative savings to hospitals and physicians function as price discounts when calculating costs. For example, if physicians could lower their overhead by 6.25 percent of gross income by trimming billing expenses, fees could be lowered by 6.25 percent and physicians would still earn the same net income for the same volume of services. We therefore estimated the minimum potential administrative savings in hospital and physician expenditures to be $40 billion by discounting projected hospital and physician costs by 11.2 percent and 6.25 percent, respectively (Table 1).

Additional savings accrue from the reduced administrative "load factor" of a public plan. In 1987, the cost of public and private insurance overhead and profits expressed as a percent of personal health care expenditures was 5.9 percent in the United States and only 1.4 percent in Canada.[9,23] If our NHP operated with the efficiency of Canada's, the administration of health insurance would cost $8 billion, less than one quarter the $35 billion projected by the Health Care Financing Administration in 1991.

As indicated in Table 1, the net cost of personal health care and insurance overhead for universal coverage under the NHP, including expanded services for the previously uninsured, would be at most $547 billion if the system operated with the administrative efficiency of the Canadian system. This is $55 billion less than the $602 billion that will be spent in 1991 under current policies that exclude approximately 35 million Americans.

Budgeting Under the NHP

We do not propose reducing the health care budget by $55 billion under the NHP. As noted above, we are uncertain how utilization patterns might respond to universal, first-dollar insurance coverage. Nor can we be completely confident that hospitals and physicians will immediately shed their excess administrative poundage and assume the leaner proportions possible under a simplified payment system. We therefore propose the following budgetary strategy for the NHP: We would set the overall health care budget for the NHP's initial year at the amount projected under current policies ($602 billion if implemented in 1991). To keep expenditures within this target, we would rely on the ability of a single payer to allocate and enforce prospective budgets for physician and hospital services. These budgets would

challenge providers to extract administrative savings and redirect resources into patient care for the underserved. The budget would allow a range of utilization responses among patients and physicians.

For example, the NHP could set total hospital operating budgets at the Health Care Financing Administration projected "baseline" 1991 level of $273 billion (Table 2), though some individual hospitals' budgets might be adjusted to reflect past underfunding or large operating surpluses. On average, a hospital able to achieve full administrative savings would have 11.2 percent of its budget to devote to more or better clinical services. Billing personnel could be transferred to clinical departments to perform clerical duties, freeing up nurses for bedside care. Hospitals unable to realize immediate administrative savings would not be penalized in the short run. However, in the longer run, the single payer within each state would evaluate hospitals' clinical performance and efficiency and modify budgets, taking account of these hospital quality measures as well as community needs. The Canadian experience demonstrates that such a budgeting process need not be cumbersome or expensive, consuming less than $2 per capita in British Columbia (D. Cunningham, British Columbia Ministry of Health, written communication, July 1990).

Prospective budgeting of physician services under fee-for-service methods would require expenditure targets or caps. On average, fees would be set at 6.25 percent below current levels, reflecting expected administrative savings to physicians. The expenditure target, however, could be set at $154 billion, 6 percent above the "baseline" projected level for 1991 (Table 2). This would allow physician payments to accommodate a net utilization increase of up to 12.25 percent, sufficient to satisfy increased demand by the uninsured and underinsured, while allowing a net increase in physician income of 6 percent. A utilization increase above 12.25 percent would trigger a compensatory decrease in fees to keep expenditures within the budget target. Such a plan allows for control of costs with a

Table 2.—National Health Program (NHP) Budget, by Category of Expenditure, in Billions of Dollars

Category	NHP	Current Policies*
Hospital	273	273
Physician	154	145
Other†	149	149
Insurance administration and profits	8	35
Subtotal	**584**	**602**
New health initiatives and transition costs	18	0
Total Budget	**602**	**602**

These are Health Care Financing Administration projections.

†"Other" includes drugs, dental and other professional services, and so forth.

minimum of the administrative waste or encumbrances of our current utilization review mechanisms.[24]

Summing the aggregate hospital operating budget of $273 billion, the physician budget of $154 billion, and the other categories of personal health care spending and administration would still leave total expenditures $18 billion below our proposed $602 billion budget (Table 2). The $18 billion balance could be used for start-up costs for the NHP, job training and placement programs for displaced administrative personnel, improved long-term care, and revitalized public health programs.

Financing the NHP

Health insurance proposals are frequently shipwrecked on the shoals of their financing; any serious proposal must specify a revenue package. Although the NHP would not result in a net increase in total health care expenditures, it would produce a major shift in payment sources toward government and away from private insurance and out-of-pocket payments. We emphasize that the average individual and business would not pay more for health care under the NHP but would pay taxes that take the place of, but do not exceed, current premium payments and out-of-pocket costs. Moreover, with the single payer's capacity to control inflation, individuals and businesses should soon enjoy reductions in the rate of increase of their health care costs.

What principle should underlie the choice of revenue sources? Health care is only one factor—sometimes a minor one—in the promotion and preservation of health. Poverty, racial oppression, substance abuse, lack of education, lack of exercise, overnutrition and undernutrition, and occupational and environmental hazards all damage health. Some of these factors can be influenced by society's revenue-generating mechanisms. For example, raising excise taxes on cigarettes and alcohol reduces their consumption and thereby improves health, particularly among teenagers and the poor. [25] On the other hand, burdening low-income families with high payments (whether taxes, premiums, or out-of-pocket dollars) reduces their disposable income and amplifies the ill effects of poverty. In contrast, a system of taxes and other payments that reduces the burden on low-income families without impeding job formation may ameliorate poverty's health consequences. Thus, funding mechanisms can be "healthy" or "unhealthy."

Health care financing in the United States is markedly regressive and hence unhealthy. The bottom income decile receives 1.3 percent of total income but pays 3.9 percent of health costs, while the top income decile receives 33.8 percent of income and pays only 21.7 percent of health costs. By comparison, in Britain the bottom decile receives 2.3 percent of income and pays 1.7 percent of health costs, while the top decile receives 24.9 percent of income and pays 25.6 percent of costs. [26] Any departure from the existing configuration of U.S. health care funding should reverse the current unhealthy pattern.

We estimate that public expenditures will account for 85 percent of health spending under the NHP, requiring $509 billion in revenues for 1991 (Table 3). We will discuss these revenues in three categories: (1) payroll taxes, (2) general government revenues, and (3) payments by individuals (Figure).

Payroll Taxes

Employer-employee payments for group health insurance (31 percent of personal health expenditures [excluding nursing-home care][27]) are, in essence, a payroll tax, [28] with the money going to an insurance company or a self-insured fund rather than to the government.

Table 3.—Public Plan's Share of 1991 Personal Health Care Expenditures Under National Health Program (NHP), in Billions of Dollars

Service	Total Cost	% Covered by NHP	NHP Cost
Hospital	273	96*	262
Physician	154	91*	140
Other	149	55†	82
New health initiatives and transition costs	18	100	18
Administration	8	85†	7
Total	**602**	**85**	**509‡**

*These figures are based on the public share of spending for these services in Canada. The shares are less than 100% because certain services, such as cosmetic surgery, life insurance examinations, and private room surcharges, are not covered benefits.[34]

†These figures are based on our "best guess" estimate, since the NHP will provide more extensive coverage of nonhospital and nonphysician services than do the Canadian provincial plans. Nonprescription drugs are an example of a product in the "other" category that will not be covered.

‡A total of $93 billion of personal health care expenditures uncovered by the NHP remain as out-of-pocket and individual private insurance premium costs.

Social Security payments for Medicare (12 percent of health expenditures [27,29]) are also a payroll tax. It is logical to combine these two sources of financing, which together account for 43 percent of health expenditures. To minimize economic disruption, we propose that a similar proportion of the NHP be funded by payroll tax.

The regressive nature of a payroll tax makes it a less-than-healthy revenue source; the employer share is often shifted to employees as lower wages or to consumers as higher prices. [30] It should be made more progressive by reducing the employee share for lower-wage employees, by raising the employee share for high-income employees (e.g., eliminating the current Social Security cap), and by reducing the employer share for small business. Employers and employees currently pay almost 2 percent of total payroll for Medicare-related Social Security taxes and approximately 10 percent for private health insurance—a combined health-related payroll tax of 13 percent. [29,31,32] Using Department of Commerce figures, we project that under the NHP, an average tax rate of 9 percent for medium and large employers, with an average 2 percent rate for employees, and half these rates for businesses with fewer than 20 employees, would raise $228 billion in revenues. [33] These precise tax rates are only initial suggestions and must be negotiated with the affected parties.

General Government Revenues

Twenty-six percent of personal health expenditures (excluding nursing-home care) comes from non-Social Security governmental revenues at the federal, state, and local levels. [27,29] Of this total, 51 percent comes from individual income taxes, 12 percent from property taxes, 12 percent from sales taxes, 12 percent from corporation income taxes, 5 percent from gasoline, tobacco, and alcohol taxes, and 8 percent from other sources. [34] Although some of these revenue sources are unhealthy, we propose leaving them intact, adhering to the principle that implementing the NHP should not demand radical economic restructuring. These revenues would generate $157 billion for the NHP in 1991. [9,29]

Payments by Individuals

The third major source of health financing consists of payments by individuals; these payments currently account for 31 percent of health expenditures (5 percent in individual insurance premiums, 24 percent in out-of-pocket payments, 1 percent other Medicare premiums, and 1 percent in other private funds). [27,29] They are the least healthy revenues because they burden lower-income families far more than they do the affluent. To the extent that they pay for services covered under the NHP, they will disappear.

We propose replacing the majority of individual payments with "healthier" revenues—taxes that reduce income disparities and discourage the use of harmful and polluting substances. The following measures, according to a Congressional Budget Office study, [35] would generate $124 billion per year and could be considered as NHP tax revenue sources: (1) a new federal income tax bracket of 38 percent for families with income higher than $170,000, (2) a cap on mortgage interest deductions for luxury homes, (3) a 0.5 percent tax on transfer of securities, (4) an increase in energy taxes to encourage energy conservation and reduce pollution, (5) an increase in excise taxes on cigarettes to 32 cents per pack and on alcohol to 25 cents per ounce, (6) an excise tax on

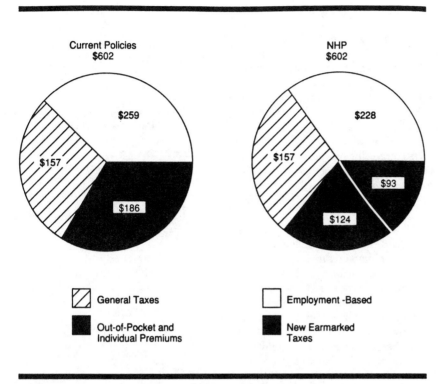

Current Policies
$602

$259

$157

$186

NHP
$602

$228

$157

$93

$124

General Taxes

Out-of-Pocket and
Individual Premiums

Employment -Based

New Earmarked
Taxes

Revenue sources. Figures are in billions of 1991 dollars. NHP indicates national health program.

Comment

In health insurance, as in many things in life, simplicity is a virtue. The NHP's approach to universal access is simple: every American automatically qualifies for equal, comprehensive health insurance under a unitary public plan. The economic premises of the NHP are also simple: funnel all third-party payments through a single payer, thereby saving billions of dollars in administrative costs and achieving cost containment through global controls rather than minute bureaucratic scrutiny.

The administrative cost reductions during the NHP's initial phase are not, as some have argued, only a one-time saving.[37] Whether in Canada or New Zealand, Sweden or Britain, single-payer systems have stabilized costs in the past decade, while U.S. health care inflation has been impervious to the most earnest attempts to control costs.[38-40] Economist Robert Evans[41] has concluded that "universality of coverage and sole-source funding are, as far as we know now, preconditions for cost control."

Global expenditure control can also enhance clinical freedom. Under the micromanagement model of cost containment, each of the multiple payers, lacking global budgetary levers, resorts to intrusive patient-by-patient utilization review.[24] Such day-to-day interference in medical practice is minimized in single-payer systems.[40] As John Wennberg[16] recently observed:

The key to the preservation of fee-for-service markets, as the Canadians seem to recognize, is not the micromanagement of the doctor-patient relationship but the management of capacity and budget. The American problem is to find the will to set the supply thermostat somewhere within reason.

The NHP would benefit most Americans, though a few powerful interest groups would suffer. It would virtually eliminate financial barriers to care for those who are currently uninsured and underinsured, ensure patients a free choice of providers, ensure physicians a free choice of practice settings, diminish bureaucratic interference in clinical decision making, stabilize health spending, and reduce the growing burden of health care costs for many individuals

sources of air and water pollutants, and (7) a tax on fossil fuels to reduce carbon dioxide emissions. Although some of these taxes are regressive, their overall effects are health promoting.

To summarize, the NHP would fund approximately 38 percent of health expenditures from a payroll tax similar to current payroll expenses for Medicare and health insurance premiums; 26 percent from existing federal, state, and local revenues; and 21 percent from new, healthy federal tax revenues that would largely supplant current out-of-pocket expenditures. Fifteen percent of expenditures would remain out-of-pocket (Figure).

A majority of Americans would accept this type of tax package if it were earmarked for health care and placed in a health care trust fund. A 1990 poll found that 72 percent would support an NHP even if it required a tax increase; however, only 22 percent would pay more than $200 extra per year.[36] Our proposal would not increase the sums paid for health care by low- and middle-income groups. It is designed to

minimize winners and losers, aside from the private health insurance industry.

Two additional principles should be incorporated in NHP funding. Per capita health spending should be equalized throughout the nation, with federal funds transferred to states under formulas adjusted for age, income levels, health status, wage, and other input costs. Finally, to protect the NHP from annual budgetary debacles in Washington, DC, it must be an entitlement program with a statutory expenditure floor as well as a ceiling. In contrast to entitlement programs restricted to poor families, the NHP would embrace the entire population and could thus command the level of support enjoyed by Social Security. Adequate increases in NHP funding (based on such factors as aging of the population, epidemics, advances in medical technology, and inflation) must be mandated by law. As suggested in our original NHP proposal,[7] an expanded program of technology assessment would help guide budgetary allocations.

and employers. Small-business owners who do not currently cover their employees would face modest cost increases, though far less than mandated by most alternative proposals. The health insurance industry would feel the greatest impact. Indeed, most of the extra funds needed to expand care would come from eliminating the overhead and profits of insurance companies and from abolishing the billing apparatus necessary to apportion costs among the various plans. Job retraining programs for displaced administrative and clerical personnel would be essential.

Although few dispute the ability of the NHP to provide universal coverage and control costs, critics have raised the specter of rationing, pointing to queues for some high technology services in Canada.[42] We do not advocate cutting U.S. health spending to Canadian levels. Even with a slower rate of growth under the NHP, U.S. health expenditures will remain well above those of any other nation. Deploying our greater resources with Canadian efficiency would permit increases in utilization and improvements in technology without skyrocketing costs. Compared with Americans, Canadians do, in fact, get more health care for their health care dollar. About half of the cost differential between the two nations is squandered on insurance overhead and paper pushing.[18,43] Stanford economist Victor Fuchs[44] has concluded that "the quantity of [physician] services per capita is much higher in Canada than in the United States . . . the data firmly reject the view that Canadians save money by delivering fewer services."

Health financing reforms unable to extract administrative savings inevitably impose added costs for expanded services. Employer mandate proposals (e.g., the Pepper Commission Plan,[1] the American Medical Association's Health Access America plan,[3] the National Leadership Commission's proposal,[2] and Massachusetts' Universal Health Care Law [*New York Times*, April 11, 1991:A1]) would leave existing insurance in place while expanding public programs for the unemployed and requiring employers to insure their workers. None of these plans offer improved coverage for

those currently insured, nor do they offer new cost control mechanisms. Hence high initial costs presage continuing inflation or far more stringent and intrusive micromanagement—probably both. Modifications of the employer mandate approach (e.g., the UNYCare proposal in New York State)[45] that attempt to meld the cost containment features of a single-payer system with a continuing role for private insurance also eschew most administrative savings, compromising the ability of such measures to expand access without raising costs.

There is slim evidence that Enthoven and Kronick's[46] "managed competition" plan—featuring competing managed care insurers and higher patient copayments—can hold costs in check.[47] Does forcing consumers to bear premium costs for higher-priced plans hold down overall costs or simply segregate the market based on ability to pay? Do low-cost plans provide care more efficiently or simply market themselves more effectively to lower-risk subscribers? Is the rubric "Consumer Choice Health Plan" appropriate for a system likely to lock the vast majority of patients and physicians into closed panel health maintenance organizations run by insurance companies? The ultimate vision of managed competition—a landscape dominated by a limited number of huge health maintenance organizations managing salaried physicians—is a more radical departure from the current health care scene than the NHP.

The objectives of the NHP are simple: (1) to minimize financial barriers to appropriate medical care, (2) to distribute costs fairly, and (3) to contain costs at a reasonable level. Once a structure is in place for meeting these basic concerns, the medical profession and society as a whole can move on to the more complicated questions: Which health services truly improve the quality of life? What share of our human and material resources should we devote to health care? How shall we reduce the toll now extracted by poverty, ignorance, and addictions? By implementing a national health program, we can turn and face the challenges ahead.

Notes

1. US Bipartisan Commission on Comprehensive Health Care. *A Call for Action.* Washington, DC: The Pepper Commission on Comprehensive Health Care; 1990.

2. National Leadership Commission on Health Care. *For the Health of a Nation.* Ann Arbor, Mich: Health Administration Press; 1989.

3. *Health Access America.* Chicago, Ill: American Medical Association; 1990.

4. Kennedy E. Senate Bill S.768. November 20, 1989.

5. Woolhandler S, Himmelstein DU. Resolving the cost/access conflict: the case for a national health program. *J Gen Intern Med.* 1989;4:54–60.

6. Grumbach K. National health insurance in America: can we practice with it? can we practice without it? *West J Med.* 1989;151:210–216.

7. Himmelstein DU, Woolhandler S. A national health program for the United States: a physicians' proposal. *N Engl J Med.* 1989;320:102–108.

8. Woolhandler S, Himmelstein DU. A national health program: a northern light at the end of the tunnel. *JAMA* 1989; 262:2136–2137.

9. Health Care Financing Administration. National health expenditures: 1986–2000. *Health Care Financing Rev.* 1987;8(4):1–36.

10. Needleman J, Arnold J, Sheils J, Lewin LS. *The Health Care Financing System and the Uninsured.* Washington, DC: Lewin/ICF; 1990.

11. Newhouse JP, Manning WG, Morris CN, et al. Some interim results from a controlled trial of cost sharing in health insurance. *N Engl J Med.* 1981;305:1501–1507.

12. Enterline PE, Salter V, McDonald AD, McDonald JC. The distribution of medical services before and after 'free' medical care: the Quebec experience. *N Engl J Med.* 1973;289:1174–1178.

13. McDonald AD, McDonald JC, Salter V, Enterline P. Effects of Quebec Medicare on physician consultation for selected symptoms. *N Engl J Med.* 1974;291:649–652.

14. Brook RH, Ware JE Jr, Rogers WH, et al. Does free care improve adults' health? results from a randomized controlled trial. *N Engl J Med.* 1983;309:1426–1434.

15. Eisenberg JM. Doctors' Decisions and the Cost of Medical Care. Ann Arbor, Mich: Health Administration Press; 1986.

16. Wennberg J. Outcomes research, cost containment, and the fear of health care

rationing. *N Engl J Med.* 1990;323:1202–1204.

17. Chassin MR, Kosecoff J, Park RE, et al. Does inappropriate use explain geographic variations in the use of health care services? *JAMA.* 1987;258:2533–2537.

18. Himmelstein D, Woolhandler S. Cost without benefit: administrative waste in US health care. *N Engl J Med.* 1986;314:441–445.

19. *Aggregate Hospital Financial Data for California: Report Periods Ending June 30, 1987–June 29, 1988.* Sacramento: California Health Facilities Commission; 1989.

20. Gonzalez ML, Emmons DW. *Socioeconomic Characteristics of Medical Practice.* Chicago, Ill: American Medical Association; 1988.

21. Iglehart J. Canada's health system faces its problems. *N Engl J Med.* 1990;322:562–568.

22. American Medical Association. The administrative burden of health insurance on physicians. *Socioeconomic Monitoring Survey Rep.* 1989;3:2–4.

23. *National Health Expenditures.* Ottawa, Ontario: Health and Welfare Canada; 1990.

24. Grumbach K, Bodenheimer T. Reins or fences? a physician's view of cost containment. *Health Aff.* 1990;9(4):120–126.

25. Last JM. Controlling the smoking epidemic. *Am J Prev Med.* 1985;1:1–3.

26. Wagstaff A, Van Doorslaer E, Paci P. Equity in the finance and delivery of health care: some tentative cross-country comparisons. *Oxford Rev Econ Policy.* 1989;5:89–112.

27. Levit KR, Freeland MS, Waldo DR. National health care spending trends: 1988. *Health Aff.* 1990;9(2):171–184.

28. Reinhardt UE. Health insurance for the nation's poor. *Health Aff.* 1987;6(1):101–112.

29. Levit KR, Freeland MS, Waldo DR. Health spending and ability to pay: business, individuals, and government. *Health Care Financing Rev.* 1989;10(3):1–11.

30. Pechman JA. *Federal Tax Policy.* Washington, DC: The Brookings Institution; 1987.

31. Bergthold LA. *Purchasing Power in Health.* New Brunswick, NJ: Rutgers University Press; 1990.

32. DiCarlo S, Gabel J. Conventional health insurance: a decade later. *Health Care Financing Rev.* 1989;10(3):77–89.

33. Bureau of the Census. *Statistical abstract of the United States 1990.* Washington, DC: US Dept of Commerce; 1990.

34. Bureau of the Census. *Quarterly Summary of Federal, State, and Local Tax Revenue, July-September 1989.* Washington, DC: US Dept of Commerce; 1990.

35. Congressional Budget Office. *Reducing the Deficit: Spending and Revenue Options.* Washington, DC: The Congress of the United States; 1990.

36. Blendon RJ, Donelan K. The public and the emerging debate over national health insurance. *N Engl J Med.* 1990;323:208–212.

37. Aaron H, Schwartz WG. Rationing health care: the choice before us. *Science.* 1990;247:418–422.

38. International comparisons of health care financing and delivery: data and perspectives. *Health Care Financing Rev.* 1989;10 (suppl):1–196.

39. Pfaff M. Differences in health care spending across countries: statistical evidence. *J Health Polit Policy Law.* 1990;15:1–24.

40. Evans RG, Lomas J, Barer ML, et al. Controlling health expenditures: the Canadian reality. *N Engl J Med* 1989;320:571–577.

41. Evans RG. Accessible, acceptable, and affordable: financing health care in Canada. In: *The 1990 Richard and Hinda Rosenthal Lectures.* Washington, DC: Institute of Medicine; 1990:7–47.

42. Board of Trustees, American Medical Association. *Study of the Canadian Health Care System.* Chicago, Ill: American Medical Association; 1989. Report V(A–89).

43. Evans RG. Split vision: interpreting cross-border differences in heatlh spending. *Health Aff.* 1988;7(4):17–24.

44. Fuchs, VR, Hahn, JS. How does Canada do it? a comparison of expenditures for physicians' services in the United States and Canada. *N Engl J Med.* 1990;323:884–890.

45. Beauchamp DE, Rouse RL. Universal New York Health Care: a single-payer strategy linking cost control and universal access. *N Engl J Med.* 1990;323:640–644.

46. Enthoven A, Kronick R. A consumer choice health plan for the 1990s: universal health insurance in a system designed to promote quality and economy. *N Engl J Med.* 1989;320:29-37,94–101.

47. Jones SB. Can multiple choice be managed to constrain health care costs? *Health Aff.* 1989;8(3):51–59.

34

Caring for the Uninsured and Underinsured: A National Long-Term Care Program for the United States—A Caring Vision

Charlene Harrington, Christine Cassel, Carroll L. Estes, Steffie Woolhandler, David U. Himmelstein, the Working Group on Long-Term Care Program Design, and the Physicians for a National Health Program

American medicine often cures but too rarely cares. Technical sophistication in therapy for acute illnesses coexists with neglect for many of the disabled. New hospitals that lie one-third empty house thousands of chronic care patients because even the shabbiest nursing homes remain constantly full.[1] If the fabric of our acute care is marred by the stain of the uninsured and underinsured, the cloth of our long-term care (LTC) is a threadbare and tattered remnant.

For millions with disabilities, the assistance that would enable independent living is unobtainable. Nursing homes offered as alternatives to the fortunate few with Medicaid or savings are often little more than warehouses. In the home, relatives and friends labor unaided, uncompensated and without respite. Geriatric training is woefully underfunded and carries little prestige.[2] Hence, too few physicians are well equipped to address remediable medical problems that contribute to disability,[3,4] while many are called on to assume responsibility for care that has more to do with personal maintenance and hygiene than with more familiar

Reprinted with permission from *JAMA, The Journal of the American Medical Association* 265, no. 21 (December 4, 1991), pp. 3023–29. Copyright © 1991 American Medical Association.

medical terrain; even when they know what should be done, the needed resources are often unavailable. The experts in providing care—nurses, homemakers, social workers, and the like—are locked in a hierarchy inappropriate for caring.

With the aging of the population and improved survival of disabled people of all ages, the need for a cogent LTC policy will become even more pressing. Yet policymakers have neglected LTC, for a number of reasons. (1) They have been unwilling to accept LTC as a federal responsibility in an era of cost containment. (2) Meeting routine living needs is a central feature of LTC, with biomedical issues often secondary. Hence, logic dictates that the system emphasize social services, not just medical ones, with social service and nursing personnel rather than physicians often coordinating care—a model that some physicians and policymakers may find threatening.[5] And, (3) LTC needs are largely invisible to policymakers because the majority of services for disabled people—of any age—are provided by "informal" (unpaid) care givers, mainly female family members, neighbors, or friends.

Long-term care services are those health, social, housing, transportation, and other supportive services needed

by persons with physical, mental, or cognitive limitations sufficient to compromise independent living. The United States has a complicated and overlapping array of financing and service programs for LTC. Financing for LTC is largely independent of financing for acute care and varies depending on whether the need is intermittent or continuous, short or long term, posthospital or unrelated to hospitalization.[6–8] Private insurance companies have made only tentative efforts to market LTC insurance and currently insure less than 1 percent of Americans.[9] Insurance for LTC is unaffordable to most who need it and rarely covers all necessary services.[10–12] Thus, about half of LTC expenses are paid out-of-pocket, with most of the remainder paid by Medicaid.

Presently the elderly spend 18 percent of their income for medical care, with out-of-pocket costs rising twice as fast as Social Security payments. Medical expenses cost the average elder 4.5 months of his or her Social Security checks.[13] The financial burden for LTC falls most heavily on disabled people without Medicaid coverage.[14] To qualify for Medicaid, families must either be destitute or "spend down" their personal funds until they are impoverished. Furthermore, Medicaid is institutionally biased, funding nursing home care far more extensively than home- and community-based services.

Age restrictions on many LTC programs arbitrarily limit access, since about a third of the LTC population is not elderly.[9,15,16] Seventy-eight percent of the disabled who receive Social Security disability benefits, 14 percent of nursing home residents, and 34 percent of the noninstitutionalized population reporting limitations in activity due to chronic conditions are under 65 years.[17,18] Children constitute 5 percent of the severely disabled, yet generally are not eligible for LTC under public programs unless they are poor.

Informal services are vital to millions but are neither supported nor encouraged by current programs. More than 70 percent of those receiving LTC (3.2 million people) rely exclusively on unpaid care givers.[19] Almost 22 percent use both formal and informal care, while 5 percent use only formal care.[18,22] Of the more than 7 million informal care givers, three fourths are women, 36 percent are themselves over 65 years old, a third are in poor health, 10 percent have given up paid employment to assume the care of their loved one, and eight of 10 spend at least 4 hours every day providing care.[9] Such personal devotion can never be replaced by the assistance of even the kindest of strangers. It must be valued and supported, not supplanted by formal care.

We believe that a government-financed program will be required in order to ensure adequate LTC for most Americans. At most 40 percent, and perhaps as few as 6 percent, of older Americans could afford private LTC insurance.[9,10,23-25] The average nursing home costs of $20,000 to $40,000 per year would bankrupt the majority of Americans within 3 years.[26]

There is growing recognition that the crisis in LTC, as in acute care, calls for bold and fundamental change. We propose the incorporation of LTC into a publicly funded national health program (NHP). We borrow from the experience in the Canadian provinces of Manitoba and British Columbia,[27] where LTC is part of the basic health care entitlement regardless of age or income.[27] Case managers and specialists in needs assessment (largely nonphysi-

cians) evaluate the need for LTC and authorize payment for services. This mechanism for directing appropriate services to those in need has allowed broad access to nursing home and community-based services without runaway inflation.

We also incorporate elements from several recent LTC proposals for the United States.[9,10,14,24,28-30] Most of these, however, have three important flaws: (1) they focus primarily on the aged and would exclude the 40 percent to 51 percent of those who need LTC but are under the age of 65 years[15,16]; (2) while most would expand Medicare, they would provide a major role for private insurers, perpetuating fragmented and inefficient financing mechanisms; and (3) they exclude nurses and social workers from certifying and prescribing nonmedical LTC services, inappropriately burdening physicians with responsibilities that are often outside their areas of interest and expertise.

Our proposal is designed as a major component of the NHP proposed by Physicians for a National Health Program.[31] The NHP would provide universal coverage for preventive, acute, and LTC services for all age groups through a public insurance program, pooling funds in existing public programs with new federal revenues raised through progressive taxation. This approach would improve access to the acute care that could ameliorate much disability, eliminate the costly substitution of acute care for LTC, prevent unnecessary nursing home placements, and provide a genuine safety net, both medical and financial, for people of all ages.

Goals for LTC

Nine principles are central to our proposal:

- Long-term care should be a *right* of all Americans, not a commodity available only to the wealthy and the destitute.
- Coverage should be universal, with access to services based on need rather than age, cause of disability, or income.
- Long-term care should provide a continuum of social and medical services aimed at maximizing functional independence.
- Medically and socially oriented LTC should be coordinated with acute inpatient and ambulatory care.

- The program should encourage the development of accessible, efficient, and innovative systems of health care delivery.
- The program should promote high-quality services and appropriate utilization, in the least restrictive environment possible.
- The financial risk should be spread across the entire population using a progressive financing system rather than compounding the misfortune of disability with the specter of financial ruin.
- The importance of "informal" care should be acknowledged, and support, financial and other, should be offered to assist rather than supplant home and community care givers.
- Consumers should have a range of choices and options for LTC that are culturally appropriate.

Coverage

Everyone would be covered for all medically and socially necessary services under a single public plan. Home- and community-based benefits would include nursing, therapy services, case management, meals, information and referral, in-home support (homemaker and attendant) services, respite, transportation services, adult day health, social day care, psychiatric day care, hospice, community mental health, and other related services. Residential services would include foster care, board and care, assisted living, and residential care facilities. Institutional care would include nursing homes, chronic care hospitals, and rehabilitation facilities. Drug and alcohol treatment, outpatient rehabilitation, and independent living programs would also be covered. In special circumstances, other services might be covered such as supported employment and training, financial management, legal services, protective services, senior companions, and payment for informal care givers.

Preventive services would be covered in an effort to minimize avoidable deterioration in physical and mental functioning. The reluctance of some individuals to seek such preventive services requires sensitive outreach programs. Supportive housing environments, though essential for many who are frail and disabled, should be financed separately as part of housing rather than medical programs. Long-term care services would supplement and be integrated with the acute care services provided by the NHP, such as medical, dental, and nursing care; drugs and medical devices; and preventive services.[31]

The public program, with a single, uniform benefit package, would consolidate all current federal and state programs for LTC. At present, 80 federal programs finance LTC services, including Medicare, Medicaid, the Department of Veterans Affairs, the Older Americans Act, and Title XX Social Services.[21] Other public programs finance LTC for the developmentally disabled, the mentally disabled, substance abusers, and crippled children. State disability insurance programs also finance some LTC. This multiplicity of programs leaves enormous gaps in both access and coverage, confuses consumers attempting to gain access to the system, and drives up administrative costs. Furthermore, the system is grossly out of balance, biased toward acute and institutional care and away from community-based health and social services. In contrast, the proposed LTC program would be comprehensive, administratively spare, and "user friendly."

Comprehensive coverage permits use of the most appropriate services and may prevent unnecessary hospitalization or institutional placement. Since most individuals needing LTC prefer to remain at home,[24,26] services should promote independent living and support informal care givers, using nursing homes as the last resort rather than as the primary approach to LTC. Services must be culturally appropriate for special population groups including ethnic, cultural, and religious minorities; the oldest old; individuals who are mentally impaired or developmentally disabled; children; and young adults.

Administrative Structure and Eligibility for Care

With a federal mandate, each state would set up an LTC system with a state LTC Planning and Payment Board and a network of local public LTC agencies. These local agencies would employ specialized panels of social workers, nurses, therapists, and physicians responsible for assessing individuals' LTC needs,

service planning, care coordination, provider certification, and, in some cases, provision of services. These agencies would serve as the entry points to LTC within local communities, certify eligibility for specific services, and assign a case manager when appropriate.

The LTC Planning and Payment Board and the local LTC agencies in each state would pay for the full continuum of covered LTC services. Each state's LTC operating budget would be allocated to the local LTC agencies based on population, the number of elderly and disabled, the economic status of the population, case-mix, and cost of living. Each local LTC agency would apportion the available budget to cover the operating costs of approved providers in its community—although the actual payment apparatus would be centralized in the state's LTC Planning and Payment Board to avoid duplication of administrative functions.

Each institutional provider, e.g., community agency, nursing home, home care agency, or social service organization, would negotiate a global operating budget with the local LTC agency. The budget would be based on past expenditures, financial and clinical performance, utilization, and projected changes in services, wages, and other related factors. Alternatively, institutional providers could contract to provide comprehensive LTC services (or integrated LTC and acute care services) on a capitated basis. No part of the operating budget or capitation fee could be used for expansion, profit, marketing, or major capital purchases or leases. Capital expenditures for new, expanded, or updated LTC facilities and programs would be allocated based on explicit health planning goals separately from operating budgets by the state LTC agency. For-profit providers would be paid a fixed return on existing equity, and new for-profit investment would be proscribed. As Physicians for a National Health Program has previously proposed,[31] physicians could be paid on a fee-for-service basis, or receive salaries from institutional providers. Physicians and other providers would be prohibited from referring patients to facilities or services in which they held a proprietary interest. Providers participating in

the public program would be required to accept the public payments as payment in full and would not be allowed to charge patients directly for any covered service. Federal and state budget allocations for LTC services would be separate from those for acute care, as in Canada.

Coverage would extend to anyone, regardless of age or income, needing assistance with one or more activity of daily living (ADL) or instrumental activity of daily living (IADL). (ADLs are basic self-maintenance activities [i.e., bathing, dressing, going to the toilet, getting outside, walking, transferring from bed to chair, or eating]; IADLs relate to a person's ability to be independent [cooking, cleaning, shopping, taking medications, doing laundry, making telephone calls, or managing money].) High-risk patients not strictly meeting this definition would be eligible for services needed to prevent worsening disability and subsequent costly institutional care. Local panels would have the flexibility, within their defined budgets, to authorize a wide range of services, taking into account such social factors as the availability of informal care.

When case management or care coordination is needed, the local agencies would assume these tasks or delegate them to appropriate providers, e.g., capitated providers offering comprehensive services. Not all those needing LTC require case management.[32] Case managers and care coordinators would work with the client, family, and other care givers to assess adequacy and appropriateness of services, promote efficiency, and respond to changing needs. Progressive decline in function characterizes many chronic illnesses, while full recovery is possible in others. Thus, change in need is a nearly universal aspect of LTC and mandates frequent re-evaluation and flexibility. In all cases, programs should encourage independence and minimize professional intrusion into daily life.

A universal need-based entitlement to LTC would replace the current irrational patchwork of public and private programs, each with its own eligibility criteria, by age, cause of disability, and income. All income groups would be covered without means testing, which is cumbersome and costly to administer, may increase costs in the long run by causing people to postpone needed care, creates a stigma against recipients, and narrows the base of political support for the program.[28] There are scant data on how to set simple eligibility standards that ensure coverage for all in need, while excluding those for whom LTC services are a luxury rather than a necessity. We have chosen an inclusive general criterion (one ADL or IADL) and have left fine tuning to local agencies able to individualize decisions.

In all, approximately 3.9 percent of the population (9.3 million people in 1985) would be eligible for covered LTC services. An estimated 3.6 percent (7.6 million persons) of the total noninstitutionalized population need assistance with ADLs or IADLs,[15] including only 8 percent of those aged 65 to 69 years but 46 percent of those aged 85 years and over.[15] Another 1.6 million people are in nursing homes and residential care facilities,[17] and 200,000 people are in psychiatric and long-stay hospitals.[33]

Utilization and Cost Controls

Removing financial barriers to LTC will increase demand for formal services. Long-term care insurance could legitimately result in a 20 percent increase in nursing home utilization and a 50 percent to 100 percent increase in use of community and home health care by the elderly.[9,24] Increases in utilization might be expected to level off after about 3 years, as occurred in Saskatchewan's LTC program.[27]

Our program would be financed entirely by tax revenues, without premiums, deductibles, copayments, or coinsurance. However, people permanently residing in residential care would use part of their basic Social Security or Supplemental Security Income to contribute to "hotel" costs. Although other cost-sharing methods raise revenues and discourage utilization, these regressive financing mechanisms disproportionately burden the poor and the sick and reduce the use of preventive and other essential services.[28,34,35]

Although we eschew financial barriers to care, utilization controls are essential since many LTC services (e.g., "meals on wheels," homemakers) are desirable to people without disabilities.

Several states' Medicaid programs have demonstrated that screening and utilization controls can both control costs and improve care by preventing unnecessary institutionalization, coordinating services, and ensuring the use of the most appropriate care.[35,36]

The local LTC agencies, each with a defined catchment area and budget, would apportion the finite resources for LTC among those in need. These local agencies, serving as the single point of entry for LTC service authorization, would work with clients and care givers to select and coordinate appropriate services from a comprehensive listing of providers. This approach relies on enforceable overall budgetary ceilings to contain costs. The local agencies would have strong incentives to support more cost-effective informal providers and community-based services that might forestall institutionalization.

Innovation in the Provision of LTC

Broad changes in the provision of LTC are essential.[37] The current system is fragmented among many acute care inpatient, ambulatory, and LTC providers. This fragmentation creates higher costs through the duplication of bureaucracy and the failure to achieve administrative economies of scale. More important, the lack of coordination compromises the quality of care. A unified financing system would foster the integration, or at least coordination, of acute care and LTC—an essential step, since virtually everyone needing LTC also needs acute care. Financing the full continuum of care from a common source might also enable a more rational targeting of resources, with emphasis on preventive services, early intervention, vigorous rehabilitation, and restorative care. Expanded community-based services would allow earlier discharge for many hospitalized patients and might forestall hospitalization for many others.

The goal of the national LTC program would be to support and assist informal care givers, not to replace them. However, informal care givers should not be expected to undertake an overwhelming burden of care and would be offered predictable respite care and other supportive services, such as counseling, training, and support groups.

The program would encourage the provision of LTC by multidisciplinary teams of social workers, nurses, therapists, physicians, attendants, transportation workers, and other providers. Collegial relationships and teamwork should be the rule, with leadership from nurses and social workers as well as from an expanded cadre of well-trained geriatricians, rather than the traditional hierarchical relationships between physicians and nonphysicians.[38]

The availability of capitated funding would foster organizations providing consolidated and comprehensive LTC and acute care services. Two LTC demonstrations that have employed such a model are the social health maintenance organizations and the On Lok Senior Health Service in San Francisco, Calif. Both provide a full range of acute, ambulatory, and LTC services with a capitated financing system.[39,40]

Although such coordinated care may be optimal,[41] individual providers could continue to operate on a contractual or fee-for-service basis. In some cases, family members or other informal care givers could be approved as providers. However, in these situations responsibility for case management and care coordination would ordinarily rest with the local LTC agency.

Innovation would be supported by earmarked extra funding that the state LTC boards would award to local agencies offering the most promising proposals. While each local agency would be required to provide a standard set of services with uniform eligibility criteria and reimbursement rates, this supplemental funding would encourage state and local agencies to develop services beyond the basic level and to seek and reward innovation. This is particularly important for improving services to different age groups, disability categories, and cultural and racial minorities.

Finally, missteps are inevitable in the course of the major reform we envision. Funding for ongoing evaluation is essential to rapidly disclose problems and allow their timely correction. Particular attention should be focused on key policy questions where current expert opinion has not been fully tested by rigorous research. In what situations does case management improve outcomes or efficiency? What organizational framework best ensures appropriate attention to both medical and social needs? What, if any, preventive measures minimize deterioration in mental or physical function? Are categories such as ADLs and IADLs optimal for targeting care?

Quality of Care

No other segment of the health care system has as many documented quality of care problems as the nursing home industry, and concern is growing about the quality of home care.[42-44] As many as one third of all nursing homes are operating below the minimum federal standards.[45] Monitoring the quality of LTC has been hindered by variability in state regulatory programs and the lack of well-validated regulatory standards and procedures.[46]

Each LTC provider (including home care agencies) would be required to meet uniform national quality standards in order to be paid by the NHP. These standards would include structural measures (e.g., staffing levels, educational requirements), process measures (e.g., individualized planning and provision of care), and outcome measures (e.g., changes in functional or mental status, incontinence, mortality, and hospital admission rates). Earmarked funds from the federal LTC budget would support urgently needed research to validate and improve these standards and to develop new approaches to quality assurance.

Each LTC organization and agency would be required to establish a quality assurance program meeting national standards and a quality assurance committee with representatives of each category of service provider (e.g., social workers, homemakers, nurses, physicians, and so forth), clients and their family members or other care givers, and community representatives. The committee would meet regularly to review quality of care and to resolve problems and disputes, with unresolved issues reported to the public regulatory system discussed below.

All regulatory activities of the current licensing and certification agencies, peer review organizations, Medicare inspection of care, and other agencies that monitor LTC would be combined

into a single program. This unified monitoring system would enforce regulations and have the power to sanction and decertify providers. This program would be administered at the federal and state levels, with input from the local LTC agencies and provider quality assurance committees. Consumer complaint systems and telephone hotlines for quality concerns would be mandated. The regulatory agency would be required to employ sufficient staff to conduct periodic surveys of each provider and to investigate complaints in a timely fashion. Providers would be required to disclose financial data and other management information such as staff turnover rates, incident rates, and patient outcome data.

Improving the training, wages, and morale of LTC workers is also crucial to improving the quality of care. Long-term care workers currently earn 15 percent to 45 percent less than comparable hospital employees (U.S. Department of Health and Human Services, Division of Nursing, unpublished data, 1988), and 20 percent of nursing home workers have no health insurance.[47] Nursing homes are not currently required to provide around-the-clock registered nursing care, few have specialized staff such as geriatric nurse practitioners, and aides are often inadequately trained. Many home care agencies have no professional staff or consultants. Wages in LTC organizations receiving payment from the NHP would be regulated to achieve parity with the acute care sector, with funding for this increase phased in over 5 years.

Funding would also be allocated for training and inservice education of LTC professionals, paraprofessionals, and informal care givers. Formal providers would be required to meet minimum training and competency standards. Augmented training is particularly important for nurses and physicians, who often lack experience in working with the frail elderly, the disabled, and the mentally impaired and in working with multidisciplinary teams to develop community services. The development of a cadre of physicians and nurses with special training in gerontology and geriatrics is essential. These professionals would play key clinical and managerial roles in integrating LTC for the elderly

with acute care, as in Great Britain and other countries.[48]

Consumer Choice

Consumer choice would be explicitly fostered by the national LTC program. Each individual eligible for LTC services would choose among the certified providers in her or his area. Individuals would select a primary provider organization and/or individual care provider, including a primary care physician, and could switch providers if they desired. An independent ombudsman would resolve consumer grievances over provider choice. Consumers and/or their delegated representatives would be encouraged to assume control over decisions regarding their care and would be given assurance that durable power of attorney and living will provisions would be honored.

Costs and Financing

Estimates of current expenditures for LTC are imprecise because of the diversity of payment sources. In 1990 an estimated $54.6 billion was spent for nursing homes, $14.1 billion for equipment and appliances, and $10.6 billion for home health services.[49] In addition, about 10 percent ($25 billion) of total hospital costs were spent on psychiatric, rehabilitative, and chronic care services.[49] Thus, the total LTC expenditures were at least $104 billion in 1990 (16 percent of total health spending), excluding informal LTC services. Public programs, primarily Medicaid, currently finance about half of formal LTC. Medicaid pays for 48 percent of nursing home care, Medicare for 2 percent, and other public payers for 3 percent.[50] Private insurance covers less than 2 percent of nursing home costs, while consumers pay 45 percent directly out-of-pocket.[50-53] Consumers pay out-of-pocket for 40 percent of home services in the United States.[64]

Our program would replace almost all of the $52 billion (all figures in 1990 dollars) currently spent each year on private LTC insurance and out-of-pocket costs with public expenditures. Additional funding would be needed, particularly in the first few years, to pay for the increased utilization of LTC for previously unmet needs. The expected utilization increases of 20 percent for nursing homes and 50 percent to 100 percent for home health care [9,24] would cost between $16 billion and $21.5 billion annually.

Further funding would be needed to improve quality through increased training, wages, and staffing levels. However, some of these costs would be offset by reduced administrative costs and improved program efficiency. Additional savings may result from reductions in disability and inappropriate hospitalizations. Precise estimates of these costs and savings are impossible. For our estimates, we assume that the net increase needed for the quality improvement measures (after subtracting potential administrative and other savings) amounts to $2 billion per year.

Overall, a total of $70 to $75.5 billion in new tax revenues ($380 to $410 per adult) would be needed to finance our program. Of this total, $52 billion represents money that is currently spent privately that would be shifted onto the public ledger. In effect, a broad-based tax would replace payments by the chronically ill. Because LTC has been seriously underfunded, $18 to $23.5 billion in truly new spending ($100 to $130 per adult) would be needed to expand care and improve its quality. Since almost every family will use such services at some point, this seems a reasonable price for financial protection and improved services for the disabled and aged.

These revenues could be raised from several sources, including the Social Security system, general taxes, and estate taxes. Expanding Social Security payroll taxes that currently fund Medicare would build upon the existing tax system and ensure a broad tax base. For example, a 1 percent increase in payroll taxes for both employers and employees would raise about $50 billion.[10] Increasing the earned income tax credit for lower-income workers to lower their payroll tax and removing the current ceiling on Social Security taxes would generate about $49 billion in additional revenue, while making such taxes less regressive.[10,28] Federal estate taxes are another logical source of funds for LTC and would have little negative impact on low-income groups. A 10 percent surcharge on gifts and estates above $200,000 would raise $2 to $4 billion, [9,10] and taxing capital gains at death would raise about $5.5 billion.[10]

Comment

Our proposed LTC program would be integrated with the NHP, creating a single comprehensive and universal public program for acute care and LTC. The program would be federally mandated and funded but administered at the state and local levels. A single state board would contract directly with providers through a network of local public agencies responsible for LTC eligibility determination and for case management and/or care coordination. All payment would be channeled through the single payment agency in each state.

Single-source payment is key to controlling costs, streamlining administration, and minimizing inequalities in care.[31-55] Private insurance duplicating the public program would be eliminated in order to decrease administrative costs, prevent insurers from electing to cover only the healthiest (hence leaving only the most difficult and expensive tasks for the public sector), and guard against the emergence of two-class care. [30-56]

Prospective global budgeting for nursing homes and community-based services would simplify administration and virtually eliminate billing and eligibility determination. Prohibiting the use of operating funds for capital purchases or profit would minimize financial incentives both for skimping on care (as under the current per-diem nursing home payment system) and for excessive intervention (as under the fee-for-service payments received by many home care providers). The separate appropriation of capital funds would facilitate rational health planning.

Current capital spending largely determines future operating costs, as well as the distribution of facilities and programs. Combining operating and capital payments under the existing reimbursement system allows prosperous providers to expand and modernize, whereas impoverished ones cannot, regardless of their quality or the needs of the population they serve. The NHP would replace this implicit mechanism for distributing capital with an explicit one. Capital funds would be allocated on the basis of a comprehensive planning process, with the involvement of health planners, community members, and providers. Priority would be given to underserved regions and populations and to the development of home- and community-based services, to correct the current bias toward institutional care. While funds for sheltered and supportive housing are more appropriately part of a housing rather than a medical care program, coordination in planning of housing and LTC is essential.

Issues of profit-making are particularly problematic in LTC, where 75 percent of the nursing homes and a growing proportion of home care agencies are proprietary.[17] There is ample documentation of LTC providers' skimping on basic services and staffing in order to maximize profits. [46-57] As previously proposed,[31] the NHP would pay owners of for-profit providers a reasonable fixed rate of return on existing equity. Since virtually all new capital investment would be funded by the NHP, it would not be included in calculating return on equity. The proprietary sector would gradually shrink because new for-profit investment would be proscribed.

We advocate fully public financing of LTC for four reasons: (1) single-source public funding facilitates cost containment through administrative streamlining and the ability to set and enforce an overall budget; (2) financial risk is spread across the entire population (who are all ultimately at risk for needing services) rather than falling only on the disabled and elderly; (3) few people today are covered by private LTC insurance, and there is little reason to believe that widespread private coverage is practicable; and (4) there is a need for clear public accountability.

Public insurance programs are far more efficient than private plans. Administration consumes 5 percent of total Medicaid spending[24] and only 2 percent of the Medicare budget. In contrast, in 1986 Blue Cross/Blue Shield and self-insured plans had overhead of 8 percent, prepaid plans averaged 11.7 percent, and commercial insurers averaged

18.9 percent.[52] Many Medicare supplemental policies (medigap insurance) have notoriously low payout ratios, 60 percent or less.[58] Payout rates for private LTC insurance are low[10] and virtually unregulated. According to the General Accounting Office, of the 33 states with minimum payout ratios for general health insurance, most do not report benefit and premium data separately for LTC insurance, only 20 states even monitor payout ratios, and 12 states have established minimum LTC insurance payout ratios.[18]

The multiplicity of public and private insurers in the United States results in exorbitant administrative costs. Health insurance overhead alone costs $106 per capita in the United States (0.66 percent of gross national product) compared with $15 per capita (O.11 percent of gross national product) in Canada.[59] Additional unnecessary administrative costs accrue to providers who must determine eligibility, attribute costs and charges to individual patients and insurers, and send and collect bills for myriad insurers and individual patients.[60] Overall, administration accounts for almost one fourth of U.S. health spending, but only 11% in Canada.[60]

Finally, public opinion strongly supports public financing of LTC. Eighty-seven percent of Americans consider the absence of LTC financing a crisis, the majority prefer public over private funding, federal administration is favored over private insurance programs by a 3 to 2 margin, and two thirds believe that private insurance companies would undermine quality of care because of their emphasis on profits.[26] While respondents want a federally financed program, they support the administration of such a program at the state level.[26]

The oft-stated view that the public wants LTC coverage but is unwilling to pay for it is inaccurate.[61] The 1987 poll conducted by the American Association of Retired Persons and the Villers Foundation found that 86 percent of the sample supported government action for a universal LTC program that would finance care for all income groups, and not just the poor. Overall, 75 percent would agree to increased taxes for LTC.[26] A 1988 Harris poll reached virtually identical conclusions.[62]

Conclusions

In summary, we recommend that LTC be incorporated into a publicly financed NHP. We urge that a comprehensive public model be adopted as a single mandatory plan for the entire population and that new public revenues be combined with existing public program dollars. This approach would ensure universal access, comprehensive benefits, improved quality, and greater cost control. Most important, the financial costs would be spread across the entire population rather than borne by the disabled themselves. Our nation has the resources to provide better care for the disabled and elderly, and it has a responsibility to develop a reasonable system of LTC. The public supports this type of approach. Health and human services professionals and the makers of public policy need the vision and courage to implement such a system.

This proposal was drafted by a 17-member Working Group, then reviewed and endorsed by 415 other physicians and other health professionals from virtually every state and medical specialty. Members of the Working Group were Charlene Harrington, RN, Ph.D., San Francisco, CA; Christine Cassel, M.D., Chicago, IL; Carroll L. Estes, Ph.D., San Francisco, CA; Steffie Woolhandler, M.D., MPH, Cambridge, MA; and David U. Himmelstein, M.D., Cambridge, MA, co-chairs; and William H. Barker, M.D., Rochester, NY; Kenneth R. Barney, M.D., Cambridge, MA; Thomas Bodenheimer, M.D., San Francisco, CA; David Carrell, Ph.D., San Francisco, CA; Kenneth B. Frisof, M.D., Cleveland, OH; Judith B. Kaplan, M.S., Cambridge, MA; Peter D. Mott, M.D., Rochester, NY; Robert J. Newcomer, Ph.D., San Francisco, CA, David C. Parish, M.D., MPH, Macon, GA; James H. Sanders, Jr., M.D., Brevard, NC; Lillian Rabinowitz, Berkeley, CA; and Howard Waitzkin, M.D., Ph.D., Anaheim, CA.

Notes

1. Holahan J, Dubay LC, Kenney G, Welch WP, Bishop C, Dor A. Should Medicare compensate hospitals for administratively necessary days? *Milbank Q.* 1989; 67:137–167.

2. Hazzard WR. A report card on academic geriatrics in 1991: a struggle for academic respectability. *Ann Intern Med.* 1991;116: 229–230.

3. Rowe JW, Drossman E, Bond E. Academic geriatrics for the year 2000: an

Institute of Medicine report. *N Engl J Med.* 1987;316:1426–1428.

4. Kane R, Solomon D, Beck J, Keeler E, Kane R. The future need for geriatric manpower in the US *N Engl J Med.* 1980;302:1327–1332.

5. Estes CL, Binney EA. The biomedicalization of aging: dangers and dilemmas. *Gerontologist.* 1989; 29:587–596.

6. Kane RA, Kane RL. *Long-term Care: Principles, Programs, and Policies.* New York, NY: Springer Publishing Co Inc; 1987.

7. Estes CL, Newcomer RJ, Benjamin AE, et al. *Fiscal Austerity and Aging.* Beverly Hills, Calif: Sage Publications; 1983.

8. Harrington C, Newcomer RJ, Estes CL, et al. *Long-term Care of the Elderly: Public Policy Issues.* Beverly Hills, Calif: Sage Publications; 1985.

9. *A Call for Action: Final Report.* Washington, DC: US Bipartisan Commission on Comprehensive Health Care; 1990.

10. Ball RM, Bethell TN. *Because We're All in This Together: The Case for a National Long-term Care Insurance Policy.* Washington, DC: Families USA Foundation; 1989.

11. Firman J, Weissert W, Wilson CE. *Private Long-term Care Insurance: How Well Is It Meeting Consumer Needs and Public Policy Concerns?* Washington, DC: United Seniors Health Cooperative; 1988.

12. Estes CL. *Long-term Care: Requiem for Commercial Private Insurance.* San Francisco. Calif: Institute for Health and Aging, 1990. Study prepared for the Annual Meeting of the Gray Panthers.

13. *Private Long-term Care Insurance: Unfit for Sale? A Report of the Chairman of the Subcommittee on Health and Long-term Care.* Washington, DC: US House Select Committee on Aging, 1989.

14. *InterStudy Long-term Care Expansion Program: A Proposal for Reform.* Excelsior, Minn: InterStudy; 1988;1.

15. L. Plante MP. *Data on Disability From the National Health Interview Survey, 1983–85.* Washington, DC: US Dept of Education; 1988. Prepared for the National Institute on Disability and Rehabilitation Research

16. *Issues Concerning the Financing and Delivery of Long-term Care 1989.* Washington, DC: Employee Benefit Research Institute; 1989. No. 86.

17. National Center for Health Statistics, Hing E, Sekscenski E, Strahan G. The National Nursing Home Survey: 1985 Summary for the United States. *Vital Health Stat [13].* 1987;No. 97. DHHS publication (PHS) 89–1758.

18. National Center for Health Statistics, Schoenborn CA, Marano M. Current estimates from the National Health Interview Survey: United States, 1987. *Vital Health Stat [10].* 1988;No. 166. DHHS publication (PHS) 88–1594.

19. Liu K, Manton KG, Liu BM. Home care expenses for the disabled elderly. *HCF Rev.* 1985;7: 51–57.

20. Stone R, Cafferata GL, Sangl J. Caregivers of the frail elderly: a national profile. *Gerontologist.* 1987;27:616–626.

21. *Developments in Aging: 1988: A Report of the Special Committee on Aging, United States Senate.* Washington, DC: US Senate; 1989;1–3.

22. Stone R. Aging in the eighties, age 65 years and over—use of community services: preliminary data from the supplement on aging to the National Health Interview Survey: United States January–June 1985. *NCHS Adv Data.* 1986;124.

23. Families USA Foundation calls for a FTC investigation of insurance industry abuse of frail elderly nursing home insurance buyers. Press release. Washington, DC: Families USA Foundation; February 26, 1990.

24. Rivlin AM, Weiner JM. *Caring for the Disabled Elderly: Who Will Pay?* Washington, DC: Brookings Institution; 1988.

25. *Source Book of Health Insurance Data: Update.* Washington, DC: Health Insurance Association of America; 1988.

26. *The American Public Views Long-term Care: A Survey Conducted for the American Association of Retired Persons and the Villers Foundation.* Princeton, NJ: R.L. Associates; October 1987.

27. Kane RL, Kane RA. *A Will and a Way: What the United States Can Learn From Canada About Care of the Elderly.* New York, NY: Columbia University Press; 1985.

28. Blumenthal D, Schlesinger M, Drumbeller PB. *Renewing the Promise: Medicare and Its Reform.* New York, NY: Oxford University Press Inc; 1988.

29. *Long-term Care Conference.* Washington, DC: Villers Foundation; 1987.

30. *Draft Proposal Long-term Care Social Insurance Program Initiative.* Washington, DC: Lewin & Associates; 1987. Prepared for Advisory Committee on Long-term Care, sponsored by the American Association of Retired Persons, Older Women's League, and the Villers Foundation.

31. Himmelstein DU, Woolhandler S, and the Writing Committee of the Working Group of Program Design of Physicians for a National Health Program. A national health program for the United States: a physicians proposal. *N Engl J Med.* 1989; 320:102–108.

32. Callahan JJ. Case management for the elderly: a panacea? *J Aging Social Pol.* 1989;1:181–195.

33. *Hospital Statistics: 1986 Edition.* Chicago, Ill: American Hospital Association; 1986.

34. Estes CL. The United States: long-term care and federal policy. In: Reif L, Trager B, eds. *International Perspectives on Long-term Care.* New York, NY: The Haworth Press; 1985:315–328.

35. *InterStudy's Long-term Care Expansion Program: Issue Papers.* Excelsior, Minn: InterStudy; 1988;2.

36. Justice D. *State Long-term Care Reform: Development of Community Care Systems in Six States.* Washington, DC: National Governor's Association; 1988.

37. Kane RL, Kane RA. A nursing home in your future? *N Engl J Med.* 1991;324:627–629.

38. Freidson E. *Professional Dominance.* Chicago, Ill: Aldine Publishing Co; 1970.

39. Newcomer RJ, Harrington C, Friedlob A, et al. *Evaluation of the Social Health Maintenance Organization Demonstration.* Wasington, DC: US Dept of Health and Human Services, Health Care Financing Administration; 1989. Publication O3283.

40. Zawadski RT. The long-term care demonstration projects: what they are and why they came into being. *Home Health Care Services Q.* Fall/Winter 1983;4:3–19.

41. Campbell LJ, Cole KD. Geriatric assessment teams. *Clin Geriatr Med.* 1987; 3(1):99–117.

42. *Hearings Before the Special Committee on Aging of the US Senate,* 99th Cong, 2nd Sess (1986).

43. *Hearings Before the US House Committee on Ways and Means,* 99th Cong, 2nd Sess (1986).

44. Kusserow RP. *Home Health Aide Services for Medicare Patients.* Washington, DC: US Dept of Health and Human Services; 1987. Unpublished rept OA101–860-0010.

45. *Report to the Chairman, Subcommittee on Health and Long-term Care, Select Committee on Aging, US House of Representatives: Medicare and Medicaid: Stronger Enforcement of Nursing Home Requirements Needed.* Washington, DC: US General Accounting Office; 1987.

46. Institute of Medicine. *Improving the Quality of Care in Nursing Homes.* Washington, DC: National Academy Press; 1986.

47. Himmelstein DU, Woolhandler S. Who cares for the care givers? Lack of health insurance among health and insurance personnel. *JAMA.* 1991;266: 399–401.

48. Barker WH. *Adding Life to Years: Organized Geriatic Services in Great Britain and Implications for the United States.* Baltimore, Md: The Johns Hopkins University Press; 1987.

49. US Dept of Commerce, International Trade Administration. *Health and Medical Services: US Industrial Outlook 1990.* Washington, DC: US Dept of Commerce; 1990.

50. *Hearings Before the Health Task Force Committee on the Budget, US House of Representatives,* 100th Cong, 2nd Sess (1987) (testimony of Nancy Cordon, assistant director for Human Resources and Community Dept).

51. Task Force on Long-term Care Policies. *Report to Congress and the Secretary: Long-term Health Care Policies.* Washington, DC: US Dept of Health and Human Services; 1987.

52. Division of National Cost Estimates, Office of the Actuary, Health Care Financing Administration. *National Health Expenditures, 1986–2000.* Washington, DC: Health Care Financing Administration; 1987;8:1–36.

53. Levit KR, Freedland MS. National medical care spending. *Health Aff.* 1988;7:124–136.

54. Price RJ, O'Shaughnessy C. *Long-term Care for the Elderly.* Washington, DC: The Library of Congress; 1990. Congressional Research Service Issue Brief

55. Harrington C, Newcomer RJ, Friedlob A. Medicare beneficiary enrollment in S/HMO. In: *Social/Health Maintenance Organization Demonstration Evaluation: Report on the First Thirty Months.* Washington, DC: Health Care Financing Administration; 1987: chap 4. Contract HCFA 85034/CP.

56. Bodenheimer T. Should we abolish the private health insurance industry? *Int J Health Serv.* 1990; 20:199–220.

57. Hawes C, Phillips CD. The changing structure of the nursing home industry and the impact of ownership on quality, cost, and access. In: Gray BH, McNerney WJ, eds. *For-Profit Enterprise in Health Care.* Washington, DC: Academy Press; 1986:492–538.

58. *Report to the Subcommittee on Health, Committee on Ways and Means, House of Representatives: Medigap Insurance Law Has Increased Protection Against Substandsrd and Overpriced Policies.* Washington, DC: US Government Accounting Office; 1986.

59. Evans RG, Lomas J, Barer ML, et al. Controlling health expenditures—the Canadian reality. *N Engl J Med.* 1989;320: 571–577.

60. Woolhandler S, Himmelstein DU. The deteriorating administrative efficiency of the US health care system. *N Engl J Med.* 1991;324:1253–1258.

61. Blendon R.J. The public's view of the future of health care. *JAMA.* 1988;259: 3587–3593.

62. Harris L. *Majorities Favor Passage of Long-term Health Care Legislation.* New York, NY: Louis Harris & Associates; 1988.

Index

About the Editors

David A. Kindig, M.D., Ph.D., is currently Professor of Preventive Medicine and Director, Programs in Health Management, University of Wisconsin School of Medicine, Madison, Wisconsin. His graduate degrees are from the University of Chicago, and he served a residency in Pediatrics and Social Medicine at Montefiore Hospital in the Bronx. As a medical student, he was National President of the Student American Medical Association. His management positions include first Medical Director of the National Health Service Corps; Deputy Director, Bureau of Health Manpower DHEW; Executive Director, Montefiore Hospital and medical Center; and Vice Chancellor for Health Sciences, University of Wisconsin–Madison. His research interests include urban and rural health, primary care, administrative medicine, equity in health care, and international health. He currently serves as a Commissioner of the Prospective Payment Assessment Commission; on the AHCPR Study Section for Research Dissemination; on the Board of the Association of University Programs in Health Administration; on Advisory Boards of several rural research centers; and as Chair of the Wisconsin AHEC Advisory Committee.

Robert B. Sullivan, M.A., M.A.B., is Research Director for the Faculty Task Force on National Health Programs at the University of Wisconsin–Madison. As a consultant from 1980 to 1989, he conducted strategic planning and feasibility studies for hospitals, medical groups, nursing homes, and other health care organizations. His health care experience, combined with a background in insurance, led to his interest in access issues and universal health programs. Mr. Sullivan holds master's degrees in health services administration and in the history of medicine, and is completing a doctorate in the history of medicine at the University of Wisconsin–Madison. His research has focused on twentieth-century health policy, with special emphasis on comparative analyses of health programs in the United States, Canada, and Europe. The recipient of a Fulbright scholarship for the 1992–1993 academic year, Mr. Sullivan is conducting research at McGill University in Montreal on the development of the health care system in Quebec since World War II.

Editorial Contributors

Pamela Spohn, Ph.D., has been on the faculty of the School of Social Work at the University of Wisconsin–Madison since 1989. After serving as principal consultant on health and welfare to the Assembly Ways and Means Committee in the California legislature for four years, she earned a Ph.D. in Social Welfare from the University of California–Berkeley. Her research interests include the organization and financing of health care, with particular emphasis on access issues. Some of her research projects have examined barriers to care created by the lack of health insurance resulting both from medical underwriting practices and from coverage gaps between the private employer-based insurance system, and Medicare and Medicaid.

Linda Reivitz, M.A.B., is Deputy Director of the Programs in Health Management at the University of Wisconsin–Madison, where she teaches health policy. She has spent much of the past 20 years in public service at both the state and national levels. In addition to holding management positions in several state government agencies, from 1983 to 1986 Ms. Reivitz was Secretary of Wisconsin's Department of Health and Social Services, and later Director of Planning for a nonprofit health care organization. She has also analyzed health policy issues as a member of the professional staff of the Joint Economic Committee in Washington, D.C. Ms. Reivitz received her master's degree in business from the University of Wisconsin–Madison in 1981.